CONTROVERSIES IN VOTING BEHAVIOR

CONTROVERSIES IN VOTING BEHAVIOR

THIRD EDITION

Richard G. Niemi
University of Rochester

Herbert F. Weisberg
The Ohio State University

A Division of Congressional Quarterly Inc.
Washington, D.C.

Library of Congress Cataloging-in-Publication Data

Controversies in voting behavior / [edited by] Richard G. Niemi,
    Herbert F. Weisberg.--3rd ed.
        p.   cm.
    Includes bibliographical references and index.
    ISBN 0-87187-706-6
    1. Elections.   2. Voting.   I. Niemi, Richard G.   II. Weisberg,
    Herbert F.
JF1001.C575   1992
324.9--dc20   92-22878
                                                         CIP

We dedicate this book (third edition) to our wives (first edition),
Shirley Niemi and Judy Weisberg

CONTENTS

PREFACE

In this third edition of *Controversies in Voting Behavior,* we have again selected what we regard as the best work in contemporary voting behavior research. Like its subject matter, the study of voting remains lively, full of controversy, and yet often enlightening. These new readings nicely capture all these elements, collectively describing the current state of the field as well as suggesting the new directions in which research is headed.

Because of new elections as well as ever-changing theoretical and methodological developments, scholarly articles on voting behavior retain their freshness for perhaps a half-dozen years. By then, a small proportion have achieved classic status; others fade into the background. With this in mind, we have focused this new edition on very recent work, though in some instances we have stretched back to the mid-1980s. As in the first two editions, we have written introductions in which we try to provide the background and context that will allow students to understand as fully as possible the research described in the readings.

When we first decided to prepare a reader on controversies in voting behavior in the mid-1970s, the field was in a state of internal disarray. The view of voting behavior as the most scientific field in the study of political behavior was coming apart under the weight of disagreements in the literature. We thought it would be useful to pull together the debates so that readers could see both what had been learned and what remained to be learned. Perhaps naively, we expected that some of these controversies would soon be resolved. After preparing a second and now a third edition, we recognize that these controversies will remain lively for a long time. Indeed, we expect this edition to be followed in due course by a fourth, a fifth, and even a sixth edition.

Controversies in Voting Behavior now has a companion reader, *Classics in Voting Behavior.* That volume covers earlier research that is essential to a complete understanding of current scholarship on voting behavior as well as for understanding certain aspects of public opinion and historical research. The two-book solution rescues us from having to provide too little of either the background now covered in *Classics* or the current scholarship now covered in *Controversies.* This also enables us to continue our practice of presenting unabridged readings in the *Controversies* volume so that the students can see the full arguments along with all the details of the methods employed.

The way in which ideas have developed permits a largely chronological division between the two readers. With one exception, *Classics* covers work from the beginning of systematic voting behavior research through the early to mid-1980s. The exception is research on long-term voting trends and historical alignments and realignments. Recent scholarship on pre-New Deal voter alignments has been fascinating, but there has not been enough of it to justify extensive, separate coverage in *Controversies*. Work on post-New Deal alignments is plentiful throughout the period, but it benefits greatly from the hindsight provided by the passage of time, so that most pre-1980s writing about the direction of recent alignments seems seriously deficient. Hence, the historical perspective section of *Classics* covers pre-New Deal voter behavior and party systems, and the corresponding section of *Controversies* covers changes in alignments since that time.

We would like to thank the many people who have helped us put this edition together. Our first thanks go to the authors of the various articles included here. Not only did they allow us to reprint their work, but they edited material, provided us with original figures, sent us copies of recent or new material, endured questions about minor typographical errors or occasional missing references, and so on. At CQ, we are especially grateful to David Tarr and Brenda Carter, who helped make the two-volume idea a reality. Shana Wagger was very helpful in keeping us on schedule while remaining cheerful even when deadlines were stretched. Jenny Philipson, Kerry Kern, and Laura Carter handled the many production details with a fine combination of skill and humor. Our copy editor, Tracy Villano, helped improve our prose. John Aldrich provided us with a skillful assessment of the overall project as well as detailed comments on our introductions. Finally, Weisberg would also like to thank the Ohio State University for a sabbatical leave that gave him more time to work on the project and the Department of Political Science at Rice University for providing a stimulating and hospitable environment for working on this book.

R.G.N.
H.F.W.

INTRODUCTION

1. THE STUDY OF VOTING AND ELECTIONS

Another presidential election, this time with a president seeking reelection after a muted victory in a foreign crisis, with domestic economic ills, and with a public dissatisfied with politics generally and with the presidential candidates in particular. The scenario is that of the United States in 1992, but it is just a variant of the scenario in many other election years. As in those other years, the public looks forward to the election as a solution for its problems but all too soon realizes that it changes little. At some point the public wonders why all this excitement about elections. One answer has been vividly provided by the break-up of communism in Eastern Europe along with the movement away from military rule in Latin America. The peoples of those countries happily embraced democracy, even if they felt some letdown when they realized that a change in regime was not a cure-all for economic woes. Still, they recognized the essential truth of Winston Churchill's comment that "it has been said that democracy is the worst form of government except all those other forms that have been tried from time to time." Democracy and free elections might not suffice to solve all problems, but their absence can be even more serious a problem. This leads us to contemplate what the functions of elections are in a democracy.

According to one textbook image, elections serve several functions in a democracy. Not only do they allow citizens to choose the government, but they also restrain political leaders who must behave in a way that maximizes their chances of reelection. Elections are thus one means of linking public attitudes with governmental policy. In addition, electing a government is a way of legitimizing its authority. Elections provide a peaceful means for political change. And they permit individuals and groups to resolve their conflicting needs peacefully. Along with this view of elections is a corresponding view of voters as choosing intelligently among the candidates. Although no one would argue that all voters are well informed, the view from this perspective is that voters as a whole make careful and informed choices.

An opposite view holds that elections are just symbolic in character. According to this position, elections are a secular ritual of democracy, and voting makes citizens consider themselves participants in the nation's governance. Voters

1

feel they have fulfilled their civic duty by voting, even if the chance that a single vote affects the election outcome is nearly nil and even if the election outcome is not really going to alter the future of public policy. Correspondingly, according to this view voters do not make intelligent, informed decisions. Few know anything about the candidates, and what they do know is often irrelevant to governance. Consequently, election results are uninterpretable. This view of elections emphasizes that voting does more to make citizens feel good than to alter political outcomes.

The controversy as to the role of voting and elections turns to a considerable extent on the actual effects of elections. Do elections matter? In the United States, do Democratic and Republican administrations pursue different policies? In other nations, is public policy different under left-wing and right-wing governments? To some extent, these are subjective questions. A Marxist would perceive little difference between Democratic and Republican policies in the United States. A monarchist in Europe might regard policies of left-wing and right-wing governments with equal disdain.

Fortunately, whether elections matter is also partly an empirical question. Government policy outputs under Democratic and Republican administrations can be compared, as can those under left-wing and right-wing governments. There is, in fact, an increasing body of such studies, and they nearly always find policy differences between governments. A variety of research, for example, shows a relationship between party leadership of government and spending on social welfare (see Hicks and Swank, 1992, and the references cited therein). Increasingly, researchers are trying to relate policy decisions directly to public opinion (Stimson, 1991), even quite specific decisions such as the rate of troop withdrawals from Vietnam during the 1970s (Page and Shapiro, 1983; Farkas, Shapiro, and Page, 1990).

Nor does it always require scholarly studies to reveal the consequences of elections. In 1964, Barry Goldwater ran for president of the United States as a conservative candidate offering "a choice and not an echo," and when he lost in a landslide President Lyndon B. Johnson instituted liberal Great Society programs such as the War on Poverty. In 1980 Ronald Reagan ran on virtually an anti-government platform, and he turned his large victory margin over President Jimmy Carter into a mandate for conservative action in restraining the growth of government domestic programs and lowering taxes. George Bush's 1988 election over Michael Dukakis was just as clearly a choice in favor of continued restraint for social welfare programs. Margaret Thatcher's 1979 victory over James Callaghan in Britain led to the denationalization of some industries that previous Labour governments had nationalized, and the reelection of Conservative governments in 1983, 1987, and 1992 reinforced that decision. These are policy consequences of elections that voters will notice. The election of black mayors in a number of U.S. cities in the 1980s—though not a policy shift as such—suggests another important kind of change; the extensive voting along racial lines in many of those mayoral elections is prima facie evidence of voter awareness of at least this difference in candidates, and it shows as well a presumption that who gets elected makes a difference.

A more difficult question is whether even these consequences make a difference in the long run. Does it really matter if there is a war on poverty, restrained growth of federal programs, or denationalization of industry? Problems seem to remain in any case. This is particularly true of economic problems. We seem to be on a roller coaster, going from severe inflation to harsh unemployment and then back again to inflation. Neither Keynesian nor supply-side economics has been able to strike a proper balance between the two. And economic problems affect the national mood, as when the long-lasting United States recession of the early 1990s led to public pessimism about the nation's future.

Significantly, the electorate has had a reaction if not an answer to this possibly unanswerable question. There seems to be a trend toward voting on the basis of perceived candidate competence. Carter's defeat in 1980 was less a mandate for Reagan's conservative policies than a rejection of Carter's inability to handle inflation, the American hostages in Teheran, and other such problems (Miller and Wattenberg, 1981). Mrs. Thatcher's reelection in 1983 reflected public satisfaction with her successful victory against Argentina in the Falkland Islands war as well as simultaneous dismay over Labour's extreme and sometimes incoherent disarmament policy. Despite the success of the U.S.-led Coalition forces in the Persian Gulf War, President Bush was in trouble with the U.S. electorate in 1992 because he was not perceived as able to translate his foreign policy successes into domestic economic solutions. Many Americans became interested in a possible independent candidacy by Ross Perot in 1992, partly because of his demonstrated successes in the business realm. In the end, it may be that there are no solutions that work, but the public knows enough to reject leaders who cannot deliver and keep those who achieve some success.

Whether in terms of policy consequences or leadership choices, elections retain their importance in democracies. They do make a difference, at least in the short run. And voters to some degree make choices on the basis of this difference. At the same time, it must be admitted that we do not yet fully understand voting and elections. Our understanding of these topics has changed a great deal in the past few decades, paralleling changes in our ways of studying them. Yet to our frequent dismay, many of the major questions in the field are not yet settled, despite the considerable attention that has been paid to them. Nevertheless, we are getting closer to answering some of these questions.

How to Study Voting

Methodology

Modern voting studies rely heavily on survey research. There are certainly other ways of studying elections, but the most direct and often the most valid way of understanding why people vote as they do is to ask them.

Readers unfamiliar with survey research are often suspicious of using small samples to describe large populations. The sampling theory underlying such work is based on mathematical probability theory. We shall not describe it fully here (see *Classics in Voting Behavior*[1] for a more complete introduction), but it is worth pointing out that with scientific sampling using random sampling procedures (in which each person has a known probability of falling into a sample), the sampling error can be calculated on the basis of the sample size. For example, samples of about 1,500 respondents (which is a common sample size for election surveys) give estimates within about a 3 percent range. Thus, a survey study finding that 58 percent of the sample favors a particular candidate really means that the odds are very high that the true population proportion favoring that candidate is between 55 (58 − 3) and 61 (58 + 3) percent. This degree of precision is usually considered adequate. Other sources of error can affect the accuracy of surveys, but at least the error due to sampling can be estimated scientifically when using probability sampling.

While we emphasize the importance of surveys, an important recent development in voting studies has been the increased use of experiments. Researchers as different in their orientations as political psychologists and formal theorists now use experiments to test their theories of voter decision-making. These studies often use small numbers of subjects and often rely on student subjects. As examples, political psychologists have shown subjects campaign brochures for candidates and have used their recollection of topics in the brochures as tests between different theories of the process of candidate evaluation (Lodge, McGraw, and Stroh, 1989) while formal theorists have tested whether subjects who are given particular utility functions end up in predicted equilibrium solutions (McKelvey and Ordeshook, 1985). We would expect this increased use of experiments to continue, even while political surveys remain the dominant mode of studying elections.

The Data Base

In *Classics in Voting Behavior*, we reviewed the history of voting behavior research from its origins in journalistic studies in the late 1930s through the mid-1980s. We stressed the importance of survey research generally, and in particular the series of University of Michigan surveys that are now associated with the National Election Studies. The NES studies are particularly valuable because many of the same questions have been used repeatedly since 1952, permitting an analysis of change over a lengthy time period. Readers unfamiliar with these studies are urged to refer to *Classics*.

What we shall do here is to provide a brief update of studies and approaches that have characterized work since the mid-1980s. Our chief vehicle for doing this is Table 1-1, which shows, for this period, the main data sets as well as representative publications based on them.

The most significant trend, begun by the early 1980s but having much fuller flower in the last half-dozen or so years, is an expansion of the number and variety of large scale data sets and therefore in the subject matter covered. There are several explanations for these developments. For one, the shift from door-to-door interviews to telephone interviews has made it easier to conduct national surveys from a single site, without the difficulty of training separate teams of interviewers in multiple communities. As a result, the national news media,

Table 1-1   Major Electoral Behavior Studies and Accompanying Reports, 1977-1992

Year	Study	Report
1977-	CBS/*New York Times* national surveys; exit polls; special surveys	M. MacKuen, R. Erikson, J. Stimson, "Question-wording and Macropartisanship," *APSR*,[a] June 1992
1981-	ABC/*Washington Post* national surveys; exit polls; special surveys	
1984	University of Michigan, National Election Study (NES) national sample, continuous monitoring	L. Bartels, *Presidential Primaries*, Princeton University Press, 1988
1984	University of Michigan, NES, national sample	M. Shanks, W. Miller, "Policy Direction and Performance Evaluation," *BJPS*,[b] April 1990
1984	University of Michigan, National Black Election Study (NBES) national sample	K. Tate, R. Brown, S. Hatchett, J. Jackson, *The 1984 National Black Election Study: A Sourcebook*, Institute for Social Research, 1988
1984	Decision/Making/Information, national sample, continuous monitoring	D. Allsop, H. Weisberg, "Measuring Change in Party Identification in an Election Campaign," *AJPS*,[c] November 1988
1984	Aldrich, Sullivan, Borgida national (Gallup) sample	J. Aldrich, J. Sullivan, E. Borgida, "Foreign Affairs and Issue Voting," *APSR*, March 1989
1968-89	State Legislative Elections, (aggregate data)	*Legislative Studies Quarterly*, February 1991 issue
1986	University of Michigan NES, national sample	
1987	National Opinion Research Center, General Social Survey national sample, black oversample	N. Nie, S. Verba, H. Brady, K. Schlozman, J. Junn, "Participation in America: Continuity and Change," 1988 MWPSA[d] Paper
1988	University of Michigan NES, national sample	P. Abramson, J. Aldrich, D. Rohde, *Change and Continuity in the 1988 Elections*, CQ Press, 1991

(table continues)

Table 1-1 *(continued)*

Year	Study	Report
1988	University of Michigan, NBES national sample	K. Tate, "Black Political Participation in the 1984 and 1988 Presidential Elections," *APSR*, December 1991
1988	University of Michigan, NES sixteen states with "Super Tuesday" primaries	P. Abramson, J. Aldrich, P. Paolino, D. Rohde. "Sophisticated" Voting in the 1988 Presidential Primaries," *APSR*, March 1992
1988	University of Michigan NES, national sample, Senate Study	*Legislative Studies Quarterly*, November 1990 issue
1990	University of Michigan NES, national sample	
1990	University of Michigan NES, national sample, Senate study	
1992	University of Michigan NES, national sample	
1992	University of Michigan NES, national sample, Senate study	

[a] *American Political Science Review*
[b] *British Journal of Political Science*
[c] *American Journal of Political Science*
[d] *Midwest Political Science Association*

political parties, and academic political scientists are able to conduct more frequent national surveys.[2] For another, the continuity of funding for the National Election Studies starting just before this period (1978) has allowed it to engage in more advanced planning of studies. This resulted in greater innovation on both legislative and presidential elections. Yet a third reason for the growth of available studies is greater cooperation between academic and commercial organizations; studies that once might have sat unused in the electronic equivalent of file drawers are now easily available to researchers through the Inter-University Consortium for Political and Social Research and other data archives.

Take the NES studies first. In 1978 and again in 1982 it was possible to conduct major surveys on the congressional elections, the first such major study since 1958. The NES Board of Overseers then decided to conduct a major study of U.S. Senate elections, with interviews for each Senate seat. Since only a third of the senators are up for reelection in any single election, studying every Senate seat required a multi-year commitment, in this instance a Senate study in 1988-90- 92. The reports on the Senate study are incomplete at this time, but we are able to represent the congressional studies in this book (see Chapter 13, as well as Chapter 15 in *Classics*).

There has been similar innovation in the study of presidential elections. In 1980 the NES conducted a panel survey across the election year, interviewing the same respondents in January-February, June-July, September-October, and November-December, along with a minor panel that was interviewed twice. In 1984 NES switched to a "continuous monitoring study" in which separate, small random samples were taken weekly throughout the election year, from January through December. Both of these designs allowed for a greater examination of voting in presidential primaries (see Chapter 19) and of attitude change through the election year than previous designs permitted.

Additionally, as Table 1-1 indicates, there are important political surveys conducted outside of the NES aegis. For example, a National Black Election Study was conducted in 1984 and 1988. Also, the major news networks have conducted "exit polls" after presidential primaries and presidential and off-year general elections. These polls focus most on how people just voted, but they include a few additional questions that are increasingly used in academic studies. Wright, Erikson, and McIver (1985), for example, have used the CBS News/ *New York Times* exit polls to establish rankings of the states in terms of their Republican-Democrat balance and their liberal-conservative balance, and Norrander (1989) has used these data to rank the states according to their proportions of political independents. The monthly polling by some of these organizations has led to long time series on political indicators; these time series have shown that some political attitudes are more variable than was previously thought to be the case (see Chapter 17 for a discussion of such change in party identification). The political parties have also sponsored some polls of these types, though, unfortunately, their data are generally less accessible to academics.[3] Some political scientists have also been able to secure funding for separate election surveys to study particular topics, as in a national survey by scholars at the University of Minnesota to test a political psychology model of the vote (see Chapter 12) and in a study by scholars at Ohio State University of split-ticket voting in Ohio (Beck, Baum, Clausen, and Smith, 1992).

There has also been greater coverage of gubernatorial and state legislative elections. Some of this has been in the form of an extensive collective of state legislative election returns, currently covering 1968 to the present (see Chapter 13 for references to its use). In addition, researchers have begun to use the media exit polls, with their large state samples, to study gubernatorial voting.

All in all, studies conducted in the last decade or so reflect a greater variety of study design than in previous years. In turn, this has enabled us to study voting, as well as related aspects of public opinion, in much greater breadth and depth than ever before.

Another development of importance has been an increasing emphasis on economics in political survey questions and analysis. New questions in the

Michigan surveys, for example, examine respondents' perceptions of a trade-off between inflation and unemployment. Economic variables are crucial to many new theories of voting, from Kramer's (1971) understanding of voting in congressional elections to Fiorina's (1981) emphasis on retrospective voting, wherein citizens decide how satisfied they are with the past performance of the parties, especially the government's handling of the economy. The result has been very much a marrying of political and economic concerns in a study of the political economy of elections.

There also has been an increasing use of sophisticated analysis methods in election studies. In part, this has been a borrowing of techniques from econometrics, such as the simultaneous equations approach, but it also includes greater use of factor analysis and many other advanced techniques. Some of the most complex pieces use covariance structure modeling (particularly Jöreskog's LISREL computer program) to test hypothesized structural and measurement models. What is surprising is that this greater methodological sophistication is not necessarily leading to greater consensus on the leading controversies in the field. Instead, the more sophisticated techniques frequently require arbitrary decisions and untestable assumptions. As a result, the debates become more advanced without leading to an incontestable conclusion.

The final development of importance in surveys about elections is an even greater expansion in their use outside the United States. In countries where the election date is not fixed (such as Canada, Britain, and a number of others), prime ministers and party leaders now consult these polls before deciding on the timing of the election. The media poll extensively during the campaigns, so much so that there are almost daily reports of new polls in countries (again such as Britain) that have short election campaigns. In some situations, especially when multiple parties are competing, polls have also been important in suggesting to people how to maximize the impact of their vote.[4]

Academic polling is also of increasing importance in many countries. Some of the early cross-national research represented attempts to replicate the Michigan surveys in other countries, often by collaboration between some of the original Michigan researchers and investigators from the country in question. These early studies frequently found that the concepts and questions developed in the American surveys were not applicable in other countries, as will be brought out in the discussion of party identification (Chapter 17). As a result, the more recent election studies have been typified by native researchers developing new questions and concepts based on their understanding of their countries. In some cases parallel developments have taken place across countries, as in frequent cross-national use of panel studies.[5]

How to Understand Voting

The Theory

We also discussed the theoretical foundations of voting behavior research in *Classics* with stress on two main approaches. The social-psychological approach, pioneered by the University of Michigan researchers in their landmark book *The American Voter* (Campbell, Converse, Miller, and Stokes, 1960), emphasizes attitudes. For example, research that seeks to apportion the extent to which a presidential victory is due to voters' party attachments, to their issue positions, or to their candidate orientation generally is in this social-psychological tradition. By contrast, the rational choice approach (Downs, 1957) postulates that voters choose their actions (such as whether to vote and how to vote) on the basis of which action gives them greater benefits. The early rational choice work was very mathematical, but increasingly the school became associated with a greater emphasis on issues as a determinant of voting.

These two approaches have remained important to the understanding of voting, but there have been additional interesting theoretical developments in recent years. For one thing, the early antagonism between the social-psychological and rational voter approaches has declined, and some studies have bridged the approaches. Increasingly, rational voter models are tested with the same empirical data used to test social-psychological models, and this has lessened the barriers between the two. For another, a new approach has been forming around what might be termed "modern political psychology." Social psychology has changed a lot since the 1950s when *The American Voter* was written. In particular, that field has experienced what is often referred to as a "cognitive revolution," as psychologists have achieved better understandings of the basis of human thoughts. Simultaneously, the field has given greater attention to human emotions and their effects on behaviors. These developments have been applied widely across the social sciences, with one result being a new field of political psychology. Political psychology perspectives on voting behavior are represented at several places in this book, especially Chapters 6, 11, and 12. It is too early to assess the impact of this new approach to voting research, but it may become a major alternative to the rational choice approach.

The Controversies

The core controversy over the years has been between two of the approaches to understanding voting behavior that are described above: the original Michigan social-psychological model and the rational choice model. A related controversy developed in the 1970s and early 1980s between the Michigan model and the "revisionist school." The revisionists generally accepted the Michigan framework but objected to particular findings, such as the lowly place accorded issues in the Michigan results and its static view of party identification. We can now add controversy over the newer political psychology approach and its sometimes dominant emphasis on candidate characteristics. While these fundamental controversies remain, research has increasingly focused on specific subjects, with the realization that each of the major approaches to voting behavior might shed light on them. It is about these subject controversies that we organize this book.

Some of the controversies are of longstanding. Yet we would emphasize that changes in the controversies have occurred. One important change in the nature of the arguments has been that in every case the controversy has now expanded to include cross-cultural and cross-time dimensions. Thus, for example, we no longer simply ask whether voters choose on the basis of party identification or issues. Instead, we ask in what circumstances each is important, knowing that each is sometimes the dominant explanation. We also ask what kinds of issues are important—both in a generic sense (whether retrospective or prospective views predominate) and in the specific sense of which issues are crucial. And we ask whether the same kinds of issues (for example, economic issues, the environment, women's issues, and so on) are significant throughout the set of countries with elections. Thus we have made some progress in our understanding of voters and elections, even though considerable controversy remains.

This book is organized around six of the major controversies. Some play off controversies reviewed in *Classics in Voting Behavior*, but often with some twist in how the debate is now framed. At times this is virtually stylistic, as when the old controversy as to how ideological the public is turned into a debate over the public's level of political sophistication. More often the controversy is now phrased in more complex terms. Thus instead of asking whether issues are important in voting, the question is one of when do they become important. In some cases, old controversies have intensified, as with the debate over stability of party identification.

One might expect that the combination of sophisticated methodology, high-quality data, and effective theories would yield a commonly accepted understanding of voting and elections. This has not been the case. Controversy remains: controversy over the reasons that more people do not vote; over how people think about politics; over the relative importance of issues and candidates in presidential elections; over whether congressional elections are primarily national or local elections; over how stable partisan attachments are; over the nature of recent changes in the party system. Controversy remains, but what could be more appropriate in the elections field? Elections are about controversy, and the study of elections will always evoke controversy.

NOTES

1. As explained in the Preface, this book is a companion volume to *Classics in Voting Behavior* (Niemi and Weisberg, 1992). Throughout this chapter and other introductions, there will be several cross-references to *Classics*.
2. We should add that this is not without hazard: telephone respondents may differ from respondents in personal interviews in ways that are not yet fully understood, accounting for some of the differences that are found between recent surveys and those of a few decades ago (Chapter 16, note 6).
3. See, for example, the useful comparison of changes in party identification during the 1984 presidential campaign as measured by a continuous monitoring poll sponsored by the Republican National Committee versus the NES continuous monitoring study that same year in Allsop and Weisberg (1988).
4. See Crewe and Harrop (1989) on the role of polls and the media in advertising "tactical voting" in the British general election of 1987.
5. A large number of non-U.S. academic surveys, as well as books and articles reporting on them, are found in de Guchteneire, LeDuc, and Niemi (1991).

FURTHER READINGS

The Role of Elections

Douglas A. Hibbs, Jr., *The Political Economy of Industrialized Democracies* (Cambridge: Harvard University Press, 1987). The economics of elections.

Bernard Grofman and Chandler Davidson, eds., *Controversies in Minority Voting: The Voting Rights Act in Twenty-Five Year Perspective* (Washington, D.C.: Brookings, 1992). Electoral success of minorities and other results of the Voting Rights Act.

Bernard Grofman, Lisa Handley, and Richard G. Niemi, *Minority Representation and the Quest for Voting Equality* (New York: Cambridge University Press, 1992). Legal and social controversies relating to minority representation in the 1990s.

Alexander M. Hicks and Duane H. Swank, "Politics, Institutions, and Welfare Spending in Industrialized Democracies, 1960-1982," *American Political Science Review* (1992) 86:forthcoming. Effect of partisanship of governing coalition, electoral competition, and turnout on social welfare expenditures in 18 countries.

Public Opinion and Public Policy

James A. Stimson, *Public Opinion in America* (Boulder, Colo.: Westview, 1991). The interpretability of the public's "mood," and its electoral connections.

Benjamin I. Page and Robert Y. Shapiro, *The Rational Public: Fifty Years of Trends in American's Policy Preferences* (Chicago: University of Chicago Press, 1992). Assessment of public opinion and its sources, with some discussion of its effects on policy.

Books Studying Voting Across a Series of U.S. Elections

Norman H. Nie, Sidney Verba, and John P. Petrocik, *The Changing American Voter,* rev. ed. (Cambridge: Harvard University Press, 1979). Revisionist look at the American voter.

Paul R. Abramson, *Political Attitudes in America* (San Francisco: Freeman, 1983). Continuity and change from 1950s to 1980s in party loyalties, political efficacy, political trust, and other political variables.

Warren E. Miller and Santa A. Traugott, *American National Election Studies Data Sourcebook* (Cambridge: Harvard University Press, 1989). Compilation of responses and crosstabs to SRC/CPS/NES political questions.

Paul R. Abramson, John H. Aldrich, and David W. Rohde, *Change and Continuity in the 1988 Elections,* rev. ed. (Washington, D.C.: CQ Press, 1991). Factors affecting voting in the 1988 and 1990 elections.

William H. Flanigan and Nancy H. Zingale, *Political Behavior of the American Electorate,* 7th ed. (Washington, D.C.: CQ Press, 1991). Textbook treatment of issues, candidates, and elections.

Herbert B. Asher, *Presidential Elections and American Politics,* 5th ed. (Pacific Grove, Calif: Brooks/Cole, 1992). Textbook treatment of voters, candidates, and campaigns.

Books Reflecting a "Rational" Model Approach

William H. Riker, *Liberalism Against Populism* (San Francisco: Freeman, 1982). Analysis of group decisionmaking, with some applications to electoral situations.

Books Emphasizing Political Psychology

Richard R. Lau and David O. Sears, eds., *Political Cognition* (Hillsdale, N.J.: Erlbaum, 1986). The cognitive revolution enters political science, with some applications to electoral situations.

Paul M. Sniderman, Richard A. Brady, and Phillip E. Tetlock, *Reasoning and Choice* (New York: Cambridge University Press, 1991).

English Language Books on Voting Behavior in Other Countries

Mark Franklin, *The Decline of Class Voting in Britain* (Oxford: Clarendon Press, 1985).

Tom Bruneau and A. Macleod, *Politics in Contemporary Portugal: Parties and the Consolidation of Democracy* (Boulder, Colo.: Rienner, 1986).

Michael Laver, Peter Mair, and R. Sinnott, eds., *How Ireland Voted: The General Election of 1987* (Dublin: Poolbeg Press, 1987).

Richard Gunther, Giacomo Sani, and Goldie Shabad, *Spain After Franco: The Making of a Competitive Party System* (Berkeley: University of California Press, 1986; revised paperback edition, 1988).

J. Kelley and Clive Bean, *Australian Attitudes: Social and Political Analyses from the National Social Science Survey* (Sydney: Allen and Unwin, 1988).

Asher Arian and Mikhal Shamir, eds., *Elections in Israel 1988* (Boulder, Colo.: Westview, 1990).

William L. Miller, *How Voters Change: The 1987 British Election Campaign in Perspective* (Oxford: Oxford University Press, 1990).

Scott Flanagan, Bradley Richardson, Joji Watanuki, Ichiro Miyake, and Shinsaku Kohei, *The Japanese Voter* (New Haven, Conn.: Yale University Press, 1991).

Anthony Heath, John Curtice, Roger Jowell, et al., *Understanding Political Change: The British Voter 1964-1987* (Oxford: Pergamon Press, 1991).

Books on Voting Behavior Across Several Different Countries

Russell J. Dalton, *Citizen Politics in Western Democracies* (Chatham, N.J.: Chatham House, 1988). Political attitudes, behavior, and party systems in France, Great Britain, Germany, and the United States.

Donald Granberg and Sören Holmberg, *The Political System Matters: Social Psychology and Voting Behavior in Sweden and the United States* (New

York: Cambridge, 1988). Attitudes and voting behavior differences related to differences in the political and party systems of the two countries.

Ronald Inglehart, *Culture Shift in Advanced Industrial Society* (Princeton: Princeton University Press, 1990). Generational changes in attitudes in the countries of the European community.

M. Kent Jennings, Jan W. van Deth, et al., *Continuities in Political Action* (Berlin: deGruyter, 1990). Follow-up to *Political Action* study of political attitudes and participation in Germany, the Netherlands, and the United States.

Mark Franklin, Tom Mackie, Henry Valen, et al., *Electoral Change: Responses to Evolving Social and Attitudinal Structures in Western Countries* (Cambridge: Cambridge University Press, 1992).

Ronald Inglehart and K. Reif, eds., *Euro-Barometer: The Dynamics of European Opinion* (London: MacMillan, forthcoming). Analysis of surveys taken throughout the European Community.

PART I: ELECTION TURNOUT

2. WHY DON'T MORE PEOPLE VOTE?

If there is one clear fact about voting in the United States in the late twentieth century, it is that fewer Americans are showing up at the polls on election day to cast their ballots than used to be the case. The trend is particularly obvious at the presidential level. Whereas 63 percent of the electorate voted during the Kennedy-Nixon election of 1960, only 50 percent turned out for the Bush-Dukakis contest of 1988. American turnout rates were already far below that of European democracies, where 90 percent or more of the electorates routinely vote at national elections (Chapter 5), as well as late nineteenth-century America, where 90 percent turnout was also typical (*Classics in Voting Behavior*, chap. 29).

The trend toward lower turnout is perplexing because it runs counter to what one would expect given the increasing educational level of the electorate. One of the most consistent findings about voter turnout in the United States is that more educated people are likelier to vote than less educated people. Yet the 1960-1988 period during which turnout fell was the same period in which the educational level of Americans sharply rose. College education became much more prevalent, while fewer people stopped their education prior to high school.

Richard Brody (1978) has labelled these parallel turnout and education trends as the "puzzle" of participation—a decrease in turnout concurrent with a dramatic increase in educational levels. This puzzle was further intensified by the effective enfranchisement of southern blacks during the same period, which again should have worked to increase the overall turnout rate.

While the turnout decline is very clear, the explanation is not. Indeed, the turnout decline has led to a growth area in the voting literature as scholars have refocused their attention on the determinants of turnout. Some researchers have tried to explain this turnout change at the individual level while others have moved to group or systemic levels. That is where we pick up this debate as to why fewer Americans are voting.

Turnout Due to Individual Factors

Understanding the decline in turnout first requires knowledge of which factors affect turnout. Turnout has actually been studied systematically for several decades. Some of the earliest empirical analyses of political behavior focused on turnout (Merriam and Gosnell, 1924; Tingsten, 1937). In some cases these studies took advantage of official data, as when several European countries and the state of Illinois tabulated voting turnout separately for men and women. In other cases they analyzed aggregate data, for example comparing turnout in election districts with high and low concentrations of a particular social group.

The advent of voting surveys provided an additional opportunity to examine the causes and correlates of turnout at the individual level. Soon the empirical correlates of voting were discovered using data from the National Election Study (NES) and other surveys (Campbell, Gurin, and Miller, 1954; Campbell, Converse, Miller, and Stokes, 1960, chap. 5; Milbrath and Goel, 1977). The most full-scale examination of who votes was provided by Wolfinger and Rosenstone (1980) in their analysis of the massive post-election surveys conducted by the Census Bureau to monitor state compliance with the Voting Rights Act.[1]

As noted, these studies routinely show that the largest correlate of turnout in the United States is education. People with more education vote at much higher rates than those with less education. Other socioeconomic status factors also correlate with voting rates; higher-income and middle-class people are more likely to vote than lower-income people. Middle-aged people are more likely to vote than younger and older people. Turnout in the northern states has been higher than in southern states. Whites have voted at higher rates than blacks, with that difference narrowing considerably since the federal government intervened with the Voting Rights Act (Bostis and Morris, 1992). Finally, the early studies found that men voted at a higher rate than women, a difference that has disappeared in more recent elections (Conway, 1991, p. 32).

It should be added here that data problems in studying turnout rates exist. Surveys always obtain a higher turnout rate than official statistics reveal. Part of the problem involves the sampling frame for surveys. For example, surveys typically exclude various institutional settings (hospitals, prisons, dormitories, and so on) which have very low turnout rates. Additionally, pre-election interviews tend to stimulate turnout, so post-election interviews with the same people find a higher voting rate (Clausen, 1968-69). Finally, some survey respondents claim to have voted when they actually did not, presumably out of a reluctance to admit to interviewers that they did not vote. Recent NES presidential election surveys have included special "vote validation" efforts in which official voting records are checked to see which respondents actually did vote. Silver, Anderson, and Abramson (1986) have analyzed the patterns of vote overreporting, finding that misreporting turnout is related to demographics, with more highly educated people most likely to claim they voted when they did not. These problems notwithstanding, many of the individual correlates of voting have been found so often, with so many different types of surveys, that the results are generally viewed as accurate.

As reviewed in *Classics in Voting Behavior* (chap. 2), the rationality of voting has been examined at the individual level starting with Downs's (1957) work. Briefly, turnout is modelled as a matter of benefits versus costs, with a person predicted to vote if and only if the benefits exceed the costs. The benefits term is based on how much difference the citizen sees between the candidates on issues, weighted by the citizen's probability of affecting the election outcome by voting. The costs include the time costs involved in going to the polls, the information costs associated with following the election, and whatever costs are associated with registration for first-time voters or people who have just moved. The costs may be small, but the probability of one individual affecting the election outcome is so tiny that nonvoting is rational for many citizens. Indeed, nonvoting seems so sensible under this formulation that analysts have felt a need to adjust the model so that voting becomes rational for some citizens. This is done by adding in one more term to the benefits side of the calculus—the sense of fulfilling one's duty as a citizen that a person acquires by voting. While this formulation is both parsimonious and elegant, it does little to account for the decline in turnout in American presidential elections since 1960. There is no obvious reason to feel that the benefits of voting have declined or that the costs have increased over this period; indeed, registration has become easier in most states, so that the costs may actually have diminished.

The early empirical attempts to analyze the post-1960 turnout decline tried to determine what percentage of the decline was due to each of several factors. Shaffer (1981) found that 86 percent of the 1960-1976 decline was due to decreases in the average age of the voting public,[2] following the campaign in the newspapers, partisanship, and external political efficacy. Abramson and Aldrich (1982) found that 70 percent of the 1960-1980 decline was due to declines in strength of partisanship and efficacy. Unfortunately, these early attempts were too simplistic. As Cassel and Luskin (1988) pointed out, not including all variables that affect turnout results in model misspecification. The explanation levels in the earlier articles seem high, but their procedures could actually account for too much, potentially explaining even more than 100 percent of the decline. Also, Cassel and Luskin emphasized that variables that increased turnout in that same period (such as increased education) must be included in the analysis. Without this, we would be in the same situation as if we were studying decreases in a person's bank balance without paying attention to deposits made during the same period.

Teixeira (1987), part of which is reprinted here as Chapter 3, provides a more complete analysis of the turnout decline, overcoming many of the Cassel-Luskin objections. Pooling all the NES election studies from 1960 to 1980 to determine the sources of the changes, he finds three demographic changes that worked to decrease turnout: a younger eligible electorate, fewer people married and living with their spouses, and a more mobile population. These factors account together for about three-eighths of the turnout decline. At the same time, he finds three other changes that account for the remaining five-eighths: a less partisan electorate (since stronger partisans are more likely to vote), fewer people being involved in the campaign through reading about it in the newspapers, and people feeling less effective in influencing government actions. This is one of the most complete modelling efforts to date, though even it can be challenged for having omitted some potentially relevant variables (such as union membership and religion).

Another fairly complete model is given in the Smith and Dolny (1989) pooled cross-section analysis over the 1956-1984 period. They find significant effects for political efficacy, strength of party identification, interest in politics, political knowledge, and following politics in newspapers along with the standard demographic predictors, but they do not succeed in accounting for the decline in turnout over the period. Miller (1992a) shows that the turnout decline is due to the post-New Deal generation, but his model is less fully specified than those of Teixeira and of Smith and Dolny.

As we are increasingly comfortable with using individual-level data in studying citizen politics, it is natural to look for individual-level determinants of the decline in turnout. The literature reviewed so far does not preclude such an effort, but neither does it suggest that this will be easy.

Turnout Due to Group and Systemic Factors

In addition to viewing turnout as due to individual factors, it can be viewed as affected by such other factors as social groups, political mobilization, and legal constraints. Indeed, these could be as important as the individual factors just considered, or even more important.

While most of the empirical turnout literature has focused on individual factors, there are several suggestions of group effects. For example, Verba and Nie (*Classics*, chap. 3) view communal participation as one mode of political participation. If working through groups is a mode of political participation, then groups can also be relevant to the turnout decision. Indeed, in a later portion of their work (Verba and Nie, 1972, chap. 10) they find that blacks participated in politics more than would have been expected on the basis of their socioeconomic characteristics. Verba and Nie explain this in terms of actions by the black community, citing as an example the role of black churches in stimulating turnout. It takes only a small step to move from that result to suggesting that social groups may be more generally relevant in turnout decisions.

Uhlaner (1989) takes this step. She argues that groups play a key role in making turnout rational. "Although the vote of a single individual has little influence on who wins, an increase of a few percentage points in some group's turnout may well change an election outcome" (p. 392). In her model, this potential provides group leaders with bargaining power that they can exert on behalf of their social group. Uhlaner analyzes this problem from the perspectives of the member, the leader, and the candidate and includes some data analysis in which turnout for union households was greater than for nonunion households, particularly in 1982 when the unions tried to send a message about Republican economics through the election. The impact of such group appeals is certainly difficult to prove empirically, but the argument of groups as a mediating factor that can spur turnout and make it more rational is very appealing on its face.

Morton (1991) has made a similar case for the importance of groups in rational turnout decisions, showing that the impact holds so long as candidates take different issue positions. She concludes that groups are not sufficient to explain turnout from a rational perspective, but "since some sort of mechanism to reduce the size of the electorate appears *necessary* to explain large positive voting using rational choice theory even when candidate positions are different and at present the inclusion of groups is the only such proposal offered, it appears that incorporating groups is a desirable approach to analyzing voting behavior" (p. 774).

Another aspect of participation involves the possibility of a political mobilization effect. The literature has spoken of political context and mobilization effects, as when party effort and/or exciting campaigns induce people to go to the polls, but these have been harder to measure and therefore to document. In a study of participation in state gubernatorial elections, Patterson and Caldeira (1983) include measures of whether the state is competitive between the major parties, measures of campaign spending, of closeness of the gubernatorial election, and of presence of a senate contest in the same election. Each of these political mobilization factors was highly significant in accounting for state turnout levels in 1978 and 1980, even after controlling for socioeconomic variables, the effects of registration laws, region, and year. Cox and Munger (1989) similarly show effects of closeness and expenditure on turnout in 1982 congressional elections.

The topic of political mobilization has been studied most for African-Americans. The early Verba and Nie work demonstrated a group mobilization effect over and above that which could be accounted for by individual factors. Several studies have attempted to update this work for the 1980s. Tate's (1991) analysis using National Black Election Study data of turnout of black Democrats in the 1984 and 1988 primary and general election found mixed effects. Jackson's candidacy increased turnout in the 1984 primaries, but not the 1988 ones. Opposition to the Reagan administration increased black turnout in the 1984 general election. Jackson supporters voted at lower rates in the 1988 general election. Race identification was not found to have a consistent effect, but church membership and involvement in black political organizations were found to provide resources promoting participation.

A related question is what happens when minorities actually obtain power. Bobo and Gilliam, in an article reprinted here as Chapter 4, look at the effects of black empowerment in U.S. cities. They use the 1987 National Opinion Research Center (NORC) General Social Survey, which included a large black oversample for a total of 544 black respondents. They find significant overall black-white participation differences in turnout and other modes of participation, but these differences disappear after controlling for socioeconomic and other demographic variables. However, blacks in areas with a black mayor ("high black empowerment areas") are more active than blacks in low-empowerment areas and whites of comparable socioeconomic status.

In their own update on these results, Nie, Verba, Brady, Schlozman, and Junn (1988) report that black educational levels increased from 1967 to 1987 more sharply than did black participation levels. In 1967 the relationship between education and participation was mild for blacks, much weaker than for whites. By 1987 the relationship was higher for blacks, comparable to that for whites. The difference was primarily due to lower educational levels: blacks without a high school education participated more than would have been predicted in 1967 while their participation level fell by 1987. Also, organizational membership decreased among blacks over this twenty-year period, as the fervor of the civil rights movement diminished. As a result of these several changes, by 1987 blacks gained less in participation from organizational affiliation than in 1967 while whites gained more. There were gains in black participation in the south; however, there were even larger gains in white participation in the south. Overall, they conclude that black "group-based mobilization has retreated in favor of individual activation rooted in educational attainment" (p. 28).

Systemic factors, such as registration laws and campaign spending, can also affect turnout rates. Analyzing the large-scale 1984 Census Bureau study, Leighley and Nagler (1990) find overall results similar to the analysis of the 1972 Census Bureau data by Wolfinger and Rosenstone (1980) in terms of the importance of education, though blacks were found more likely to vote in the 1984 data. They also test the effects of several systemic variables when the individual variables are kept in the analysis. The individual level predictors remain significant. Senate expenditures do stimulate turnout, but the closeness of presidential, gubernatorial, and senatorial elections are not significant in the predicted directions. Party competition and urbanization are also not significant.

Similarly, there is a focus on legal, party competition, and organizational factors affecting turnout in the comparative literature. Powell's work is an excellent example. In a study of turnout in thirty western democracies (Powell, 1980), he found that compulsory voting laws and state-run registration systems are legal factors that affect turnout differences between different nations. A competitive party system also affects turnout, as does a strong linkage between the parties and national cleavage groups (such as the cleavage between religious and other parties in the Netherlands).

Powell (1986), in an article reprinted here as Chapter 5, tries to account for the lower turnout in the United States than in other industrial democracies using both aggregate data and survey data. At the aggregate level, he focuses on such variables as nationally competitive election districts (whether the electoral system encourages parties to contest elections vigorously, even in districts where a contesting party is weak, which is not the case in the United States) and party-group linkages (the extent to which group affiliations are related to voters' party choice, which again is low in the United States). At the individual level, he examines attitudinal variables and demographic variables, such as age and education. Putting these several factors together, Powell is able to estimate that the advantages of the United States on individual attitudinal variables and especially education is more than compensated for by the disadvantages of the United States on competitiveness of electoral districts and especially group-party links, leading to a net 10 percent lower turnout.

In a paper focusing only on turnout in Western European nations, Lewis-Beck and Lockerbie (1989) put forward a model viewing turnout as a function of social structure (age, gender, social-economic status, and marital status), cognitive mobilization (education, sophistication, and information), politicization (partisan strength), and campaign issues (the issues of a particular election). Survey data in Britain, France, Germany, and Italy do not show that personal financial difficulties lead to greater election turnout. However, there are significant prospective economic effects in each country. Governments are rewarded when voters see good economic times ahead, while fear of bad economic times leads to unconventional participation, namely protest. This exact model has not been applied to the United States, but the possibility of differential effects of different economic conditions is worth exploring.

The focus on systemic variables is also echoed in the historical American literature, such as that reviewed in the discussion of the effects of voting law changes on turnout in the 1890s in *Classics* (chaps. 28-30). Turnout declines during that period were due to such factors as the imposition of registration requirements (partly because that made fraudulent turnout less likely) and the adoption in the south of poll taxes, literacy tests, and other discriminatory devices to disfranchise blacks (and, not coincidentally, poor whites). Burnham (*Classics*, chap. 29) also argues that the decline was due to the American party system being taken over by the elite, without the socialist party alternative that was provided in most European nations at that time.

Regardless of the many arguments on this side of the debate, it is interesting that none of the works reviewed in this section explicitly attempts to account for the turnout decline in the United States after 1960. There are attempts to measure the effects of group and systemic factors, but none connecting that with the turnout decline per se.

Conclusion

The late 1980s and early 1990s have been an era of democracy. Tumultuous political change has occurred throughout many regions of the world. Regimes have toppled. Latin American nations have moved from military rule to democracy. Eastern European nations have switched from communism to democracy. Yet in this era of worldwide democracy, it is ironic that fewer and fewer Americans find it worth their time or effort to participate in elections, even in those for president.

Ideally, our search for understanding the determinants of turnout will lead to an understanding of the turnout decline over the past three decades along with recommendations on how to increase voting rates. Unfortunately, we have not progressed very far in this direction. Clearly turnout in the United States should benefit from the present high level of education, but somehow that high level coexists with low turnout. Logically, the systemic factors reviewed in the second half of the chapter must account for much of this discrepancy. Registration laws in the United States combined with other features of the voting system (particularly the weak link between social groups and political parties) seem to be a major part of the explanation.

Moving from this understanding to reforms to increase voting participation is very difficult. Changes in voting rules inevitably affect the distribution of political power in a society. Each political party worries about the effects of voting reforms on its election totals. At present in the United States, the Democratic party has been most eager to pass laws to facilitate registration (most recently with the "motor voter" bill that would require states to allow people to register to vote as they file for drivers licenses), presumably because it feels that it would gain most from mobilizing the unregistered. Correspondingly, the Republican party has been unwilling to go along with this reform, fearing electoral fraud, desiring to maintain the quality of the electorate, and probably realizing they could lose from the resulting mobilization of the unregistered. The voting literature does not necessarily agree with the parties that higher voting rates would have a partisan effect (see especially Wolfinger and Rosenstone, 1980, and DeNardo, 1986, for the counter-argument), but the partisan disagreement certainly makes clear that higher turnout rates are not universally favored. What the implications of this are for the future of American democracy in this era of worldwide democracy remain to be seen.

NOTES

1. The Voting Rights Act of 1965 was intended to achieve equal rights for African-Americans; it was later extended to other minority groups. See, among others, Thernstrom (1987); Parker (1990); Grofman, Handley, and Niemi (1992).
2. The decrease in average age was due in part to changing demographics and in part to the adoption of the 26th Amendment (in 1971) that permitted 18-20 year olds to vote.

FURTHER READINGS

Explanations of Turnout Decline

Paul R. Abramson and John H. Aldrich, "The Decline of Electoral Participation in America," *American Political Science Review* (1982) 76:502-21. An accounting for the reasons underlying the turnout decline.

John H. Aldrich and Dennis M. Simon, "Turnout in American National Elections." In *Research in Micropolitics,* vol. 1, ed. Samuel Long (Greenwich, Conn.: JAI Press, 1986). Review of turnout literature.

Richard A. Brody, "The Puzzle of Participation." In *The New American Political System,* ed. Anthony King (Washington, D.C.: American Enterprise Institute, 1978). Turnout declined during a period of increasing education.

Carol Cassel and Robert Luskin, "Simple Explanations of Turnout Decline," *American Political Science Review* (1988) 82:1321-30. Methodological demonstration that previous explanations of the turnout decline are flawed.

Warren E. Miller, "The Puzzle Transformed: Explaining Declining Turnout," *Political Behavior* (1992) 14:1-43. Generational explanation of the turnout decline.

Voter Validation

Brian Silver, Barbara Anderson, and Paul Abramson, "Who Overreports Voting?" *American Political Science Review* (1986) 80:613-24. Develops new calculation system for determining sources of vote misreporting.

Groups and Voter Turnout

Katherine Tate, "Black Political Participation in the 1984 and 1988 Presidential Elections," *American Political Science Review* (1991) 85:1159-76. Black participation was stimulated by support of Jesse Jackson and by church membership and involvement in black political organizations.

Carole J. Uhlaner, "Rational Turnout: The Neglected Role of Groups," *American Journal of Political Science* (1989) 33:390-422. Turnout is rational because of the mediating role of groups.

Factors Affecting Turnout

Stephen Bennett and David Resnick, "The Implications of Nonvoting for Democracy in the United States," *American Journal of Political Science* (1990) 34:771-802. Analyzes the extent to which voters and nonvoters differ on policy matters.

Jan E. Leighley, "Social Interaction and Contextual Influences on Political Participation," *American Politics Quarterly* (1990) 18:459-75. Effects of personal discussion networks on turnout.

Jesse Marquette and Katherine Hinckley, "Voter Turnout and Candidate Choice," *Political Behavior* (1988) 10:52-76. Turnout and vote should be modelled as a single choice decision rather than as two separate decisions.

Samuel C. Patterson and Gregory A. Caldeira, "Getting Out the Vote: Participation in Gubernatorial Elections," *American Political Science Review* (1983) 77:675-89. Mobilizing factors of campaign activism and competitiveness explain more turnout variations than do socioeconomic characteristics.

Peverill Squire, Raymond E. Wolfinger, and David P. Glass, "Residential Mobility and Voter Turnout," *American Political Science Review* (1987) 81:45-65. Mobility diminishes turnout.

A. Wuffle, "Should You Brush Your Teeth on November 6, 1984? A Rational Choice Perspective," *P.S.* (1984) 17:577-81. Turnout decisions should be seen as a matter of habit.

Cross-National Studies of Turnout

Robert Jackman, "Political Institutions and Vote Turnout in the Industrial Democracies," *American Political Science Review* (1987) 81:405-23. Complements the Powell chapter in this volume with an analysis of turnout differences outside of the United States.

Michael S. Lewis-Beck and Brad Lockerbie, "Economics, Votes, Protests: Western European Cases," *Comparative Political Studies* (1989) 22:155-77. Effects of the economy on voting and unconventional participation.

3. THE POLITICS OF TURNOUT DECLINE

Ruy A. Teixeira

The results of the previous chapter [of Teixeira's book] showed that turnout decline in the 1960-1980 period could not be substantially attributed to social structural change. This chapter looks at the other set of factors possibly relevant to decreased turnout: those tapping the connections of individuals to the political system—what I have called sociopolitical characteristics. The three characteristics to be examined are partisanship, political efficacy, and campaign newspaper reading. Analyzing their relationship to turnout decline will test the possibility that the key change lay in the disconnection of individuals from politics—the erosion of certain attitudinal/behavioral commitments to the political system—which made elections less meaningful for Americans.

Social Structure, Sociopolitical Characteristics, and Turnout

Table 3-1 shows the results when the three sociopolitical variables are successively added to the full social structure turnout model. As can be seen from the difference in the scaled deviance row of the table, each of these variables substantially improves the goodness of fit of the model. This indicates that all three sociopolitical characteristics have effects on turnout that are independent of those traceable to an individual's demographic position.

The second column displays the coefficients of variables after the first characteristic, partisanship, is added to the model. There are several things worth noting about these results:

(a) A number of the parameter estimates are essentially unaffected by the presence of partisanship, including, interestingly enough, those for the education variable. This indicates that previous estimates for these variables were not capturing, through intercorrelation, any of the effect on turnout actually attributable to partisanship.

Source: Ruy A. Teixeira, *Why Americans Don't Vote: Turnout Decline in the United States 1960-1984,* New York: Greenwood Press, 1987.

Table 3-1   Social Structure, Sociopolitical Characteristics, and Turnout: Coefficients of Variables in Multivariate Models

	All Social Structure	+ Partisan-ship	+ Efficacy	+ Newspaper Reading
Education [a]				
12 years	.496*	.521*	.457*	.396*
13-15 years	.779*	.781*	.672*	.566*
16 or more	.961*	.965*	.836*	.690*
Age				
25-28 years	.097	.074	.093	.065
29-32	.294*	.259*	.271*	.214*
33-36	.444*	.387*	.380*	.316*
37 or more	.712*	.615*	.634*	.535*
Marital Status				
Married-SP [b]	.280*	.284*	.259*	.229*
Residential Mobility				
Not mobile [c]	.417*	.413*	.421*	.422*
Occupation				
Blue collar [d]	.064	.071	.062	.058
White collar and other	.240*	.233*	.233*	.220*
Family Income				
Nonpoor [e]	.165*	.194*	.157*	.141*
Sex				
Male	.092*	.094*	.095*	.060*
Race				
White	.108*	.180*	.160*	.107*
Region				
Non-south	.319*	.315*	.296*	.296*
Partisanship				
Interval scale [f]		.454*	.419*	.383*
Political Efficacy				
Interval scale [f]			.291*	.254*
Newspaper Reading				
Some articles				.321*
Many articles				.577*
Intercept	−1.29*	−1.81*	−1.98*	−1.98*
Scaled deviance (SD)	9283	8933	8695	8484
Degrees of freedom (DF)	8273	8272	8271	8269
Difference in SD [g]		350**	238**	211**
Difference in DF [g]		1	1	2

(notes follow)

Table 3-1 *(continued)*

Note: Unweighted $N = 8,289$.

[a] 0-8 and 9-11 years of education have been combined, since no significant difference was found between these categories when the sociopolitical variables were controlled for.

[b] SP = spouse present.

[c] Mobile is defined as within two years.

[d] Blue collar includes service workers.

[e] Poor is defined as less than $5,000 in 1960 dollars.

[f] These scales are both 0,1,2 scales.

[g] Differences are between the current model and the one immediately previous. The SD difference is distributed approximately as chi-square with degrees of freedom equal to the DF difference between the models (number of extra parameters fitted in the current model).

* coefficient is at least twice its standard error.

** chi-square is significant at .05 level.

(b) Partisanship was evidently exerting a suppressor effect on income and race, since these estimates go up when the former variable is added to the model. This means that nonwhites and poor people tend to be more highly partisan than whites and the nonpoor, respectively.

(c) The estimates for the age coefficients go down significantly when partisanship is added to the model. This indicates that older people tend to be more partisan, so previous estimates of age's effect had captured some of the effect on turnout properly attributable to partisanship.

The third column presents a model in which political efficacy is added to the model just described. The estimates most affected by this addition are those for the education variable. They are substantially attenuated, indicating a strong correlation between efficacy and education (i.e., the higher educational levels have higher levels of political efficacy). Most other estimates are moderately attenuated, although some, like mobility, occupation, and sex, are essentially unchanged. In addition, there appears to have been a weak suppressor relationship between age and efficacy, with the estimates for most age groups becoming somewhat higher with efficacy in the equation. This indicates that the youngest age group tends to be slightly more efficacious than these other groups.

The final column adds the newspaper reading variable to the model. The resultant estimates for partisanship and efficacy are modestly attenuated, indicating some positive correlation between these characteristics and newspaper reading. In addition, as one might expect, the education estimates drop sharply, with the drop being greater the higher the educational level. This means that as education increases, the amount of campaign newspaper reading does as well. The age estimates display the same pattern, showing that growing older also increases the extent to which campaigns are followed in the papers.

The largest decreases for other estimates are for the sex and race variables. The coefficient for sex actually declines to the point where it is, by usual t test criteria, statistically insignificant. Other estimates are slightly attenuated or, like mobility and region, essentially unchanged.

In conclusion, the addition of the three sociopolitical characteristics to the turnout model decreases the scaled deviance by almost 800, while fitting only four parameters. This is a large increase in goodness of fit, considering the small number of degrees of freedom used up. These characteristics may therefore be assumed to be important determinants of an individual's likelihood of voting.

Social Structure, Sociopolitical Characteristics, and Turnout Decline

This section follows the same procedure used in the previous chapter [of Teixeira] for examining the relationship between turnout decline and variables newly introduced into the model. Variables will be added to a model that initially includes all characteristics examined previously (in this case, the nine social structural attributes), plus the five dummy variables representing time period. These dummies will then be examined, both for the pattern and magnitude of changes, so that the role of sociopolitical characteristics in turnout decline can be assessed. If the coefficients of the time dummies are attenuated to the point where they are statistically insignificant, this would indicate that, with the addition of these characteristics, adjusted turnout decline has largely been accounted for.

Table 3-2 displays the time dummy estimates for a series of turnout models that include these dummies. The first column shows the model with time only. These estimates model the decline in turnout as it was reported in the data. The second column reports the coefficients for a model including all demographic variables. As discussed in the previous chapter, the estimates here represent the net amount of turnout decline that remains unexplained, once the upward push from socioeconomic upgrading is balanced against the downward pressure from other sources of social structural change.

The third column shows the time coefficients when the partisanship variable is added to the equation. Except in the case of 1964, these coefficients are markedly smaller than they were in the previous model. This indicates that distributional change on this variable can explain some of the adjusted turnout decline not accounted for by demographic change. It is still true, however, that the estimated effect of time is higher than in the initial model that included no individual attributes. Thus the puzzle is far from solved by the addition of the partisanship variable.

The next column reports the results when political efficacy is added to the model. These results are striking. The addition of this single variable drastically reduces the time estimates, especially from 1968 on. None of the estimates are above .2 and only two are above .1 (and one of these two is just barely above that level). This contrasts with the previous model, in which three and four estimates, respectively, were above these levels. The seriousness of these changes is underscored by the fact that only the 1980 coefficient remains statistically significant by t test criteria. In addition, removing time from the model increases the scaled deviance by only 7—an insignificant amount—indicating that time has lost most of its ability to predict the likelihood of turnout. It is fair to conclude, therefore, that (a) the decline in political efficacy can be held responsible for a substantial portion of adjusted turnout decline during the

Table 3-2   Social Structure, Sociopolitical Characteristics, and Turnout Decline: Coefficients of Time Dummies in Different Models

Year	Time Only	Time, All Demographic +	Partisan- ship +	Efficacy +	Newspaper Reading +	Interactive Model
1964	−.052	−.057	−.086	−.039	−.040	−.020
1968	−.113*	−.217*	−.196*	−.074	−.061	—
1972	−.196*	−.267*	−.218*	−.104	.004	.283*
1976	−.249*	−.300*	−.240*	−.084	−.032	.283*
1980	−.255*	−.338*	−.296*	−.140*	−.047	—
Intercept	.816*	−1.06*	−1.59*	−1.88*	−1.96*	−2.12*
SD	10660	9216	8893	8688	8482	8409
DF	8283	8268	8267	8266	8264	8261
SD difference [a]		1444**	323**	205**	206**	b
DF difference [a]		15	1	1	2	b
SD minus time [c]		70**	40**	7	2	—

Note: SD = scaled deviance; DF = degrees of freedom. Unweighted N = 8,289; 1960 is reference category for time variable.

[a] Differences are between the current model and the one immediately previous. The SD difference is distributed approximately as chi-square with degrees of freedom equal to the DF difference between the models (number of extra parameters fitted in the current model).
[b] Previous model is not hierarchically nested within current model.
[c] This quantity is the difference in scaled deviance when time is removed from a given model. It is a chi-square statistic with five degrees of freedom.

* coefficient is at least twice its standard error
** chi-square is significant at .05 level

1960-1980 time period, and (b) adjusted turnout decline itself is close to being accounted for.

The fifth column shows the time dummy estimates when the last sociopolitical characteristic, campaign newspaper reading, is added to the model. These results are also quite striking. The estimates after 1968 all decline by a factor of .1 or more, and all of the time estimates are now considerably under the .1 level.[1] The 1980 coefficient, in particular, is under .05 and no longer has a statistically significant t test. It is thus evident that the decline in campaign newspaper reading is also an important factor in explaining declining turnout.

In addition, the increase in scaled deviance produced by removing time from the model is now only two. This indicates that at this point in the modeling process, the explanatory power of time is small indeed. Thus the effect originally estimated for time, which reflected the differences in turnout levels across elections, has now been absorbed by other variables in the model.

These results therefore suggest that the three sociopolitical characteristics just introduced into the model can explain most of adjusted turnout decline not attributable to demographic factors. This means that even with the turnout-promoting effect of socioeconomic status (SES) upgrading taken into consideration, a combination of social structural and sociopolitical change can largely account for the fall in participation over the two decades in question (an estimate of the extent of this accounting will be offered shortly). . . .

[An interactive model was also estimated, to see if interaction effects were of importance in explaining turnout decline. Although some significant interaction effects were found, these effects, as well as the new estimates for the time parameters, were found to be basically uninterpretable, and thus not useful for analyzing decreased participation.]

Decomposing Turnout Decline

It is now appropriate to answer two questions: (1) What is the nature of the story being told by the best model available? According to the model, which factors are responsible for how much of the fall in turnout? (2) How well does the model explain the decline in turnout over the period in question? What proportion of this decline can the variables in the model account for?

These questions will be answered using the additive model. This is the model that includes all the variables discussed so far: nine social structural and the three sociopolitical ones introduced in this chapter. The model will not include the time dummies, since they represent unexplained variation in turnout levels, and hence are not relevant to either of the two questions.

The decline in turnout covered will be that for the entire period. This entails looking at the turnout differential between the two years that form the end points of the period: 1960 and 1980. Although other differentials could be examined, this is the most important one and will be looked at first, as has been the practice in the rest of the turnout decline literature (Abramson and Aldrich, Cassel and Hill, Shaffer, etc.). I emphasize, however, that this is not the last step in partitioning turnout decline—as has also been the practice in the literature, unfortunately. There are other parts of the story that cannot be told simply by looking at the 1960-1980 differential, and they will not be neglected in this analysis.

The decomposition of the turnout differential between 1960 and 1980 was accomplished by first substituting the 1960 means of the independent variables into the model (coefficients displayed in the last column of Table 3-1), then the 1980 means, and then subtracting the first set of terms from the second. This produces the three equations shown below.

$$\overline{y}_{60} = a + \Sigma b_i (\overline{x}_{60})_i \qquad (1)$$
$$\overline{y}_{80} = a + \Sigma b_i (\overline{x}_{80})_i \qquad (2)$$
$$\overline{y}_{60} - \overline{y}_{80} = \Sigma b_i ((\overline{x}_{60})_i - (\overline{x}_{80})_i) \qquad (3)$$

The left side of equation (3) represents the difference in predicted probit between 1960 and 1980. The right side parcels out this difference by variables entered in the model. For each variable there is a term that multiplies the coefficient for that variable by the difference in means for the variable between 1960 and 1980. This represents the contribution of that particular characteristic, or category of a characteristic, to the overall difference in predicted probit, and thus to the 1960-1980 turnout differential predicted by the model.

Finally, the overall probits generated for 1960 and 1980—left side of equations (1) and (2)—can be translated into percentages to get the predicted turnout levels for the two elections. The difference between the 1960 and 1980 figures represents the percentage of decline in turnout predicted by the model. This can then be compared with the decline observed in the data to see what proportion of this decline is accounted for by the model.

The results of this sequence of steps are shown in Table 3-3. The first two columns of the table display the predicted probit decline and the percentage of overall predicted probit decline attributable to a given characteristic, or set of characteristics. These characteristics are divided into three groups: SES characteristics, non-SES demographic characteristics, and sociopolitical characteristics. Each of these groups is worth commenting on separately.

The first group, SES characteristics, consists of education and a category combining occupation and income. All quantities are negatively signed, indicating that these characteristics made negative contributions to turnout decline (i.e., actually served to promote, rather than depress, turnout levels). Education is far and away the crucial factor here, its influence being more than three times as great as occupation and income put together. This is as would be expected, given the superior strength of education as a predictor of turnout and the larger amount of distributional change on this variable over the time period.

Together, the SES characteristics increased the predicted probit by .166, 65.7 percent, in magnitude, of the total probit drop. Translated into percentage terms, this means that, had all other factors remained constant, SES-upgrading would have increased turnout by 3.9 percent. This is nearly half of the turnout decline reported in the data (8 percent), making these countervailing forces substantial ones indeed.

The second group of characteristics includes all demographic characteristics except the socioeconomic ones just mentioned. The three characteristics that make substantial contributions are listed separately—marital status, residential mobility, and age—while the three that make minor contributions are combined into a single category (race, region, sex). Age, according to the model, plays the strongest role in turnout decline, accounting for more than a quarter of the drop in predicted probit. Marital status and mobility account for, respectively, about 18 percent and 13 percent each. Finally, race, region, and sex, as a group, explain less than 6 percent of the drop.[2]

All the non-SES demographic characteristics together decreased the predicted probit by .158, or about 63 percent of the drop predicted by the model. Thus distributional change on these variables made a strong contribution to declining participation. Interestingly, this contribution to turnout decline from non-SES social structural sources is just about equal in magnitude to the upward push or turnout from the SES sources.

The final group of characteristics consists of the three sociopolitical variables introduced in this chapter: partisanship, political efficacy, and campaign newspaper reading. Partisanship plays the weakest role of the three in turnout decline, accounting for about 18 percent of the predicted probit drop. Efficacy and newspaper reading, on the other hand, play strong and roughly equal roles in

Table 3-3   Explaining the Turnout Differential Between 1960 and 1980

Variable	Predicted Decline	Percent of Predicted Decline	Percent of SES-Adjusted Decline
Socioeconomic characteristics			
Education	−.127	−50.3	—
Occupation, income	−.039	−15.4	—
All SES	−.166	−65.7	—
Non-SES demographic characteristics			
Age	.066	26.2	15.8
Marital status	.045	17.8	10.7
Residential mobility	.033	13.0	7.9
Race, region, sex	.014	5.5	3.3
All non-SES demographic	.158	62.5	37.7
Sociopolitical characteristics			
Partisanship	.046	18.2	11.0
Newspaper reading	.104	41.1	24.8
Political efficacy	.111	43.9	26.5
All sociopolitical	.261	103.2	62.3
Total probit drop	.253	100.0	100.0

Note: Percentage point decline in turnout predicted by model: 7.0; percentage point decline in turnout reported in ANES survey: 8.0; percent of turnout differential explained by model: 87.5.

turnout decline—about 44 percent and 41 percent of total probit drop, respectively. Together, the three variables account for over 100 percent of the decline predicted by the model.

These results are rearranged in the next column. This rearrangement uses the concept of SES-adjusted turnout developed earlier. To reflect the fact that SES upgrading served to promote turnout, and thus made the amount of turnout decline to be explained larger than that observed in the data, the predicted probit increase from these characteristics (.166) is added to the overall probit drop (.253) to produce the amount of probit decline actually explained by the other, non-SES variables in the model (.453). The probit drop from individual characteristics, or sets of characteristics, is then divided by .453 to find the proportion of adjusted decline accounted for by these variables. These proportions are what is shown in column three.

These figures make the findings from the decomposition somewhat more intelligible. Here the positive contributions to turnout decline add up to 100 percent, rather than well over 100 percent, as in the previous column. As can be seen from the table, these contributions now break down into 62 percent from sociopolitical sources and 38 percent from non-SES demographic sources. This is roughly a 5:3 ratio.

These results cast some interesting light on previous research into this topic. Abramson and Aldrich, for instance, attributed about two-thirds of the 1960-1980 turnout differential to the combined effects of partisanship and efficacy. Looking at the decomposition of nonadjusted, or net, turnout decline in Table 3-3 (column two), these two variables account for about 62 percent of decline—a comparable figure. However, these two characteristics, considered in the context of the *adjusted* fall in turnout, only explain 37.5 percent of the drop, a less impressive figure. This illustrates how an overly simple model can appear to come close to solving the puzzle, but only does so at the price of serious incompleteness. Once the incompleteness is rectified, as above, it becomes clear that what seemed fairly close to a solution was actually rather far away.

In contrast to previous research, then, the model developed here presents a solution that (a) despite taking into account the true extent of the puzzle, by controlling for socioeconomic upgrading, (b) still does an equally good, or even better, job of solving it. Within the context created by this SES-upgrading, it becomes apparent that factors such as age, newspaper reading, marital status, and mobility must be considered *in addition to* partisanship and efficacy if the fall in turnout is to be adequately explained. Looked at in this way, each of the variables becomes a piece of the puzzle's solution, all of which must be put together to form a complete solution. Two or three pieces cannot stand alone. This is the essence of the story being directly told by the model.

Thus far the discussion has been focused on answering the first question asked about the decomposition: how does it allot responsibility among the different factors influencing turnout decline? But this accounting procedure is essentially internal to the model. It is now appropriate to answer the second question: what proportion of observed turnout decline can be explained by the variables in the model? This measures the model against the crucial external standard by which its usefulness can be judged.

These results are summarized at the bottom of Table 3-3. The fall in turnout predicted by the model is 7 percent, whereas the decline observed in the data is 8 percent. This means that the model accounts for about 88 percent of turnout decline, even with SES-upgrading controlled for. This compares favorably with figures reported by other researchers (Shaffer, 1981; Abramson and Aldrich, 1982), despite the "advantages" these analysts had by not controlling for upgrading. Thus not only is the model thorough in the range of factors considered, but its predictions are able to explain almost all of the observed decline in turnout as well.

Additional Interpretation

The results presented in Table 3-3 may be further interpreted in the following way. There were really three processes of change taking place between 1960 and 1980, which correspond to the three divisions within the table. First, there was socioeconomic upgrading, which made America, in the popular view, more of a "middle-class" society. This apparently facilitated access to the electoral arena, just as would be expected from the standard literature on turnout. But this was not the only change taking place. While the electorate was becoming more "middle-class," it was also becoming younger, more mobile, and more likely to be single. This decline in the social "rootedness" of the electorate made it harder, in the aggregate, for Americans to handle the voting process. The impact of the two processes of change, as can be seen in column two of Table 3-3, was similar in magnitude, so they roughly canceled each other out. Voting, therefore, became neither significantly easier nor significantly harder as a result of social structural change over the two decades.

The final set of changes involved the links of Americans to their political system. A process of disconnection took place that weakened the individual-level commitments of citizens to the political system and political action. This disconnection made elections less meaningful for voters, thereby weakening their motivation to vote. Unlike the other two processes of change, however, there was nothing to counterbalance the effects of this process. The resultant, therefore, of the three types of changes was the depression in turnout levels over the twenty-year time period.

The imagery of core and periphery provides a helpful way of reformulating this point. If there is both a demographic and a political core of the population, relative to the electoral system, then it may be said that one of these cores—the demographic one—remained about the same between 1960 and 1980. The political core, on the other hand, shrank, owing to the process of disconnection just mentioned. Thus, although the demographic core was stable, the political periphery expanded. This political peripheralization may be viewed as the driving force behind the decline of turnout in the United States.

Conclusion

This section began by examining the role of sociopolitical characteristics in turnout decline. It was found that the addition of three variables, partisanship, political efficacy, and campaign newspaper reading, to the social structural model developed previously allowed for the successful elimination of significant effects attributable to time (i.e., effects on turnout levels not traceable to variables included in the analysis). This meant that within the framework of the model, adjusted turnout decline had substantially been accounted for.

. . . The additive model, which included the nine social structural and three sociopolitical variables, was used as a basis for decomposing predicted turnout decline and comparing predicted to observed decline.

This decomposition, based on the 1960-1980 turnout differential, revealed that the upward pressure on voting levels from SES—primarily educational—upgrading was strong, amounting to about two-thirds of total probit decline predicted by the model. This meant that because (a) families had more real income, (b) occupational shifts lowered the proportions of housewives and blue-collar workers, (c) educational attainment went up dramatically, turnout—had nothing else changed save the distribution of the population into socioeconomic categories—would have gone up substantially instead of decreasing.

Taking this fact into consideration, it was found that six changes in American society were largely responsible for the difference in turnout levels between the 1960 and 1980 elections. The first three had to do with the decline in the extent to which the electorate was socially rooted: (1) the voting pool in 1980 was younger than in 1960; (2) the proportion of the population living "tradition-ally"—that is, married and living with their spouses—was much smaller in 1980 than in 1960; and (3) citizens were more mobile in 1980 than in 1960. Together, these changes accounted for about 38 percent, or three-eighths, of the turnout differential between these two years.

The other three societal changes tapped ways through which individuals were linked to the political system and political action: (1) through party identification—voters were less partisan in 1980 than at the beginning of the period; (2) through campaign involvement—a far smaller proportion of the elec-torate in 1980 followed the campaign in the newspapers than did in 1960; and (3) through a belief in the effectiveness of political action—people felt less efficacious, or powerful, relative to governmental actions and public officials in 1980 than in the earlier years. Together, the erosion of these political ties accounted for about 62 percent, or five-eighths, of the difference in turnout levels between 1960 and 1980. . . .

The Changing American Nonvoter, 1960–1980

The key findings presented thus far have been the following. First, there was a cluster of results concerning the influence of demographic change on turnout levels. It was determined that increased educational attainment—as well as an upgrading of the income and occupation distributions—acted to push turnout upward. (Americans became more "middle class.") But, at the same time, the proportions of the electorate that were young, residentially mobile, and single increased, acting to depress turnout levels. (Americans became less socially "rooted.") The effects of these two sets of changes were of the same magnitude, so the net impact of demographic change on turnout was negligible.

It was therefore determined that the crucial factors in reducing turnout levels lay in the political realm. Three factors were identified as being of salience: (1) decline in citizens' perception of their ability to influence government actions (decreased political efficacy); (2) decline in campaign involvement (decreased campaign newspaper reading); and (3) decline in partisanship (decreased party identification). These three trends were identified as part of a process of political disconnection or "peripheralization" that reduced the meaningfulness of electoral participation to Americans.

These two sets of changes involved in turnout decline—social structural and sociopolitical—each have substantive implications.

Implications of Structural Change

It has long been a popular view that the pool of American nonvoters is concentrated among the lowest socioeconomic segments of society. Burnham (1982) says "the 'party of non-voters' is concentrated among the poorest and most dependent social classes." He goes on to attribute the growth of this party to the failure of the system to meet the needs of the socioeconomically deprived, who join this party in ever larger numbers. Beliefs along these lines underpin most of the more extravagant claims for the political potential of mobilizing nonvoters.

Because these potential voters are increasingly from the "lower class," and therefore, presumably, left of center, their mobilization would decisively change the complexion of American politics (Rogers, 1984).

There are two problems with this view. First, because the sets of changes relevant to turnout levels include (a) socioeconomic upgrading, (b) other demographic changes not necessarily heavily grouped on socioeconomic categories (increased proportions young, mobile, single), and (c) political changes that made their impact felt across the population, there is no compelling reason to believe that the pool of nonvoters has become increasingly skewed toward the lowest socioeconomic categories. And, in fact, this does not appear to be the case (see Table 3-4). An elementary measure of disproportionality, for instance (ratio of proportion of nonvoting population in a given category to proportion of overall population in that category), for 1960 and 1980, reveals relatively little change over time (1.48 to 1.52 for high school dropouts; 1.39 to 1.26 for poor people).

What did happen between 1960 and 1980, as a result of the trends detailed in this investigation, was a decrease in the extent to which nonvoters were concentrated—in an absolute sense—in the lowest socioeconomic categories. This is because there are proportionally fewer people in these categories—thus fewer nonvoters for socioeconomic reasons—*and* more people moving into the nonvoting pool for non-socioeconomic reasons. The net result of these two trends was a substantial shift in the profile of the American nonvoter.

The data in Table 3-4 illustrate this shift. While in 1960, 72 percent of nonvoters had less than a high school education, by 1980 this figure had dropped to only 39 percent. Similarly, in 1960, 60 percent of nonvoters were poor, whereas only 44 percent were in 1980. On the other side of the coin, about 7 percent of nonvoters were under age twenty-five in 1960, whereas 25 percent were in 1980. Or, 37 percent and 26 percent were mobile and single, respectively, in 1960, but by 1980 each of these categories captured half of the nonvoting population.

Thus, although in 1960 it might have been quite reasonable to describe the American nonvoter as a poor high school dropout, this description is no longer so compelling in 1980. The pool of nonvoters is much more dispersed among socioeconomic categories, and other categories as well. Nonvoters, then, cannot be easily typecast as residing on the absolute lowest rungs of the social structure.

Nor, as mentioned earlier, has their relative representation among the lowest socioeconomic categories changed much. But it is still the case that there *are* skews, socioeconomic and otherwise, in the distribution of nonvoters. That is, nonvoters are not a faithful demographic representation of the general population, but are disproportionally concentrated in certain categories. From this viewpoint, it could be argued that, despite the failure of the nonvoting population to display an overwhelmingly depressed socioeconomic profile, these skews are strong enough to make a general mobilization of nonvoters politically dramatic (if no more dramatic than it might have been twenty years ago).

This is where the second problem comes in. Skews in partisan bias and political views by demographic category are not strong enough to make such a scenario plausible. Wolfinger and Rosenstone (1980, pp. 80-88), estimate, for instance, that a general increase of 9 percent in the turnout rate would only

Table 3-4 Comparing the American Nonvoter, 1960 and 1980: Proportions of Voters and Nonvoters in Selected Population Categories

	1960			1980		
	All	*Voters*	*Non-Voters*	*All*	*Voters*	*Non-Voters*
Education						
0-12 years	.486	.424	.724	.257	.204	.390
12	.290	.322	.171	.354	.346	.375
13-15	.120	.132	.070	.211	.224	.179
16 or more	.104	.123	.035	.177	.225	.057
Age						
18-24 years	.033	.023	.068	.145	.104	.246
25-28	.086	.074	.130	.103	.086	.146
29-32	.085	.076	.119	.088	.085	.094
33-36	.103	.111	.070	.088	.089	.087
37 or more	.694	.715	.612	.576	.636	.427
Marital status						
Not married-SP [a]	.198	.183	.255	.394	.353	.496
Married-SP	.817	.802	.745	.606	.647	.504
Residential mobility						
Mobile within two years	.254	.225	.366	.332	.264	.501
Not mobile	.746	.775	.634	.668	.736	.499
Occupation						
Housewives	.249	.218	.369	.160	.152	.179
Blue collar [b]	.284	.280	.298	.237	.202	.323
White collar and other	.467	.502	.333	.603	.646	.499
Family income						
Poor [c]	.434	.390	.604	.347	.311	.437
Nonpoor	.566	.610	.396	.653	.689	.563
Partisanship						
Independent, apolitical	.126	.092	.255	.147	.100	.263
Weak partisan, leaner	.512	.519	.482	.589	.585	.600
Strong partisan	.363	.389	.263	.264	.315	.136
Political efficacy						
Low efficacy	.153	.103	.344	.319	.257	.471
Middle efficacy	.235	.221	.287	.340	.340	.340
High efficacy	.612	.676	.369	.341	.402	.189
Campaign newspaper reading						
No articles	.198	.135	.436	.290	.208	.491
Some articles	.249	.238	.293	.447	.471	.387
Many articles	.553	.627	.271	.263	.320	.122

[a] SP = spouse present.
[b] Blue collar includes service workers.
[c] Poor is defined as less than $5,000 in 1960 dollars.

produce a .3 percent increase in Democratic sympathies. This finding does not reflect the fact that there are no demographic skews, or no partisan skews by demography, but rather that the combined impact of these skews is not large enough to make a big difference when the number of voters is simply increased at random by drawing from the nonvoting population.

Thus the view that the contemporary pool of nonvoters is increasingly huddled at the bottom of the social structure, ready to transform the nature of American politics in a predetermined direction, is shown to be of questionable plausibility. Instead, nonvoters are spread across demographic and partisan categories, and their political impact could therefore vary widely, depending on which *parts* of that population are mobilized into the electoral arena. In implicit recognition of these facts, (a) tendencies across the political spectrum are seeking to reach nonvoters through voter registration and other efforts—these potential voters are no longer seen as naturally belonging to the Democrats or the left (Perlez, 1984); and (b) where these efforts are being pursued, they are of a *targeted* nature, seeking to reach subpopulations of nonvoters whose probability of voting "right" is greater—and, it is hoped, overwhelmingly greater (i.e., Democratic registration of blacks)—than the overall pool of abstentionists.

To put a finer point on it, when the advantages of higher turnout are alluded to, in partisan terms, it should always be kept in mind that such advantages are mostly dependent on which *part* of the nonvoting pool is under consideration. It makes perfect sense to contend, for instance, that higher mobilization of a population group that votes 60 percent Democratic will benefit the Democrats. It makes less sense to insist that high turnout per se will automatically benefit the Democrats, or that high turnout is necessarily the "key" to any given election. After all, to mobilize more of a population group that votes 60 percent Democratic presupposes that one *has* a population group that votes 60 percent Democratic. As recent history attests (witness the decline in union member support for the Democrats), these groups can be hard to come by. The turnout "key" thus becomes inseparably linked with the general political problem of reaching the groups most likely to be one's supporters among the electorate.

Implications of Political Change

The implications of the political changes relevant to turnout decline—the generalized disconnection from the political world—may be better understood by recalling an observation made earlier about comparative differences in turnout rates. These differences, where the U.S. turnout rate is generally far lower than that of other industrialized democracies, have been attributed to the facts that (a) registration is state sponsored in these other countries, thereby making it considerably easier for the individual citizen to qualify to vote; and (b) political parties in these nations play a much stronger role in commanding voter loyalty and mobilizing citizens to go to the polls.

These comparative differences may be summed up by saying that voting is, to a large extent, a collective responsibility in other democracies. The state and the political parties actively attempt to engage citizens in the electoral process, thereby taking a considerable amount of the burden of voting off the shoulders of the individual. In contrast, in the United States, the state plays almost no role, and the parties, comparatively little, in mobilizing the voter into the electoral arena. It is the individual responsibility of the voter to register, find out enough to differentiate between candidates, make a decision, and act to ratify that decision by casting his or her ballot.

This observation may be related to the research findings in the following manner. Let us recall that the two political factors most important in explaining turnout decline were the decreases in political efficacy and campaign newspaper reading. One is an attitude and the other is an activity, but they both tap important ways that individuals interface with an election campaign. The first, political efficacy, expresses the extent to which an individual feels that his or her individual actions have any effect on government actions. The second, campaign newspaper reading, measures the extent of an individual's campaign involvement through the medium of the papers.

Thus two critical ways in which individuals linked themselves to the voting process changed. On the one hand, far fewer people felt that their political actions—of which voting is the most common example—were effective in influencing the government. Thus this crucial individual motivation to vote was undermined. On the other hand, people ceased taking the trouble to follow the campaign in the papers because of some combination of changing media environment and general political withdrawal. This made the individual voter, whose responsibility it was to be informed about and involved in the campaign, less informed and involved, and thus less inclined to vote.

In a sense, voters were "dropping out" of politics at the individual level, both attitudinally and behaviorally. Their commitments, such as they were, to the political system were eroding. In a society like the United States, where voting is heavily dependent on individual responsibility and motivation, this naturally produced a decline in the voting rate. No collectives stood willing (or perhaps even able) to pick up this slack in the electoral system and ensure turnout at the polls. Thus not only is the United States a society in which the turnout rate is traditionally low because of the lack of collectivities that organize the act of voting for citizens, but it is also a society whose *decline* in turnout rates is bound up with the system of individual responsibility for voting.

In one sense, this story may be looked at as good news. It does not appear that the decline in turnout is linked to some form of radical revulsion with democracy or contemporary society, but rather to the erosion of this individually focused system of voter participation. It was perhaps inevitable that this system should weaken under the press of historical events (as the findings in this investigation suggest that it has). But it hardly implies that this weakening could or will evolve to the point of political collapse.

In another sense, the story, if it does not qualify as bad news, certainly poses a thorny problem. How can the problem of low voter turnout be dealt with in the context of an individual system of electoral participation (not well designed for high voter turnout in the first place) that has been seriously weakened by social and political developments?

There are two possible ways this problem could be dealt with. The first way would be through revamping the individual system of voting responsibility, so that it works more like it did in the 1950s than in the 1970s. This could be done by somehow recreating the "system of the 1950s" (described in chapter 1 [of Teixeira]) or by introducing a new individually oriented system of electoral participation that, although structured differently from the system of the 1950s, works as well in promoting turnout.

The second way the voter turnout problem could be addressed would be by replacing the individual system of voting responsibility with a collectively oriented one, such as most European countries have. This would entail a much more active role for the state and political parties in the United States in registering voters and mobilizing them to go to the polls.

Movement in the first direction seems more likely. However, even if there are changes that favor the individual system of electoral participation, there is the possibility that these changes might not really work. The individually oriented participation system is basically a weak one, and it is possible that it works (relatively) well only under certain historical conditions. If this is true, once the historical conditions have passed, the system may prove difficult to resuscitate or restructure.

Movement in the second direction, toward a collectively oriented system of electoral participation, although less likely to occur, would put voter turnout on a firmer foundation. Such a system would be relatively robust and provide an organized, ongoing way of getting voters to the polls. Precisely because of its organized and ongoing character, however, it requires more of a conscious social will to put in place. . . .

NOTES

1. Note that the time dummy coefficient for 1968 is the greatest in magnitude. This partially reflects the problem with the mobility variable, where the proportion mobile in the data is considerably lower for 1968 and 1972 than the actual population proportions. This means that the time estimates for these years are more negative (by at least 0.3) than they should be. With this taken into account, the magnitude of the 1968 coefficient is no longer so anomalous. It should also be noted, however, that taking account of this factor would indicate that the 1972 estimate should be at least +.03, making 1972 somewhat different from the other years.
2. It is also possible that this 6 percent considerably overestimates the contribution from this category. In Table 1-1 [of Teixeira] the proportion nonwhite seems unusually high, relative to the figures for the other years. This may reflect measurement error (or, really, its decline), since the question on race for 1980 was a different and more thorough one than in the previous surveys. Thus the increase in proportion nonwhite in the data may be somewhat inflated—and therefore the contribution of racial distributional change to turnout decline inflated as well.

4. RACE, SOCIOPOLITICAL PARTICIPATION, AND BLACK EMPOWERMENT

Lawrence Bobo and Franklin D. Gilliam, Jr.

In the early 1970s students of black political behavior reached consensus on two points: (1) that blacks tended to participate more than whites when differences in socioeconomic status were taken into account (Milbrath and Goel, 1977; Olsen, 1970; Verba and Nie, 1972) and (2) that a strong sense of "ethnic community," or group consciousness, was the stimulus to heightened black participation (Guterbock and London, 1983; Shingles, 1981; Verba and Nie, 1972). Much of the data supporting this view of black political behavior comes from the late 1950s and 1960s. Over the ensuing 20 to 30 years, however, blacks made enormous strides in socioeconomic status and political influence. For example, Williams and Morris (1987, p. 137) recently reported that the number of black elected officials rose from "fewer than 103 in 1964 to 6,384 in 1986." As a result of such changes it is appropriate to reexamine theoretical and empirical notions about black-white differences in sociopolitical behavior.

It is plausible to speak of substantial—though far from ideal (Jennings, 1984)—"black-political empowerment." Increases in the control of institutionalized power by blacks is likely to have considerable impact on the level and nature of black sociopolitical behavior. Our purpose is to develop and test theoretical ideas about the effects of empowerment on racial differences in participation. The research is based on data from the 1987 General Social Survey, which involved a national probability sample of adults, a large black oversample (total black N = 544), and a replication of the battery of sociopolitical behavior measures from Verba and Nie's (1972) classic study.

Background

Patterns and Theories of Black Participation

Previous attempts to explain black-white differences in participation have focused on sociodemographic, psychological, and structural factors. Some of the

Source: *American Political Science Review* (1990) 84:377-93. Reprinted with permission of the publisher.

earliest research explained racial differences in political behavior on the basis of blacks' lower average levels of education, occupational status, and income (Matthews and Prothro, 1966; Orum, 1966). This approach is commonly known as the "standard socioeconomic model" (Verba and Nie, 1972) and is a baseline model for most research on participation. This model, however, was confounded by the frequent empirical finding that once controls for socioeconomic status were introduced, blacks actually participated at higher rates than whites.

Two psychological theories have been advanced to explain this pattern. The first, compensatory theory, grows out of a more sociological tradition concerned with both political and social participation. This view posits that blacks join organizations and become politically active to an exaggerated degree in order to overcome the exclusion and feelings of inferiority forced on them by a hostile white society (Babchuk and Thompson, 1962; Myrdal, 1944; Orum, 1966).

The second theory, the ethnic community approach, holds that membership in disadvantaged minority communities leads people to develop strong feelings of group attachment and group consciousness. One product of these feelings is the emergence of group norms that call for political action to improve the status of the group (Antunes and Gaitz, 1975; Miller et al., 1981; Olsen, 1970; Verba and Nie, 1972). In particular, very high levels of participation were found for blacks who exhibited a political orientation characterized by low levels of trust in government and high levels of personal efficacy (Guterbock and London, 1983; Shingles, 1981). The extraordinary levels of participation among blacks, then, reflected mainly the actions of the "politically discontented" among them who were acting on community norms.

Tests of these theories have suffered from several methodological limitations (Walton, 1985, pp. 78-82). These shortcomings include small numbers of black respondents (e.g., McPherson, 1977; Olsen, 1970; Orum, 1966) and indirect measures of central concepts (e.g., Verba and Nie's group consciousness measure). Even the most recent tests of these ideas are based on data gathered in the 1960s (Guterbock and London, 1983; Shingles, 1981). More troubling at a conceptual level is the fact that these theories were designed to explain black sociopolitical behavior at the time when blacks were struggling for basic inclusion in U.S. society and politics.

Profound changes in the social and political status of blacks, however, call into question the applicability of such theories. Specifically, what should we expect about contemporary racial differences in political behavior? Should we expect, for example, that the politically discontented continue as the most active group of blacks?

Black Political Empowerment

Understanding black participation in the contemporary period, we believe, requires taking into account the likely effects of black political empowerment. By political empowerment—or political incorporation, as some have called it (Browning, Marshall, and Tabb, 1984)—we mean the extent to which a group has achieved significant representation and influence in political decision making. The business of U.S. politics is transacted on several levels. Black gains in public officeholding, however, have primarily been at the state and local levels (Joint Center for Political Studies, 1988, p. 8). Blacks have made tremendous strides in obtaining seats in state legislatures and on city councils and school boards (p. 13). The most notable black gains, we believe, have been at the mayoral level (see Persons, 1987). In major cities such as Atlanta, Detroit, Gary, Los Angeles, and others, black mayors have controlled city hall for more than a decade. Conceptually, we focus on whether blacks have captured the mayor's office because it involved the highest degree of local empowerment, usually signaling both a high level of organization among elites in the African-American community and a relatively high degree of control over local decision making (Browning, Marshall, and Tabb, 1984; Nelson and Meranto, 1977).

There are two interrelated reasons why such empowerment should influence mass sociopolitical participation. First, empowerment should influence participation because sociopolitical behavior has a heavily instrumental basis. Like Wolfinger and Rosenstone (1980), we believe that people participate because the perceived benefits of doing so outweigh the perceived costs. Second, empowerment should influence participation because macro level aspects of a person's sociopolitical environment affect cost-benefit calculations. There is a large literature on the effects of political contexts on cost-benefit calculations relevant to participation. Studies have emphasized legal factors (Ashenfelter and Kelley, 1975; Wolfinger and Rosenstone, 1980), electoral factors (Gilliam, 1985; Patterson and Caldeira, 1983), organizational factors such as mobilization efforts by political parties (Flanigan and Zingale, 1979; Key, 1949), and cues from political figures indicating likely policy responsiveness (Bullock, 1981; Whitby, 1987). Our primary interest is in this latter type of contextual influence. We hypothesize that where blacks hold more positions of authority, wield political power, and have done so for longer periods of time, greater numbers of blacks should see value in sociopolitical involvement.

We expect, then, that the greater the level of empowerment, the more likely it is that blacks will become politically involved (Hamilton, 1986). Empowerment should increase participation because of its effects on several social psychological factors, in particular, its impact on levels of political trust, efficacy, and knowledge about politics. Blacks in high empowerment areas should feel more trusting of government, express higher levels of efficacy, and become more knowledgeable about politics than blacks in low empowerment areas. All of which should, in turn, contribute to higher levels of participation.

The impact of empowerment on levels of trust and efficacy among blacks should also change the nature of *black-white differences* in the extent and correlates of participation. In areas of high black empowerment, blacks should participate at rates equal to, or greater than, whites (all other things being equal). In areas of relatively low black empowerment, blacks should participate at rates lower than whites. Furthermore, black empowerment should bring greater similarity between blacks and whites in the relationship of political orientations to sociopolitical participation. Earlier research found that the most active blacks were politically discontented; that is, they exhibited a combination of low levels of trust in government and high levels of personal political efficacy. In contrast, the most active whites were found among those aptly labeled "politically engaged"—those individuals with high levels of trust and high levels of efficacy. Growing black empowerment suggests a shift of the most active blacks to the same type of "engaged" orientation of the most active whites.

Data and Measures

The data come from the National Opinion Research Center's 1987 General Social Survey (GSS; Davis and Smith, 1987). This is a nationally representative multistage probability sample of English-speaking adults living in the continental United States. The main GSS sample included a total of 1,466 respondents, with 191 blacks, 1,222 whites, and 53 nonblack nonwhites (excluded from all analyses), with an overall response rate of 75.4%. The 1987 GSS also includes a large black oversample (N = 353). The oversample had a response rate of 79.9% and brings the total black sample size to 544. There were no statistically discernable differences in age, sex, education, family income, occupational prestige, or regional distribution between blacks in the oversample and blacks in the main GSS.

Level of Empowerment.   Respondents from primary sampling units (PSUs) where the largest city had a black mayor at the time of the survey are scored as living in high-black-empowerment areas. Individuals living in PSUs without a black mayor or in PSUs with black mayors only in a smaller city, were scored as low-black-empowerment areas.[1]

Sociopolitical Participation.   Since individuals may act to influence political decision making significantly through means other than voting, our research focuses on broad measures of sociopolitical involvement; that is, our goal is to understand general patterns of participation, not merely electoral turnout. Fortunately, the 1987 GSS replicated the large battery of sociopolitical behavior measures developed by Verba and Nie (1972). Full wording for the 15 individual participation measures is shown in the Appendix. Verba and Nie found that these 15 indicators reflected four major models of sociopolitical involvement: voting, campaigning, communal activity (membership in groups and organizations that work to solve problems of broad social importance), and particularized contacting (direct contact concerning a personal matter with an elected official). We find a similar factor structure for the 1987 data and thus employ scales for these four major modes of participation, as well as a summary participation index, as our main dependent variables. For most analyses we rely on the summary participation index (we note differences across the modes when relevant). Details on scale reliability and index construction are reported in the Appendix.

Analysis and Results

Previous research suggests that blacks should participate at lower rates than whites but that this pattern is reversed after introducing controls for socioeco-

Table 4-1   Race Differences in Sociopolitical Participation: Participation Items by Race

Participation Items	Blacks (%)	Whites (%)	Difference (%)
Voting			
Local voting	76	82	−6%**
	(534)	(1,208)	
1980 national election	65	70	−5%*
	(512)	(1,187)	
1984 national election	61	71	−10%**
	(513)	(1,187)	
Campaigning			
Persuade others	42	48	−6%
	(539)	(1,215)	
Donate money	16	24	−8%**
	(539)	(1,215)	
Attend meeting	22	19	3%
	(540)	(1,214)	
Work	21	28	−7%*
	(540)	(1,217)	
Member political club	3	4	−1%
	(544)	(1,222)	
Communal activity			
Local problem solving	32	34	−2%
	(538)	(1,219)	
Start local group	16	18	−2%
	(536)	(1,218)	
Contact local officials	17	26	−9%
	(539)	(1,215)	
Contact nonlocal officials	10	25	−15%**
	(539)	(1,222)	
Community group activity	39	42	−3%
	(544)	(1,222)	
Particularized contacting			
Contact local officials	8	10	−2%
	(539)	(1,214)	
Contact nonlocal officials	5	8	−3*
	(539)	(1,215)	

Note: Base numbers of cases are in parentheses.
*$p < .05$.
**$p < .001$.

nomic status. The results presented in Tables 4-1 and 4-2 confirm the first of these expectations and disconfirm the latter. Whether examining the individual indicators of participation (Table 4-1) or the scaled measures of voting, campaigning, communal involvement, and particularized contacting (Table 4-2), blacks generally participate at lower rates than do whites. Of the 15 individual

Table 4-2 Race Differences in Sociopolitical Participation: Participation Scales by Race

Modes of Participation Scales	Unadjusted Means		Adjusted Means	
	Blacks	*Whites*	*Blacks*	*Whites*
Voting	−16.59	3.64**	2.69	−.39
Campaigning	−8.71	1.35	5.37	−.79
Communal activity	−16.38	2.56**	4.58	−.67
Particularized contacting	−10.75	1.67*	−3.70	.70
Summary index	−18.40	2.86**	4.86	−.71

Note: Adjusted means are corrected for socioeconomic status (education, occupational prestige, and family income) and demographic factors (age and sex).

*$p < .05$.
**$p < .001$.

measures 14 show that whites are more active than blacks, with eight of these differences reaching statistical significance. Blacks are consistently less active than whites on the measures of voting. The black-white differences tend to be smaller for campaign involvement, which is usually regarded as a high-initiative political behavior.

Blacks have lower participation scores than whites on all of the major modes of participation scales—voting, campaigning, communal activity, and particularized contacting—as well as on the summary participation index. (The scales are scored to have a mean of approximately zero, hence negative scores indicate below-average rates of participation). Four of these five comparisons show a significant difference favoring whites, with the campaigning scale providing the only exception. The last two columns of Table 4-2 report mean participation scores after adjusting the scales for the respondents' education, occupation, family income, age, and sex.[2] None of the adjusted scale comparisons shows a significant black-white difference, indicating that the compositional differences in socioeconomic status—especially education—accounts for lower average black participation.[3]

Similar black-white rates of participation, net of socioeconomic and demographic factors, still leave open the possibility of empowerment effects on participation. We hypothesized that the level of black sociopolitical involvement would be higher in areas where blacks were politically empowered and that racial differences would favor blacks over whites in high-black-empowerment areas. The results reported in Table 4-3 strongly support these hypotheses. The top half of the table shows that blacks in high-empowerment areas are significantly more active (32.65) than blacks in low-empowerment areas. In addition, blacks in low-empowerment areas are significantly less active than comparable whites (−33.96). The black-white difference in high-empowerment areas favors blacks but does not reach statistical significance. Most important, as the bottom half shows, after we adjust the summary participation index for socioeconomic status,

Table 4-3 Black Political Empowerment, Race, and Participation

Race	Mean Participation Score, Level of Black Empowerment		
	Low	High	Difference
Summary Participation Index			
Blacks	−29.26	3.39	−32.65***
	(358)	(182)	
Whites	4.70	−8.64	13.34
	(1,047)	(170)	
Difference	−33.96***	12.03	
Adjusted Summary Participation Index			
Blacks	−2.05	17.90	−19.95*
	(294)	(159)	
Whites	1.19	−12.45	13.64
	(930)	(152)	
Difference	−3.34	30.35**	

*$p < .05$.
**$p < .01$.
***$p < .001$.

age, and sex, blacks in high-empowerment areas are indeed more active than comparable whites.[4] There is no racial difference in participation, net of socioeconomic status, age, and sex, in low-empowerment areas.

We have argued that empowerment influences black participation because it is a contextual cue of likely policy responsiveness to black concerns. If so, the empowerment effect on participation should work through those psychological factors that facilitate political involvement; that is, level of empowerment should influence participation because it increases attentiveness to politics among blacks as well as increasing their levels of political trust and efficacy. The results shown in Table 4-4, which presents mean item and scale scores for the measures of political knowledge, trust, and efficacy, unequivocally support the first of these hypotheses but speak equivocally regarding the impact of empowerment on levels of trust and efficacy. In percentage terms, blacks living in high-empowerment areas are significantly more likely to name the local school board president correctly (38% vs. 25%), their representative (31% vs. 22%), and the state governor (75% vs. 61%) than blacks living in low-empowerment areas.[5] The impact of empowerment on trust and efficacy appears to be localized in nature. Blacks in high-empowerment areas trust local officials more and expect to have greater influence with them than do blacks in low-empowerment areas. However (not too surprisingly), the sort of "local" empowerment we tap here does not change trust in the federal government or improve blacks' views of the motivations of politicians in general.

Table 4-4 Mean Political Knowledge, Trust, and Efficacy by Black
Political Empowerment and Race

| | Empowerment Level | | | |
| | Blacks | | Whites | |
Knowledge, Trust, and Efficacy	Low	High	Low	High
Correctly name school board head	1.25[a]	1.38	1.35[b]	1.14
Correctly name congressman	1.22[a]	1.31	1.41[b]	1.29[c]
Correctly name governor	1.61[a]	1.75	1.81	1.79[c]
Political knowledge scale	4.07[a]	4.44	4.57[b]	4.22[c]
Local trust[d]	2.33[a]	2.50	2.68	2.74[c]
Federal trust[d]	2.10	2.10	2.36[b]	2.49[c]
Political trust scale	2.22	2.30	2.52	2.62[c]
Local influence[e]	2.26[a]	2.48	2.51	2.55[c]
Local officials care[e]	2.88	2.83	3.03[b]	2.90[c]
Political efficacy scale	2.57	2.65	2.77	2.72[c]

[a] Significant difference by empowerment among blacks.

[b] Significant difference by empowerment among whites.

[c] Significant difference between blacks and whites on item or scale.

[d] The two political trust items are modestly correlated ($r = .36, p < .001$) and are worded as follows. Local trust: "How much of the time do you think you can trust the local government here in [respondent's local government unit] to do what is right—just about always, most of the time, only some of the time, or almost never?" Federal trust: "How much of the time do you think you can trust the government in Washington to do what is right—just about always, most of the time, only some of the time, or almost never?"

[e] The two political efficacy items are modestly correlated ($r = .39, p < .001$) and are worded as follows. Local influence: "How much influence do you think people like you can have over local government decisions—a lot, a moderate amount, a little, or none at all?" Local officials care: "If you had a complaint about a local government activity and took that complaint to a member of the local government council, would you expect him or her to pay a lot of attention to what you say, some attention, very little attention, or none at all?" Scoring of all items has been reversed for these analyses.

These results also illuminate black-white differences in participation. Whites in high-black-empowerment areas are often less politically knowledgeable than whites in low-black-empowerment areas. Specifically, among whites, those living in high-black-empowerment areas were significantly less able to name the local school board president (14% vs. 34%) or their representative (29% vs. 41%) but were just as able to name the state governor (80% vs. 82%). The level of black-empowerment does not, however, consistently influence whites' feelings of trust and efficacy. In sum, whites tend to pay less attention to local politics when blacks control local offices but do not become generally less trusting or efficacious as a result.

We can gain greater leverage on how empowerment affects behavior by considering whether it also helps shape basic political orientations involving the intersection of political trust and efficacy (Gilliam and Bobo, 1988). Previous research found that the most active blacks were politically discontented—those

Table 4-5 Political Orientation, Empowerment, and Participation Among U.S. Blacks and Whites, 1987

Variables by Race	Politi-cally Engaged	Politi-cally Discon-tented	Politi-cally Obedient	Politi-cally Alienated	Total	Number of Cases	f-ratio	d.f.
Political orientation (%)								
($x^2 = 70.87$, d.f. $= 3$, $p < .001$)								
Blacks	25	20	22	32	100	531	—	—
Whites	42	12	26	19	99	1,208	—	—
Black empowerment (%)								
Blacks ($x^2 = 9.71$, d.f. $=3$, $p < .05$)								
Low	22	21	21	36	100	350	—	—
High	32	18	24	26	100	181	—	—
Whites ($x^2 = 3.41$, d.f. $= 3$, n.s.)								
Low	41	13	26	20	100	1,038	—	—
High	44	9	29	18	100	170	—	—
Participation[a]								
Unadjusted								
Blacks	17.40	−13.35	−37.33	−33.21	—	530	10.29	3/526
Whites	33.51	32.19	−34.12	−27.48	—	1,206	45.69	3/1,202
Adjusted								
Blacks	39.37	3.03	−5.55	−12.87	—	444	9.42	3/443
Whites	20.44	25.90	−26.58	−26.24	—	1,074	27.04	3/1,070

[a] Summary participation index means.

who combined high feelings of efficacy with low feelings of trust—but that the most active whites were highly efficacious and highly trusting. We hypothesized that in the modern period the most active blacks should maintain the same sort of "engaged"—high efficacy and high trust—orientation characteristic of politically active whites and do so, in part, because of improved levels of black political empowerment. In the main, the results of Table 4-5 support these hypotheses.[6] To be sure, blacks are less likely than whites (25% vs. 42%) to fall into the politically engaged group (rows 1-2) and are more likely than whites to appear among the alienated who lack in both trust and efficacy (32% vs. 19%). However, rows 3-6 show that blacks in high-empowerment areas are more likely to be among the politically engaged than blacks in low-empowerment areas. Moreover, rows 7-10 show that politically engaged blacks are the most active segment of the black community. Indeed, after we have controlled for socioeconomic status, age, and sex, politically engaged blacks score as more active than politically engaged whites. This is a sharp reversal of the patterns for blacks found in earlier research.[7]

Empowerment increases black participation. It appears to do so because it increases attentiveness to politics and because it contributes to a more engaged

Table 4-6   Regression Models of Summary Participation Index

Independent Variables	Blacks			Whites
	Model 1	Model 2	Model 3	
Constant	−265.63***	−250.89***	−331.83***	−283.02***
Variables				
Empowerment	23.31**	19.02*	9.14	−4.66
	(.12)	(.10)	(.05)	(−.01)
Political orientations				
Engaged	—	31.63**	31.89**	−.53
		(.15)	(.15)	(−.00)
Obedient	—	−10.36	−7.96	−45.81***
		(−.05)	(−.03)	(−.19)
Alienated	—	−16.88	−18.19	−45.49***
		(−.08)	(−.09)	(−.18)
Political knowledge	—	—	36.49	25.26***
			(.38)	(.24)
Social background				
Age	1.84***	1.78***	1.24***	1.26***
	(.33)	(.32)	(.22)	(.21)
Education	10.89***	10.17***	7.13***	8.04***
	(.39)	(.36)	(.25)	(.24)
Occupation	.78*	.68*	.38	.65**
	(.11)	(.09)	(.05)	(.09)
Family income	.01	.01	−.08	.30
	(.00)	(.00)	(−.01)	(.05)
Region (South = 1)	15.54	16.82*	9.25	−4.52
	(.08)	(.09)	(.05)	(−.02)
Sex (female = 1)	1.60	−.04	−5.35	5.04
	(.01)	(−.00)	(−.03)	(.02)
"Urbanicity"	−.07	.10	.92	−.08
	(−.00)	(.00)	(.02)	(.00)
Adjusted R^2	.22	.25	.37	.30
Number of cases	437	437	437	1,040

*p < .05, two-tailed test.
**p < .01, two-tailed test.
***p < .001, two-tailed test.

orientation to politics. Still unclear is whether empowerment exerts direct effects on participation, or works largely through its impact on knowledge and political orientation. Table 4-6 reports the results of Ordinary Least Squares (OLS) regression analyses of participation, which indicate that among blacks the effect of empowerment on participation is mediated modestly by its influence on political orientations and powerfully by its influence on political knowledge. Model 1

Table 4-7 Predicted Mean Participation Scores by Race, Empowerment, and Political Orientation

| | Empowerment Levels | | | |
| | Blacks | | Whites | |
Political Orientation	Low	High	Low	High
Politically engaged	18.11	36.59	38.25	20.03
Politically discontented	−21.29	24.50	33.77	35.91
Politically obedient	−43.99	−21.02	−27.50	−46.22
Politically alienated	−49.50	−3.10	−31.96	−37.75

shows that among blacks empowerment has a significant positive effect on participation, net of education, family income, occupation, age, sex, region of residence, and "urbanicity." (We added region and "urbanicity" to ensure that the empowerment effect was not merely capturing north-vs.-south or size-of-place effects.) However, model 2 shows that by adding a series of dummy variables representing political orientations, the coefficient for empowerment remains significant even though it decreases by about 18%, from 23.31 to 19.02. On adding political knowledge to the model (model 3), the coefficient for empowerment is cut by more than half and becomes insignificant. Hence, all of the impact of empowerment on participation is indirect via its tendency to encourage more engaged political orientations and greater attentiveness to politics among blacks.[8] We should note that political orientations bring a significant increase in variance explained (3%), with the politically engaged blacks scoring as significantly more active than the politically discontented. Furthermore, the political knowledge scale brings a substantial increase in variance explained (12%) and has the single strongest direct effect (partial beta = .38, p < .001) on summary participation scores among blacks.

The final column of Table 4-6 shows that empowerment has no effect on white participation; but, as with blacks, political orientations and political knowledge strongly influence levels of participation. We should note that political knowledge has a stronger effect on participation among blacks than it does among whites. Viewed in this light, the effect of empowerment on black levels of political knowledge is of signal importance.

A more concrete view of rates of participation can be seen in Table 4-7, which shows predicted participation scores for blacks and whites under the OLS models in columns 3 and 4, respectively. First, blacks in high-empowerment areas are more active than those in low-empowerment areas regardless of political orientation. Second, blacks in high-empowerment areas are more active than their white counterparts among the engaged, among the obedient, and among the alienated. Only among the politically discontented, once regarded as the most politically active segment of the black community, do blacks in high-empowerment areas participate at lower rates than comparable whites. This suggests that otherwise efficacious blacks who do not trust black politicians in their communities are especially likely, relative to similar whites, to withdraw from politics. Third, blacks in low-black-empowerment areas, regardless of orientation, tend to be less active than whites in the same areas.

Discussion and Conclusions

Our results show, first, that where blacks hold positions of political power, they are more active and participate at higher rates than whites of comparable socioeconomic status. Second, black empowerment is a contextual cue of likely policy responsiveness that encourages blacks to feel that participation has intrinsic value. This conclusion is based on the finding that empowerment leads to higher levels of political knowledge and that it leads to a more engaged (i.e., trusting and efficacious) orientation to politics.

An alternative interpretation of these results holds that black empowerment is the outcome of higher participation brought about by registration and turnout drives when a viable black candidate emerges. This explanation of our results is unconvincing on logical and empirical grounds even though we agree that the mobilization of black voters is a necessary component of the accomplishment of empowerment (Browning, Marshall, and Tabb, 1984). First, blacks are not newcomers to elective office in most of the "empowered" areas in our sample, and our dependent variables are general patterns of individual behavior. Hence, it is unlikely that we have found merely the short-term effects of black voter mobilization efforts. What is more, the effects of empowerment are not restricted to electoral turnout. Second, if the association between empowerment and participation were merely the result of voter mobilization drives by black candidates, we should have found strong direct effects of empowerment on participation among blacks. Instead, the data show that empowerment works through the psychological factors of political orientation and (especially) level of actual political knowledge. We suggest that black empowerment, whatever heightened mobilization this feat initially requires, has broad and lasting consequences on how often, and why, blacks become active participants in the political process. One sign of the potential for such effects is that whites, too, are affected. Recall the finding that whites in high-black-empowerment areas are less politically knowledgeable than whites in low-black-empowerment areas.

These results call for changes in our empirical and theoretical ideas about black sociopolitical behavior. Studies of sociopolitical participation based on data from the late 1950s and into the 1960s found that blacks participated less than whites, that blacks were more active than whites at any given level of socioeconomic status, and that greater black involvement was rooted in group consciousness and a sense of political discontent. Substantively, these patterns were correctly read as showing that (1) blacks were fighting for basic civic inclusion and to obtain the larger goal of improving the material status of the group and (2) that full understanding of patterns of sociopolitical participation in the United States required one to take race into account.

The significance of race for sociopolitical behavior has evidently changed. On the one hand, we find that blacks generally participate at the same rate as whites of comparable socioeconomic status and that the politically engaged are the most active segment of both groups. It is tempting to conclude, therefore, that the importance of race for patterns of sociopolitical participation has greatly declined. On the other hand, blacks are more active than comparable whites in areas of high black political empowerment. In addition, level of empowerment shapes both blacks' likelihood of adopting an "engaged" orientation to politics and their basic levels of knowledge about political affairs. These psychological orientations to politics, in turn, powerfully affect a person's level of sociopolitical involvement. It is more accurate, then, to conclude that race now shapes sociopolitical behavior in different ways and for somewhat different reasons than held in the past.

In our judgment, these differences reflect broad legal-political-economic changes that improved the general social standing of many blacks and, most directly, brought a tremendous increase in the number and influence of black elected officials. To be sure, the core political goals of blacks have steadily been full and fair inclusion in all domains of U.S. society (Hamilton, 1984; Jones, 1972; Walton, 1985). When the pathways to these objectives were fundamentally blocked, different strategies and orientations were necessary than now seem appropriate in a context of significant wielding of institutional power by blacks. With the goal of basic civic inclusion largely accomplished, the black political agenda has shifted to the goal of maintaining, exploiting, and expanding the political and economic resources available to the black community (Hamilton, 1986).

Nonetheless, the degree of black political empowerment and general social progress must be kept in perspective. Blacks gained control of mayoral offices at a time when the power of urban political machines continued to decline, when population and commerce were shifting to suburban areas (Wilson, 1980), and when federal programs became less generous (Moore, 1988). Hindrances to black empowerment in the form of cumbersome voter registration procedures, district boundaries that dilute the black vote, gerrymandering, hostility to black candidates among a significant number of whites (Williams and Morris, 1987), and the cooptation of some black leaders (Browning, Marshall, and Tabb, 1984; Jennings,1984) are still problematic. In addition, the persisting social segregation and economic disadvantages of blacks (Farley and Allen, 1987; Wilson, 1987) constitute structural bases for black racial identity formation (Allen, Dawson, and Brown, 1989) as well as for sharp black-white political polarization over race relations issues (Bobo, 1988), social welfare policy attitudes (Bobo, n.d.; Gilliam and Whitby, 1989), and basic life satisfaction (Thomas and Hughes, 1986). Black progress and political empowerment are still partial and incomplete even though they have advanced far enough to affect how often, and why, blacks become politically active.

Further investigations of changing black sociopolitical behavior and the influence of black empowerment will require studies with larger samples of blacks. Future research should develop direct indicators of whether black respondents think black officials are more responsive to their needs than white officials (Jackson and Oliver, 1988). Full exploration of these ideas will require data on whether black officials have the inclination and resources to produce desired outcomes for their constituents (Eisinger, 1982). Tapping the reactions of whites to black elected officials is a necessary component of this research. In addition, the empowerment model may be extended to other U.S. minority groups. The growing electoral power of Latinos, for example, might be fruitfully studied within the empowerment framework we developed here.

Appendix

Wording of Participation Items

Voting. (1) "Now in 1980, you remember that Carter ran for President on the Democratic ticket against Reagan for the Republicans, and Anderson as an independent. Do you remember for sure whether or not you voted in that election?" (2) "In 1984, you remember that Mondale ran for President on the Democratic ticket against Reagan for the Republicans. Do you remember for sure whether or not you voted in that election?" (3) "What about local elections—do you always vote in those, do you sometimes miss one, or do you rarely vote, or do you never vote?"

Campaigning. (1) "During elections do you ever try to show people why they should vote for one of the parties or candidates? Do you do that often, sometimes, rarely or never?" (2) "In the past three or four years, have you contributed money to a political party or candidate or to any other political party or candidate or to any other political cause?" (3) "In the past three or four years have you attended any political meetings or rallies?" (4) "Have you done work for one of the parties or candidates in most elections, some elections, only a few, or have you never done such work?" (5) "Would you tell me whether or not you are a member of political clubs? [If yes,] Do political clubs to which you belong do anything to try to solve individual or community problems? [If yes,] Have you ever done any active work for political clubs? I mean, been a leader, helped organize meetings, or given time or money?"

Communal Activity. (1) "Have you ever worked with others in this community to try to solve some community problem?" (2) "Have you ever taken part in forming a new group or a new organization to try to solve some community problem?" (3) "Have you ever personally gone to see, or spoken to, or written to—some member of the local government or some other person of influence in the community about some need or problem? [If yes,] Was this need or problem primarily of concern to you, your friends and family, or was it an issue of wider concern?" (4) "What about some representative or governmental official outside of the local community—on the country, state, or national level? Have you ever contacted or written to such a person on some need or problem? [If yes,] Was this need or problem primarily of concern to you, your friends and family, or was it an issue of wider concern?" The final component of the

Table 4-8 Descriptive Statistics for Participation Dependent Measures

Participation Measures	Minimum	Maximum	Mean	Standard Deviation	Average Correlation	Alpha
Voting						
(N = 1,699)	−181.40	89.71	.986	100.02	.64	.85
Campaigning						
(N = 1,746)	−75.42	435.85	−.005	102.10	.35	.73
Communal activity						
(N = 1,748)	−89.31	414.37	.016	105.69	.35	.72
Particularized contacting						
(N = 1,744)	−40.88	426.78	.000	105.38	.28	.46
Summary index						
(N = 1,745)	−145.45	380.91	.000	100.00	.24	.56

communal activity item is a composite measure based on responses to questions concerned with *membership* in any of 15 possible voluntary associations (fraternal groups; service clubs; veterans groups; labor unions; sports groups; youth groups; school service groups; hobby and garden clubs; school fraternities and sororities; nationality groups; farm organizations; literary, art, discussion, or study groups; professional or academic societies; church affiliated groups; and any other groups), whether those groups worked to solve individual or community problems, and whether the respondent had been actively involved in the organization.

Particularized Contacting. See items 3 and 4 in the Communal Activity section for question wording. Those who had contacted a local official or a nonlocal official on a personal matter are given high scores.

Creation of Participation Scales and Index

The participation measures were factor-analyzed using a principal components extraction and an oblique rotation, resulting in a four-factor solution. The factors identified correspond to Verba and Nie's (1972) voting, campaigning, communal involvement, and particularized contacting modes. We created scales for the items loading on each major mode by weighing each item by its factor loading, summing and standardizing the measure and then multiplying it by 100. For each major mode this yields a scale with a mean of approximately 0 and a standard deviation of approximately 100. The summary participation index is based on a higher-order factor analysis using the four major mode scales, and the major mode scales are all positively intercorrelated. Each scale was weighed by its respective factor score and the sum of these was then standardized and multiplied by 100. Descriptive statistics for each measure are shown in Table 4-8, along with average interitem correlations and alpha coefficients. More complete details on scale and index creation can be obtained by writing to us.

NOTES

1. The PSUs scored as high-empowerment areas include Atlanta, Baltimore, Birmingham, Chicago, Dayton, Detroit, Los Angeles, Newark, Philadelphia, Richmond, and Washington. All other PSUs were scored as low-black-empowerment areas. We identified areas with black mayors using Joint Center for Political Studies (1986). Ideally, we would like to employ a more refined empowerment measure that could, for example, distinguish areas where blacks have held the mayor's office for several consecutive terms (e.g., Atlanta, Los Angeles, Detroit) from areas where this is a more recent, contested, and still-vulnerable accomplishment (e.g., Philadelphia, Chicago). We decided against such an approach because even with our relatively large black sample, we have too few black respondents in many PSUs to test for such differences efficiently and reliably.

2. Age and sex were included because our sample of blacks tends to be younger and include more women than the white sample. The adjustments were made by estimating an Ordinary Least Squares regression equation, pooled across race and weighted for the black oversample, of the form

$$y^* = b_0 - b_1^*(\text{educ}) - b_2^*(\text{occu}) - b_3^*(\text{faminc}) - b_4^*(\text{age}) - b_5^*(\text{sex}),$$

where y^* = adjusted participation score, b_0 = intercept, b_1-b_2 = OLS regression coefficients, educ = respondent's level of education, occu = respondent's (spouse's if respondent is not employed) occupational prestige (NORC Hodge-Siegel-Rossi scale), faminc = family income, age = respondent's age, and sex = dummy variable for sex (male = 0, female = 1).

3. Two possible complexities should be noted. First, we also found no pattern of significantly higher black participation at specific status levels; that is, we created socioeconomic status group quartiles based on a combination of education, occupational prestige, and family income. Black-white comparisons within the quartile groups using the adjusted participation scales revealed only one significant difference out of 16 possible comparisons (4 quartile groups by 4 participation scales), and this one favored whites over blacks. Second, political behaviors tend to be overreported (Abramson and Claggett, 1986; Presser, 1984), a tendency that may be exaggerated by our reliance on retrospective reports. But recent analyses suggest no substantial racial differential (Anderson and Silver, 1986) and also suggest that validation data do not paint a substantially different picture of the determinants of participation than do self-reports in surveys (Katosh and Traugott, 1981). Hence, we believe these data accurately gauge black-white differences in patterns of sociopolitical involvement and the relationship of participation to other factors.

4. In general, analyses of the major mode of participation scales support the summary index results shown in Table 4-3. Blacks in high-empowerment areas score as more active than comparable whites, net of socioeconomic status, age, and sex, for the voting, campaigning, communal activity, and particularized contacting scales. This difference is significant in the cases of voting (29.10, $p < .01$) and communal activity (24.92, $p < .05$), of borderline significance for campaign activity (22.68, $p < .08$), and in the right direction but insignificant for particularized contacting of officials (4.16). Among whites, those living in high-black-empowerment areas are significantly less likely than those in low-black-empowerment areas to report voting ($-18.79, p < .05$) and communal activity ($-17.61, p < .05$). Blacks in high-empowerment areas score as more active than blacks in low-empowerment areas for each major mode of

participation scale, with this difference reaching significance for campaigning (28.50, $p < .01$) and voting (15.37, $p = .09$).

5. Ordinary Least Squares regression analyses show that level of empowerment significantly increases scores on the political knowledge scale net of education, family income, occupation, age, sex, region (north vs. south), and size of place. (We included the two latter variables in order to assure that the empowerment variable was not simply capturing north-vs.-south or size-of-place differences.) Specifically, empowerment adds 1.6% to the total variance explained in political knowledge among blacks ($F = 8.33$, d.f. $= 1/434$, $p < .01$) and has the third largest effect in the equation (partial beta $= .13$, $p < .01$), following those for level of education (partial beta $= .30$, $p < .001$) and age (.25, $p < .001$).

6. The sort of political orientation typology we employ here, which distinguishes the politically engaged (high-trust, high-efficacy), the politically discontented (low-trust, high-efficacy), politically obedient (high-trust, low-efficacy), and politically alienated (low-trust, low-efficacy) is well established (Guterbock and London 1983; Shingles 1981). Cells of the political orientation typology were created by dichotomizing the political trust and political efficacy scales at the black median (in order to assure adequate numbers of black respondents in each category) and then cross-classifying the trust and efficacy variables.

7. Analyses of the separate major mode of participation scales support the results reported in Table 4-5. Among blacks, there are significant differences by the orientation typology on the adjusted voting ($F = 4.09$, d.f. $= 3/429$, $p < .01$), campaigning ($F = 8.65$, d.f. $= 3/443$, $p < .001$), and communal activity scales ($F = 5.53$, d.f. $= 3/443$, $p < .01$), but not on the adjusted particularized contacting scale ($F = .16$, d.f. $= 3/443$, n.s.). Politically engaged blacks, net of socioeconomic status, age, and sex, are the most active orientation type among blacks in terms of voting, campaigning, and communal activity. Thus, even for very-high-initiative behaviors such as campaigning and communal activity, politically engaged blacks are more active than the politically discontented.

8. The effect of empowerment on black participation is most consistent in the electoral arena, that is, for voting and especially for campaigning activity. The empowerment variable has a small but significant zero-order correlation with black voting ($r = .12$) and campaigning ($r = .16$), a borderline correlation with communal activity ($r = .09$), and no relation to particularized contacting. Multiple regression analyses show that empowerment has a borderline effect on voting (partial beta $= .07$, $p = .10$), net of socioeconomic status, age, sex, region, and size of place. This borderline effect is eliminated on introducing the political orientation and knowledge variables. Empowerment has a highly significant effect on campaigning (partial beta $= .17$, $p < .001$), net of socioeconomic status, age, sex, region, and size of place. Furthermore, empowerment has a significant direct effect on campaigning (partial beta $= .11$, $p < .05$) even after controlling for political orientations and political knowledge. The multiple regression analyses showed no net effect of empowerment on black levels of communal activity or particularized contacting of officials.

5. AMERICAN VOTER TURNOUT IN COMPARATIVE PERSPECTIVE

G. Bingham Powell, Jr.

Seen in comparative perspective, American voter turnout presents an interesting paradox. Americans seem to be more politically aware and involved than citizens in any other democracy, yet the levels of voter turnout in the United States are consistently far below the democratic average. The resolution of the paradox lies, apparently, in the nature of voting as a form of participation.

In their study of different forms of political participation in seven nations, Verba, Nie, and Kim (1978) suggest a distinction between two types of forces that shape political activity. On one hand, there are the attitudes and characteristics that individuals bring to the participatory arena. Participation is, in general, facilitated by greater socioeconomic resources and by general levels of political awareness and self-confidence. On the other hand, participation is also facilitated or hindered by the institutional context within which individuals act. Legal rules, social and political structures, and configurations of partisanship all present the individual with conditions that shape his or her choices, and are relatively difficult for the individual to change. Analysis of the different types of participation suggests that voting is particularly likely to be dominated by institutional factors.

The present analysis attempts to explain the paradox of American voter participation in terms of the conjunction of the two types of forces cited above. Americans do possess political attitudes that encourage their voting activity. If citizens in other democracies possessed the American configuration of attitudes, their voter participation would on average increase. However, the American attitudinal advantage is only a marginal enhancer of voting. Its effects are limited, first, because in recent years the American attitudinal advantage has declined, and, more importantly, because voting is so powerfully shaped by institutional context. In comparative perspective, the American registration rules, electoral system, and party system inhibit voter participation, outweighing by far the attitudinal advantage.

The subsequent discussion is divided into three sections. The first of these

Source: *American Political Science Review* (1986) 80:17-43. Reprinted with permission of the publisher.

presents aggregate evidence on American advantages in social and attitudinal resources compared with other modern democracies, and contrasts these with the putatively disadvantageous institutional conditions. The second section uses econometric analyses of survey and aggregate data to estimate the relative importance of specific individual and system characteristics that affect voter participation. The third section analyzes the contributions made by each type of factor to relative American voter turnout by combining the estimates of the impact of various individual and institutional attributes with the evidence on the relative American advantages and disadvantages.

The Cultural and Institutional Environment for Voting

Table 5-1 presents some evidence that allows us to characterize the American political cultural environment in comparative perspective. The table is divided into several sections. The first compares the democratic publics on some attitudes often demonstrated to be associated with political participation. The second section compares the citizens' reports of three forms of political activity that might be expected to be related to their likelihood of voting. The third section compares the electorates on some demographic characteristics expected to be related to voter turnout.

Although attitudes facilitating participation declined in the United States in the late 1960s (Abramson and Aldrich, 1982; Nie, Verba, and Petrocik, 1976), comparison with political attitudes in the European nations still shows the American public to good advantage. Partisanship has declined, but is still equal to or above average. Eighty-three percent of Americans named a party they usually felt close to, placing the United States behind only the Netherlands and Finland in a twelve-nation comparison. On the other side of the partisanship scale, 14% said they felt very close to their party, a figure slightly behind only two other countries (Austria and Italy), although a drop from the America of the early 1960s.

Despite the drop in political confidence, the United States still led all countries in the number of citizens believing that they had some say in government. In general political interest, the 90% of Americans who reported at least some interest were comparable to their counterparts a decade earlier, and well ahead of the cross-national average. Only in the decline of political trust did the Americans drop from a leading position to one well back. The United States ranked ahead of only Italy in trust of the national government in 1974. (While most of the other attitude levels stabilized in the mid-1970s, and did not decline further, trust actually dropped an additional 8% between 1974 and 1980.) But political trust, although related to voter participation in America, was the least important of the four attitude variables in the American attitude studies.[1] We must conclude, therefore, that despite the decline in the period from 1960-1975, American political attitudes should still facilitate more political participation than political attitudes in other democracies.

This conclusion is strongly supported by the second section of the table, which compares three other measures of political activity: (1) discussing politics

Table 5-1 The Cultural Environment for Voter Participation: America Compared to Other Industrial Democracies in the 1970s

Variables	United States %	Averages from Other Industrial Democracies 11 Nations %	Averages from Other Industrial Democracies 7 Nations %	Rank of the United States
Attitudes Facilitating Voter Turnout				
Partisanship: mention a party they usually feel close to	83	73	77	3/12
Efficacy: reject: "People like me have no say in what the government does."	59	—	33	1/8
Trust: trust the national government to do what is right most or all of the time	34	—	47	7/8
Interest: possess at least some interest in politics	91	—	75	1/8
Other Forms of Political Activity				
Discussion: discussed politics with others	89	68	74	1/12
Persuasion: tried to convince others during elections	40	—	27	2/8
Party work: worked for a party or candidate during an election	30	—	14	1/8
Demographic Characteristics Facilitating Participation				
Education: beyond lower (ninth grade) education	79	—	39	1/8
Occupation: white collar jobs in work force	64	49	48	1/12
Age: over age 34 among population of voting age	64	66	66	11/12

Sources: Occupation from Taylor and Jodice, 1983. Age from United Nations, 1979-1983. Other Democracies (Austria, Britain, Finland, Germany, Italy, Netherlands, Switzerland, Belgium, Denmark, France, and Ireland): Political Action Study (Barnes et al., 1979) and Euro-Barometer (Rabier and Inglehart, 1981).

with other people, (2) trying to convince others to vote for a party or candidate during an election campaign, and (3) working for a party or candidate during elections. Nearly 90% of the American public reports discussing politics at least some of the time, compared to an average of only 68% across the 11 European nations. (Comparisons at the most active end of the discussion measure yield similar comparative results.) Thirty percent of the American citizens report having worked during a campaign at some time, more than double the average for seven European nations in which this question was asked. In reporting having tried to convince others during election campaigns, the Americans trail only the West Germans, with 40% affirming such activity, in comparison to an average of 27% in seven other countries. These American results parallel other studies of the American electorate quite closely. The strong relative position of the American public in attitudes that facilitate participation and in various measures of political activity other than voting also appears in other comparative studies, particularly in the five-nation Civic Culture study (Almond and Verba, 1963), and in the seven-nation Participation and Equality study (Verba et al., 1978).

The last section of Table 5-1 compares the American and European mass publics on three important demographic characteristics that have been shown to be related to political participation propensities. The American participation studies, as well as the comparative studies, have demonstrated that possession of greater social and economic resources, particularly higher levels of education, is associated with attitudes and behavior that facilitate participation. While these comparisons must not be taken completely literally, given differences in occupational structure and in educational quality and content, they help explain the relatively high levels of political awareness and involvement in the United States. The average educational level is much higher in the United States than in most of Western Europe (reflecting the much older American concern for mass education, as opposed to the European elite emphasis). The American citizen is also more likely to hold a white-collar or professional job than his European counterpart, although here the differences are not quite so marked, as all these nations are relatively economically developed.

Only in its age structure do the demographics of the American public tell against political participation. Many studies have shown that the youngest segment of the electorate, in general those under age 35, tends to participate less in most forms of political activity.[2] At the time of the 1970 censuses, the proportion of young voters in the American electorate was above average, although the differences were not very great. The gap increased notably by the 1980 census, due in part to reluctance in a few European nations to lower the voting age to 18, but primarily to the "bulge" of young people entering the American electorate in the late 1960s and the 1970s. This demographic change, as we shall discuss later, did increase the gap in turnout between the United States and the other democracies. As late as 1970, however, the age gap was slight.

The picture of American political attitudes and demographic characteristics that emerges from Table 5-1 leads us to expect high levels of American voter participation. However, the institutional factors facing the American voters are for the most part highly inhibiting, compared with those in the other industrial nations. The following discussion summarizes these differences from the American point of view. The full distribution for the 20 contemporary democracies is presented in Appendix 5-1.

As has been emphasized in previous comparative studies of voter participation (Crewe, 1981; Glass, Squire, and Wolfinger, 1984; Powell, 1980), the legal situation is of great importance. In some nations, legal sanctions are used to encourage voters to go to the polls. While the nature of the penalties and the level of enforcement varies within and across countries, there is no doubt that such sanctions tend to increase voter turnout. Such mandated voter participation has not been used in the United States, but is present in Australia, Belgium, Greece, and Italy as well as in parts of Austria and Switzerland.

Moreover, the registration laws make voting more difficult in the United States than in almost any other democracy. In 16 of the democracies examined, initiative for registering eligible voters is taken by the government in some fashion. In Australia and New Zealand the citizens must take the initiative; however, they are legally required to do so, and subject to fines or other penalties for failing to register. Of the 20 democracies outside the United States, only France leaves voter registration to voluntary initiative of citizens (Herman, 1976). In France citizens are required to register in their community and to obtain identification cards, which facilitates voter registration. In the United States registration is entirely the responsibility of the citizens and no set of requirements brings them to the registration site. Moreover, although the residency requirement in the United States has now been limited to 30 days before a federal election, only a handful of states with small populations have day-of-voting registration. Other states vary greatly in their registration hours and places, and in the degree to which these facilitate registration (see Rosenstone and Wolfinger, 1978), but all require the voter to re-register if he or she has changed residence since the last election. As the 1980 census showed that 47% of the population had moved in the past five years, it would seem that about half the eligible citizens must, in effect, make a double effort to vote in a presidential election: first the effort to register, then to vote.

A feature of the institutional context that has been the subject of much debate and analysis among American political scientists, but whose comparative implications are harder to measure and assess, is the competitive context. Intuitively, it would seem that in elections in which the outcome was expected to be close, citizens would feel more reason to participate and, perhaps more importantly, party organizations and activists would feel more incentive to get their voters to the polls.

In Appendix 5-1, and in the statistical analysis in the next section, two possible aspects of such competition are examined. First, we consider the frequency with which control of the national chief executive, by a party or coalition of parties, changed after an election in the twenty-year period from 1961 through 1980. By this measure, there is no doubt that the environment of the American presidential election was among the most competitive in any democracy. In the United States, party control of the presidency changed hands following four of the six elections between 1960 and 1980. We must note, however, that there were few changes in party control of the national legislature in the United States in this period, with the Democrats maintaining control of the House and losing control of the Senate only in 1980.

The second aspect of competitiveness concerns the possible influence of the electoral constituencies on competition in different parts of a country. The idea is simply that the electoral constituencies help determine whether parties and voters have equal incentive to get voters to the polls in all parts of the country, or whether there may be reason to neglect less evenly balanced regions in turning out the vote. Where the chief executive is chosen by simple majority or plurality vote, all regions should be equally important (e.g., France). In countries where the chief executive is chosen by the legislature, as in the various parliamentary systems, the question becomes the nature of the constituencies electing the legislators. With proportional representation from the nation as a whole or from large districts, parties have an incentive to mobilize everywhere. With single-member districts, some areas may be written off as hopeless.

Various American studies have found such effects in races for state legislative seats and governor (Caldeira and Patterson, 1982; Patterson and Caldeira, 1983; and references cited therein). Studies in Britain and Canada (Denver and Hands, 1975; Irvine, 1976) also suggest effects that dampen participation in some districts. In this intranational consideration of competitiveness, we would expect the American situation to be most like those in the single-member district countries, as the state acts as the electoral unit in the electoral college, and its electoral votes are delivered as a block, rather than proportionally. We must note, however, that American states shift support in quite volatile fashion. In 1972 about two-thirds of the states went for a candidate by a margin of over 20%, but in 1976 only 4% did so, while in 1980 20% did so.

Another important aspect of the partisan context is the linkage between political parties and social groups. For a variety of reasons, we expect voter turnout to be higher in countries having sharper partisan-group differentials in support. Partisan choice should seem simpler to the less involved; cues from the personal environment of the individual (friends, family, and co-workers) should be more consistent; party organizers can more easily identify their potential supporters in making appeals and in helping voters to the polls on election day. The last column in Appendix 5-1 shows a measure of the differential ties between voters' membership in social groups and their partisanship. In some countries, as in Sweden or the Netherlands, to know a voter's occupation or religion enables us to predict his or her voting preference to a very great degree. In Sweden in 1964, for example, about 84% of those with manual labor occupations supported the Social Democrats or the Communists, while only about 32% of the voters with white-collar or farm occupations did so, yielding a "class voting" index of 52. In the United States in the same year the manual labor support for the Democrats exceeded white-collar support by only about 17%. Indices of partisan support based on occupation, religion, and church attendance were calculated from surveys in 20 countries. Appendix 5-1 shows the highest of these indices.[3]

As shown in Appendix 5-1, the party-group support differentials in the

United States were only about half as great as those in the average democracy. In fact, the United States had one of the lowest levels of party-group support of any modern democracy. As the bases of the old Roosevelt coalition continued to crumble during the last 20 years, the vote scores on party-group differences fell even faster than these numbers, based on party identification, would indicate (see Abramson, Aldrich, and Rohde, 1983).[4]

While the party-group linkage measure seems to tap an important feature of the party system for voting mobilization, it would be desirable to have explicit measures of the strength of comparative party organizations. We would expect dense, penetrative, nationally-oriented party organizations to be most effective in getting voters to the polls in national elections. Unfortunately, there seems to be no reliable quantitative studies of party organization strength across nations. The only comparative study that even attempts to describe party organization in these terms is Janda's work (1980), which relies on expert coding estimates for 12 of the nations being considered here. The time period was the early 1960s.

The Janda study results are suggestive, and can be summarized here briefly. They portray the American party system as slightly above average in the sheer magnitude and extensiveness of party organization, but highly decentralized and with very weak ties to other social organizations. The results regarding extensiveness are interesting, but most of the major parties scored close to the maximum on the measures reported. There was not much variation across nations on the variable; the slight American advantage resulted from weak scores by some of the smaller parties in multiparty systems. I have not been able to discover comparative survey results on voters' reports of contacts by parties or other measures of comparative party effort.

The measures of centralization and organizational ties between parties and social organizations, called "penetration" in the Janda study, differentiate the democracies more sharply. The American parties are highly decentralized, especially in the selection of legislative candidates. On a combined measure of organizational structure, funding, and candidate selection, the United States ranks lowest of the 12 modern democracies in the degree of centralization. On the "penetration" measure, examining the ties between parties and such organizations as trade unions, religious bodies, and ethnic groups, the American parties ranked ahead of only the Irish parties. This measure seems to be the organizational counterpart of the party-group linkage measure based on partisan behavior, and empirically is closer related to it. We would expect that the lesser capacity of American parties to make use of other social organizations to spread their messages and to get voters to the polls would hinder their mobilization efforts.

We can summarize the description of the institutional environment for voting in the United States in comparison with other democracies by saying that it is the inverse of our description of the cultural environment. With few exceptions (age structure and political trust), the evidence on American political culture suggests that it should facilitate all kinds of individual political activity. With one exception (experience of party changes in national control of the executive), the institutional factors would seem to make the act of voting more difficult, and to impede the ability of parties and activists to mobilize supporters through appeals or through election day efforts to get them to the voting booth.

Estimating the Impact of Individual and Institutional Variables on Voter Turnout

While the evidence in the first section suggests reasons for America's exceptional pattern of an involved, but nonvoting citizenry, we need much more precise estimates of the relative importance of factors at the individual and system levels believed to affect voting. As it is likely that variables at both the individual and system levels are significant, the ideal analysis would consider both types of factors simultaneously. Unfortunately, we do not have comparable attitude surveys for half of the industrialized democracies. For the moment, therefore, we shall develop separate models of voter turnout. One of these models will be based on aggregate analysis of system-level variables, using the full set of 20 industrialized democracies. The second will be based on individual surveys from nine nations. In conclusion we shall consider on a preliminary basis the interaction of levels.

Comparisons of American Voter Turnout

The first step is to measure American voter turnout in comparative perspective. The problem is fraught with technical difficulties, but the overall situation is quite clear. In comparison with other democracies, the United States has relatively low participation of its citizens in major national elections. Average turnout in presidential elections in the United States as a percentage of the voting-age population was 54% in the period from 1972 to 1980. In the other 20 industrialized democracies the average turnout was 80%. American national voter participation exceeds only that of Switzerland. Among the nations that did not have compulsory voting, average voter turnout was 77% of the population of voting age, nearly 50% higher than turnout in the United States. This comparison is probably the most valid and reliable of those available. Detailed data are shown in Appendix 5-1. Similar comparisons may be found in Crewe (1981), Glass et al. (1984), and Powell (1980).

These comparisons rely on official reports of votes in the election that determines most directly the control of the chief executive. In the United States and France, these are presidential elections; in the other industrialized democracies, the most comparable elections are for the national legislature. The major problem in comparison is the denominator of the voting ratio: the eligible population. As turnout tends to be quite stable from election to election, the use of averages does not conceal many changes, but does help even out small errors in the census survey-based estimates of the voting age population at the time of the election. Appendix 5-3 discusses problems for comparison created by resident aliens in the population.

An important point to recognize about American voter turnout in comparative perspective is its close relation to voter registration. The United States is unique in the low registration rate of its population of voting age. Comparisons of turnout as percentages of either voting-age or registered populations lead to similar numbers in most countries, but radically different ones in the United States. In the United States perhaps two-thirds of eligible citizens are registered; of the other democracies, only in Switzerland are less than 90% of the citizens of voting age registered.

A final comparative point considers the time perspective. In most countries voter turnout changed little from the 1960s to the 1970s, remaining rather stable from election to election. In the United States, however, turnout dropped notably, for reasons various scholars have discussed elsewhere. These changes only served to widen the gap in electoral participation between the United States and the other democracies. They did not create the gap, nor, in fact, did the decline in American turnout even change its rank against any other country.

Aggregate-Level Explanations of Voter Turnout

I have collected data on most of the contextual and institutional factors described in the previous sections for the modern democracies. We can use these to attempt to explain differences in turnout across the democracies. As the institutional conditions do not change very often, it seems more appropriate to compare country averages than to enter individual elections as separate cases. Table 5-2, then, presents the model for voter turnout as a percentage of the population of voting age. Theoretically, we would expect that in the presence of compulsory voting, other factors encouraging participation have less effect. The countries where voting is compulsory are therefore deleted in the models in Table 5-2. (If we include them and a dummy variable for compulsory voting, the latter is powerful and significant, while the other aggregate coefficients are slightly depressed.)

The figures for the 1960s and 1970s are shown separately, as we hope to have more confidence in the results that are consistent at the two time periods. With a few minor exceptions, the independent variables are also measured separately at the two time points. Spain is not included in the first decade, as it did not become a democracy until the late 1970s. (Absence of party-group linkage data for Switzerland before 1972 and Israel in the 1970s forces us to use the same figure for both decades.) Switzerland is included as a dummy variable because of the unique nature of its collective executive and other special features of Swiss democracy.[5] A dummy variable is also included for the U.S., with its special registration conditions.

If we consider the general aggregate models emerging from Table 5-2, we see that they are reasonably stable and consistent across the time periods. (With few exceptions, they are also consistent with the analysis of voter turnout in 20 democracies reported in Powell, 1980, 1982.) The coefficients for intranationally competitive electoral laws and party-group linkages are rather similar in both time periods; party-group linkages are particularly strong and significant. The impact of changes in the chief executive is both weaker and less consistent. The unstandardized age coefficients are larger in the second decade, presumably reflecting the lowering of the voting age in most of the democracies in the 1970s, increasing the weight of an under-34 component. The dummy for Switzerland

Table 5-2 Aggregate-Level Explanations of Voter Turnout: Predicting Average Turnout as Percent of the Population of Voting Age in Democracies Without Compulsory Voting

Predictor Variable	Regression Coefficient	Standard Error	Standardized Beta
Voter Turnout in the 1960s: 1960-1970			
Age: Percent over age 34	.01	.32	.00
Automatic registration	3.70	2.51	.23[a]
Frequent changes in executive	.43	1.58	.03
Nationally competitive election districts	1.89	1.45	.22[a]
Party-group linkage index	.38	.15	.41[a]
United States dummy	−1.71	7.74	−.04
Switzerland dummy	−30.11	5.61	−.75[a]
$N = 15$ $R^2 = .90$			
Voter Turnout in the 1970s: 1971-1980			
Age: Percent over age 34	.38	.28	.13[a]
Automatic registration	.33	1.97	.02
Frequent changes in executive	1.26	1.23	.11
Nationally competitive election districts	1.78	1.09	.18[a]
Party-group linkage index	.45	.18	.33[a]
United States dummy	−12.30	6.46	−.25[a]
Switzerland dummy	−38.50	4.89	−.79[a]
$N = 17$ $R^2 = .94$			

[a] Significant at the .05 level.

Sources: Sources and data coding shown in Appendix 5-1.

reflects the significantly lower turnout in the Swiss system in both decades, although the gap has increased over time. The presence of automatic registration facilitates turnout; its effects are stronger if we delete the U.S. dummy. (The increasingly negative U.S. dummy is discussed below.)

The implications of these data are that voter turnout in the United States is severely inhibited by its institutional context. The only feature of the institutional context where the United States seemed to enjoy a clear-cut advantage was in the frequent changes in chief executive—a variable that was insignificant in each decade in the aggregate analysis (considering the Swiss case as unique, rather than occupying the end of a continuum, in this regard). The U.S. was disadvantaged by voluntary registration, unevenly competitive electoral districts, and very weak linkages (perceptual and organizational) between parties and social groups. The distance of 23 points between American party-group linkages and those in the average democracy would alone have been predicted to depress turnout by about 10%, based on the average coefficient in Table 5-2.

These models also work very similarly if we use turnout as a percent of the registered electorate as the dependent variable. The major difference is a reversal in sign of the automatic registration variable. That is, the presence of automatic registration facilitates voting participation of the age-eligible population, but leads to lower turnout among the registered. Such effects probably reflect the differing degrees of interest and partisanship required to enter the pool of the registered in the two kinds of registration situations. It is consistent with the well-known fact that turnout of registered voters is actually very high in the United States.

One variable not shown in the table is worthy of comment. While comparable education statistics were not available, I did attempt to use a measure of the percent of the labor force in white-collar occupations to get at the greater socioeconomic resources and skills available in some populations. The white-collar variable was positively related to aggregate levels of political discussion, in the 14 nations for which I had such a measure, at a significant and positive level ($r = .53$), just as we would predict from participation theory and from the individual models examined in the next section. However, the percent white-collar was negatively related to voter turnout ($r = -.18$), and when entered into the multiple regression with the institutional variables tended to be reduced toward zero. Accordingly, the white-collar variable is deleted in Table 5-2; its effects in mobilizing awareness are not sufficient to make an impact on turnout in the aggregate data analysis.

The analysis in Table 5-2 makes it possible to estimate the effects of the institutional variables in shaping voter turnout in modern democracies. I would emphasize, however, that we must be careful in the substantive interpretation of the institutional variables. The variables for intranational constituencies that enhance competition, and those for party-group linkage are the major source of concern. They are getting at some institutional property of the systems that affect turnout, to be sure. But these two variables are themselves related, and, in the subset of 12 countries for which we have the rather doubtful data, both are related to party organizational structure—especially party penetration of social groups. The party organization variables are not entered in the models, because of the limited number of cases and dubious nature of the data. If we do analyze those 12 countries, we find that centralization and penetration of social groups are strongly associated with turnout and with party-group linkage. Extensiveness, which has little variance, is not related to turnout. In multiple regression analysis, however, party-group linkage tends to reduce the impact of centralization and penetration to insignificance. Given the measurement problems, it is unwise to be confident about which of these aspects of the party and electoral system are the ones shaping turnout.

Individual-Level Explanations of Voter Turnout

Our analysis of voter turnout at the individual level relies on comparative survey studies. We would like to know two things. First, are the processes of voter involvement in the United States similar to those in other countries despite the differences in context? Second, if not, are there reasonably similar processes operating in other democracies, so that we could estimate the relative importance of various individual-level variables if the United States did have electoral and party contexts more comparable to those in other countries?

One difficulty should be noted first. We know that American survey studies consistently report greater levels of participation than do aggregate statistics. The difference reflects in part the population reached by the completed survey, and in part a tendency of citizens to overreport their participation. Judging by analysis of the voter validation studies conducted by the University of Michigan Survey Research Center (SRC) in 1964, 1976, and 1980, the overstatement of participation of some 18% in the 1970s reflects about an 11% net overreporting by citizens, and a problem of about 7% in the survey reaching parts of the population of voting age (Clausen, 1968-1969; Katosh and Traugott, 1981). Citizen surveys in most other modern democracies do not show as large an overstatement as do the American studies. However, the percentage of nonvoters who report voting in other countries seems not dissimilar to that in the United States—about one-fourth to one-third the nonvoters in the sample. (This statement is an informed guess, based on comparison of official and reported turnout across 14 surveys; the proportions due to sampling and response errors cannot be estimated accurately.) It is reassuring for our purposes that the relative rank of the United States among the nations which we shall be comparing here is the same using either survey or official statistics, with the United States ahead of Switzerland, but behind the other nations.

Table 5-3 uses standard demographic variables plus party identification (ID) to predict political discussion and voting in the most recent national election from surveys in nine nations, including the United States. The left side of the table shows the model for voter turnout; the right side shows a model for political discussion. On the far left side of the table we see categories of increasing education and age, as well as entries for sex and party identification. The cell entries show the increased probability of voting as we move, for example, from one education group to the next, in comparison with the base-line group. In the United States there is on average no increased probability of voting as we move from sixth grade to ninth grade education, but an increase of 10% as we move from ninth grade to the eleventh grade, and another 17% for actually completing high school. Turnout among the college educated is 35% greater than among those with a primary education only. We can compare these sharp education effects with the average effects in the other eight nations: a consistent, but small, increase of 2-3% as we move up the comparable categories, with turnout among the college educated only 10% higher than among those with a primary education. The American voter participation process is obviously far more affected by education levels than the process in other nations.

Table 5-3, and Table 5-4, show the unstandardized regression coefficients (multiplied by 100) from the ordinary least squares regression equations that predict voting using demographic and attitudinal variables. The dummy variables for each group category allow us to make direct comparisons with the base-line category and observe possible curvilinear effects, while controlling for other variables in the equations. Because voting is dichotomous, however, there is a potential problem of misestimating the magnitude of the coefficients by using multiple regression. The use of LOGIT or PROBIT provides reliable estimates with such dichotomous dependent variables. All the equations in the individual

Table 5-3 Individual-Level Explanations of Voter Turnout: Predicting the Increase in Probability of Voting and Talking Politics in Nine Nations

| | *Predicted Increment in Activity Relative to Base-line Group in the Category*[a] | | | |
| | *Percent Who Voted in Last National Election* | | *Percent Who Discussed Politics* | |
Independent Variables	*United States*	*Eight-Nation Average*	*United States*	*Eight-Nation Average*
Education Level [b]				
Basic	—	—	—	—
Lower	(0)	2	10	11
Extended lower	10	4	16	17
Middle	27	7	24	25
Post-secondary	35	10	29	28
Sex				
Male	—	—	—	—
Female	−6	−1	−5	−12
Age				
20-25	—	—	—	—
26-29	9	21	(5)	(1)
30-39	21	25	(5)	(0)
40-49	25	30	(3)	(−1)
50-59	32	(30)	(5)	(−2)
60+	40	(30)	(−2)	−8
Party Identification				
No	—	—	—	—
Yes	18	17	13	13

[a] These numbers are 100 x the unstandardized regression coefficients in regression equations with dummy variables for each group except the base-line group in each category. Coefficients in parentheses are not significant at the .05 level. As demonstrated in Appendix 5-2, LOGIT and PROBIT models provide nearly identical estimates. The eight nations are Britain, West Germany, Netherlands, Austria, Italy, Switzerland, Finland, and Canada. (Coefficients are averaged, not taken from a single pooled data equation.) For Canada the analysis uses federal party identification in 1974 and the same education categories that were used in the United States.

[b] The education variable is based on codes constructed for each country that attempt to identify comparable levels across countries. See Barnes et al. (1979), pp. 584-588. In the U.S. the levels correspond to the following categories: Under 7 grades completed, 7-9 grades, 10-11 grades, Completed High School, and Post High School.

level analysis have been reestimated using LOGIT and PROBIT. In fact, as usually seems to be the case, the solutions are virtually identical for those with ordinary multiple regression. Appendix 5-2 demonstrates the extremely similar predictions from the three models. As multiple regression provides more readily interpreted coefficients, it is used in Tables 5-3 and 5-4. The results of this analysis emphasize the robustness of regression results when dealing with dichotomous dependent variables, and suggest that the concern frequently expressed by readers on this score is seldom justified.

For readers accustomed to standardized regression coefficients, I can report that comparing, for example, average regression coefficients for a Socioeconomic Resource Level (SERL) variable of education and income, as used by Verba et al. (1978), in the equations yields a standardized beta coefficient of .33 between SERL and vote in the U.S., and only .05 between SERL and vote in 10 other nations.

The greater power of education effects in the United States might lead us to suspect that the education variable was being measured inadequately or differently in different countries. While we cannot disprove this possibility, some persuasive evidence that it is not so is offered in the two right-hand columns of Table 5-3. Here, the model is applied to a dichotomous measure of political discussion. The discussion results are striking for the great similarity between the impact of education in the United States and the other democracies, and are a tribute to the comparability of the Barnes and Kaase (1979) coding of education level. Not only does the probability of discussing politics rise with each increment of education, but the effects are extremely similar across countries.[6] This comparison seems powerful evidence that the voting participation process, but not the general process of personal involvement, is quite different in the United States.

Not only education, but age, shows a different relationship to voter turnout in the United States and the other countries. In the United States, each age increment shows increased probability of voting. In the other nations, the effects are very great going from the first to the second age group, but quite weak thereafter. On the other hand, the effect of party identification on voter turnout, and on discussion, is about the same in the United States as in the European average. Women voted somewhat less often than men in the United States, while the average difference was very small in other countries. Political discussion showed a sex gap in all countries, but the American difference was much less than that in the other democracies.[7]

The comparison of averages in Table 5-3 does, of course, blur differences among the non-American nations. Moreover, we need clearer evidence on the attitudinal processes involved in getting voters to the polls. In Table 5-4 we see individual participation models for the eight nations in the 1973-1976 Political Action study plus Canada in 1974, and including measures of interest and efficacy variables used in many American studies. For the sake of simplicity, political trust is not included here; its effects are quite weak, although in the predicted direction in most countries. The top of the table shows, again, the increased amount of voting participation expected from each increment of education, controlling for interest and efficacy as well as for sex, age, and party identification. Toward the bottom of the table we see the predictions for interest and efficacy. Each of the nine nations is presented separately, as we are not controlling for system-level effects. (The efficacy variable is a two-question variable, including the "no say" item shown in Table 5-1, exactly as used in Abramson and Aldrich, 1982.)

Table 5-4 Individual-Level Explanations of Voter Turnout: Predicting the Increase in Probability of Voting from Demographic and Attitudinal Variables in Nine Nations

Independent Variables	Predicted Increment in Voter Turnout Relative to Base-line Group (%)[b]								
	U.S.	Britain	W.Ger.	Neth.	Switz.	Fin.	Canada	Austria	Italy
Education Level[a]									
Basic	—	—	—	—	—	—	—	—	—
Lower	-5	-3	0	-1	10*	-3	1	1	0
Extended lower	2	-2	2	2	7*	0	5	1	3
Middle	15*	1	4	7	9*	5	9*	-0	0
Post-secondary	21*	6	3	7	15*	4	5	2	-4
Sex									
Male	—	—	—	—	—	—	—	—	—
Female	-3	1	-0	8*	-4	0	-0	1	0
Age									
20-25	—	—	—	—	—	—	—	—	—
26-29	10*	12*	14*	13*	9*	25*	3	40*	48*
30-39	19*	26*	16*	9*	16*	32*	6	39*	51*
40-49	23*	36*	15*	15*	23*	31*	15*	40*	51*
50-59	29*	34*	16*	19*	25*	35*	10*	40*	52*
60+	37*	33*	15*	21*	20*	35*	15*	40*	52*
Party Identification									
No	—	—	—	—	—	—	—	—	—
Yes	13*	24*	8*	33*	21*	9*	4*	4*	3*

Political Interest

Not at all	—	—	—	—	—	—	—	—	—
Not much	17*	9*	5*	8*	19*	9*	24*	2	2
Somewhat	30*	15*	7*	12*	34*	15*	34*	1	4*
Very	32*	18*	8*	8*	33*	14*	36*	2	−0

Political Efficacy

Low	—	—	—	—	—	—	—	—	—
Mixed	6*	3	2	2	8*	1	−1	1	−3*
High	9*	6*	1	7*	6	−0	−0	1	−4*

Reported turnout (%)	74	79	94	85	59	90	82	96	95

aSee Note to Table 5-3 for education levels.

bSee Note to Table 5-3 for source of estimate.

* Indicates that turnout of group was significantly above base-line group (.05). N of cases from 1030 to 2149.

The data in Table 5-4 are complex, but rich in information. The first point to note is that the individual voter participation processes in Austria and, especially, Italy (shown at the far right of the table) are rather different from those in the other countries. The attitudinal variables, particularly interest, but also efficacy, education, and even party identification, have much less effect in these two countries. And age is notable for the very great increase between the 21-24 group and the next older one, with very little subsequent change. It seems likely that voter participation in Austria and Italy is dominated primarily by institutional effects. Both countries have substantial compulsory voting, and Austria has an extremely well-organized and penetrative party system, so these patterns are not too surprising. Moreover, the extremely high reported turnout levels of 95% leave limited room for attitudinal effects to have play.

The second point to note about Table 5-4 is that the six "middle" countries, with automatic registration but without compulsory voting, manifest voter process models that seem rather similar. Naturally, we do find substantial variation—as we would expect from the measurement and language differences, the rather small subgroups in some categories, and the very high reported turnout levels (over 90% in Germany and Finland). But in each country we see sharp, slightly curvilinear effects of political interest and, less consistently, efficacy. Party identification, although varying in magnitude, is a significant direct predictor of turnout in each country.[8] Age has a generally positive and curvilinear effect, although the timing of drop-off varies. Sex is an insignificant predictor of turnout in all countries except the Netherlands, after interest and party identification are taken into account. Finally, we see that after political interest and efficacy have been included in the model, education has very weak and often insignificant effects on turnout. In most countries a somewhat weak initial effect of education (summarized in Table 5-3) is further reduced by taking account of political interest. Scattered and collectively significant small effects do remain, particularly at the middle and higher education levels.

Considering the American model in comparison with the other six nations without compulsory voting suggests both commonality and difference. On the one hand, attitudinal effects are rather similar. Party identification has an effect which falls about at the average of the other democracies. Interest is similar in strength, if on the higher side, and similar in its curvilinearity (not much impact by the increase from "somewhat" to "very" interested). Efficacy has an effect in the United States that is somewhat above the democratic average. Sex is insignificant in its effect on turnout after attitudinal variables are taken into account.

On the other hand, the direct effects of age and, especially, education are much greater in the United States than in any of the other countries. The age variable is notable for its continuing impact as we move to increasingly older groups. The impact is about average as citizens age from 20 to 39, but continues in the U.S., while becoming weaker in the higher age categories elsewhere. It seems likely that the lesser mobility of the older age groups, in conjunction with the unique American registration system, plays a major role in accounting for this continuing impact of age in the United States (Squire, Glass and Wolfinger,

1984; Wolfinger and Rosenstone, 1980, chap. 3). Unfortunately, a variable for length of residence is not included in the eight-nation study.

Most distinctive of all is the direct impact of education on American voter turnout. While the effect of education shown in Table 5-3 is reduced somewhat with interest and efficacy in the model, the direct effects are still quite powerful, with high school graduation worth 13% and college work another 6%. Not only does the United States have the most educated citizenry, but education has much more direct impact on voter turnout.[9] It seems very likely, although we cannot demonstrate it directly, that the difficulty of registration in America is also responsible for this remarkable distinctiveness of American voting processes. The great weakness of the party system in its organization and linkage to social groups may also enhance the value of personal characteristics and resources.

Of course, the overwhelming point to make about the models shown in Tables 5-3 and 5-4, when compared to the evidence on the cultural environment from Table 5-1, is that they all lead us to expect high voter turnout in the United States. The American electorate is highly educated, has above average levels of party identification, and is more interested and more efficacious than citizens in other democracies. The relatively low levels of trust are not as important as these other American advantages.

These individual-level modeling efforts redirect our attention to contextual factors operating largely, it would seem, at the national level. It is possible, of course, that incorporation of attitudinal and demographic variables here unmeasured would succeed in explaining the differences across nations in level of voter turnout. It would be especially reassuring to see a variable for citizen duty available across countries.[10] But the comparisons with political discussion suggest that the present variables, at least, are being measured fairly well, and that they do not account for the relatively low levels of American voter participation.

Effects of Misspecification in the Aggregate- and Individual-Level Models

Thus far we have estimated the importance of aggregate and individual characteristics in predicting voter turnout in separate models. To use the estimates in evaluating the factors depressing or encouraging American voter turnout, we need some assurance that each model is being reasonably well specified, despite absence of the variables in the other model. We cannot fully solve this problem without comparable attitude surveys in all the democracies, but we can gain some confidence by conducting the individual and aggregate analysis jointly in the subset of countries for which we have both kinds of data, and within which the individual models were fairly similar. We can pool the 7000 cases in the six countries that have both automatic registration and voluntary voting, replace the names of countries with their values on aggregate contextual variables, and estimate the coefficients with both individual and contextual variables operating together.

The problem in this approach is that we still have only six countries, despite 7000 cases, and some of the contextual variables interact badly, creating unstable estimates. Nor do we have the degree of freedom to enter many contextual variables simultaneously. We can, however, get some sense of the specification problem by using only a few of the aggregate variables. We can first run the model with these variables only, then add the attitudinal variables and see if the estimates change greatly. The process is reversed to ascertain the stability of the attitudinal estimates. The results of these procedures are relatively reassuring.

Consider first the aggregate coefficients. I ran the model with dummy variables for Switzerland, the age categories, and district competitiveness (coded single-member district, multi-district proportional representation [PR], national PR). Then I added the full set of individual-level variables for education, party identification, interest, and efficacy. The estimates for district competitiveness increased slightly after adding the individual-level variables. (The resulting model is that shown in Appendix 5-2.) Repeating this analysis using party-group linkages rather than district competitiveness also led to an increase in the party-group linkages coefficient by about 20% after including the attitudinal variables. Although the size of the coefficients is, naturally, rather different than the results in Table 5-2, because of the small number of cases and the inclusion of only one variable at a time, the analysis suggests that we can use the estimates from Table 5-2 without being too worried that they are badly biased by the absence of the attitudinal variables. Naturally, we would prefer to use the estimates based on the full set of democracies, rather than the six in the survey.

The results for the individual variables are also fairly robust, but show some need for caution. If we pool the six countries and run the individual-level variables alone, we get estimates for party identification, interest, and efficacy that are fairly similar to results including the aggregate variables (either as in Appendix 5-2, or with dummy variables for five of the countries). But the education effects, always somewhat weak and inconsistent in these countries, are estimated to be weakly negative after interest and efficacy are taken into account. Not until we include a variable for district competitiveness, or the country dummies, do we get the weakly positive education estimates we might expect from averaging the coefficients in Table 5-4.

The results of this exploration of the specification problem suggest that we can use the estimates directly from Table 5-2 for the contextual variables. But estimates for the individual-level variables must either explicitly include contextual variables, as in Appendix 5-2, or use country dummies or an averaging procedure that implicitly takes account of such effects.

Estimating the Effects of Cultural and Institutional Setting on Relative American Voter Turnout Levels

The coefficients estimated in the previous section can be used to analyze the effect of individual and institutional variables on levels of voter turnout in the United States as compared with other democracies. We must, however, keep in mind the unique nature of the American model, as shown in Tables 5-3 and 5-4. Because of the unique difficulty of registration in the United States, if for no other reason, it is difficult to be sure how the contextual variables affect American participation under present conditions. We shall approach the problem by using the coefficients estimated in the previous section to predict how turnout in the average modern democracy would change if its attitudinal and competitive conditions were similar to those in the United States.

Beginning with the individual-level variables, we have estimated the increment to turnout created by increased levels of party identification, education, interest, and efficacy. By comparing the percentage of the American citizenry with those characteristics with the percentage in the average democracy, we can multiply the difference by the estimated turnout increment to see the predicted effect of the average democracy developing a political culture similar to the American. For example, 84% of the American respondents stated a party identification, compared to 78% of those in the other democracies. If we multiply the 6% American advantage in party identification by the predicted increment of 14% (from Appendix 5-2) for individuals in the average democracy having a party identification, we estimate that increasing party identification in other countries to the American level would increase their average voter turnout by .85%—a bit under a 1% gain in turnout. In the case of education, interest, and efficacy, we do the analysis for each category above the baseline category, and sum the results to see the impact of the full distribution on the expected levels of voter turnout. The analysis is shown in the top half of Table 5-5.

While the analysis is somewhat complex, the results are simply summarized. If citizens in the average democracy were as interested in politics as Americans, voter turnout would increase by 2.2%; American levels of efficacy would increase turnout by .5%. The education coefficients estimated in Appendix 5-2 would increase turnout by 1.6% if the average democracy reached American education levels. These education estimates, as noted, are somewhat unstable; using average increments from Table 5-4 leads us to predict a 2.7% increase; using a model with country dummies leads to a figure between these. We should note that while the education coefficients are small, the huge American advantage in education levels has a notable effect. Over all, the United States is advantaged by its political culture. If the average democracy had a political culture as facilitating to voter turnout as American education and attitudes, we would expect turnout to increase by about 5%.

We can do the same thing with the institutional factors, using the models in Table 5-2. The presentation and analysis are slightly simpler here, because we use the linear estimates from Table 5-2, and can make predictions on average differences between the U.S. and the average democracy. If the other democracies had the American levels on competition-encouraging constituencies and party-group linkages, their turnout would be predicted to decrease by about 13%. The weak American linkages between parties and groups (and the associated weak party organizations) would reduce turnout by 10%. The low competitiveness of some American electoral constituencies would reduce turnout by about 3%. (The variable for changes in the chief executive, insignificant in both decades as shown in Table 5-2, is not included.) The age level increased turnout in the 1960s by a small amount, but decreases it about 2% in the 1970s, with the American lowering of voting age and the age bulge among the young. The net effect of all the variables in Table 5-5 is to lower turnout by about 10%, the American

Table 5-5 Predicting Changes in Voter Turnout if the Average Democracy
Had Automatic Registration but Individual and Institutional
Characteristics Similar to the United States

Independent Variables	Distributions on Independent Variables[a] (%)		United States Advantage in 1970s (%)	Estimated Regression Coefficient[b]	Predicted Change in Turnout in Average Democracy (%)
	Other Nations	United States			
Education					
Basic	36	5	—	—	—
Lower	22	16	−6	−.011	.07
Extended lower	21	13	−8	−.003	.02
Middle	11	31	20	.026	.52
Higher	10	35	25	.039	.98
Party Identification					
No	22	16	—	—	—
Yes	78	84	6	.142	.85
Political Interest					
None	17	9	—	—	—
Not much	27	21	−6	.118	−.71
Some	38	44	6	.189	1.13
Very much	17	26	9	.197	1.77
Political Efficacy					
No	49	34	—	—	—
Some	29	29	0	.024	0
Yes	22	37	15	.033	.50
Age					
Over 34 years	63	58	−5	.380	−1.90
Nationally competitive election districts scale	2.76	1	−1.76	1.800	−3.20
Party-group linkage index	36	13	−23	.450	−10.40

Net predicted changes due to:

Individual level variables of education, party, interest, efficacy	5.1
Aggregate age distribution	−1.9
Institutional variables	−13.6

[a] Institutional variables from Appendix 5-1, excluding compulsory voting nations. Attitudinal variables for the countries in Appendix 5-2.

[b] Coefficients from Table 5-2 and Appendix 5-2.

Sources and Variables: See Tables 5-1, 5-2, 5-3, and Appendices 5-1 and 5-2.

attitudinal advantage being outweighed by the institutional disadvantage on a 13 to 5 basis, with age adding another 2% disadvantage.

If we make the more heroic assumption that adopting automatic registration would create an American voting process like those in the other democracies, we would predict, then, that such registration would lead to American turnout levels some 10% below those of the cross-national averages. Recalling that turnout in the countries without compulsory voting (other than Switzerland) averaged 80%, we see that such changes would mean American turnout of the age-eligible would be increased from 54% to 70%. As discussed in Appendix 5-3, the presence of resident aliens, ineligible to vote, would limit this by at least 2%, to about 68%. Given the American institutional disadvantages (apart from registration), the U.S. would still have one of the lowest turnout levels of any democracy, tied with Canada and ahead of Switzerland, but the gap would be far less.

In comparison to present American voter turnout levels, the analysis implies that if the United States adopted automatic registration, or something similar, turnout might be increased by 14%.[11] This estimate is not inconsistent with that based on cross-state comparisons by Rosenstone and Wolfinger (1978), predicting that voter turnout in the early 1970s would have increased by about 9% if all states had had registration laws as facilitating as those in the most permissive states. It also fits reasonably well with the point made by Glass et al. (1984) that average turnout in states with election-day registration in the 1980 election was about 66%, some 13% above the national average. None of these states, of course, had automatic or compulsory registration. (The 1980 comparison, however, does not consider other attitudinal and institutional characteristics of the states with election-day registration.)

As Glass et al. (1984) and others have argued, getting most American citizens registered would lead to a major increase in American voter turnout. However, the present analysis suggests that it would not lead the U.S. to overtake most other democracies in voter turnout. Assuming that the U.S. does not wish to introduce compulsory voting, the other institutional factors are probably hard to implement. To make the presidential elections competitive across the country by doing away with the electoral college would probably help somewhat, but not as immediately as the 3% constituency factor in the model indicates, as it is surely capturing some party system effects. And the single-member district effects at legislative and lower levels would remain.

A final point here concerns changes over the last two decades. As has been noted by various scholars, the attitudinal characteristics that enhance participation in the U.S. have declined sharply since the early 1960s. If the 1960-64 levels of American education, partisanship, interest, efficacy, and trust are compared to the European averages of the 1970s (shown in Table 5-1) the U.S. ranks first in each measure by far. As we saw in Table 5-4, these individual characteristics are particularly important for voting in the American context. The most negative U.S. dummy coefficient in the 1970s in Table 5-2 seems to reflect the degree to which the attitudinal advantages compensated for the difficult U.S. registration conditions in the 1960s, but not in the 1970s.

Concluding Comments

In closing it is perhaps useful to separate the firm conclusions of this analysis from the more speculative ones. Comparison of voter turnout in the United States with voter turnout in other industrialized democracies leads to four observations in which we can be quite confident:

(1) Measured as a percentage of the population of voting age, voter turnout in the United States is very low in comparison with the other democracies. It was well below average in the 1960s and has declined even further, while average turnout in the other democracies has been stable at about 80%.

(2) The American attitudinal environment is, nonetheless, rather favorable to citizen participation of all kinds, including voting, although less so than in the early 1960s.

(3) The American legal and institutional environment is inhibiting to voter participation.

(4) As a form of participation, voting is particularly influenced by institutional factors, although attitudes are relevant.

Some other forms of participation, such as political discussion, are much less influenced by the institutional setting, and Americans are comparatively highly active in these forms of political involvement.

Although we cannot be quite as confident, it seems very likely that the unique American registration laws, which require frequent citizen initiatives from a mobile population, play a substantial role in depressing American voter turnout. It is also likely that these laws are responsible for the unusual degree to which education and other socioeconomic resources are directly related to voter turnout in the United States, even beyond their role (found virtually everywhere) in creating the attitudes of interest and efficacy which encourage participation.

The specific weights that have been attributed to the various factors are much more speculative, for a variety of technical reasons. This analysis suggests that in comparative perspective, the United States would be advantaged about 3% by its configuration of attitudes (especially political interest) and another 2% by its education level, but disadvantaged 2% by the age levels, 13% by the other institutional and party system factors, and up to 14% by the registration laws. There has been a marked decline in the attitudinal advantage over the last two decades. Although the amount of its effect is somewhat in doubt, the registration laws are probably the most easily altered factor, as well as perhaps the most important. Changing these laws would still leave the United States with below-average voter turnout, but the gap between the United States and the cross-national average would be greatly reduced. Changing the structure of party competition to mobilize lower class voters, for example, is probably much more difficult, although blacks represent an obvious target of opportunity for the Democratic party.

A full-scale analysis of the consequences of voter turnout is beyond the scope of this paper. We can, however, briefly conclude with a comment on two aspects of the problem: system legitimacy and voter quality. A substantial debate exists in the democratic theory literature concerning the implications of high levels of voter turnout for the legitimacy and stability of democratic systems. On one hand, theorists favoring citizen participation have argued that higher levels of turnout reflect and encourage political legitimacy and citizen support. On the other hand, theorists concerned about democratic stability have pointed to the often undemocratic values of the less educated, and the high levels of turnout in such unstable systems as Weimar Germany and postwar Italy, to argue the dangers of high voter turnout levels.

Recent empirical analysis suggests that the theorists favoring participation have the best of the argument. Analysis of voter turnout in 29 democracies clearly shows a strong association between higher turnout and less citizen turmoil and violence. After controlling for various economic, constitutional, and party system variables, higher levels of turnout still seemed associated with less frequent citizen riots and protests, although not related to deaths by political violence or the overthrow of democracy (Powell, 1982, chap. 10). On the other hand, the countries with higher levels of turnout, at least among the more industrialized countries, did tend to have less durable tenure of the chief executive. From the American perspective, where a presidential system usually creates substantial executive durability in any case, the balance of the evidence would seem to favor higher levels of citizen voter involvement. There should be some channeling of citizen discontent out of the streets and through legitimate political channels without loss of executive stability.

The argument about the quality of the voter can be approached from two directions. On one hand, because of the effects of social and economic resources under the present system, there is little doubt that adopting automatic registration or other measures to encourage turnout of the less well-off would bring to the polls a total electorate somewhat less interested, efficacious, and informed than the present voters. We do not want to overstate this fact, because we have already estimated that such changes would only increase turnout to less than 70%, and some small effects of interest and education in encouraging voters remain. But some decrease in the present levels of voter sophistication (not exactly overwhelming in ideal terms) would probably occur. On the other hand, we must recall that by comparative standards, the American electorate is extremely interested and involved. Even the total mobilization of all American citizens would mean a voting group that is more interested, efficacious, and more likely to engage in political discussion and other activity than are present voters in most other democracies.

NOTES

1. For average gammas between attitude variables and turnout in the United States between 1960 and 1976, see Miller, Miller, and Schneider (1980). The correlation between trust and turnout is .12, compared to .37 for efficacy and .50 for interest.

2. See Niemi, Stanley and Evans (1984), and the references therein. For sake of simplicity, I am here ignoring the slight turnout decline among the oldest age groups.

3. See Crewe (1981) and Powell (1980) for alternative measures. See Powell (1980) for most sources used to estimate party-group linkages. These data were extended with data from the political action surveys and Euro-barometer (Rabier and Inglehart, 1981) study cited above, and with calculations from tables appearing in Flanagan (1984), Holmberg (1981), Levine and Robinson (1976), Linz (1980), and Valen (1979).

4. The one demographic group in the United States with highly differential party support is black Americans. I have not included black support in the American party-group linkage calculations for two reasons. First, because groups as small as 10% of the population are not included in the analysis for other countries, and would increase the linkage numbers in most countries if they were. Secondly, although Verba et al. (1978, chap. 10) and others have shown that blacks do overparticipate as a social segment, relative to expectations from their socioeconomic resources, they seem relatively unmobilized considering their potential value to the Democratic Party. While this may be changing in 1984, it suggests that party-group linkages depend on party mobilization efforts to take advantage of differential group linkages, and are not purely individual-level phenomena.

5. For a more extensive discussion of the Swiss case see Powell (1980) and Appendix 5-3.

6. See the very comparable relationships between socioeconomic resources and "political involvement" reported by Verba et al. (1978, p. 75) in their seven rather different nations, and the marked contrast they, too, found with voting participation.

7. See also Almond and Verba (1963) and Verba et al. (1978, chap. 12) for similar findings on differences between males and females.

8. Measurement of partisanship is a matter of current controversy too complex to review here. In fact, it seems surprising that the results for partisanship and turnout are as consistent as they are, given the different meanings and stability associated with partisanship across countries. But the coefficients in Table 5-4 do show some notable differences in the impact of party identification on turnout. Measurement problems may well be responsible. The present analysis has been replicated using a measure of partisan intensity rather than a simple dichotomous partisan identification variable, with very similar results. In the case of Canada, it should be noted that the general political interest question was not available in the Canadian study. A question about interest in the campaign was used instead, which had a particularly weakening effect on the original Canadian party identification coefficient. However, that coefficient was well below average even without the other attitudinal variables. Efforts to use a provincial or combined party identification measure for Canada, rather than the federal party identification used here, did not change the results.

9. For similar results in a different study, using different surveys, see Verba, Nie, and Kim (1971, pp. 75-79).

10. American voting research suggests that citizen duty is the best predictor of voter turnout, and has not changed greatly in magnitude or power over the past 20 years (Miller et al., 1980). I have not been able to find comparative studies using citizen-duty variables in other countries. The Almond-Verba study (1963) does examine responses to a question on obligations that citizens owe their countries. Americans and Germans report rather similar frequencies of mentioning voting as an obligation—levels higher than the British, Italian, and Mexican respondents. It seems unlikely that duty is a more powerful mobilizer in Europe than in the United States.

11. It must be emphasized repeatedly, of course, that other, unmeasured, attitudinal and

institutional variables may account for part of the difference. We have, for example, no measure of citizen mobility. Although its effects should be less under conditions of automatic registration, we would still expect less turnout from the highly mobile. This and other unknown factors are included in what here is ascribed to registration laws. For that reason the estimate may well be on the high side.

Appendix 5-1 Voter Turnout and Institutional Characteristics of Twenty Democracies in the 1970s

Country	Average Turnout as Percent Eligible	Average Registered as Percent Eligible	Compulsory Voting	Eligible Required to Register	Frequency of Change in Chief Executive[a]	Type of Electoral District[b]	Average Strength of Party-Group Linkages
Australia	86	91	Yes	Yes	3	1	33
Austria	88	96	No	Automatic	3	3	42
Belgium	88	95	Yes	Automatic	2	3	51
Canada	68	93	No	Automatic	4	1	29
Denmark	85	98	No	Automatic	4	4	43
Finland[c]	82	100	No	Automatic	2	3	48
France (presidential election)	78	91	No	No	3	4	33
West Germany[d]	85	94	No	Automatic	2	4	34
Ireland	77	100	No	Automatic	4	2	25
Israel	80	100	No	Automatic	2	4	—
Italy	94	100	Yes	Automatic	2	3	40
Japan	72	100	No	Automatic	1	2	30
Netherlands	82	98	No	Automatic	2	4	45
New Zealand	83	95	No	Yes	3	1	40
Norway	82	100	No	Automatic	3	3	37
Sweden	88	97	No	Automatic	3	4	42
Switzerland	44	85	No	Automatic	1	3	43
United Kingdom	75	100	No	Automatic	4	1	33
United States (presidential election)	54	61[e]	No	No	4	1	13
Spain	78	100	No	Automatic	—	3	42

[a] 4 = Chief executive changed party hands 50% of elections 1960-80; 3 = clear changes, but under 50%; 2 = partial changes only; 1 = no changes in parties controlling chief executive.

[b] 4 = national election PR or national pool for some legislative seats, or simple national presidency vote; 3 = large district PR; 2 = PR with three to five members per district; 1 = single member or winner-take-all districts.

[c] Excludes Finns living outside of Finland from voted, registered and eligible.

[d] Excludes West Berlin (not eligible to vote in West German elections).

[e] Estimated from University of Michigan Survey Research Center study.

Sources: For registered and voted, Mackie and Rose (1982) and *European Journal of Political Research*. Age-eligible population calculated from United Nations Demographic Yearbooks, 1979, 1981, 1983 (based on census data, interpolated to election year).

Appendix 5-2   A Comparison of Three Models of Multivariate Analysis of Voter Turnout in Six Nations: Regression, LOGIT, PROBIT

Independent Variables	Slope Coefficients			Predicted Turnout (%)			Simple Turnout (%)
	Regression	LOGIT	PROBIT	Regression	LOGIT	PROBIT	
Intercept	.347	4.15	4.08	84	84	84	84
Education[a]							
Basic	—	—	—	83	83	83	85
Lower	−.011	−.009	−.016	82	83	83	82
Extended lower	−.003	.021	.014	83	83	83	82
Middle	.026	.137	.139	86	86	86	83
Post secondary	.039	.206	.208	87	87	87	88
Age							
20−25	—	—	—	66	67	66	65
26−29	.113	.342	.402	77	77	77	77
30−39	.173	.581	.662	83	83	83	84
40−49	.221	.787	.887	88	88	88	88
50−59	.218	.783	.890	88	87	88	87
60+	.217	.785	.895	87	88	88	87
Party ID							
No	—	—	—	73	74	74	68
Yes	.142	.516	.583	87	87	87	88
Interest							
Not at all	—	—	—	70	72	72	66
Not much	.118	.353	.404	82	82	82	79
Somewhat	.189	.671	.747	89	89	89	90
Very	.197	.805	.863	90	91	90	94
Efficacy							
Low	—	—	—	82	82	82	81
Mixed	.024	.107	.123	85	85	85	86
High	.033	.148	.174	86	86	86	88
Electoral							
SMD	—	—	—	75	74	74	81
Multi-District PR	.112	.522	.575	87	86	86	75
National PR	.125	.628	.685	88	88	88	92
Switzerland							
No	—	—	—	87	87	87	87
Yes	−.250	−.882	−.997	62	62	62	62

Note: Based on pooled data from Britain, West Germany, Netherlands, Switzerland, Finland, and Canada. N = 7191. Excludes cases missing on any variable. LOGIT and PROBIT from MVS/OS version of SPSSX; the program adds 5 to the PROBIT and divides by 2 and adds 5 to LOGIT; account is taken of this in the predictions.
[a] See the note to Table 5-3.

Appendix 5-3 How Alien Residents Affect Voting Turnout Figures

The problem of fair comparison of voting turnout figures raises many theoretical and technical issues. One of these is worth special comment here: alien residents in the population. In most democracies voting eligibility is limited to citizens. Population figures, on the other hand, usually include noncitizens resident in the country for a year or more. Countries vary substantially in the percentage of such aliens, largely depending on the presence of jobs and ease of access to draw alien workers and their families, but also depending on their naturalization policies in denying or facilitating attainment of. citizenship by resident aliens. If we accept the legitimacy of the denial of voting eligibility to aliens, then the countries with substantial alien populations are penalized in column 2 of Appendix 5-1. Unfortunately, we do not have good data on percentage of residents counted by census who are aliens of voting age, and cannot systematically adjust our turnout data to remove them. For the United States we do have census estimates based on self-reported citizenship. This percentage probably understates noncitizenship; we do not know by how much. The census study figures (U.S. Bureau of Census, 1978, 1982) indicate 3-4% of the population of voting age in the United States were noncitizens in the 1970s. Adjusting the U.S. turnout figures to exclude these noncitizens would increase turnout of age-eligible Americans by 2%—closing only slightly the gap between American turnout and the democratic average. As we can see in Appendix 5-1, this adjustment would not alter the position of the U.S. relative to most other democracies.

Moreover, while it is clear that some countries in Appendix 5-1 have fewer aliens than the United States, figures for West Germany, France, Belgium, and Switzerland indicate that they had more aliens in the resident population than did the United States (Britain also had more, but special provisions affecting immigrants from the Commonwealth enfranchised many of them rapidly.) The best figures and most aliens were for Switzerland, where the foreign worker population increased from 10% in 1960 to 16% in 1970. Moreover, a 1975 study indicated that 80% of these Swiss immigrants had lived in Switzerland for more than seven years, although very few were able to become citizens under the difficult Swiss rules, which include a twelve-year residency requirement (Miller, 1981). Excluding aliens from both Switzerland and the United States brings Swiss turnout nearly to the American level, and accounts for virtually all of the Swiss unregistered population of voting age. Thus, the resident alien problem does not seem to be a serious problem in American comparisons with other democracies, although Switzerland is rather sharply affected. (The slight decline in turnout as percent of resident age population in West Germany in the 1970s may well also be caused by foreign workers.)

PART II: POLITICAL SOPHISTICATION

6. WHAT DETERMINES HOW VOTERS THINK ABOUT POLITICS?

For more than twenty years after publication of *The American Voter*, a considerable volume of research on public opinion and voting behavior focused on the level, or distribution, of ideological thinking in the American electorate. As Kinder (1983, pp. 389-90) pointed out, a good deal was learned about public opinion in the process, but, by the mid-1980s, it was time to move on to new questions. To some extent, this has happened, although questions about the extent of ideology have not disappeared. New work is still devoted to the question of "fundamental" knowledge, sometimes with a slightly new twist, such as the degree to which individuals view liberalism and conservatism as bipolar concepts. The concern with the overall ideological level of the electorate has not been replaced by a clear, new focus. Nevertheless, there is a detectable new theme to recent work, involving the nature of political thinking and the factors that influence the various degrees of sophistication. This chapter is organized around that theme.

We note at the outset that answers to the new questions are not entirely independent of answers to the old question. Not surprisingly, for example, those who claim that the original view was incorrect—that is, those who argue that voters were relatively sophisticated in the 1950s—tend not to be concerned with variations in levels or types of political thinking. Nonetheless, as we shall see, overall voter sophistication and variations in how voters think about politics are distinguishable phenomena.

The Original View Reinforced: Voters Are Unsophisticated

The most forceful statement of this view is by Eric Smith (1989) in his aptly-named book, *The Unchanging American Voter*. In order to understand his position, recall how *The American Voter* (Campbell, Converse, Miller, and Stokes, 1960) characterized the political sophistication of the electorate of the 1950s. They asked people "What do you like about the Republican party? What do you dislike about the Republican party?" and similar questions about the Democratic party, about the Republican presidential nominee, and about the

Democratic presidential nominee. The answers to these eight like/dislike questions were then coded in terms of the respondent's "level of conceptualization." Citizens who responded in ideological—chiefly liberal/conservative—terms or in terms of broad ideas that are inherently ideological, such as attitudes toward change, were coded as ideologues and were treated as having the highest level of conceptualization. Next came those who viewed politics as a matter of group benefits, seeing one party (or candidate) as particularly good (or bad) because of how they treated a particular social group ("the Republicans are good for business," "the Democrats are good for workers"). The third category, termed nature of the times, consisted of those who responded in vague generalities about the times or with isolated, single issues; and the fourth category was reserved for those whose eight answers were totally devoid of any issue content. *The American Voter* viewed voters as unsophisticated in that few voters were ideologues and most were in the bottom two categories.

As should be clear from its title, *The Unchanging American Voter* essentially agrees with the conclusions of *The American Voter*, though Smith does not fully embrace its methods. With respect to the levels of conceptualization, for example, Smith (p. 104) argues that "the principal uses of the levels indexes have been to assess the number of ideologues in the population and to assess the change in that number over time. Neither use is justified. . . . The levels indexes do not work."

Smith (chap. 2) argues that the levels of conceptualization are not valid measures of different modes of thinking; psychologists, he says, have not developed any such concepts to distinguish different kinds of political thought. However, the levels measure *sophistication*, "albeit crudely," and then "only because they reflect the number of responses, which measure sophistication" (p. 76).[1] In any event, whatever they measure, they are riddled with random measurement error, though the underlying characteristics are highly stable (chap. 1). And the latter point "supports *The American Voter's* conceptual permanence thesis" (p. 42)—that is, the notion that some voters simply lack the cognitive ability to understand abstractions such as liberalism and conservatism, while a small number hold ideological ways of thinking consistently over time.

If this conceptual permanence thesis is indeed correct, two testable propositions follow. First, the electorate is relatively unsophisticated. Smith hardly dwells on this point, but it is clear that he regards the electorate's lack of factual information and lack of recognition of ideological terms as good evidence in support of it. Second, there is little change in the sophistication of the electorate across time; despite the normal ups and downs of political interest, reflecting the varying prominence of political events, sophistication marches along at a relatively constant state.

Smith argues that, in fact, the sophistication level of the American electorate has not changed over a long period of time—probably at least since the 1940s when reasonable survey evidence became available, and certainly not in the 1960s, a period in which other researchers have detected important changes. Smith's argument rests on three pieces of evidence. First, as we have already noted, is the high individual-level stability of the underlying traits measured by the levels of conceptualization. Second is a showing (pp. 98-101) that most of the change in the distribution of the "levels" between 1960 and later was due to candidate images, which Smith regards as a false indicator of sophistication. Third, in a section we reprint here as Chapter 7, is evidence that there has been remarkably little change over the years in awareness of a number of information and ideological-recognition items.

However, Smith is not the only recent author to argue that voters are unsophisticated and that apparent evidence to the contrary is flawed or misleading. Neuman (1986, p. 9) notes that "apathy dominates American mass politics" and that "this has probably been true since the time of Alexis de Tocqueville." Like Smith, he cites a variety of results tending to show voter ignorance and ideological unawareness right up into the 1980s (chap. 2). Unlike Smith, he emphasizes the lack of attentiveness of the bulk of the population rather than inherent, cognitive limitations. Indeed, he notes (p. 186) that "the great majority of the population . . . can be alerted if fellow citizens sound the political alarm," and cites Vietnam, Watergate, civil rights, and women's rights, as well as "a multitude of more narrowly defined issues" as recent concerns over which citizen awareness has rocketed to public attention (and then quickly receded).

Others find evidence for constant, low levels of voter sophistication levels in the distributions of the levels of conceptualization over a period now approaching three decades (Table 6-1). This coding of the levels is based on a full reading of the responses to the "likes/dislikes" questions and is thus comparable over the entire series.[2] In summarizing the results, Knight (1990, p. 72) observes the well-known increase in the top category in 1964, but she then emphasizes the absence of any increase in the 1980s despite "the apparent ideological nature of the Reagan campaigns." She interprets the evidence as indicative both of a "limited capacity for ideological thinking" and "one which is relatively impervious to the campaign environment" (p. 72).

Still other work speaks to the unchanging character of voters' ideological capacities, indirectly supporting the view of an unsophisticated electorate. This includes work on the correlates of ideological thinking. For example, if education were highly correlated with sophistication, we would expect the overall level of sophistication to have increased in the past few decades as new generations came of age with greater education than their predecessors. Yet, as we have seen, there was no steady increase in sophistication in the 1960s and 1970s. And recent studies at the individual level indicate that, indeed, the relationship between education and sophistication is surprisingly weak (Smith, 1989, chap. 5; Luskin, 1990, pp. 345-49).[3]

Another bit of indirect evidence comes from a recent report by Hagner and Pierce (1991). In responding to Smith's work, they looked at what they called the "superficiality hypothesis"—that responses to the likes/dislikes questions are heavily laden with reports of the dominant campaign themes as seen on television. They found relatively few such responses and a "remarkable level of stability" (p. 24) in the proportion of such responses from 1976-1988.[4]

Table 6-1 Distribution of the Levels of Conceptualization, 1956-1988

Levels of conceptualization	1956	1960	1964	1968	1972	1976	1980	1984	1988
Ideologues	12%	19%	27%	26%	22%	21%	21%	19%	18%
Group benefit	42	31	27	24	27	26	31	26	36
Nature of the times	24	26	20	29	34	30	30	35	25
No issue content	22	23	26	21	17	24	19	19	21
Total	100%	99%	100%	100%	100%	101%	101%	99%	100%
N	(1,740)	(1,741)	(1,431)	(1,319)	(1,372)	(2,870)	(1,612)	(2,257)	(2,040)

Source: Knight (1990, p. 72), updated with 1988 values supplied by Kathleen Knight.

The Original Criticisms Reinforced: Voters Are Relatively Sophisticated

All of the work reviewed so far indicates limited and unchanging cognitive capabilities. Another set of work views voters as unchanging but as moderately sophisticated. This work, beginning in Europe and extending to the United States in the late 1970s (see *Classics in Voting Behavior*, chap. 4), is based on the observation that a large proportion of the electorate can place themselves on a liberal/conservative scale (left/right in Europe) and that this placement is meaningfully related to attitudes and voting (for example, Levitin and Miller, 1979; Knight, 1985; Jacoby, 1986).

Researchers who focus on liberal/conservative self-placement generally believe the electorate to have greater knowledge and understanding than do those who rely on open-ended material.[5] That they have observed little change in ability or willingness to place oneself (or major political actors) on the scale reinforces their view that the electorate was more sophisticated even at the time of the first major election studies. In part this may be an artifact of the short time in which liberal/conservative scales have been used; time series based on identical questions extend only to the early 1970s. But in this period there has been no hint of significant changes. In fact, few studies have even bothered to compare overall placement percentages. Fuchs and Klingemann (1989, p. 210), however, show comparisons between the United States, Germany, and the Netherlands in both 1974 and 1980, with no change in the between-country ordering and little change within countries. Niemi, Mueller, and Smith (1989, p. 21) find that, in the National Election Studies between 1972 and 1986, the percentage who fail to place themselves varies between 21 and 34 percent, but with no obvious pattern. Fleishman (1986) notes only a small decline in self-placement in 1980 and 1982, albeit in the presence of an explicitly ideological presidential candidate.[6]

Another stream of work focuses on the stability of survey responses and, to a lesser extent, on the correlations (interpreted as "constraint") among attitudes. It can be traced back to Achen's (1975) article on the unreliability of survey questions. We will not review all of that work here (see *Classics*, chap. 4), but we will note some recent, supportive research.[7]

Krosnick has been at the forefront of recent work showing that attitudinal *in*stability is caused, in part, by question formats. He argues that contrary to conventional wisdom, symbolic attitudes, such as party identification, are not inherently more stable than nonsymbolic attitudes. In a variety of experimental studies, Krosnick and Berent (1991) find that use of a "branching" format for issue questions—that is, the same format used in the traditional party identification question—leads to much greater stability than formats typically used with policy items.[8] In another report, which directly addresses the matter of voter sophistication, Krosnick (1991, p. 561) calculates stability coefficients for a variety of attitudes using panel data from the 1950s and 1970s and from 1980. All coefficients are high, and there are no significant differences among the three panels.[9]

Green's (1988) work also supports a view of relatively sophisticated voters. In contrast to Conover and Feldman (1981), Green suggests that individuals view liberals and conservatives as polar opposites. That is, once measurement error is taken into account, thermometer scores show that people who like conservatives dislike liberals, and vice versa. His evidence is limited to two election years in the 1970s, but the nearly identical results in those years as well as the overall high level of understanding suggested by his results would lead us to conclude that voters do not require special circumstances or events to view the world in a sophisticated way. Using a quite different approach, Fuchs and Klingemann (1989, pp. 220-21) also suggest that interpretations of left and right are largely bipolar, although the tendency is marginally less for the United States than for Germany and the Netherlands.[10]

In short, a host of works suggest that the way in which voters think about politics is relatively unchanging. But these views are sharply contrasting—one set viewing the electorate as largely unsophisticated up to and including the present, and another set viewing the electorate as having coherent, even quite ideological perspectives at least since the 1950s.

A New View: The Level of Political Sophistication Depends on the Political Environment

It is obvious, of course, that voters' outlooks depend to some degree on the political environment. Candidate images, for example, naturally vary with the comings and goings of particular individuals. Certain issues, such as Iraq and Desert Storm, are on the agenda for very short periods of time, and even issues such as the Vietnam War are not really long-run concerns of the electorate. More significant, however, is the argument that the way in which voters respond to politics, in some more abstract sense, varies along with political stimuli.

Evidence that individuals change in ways other than in their surface responses about current personalities and issues first appeared in the 1964 National Election Study, though it became most apparent when data were available through the early- to mid-1970s. That work is reviewed in *Classics* (chap. 4), but it is important to repeat one point here—namely, that evidence of change was widespread. For example, increases in levels of constraint may have been a methodological artifact (see *Classics*, chap. 7), but the larger number of ideologues (Table 6-1) was not; also, observed stability on many items was unchanged from the 1950s, but stability on certain new items was much greater (Converse and Markus, 1979).

Further evidence of a change in the level of voter sophistication, as well as an explanation for the change, was provided by Carmines and Stimson (1989, chap. 5). They argued that Americans' political attitudes were restructured in the 1970s around the theme of race. Though a portion of their analysis is bedeviled by the same change in question format that plagued others' work, they show that attitudes on racial issues were more highly constrained than attitudes on nonracial matters and that the difference grew over time. Moreover, they suggest that "the change in levels of attitudinal consistency was rooted in real-world political events" (p. 135).[11]

Another widely held explanation for increased sophistication in the mid-1960s and beyond is that politics became more salient to ordinary voters. However, as plausible as this explanation is, there has been surprisingly little evidence to support it. Indeed, seemingly contrary evidence has sometimes been reported, as when Niemi and Westholm (1984, p. 75) found little relationship in the United States between political interest and attitudinal stability. Recently, however, in a study of the origins of sophistication, reprinted here as Chapter 8, Luskin found that interest, along with intelligence, is a major contributor, even in the presence of controls for education, media usage, and other variables. Thus, to the extent that interest drives the relationship, the public may be capable of much greater sophistication than it ordinarily demonstrates.

Of course, a capacity for high-level thinking does not mean that large numbers will demonstrate sophisticated thought at any one time, or that, over a period of time, all or most voters will show signs of sophistication. Luskin himself appears somewhat pessimistic in saying that interest in politics and therefore sophistication levels are quite stable (p. 132). Neuman (1986), too, seems somewhat ambivalent, arguing both that "the great majority of the population . . . can be alerted if fellow citizens sound the alarm" (p. 286) and that the idea of issue publics—that is, that at any one time, there are many small groups of people intensely interested in particular public policies—does not fit the empirical evidence (pp. 67-73).[12] In any event, to the degree that voters are responsive to the political environment, the *potential* exists for greater sophistication than is typically apparent. It also follows that there should exist certain periods at which the level of sophistication is noteworthy, although the difficulty of defining and measuring sophistication across long periods of time makes this a difficult proposition to test.

Another, more compelling, line of work also suggests that the extent to which voters view the political world is dependent on their environment. This work extends back to the 1960s, when it was discovered that party identification does not mean the same thing for Americans and Europeans and that in Europe, class, religious, and agrarian-industrial cleavages were more important bases for political conflict. Later, it was discovered that Europeans more often view partisan conflict in terms of a left/right dimension and that they can more often give meaning to that continuum (*Classics*, chap. 4).

Recent work has supported and amplified the view that Europeans are more responsive to the left/right dimension. Fuchs and Klingemann (1989), for example, find Americans much less likely than German and Dutch voters to recognize and understand left/right terminology and consistently less likely to give substantial meaning to the left/right continuum. They also find that German and Dutch voters are more likely to view the dimension in a bipolar fashion (pp. 220-22). Similarly, Granberg and Holmberg (1988) found that opinions on issues are more constrained in Sweden than in the United States (chap. 4), caused, perhaps, by the considerably greater consensus in Sweden on the positions taken by the political parties (chap. 2). They also reinforce Niemi and Westholm's (1984) finding of greater attitudinal stability in Sweden.

Though the contrast between the United States and Europe is the most striking, there are differences among European electorates as well. In an early study, Klingemann (1979a) found the Netherlands and Germany to be especially high on ideological thinking. For example, on a measure combining active use with recognition and understanding of ideological terms, he found that 59 percent and 67 percent, respectively, had at least a minimal conceptual understanding in contrast to 47 percent and 33 percent in Austria and Great Britain, respectively (p. 246). More recently, Westholm and Niemi (1992) added a new element by finding sharp differences among European countries (as well as with the United States) in the manner and extent to which left/right self-placement is transmitted intergenerationally.

Thus, one strain of recent work emphasizes variability in levels of political sophistication, both across time and across political systems. The stimuli with which individuals are presented—the kinds of issues that are salient, the nature of elite arguments, and the type of political system—conspire, as it were, to create unsophisticated electorates in certain times and places and much more sophisticated electorates in other circumstances.

Another New View: How People Think About Politics Varies across Individuals

Most political scientists view sophistication as a good thing; implicitly or explicitly, they see a high level of sophistication as better than a low level, perhaps for the individual and certainly for society. However, some researchers have begun to ask *how* individuals understand politics, with considerably less concern for whether or not they display a high level of sophistication. In fact, researchers adopting this perspective usually acknowledge that most people do not have highly sophisticated political views; nonetheless, they argue, voters do have political perceptions that can be meaningfully characterized and that allow those voters to interpret and engage in political discourse. Thus, our effort should be one of trying to understand correctly how it is that most people do think about politics.

This approach has some similarities with Lane's early work about personal ideologies (see *Classics*, chap. 4), but it draws its label and many of its ideas from cognitive psychology (especially "schema theory"). Schema theory begins by asking how it is that people organize their political thinking. The answer is best conceived of as "a cognitive structure that contains knowledge about the attributes of a concept, specific instances and examples, and their interrelationships" (Hamill and Lodge, 1986, p. 70). These "knowledge structures" (Lau, 1986, p. 95) may be very sophisticated and, for political matters, be based on abstractions such as liberals and conservatives. But they may just as well be simpler and based on properties such as class, race, issues, parties, or personalities (for example, Conover and Feldman, 1984; Hamill, Lodge, and Blake, 1985; Lau, 1986). Moreover, a person does not necessarily have just one schema in the way that an individual presumably falls at one point on a measure of sophistication (Lau, p. 112).

Schema are not studied so much for their own sake as for understanding how individuals process information; a prototypical example is Conover and Feldman's (1989) study of how individuals acquired information about candidates' issue positions during the 1976 campaign. Schema are considered dynamic by their very nature; they are the basis on which information is acquired, stored, and processed, but they themselves change as more information is absorbed. Lodge, McGraw, and Stroh (1989) make this an explicit part of their "impression-driven" model of information processing, in which there is "a counter in working memory that integrates new information into a 'running tally' of one's current impression" (p. 401).

Just as there is no single way to measure sophistication, there is no agreed-upon operationalization of the schema concept. There does seem to be some consensus that the appropriate methodology should allow individuals to reveal their own way of interpreting information. Thus, for example, Miller (1991, p. 1375) notes the use of "open-ended questions, rank-ordered lists, free selection of n choices from a longer list," and Conover and Feldman (1984, pp. 101-02) suggest that one way of measuring schema is to use some sort of rating task. Beyond that, however, methods differ widely. Conover and Feldman (1984) based their schema on a Q sort, in which individuals sorted statements according to the degree to which they reflected the hypothesized domains. Lodge and Hamill (1986) identified "partisan" schema through a combination of political interest questions and ability to classify prominent political leaders as Republican or Democratic. Allen, Dawson, and Brown (1989) defined closeness to African-American mass or elite groups by respondents' feeling of closeness to poor blacks, black elected officials, and so forth. Interestingly, some studies have used the very same questions used to determine the levels of conceptualization. Lau (1986), for example, used all of the likes/dislikes questions to create group, party, issue, and candidate schema. Miller, Wattenberg, and Malanchuk (1986) used the candidate questions to identify five categories of responses about candidate personalities.

The schema approach has recently been attacked as devoid of new ideas and as often involving little more than the substitution of a new label to describe old ideas (Kuklinski, Luskin, and Bolland, 1991). While there is much in this critique with which we agree,[13] we note that the critics are *not* arguing that cognitive structures are independent of the environment. Indeed, one of the positive points that Kuklinski, Luskin, and Bolland see in schema theory is an emphasis on information processing (p. 1347). Thus, however one evaluates schema theory, the emphasis on information intake and development is very different from the focus on fixed mental capabilities that characterizes work reviewed at the beginning of this chapter and fits nicely with more recent work emphasizing the responsiveness of voters's perceptions to the political environment.

Schema theory has also been of value in reinforcing and enhancing the view that many people have a structure for interpreting political information—even a shared structure—in the absence of well-developed ideologies. In some respects this is not a new idea at all. Following Lane's (1962) ideas, for example, we noted that the second level of conceptualization ("group benefits") might well represent a class ideology (or what might now be called a schema) used by working class voters to interpret political stimuli (*Classics*, chap. 4), and Luskin argues that the original coding of the levels might differentiate too finely among nonabstract responses (1987, p. 882; see also Knight, 1990, pp. 79-80). Nonetheless, because "political schema measures do not assume any ordering between, or make any value judgments about, the different schema" (Lau, 1986, p. 113), those who take this perspective may have heightened our awareness of the ways in which *all* individuals understand and respond to political stimuli.[14]

Conclusion

One thing we know with certainty: there is ordinarily, even when politics is at its most salient level, a wide range of sophistication. Many voters do not understand, much less actively use, abstract principles to organize their political thoughts. This holds whether we think in terms of the liberal/conservative dimension or search for individualized abstractions. In addition, partly as cause and partly as consequence, many individuals are surprisingly innocent of basic facts about political matters and, in ordinary times, strikingly indifferent to them as well.[15]

A second thing is equally certain. There is a distribution of sophistication, just as there is of political knowledge and political interest. Most voters are not so ignorant or indifferent as to have no political opinions whatsoever or to respond only randomly to survey inquiries. In fact, many use the terms of ideological discourse, even if they are less than certain of their meaning. Of course, at the "bottom" end of the distribution, the extremely negative characterizations are true. But to see the entire electorate in those terms is as misleading as it is to think that the whole population is highly sophisticated.

But if most individuals are neither highly sophisticated nor abysmally ignorant, how do they view politics? We are only now beginning to get some answers, as researchers move away from an exclusive concern with how many in the electorate are ideological to the study of why and how less ideological individuals process and interpret political information. What is most clear so far is that almost all individuals have some systematic means of interpreting political matters and that those means involve a variety of connections or relationships among ideas rather than a single, common perspective. Some voters see politics heavily in partisan terms, others interpret matters largely by means of a racial, religious, or class perspective, and still others are mostly attuned to candidate qualities, whether personality traits, instrumental characteristics such as competence, or purely affective features such as charm and looks.

What is less clear is how to make use of the variety of ways in which people think about politics. One way of beginning this task might be to think more explicitly about the degree to which individuals respond to their political environments. We reviewed a fair amount of evidence suggesting that the way in which voters react to politics depends on their surroundings—the nature of the party system, the issues that confront them, and specific candidates and the nature of their rhetoric. A better understanding of the way in which these factors influence people would perhaps be a start toward a political theory of political sophistication.

NOTES

1. Smith published his initial analysis of the levels in Smith (1980). That article and his recent book have stimulated a number of vehement rebuttals. Cassel (1984, pp. 422-26), for example, criticizes Smith for using change scores and finds that expected relationships with other variables are more substantial when the conceptualization index itself is used. Jacoby (1986) and Knight (1990) find systematic differences in the way in which those at various levels respond to measures of liberalism/conservatism. Hagner and Pierce (1991) criticize Smith on a number of grounds, including what they regard as a misinterpretation of change in the party versus candidate components of the levels index. On the matter of psychologists' work, see Hagner and Pierce (1991, pp. 11-12) and Luskin (1990, p. 332). About the only point of agreement between Smith and his critics is that there is a fair amount of unreliability in the levels measure.

2. Coding of the levels has sometimes been based on so-called "master codes" designed by the Michigan research team and applied by each study's staff of coders. That operationalization has been criticized for missing some of the subtleties of the original measure and for overestimating the number of ideologues. See Smith (1980, p. 686) and Hagner and Pierce (1982, p. 785).

3. Similarly, Converse (1975, pp. 103-04) found an unexpectedly small relationship between education and attitude stability, and Junn (1991, pp. 203-08) found conflicting results about the effects of education on political knowledge.

4. In arguing that sophistication levels are relatively constant, one must necessarily make mention of the largely artifactual change in measured attitudinal constraint between 1960 and 1964. See *Classics*, chaps. 4-7.

5. It is widely recognized, of course, that "ideological identification" is not the same as "ideological sophistication"—that is, that many who can place themselves on a dimension do not fully understand it, much less actively use it in their day-to-day

discourse. See, for example, Jacoby (1986), Knight (1984; 1990, pp. 73-77); Fuchs and Klingemann (1989).

6. Of course, as Fleishman and others (for example, Dalton, 1988, chap. 7) have pointed out, the meaningfulness of the liberal/conservative dimension may change over time, as the old issues that defined the concepts become irrelevant and new issues are not yet integrated into the traditional framework. In fact, what may happen is that current issues ultimately define a completely new dimension and the old one simply fades into oblivion.

7. It is perhaps an over-interpretation to say that these authors view the electorate as relatively sophisticated inasmuch as they make very important, but relatively circumscribed, statements. For example, to say that voters have stable opinions that are untapped because of faulty survey instruments is not to say that voters are highly sophisticated in all respects (for example, that they understand and make active use of abstract, ideological concepts). Nonetheless, these authors convey a sense of a relatively high level of voter knowledge and reasoning ability.

8. Zaller's (1988) experiments also show that over-time stability is affected by question format, although his work emphasizes individual differences in reactions to policy questions.

9. Krosnick by no means argues simplistically that everyone has firm views on all political matters. He shows, for example, that the importance individuals attach to issues is an important determinant of over-time stability (Krosnick, 1990).

10. On the other hand, Knight (1990) shows that viewing liberals and conservatives in a bipolar fashion is strong only among those who are ideologues on the levels of conceptualization index, even when scores are corrected for differential tendencies to rate groups relatively high or low. See also Jacoby (1988) and Stimson (1975). It is not clear, however, whether these authors' results mean that how voters view the political world is responsive to the environment.

11. While attitudinal consistency, or the extent to which one's ideas are constrained, is widely regarded as an important element of sophistication, Luskin (1987), Wyckoff (1987), and Smith (1989, chap. 3) have all suggested that correlations among responses to policy questions may not be a good measure of consistency (and therefore of sophistication). Wyckoff, for example, suggests that correlational analysis is biased toward a conventional (that is, elite) understanding of how ideas should fit together. Wyckoff also suggests that attitudinal stability is not a valid measure of sophistication. Both approaches continue to be used, though now researchers are more careful to indicate just what their findings mean and do not mean.

12. On the basis of a more thorough analysis of the importance of issues, Krosnick (1990) finds substantial support for the issue-publics perspective.

13. The idea of an on-line model of information processing (Lodge, McGraw, and Stroh, 1989), for example, is highly reminiscent of Fiorina's view of party identification as a "running tally" (1981, p. 84) of partisan observations and evaluations.

14. Still, the relationship between sophistication and modes of information processing is somewhat ambiguous. On the one hand, Rahn, Aldrich, Borgida, and Sullivan (1990; Chapter 12 in this volume) find that sophistication is unrelated to the way in which individuals form impressions of presidential candidates, and both Lau (1986, pp. 115-16) and Miller, Wattenberg, and Malanchuk (1986, pp. 526-27) find that education (usually considered a component of sophistication) is unrelated to the use of an issue schema. On the other hand, the latter two studies find that higher levels of education are associated with greater use of certain kinds of personal evaluations. To make

matters more confusing, Lodge and Hamill (1986, p. 508) define schematics (that is, individuals who hold a particular schematic view) on the basis of sophistication.

15. We think this point is acknowledged even by those who view the electorate in a relatively positive light. See note 6 above.

FURTHER READINGS

Measurement and Degrees of Political Sophistication

Carol A. Cassel, "Issues in Measurement: The 'Levels of Conceptualization' Index of Ideological Sophistication," *American Journal of Political Science* (1984) 28:418-29. Smith erroneously used change scores, leading him to underestimate the reliability and validity of the levels index.

Donald Philip Green, "On the Dimensionality of Public Sentiment toward Partisan and Ideological Groups," *American Journal of Political Science* (1988) 32:758-80. Contrary to Conover and Feldman, the public views Democrats/Republicans and liberals/conservatives as polar opposites.

Jon A. Krosnick, "The Stability of Political Preferences: Comparisons of Symbolic and Nonsymbolic Attitudes," *American Journal of Political Science* (1991) 35:547-76. Differences in stability of symbolic and nonsymbolic attitudes can be attributed to differences in survey questions.

Robert C. Luskin, "Measuring Political Sophistication," *American Journal of Political Science* (1987) 31:856-99. Excellent critique of various classes of and specific measures of sophistication.

Schema Theory and Related Models

Pamela Johnston Conover and Stanley Feldman, "Candidate Perception in an Ambiguous World: Campaigns, Cues, and Inference Processes," *American Journal of Political Science* (1989) 33:912-40. How voters use various cues to infer candidate stands on issues.

James H. Kuklinski, Robert C. Luskin, and John M. Bolland, "Where's the Schema? Going Beyond the 'S' Word in Political Psychology," *American Political Review* (1991) 85:1341-55. Schema theory has contributed little to political psychology; suggestions for greater use of cognitive psychology.

Richard R. Lau, "Political Schemata, Candidate Evaluations, and Voting Behavior," In *Political Cognition*, ed. Richard R. Lau and David O. Sears (Hillsdale, N.J.: Erlbaum, 1986). Measures schema with likes/dislikes questions; compares schema to the levels index; presence of schema affect perceptions of candidates.

Milton Lodge, Kathleen M. McGraw, and Patrick Stroh, "An Impression-Driven Model of Candidate Evaluation," *American Political Science Review* (1989) 83:399-419. Experimental studies of the ways in which individuals form impressions of candidates and campaign material.

Comparative Studies of Ideology

Russell J. Dalton, *Citizen Politics in Western Democracies* (Chatham, N.J.: Chatham House, 1988). Chapter 7 shows a dimensional analysis of "Old Politics" and "New Politics" cleavages.

Dieter Fuchs and Hans-Dieter Klingemann, "The Left-Right Schema," In *Continuities in Political Action*, M. Kent Jennings, Jan W. van Deth, et al. (Berlin: deGruyter, 1990). Understanding of and meaning given to the left/right dimension in the United States, Germany, and the Netherlands.

Donald Granberg and Sören Holmberg, *The Political System Matters: Social Psychology and Voting Behavior in Sweden and the United States* (New York: Cambridge, 1988). Emphasizes how the United States and Swedish political systems affect issue consistency, perceptions of party positions, vote changes, and so forth.

Anders Westholm and Richard G. Niemi, "Political Institutions and Political Socialization: A Cross-National Study," *Comparative Political Studies* (1992) forthcoming. Transmission of left/right orientation and party identification in the United States and seven European countries.

7. CHANGES IN THE PUBLIC'S POLITICAL SOPHISTICATION

Eric R. A. N. Smith

Neither the level of conceptualization indexes nor the attitude consistency measures works [according to Smith's book, chaps. 1-3]. Neither is capable of measuring change over time in the public's political knowledge and sophistication. So what does work? How can one measure change in the way the public thinks about politics? And what do such measurements indicate about change in the public's knowledge and sophistication? These are the questions I address in this chapter.

Preliminary Considerations

There are few measures of political knowledge and sophistication that are available over any extended number of survey years, and all of the measures have problems. This unfortunate state of affairs is in some ways the result of progress in research. In the early years of survey research, there were a fair number of information questions. Indeed, one of the most important early findings of survey researchers was how little the public knew about politics (Erskine, 1962, 1963a, 1963b, 1963c; Hero, 1959; Hyman and Sheatsley, 1947; Kriesberg, 1949; Metzner, 1949; Patchen, 1964; Robinson, 1967; Withey, 1962). The public's lack of information was so well established that scholars lost interest in studying the subject. Because survey questions asked of national samples are scarce and valuable resources, fewer questions were asked to assess the public's knowledge, and more questions were asked about other, more interesting topics—many suggested by *The American Voter*.

Throughout the 1950s and 1960s, the number of political knowledge questions dwindled. The Gallup Poll, for instance, used to ask such questions as "How many senators are there from your state?" and "Can you tell me what is

Source: From *The Unchanging American Voter* (Berkeley, Calif.: University of California Press, 1989), 159-176, 190. Copyright © 1989 The Regents of the University of California.

meant by the term 'Electoral College'?" By 1960, it had abandoned the practice (Gallup, 1972). Erskine (1963a, p. 133) noted this decline in her comprehensive review of "all available questions" on political textbook knowledge. She found 110 questions over the 1947-1962 period. In the first four years, 46 questions were asked; in the next four years, 42 questions appeared; in the next four, only 18 questions were used; and by the last four years, from 1959 to 1962, just 4 questions were asked. In other words, over that sixteen-year period, information questions virtually vanished.

Another reason for the scarcity of questions about political information is that they are hard to ask. Because people know so little about politics, factual questions with right or wrong answers are often embarrassing to respondents. They cause problems in the interview situation, and are therefore difficult to ask. As an example of this, consider the fate of the information questions asked in the CPS 1972 National Election Survey. There were only a few questions asking the most basic facts—how many times can a person be elected president, how long is a senator's term, which party had a majority in the House of Representatives before and after the election. Interviewers later objected to these questions because respondents had complained to them. The interviews were supposed to be about the respondents' opinions, not about their knowledge. Apparently, some respondents got upset. Consequently, most of the information questions were not repeated in later years.

The result is that few information questions were repeatedly asked across the years. As Converse (1975, p. 101) remarked, this lack of a record of the public's information level is "deplorable." The CPS National Election Surveys contain a few such questions, but none is very good. The NORC General Social Surveys do not have any political information questions. The Gallup and other private surveys have occasional information questions, but because those organizations focus on contemporary politics, few questions are repeated, and only one of them (recall of congressman's name) is repeated systematically over a long time span. In short, if one wants to examine changes in the public's knowledge over time with direct questions about factual information, one has to make do with a very small set of questions.

Aside from the lack of repeated information items, there is another more subtle difficulty in looking at the changes in people's knowledge. Many items are not quite comparable over time. Circumstances that make some items more or less difficult to answer correctly change from year to year. At first this idea might seem to be the same as the thesis argued by *The Changing American Voter*, namely, changes in the environment cause changes in political sophistication. It may sound similar, but it is not. The claim is that changes in the environment cause changes in the difficulty of specific information items. The two ideas are quite different. To see the distinction, consider how we use information items to measure political knowledge. We select a small set of items, usually no more than three or four. Each item asks for a specific piece of information. However, we are not actually interested in those pieces of information, but rather in what we can infer beyond those three or four facts. We care not about the individual's knowledge of those specific facts, but about how much the individual knows about politics in general. We use the small set of items to infer how much the respondent knows about the realm of politics.

By way of example, consider the 1968 questions asking what type of government the People's Republic of China has and whether the PRC was a member of the United Nations. Knowing those facts is not what we care about. If two people know exactly as much as one another except that one person knows these two additional facts, we would think them equally sophisticated. We would not really care about the difference. Yet if one person knows both facts and the other does not, it is a good bet that the one who knows about China also knows a good deal more about a wide range of other political issues. In short, when we measure information, we have little reason to be interested in the content of the scale. Our interest lies in what we can use the scale to measure—general political information.

There are, of course, cases in which researchers are interested in specific facts. For instance, those who study congressional elections care about whether respondents know the candidates' names. In this and similar cases, the researcher's interest is not in general political knowledge. These examples of interest in specific items are irrelevant to this inquiry.

It follows that environmental changes that affect *only* the item in question and not the individual's overall information level are changes that must be ignored. That is, when circumstances change so that a specific fact becomes better or less well known, but nothing else changes, we want to be able to identify that change and adjust for it when making comparisons over time. For example, consider what might happen if a question about the government of South Africa had been repeatedly asked since the 1950s. Up until the recent surge of news about the movement for freedom and civil rights for South Africa's blacks, few Americans would be likely to know much about South Africa. Now that the antiapartheid movement is getting lots of media attention, the number of people who know about the country has certainly risen. But does that mean that the public is becoming more sophisticated? It does not. Just as South Africa is gaining in recognition, Afghanistan, Biafra, Bangladesh, and other foreign media hot spots of the past are fading. Overall knowledge has not really changed. Instead, some facts are becoming more widespread, and others are becoming less so.

In sum, the political environment can change in ways that cause the relationship between an information item and the individual's total knowledge to change. Put more technically, the item's "difficulty" can change.[1] When these changes occur, the inferences one can draw from the item must also change. Although it is not easy to do, one must try to identify changes that affect only the item and to adjust our over-time comparisons for those changes. That is, one must try to get past superficial changes in the method of measuring information so changes in general information over time can be measured.

The criteria for selecting information items were (1) an item had to be repeated at least two or more times, (2) at least one of those times had to be 1960 or earlier, and at least one had to be 1964 or later, and (3) the item had to be repeated in an identical or nearly identical format. That is, the time series had to include the 1960-1964 gap so that the great leap forward thesis could be tested.

The condition that the items had to be identical is, of course, necessary for any sort of comparisons across time.

These conditions eliminated almost all available information items. Few of the SRC/CPS National Election Study items were repeated more than once, and even fewer included both sides of the 1960-1964 gap. For instance, the question about what sort of government the people of mainland China have was asked only in 1964 and 1968. Because it does not include the critical early 1960s, it was not included.

The problem of differently worded questions being asked at different times also eliminated some measures. The most important measure to be rejected because of changes in question wording is the party difference scale used in Chapter 2 [of Smith]. This scale counts the number of differences between the Democratic and Republican parties that each respondent sees on a series of issue questions (the same issue questions used to measure attitude consistency). The problem is the same as the one with attitude consistency. The wordings of the questions were changed between 1960 and 1964, with the result that the relationships between the party difference scale and all other measures sharply changed. As a consequence, the party difference scale is not comparable across the 1960-1964 gap. Although the scale seems to be an excellent measure for use in cross-sectional analyses, it cannot be used in a time series investigation.[2]

Measures of Political Knowledge

The best information measure available is the number of responses to the like/dislike questions. The assumption underlying this measure is that the more one knows, the more one will have to say when asked open-ended questions about the parties and candidates. The statistics presented in Chapter 2 [of Smith], as well as those presented by Kessel (1980, chap. 7 and app. A) attest to the measure's validity and reliability. Because this measure is available over the entire time span of this study, it can be used to assess changes in the public's political thinking.

There are, of course, problems with the number of responses as a measure of political knowledge and sophistication. The first problem, noted earlier and also pointed out by Kessel (1980, p. 275), is that a more talkative person will receive a higher score irrespective of his or her knowledge of politics. Although I doubt that this is much of a problem, there is no way of estimating the bias introduced by talkativeness. However, there is no reason to expect talkativeness to change over time. Thus because our interest here is in using this measure for comparisons over time, this problem is not a cause for worry. A constant source of bias over time (talkativeness) will not affect over-time comparisons.

A second problem, related to the first, is that the number of responses is not directly a measure of knowledge. No answers are graded right or wrong. This is in no sense a direct test of what the respondent knows. Thus talkativeness can intrude, and so can other influences. For instance, interest in politics can cause people to say more, irrespective of their normal talkativeness or of their knowledge of politics. Still, although the number of responses has problems, they do not seem to be overwhelming.

Table 7-1   Mean Number of Responses by Year

	1956	1960	1964	1968	1972	1976
Party response	3.5	3.3	3.1	3.7	2.9	3.0
Candidate response	4.1	4.1	4.5	4.5	4.1	4.4
Total	7.6	7.4	7.6	8.2	7.0	7.0

Source: Data are from the CPS 1956-1976 American National Election Studies.

The mean number of responses by each respondent to the party questions, the candidate questions, and the two combined from 1956 through 1976 are shown in Table 7-1. Although there is a little fluctuation up and down in each of the three time series, there is no overall trend in any of them. The average number of responses to the party questions moves around between 2.9 and 3.7. The average number of candidate responses varies more narrowly, between 4.1 and 4.5. Neither measure shows the electorate becoming either more or less knowledgeable and sophisticated between 1960 and 1964, the period of the great leap forward in sophistication according to *The Changing American Voter*. The number of party comments declines slightly from 3.3 to 3.1, and the number of candidate comments rises slightly from 4.1 to 4.5. The picture is one of an unchanging American voter.

Another measure of political knowledge is recall of the names of candidates in contested congressional elections. This measure has an advantage in that it asks for a specific piece of information, and one can identify right and wrong answers. Yet this measure has its own problems, the major one being that various political factors that influence how well representatives and their challengers are known have been changing over time. For instance, hotly contested, close elections make both contestants better known because of the campaign spending, media attention, and so forth. Yet the number of close elections for the House has declined sharply since the 1950s (Burnham, 1975; Mayhew, 1974). The result may be that fewer people know their representatives than would had the number of close elections remained the same over the years.

Another factor is the effort that members of the House put into building their reputations in their districts. As Fiorina (1977), Mayhew (1974), and others have shown, politicians are spending far more time and effort than they used to wooing their constituents (Jacobson, 1987a, chap. 3). They visit their districts more often. They send more mail home. They spend more staff money on casework and playing the ombudsman role. These factors may contaminate long-term trends in candidate recall. Thus although recall is a fairly good measure of information (and one of the few that was asked repeatedly), it is hardly a perfect measure. It may work reasonably well with cross-sectional data, but using it for comparisons in time series involves some risks.

Keeping these qualifications in mind, consider the data on recall to see if they reveal any trends. Three different sets of recall data are shown in Table 7-2,

Table 7-2   Recall of Candidates' Names in Contested House Elections

| Year | Ferejohn (1977) CPS Voters Only | | Cover (1976) CPS All Respondents | | Gallup (1972) |
	Incumbents	Non-incumbents	Incumbents	Non-incumbents	Incumbents
1942					50%
1947					42
1957					35
1958	58%	38%	44%	28%	
1964	63	40	52	32	
1965					43
1966	56	38	40	23	46
1968	64	46	50	34	
1970	55	31	35	16	53
1972	50	31	36	19	
1974	57	32	34	16	
1978	61	38			

Note: The Ferejohn data are based on voters in contested seats. The Cover data are based on all respondents in seats contested by incumbents. The Gallup data are based on all respondents irrespective of whether their congressional races are contested or not or whether incumbents are running.

Source: Both the Ferejohn and Cover data are from the CPS 1956-1978 American National Election Studies. The Ferejohn data are calculated by Ferejohn (1977, p. 170) and Crotty (1984, p. 218). The Cover data are computed by Cover (1976, p. 58) and Mann (1978, p. 27). The Gallup data are from Gallup (1972).

two from CPS data and one from Gallup data. The first set, collected by Ferejohn (1977), is based on voters in contested congressional districts. The second set, collected by Cover (1976), is based on both voters and nonvoters in all districts in which incumbents ran for re-election. The third set, from the Gallup Poll, is based on all respondents to the poll and thus includes both contested and uncontested seats.[3]

Scanning down each column of figures reveals a fair amount of fluctuation. Ferejohn's figures for recall of incumbents, for instance, vary from 50 to 64 percent. The one pre-1964 data point, 58 percent correct recall, is exactly the same as the average of the 1964 and later figures. That is, there is no difference between recall in the pre- and post-1964 periods. The other time series point to the same conclusion. None of the three data sets reveals any increase in recall over time. In fact, while the Ferejohn and Gallup data show no trends of any kind, the Cover data show an actual decline in recall starting in 1970. Mann (1978, p. 27) suggested that the decline is concentrated among nonvoters. Yet whatever the source of the decline, two data sets show no change over a thirty-year time span, and one data set shows a decline. There is certainly some fluctuation from one year to another. For instance, recall during presidential election years seems to be somewhat higher than during other years, but nothing here suggests any increase in knowledge over time. So again the finding is that the American voter is unchanging.

Another often used measure of political information is based on the respondents' knowledge of control of the House of Representatives. In every presidential election year since 1960, the CPS National Election Studies have included a pair of questions asking which party had a majority in the House before and after the election. This seems to be a much more useful measure of political information. It clearly measures knowledge that is needed to follow what is happening in Washington. Not knowing which party is running one of the houses of Congress makes it extremely difficult to blame or reward the party in power. Therefore this knowledge is required to vote rationally.

The problem with knowing which party controls the House is that voters apparently confuse control of the White House with control of Congress. Arseneau and Wolfinger (1973, p. 3) first suggested this when they were looking at data on which party controlled the House prior to the election. They found that although 69 percent of the sample knew the right answer in 1966, only 50 percent did in 1970. They interpreted the sharp drop as being caused by the change from unified control of government by the Democrats in 1966 to divided control in 1970. Indeed, as Arseneau and Wolfinger point out, the figure of 50 percent knowing the right answer in 1970 closely matches the 47 percent who knew the right answer in 1958 when the government was last under divided control (see Stokes and Miller, 1962). In other words, Arseneau and Wolfinger were arguing that the 1966-1970 difference in knowledge was caused by the items becoming easier to answer. There was no overall change in knowledge; it was just easier to know the right answer in 1966.

Another variation on this problem of confusion is that voters may confuse control of the House with control of the Senate. In 1980, when the Republicans won control of the Senate for the first time since the 1950s, only 14 percent of the sample knew that the Democrats controlled the House both before and after the election (see Table 7-3). This startlingly low level of information certainly resulted from the Republicans' victory in the Senate and the enormous amount of media coverage it received. For my purposes, the implication is that one has to be careful using these items in comparisons across time.

The specific information index used is the same one used in Chapter 2 [of Smith], that is, the number of correct answers given to the questions about which party had a majority in the House before and after the election. The bottom row of Table 7-3 reveals that the percentage who knew both answers rose from 43 percent to 60 percent from 1960 to 1964, and then returned to the upper 40 percent range until the 1980 election reduced the people to utter confusion. Here is evidence that the public became more knowledgeable between 1960 and 1964. Is it reliable?

There are two reasons not to accept this evidence without corroboration. First, by 1968, the level of knowledge had returned to the 1960 level. That is, this index does not match the level of conceptualization indexes. According to the levels indexes, the public became more sophisticated between 1960 and 1964, and remained that way through the 1970s. According to the index of information about the control of the House, 1964 was an isolated year in which the people temporarily knew more. Although it shows a surge from 1960 to 1964, it does not

Table 7-3   Knowledge of Control of the House

	1960	1964	1968	1972	1976	1980
Know neither	32%	17%	27%	29%	31%	28%
Know one	25	23	28	23	20	59
Know both	43	60	45	48	49	14
N	1,932	1,450	1,348	1,119	2,403	1,405

Note: The questions were "Do you happen to know which party elected the most members to the House of Representatives in the elections (this/last) month? Which one?" and "Do you happen to know which party had the most members in the House of Representatives in Washington before the elections (this/last) month? Which one?" Both incorrect responses and "Don't know" responses were counted as incorrect.

Source: Data are from the CPS 1960-1980 American National Election Studies.

support the thesis of *The Changing American Voter*; rather, it contradicts it by falling in 1968.

Second, Lyndon Johnson's 1964 landslide was accompanied by a huge increase in the margin by which the Democrats controlled the House (thirty-seven seats). The media response to the Democrats' newly dominant position may well have resulted in the surge of knowledge about the House majority. One might initially object that the same jump in knowledge did not occur eight years later, when Richard Nixon had a similar landslide. However, in that case there was relatively little change in Congress. The Republicans gained only twelve seats in the House, and they actually lost two seats in the Senate. So although the media presented it as a huge triumph for Nixon, it was obviously not a triumph that extended to Congress. Because the media were not talking about the huge gain in Congress, one should not expect to see a gain in information in 1972.

In sum, these items about control of the House do not provide a basis for saying that the public's knowledge and sophistication changed over the 1960s and 1970s. Even if one accepts the data at face value and ignores the obvious problems in making comparisons across time, one is still left with a one-time surge in knowledge in 1964. *The Changing American Voter*'s thesis of a new level of sophistication following 1964 is just not supported.

A different way of measuring how much people know about politics is to find out whether they see any important differences between the Democratic and Republican parties. The assumption underlying this method is that there really are important differences between the parties. If one makes this assumption, one can take the percentage of people who say that there are important differences as a measure of the public's political knowledge.

There may be a problem with this measure as well. At some times, the differences between the parties, especially as they are represented by their presidential candidates, are larger than at other times. For instance, the differences between the parties (as represented by the candidates) in 1964 or in 1980 were far greater then the differences in 1960 or in 1968.

Whether this is a problem is not clear because it seems that this type of

Table 7-4   Perception of Important Differences Between the Parties

	1952	1960	1964	1968	1972	1976	1980
Percent seeing important differences	50	50	51	52	46	47	58

Note: In 1952, the question was "Do you think there are any important differences between what the Democratic and Republican parties stand for, or do you think they are about the same?" In 1960, 1964, and 1972-1980, it was "Do you think there are any important differences in what the Republicans and Democrats stand for?" In 1968, it was "Do you think there are any important differences between the Republican and Democratic parties?" Responses of both "No difference" and "Don't know" are combined as no difference.

Source: Wattenberg, 1984, t. 4.1, p. 52. Data are from the CPS 1952-1980 American National Election Studies.

change may be closer to *The Changing American Voter*'s idea of environmental change than to the item-specific notion of change discussed previously. That is, if voters become aware of more differences between the parties, it seems reasonable to infer that they have gained a fair amount of information about the policy positions of the two parties. This is not a narrow increase in information that is specific to one item. Thus it seems that changes in this measure reflect real changes in the public's knowledge of politics. For this reason, one should probably conclude that this is one of the better information scales.

The public's perception of differences between the parties, shown in Table 7-4, does not change much over time. From 1952 through 1976, the percentage of those seeing differences ranges from 46 to 52 percent—a fairly narrow range presumably reflecting nothing more than sampling error. The only year that stands out is 1980, when the proportion of those seeing a gap jumps to 58 percent. Although it is easy to attribute the higher 1980 figure to Ronald Reagan, it is not so clear why a similarly high figure was not found in 1964. In any event, insofar as the perception of differences measures knowledge and is comparable over time, these data indicate that there was no change over time. In particular, there was no sudden surge to a new level of understanding in 1964. Again, the evidence leads to rejection of *The Changing American Voter*'s thesis.

The foregoing measures are all somewhat distant from the notion of "sophistication" as supposedly reflected in the level of conceptualization indexes. The names of the candidates for Congress, which party controls the House, whether there are differences between the parties, and so forth are not at all the same as whether one thinks in an ideological way. Two more direct measures of ideological thinking, or more precisely, knowledge of ideological terms, are available. The first is the question, which party is more conservative. Presumably, those who report that the Republicans are more conservative understand the meaning of the term better.

Here again the contrast between the particular candidates in each election might make the answer more or less obvious from one election to the next. For instance, one might expect the 1964 and 1972 elections—each with its own blatantly ideological candidate—would yield a higher number of correct answers. It might be easier to attach the ideological labels to the candidates. However, if voters learned more than just which labels went with which candidates, if they learned something about what those labels meant, this would be a good measure over time.

Table 7-5 shows the percentage of those identifying the Republican party as the more conservative of the two. There is again some fluctuation from the one election to the next. Somewhat unexpectedly, there is a very slight downward trend. In the three elections in the 1960s, from 81 to 88 percent of the voters knew which party was more conservative; in the two elections in the 1970s, only 79 and 75 percent of the respondents gave the right answer. In addition, the 1964 and 1972 elections do not stand out. If anything, in both years, fewer people got the answers right than had done so four years previously. (The 1960-1964 difference, however, is a trivial 4 percent.) Once again, the data give little comfort to *The Changing American Voter* thesis.

The second more direct measure of knowledge of ideological terms (and thus possibly of ideological thinking) is the proportion of people who recognize and understand what the term "conservative" means. In 1960, respondents to the SRC/CPS National Election Study were asked to identify the more conservative party and then asked, "What do you have in mind when you say that the Republicans (Democrats) are more conservative than the Democrats (Republicans)?"

Converse (1964, p. 219) found that about half the population reasonably understood the liberal-conservative distinction. Using the same question from the 1964 study, Pierce (1970) replicated Converse's measure and came up with exactly the same result—half the population understood the term. Twenty years later, Luttbeg and Gant (1985) replicated the Converse-Pierce measure and again got the same result—half the population understood the liberal-conservative distinction.

A fourth replication of the strata of knowledge and understanding was conducted by Jennings and Niemi (1974, pp. 110-13). Using data from a national representative sample of high school students and their parents who were surveyed in the spring of 1965, Jennings and Niemi found that 45 percent of the parents fell in the top two levels of "reasonable" understanding. Because the Jennings and Niemi sample is of parents with high school students, it does not match the other representative national samples. Still, the 45 percent figure is in line with the other research.

In addition to the replications of the "strata of knowledge and understanding" measure, there is one other measure of how many people understand the liberal-conservative distinction. In June, 1940, the Gallup Poll asked people to explain what the terms "liberal," "conservative," and "radical" mean. The questions were of the form, "Please tell me in your own words what you consider a liberal in politics." [4] In scoring the answers, the Gallup Institute used the same general approach as did Converse and his colleagues twenty years later; they were "careful to give the voters the benefit of any reasonable doubt" (Benson 1940, p. 131). Unfortunately, Gallup did not report the results for each individual question; instead, they grouped the three questions together into a scale and reported the "average." Still, this scale of understanding of the liberal-conserva-

Table 7-5 Knowledge of Which Party Is More Conservative

	1960	1964	1968	1972	1976
Republicans	85%	81%	88%	79%	75%
Democrats/Don't know	15	19	12	21	24
N	1,308	1,045	958	800	1,996

Note: The question was "Would you say that one of the parties is more conservative than the other at the national level?" (If yes) "Which party is more conservative?" (If no) "Do you think that people generally consider the Democrats or the Republicans more conservative, or wouldn't you want to guess about that?"

Source: Data are from the CPS 1960-1976 American National Election Studies.

tive distinction is reasonably comparable with the scale later developed by the Michigan researchers.[5]

The results of this 1940 Gallup Poll are startlingly similar to those obtained by the strata of knowledge measure. Forty-eight percent of the 3,054 respondents gave "correct" responses, 14 percent gave answers that were deemed "doubtful," and 38 percent either did not answer or gave answers that were obviously incorrect. In short, the Gallup results match the CPS results.

Thus these are three replications of the strata of knowledge and understanding measure—1960, 1964, and 1980. And there is one earlier problematic time point—1940. So not only does this cover a forty-year time span, but it also covers the supposedly crucial 1960-1964 gap quite well. All four times the measure yielded the same answer. There was no change in the public's understanding of the liberal-conservative distinction.

Whether people are able to use ideological terms in their thinking and whether they do in fact use them are different. Nevertheless, it certainly seems odd that there was a huge increase in the number of those who thought in ideological terms while there was no corresponding increase in the number who could think in those terms. Like all the other measures discussed, this one provides no basis for saying that there was an increase in the public's sophistication during the 1960s.

Finally, there are a few scattered items that can be culled from the Gallup Poll. In examining the public's knowledge of foreign affairs, Smith (1972) sought to discover whether the public had become more knowledgeable over the years. He faced the same lack of information items. Nevertheless, from the few items he was able to find, Smith concluded that little had changed since the 1940s.

Smith's (1972, pp. 271-72) collection of information questions from the Gallup Poll consisted of recall of congressmen's and senators' names and the following items:

In 1950, a year of war in Asia for the United States, 66 percent of the American public could correctly identify the U.S. Secretary of State . . . (AIPO: Dec. 1950). Sixteen years later, in 1966, another war year in Asia for the

United States, the figure was approximately the same—65 percent (AIPO: March, 1966). . . . A prominent writer on foreign affairs, Walter Lippman, was correctly identified in May, 1945, by 40 percent of the public . . . (AIPO: May, 1945), and by 32 percent in 1963 (AIPO: July, 1963). . . . In 1965, 20 percent of the public had a reasonably correct idea of the magnitude of China's population; in 1952, using any figure between 300 million and 700 million as a reasonably correct estimate of its purported 500 million population at that time, a corresponding figure of 24 percent was obtained (AIPO: Feb., 1952).

Beyond Smith's few items, there exists only one other Gallup Poll question that was asked with nearly identical language on both ends of the 1960-1964 gap: "Can you tell me what the term 'filibuster' in Congress means to you?" [6] In 1947, 48 percent of the respondents gave responses judged to be reasonably correct; in 1949, 54 percent were correct; and in 1964, the figure was the same—54 percent. These data may indicate a decline in knowledge because when the 1964 question was being asked, there was an important civil rights filibuster going on; yet when the two earlier questions were asked, there was no current filibuster, nor had there been one recently. Thus the finding is either no change or a decline in knowledge, depending on how one wishes to interpret the data.

Although these items hardly make up an impressive data set, they tell the same story that all the other data have told. Little or nothing has changed. So this is still more evidence that the political knowledge of the American voter did not grow. The alleged transformation of the American voter between 1960 and 1964 did not happen. None of these measures shows any trend of increasing knowledge and sophistication.

The Structure of the Information Items

My interest in measures of political information is not in the content of each specific information item. I do not care about whether respondents can recall the names of their representatives, but about what that recall implies about the respondents' general political knowledge. Thus I need to know whether the various items are, indeed, all measuring the same unobserved "knowledge."

In order to show that the information items and scales all measure a single latent variable, one can investigate the items with factor analysis. If a single factor underlies all the observed information measures, it will go a long way toward showing that they are all tapping the same phenomenon.

Even though a factor analysis yields but a single factor, it does not prove that a single variable causes all the observed variables. As Piazza (1980) argued, in addition to a factor analysis, one must also look at the relationship of the variables to other variables not included in the factor analysis. I do that in Chapter 5 [of Smith].

Seven items in the CPS National Election Studies were used for the factor analysis: the number of party responses, the number of candidate responses, which party was thought to be more conservative, the party difference index, the information index based on knowing which party controlled the House of Representatives before and after the presidential election, an index based on recall of candidates for the House, and a count of the number of "don't knows" in response to the issue items in the surveys.[7] The DK count is intended to measure the respondent's range of opinions—one of Converse's characteristics of a sophisticated person.

Only five of these items are used in the time series discussed in the rest of this chapter. The other items, the party difference index and the DK count, cannot be used in the time series because their construction changed radically between 1960 and 1964 and again between 1968 and 1972. The purpose for including them in the factor analysis is to validate the measures of political knowledge more thoroughly. None of the results changes much when either the party difference index or the DK count or both are dropped. In fact, dropping the difference index improves the performance of the factor analysis in 1960 and 1964.

The results of the maximum likelihood factor analyses for each year are shown in Table 7-6. The table shows only the factor loadings for the first factor in each year because all the solutions had only one factor. The eigenvalues at the bottom of Table 7-6 show the strength of the first factors. All the eigenvalues are 2.8 or greater. They indicate that the factors explain from 46 to 73 percent of the variance in the observed variables—an impressive standard.

The eigenvalues of the second factors are presented in Table 7-6 to show that they are all of trivial size. None even approaches 1.0, which is the conventional threshold for including factors (Harman 1976). The first factor clearly dominates in every year.[8]

The factor loadings are also all very strong. The only weak ones are for the party difference index from 1956 to 1964 and the candidate recall index. The change in the party difference index loadings is easy to explain. The index, based on the issue scales, changed whenever the issue scales were changed. In 1972 and 1976, it was constructed from the seven point issue scales (see Appendix 2 [of Smith]), and this accounts for its rise from low loadings to very strong ones.

The candidate recall indexes do not work particularly well. In two of the three years in which they are available, their loadings fall under the .40 rule-of-thumb threshold for including variables in factor analyses. As shown in Chapter 5 [of Smith], the recall questions behave differently from the other indexes in a couple of important respects. Thus a fair conclusion seems to be that recall of candidates' names is the weakest of all the information items and is the least closely related to general political information.

Despite the weakness in the recall questions and in the party difference index in the early years (an index I am not using in the time series), the overall picture provides strong support for the position that the information items are all measuring the same phenomenon. Thus there is a good set of information items available on the CPS National Election Surveys—a valuable and untapped resource.

[After a section on "The Causes and Correlates of Sophistication," Smith concludes:]

To summarize, education increased, and that should have led to a rise in sophistication. However, interest in politics and use of newspapers and magazines

Table 7-6 Maximum Likelihood Factor Analysis of Information Items

	1956	1960	1964	1968	1972	1976
Number of party responses	.72	.65	.64	.67	.65	.73
Number of candidate responses	.75	.73	.60	.65	.63	.68
Conservative party question	—	.45	.51	.49	.48	.57
Information index	—	.51	.56	.48	.48	.59
Recall of candidates	—	—	.43	.39	.31	—
Difference index	.35	.35	.24	.54	.72	.67
DK count	.55	.53	.57	.62	.56	.58
Eigenvalue	2.91	3.04	2.84	3.36	3.63	4.32
Percent variance explained	73%	51%	46%	48%	52%	72%
Second eigenvalue	.13	.15	.34	.31	.31	.24
N	1,762	1,100	1,405	1,328	1,095	1,881

Source: Data are from the CPS/SRC 1956-1976 American National Election Studies.

to follow politics fell slightly, and external political efficacy and strength of party identification fell quite a bit. Those findings should lead us to expect a decline in sophistication, although perhaps only a slight one.

On balance, one should not be surprised to find no change at all. That is, the findings in this section are consistent with those about the direct measures of knowledge and sophistication discussed in the first section of this chapter—namely, the political knowledge and sophistication of the American electorate remained unchanged between the late 1950s and the late 1970s. When we abandon the more complicated and methodologically flawed measures discussed in the earlier chapters, the levels of conceptualization and attitude consistency, there is no evidence at all of a changing American voter. To the contrary, what we find is the unchanging American voter.

NOTES

1. In more formal terms, the relationship between a test item and the overall characteristic one wants to measure can be represented by an "item characteristic curve." For a discussion of this relationship, see Bejar (1983), Lord and Novick (1968), or Osterlind (1983).
2. I do, however, include it in my upcoming factor analysis of information items.
3. All three data sets are reported by Mann (1978). The Ferejohn data are supplemented by Crotty and Jacobson (1980). The Gallup data are supplemented by additional time points from Gallup (1972).
4. The terms "radical" and "conservative" were used in the other two questions. See Benson (1940).
5. In addition to the fact that Gallup did not use the same coding procedures as CPS in analyzing their data, sampling procedures in 1940 were somewhat different from those in the 1956-1976 period. See Glenn (1970).

6. The quoted question was reported in the April 5, 1947, Gallup Poll. In the February 11, 1949, version, the first word in the question was changed to "Will." In the March 25, 1964, version, the "in Congress" was dropped. None of these changes seems significant.
7. The issue items were the ones used as the base for the party difference index. The questions were, of course, not the same. In the DK count, respondents were asked to place themselves. In the party difference index, respondents were asked to place the parties or asked which party was closest to them. The exact construction of both indexes varies by year. See Appendix 2 [of Smith].
8. Examination of the plots supports this conclusion. The other factors are all trivial and all similar to the second factor. The plots look like classic examples of clean first factors.

8. EXPLAINING POLITICAL SOPHISTICATION

Robert C. Luskin

It is in the nature of representative democracy that only a small proportion of the population can participate in politics to the fullest. The number of citizens far exceeds the number of offices. Even as ordinary citizens, however, many people do less than they could. Not everyone votes, even where voting is easy. In the United States, where registering to vote takes forethought and initiative, voting turnout just barely clears 50%, even in presidential elections. Still smaller percentages take an active part in the campaign or attempt to influence public officials between elections. Participation, alas, is a variable.[1]

The quality of participation also varies. The more strenuous forms of activity are as a rule firmly grounded in perceptions of self, group, or societal interest. Few people write their congressman or member of Parliament without definite reason. But voting, because easier and more common, is more capricious. Voters respond to the personalities and personal characteristics of the candidates as much as to policy issues.[2] So far as they do take policy into account, they may do so ineptly, either mistaking their interests (as others would see them, and as they themselves would presumably see them with further thought or better information) or mistaking the policies that best serve their interests (even as they themselves do see them). Under any construction that does not make the accurate perception and efficient pursuit of one's interests tautologously perfect, people inevitably make errors, and some people make more than others.

At bottom, these variations in citizen performance reflect variations in cognition. Some people know and have thought much more about politics than others: their "political belief systems" are more elaborate. This was the variable the famed "levels of conceptualization" (Campbell, Converse, Miller, and Stokes, 1960) were designed to measure, the variable about which Converse (1964) was writing in "The Nature of Belief Systems in Mass Publics." Terminology varies, but the name on which the literature seems to be settling is *political sophistication*.

Source: *Political Behavior* (1990) 12:331-361. Reprinted with permission of Plenum Publishing Corporation.

Sophistication and Its Consequences

More precisely, a person is politically sophisticated to the extent to which his or her political cognitions are numerous, cut a wide substantive swath, and are highly organized, or "constrained." [3] Some psychologists write in this vein of *cognitive complexity* (Schroder, Driver, and Streufert, 1967; Tetlock, 1983, 1984), meaning the extent to which a person's cognitions of some stimulus domain are both highly *differentiated* (roughly, numerous and wide-ranging) and highly *integrated* (organized or constrained). Others refer equivalently to *expertise* (Larkin, McDermott, Simon, and Simon, 1980; Fiske, Kinder, and Larter, 1983), meaning the extent to which the person's knowledge of the domain is both extensive and highly "chunked." Political sophistication is political cognitive complexity, political expertise (Luskin, 1987b).

This is also the continuum behind the frequently drawn distinction between ideological and nonideological belief systems. *Ideology*, in the sense of this literature, is the high end of sophistication: a political belief system that is particularly large, wide-ranging, and organized is an *ideology*. But all this focus on ideology is unfortunate. It is a person's actual degree of sophistication, not merely whether or not it exceeds some high and necessarily arbitrary threshold, that matters.

As matter it does. Both theory and scattered evidence suggest that the more politically sophisticated are apt to be more interested in politics (a theme on which I shall expand presently); more participatory in voting and other political activities (Verba and Nie, 1972; Klingemann, 1979b; Inglehart, 1979); better at spotting and pursuing their political interests (for inferential evidence of which, see Converse, 1964; Chong, McClosky, and Zaller, 1983); more resistant to persuasive appeals (Scott, 1963; Chaiken and Baldwin 1981); and less susceptible to agenda setting and priming by the media (Iyengar, Peters, and Kinder, 1982; though cf. Iyengar and Kinder, 1987); more easily persuaded by reasoned argument and less easily by mere symbolic display (Chaiken 1980; Petty and Cacioppo, 1979, 1984); and more attentive to policy issues and less to the candidates' personas in deciding how to vote (Miller and Miller, 1976; Wyckoff, 1980; Knight, 1985). [4]

I have phrased all this at the individual level, but it obviously follows that the aggregate distribution of sophistication affects the whole quality of democratic politics. The less sophisticated the public, the less alert to its interests, the less active and unswerving in pursuit of them, and the less resistant to manipulation from above—the further, in short, from the democratic ideal. [5] If, as Converse (1964) has argued, the distribution is invariably clumped toward the bottom, that limits the kinds of political behavior we can realistically expect or prescribe.

The Nature of This Research

The greatest single portion of the literature has focused on the descriptive aspect of this distributional question: How sophisticated or unsophisticated a public? A somewhat more pregnant question, consuming the next greatest share of attention, is whether the American public has become dramatically more sophisticated since the early 1960s. These long roaring disputes may at last be dying down. The evidence, read aright, is clear. "By anything approaching elite standards, the American public is extremely unsophisticated about politics and has not become appreciably more so.... Other publics ... are similarly unsophisticated" (Luskin, 1987b, p. 889; see also Kinder, 1983).

But though this finding obviously compels some doleful premises for descriptive democratic theory, it still leaves a loophole for lofty prescription. The publics we have studied may not be very sophisticated; they may not have become markedly more sophisticated over the periods we have observed; yet they may nonetheless be capable of becoming so. The remaining question, then, is how far a largely unsophisticated public can become or be made more sophisticated, and by what means. Beyond this, in turn, lies the question of how the distribution is generated.

On this score, the literature is not only scant but theoretically underdeveloped. What variables *affect* sophistication, and why? Which of its correlates are causal, which consequential or spurious? *How* do the variables that affect it affect it? Are their effects constant or variable? If variable, how do they vary? Does sophistication affect any of its causes in turn? The questions have scarcely been raised.

This is largely true even of the best previous analyses, in Neuman (1986), Hamill and Lodge (1986), and Hamill, Lodge, and Blake (1985).[6] It is not just that the theory behind their models is veiled; the theory might be inferred if the models were sufficiently compelling. But they are not. Neuman blurs interest and attentiveness with sophistication, then regresses this composite on a fourteen-variable medley, the majority of whose members seem remote causes at best. Hamill and Lodge lump education with intelligence and media usage and political interest with political activity. The cleanest and most sensible specification is Hamill, Lodge, and Blake's. Their variable list reads very like the roll of my sophistication equation, below. But even this model is single-equation and linear, and mistaken, as I shall argue, in both respects.

It should also be mentioned that these studies estimate their models on small, local, nonprobability samples.[7] The Stony Brook studies (Hamill, Lodge, and Blake, 1985; Hamill and Lodge, 1986) are experiments, designed to examine sophistication's effects on information processing, and well suited for that purpose. But the study of sophistication's own dependence on other variables is another story. The process of becoming more or less sophisticated is too secular for laboratory manipulation. For this purpose, experiments offer only the hope of more precise measurement to offset their cost in external validity.

I want here to offer a more explicitly reasoned model. For theoretical reasons, developed below, the model is multiequation and nonlinear. I separate intelligence from education, interest from media usage, and the latter two from sophistication. And I estimate the model on a national probability sample, from the 1976 American National Election Study (ANES). I split the sample randomly in two, reconnoitering the first half to help guide the model and using the second for the "official" estimation. The results speak to the questions of what variables affect sophistication, under what conditions, and by how much. It will hardly give away the ending to say that they contain some surprises.

The Sophistication Equation

As a very general matter, the conditions that promote any particular behavior can be grouped under the headings of *opportunity*, *ability*, and *motivation*. Bedouins in the Sahara do not become champion swimmers; ordinary people who enjoy music do not compose great symphonies; professors with research assistants do not do their own leg work. They lack the opportunity, the ability, and the motivation, respectively.[8]

Where the behavior at issue is the acquisition and structuring of political information, opportunity lies in the information to which one is exposed, so that the headings effectively become information, ability, and motivation. To become highly sophisticated, we must encounter a certain quantity of political information, be intellectually able enough to retain and organize large portions of the information we encounter, and have reason enough to make the effort. In this light, the sophistication should include:

Interest in politics: Internal motivation is "interest." People with a keener interest in politics notice more of the political information they encounter and think more seriously about the political information they notice (Chaiken, 1980; Petty and Cacioppo, 1979). They also seek more political information—an indirect effect we shall come to—but even under a uniform quota, they would tend to consume more.

Education: Education, too, may be motivational in part. In educated society, the blankest ignorance of politics may be a solecism. Yet it is hard to believe that the social penalties for ignorance can be dire or that the level of knowledge at which they cease to apply can be terribly high. No, most of education's effect must be informational. Classes, informal discussions, and readings expose many students to large quantities of political information. Retention is of course another matter, but the lengthier the schooling, the greater, on average, the exposure.

Exposure to political information in the print media (EPIPM): The most obvious source of political information is the mass media. But for all their reach, the electronic media convey surprisingly little. Broadcast news is brief and shallow, and much watching and listening wholly or intermittently nominal, a mere accompaniment to other activities (Robinson, 1977; Stevenson and White, 1980). Entire newscasts float by, essentially unattended. What does penetrate, since most people use the media for entertainment, not information (Stephenson, 1967), may be on the order of Nancy Reagan's wardrobe. Majorities of TV network news audiences, interviewed shortly afterward, cannot recall a single story covered (Neuman, 1976; Patterson and McClure, 1976; Patterson, 1980). Newspapers, by virtual default, are "the chief source of remembered information" (Graber, 1984, p. 85). Small wonder, then, that the relationship between exposure to political information in the electronic media and political information holding is generally slight to negative (Clarke and Fredin, 1978; Kent and Rush,

1976; Chaffee, Jackson-Beeck, Duvall, and Wilson, 1977; Robinson, 1972; McClure and Patterson, 1976; Patterson and McClure, 1976; Patterson, 1980). In the first half of the present data, too, the inclusion of television and radio reduces the media exposure coefficient and the R^2. Thus, to give the variable a fair chance, I have confined it to the print media.

Intelligence: We need not see cognitive ability as unidimensional to find intelligence, defined as the central tendency of cognitive abilities, a useful concept (Carroll and Maxwell, 1979). Experiments confirm that brighter subjects do better at learning, retaining, and extrapolating from information of any complexity (Baron, 1982; Campione, Brown, and Bryant, 1985). The more complex, the steeper the gradient. Thus, brighter people should accumulate more, and more complex, information about politics, other things (most notably interest) being equal (White, 1969; Harvey and Harvey, 1970; Renshon, 1977; Graber, 1984). Indeed, the dependence on intelligence should be greater for political than for many other sorts of knowledge, because politics is more abstract and remote— simply "harder material"—than, say, sports or cooking.

Occupation: In larger proportion, those willing to spend the time and effort to obtain large quantities of political information may be "those who need the details for other purposes: e.g., a farmer who needs to know about trade legislation in order to determine what proportion of his land should be planted in crops" (Popkin, Gorman, Phillips, and Smith, 1976, p. 788). The more politics impinges on one's work—the more political, governmental, or conditioned by government policies it is—the more politically sophisticated it may be necessary, profitable, or professionally advantageous to be. In addition, more politically impinged occupations provide more political information. Information about what the government is doing or is likely to do, at least in certain policy domains, and about what effects its actions are likely to have, marches even unbidden across the desks of many corporate executives, for example (Popkin et al., 1976).

Further Equations, Additional Variables

Not all these variables can be taken as exogenous. Sophistication depends on interest, but interest also depends on sophistication. We need only think of our likely reaction to the prospect of reading some potentially informative text, on advanced topology, for instance, for which we utterly lack the technical background. Intelligibility is a function of prior knowledge (Bransford and Johnson, 1972; Dooling and Lachman, 1971; Chiesi, Spilich, and Voss, 1979), and unintelligibility the nemesis of interest. There is a "cognitive element to information costs" (Converse, 1975, p. 97). But if interest is therefore endogenous, EPIPM must be endogenous, too, because people who are more interested in a subject tend to read more about it.

Hence we must write two further equations, for interest and EPIPM. For the interest equation, two additional variables suggest themselves:

Parental interest in politics: Through both observational learning and direct reinforcement, children should tend to absorb the political enthusiasm or apathy of their parents. By adulthood, the influences of other people and experiences

Figure 8-1   The Model

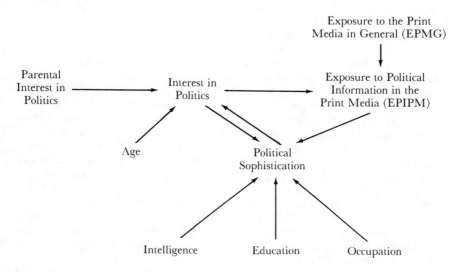

have diluted the effect, but some correspondence remains (Jennings and Niemi, 1974; 1981; Brody and Sniderman, 1977).

Age: For various reasons—declining competition from more pressing concerns, "mere exposure" (Zajonc, 1968) perhaps—political interest should and apparently does increase monotonically with age (Glenn and Grimes, 1968).

Education or occupation, sex or race? Several other variables may seem to enter the model at this point. Incentives to learn about politics may eventually be internalized in "interest," and to the extent that this occurs, the variables that control the incentives—occupation and, more arguably, education—should be in the interest equation. Another possibility is that sex or race has an effect, the residue of historical exclusion and discouragement. When added, however, these variables all have thoroughly insignificant effects.[9] The social barriers that may once have dampened blacks' and women's interest must no longer be steep enough to do so, and the internalization of educational and occupational incentives must occur through their effects on sophistication.[10]

For the EPIPM equation, the pool is unfortunately thinner. Only one additional variable suggests itself:

Exposure to the print media in general (EPMG): People obviously cannot get political news from newspapers or magazines without reading them, and the more regularly they read them, the more often they will at least bump into the political information they carry.

This, then, in causal outline, is the model. Note from the diagram in Figure 8-1 that these direct effects we have been positing imply indirect effects as well. Sophistication affects EPIPM through interest; EPIPM affects interest through sophistication; age, parental interest, and EPMG affect sophistication through interest and EPIPM.[11]

A Question of Form

Alas for convenience, the reasoning with which we launched these hypotheses suggests something other than the usual linear equations. People somehow kept from birth from all political information will not know anything about politics, no matter how cognitively able they are or how interested in the subject they might (hypothetically) be. Neither will people who have no reason or desire to give politics their attention, no matter how able they are or how much political information there is about them. And neither will people in comas, no matter how much political information passes in front of them and no matter how interesting they might (hypothetically) find it. No one factor—neither information, nor motivation, nor ability—can have an effect unless the other two are nonzero. The greater the others, the greater the effect. Motivation makes a bigger difference for the abler and more information-exposed, information a bigger difference for the abler and more highly motivated, ability a bigger difference for the more highly motivated and information-exposed. In short, we expect the effects to be positive and increasing functions of the other variables.

The simplest and most tractable form consistent with this reasoning is the multiplicative. Letting y_1 = sophistication, y_2 = interest, y_3 = EPIPM, x_1 = education, x_2 = occupation, x_3 = intelligence, x_4 = age, x_5 = parental interest, and x_6 = EPMG, we write

$$y_{i1} = \gamma_{10} y_{i2}^{\beta_{12}} y_{i3}^{\beta_{13}} x_{i1}^{\gamma_{11}} x_{i2}^{\gamma_{12}} x_{i3}^{\gamma_{13}} u_{i1}, \quad (1.1)$$

where the β's and γ's are unknown parameters, u_1 is a stochastic disturbance, and the i subscript distinguishes the ith observation ($i = 1, 2, \ldots, N$). First-half estimation of the Box-Cox model in the same variables supports this specification over the linear alternative.[12]

Now, for continuous y's, interest's (y_2's) direct effect on sophistication (y_1)—the immediate change that could be expected in y_1 for each unit change in y_2, if y_2 could be manipulated independently of y_1 and y_3—is

$$\partial E^{\circ}(y_{i1}|y_{i2},y_{i3},x_{i1},x_{i2},x_{i3})/\partial y_{i2} = \beta_{12}\gamma_{10}^{+}y_{i2}^{(\beta_{12}-1)} y_{i3}^{\beta_{13}} x_{i1}^{\gamma_{11}} x_{i2}^{\gamma_{12}} x_{i3}^{\gamma_{13}}, \quad (2)$$

where E° denotes the hypothetical expectation from (1.1) if u_1 were independent of y_2 and y_3 (see Goldberger, 1964, p. 387), and the "adjusted scale factor" $\gamma_{10}^{+} = (\exp \frac{1}{2}\sigma_1^2)\gamma_{10}$.[13] Given that the variables are always > 0 and that γ_{10} (and thus γ_{10}^{+}) > 0, this effect is nonzero iff (if and only if) $\beta_{12} \neq 0$, positive iff $\beta_{12} > 0$, and negative iff $\beta_{12} < 0$. If positive, it is an increasing function of y_2 iff $\beta_{12} > 1$, a decreasing function of y_2 iff $\beta_{12} < 1$, and constant with respect to y_2 iff $\beta_{12} = 1$. Again if positive, it is an increasing function of some other explanatory variable, say x_1, iff $\gamma_{11} > 0$, a decreasing function of x_1 iff $\gamma_{11} < 0$, and constant with respect to x_1 iff $\gamma_{11} = 0$. The theoretical expectation that the effects are all positive and increasing functions of the other explanatory variables thus becomes a stipulation that the β's and γ's be positive.

For simplicity, we cast the other equations similarly, a choice that seems as good as any for interest and theoretically attractive for EPIPM. Politically apathetic readers may ignore the political content of the newspapers and magazines they read, while even the most avid spectators cannot get political information from newspapers and magazines unless they read them. Each variable's effect should increase with the value of the other. Hence, the rest of the model is

$$y_{i2} = \gamma_{20} y_{i1}^{\beta_{21}} x_{i4}^{\gamma_{24}} x_{i5}^{\gamma_{25}} u_{i2} \qquad (1.2)$$

$$y_{i3} = \gamma_{30} y_{i2}^{\beta_{32}} x_{i6}^{\gamma_{36}} u_{i3}. \qquad (1.3)$$

Measurement

The measurement of most of these variables is straightforward or at least conventional and needs no extended comment. Age and education are scored in years, the latter up to 17 for postgraduate study. To avoid zeros (which would snarl estimation), people with no formal schooling are scored at .01. EPIPM is gauged as the sum of the frequencies with which the respondent reads about politics in newspapers and about the campaign in magazines, EPMG as whether or not he or she reads a daily paper. Interest is indicated by the extent to which the respondent "follow[s] what's going on in government and public affairs most of the time, whether there's an election going on or not," as opposed to not being "that interested." The general scheme is to score the polytomies by $(1, 2, \ldots, C)$, where C is the number of categories, and the dichotomies (occupation and EPMG), whose bottom categories seem closer to absolute zero in relation to the category above, by $(.5, 1.5)$.[14]

Only three variables need further discussion, the first of course being sophistication itself. The measure of sophistication is a compound of three elements: two measures of *integration* (I_1 and I_2) and one measure of differentiation (D). The first two are streamlined, trichotomous versions of Campbell et al.'s (1960) "levels of conceptualization" (LC)[15] and Converse's (1964) typology of "recognition and understanding" (RU), based, respectively, on the questions soliciting open-ended evaluations of parties and candidates and the questions asking respondents to say which party is (or is generally seen as) more conservative and what they mean (or is generally meant) by that. The present versions distinguish only (1) responses abstract enough to have at least the scent of "ideology," (2) narrower but still substantive responses, referring to clearly defined issues or groups, and (3) vague, policy-irrelevant, or empty responses.[16] Both are scored (0, 1, 2). The third element D is simply the number of policy issues, out of a total of 11, covering much of the landscape of then current political debate, on which the respondent can both locate him- or herself and correctly locate the parties (the Republicans to the right of the Democrats).[17] The combination

$$S = (I_1 + I_2 + 1)(D + 1),$$

thus yields a scale from 1 to 60.[18]

I claim several advantages for this measure. First, the original LC and RU measures make some dubious distinctions—between Levels B (group references) and C (mostly specific issue references) in the former and among the three lowest strata (mildly different manifestations of ignorance) in the latter. I_1 and I_2 avoid these distinctions. Second, devices like the LC, by far the most popular sort, overrate respondents who use terms like "liberal" and "conservative" without understanding them much (Smith, 1980, 1981). Devices like Converse's RU, on the other hand, overrate respondents who understand the terms but do not apply them much. Thus, the combination $I_1 + I_2$ is better than either I_1 or I_2 individually. Third, the more direct admeasurement of differentiation in D, a novel feature, lifts S above $I_1 + I_2$. In all, S performs handsomely (see Luskin, 1987b, for details).

A second refractory variable is occupation qua political impingement. As a rough first swipe, I attempt only the dichotomous distinction between more and less politically impinged occupations. By way of illustration, I place factory and clerical workers, computer specialists, and even teachers outside the social sciences in the low-impingement category and lawyers, physicians, entrepreneurs, and most administrators in the high-impingement category.[19] This measurement is admittedly crude but at least addresses the right variable. The norm is to score occupation by status, but status is not what should matter; political impingement is.

The most elusive variable, however, is intelligence. Few national probability samples provide much to work with. Education, the most frequent stand-in, is conceptually and empirically too different. We all must know people who never went to college but are mentally nimble and lithe; certainly, we all must know dull-witted students who will nonetheless get their degrees. Education may sharpen ability but is far from the same thing. The General Social Survey (GSS) conducted at irregular intervals by the National Opinion Research Center at the University of Chicago has frequently included a vest-pocket measure of intelligence in the 10-item Gallup-Thorndike vocabulary test, but lacks the political items to cover the rest of the model. Neuman (1986) makes passing use of a similar test in the 1973 Bay Area Survey, and Lodge and his colleagues (Hamill, Lodge, and Blake, 1985; Hamill and Lodge, 1986; among other studies) have applied lengthier ones in their experiments, but these data are all from small, local, nonprobability samples, as previously noted.

The only real option, in a national probability sample extensively questioned about politics, is the interviewer's rating, at the end of the ANES interviews, of the respondent's "apparent intelligence," a measure with obvious problems. Interviewers are hardly expert judges, and their ratings may in part be seepage from other variables. Following an interview about politics, interviewers may rate more politically sophisticated respondents as more intelligent. Or they may rate more highly educated respondents as more intelligent, on the assumption that they must be.

Still, a variety of circumstantial evidence suggests that the interviewer ratings do catch something that behaves plausibly like intelligence. A panel on an earlier survey found a same-interviewer reliability of .7 and an inter-interviewer reliability of .6 (Campbell, Converse, and Rodgers, 1976). And the correlations between "intelligence" and sophistication (.41) and between "intelligence" and education (.58) are no higher than might be expected if "intelligence" measures only intelligence, which should after all be substantially correlated with both. Indeed, the correlation with education accords beautifully with correlations between education and IQ scores, which cluster fairly tightly around .6 (Duncan, 1968).

The most direct—and reassuring—evidence, however, comes from a panel on the 1987 GSS survey. The interviewers rated the respondents' intelligence on much the same scale as the ANES interviewers do, and in a paper and pencil questionnaire administered after the interview, respondents took both the usual 10-item Gallup-Thorndike test and a second 12-item test due to Cattell. There is no reason to expect these interviewers to be any more expert at judging intelligence or any less swayed in their judgments by the respondent's possession or lack of diplomas than their ANES counterparts, and since the interview schedule for this special panel is heavily political (focusing on tolerance), the ratings may be deflected toward sophistication, just as the ratings in the ANES study may be. Yet, for all the likely error and confounding, the interviewer ratings are as highly correlated with the Gallup-Thorndike measure as the Gallup-Thorndike and Cattell measures are with one another, at .40 (Gibson and Wenzel, 1988).[20]

In all, the interviewer ratings seem about as empirically valid as most of the attitudinal measures we unabashedly use all the time. This may be something of a

Table 8-1   Minima, Maxima, and Means

	Minimum	Maximum	Sample* Mean
Political sophistication	1	60	16.740
Interest in politics	1	4	2.902
EPIPM	1	7	3.662
Education	.01	17	11.756
Occupation	.5	1.5	.690
Intelligence	1	5	3.320
Age	17	87*	44.904
Parental interest in politics	1	5	2.798
EPMG	.5	1.5	1.208

* The maximum value of age and all the sample means are for the second half-sample. The other minima and maxima are fixed by construction.

backhanded compliment, and I do not even wish to insist that it is perfectly true. In the end, it is simply a case of *faute de mieux*. A more objective, psychometric measure would be nice, but for now this is all we can do, and the importance of separating intelligence from education makes it worthwhile.

Table 8-1 provides a summary and reminder of these scorings in the form of the variables' minima, means, and maxima.[21]

Estimation and Results

Logarithmic transformation renders (1.1), (1.2), and (1.3) linear in the parameters (with the innocuous exceptions of γ_{10}, γ_{20}, and γ_{30}), and the usual rank condition confirms identification, so that any standard simultaneous equations estimator will serve. Table 8-2 presents the two-stage least squares (2*SLS*) estimates, their asymptotic standard errors, and the R^2s.[22]

Dire Effects

The estimates generally conform to expectation. All but three are significantly greater than zero, as predicted, although the insignificant ones are thoroughly insignificant.[23] Neither EPIPM nor education seems to affect sophistication, nor does age seem to affect interest. We shall return to these negative results presently.

Assessing the nonzero effects is difficult, because they vary. Interest's effect on sophistication depends significantly on occupation, intelligence, and interest itself (and insignificantly on education and EPIPM). How influential is interest? To some extent, the answer can only be, it depends. Yet some effects are generally much bigger than others, even so. A partial but useful summary is the greatest possible difference (hereafter, GPD) that any change in the explanatory variable can be expected to make to the dependent variable.[24] The GPD for interest's (y_2's) effect on sophistication (y_1) is

$$\gamma_{10}^+(4)^{\beta_{12}} y_{i3}^{\beta_{13}} x_{i1}^{\gamma_{11}} x_{i2}^{\gamma_{12}} x_{i3}^{\gamma_{13}} \; - \; \gamma_{10}^+(1)^{\beta_{12}} y_{i3}^{\beta_{13}} x_{i1}^{\gamma_{11}} x_{i2}^{\gamma_{12}} x_{i3}^{\gamma_{13}}, \qquad (3)$$

where 1 and 4 are interest's minimum and maximum. Note the continued presence of y_3, x_1, x_2, and x_3. The nonlinearity has been integrated out, but the nonadditivity remains. At least for specific values of these other variables, however, the GPD tells what y_2 can do to the expected value of y_1. Table 8-3 shows the estimated GPDs when the other relevant variables are all at their minima, all at their means, and all at their maxima.[25]

These figures show that interest has a huge effect. Even when other variables are discouraging—for unintelligent people whose work has little to do with politics—a maximum change in interest boosts expected sophistication by some 15 points, against a range of 59. This figure increases to 30 for people of average intellect and employment and to 44 for highly intelligent people in politicizing occupations. Intelligence has a smaller and more conditional effect, beginning to make a notable difference only when interest and occupation are near their means. When they are at their maxima, however, it can produce an increase or decrease of 22 points. Brains, in the absence of interest, do not count

Table 8-2   Structural Parameters

Equation	Explanatory Variable	Parameter	Standard Error
Sophistication			
	Constant	1.750	.418
	(adjusted)	(2.331)	
	InteRest	1.680	.587
	EPIPM	−.075	.306
$N = 740$	Education	.016	.075
$R^2 = .299$	Occupation	.176	.066
	Intelligence	.381	.199
InteRest			
	Constant	.838	.120
	(adjusted)	(.906)	
$N = 744$	Sophistication	.427	.034
$R^2 = .270$	Age	.005	.034
	PaRental inteRest	.067	.029
EPIPM			
	Constant	.799	.073
	(adjusted)	(.918)	
$N = 846$	InteRest	1.389	.101
$R^2 = .441$	EPMG	.180	.043

for much, but granted some interest, they count for a good deal. Occupation's effect is much smaller and more conditional in turn. Only for the most intelligent and interested does having a politically impinged occupation mean much. Finally, the GPDs due to education and EPIPM are just plain small. Nor of course can we put much stock in even these small numbers, since the parameter estimates are insignificant by miles.

Interest, for its part, depends largely on sophistication, which can make an enormous difference regardless of age or parental interest. Parental interest also makes a difference, but a smaller one, and only at higher levels of sophistication. EPIPM depends almost entirely on interest. Major differences in interest make a huge difference to EPIPM, even without much exposure to the print media in general. For people who are intensely interested in politics, but only for them, EPMG can also make an appreciable difference.

Total Effects

The multiplicative structural equations (1.1), (1.2), and (1.3) imply multiplicative reduced forms. For sophistication (y_1), for instance,

$$y_{i1} = \pi_{10} x_{i1}^{\pi_{11}} x_{i2}^{\pi_{12}} x_{i3}^{\pi_{13}} x_{i4}^{\pi_{14}} x_{i5}^{\pi_{15}} x_{i6}^{\pi_{16}} v_{i1}, \tag{3}$$

where the π's, known functions of the structural β's and γ's, are parameters and v_1, a known function of the structural β's and u's, is a disturbance.[26] Taking

Table 8-3　Greatest Possible Differences (Direct)

Dependent Variable	Explanatory Variable	GPD When the Other Explanatory Variables Are at Their:		
		Minima	*Means*	*Maxima*
Sophistication				
	Interest	15.390	30.171	44.810
	EPIPM	−.260	−2.911	−6.726
	Education	.204	−2.149	5.442
	Occupation	.354	3.924	8.718
	Intelligence	1.407	10.922	22.774
Interest				
	Sophistication	4.367	4.700	4.902
	Age	.008	.028	.050
	Parental interest	.103	.348	.603
EPIPM				
	Interest	4.743	5.558	5.780
	EPMG	.175	.773	1.212

expectations and derivatives gives the exogenous variables' *total* effects—their effects controlling only for the other exogenous variables (hence leaving the intervening endogenous ones free to operate). For example, education's (x_1's) total effect is

$$\partial E(y_{i1}|x_{i1},x_{i2}\ldots,x_{i6})/\partial x_{i1} = \pi_{11}\pi_{10}^{+}x_{i1}^{(\pi_{11}-1)}x_{i2}^{\pi_{12}}x_{i3}^{\pi_{13}}x_{i4}^{\pi_{14}}x_{i5}^{\pi_{15}}x_{i6}^{\pi_{16}}, \quad (4)$$

where the adjusted scale factor $\pi_{10}^{+} = (\exp \frac{1}{2}\sigma_1^2)\pi_{10}$, where σ_1^2 now denotes $E(ln\ v_{i1})^2$.[27]

The π's must be positive, if the β's and γ's are,[28] and the total effects should consequently be positive and increasing functions of the other exogenous variables.[29] We can estimate the π's by implication from the 2SLS estimates of the β's and γ's, obtaining the asymptotic standard errors as in Goldberger, Nagar, and Odeh (1961).[30]

Table 8-4 shows that all the significant estimates are indeed positive, although not all are significant. Intelligence, occupation, and parental interest affect sophistication. Education, age, and EPMG do not. EPMG arguably affects EPIPM, while intelligence, occupation, and parental interest affect both EPIPM and interest. Education and age affect neither. With the possible exception of EPMG's effect on EPIPM, which only scrapes significance at the conventional .05 level, these results are no surprise, given the structural results in Table 8-2.

Table 8-4 Reduced-Form Parameters

Equation	Explanatory Variable	Parameter	Standard Error
Sophistication			
	Constant	2.484	1.708
	(adjusted)	(3.182)	
	Education	.049	.178
	Occupation	.538	.251
	Intelligence	1.165	.251
	Age	.024	.157
	Parental interest	.323	.139
	EPMG	−.041	.170
Interest			
	Constant	1.235	.490
	(adjusted)	(1.334)	
	Education	.021	.076
	Occupation	.230	.112
	Intelligence	.497	.112
	Age	.015	.101
	Parental interest	.205	.067
	EPMG	−.018	.073
EPIPM			
	Constant	1.072	.603
	(adjusted)	(1.210)	
	Education	.029	.106
	Occupation	.319	.155
	Intelligence	.691	.160
	Age	.021	.128
	Parental interest	.285	.090
	EPMG	.156	.118

Again the best way of sizing up the effects is by the corresponding GPDs. Now, however, the appropriate GPDs are total, instead of direct: differences of expectations based on the reduced form. The total GPD that education (x_1) can make to sophistication (y_1) is

$$\pi_{10}^{+}(17)^{\pi_{11}} x_{i2}^{\pi_{12}} x_{i3}^{\pi_{13}} x_{i4}^{\pi_{14}} x_{i5}^{\pi_{15}} x_{i6}^{\pi_{16}} - \pi_{10}^{+}(.01)^{\pi_{11}} x_{i2}^{\pi_{12}} x_{i3}^{\pi_{13}} x_{i4}^{\pi_{14}} x_{i5}^{\pi_{15}} x_{i6}^{\pi_{16}},$$

where .01 and 17 are education's minimum and maximum. Table 8-5 presents the estimated total GPDs when other exogenous variables are at their minima, means, and maxima.

Here we see that with interest factored out, sophistication depends heavily on intelligence. Even for people from politically uninvolved families and in politically impinged jobs, a maximum difference in intelligence makes a perceptible difference to sophistication. For people from highly politicized families and in

Table 8-5 Greatest Possible Differences (Total)

Dependent Variable	Exogenous Variable	GPD When the Other Exogenous Variables Are at Their:		
		Minima	Means	Maxima
Sophistication				
	Education	.810	5.611	17.445
	Occupation	1.484	12.224	25.485
	Intelligence	10.164	24.608	48.351
	Age	.074	.704	2.195
	Parental interest	1.255	8.821	23.151
	EPMG	−.085	−.824	−2.515
Interest				
	Education	.181	.445	.753
	Occupation	.308	.815	1.163
	Intelligence	1.311	2.059	2.868
	Age	.027	.075	.126
	Parental interest	.418	.966	1.464
	EPMG	−.021	−.061	−.102
EPIPM				
	Education	.195	.776	1.632
	Occupation	.339	1.499	2.488
	Intelligence	1.650	3.524	5.648
	Age	.028	.207	.284
	Parental interest	.470	1.718	3.096
	EPMG	.151	.645	1.325

politicizing jobs, it makes an enormous difference. Occupation and parental interest are less important. Neither has much influence when other variables are unpropitious. Occupation makes little difference for unintelligent people from apolitical families, and the politicization of the family makes little difference for unintelligent people in politically uninvolving occupations. Both, however, gain some modest effect as the other variables approach their averages, and a sizable one by the time the other variables approach their maxima. For highly intelligent people in politically impinged occupations, growing up in a family that is keenly versus not much interested in politics can raise or lower expected sophistication by 25 points, and for highly intelligent people brought up in highly politicized families, working in a politically impinged versus a politically insulated occupation can account for a similar difference. Finally, the lower portions of the table show that intelligence dominates the other reduced form equations as well. Occupation, parental interest, and EPMG (in the case of EPIPM) have some impact, but not nearly so much.

Discussion

I offer this analysis with some diffidence, given its reliance on the interviewer ratings of intelligence. These may indeed bear some responsibility for the results, in which intelligence looks quite important and education unimportant. They may inflate intelligence's effect, perhaps at the expense of education's. And the conservative reader may wish to regard the estimates above and interpretations below as more than usually tentative. Further studies, with better measures, will tell how far they're right. Yet, for various reasons I do not think we should discount on this basis too much. I have already cited evidence that the interviewer ratings are more valid and reliable than they may appear; other evidence supports the estimated effects more directly. But let us return to this question.

By far the most influential variable, unsurprisingly, is interest. We learn about the things we care about. The next most influential, after intelligence, is occupation, a result that needs more comment. The usual pattern is for education's effect to survive a control for occupation but not vice versa (Converse, 1974), but here we see that with occupation scored by political impingement rather than by status—and with intelligence also controlled—it is occupation's effect, not education's, that survives. At the same time, the effect is relatively tame, contrary to Popkin, Gorman, Phillips, and Smith (1976). This is *not* because occupation is handicapped by exclusion from the interest equation. When added, it has no effect. Occupation's effect on interest seems to be through sophistication, an effect the model already reflects. On the other hand, the effect might well be larger, could political impingement be measured more finely.

Two further positive findings deserve underlining. The first is that interest depends on sophistication as well as vice versa. The effect, indeed, is gigantic. And since interest affects other political variables (posterior to the model, except for EPIPM), the effect redounds to sophistication's importance, both in the causal scheme of things and (therefore) as an object of inquiry. The second point is that intelligence, through sophistication, has a sizable effect on interest and EPIPM as well. Clearly, this is a variable that deserves more attention, beginning with better measurement.

The most interesting findings, however, are null. Education, in the conventional wisdom, is "probably *the* prime predictor of dependent variables reflecting political interest, participation, and mobilization" (Converse, 1974, p. 730). Studies showing association between education and sophistication, in particular, are legion. Why, then, does education fail so abjectly here? Two simple explanations can be quickly dismissed. The absence of effect is not just an idiosyncrasy of the second half-sample. The estimate was similarly insignificant in the first half, and I gave the variable this second chance only in deference to its place in the literature. Nor does education affect sophistication through interest, as we have seen.

It is possible, on the other hand, that education has some effect outside the model. It may not affect sophistication directly. It may not affect sophistication through interest. But it may still affect sophistication through intelligence, occupation, or EPMG. Let us consider this possibility more closely. Education cannot have much effect through EPMG, because EPMG's own effect is minor. It can have some through occupation, but probably not too much because occupation's effect is only moderate, and political impingement is only moderately tied to education. The largest of these submerged effects is presumably through intelligence. Certainly education and intelligence are correlated. But why? Education may sharpen the intellect, but students who are brighter to begin with are apt to go further in school. In addition, intelligence and education share a same-signed dependence on many of the same (or different but positively correlated) "third" variables, including parental intelligence, aspirations, and class. To the extent that the correlation is due to intelligence's effect on education and their mutual dependence on other variables, rather than to education's effect on intelligence, education's hidden effect must be small.

For now, we can only speculate. To estimate such poor effects, we should have to push the model's rear boundary back, making intelligence, occupation, EPMG, education itself (depending as it does on intelligence), and probably other variables not yet in the model endogenous. But many of the requisite variables—parental intelligence and child-rearing practices in the intelligence equation, for instance—lie hopelessly beyond the capacity of these or any other current data on sophistication to operationalize.

Even short of estimating some such larger model, however, there is reason to think education's effect overrated. Closer-range studies, of students in school, show little political learning. High school civics courses leave only the lightest imprint (Langton and Jennings, 1968). Seniors know more than they did as freshmen (Torney, Oppenheim, and Farnen, 1975; Merelman, 1971; Andrain, 1971), but most of the gain is probably due to maturation, information from other sources, the politicization that results from being part of a panel study about politics, and improved guessing ability (Merelman, 1981). Beck (1977), surveying the literature, concludes (p. 139) that "research has failed to show that the school, either as an institution or in terms of the individual teachers within it, has much influence on the political learning of students."

Why, then, do so many cross-sectional analyses of adult samples show a relationship between education and sophistication? The simplest explanation is the paucity of controls. The studies showing an education effect do not always partial on interest, and never on intelligence or occupation qua political impingement. So "education's" effect may really be intelligence's, occupation's, and interest's. Education may be taking credit for other variables' work. Students must pick up some political information in school, but apparently do not wind up knowing much or more, other things being equal, the longer they spend there. This makes perfect sense, once we recognize that the problem of becoming politically sophisticated by these standards is not one of scouring a barren environment for obscure information. In the schools, in the media, on the job, in ordinary conversation—messages involving terms like "liberal" and "conservative" or referring to the parties' positions on prominent issues are almost hard to avoid. The problem is one of absorbing, retaining, and organizing the information one meets—a problem of motivation and ability.

Again, this pattern could have been accentuated or produced by the measurement of intelligence. But that particular cloud would look more threatening if other recent studies, some with better measures, did not show similar results. Intelligence has an important effect both in Hamill, Lodge, and Blake (1985) and Neuman (1986, Figure 5.4); education looks somewhat more important than intelligence in Neuman, I suspect because he does not control for interest, but much less important in Hamill et al. Graber (1984, p. 196) concludes on the basis of her in-depth analysis of 21 Chicago-area residents that intelligence and "experience" (primarily occupation) predict sophistication better than education. These analyses have weaknesses of their own, as previously noted, but the generally strong showing of intelligence and generally weak showing of education suggest taking the estimates here at something not too far from face value.

How far these results generalize to other dependent variables is uncertain, but they at least cast a shadow on education's effects. The selection of education as column variable or regressor is too conventional and too easy. Education, defined as years of schooling, is easy to measure. And it is certainly related to participation and other "variables of extent." But to what degree are education's effects really education's? Does education affect participation, or is the effect really sophistication's or (one step back) intelligence's? Arguments for education effects are often really arguments of intelligence, interest, sophistication, or occupation effects. It is time to unconfound these variables.

EPIPM's failure may be of similar cloth. Again the result is not merely a quirk of the half-sample. In the first half, too, the EPIPM parameter estimate was insignificant, and only (shaken) faith kept it in the equation. Again there may be excuses. It may be thought, for example, that the exclusion of the broadcast media is to blame. But the information that comes over the airwaves is very dilute and lightly attended, and including the broadcast media *worsens* the variable's performance. Or it might be argued that it is cumulative rather than current exposure that matters. Sans measurement of cumulative exposure, we can only guess about this, but my guess is that a past perfect version of the variable could not diverge sufficiently from the present tense to produce the very different results. And again, too, the finding of negligible effect finds some company in previous research (Robinson, 1972; Chaffee, Jackson-Beeck, Duvall, and Wilson, 1977; Hamill, Lodge, and Blake, 1985).

Hence I believe the lack of effect is authentic. EPIPM and sophistication are related, of course, but mainly as a result of EPIPM's and sophistication's mutual dependence on interest and EPIPM's dependence on sophistication through interest. People obviously acquire political information from newspapers and magazines, even radio and television. But they do not acquire much more, the more often they read, watch, or listen to the news, with intelligence, occupation, and interest held constant. It does not take much time with the newspapers, magazines or newscasts for an able, motivated person to maintain a relatively high level of sophistication. The key is paying serious attention to and thinking seriously about the information one encounters, in the media and elsewhere.

People *are* influenced, to be sure, by what they see and hear. News coverage may set agendas, shifting public attention from some events and problems to others (Iyengar, Peters, and Kinder, 1982; Iyengar and Kinder, 1987). Despite selective exposure and perception, political advertising may change some attitudes. But such effects do not imply much effect on sophistication. Think of a belief system as a canvas, with the most elementary cognitions as individual marks or strokes. Some canvases contain only widely scattered, incoherent dots and squiggles. Others are dense with meaningful elements, themselves organized into meaningful scenes. News coverage or political advertising may alter the hue or arrangement of particular elements, but is unlikely to transform a sparsely filled Jackson Pollock into a Breugel or a Grandma Moses.

The failure of age is a different story. Perhaps competing demands on time and attention do not really diminish with age. Or perhaps they do, but do not really deter interest (as opposed to activity). Either would be consistent with some previous results. Klingemann (1979a) finds only a small correlation between age and sophistication. Wolfinger and Rosenstone (1980, p. 50) find "no consequential relationships between age and such 'motivational terms' as interest in the campaign and in politics, use of the mass media, and political information." On the other hand, age, unlike education and EPIPM, shows up with a significant parameter estimate in the first half-sample (the only difference in significance between halves). Is its failing to do so in the second half mere eccentricity? Reestimating the model on additional data should yield a firmer conclusion.

These empirical successes and failures follow a pattern. Sophistication depends, above all, on motivation (interest, occupation, and, indirectly, parental interest). It also depends on ability (intelligence). But the big informational variables (education and EPIPM) have little effect. Education probably has some effect outside the model, but mostly through ability (intelligence), not the dissemination of political information. Of the variables that succeed, only occupation is even partly informational, and it has a powerful motivational side as well. Sophistication, in these results, is much less a function of the information to which people are exposed than of what they can and are motivated to make of it. The readiness is pretty nearly all.

All this makes for a gloomy forecast. Most of us probably believe—I myself believe—that where sophistication is concerned, more is better. The balance of evidence suggests, however, that mass publics everywhere are woefully unsophisticated by anything approaching elite standards (Converse, 1975; Kinder 1983; Luskin, 1987b). Is there any prospect for improvement? From the time of John Stuart Mill at least, most hope has lain with education (see Thompson, 1970). But if education had the effect it is supposed to have, the revolutionary spread of education since the 1950s should have brought a similarly dramatic increase in sophistication. That there now seems to have been little such increase (Converse, 1975; Kinder, 1983; Luskin, 1987b) is another reason for crediting the estimates above. If accurate, moreover, the estimates suggest that we cannot expect much from education in the future, either. Education's effect outside the model may produce small increases in aggregate sophistication—it may in fact be responsible for the small increases that seem to have occurred—but it can only do so much.

A fairer prospect may lie with occupation. The growth of government and the increasing professionalization and bureaucratization of society have brought increasing proportions of the work force into politically impinged occupations and will probably continue to do so. Indeed, the small increases in aggregate sophistication since the 1950s may owe more to increases in political impingement than to increases in education. Still, occupation's effect seems only moderate and probably cannot be expected to tilt the distribution of sophistication very far.

Other variables have larger effects but little prospect of aggregate change. Aggregate intelligence may increase with better pre- and postnatal nutrition, higher average education, and so forth, but surely not very much. Interest in politics—as opposed to a particular campaign—should be quite stable, due in part to the inertial drag or pull of prior ignorance or sophistication. None of the model's variables both has a big effect on sophistication and promises to change very much in the aggregate.

"Constructively," as opposed to "reconstructively," [31] there does not seem to be much we can do. At most, we can expect a gradual and very limited increase, as education continues to spread and the proportion of politically impinged occupations continues to grow. To hope for more, we should have to change the parameters, not just the variables, by changing the system. But such structural changes may be impracticable or undesirable on other groups. Sufficiently small polities, for example, may encourage involvement by making the stakes more vivid. But the interrelatedness and international tensions of the modern world make city-states unattainable. And even under a more facilitative regime, the combination of limited cognitive resources and competing attentional demands may keep politics a minority pursuit, as it seems to have been even in ancient Athens (Dahl, 1984). This is not the place to dilate on democratic theory, but these results suggest that a highly sophisticated, participatory public is not even feasible prescription. How distressing this is, is unclear. But theory, if these results are right, must accommodate itself to the fact.

NOTES

1. For recent reviews of the levels of public participation in democratic politics, see Crewe (1981) and Powell (1982, 1986).

2. The literature attempting to weigh issue versus candidate or party-oriented voting is all atangle—the weights depend on the definitions of the variables and the specification of the model (compare Page and Jones, 1979, with Markus and Converse, 1979)—but it seems to me a fair reading that raw partisanship and reactions to the candidates' personas generally have more influence than perceptions of the candidates' stands on the issues. For a recent review, see Asher (1988, pp. 203-205 and passim).

3. Many authors confuse "constraint" with the statistical patterning of attitudes across individuals. Here, and as Converse (1964) originally intended it, constraint means cognitive organization, of which the statistical patterning of attitudes across individuals is merely an aggregate measure, and an extremely dilute one at that (see Luskin, 1987b).

4. For some brief arguments and further references in support of these propositions, the reader may wish to consult Luskin (1987a).

5. The less, too, it appears, a less sophisticated public will support the application of democratic norms like majority rule and the freedoms of speech and assembly to specific cases (McClosky, 1964; Gibson and Bingham, 1985; McClosky and Zaller, 1984).

6. Hamill et al.'s is not explicitly an analysis of sophistication. One of their dependent variables, however, "partisan schema usage," is almost a doppelganger for D, below, and the other two, class and ideological schema usage, have a similar thrust. These are all measures of what Fiske and Taylor (1984) call *schema development*, an object-specific version of sophistication, and for objects sufficiently prominent, like the parties, the development of different political schemas should be highly intercorrelated, and highly correlated with sophistication as a whole (Luskin, 1987b; Bolland, Kuklinski, and Luskin, 1987).

7. This is not entirely true of Neuman, some of whose analyses use ANES data. His most important analysis, however, displayed in his Figure 5.4, is based on a small, nonprobability subset of a Bay Area sample.

8. One cannot help but think, in this connection, of the detective's criteria for suspects: means, motive, and opportunity. Sniderman (1975) places the variables affecting a person's adoption of a particular opinion under similar rubrics.

9. Altogether they boost the R^2 for the interest equation (1.2), below, by .005.

10. It is in fact education's association with sophistication that those who see an education-interest connection frequently seem to have in mind (Rosenstone and Wolfinger, 1978, p. 28, for example).

11. A number of macro-level variables—the ideational richness of the debates among rival elites and the magnitude of the policy difference between them, the frequency and vehemence of wars, depressions, race riots, and other politicizing events—may also affect interest and sophistication (and EPIPM) over time or across politics (Field and Anderson, 1969; Nie, Verba, and Petrocik, 1976; Miller and Levitin, 1976; Miller et al., 1976), but are constant for a given public at a given time.

12. There are actually several Box-Cox models of varying complexity (Box and Cox, 1964). The one estimated here is

$$\frac{(y_{i1} - 1)^q}{q} = a_0 + a_1 \frac{(y_{i2} - 1)^q}{q} + a_2 \frac{(y_{i3} - 1)^q}{q} + a_3 \frac{(x_{i1} - 1)^q}{q} \quad (N1)$$

$$+ a_4 \frac{(x_{i4} - 1)^q}{q} + a_2 \frac{(x_{i5} - 1)^q}{q} + e_{i1}$$

where q and the a's are unknown parameters and e_i is a disturbance. For $q = 1$, (N1) is linear and additive; as $q \gg 0$, it becomes multiplicative. Thus estimating q (by maximum likelihood) tells which form the data prefer, although the indication is admittedly rough, since the estimation takes no account of other equations. For (N1), the estimated q is 0.21, which sustains the multiplicative form.

13. I assume here that u_{i1} is lognormal with $E(ln\ u_{i1}) = 0$ and $E(ln\ u_{i1})^2 = \sigma_1^2$ for all i, from which it follows that $E(u_{i1}) = exp\ \frac{1}{2}\sigma_1^2$ (Aitchison and Brown, 1957). The alternative assumption that $E(u_{i1}) = 1$ would obviate the adjustment at this stage, only to necessitate equivalent steps later, in the estimation of $ln\ \gamma_{10}$ (and then γ_{10}), since $E(ln\ u_{i1})$ then $\neq 0$ (cf. Goldberger, 1968).

14. In multiplicative equations, the variables' zero-points matter, although small differences in assigned values make only small differences to the estimates.

15. Smith (1980) has criticized this whole line of measurement. While concentrating his fire on Nie, Verba, and Petrocik's (1976) measure, he impugns the validity of the original *LC* as well. This wilder charge has been answered by Hagner and Pierce (1982; also Pierce and Hagner, 1982) and Knight (1985). But even Smith's evidence against the Nie et al. measure (whose face validity is lower) is less telling than may at first appear (Cassel, 1984). The measure here resembles Nie et al.'s in working from the ANES "master codes," but improved on theirs in other ways. Empirically, it performs reasonably well (Luskin, 1987b).

16. These measures are premised on the relationship between cognitive organization and abstraction, baldly asserted by Campbell et al. (1960) and Converse (1964), but amply supported by cognitive psychology (Bousfield, 1953; Tulving, 1961; Buschke, 1976).

17. This is a fairly condensed description of I_1, I_2 or D. See Luskin (1987b) for additional details.

18. The combination is multiplicative because the concept is conjunctive: Sophistication requires integration *and* differentiation. The additions of 1 prevent respondents with a score of 0 on either $(I_1 + I_2)$ or D from receiving the same score $(= 0)$ on S regardless of their score on the other.

19. The high impingement category contains the ANES occupation codes 001-002, 016-025, 030-031, 055, 061-072, 086, 091-100, 115-122, 132-133, 184, 201-202, 210-215, 222-223, 230, 235-245, 265, 270-271, 801-802, and 963-965.

20. Their correlation with the Cattell measure is .28.

21. Not-really-quite-interval data may seem to urge a multiequation probit model, but the measures of EPIPM and especially sophistication are too finely discriminated to make this attractive, and the difficulty of incorporating nonlinearities in the endogenous variables is a further discouragement. Another line of attack would be a covariance structure model, to cope with measurement errors. Again, however, the representation of nonlinearity is a problem, as is the scarcity of indicators.

22. 2SLS provides estimates of the exponential parameters $(\gamma_{11}, \gamma_{24}, \beta_{32}$, etc.) and the logged scale factors $(\gamma_{g0}^* = ln\ \gamma_{g0}, g = 1, 2, 3)$. To recover estimates of the scale factors themselves, we set $\hat{\gamma}_{g0} = exp\ \hat{\gamma}_{g0}^*$, where the " $\hat{}$ s" indicate estimates. Then, to estimate the adjusted scale factors, we set $\hat{\gamma}_{g0}^+ = (exp\ \frac{1}{2}\sigma_g^2)\hat{\gamma}_{g0}$, where σ_g^2 denotes the 2SLS-derived estimate of the logged disturbance variance $\sigma_g^2 = E(ln\ u_{ig})^2, g = 1, 2, 3$. The R^2s are computed as the r^2s between the actual and 2SLS-predicted dependent variables.

23. All significance statements refer to the asymptotically appropriate one-tailed test at the .05 level.

24. Although to refer to the great *possible* difference is implicitly to take the variables' maxima and minima seriously, the device applies beyond discrete or limited variables.

Even with more nearly continuous and unbounded measures, we should be able to examine greatest *likely* differences, substituting relatively extreme values (those lying so many standard deviations above or below the means, e.g.) for absolute maxima and minima. See Luskin (forthcoming).

25. In speaking at once of maxima and minima and of the variables' being at their means, I am presuming the existence of values between but not beyond the actual scores, a stance of convenience I take throughout.

26. In matrix notation, the logged versions of (1.1), (1.2), and (1.3) are

$$B \ln y_i + C \ln x_i = w_i,$$

where $\ln y_i$, $\ln x_i$, and $w_i = \ln u_i$ are the 3×1, 7×1, and 3×1 vectors of the ith observation on the endogenous and exogenous variables and disturbances, respectively, and B and C are the 3×3 and 3×7 matrices of parameters associated with the endogenous and exogenous variables. (The first element of $\ln x_i$ is 1, and the first row of C consists of $\ln \gamma_{10}$, $\ln \gamma_{20}$, and $\ln \gamma_{30}$.) The logged reduced form equations, therefore, are

$$\ln y_i = P \ln x_i + e_i,$$

where

(N2) $$P = -B^{-1}C$$

and $e_i = B^{-1}w_i$. Exponentiating again, row by row, yields the (unlogged) reduced-form equations. In (3), *supra*, for instance, the π's are the first row of P, except for π_{10}, which is the antilog of the first element, and $v_{i1} = \exp e_{i1}$.

27. The linear relationship $e_i = B^{-1}w_i$, together with our assumptions about u_i, implies that $E(v_{i1}) = \exp \frac{1}{2}\sigma_1^2$ (where again σ_1^2 now denotes $E(\ln v_{i1})^2$), and thus that

$$E(y_{i1}|x_{i1}, x_{i2} \cdots, x_{i6}) = \pi_{10}^+ x_{i1}^{\pi 11} x_{i2}^{\pi 12} x_{i3}^{\pi 13} x_{i4}^{\pi 14} x_{i5}^{\pi 15} x_{i6}^{\pi 16}.$$

28. By (N2).

29. By (4), parallel as it is to (2).

30. The estimates of the unlogged constants require an additional step, and the estimates of the adjusted constants yet another, as in note 22.

31. A distinction I am taking from Thompson (1970).

PART III: VOTE DETERMINANTS

9. WHAT DETERMINES THE VOTE?

Most fundamentally, the study of voting behavior focuses on what determines the vote. Is voting mainly based on the issues of the day? Are reactions to political candidates of paramount importance? To what extent is voting just a matter of following party loyalties? And is it possible to assess the relative importance of those three factors: issues, candidates, and party?

The earliest controversy in this field (*Classics in Voting Behavior*, chap. 9) was whether or not issues matter in voting. Analyses of the first national voting studies in the United States (for example, Campbell, Converse, Miller, and Stokes, 1960) could be read as saying that voting is based on party and candidates, but not issues. However, the revisionist literature of the 1960s instead emphasized the role of issues. This controversy was resolved by repeated demonstrations of the importance of issues in voting, but the relative importance of different determinants of the vote remained open to dispute.

There was an optimistic moment in the 1970s when it seemed that the use of the right survey design and analytical model would lead to a final statistical determination of the relative importance of issues, candidates, and party in affecting voting. However, such models proved controversial in their own right, reaching opposing conclusions as to whether issues or party predominated (*Classics*, chap. 9). There is now increased recognition that different voters weigh these factors differently, as in Rivers' (1988) demonstration that some voters weigh ideology more and others weigh party identification more in their voting decisions. As a result, there has been less emphasis on statistical decomposition of the vote in the post-1979 literature.

The main exception is the work by Miller and Shanks (1982) and Shanks and Miller (1990, 1991) on the elections of the 1980s. The Miller and Shanks studies posit a particular order in which factors affect voting (individual demographics first, next policy predispositions, then party identification, and so on), and then solve for the relative importance of the factors given that ordering. The results are interesting, as when agreement with the policy status quo is found to be the most important part of understanding Bush's 1988 victory, with positive evaluations of the country and of the Reagan presidency also contributing. Yet, positing a single order for the variables rather than testing between alternative reasonable models makes it difficult to assess how much these results depend on their assumptions. Thus, even this work has not resulted in firm conclusions regarding the relative importance of candidates, issues, and party in the vote decision.

Instead, the recent literature on vote determinants has focused on two specific factors, issues and candidates, with attention to how each affects voting. In part, this debate reflects two different approaches to studying politics: the renewed emphasis on issues is largely based on the influence of rational choice perspectives borrowed from economics, while the increased attention to the candidate factor is mainly due to the influence of cognitive perspectives borrowed from psychology.

Issues: The Rationality of Performance Evaluations and Economics

The contemporary issue voting literature is concerned not with whether issues matter but with which issues matter and how they matter. When the revisionists first argued that issues mattered in elections, they worked from a simple model in which voters evaluated candidate promises, choosing the candidate whose issue position was closer to their own. As the field has become more sophisticated, several implicit assumptions have been challenged, particularly the reliance on promises, on voting for the most proximate candidate, and on not distinguishing among types of issues. By contrast, the current research focuses on issue voting in such guises as retrospective voting, directional voting, foreign policy voting, and especially economic voting.

Much of the contemporary issue voting literature focuses on the role of economics in elections. There are actually several different aspects to this literature, not all of which are directly relevant to our present concern. The first argument is that government approval (often operationalized by a question on approval of the president or prime minister) is strongly influenced by the status of the economy, either the respondent's own financial status or the overall economic situation. The second argument is that the state of the economy affects voting, although along with this is a countertheme that administrations manipulate the economy near election dates so as to maximize their chances of reelection. The final argument is that left and right parties differ in their economic policies, so that the electorate is indeed making real economic choices when it votes. In terms of voting determinants, all this amounts to a strong case for the importance of economic issues in voting. We shall not consider the full case here but focus instead on the extent to which economic variables influence voting itself.

An extensive literature at the aggregate level shows that public support for political authorities is affected by economic variables (for example, MacKuen, Erikson, and Stimson, 1992b), and there is also evidence (for example, Fair, 1978, 1988) that economic variables influence the vote. In addition to this aggregate analysis, individual-level analysis lends some support to the economic influence literature, though several individual studies, especially in the 1970s, did not find economic effects. Kramer (1983) has explained this discrepancy by arguing that changing economic conditions (which can be observed in aggregate studies) affect voting, but voters in any single election experience similar economic conditions (so economic voting may not be observed at the individual level). Still, Kiewiet (1981, p. 459) finds that "there was a mass of (survey) evidence showing voters reacting to their concern over unemployment by voting more Democratic." Also, Fiorina (1981) and Lewis-Beck (1988) show that a variety of economic factors—both retrospective judgments about past performance and expectations about future behavior—influence voting behavior.[1] Kinder, Adams, and Gronke (1989) demonstrate effects of national, group, and individual economic well-being on voting, with national economic voting being most common. These studies also demonstrate convincingly that economic factors retain their explanatory power when noneconomic variables are included in the equations.

The Markus chapter in this section (Chapter 10) illustrates the type of analysis that is done in using survey data to study economic voting among the electorate. It tests between the alternative hypotheses that people vote their own economic interest ("pocketbook" voting) and that people vote on the basis of the national economy ("sociotropic" voting). Markus is able to pool together survey data for eight election years to observe the effects of changing economic conditions on the vote (and thus handle the problem that Kramer pointed out). The results show that the economy indeed affects voting, especially at the individual level. The conclusion of the paper appropriately raises two more important themes— the prediction of election outcomes and the role of the campaign. If the election outcome can be predicted well by the state of the economy, then the campaign itself may be viewed as irrelevant. The final section of this introduction turns to some other issues involved in predicting outcomes.

The work on economic issues and voting has not gone completely unchallenged. For example, a study by Madsen (1980) found little relationship between economic conditions and voting in Denmark and Norway, one by Whiteley (1980) discovered no relationship in Great Britain, and Paldam (1991) showed that, in general, such models are only true for some countries and some time periods. Nevertheless, the great majority of studies do document economic effects. Moreover, studies finding effects of the economy cover a wide variety of contexts: the U.S. presidency, the American Congress (see also Chapter 13 of this book), and governmental leaders in Britain, France, and other countries (Norpoth, Lewis-Beck, and Lafay, 1991). Additionally, Chubb (1988) found effects of the national economy on state legislative races and of both the national and state economies on gubernatorial contests.

As noted above, both economists and political scientists have now "turned around" the economic effects equations, arguing that there are political influences on economic policy. Unemployment, inflation, transfer payments (for example, social security), trade agreements, and so on are all thought to be used to generate support for the incumbent administration. A specific example of such tactics is when administrations time increases in transfer payments to fall close to the election date. In some instances the influence is benign, as when "governments pursue macroeconomic policies broadly in accordance with the objective economic interests and subjective preferences of their class-defined core constituencies"

(Hibbs, 1977, p. 1467). But others view at least some government actions as manipulations in the worst sense of the term. Tufte (1978, p. 143), for example, charges that:

> The electoral-economic cycle breeds a lurching, stop-and-go economy the world over. Governments fool around with transfer payments, making an election-year prank out of the social security system and the payroll tax. There is a bias toward policies with immediate, highly visible benefits and deferred, hidden costs—myopic policies for myopic voters. Special interests induce coalition-building politicians to impose small costs on the many to achieve large benefits for the few. The result is economic instability and inefficiency.

Still, a number of efforts to identify a general political-business cycle have concluded that none exists (Thompson and Zuk, 1983; Dinkel, 1981; Golden and Poterba, 1980; Paldam, 1981; Beck, 1987; Lewis-Beck, 1988, chap. 9; though see Grier, 1989). Even if one looks for effects only in the immediate preelection period, positive results are not always found (Beck, 1982b; Brown and Stein, 1982). Williams (1990) is able to demonstrate that federal monetary policies are affected by the election cycle and by presidential popularity and that there are party differences in real income, but other macroeconomic effects of political manipulation are limited. And Hibbs's attempt to link left- versus right-wing parties with differing unemployment levels has been questioned in separate and quite distinct analyses (Beck, 1982a; Madsen, 1980, 1981). It would appear, as Golden and Poterba (1980, p. 713) conclude, that political leaders try to influence economic outcomes, but whether they do so successfully is not yet clear.

The discussion so far in this chapter may suggest that issue voting is virtually synonymous with economic voting. That is not the case, though certainly the economic voting literature is unusually well developed. When the early literature (Campbell et al., 1960) found no evidence of issue voting at all in survey data, demonstrating any type was important. Consequently, when initial effects of economic factors were discovered, such studies burgeoned. However, a broader range of issue voting beyond economic voting has now been confirmed.

Perhaps the most influential treatment of issue voting in the 1980s was Fiorina's (1981) emphasis on retrospective effects. Fiorina showed that evaluations of past party performances were more important in voting than candidates' promises for the future. This approach was tested further by Miller and Wattenberg's (1985) analysis of the comments of National Election Studies (NES) respondents to the open-ended questions asking what they like and dislike about each presidential candidate. They coded these comments in terms of whether the references were retrospective or prospective and whether they were directed to performance or policy matters. Incumbents were indeed judged primarily on retrospective performance grounds, though challengers were judged more in terms of prospective policy, and prospective performance predominated in races in which an incumbent did not run for reelection. In any case, shifting attention away from issue voting as choosing exclusively on the basis of future promises has led to further expansion of our image of issue voting.

Note that retrospective voting is closely related to the economic voting discussion above since the emphasis on economic variables is usually explicitly retrospective (cf. Lewis-Beck, 1988). That is, when people vote on the basis of their satisfaction with the economy, they are directly evaluating the performance of the government. Thus, the economic voting literature showed that one particular type of retrospective evaluation is important, while Fiorina's work showed that other retrospective effects are also important. Other studies (Lewis-Beck, 1988; Lockerbie, 1991), however, show prospective effects in addition to the retrospective evaluations.

In many ways, the ultimate test of issue voting is in the foreign policy realm. The original view of *The American Voter* (Campbell et al., 1960) was that most issues were unimportant in voting, with public understanding of foreign policy issues even weaker than that for domestic issues. The literature of the 1960s and 1970s argued that issues are important in elections, but the denouement is the demonstration in the Aldrich, Sullivan, and Borgida chapter (11) that even foreign policy issues matter under the appropriate circumstances.

It is perhaps significant that Aldrich and his colleagues used a specially-designed survey. The choice of issue questions in NES surveys is constrained in that the same issues have usually been followed across elections. This is advantageous for studying changes in issue positions, but it is at the expense of issues that are important in a particular election year. As a result, the examination in NES-based analyses of the role of issue voting is probably on the conservative side. If the emphasis in developing questions were on short-term policy matters that occur during the campaign rather than just on long-term items, even more policy voting should be expected.

The Aldrich, Sullivan, and Borgida chapter is motivated from the perspective of social psychology rather than from the rational choice perspective that underlies most work on the role of economic issues. This perspective is particularly evident in its emphasis on issue accessibility, showing that foreign problems were accessible to the public in several presidential elections, partly because candidates campaigned on foreign policy matters. The social psychology approach has been even more influential for the current understanding of the candidate factor in elections, as will be shown in the next section of this chapter.

Issue voting has been investigated most frequently under Downsian (1957) formal models, which assume that individuals vote for the candidate nearest to the voter on a spatial dimension. This is considered a "proximity" theory in that closeness on the issues to the voter is what counts. Rational choice theorists have championed this spatial approach, which has led to considerably more emphasis on issue voting than was the case in the earliest voting behavior literature. An important alternative spatial theory has been developed by Rabinowitz and Macdonald (1989) using what they term "directional" theory. Under this approach, closeness to the candidate does not matter; what does matter is agreeing with the candidate on the direction of change. That is, a voter may want a more liberal social policy in a particular area and may therefore prefer a candidate who wants liberal change in that area over a candidate who prefers conservative change, even if the conservative candidate's position is closer to the voter.

Rabinowitz and Macdonald find support for this directional model in the 1984 NES survey.[2]

While researchers now agree that issues affect voting, there remains some disagreement as to whether voters weigh each issue equally or attach considerably more weight to some issues. The standard NES open-ended question asks respondents which national problem is important to them. Also, several studies have followed the issue scales with a question asking about the importance of the issue to them personally. It would be reasonable for voters to give greater weight to the issue they find most important and to the issues that are more important to them personally, but studies differ widely in their findings. Rabinowitz, Prothro, and Jacoby (1982) used the 1968 Comparative State Elections Project in which respondents were asked which issue was most important to them after they were asked about their attitudes on each separate issue. They estimate a regression model to determine the importance of each issue in affecting candidate evaluation, with an added weight if that issue is cited by the respondent as the most important one. That weight is significant, showing that salient issues are weighted more by voters. In contrast, Niemi and Bartels (1985), using a standard spatial model except that issues were weighted by a salience score, found no evidence that salience helped account for voting decisions. Krosnick (1990) found that issues considered more important to respondents personally have a greater impact on their candidate preferences (as measured by regression coefficients). Also, respondents viewing an issue as important to them personally were more likely to cite that issue as a reason for voting for or against one of the presidential candidates.

Candidates: The Psychology of Emotions and Cognitions

The early literature on voting behavior paid relatively little attention to the candidate factor. This lack of attention was ironic, given the extremely high relationship between candidate preference and vote. As one would expect, voters (in two candidate elections) virtually invariably vote for the candidate they like more (Brody and Page, 1973; Kelley and Mirer, 1974). Also, this lack of research emphasis on candidates was ironic, given the fact that political elites and citizens both obviously care about who the candidates are. The media certainly focus attention on the candidates and, in recent years, especially on their character (as with Gary Hart in 1987 and Bill Clinton during the 1992 primaries). Many citizens indicate they vote on the basis of the candidates rather than parties.[3] Still, pure candidate voting has seemed to bear a stigma in the voting behavior literature.

Actually, the original University of Michigan work accorded an important status to candidate voting. Along with party orientation and issue orientation, candidate orientation was treated as one of three coequal determinants of the vote in *The Voter Decides* (Campbell et al., 1954). *The American Voter* (Campbell et al., 1960) clearly showed that the candidate factor was very important in the Eisenhower wins of the 1950s. However, the importance of the candidate factor in Eisenhower's victories became caricatured as a focus on personal characteristics, such as Eisenhower's smile, making voting on the basis of the candidates seem less rational than voting on the basis of the issues. Stokes (1966) established that the considerable variation that exists in presidential election outcomes could be traced to the candidate factor, but candidate voting was still seen as less appropriate than issue voting.

The elections of the 1970s and especially the 1980s changed this view of the candidate factor. Empirical studies found that these races turned on such candidate-related matters as competence (George McGovern's defeat in 1972 according to Popkin, Gorman, Phillips, and Smith, 1976; Jimmy Carter's defeat in 1980 according to Markus, 1982), integrity (Carter's victory in 1976 in the aftermath of Watergate and Jerry Ford's pardon of Richard Nixon), and strength of leadership (Ronald Reagan's reelection in 1984). The defeated candidate had an advantage on issue questions in some of these elections, but the candidate factor worked in the opposite direction.

These results have led to a reconsideration of the rationality of candidate voting. Voting against a candidate who is not seen as competent should not be viewed as irrational; nor should voting against a candidate who is seen as a weak leader. Voting on the basis of the issues is usually seen as the ultimate form of rational voting, but it is less rational if the candidate who is preferred on the issues is not thought to be competent enough or a good enough leader to execute his policies if elected. Also, assessments of candidate competence and trust can be useful as prognoses as to which candidate will react better to the new issues, concerns, and crises that will arise in the next four years. Thus, candidate voting, properly conceived, can be every bit as rational as issue voting.

But the renewed focus on candidate voting was not just due to particular election campaigns. Social psychology studies of person perception were also being applied to the study of voting behavior. There are at least two separate strands from social psychology being borrowed: the study of emotions and the study of cognitions. Both emotions and cognitions are being given greater consideration in social psychology, though there is vigorous debate as to which precedes the other (Zajonc, 1980; Lazarus, 1982). Also influential has been the cognitive literature's view of typical citizens as "cognitive misers," making political judgments and decisions even though they have a limited capacity for dealing with information and therefore use shortcuts, cues, and previously acquired information as the basis of their decisions. Finally, these studies often reflect the social psychologist's interest in contrasting decision making by novices with that of "experts," in this instance political decision making by nonsophisticates and by people who pay attention to politics.

Social psychologists helped design two new batteries of survey questions for the NES surveys of the 1980s. One set focuses on candidate traits, asking people whether they perceive each candidate as honest, hard working, and so on. The other set focuses on affect toward the candidates, asking whether particular candidates make the respondent feel proud, afraid, and so on. Several researchers have used these candidate trait and affect questions to explore the candidate factor in more detail than was possible in the pre-1980 studies.

One popular way to analyze these item batteries is to factor analyze the inter-item correlations to look for underlying patterns. For example, answers to a dozen candidate affect questions could be correlated with one another. A high correlation between a pair of questions indicates that they measure the same underlying factor. A strongly negative correlation indicates they measure opposite aspects of the same factor. A zero correlation indicates that the questions measure different underlying factors. Factor analysis searches for a solution for all the questions at once, looking for a set of unobserved underlying factors that can account for the observed intercorrelations among the different questions.

While the literature includes some different results, the usual findings (Kinder, 1986) are that there are four factors underlying the candidate trait questions: competence, leadership, integrity, and empathy ("caring about people like me").[4] And the usual findings about the candidate affect questions (Abelson, Kinder, Peters, and Fiske, 1982) are that they fall on two separate factors: one involving the traits that are stated positively (such as proud and hopeful) and the other involving the traits that are stated negatively (such as angry and afraid). In a more theoretical treatment based on the Gray-Tellegen two-factor model of emotional appraisal, Marcus (1988) treats the positive affect factor as measuring "mastery" and the negative affect factor as measuring "threat."

Once the underlying factors were identified, the next research topic became how these factors interrelate with vote choice. The simplest model just uses the candidate trait and affect factors as predictors of overall candidate evaluations. That is, ratings of candidates on the thermometers are explained in terms of the trait and/or affect factors. An example of this is Markus's (1982) analysis of change across the waves of the 1980 NES panel study, though his model also considers the reverse—that is, the effects of the overall evaluations on perceptions of candidate traits. As another example, Ragsdale (1991) shows that the affect questions have a greater impact on presidential approval than do issue questions, though there is a question of causal direction here: whether the emotions precede presidential approval or whether they are caused by presidential approval (or share a joint cause).

Political psychologists have been developing more complex models as well. Thus, Marcus (1988) shows that perceived leadership competence of Reagan and relative judgments of Reagan and Mondale on mastery had the greatest direct impact on 1984 presidential vote intention, with party identification and relative judgments of the nominees on the threat factor having the next greatest impacts, and policy appraisals having surprisingly little direct effect. One of the most complete modeling efforts from a political psychology perspective is that by Rahn, Aldrich, Borgida, and Sullivan, reprinted here as Chapter 12. Their analysis of the 1984 presidential election is directly based on a theory of candidate appraisal. However, they also incorporate in their equations many of the components found in more conventional studies, making their analysis more persuasive to those not schooled in the candidate psychology approach. It should be noted, however, that the theoretical understanding they give to the conventional components is often quite different from that found in other studies.

The purest political psychology studies of candidate evaluation focus on understanding the processes by which evaluations occur. For example, Lodge,

McGraw, and Stroh (1989) test between a "memory-based" model in which people needing to make an evaluation first retrieve all their recollections about the candidate from memory and then compute a summary evaluation, and an "impression-driven" or "on-line processing" model in which people carry with them a running-tally evaluation that they update as the occasion arises (Hastie and Park, 1986). The current position in social psychology is that memory-based models assume greater effort than is likely for most people, so that impression-driven models are more likely to hold or to hold for more people. The Lodge, McGraw, and Stroh work is based on experimental subjects who were given a campaign brochure for a fictitious candidate with different instructions designed to emphasize only one model. A memory task (based on the ratio of positively to negatively evaluated policies attributed to the candidate) had little effect on candidate appraisal, except for subjects in the memory-based condition of the experiment. An on-line evaluation measure (the sum of the likes and dislikes for the candidate's issue positions) had a much more significant impact overall, especially for subjects in the impression-driven condition. Lodge, McGraw, and Stroh conclude that the on-line model should be assumed when political scientists measure and model the candidate evaluation process. In a later study, McGraw, Lodge, and Stroh (1990) show that political sophisticates make greater use of on-line processes, while nonsophisticates, who are less able to process political information, end up making greater use of memory-based processing.[5]

Another theme in the analysis of the candidate factor has been the effect of candidate appearance. Rosenberg, Bohan, McCafferty, and Harris (1986) showed subjects pictures of candidates who differed in physical attractiveness. With party and issue position controlled, appearance was highly significant. For example, in one of their studies the candidates with highly rated physical appearances won 59 percent of the vote.

While the early work on candidate traits was based on United States data, the same approach has been applied to other nations. Brown, Lambert, Kay, and Curtis (1988) applied it to Canada, as did Bean and Mughan (1989) to Australia and Britain. What is most fascinating in these applications is that these nations do not have presidential systems of government. Traditional accounts of parliamentary systems have given little attention to the electoral role of the prime minister, but Bean and Mughan in particular demonstrate vote gains of 6.6 percent for Margaret Thatcher in Britain in 1983 and of 4.3 percent for Bob Hawke in Australia in 1987 due to their advantages in leadership images. These results suggest that political leadership effects are not limited to presidential systems, though it is not possible to test whether such leadership effects are new or whether they also were present for prime ministers in a pre-television era.

Most analyses of vote determinants have been in general elections, but there is also a small amount of research on primaries. Presidential primaries in the United States are particularly fascinating elections. For one thing, the usual importance of party identification is muted since voters in a party's primary are generally from that party (or are Independent). For another, voters have much less familiarity with the candidates and their issue positions. Also, the usual strong relationship between candidate preference and vote is diminished for strategic reasons—some voters who prefer one candidate in a multicandidate primary may view that candidate as unelectable in the general election and therefore vote for another candidate.

Bartels (1985, 1987, 1988) examined some of these relationships for the primaries of 1976-1984. In Bartels (1985), he analyzed the 1980 NES study, which included national surveys in January-February and in April. These surveys asked people their first choice for the party nomination as well as who they thought most likely to win that nomination. Psychological processes, however, are likely to make people think their preferred candidate is more likely to win (a "projection" effect) and to make them like the candidate they consider most electable (a "bandwagon" effect); as a result, it is difficult to pull apart the role of expectations and preferences in the surveys. Bartels developed a model that allowed him to estimate these effects, finding that expectations and preferences affected each other in the Carter and Bush campaigns early in the year, while projection effects remained for Carter and Reagan by April without a bandwagon effect by that stage of the campaign.

The 1984 NES study went further than that in 1980 by taking weekly national samples through the primary season. The surveys included candidate thermometers as well as questions about each candidate's chances of winning the nomination. Bartels (1987) uses these questions to develop a model in which preferences for Gary Hart are based on the interaction between predisposition toward Walter Mondale (estimated from demographic and political variables) and perceptions of Hart's chances (estimated from a combination of objective and subjective factors). The success of a model of Hart preferences that does not take Hart directly into account suggests that the Hart success in the early 1984 primaries was more a stop-Mondale movement than a pro-Hart phenomenon. Bartels's results are of interest in many ways. For one, they show how conventional methods can be modified for use in studying other elections. Second, they show the importance of strategic considerations in studying the candidate factor. Finally, they show that systematic analysis of the nomination season can yield important results, so that further studies of presidential primaries are warranted.[6]

All in all, the increased attention to the candidate factor fits well with the view that American elections are increasingly candidate-centered. As the party system has dealigned (see Chapter 20), electoral competition at the general election is increasingly between candidates rather than parties. Meanwhile, the political party elites have lost control over the presidential nomination process, with entrepreneurial candidates being able to win the nomination through the primary system. Together, these effects have made the candidates more and more important in voting, so that the study of reactions to the candidates is all the more important.

Predicting Election Outcomes

The more we know about the determinants of voting, the better we are able to predict election outcomes. When we develop models of voting that are successful at the aggregate level (as are the economic models described above), the natural question is whether the resultant equations can be used in a predictive sense. As a result, several models for predicting election outcomes have been constructed.

The simplest presidential election models attempt to forecast the national outcome or vote percentages. A choice that must be made in such models is whether to use survey measures or aggregate data. The president's approval level is one relevant survey-based measure that can be incorporated into such equations (Brody and Sigelman, 1983). Another survey measure that is being used increasingly is sometimes called a "national mood" question—whether the public feels that the country is on the right track or whether it is on the wrong track. Given the emphasis on the economy in the issue-voting literature, measures of economic optimism are also relevant for such models. It is possible to use survey-based measures of economic optimism, but it is more common to utilize official statistics, predicting that support for the president's party will depend on the performance of the national economy. In an early example of this type, Hibbs (1982a) predicted the outcome of a number of post-War elections on the basis of change in real per capita disposable income over the four-year term. More recently, Erikson (1989a) has shown that per capita income change is an excellent predictor of presidential election outcomes over the entire post-World War II period. Some models combine survey and aggregate data, as in an effort by Lewis-Beck and Rice (1984) to forecast on the basis of presidential popularity and economic change in the second quarter of the election year.

There are many assumptions implicit in work of this type. For one thing, it assumes that the political parties are able to nominate candidates who can take advantage of the situation. As a counter-example, one might find that the economy is doing so poorly that the incumbent party would be expected to lose but the out-party is not able to nominate an effective candidate. This can happen when nomination procedures give an advantage to ideological candidates who do not have widespread appeal, which is one interpretation of the Democratic party nomination procedures starting in 1972 (Polsby and Wildavsky, 1991). Yet, Jacobson and Kernell's (1983) concept of "strategic politicians" suggests that ambitious politicians wait to run until they believe they have a good chance of winning, and so will base their decision to run partly on the state of the economy itself. This strategy works well except when economic changes occur too late in the election cycle for politicians to change their plans, as when the economy sours too late for effective challengers to enter the race (such as in 1992). Such instances work against the predictive success of economic models, so the high degree of success of such models properly implies that those instances are the exception rather than the rule. Furthermore, caution is always necessary when dealing with a small number of cases (here election years) and a very large number of possible predictors; finding one predictor that is highly successful in such a situation may just be a matter of chance (Mock and Weisberg, 1992).

The more complicated forecasting models attempt to predict statewide vote totals in presidential elections, as in Rosenstone (1983). He first determined which variables are related to statewide vote totals and then used them in a forecasting model. He found effects associated with New Deal social welfare issues and racial issues, economic conditions (change in real disposable income compared to a year earlier), public views of current wars, whether the president and/or vice-president are incumbents, home-state and region effects, and recent party success in congressional elections. The model predicts well, with an average state error of three percent for 1948-1980. This model is highly successful, but it requires a large amount of information including survey and nonsurvey measures. More recently, Campbell (1992) showed that a good forecast could be obtained at the state level with fewer variables, though again the number is much higher than in the models predicting national vote totals. However, the Campbell model uses trial-heats (candidate standing in September Gallup Polls) rather than political issues, and so is a forecasting model more than an explanatory model.

Conclusion

Are the insights from social psychology on candidate evaluation as important as those from economics on issue voting? Some of the newer candidate evaluation articles are structured as tests between the two approaches. However, we would view the tests to date as flawed. Each theory has its proponents, and tests designed by those proponents are rarely fair tests. Indeed, we would suspect that the tests conducted to date by political psychologists would not even be deemed relevant by rational-choice theorists. There may eventually be fairer tests between these approaches, but just as we noted at the beginning of this chapter that a final statistical apportioning of the influence due to partisanship and issues was unlikely, we suspect that any final determination of the relative importance of issue (or specifically economic) and candidate factors should not be expected. When different theories are based on completely different paradigms for understanding politics, it is virtually impossible to design a fair test between them.

Recent psychological approaches nonetheless serve as a corrective against overly simplistic models. Just as the early Michigan approach was thought to emphasize partisanship at the expense of issues, the rational choice approach emphasized issues at the expense of any attention to the candidate factor. Indeed, decisions based on candidate characteristics were often seen as irrational, or at least of questionable quality. Newer candidate studies have managed to change this perspective by emphasizing factors related to presidential performance. In addition, many of their models, or their key ideas, are easily integrated into the kind of framework used earlier, as illustrated by the Rahn et al. article reprinted in this section.[7]

Thus, in the end we would argue that multiple approaches to what determines the vote all provide valuable insights, though on different aspects of the voting equation. As was the original Michigan view, partisanship, issues, and candidates all play important roles in elections, though we now have a much better understanding of how each illuminates different processes, different voters, and different elections. Deciding which is more important in some overall sense seems like a plausible goal, but in practice it is likely to be chimerical.

NOTES

1. Other individual-level analyses have concentrated on congressional voting with some positive results. See Chapter 13.
2. Another alternative spatial model is a variant in which voters are uncertain about candidates' issue positions. Bartels (1986) showed that this model yields better predictions than a standard proximity model.
3. Many observers would consider candidates a more important correlate of voting than issues. For example, Luskin (1990, p. 353, note 2) concludes: "The literature attempting to weigh issue versus candidate . . . or party-oriented voting is all atangle—the weights depend on the definitions of the variables and the specification of the model (compare Page and Jones, 1979, with Markus and Converse, 1979)—but it seems to me a fair reading that raw partisanship and reactions to the candidates' personas generally have more influence than perceptions of the candidates' stands on the issues."
4. Miller, Wattenberg, and Malanchuk (1986) obtained somewhat similar factors in their analysis of open-ended comments given in response to the candidate likes and dislikes questions, dimensions which they call competence, reliability, integrity, and charisma, plus an extra factor for purely personal comments.
5. It is interesting to note that sophisticated respondents, who presumably are more interested in the subject and are more capable of retaining a large volume of information, more frequently use shortcuts. This is reminiscent of Stimson's (1975) finding that a simple, liberal/conservative ideological framework was most often used by those with more education and interest.
6. In addition to strategically voting for a candidate who is better able to win the general election, voters may also vote for their second (or even lower) choice rather than their most preferred candidate so as to stop another candidate they like even less. Abramson, Aldrich, Paolino, and Rohde (1992) find evidence of such "sophisticated voting" in the 1988 NES Super Tuesday Study. The same phenomenon has been studied under the rubric of "tactical voting" in Great Britain (for example, Heath, Curtice, Jowell, 1991. chap. 4; Niemi, Whitten, Franklin, 1991).
7. Ironically, the similarity between some work derived from economic and from psychological theories sometimes leads to the criticism that candidate models fail to bring a new perspective to voting research; see our discussion of schema theory in Chapter 6.

FURTHER READINGS

Economic Factors

Michael S. Lewis-Beck, *Economics and Elections: The Major Western Democracies* (Ann Arbor: University of Michigan Press, 1988). Cross-national study of economic factors in voting.

Donald Kinder, Gordon Adams, and Paul Gronke, "Economics and Politics in the 1984 American Presidential Election," *American Journal of Political Science* (1989) 33:491-515. Evaluations of the national economy are more important than personal or group economic well-being.

John Williams, "The Political Manipulation of Macroeconomic Policy," *Ameri-*

can Political Science Review (1990) 84:767-96. Monetary policies are affected by the election cycle; other macroeconomic effects of political manipulation are limited.

Helmut Norpoth, Michael S. Lewis-Beck, and Jean-Dominique Lafay, eds. *Economics and Politics* (Ann Arbor: University of Michigan Press, 1991). Studies of economics and voting (or executive popularity) in the United States, western Europe, and elsewhere.

Michael B. MacKuen, Robert S. Erikson, and James A. Stimson, "Peasants or Bankers? The American Electorate and the U.S. Economy," *American Political Science Review* (1992) 86:forthcoming. Voters react prospectively to the economy.

Multicandidate Elections

Larry Bartels. *Presidential Primaries and the Dynamics of Public Choice* (Princeton, N.J.: Princeton University Press, 1988). Effects of uncertainty and expectations in low information elections.

Paul R. Abramson, John H. Aldrich, Phil Paolino, and David Rohde, " 'Sophisticated' Voting in the 1988 Presidential Primaries," *American Political Science Review* (1992) 86:55-69. Voters support candidates both for reasons of preference and perceived viability.

Richard G. Niemi, Guy D. Whitten, and Mark N. Franklin, "Constituency Characteristics, Individual Characteristics and Tactical Voting in the 1987 British General Election," *British Journal of Political Science* (1992) 22:229-40. Strategic voting was relatively frequent and was closely related to partisan strength, education, and constituency characteristics.

Candidates

George Marcus, "The Structure of Emotional Response: 1984 Presidential Candidates," *American Political Science Review* (1988) 82:737-62. Applies a theory of emotions to reactions to presidential candidates.

Clive Bean and Anthony Mughan, "Leadership Effects in Parliamentary Elections in Australia and Britain," *American Political Science Review* (1989) 83:1165-79. Candidate effects exist even in two parliamentary systems.

Milton Lodge, Kathleen McGraw, and Patrick Stroh, "An Impression-Driven Model of Candidate Evaluation," *American Political Science Review* (1989) 83:399-419. Voters keep "running impressions" of candidates rather than undifferentiated sets of memories.

Lyn Ragsdale, "Strong Feelings: Emotional Responses to Presidents," *Political Behavior* (1991) 13:33-65. Compares explanatory power of rational voter model and candidate-based model.

Issues

Shanto Iyengar and Donald R. Kinder, *News That Matters* (Chicago: University of Chicago Press, 1987). A series of experiments suggests that television news has important effects on public opinion.

Jon A. Krosnick, "The Role of Attitude Importance in Social Evaluation: A Study of Policy Preferences, Presidential Candidate Evaluations, and Voting Behavior," *Journal of Personality and Social Psychology* (1988) 55:196-210. The importance of issue importance.

George Rabinowitz and Stuart Macdonald, "A Directional Theory of Issue Voting," *American Political Science Review* (1989) 83:93-121. Direction (from neutrality) rather than location on a continuous dimension is what determines voters' decisions.

J. Merrill Shanks and Warren E. Miller, "Policy Direction and Performance Evaluation: Complementary Explanations of the Reagan Elections," *British Journal of Political Science* (1990) 20:143-235. Analysis of the 1980 and 1984 NES surveys.

J. Merrill Shanks and Warren E. Miller, "Partisanship, Policy, and Performance: The Reagan Legacy in the 1988 Election," *British Journal of Political Science* (1991) 21:129-97. Suggests that various beliefs about the 1988 election, including Bush being more popular than Dukakis, were largely myths.

Election Forecasts

Robert S. Erikson, "Economic Conditions and the Presidential Vote," *American Political Science Review* (1989) 83:567-73. The economy is an important predictor of presidential election outcomes.

James E. Campbell, "Forecasting the Presidential Vote in the States," *American Journal of Political Science* (1992) 36:386-407. Predicting state votes for president, 1948-1988.

Michael S. Lewis-Beck and Thomas W. Rice, *Forecasting Elections* (Washington, D.C.: CQ Press, 1992). Models for forecasting presidential, congressional, and other elections.

10. THE IMPACT OF PERSONAL AND NATIONAL ECONOMIC CONDITIONS ON THE PRESIDENTIAL VOTE: A POOLED CROSS-SECTIONAL ANALYSIS

Gregory B. Markus

Interview with a New York City woman in 1956:

Q: "Is there anything in particular that you like about the Republican party?"
A: "My husband's job is better." (Laughter.)
Q: "How do you mean?"
A: "Well, his investments in stocks are up. They go up when the Republicans are in. My husband is a furrier, and when people get money they buy furs."

—As quoted in *The American Voter*
(Campbell et al., 1960, p. 243)

Introduction

Individual voting decisions and, consequently, election outcomes may be influenced by a myriad of factors: prevailing attachments to political parties, ideological and policy considerations, the personal characteristics and traits of the contenders for office, regional loyalties, group memberships, candidate debates, media imagery, and more. Angus Campbell and his colleagues (1960) added to this list a factor they labeled "the nature of the times."

Those researchers found, as have others since, that although many Americans have only the fuzziest of notions about many aspects of politics and government, they do have a sense of whether "times are good" or "times are bad," and they tend to vote accordingly. Some fairly elaborate theories of voting behavior have sprung from this idea (see, e.g., Key, 1966; Fiorina, 1981; Kiewiet and Rivers, 1984), but stated in its simplest form, the contention is that, other things being equal, "voters give greater support to candidates of the incumbent party when the election is preceded by a period of prosperity than when times have been poor" (Kiewiet and Rivers, 1984, p. 370).

Empirical investigations of this seemingly straightforward idea have been plentiful—some might say *too* plentiful (for reviews of this literature, see Kramer,

Source: *American Journal of Political Science* (1988) 32:137-54. Reprinted with permission of University of Texas Press. Copyright © University of Texas Press.

1971; Monroe, 1979; Kiewiet and Rivers, 1984). Yet as often happens, the attempts to resolve one research question have succeeded primarily in raising others.

Pocketbooks and Sociotropes

Perhaps foremost among these second-generation questions is the one about *whose* economic condition is the relevant datum for voters. Generally speaking, there are two (not necessarily dissonant) school of thought on this matter.

One school assumes, implicitly or explicitly, that individuals consider their own personal economic predicaments—that they are "pocketbook voters" whose support for the incumbent or his party varies directly with their personal financial well-being. "Typically, there is a perception of the economic state of the immediate family, which is an index of the 'goodness' or 'badness' of the times," wrote the authors of *The American Voter*. "The possibility that what happens to some may not happen to others in the same way seems too differentiated a view of society or politics to have much role in the evaluation process. And, of course, once the nature of the times is assessed, the leap to party culpability is simple and direct" (Campbell et al., 1960, p. 240).

The other school argues that voters are "sociotropic," that is, that their political judgments are shaped by evaluations of the *nation's* economic health, not just their own (Kinder and Kiewiet, 1979, 1981; Feldman, 1982; Weatherford, 1983).[1] The sociotropic model does not presume that voters engage in sophisticated analyses of macroeconomic policy. All that is required is that voters develop "rough evaluations of national economic conditions"—evaluations that are at least partly independent of their own personal circumstances—"and then credit or blame the incumbent accordingly" (Kinder and Kiewiet, 1981, p. 132).

Kinder and Kiewiet explicitly rejected any necessarily altruistic motivation for sociotropic voting, since citizens may well believe that improved macroeconomic conditions will benefit themselves personally in the long run. Even so, the adjective "sociotropic" implies an orientation toward societal goals or needs as opposed to purely individualistic or selfish ones (see Meehl, 1977), and the use of such evaluative terms may confuse the argument unnecessarily.

Whether voters respond to the macroeconomic "nature of the times" or whether they instead vote on the basis of their personal economic circumstances can have significant political implications. Consider two policy alternatives. Policy A would raise the incomes of the richest 10 percent of the population by \$10,000 per capita and lower the income of the bottom 90 percent by \$1,000 each, for a net increase of $.10(\$10,000) + .90(-\$1000) = +\$100$ per capita. Policy B, on the other hand, would decrease the income of the top 10 percent by \$1,000 each and raise the income of the remaining 90 percent by \$100 each, for a net increase of $.10(-\$1000) + .90(\$100) = -\$10$ per capita.

Purely pocketbook-oriented citizens would favor Policy B by a nine to one ratio and would oppose Policy A by an equal margin. In contrast, if citizens were strictly sociotropic—that is, if their policy preferences were based solely on net changes in national income and not at all on their personal circumstances or other considerations—then they would unanimously support Policy A and unanimously disapprove of Policy B. Hence, sociotropic voting—at least by some definitions—can lead to outcomes that might not be considered desirable according to certain "sociotropic" theories of justice (e.g., Rawls, 1971, esp. p. 302).

Of course, other conceptions of sociotropism—ones that take into account redistributive consequences of policies, such as how many individuals or which groups are benefited—would yield different results. And one can also construct examples in which pocketbook voting leads to socially undesirable outcomes—most notably, the classic prisoner's dilemma or, equivalently, the collective goods problem (see, e.g., Barry and Hardin, 1982). Clearly the rudimentary distinction between pocketbook and sociotropic motivations that has characterized research to date (including the present study) would benefit from further specification and elaboration. But equally clear, I think, is that it is worthwhile to distinguish the effects of prevailing macroeconomic conditions on the vote from those of personal financial predicaments.

The Kramer Specification

Unfortunately, research to date has not been able to do that. As Kramer (1983) demonstrated, studies based solely on aggregate economic and political statistics cannot distinguish pocketbook from sociotropic voting. The existence of a reliable relationship between, say, changes in real personal income per capita and aggregate support for the incumbent is equally compatible with either model. Such a result demonstrates that election outcomes depend upon economic factors but provides no insight into the decision calculus underlying individuals' votes.

A number of researchers have attempted to provide that insight by working directly with individual-level survey data (e.g., Fiorina, 1981; Lau and Sears, 1981; Kinder and Kiewiet, 1979, 1981; Kiewiet, 1981; Weatherford, 1983; Feldman, 1982). These studies differ from one another in some important respects, but generally speaking they subscribe to a common analytical strategy. That strategy involves selecting a measure of individuals' perceptions of their personal economic situations, a measure of their evaluations of the state of the economy, and then assessing the impact of both kinds of attitudes on electoral preferences.

In principle, this approach makes sense. In practice, it has been less than completely successful for two reasons. The first problem arises from the nearly universal practice of analyzing microdata strictly on an election-by-election basis.[2] Cross-sectional studies cannot address the effects on voting of temporal changes in objective national economic conditions because, in any given election, the state of the economy is a constant, not a variable.

Of course, *perceptions* of national economic health do vary across voters in an election, but the cross-sectional variation in those perceptions is small relative to the variation that occurs through time as well as across individuals. Moreover, much of the cross-sectional variation in beliefs about the state of the national economy is likely to be either spuriously related to the vote (i.e., influenced by long-held partisan identifications) or else attributable to error arising from the inevitably imprecise measurement of attitudes (Kramer, 1983).[3]

The second shortcoming of the microdata studies concerns the commonly used survey measure of changing personal financial circumstances. That measure is a single item that has appeared (with minor variation) in every Survey Research Center or Center for Political Studies presidential election study since 1956: "We are interested in how people are getting along financially these days. Would you say that you (and your family living with you) are better off or worse off than you were a year ago, or are you about the same?" [4]

In his unusually influential and provocative article, Kramer (1983) argued that the principal deficiency of this type of survey item is that it does not measure the variable of interest. According to Kramer, voters respond solely to *governmentally induced* changes in their incomes. What the survey item taps, however, are *total* changes in voters' incomes, regardless of the origins of those changes. At the individual level, fluctuations in total income reflect the effects of life-cycle differences in earning power, changing health and personal circumstances, windfalls, casualty losses, exogenous macroeconomic shocks (such as OPEC-induced energy shortages), and other "politically irrelevant" (Kramer's term) factors.

To the extent that the observed measure is contaminated by "politically irrelevant" sources of variation, ordinary least squares estimates of the parameters of interest will be statistically inconsistent—a classic case of "errors in variables," as econometricians refer to the problem. Kramer (1983), therefore, concluded that "individual-level survey data, at least when analyzed with the usual methods, are not really very useful for studying the effects of short-term economic fluctuations on individual voting decisions" (p. 94).

If that were not enough, Kiewiet and Rivers (1984) contend that the survey item probably does not even gauge *total* income changes very accurately: "it is a rather crude instrument for measuring smaller income fluctuations" (p. 379). Any measurement error in the survey responses further contributes to bias in estimates of the economics-politics connection.

To recapitulate, (1) aggregate-level analyses cannot distinguish between pocketbook and sociotropic voting. Micro-level studies, on the other hand, suffer because (2) they are almost exclusively cross-sectional and, therefore, cannot address the impact of temporal changes in the economy on voting; (3) the survey measure of personal economic well-being taps total income changes, not just the governmentally induced portion of those changes that, Kramer contends, is the variable of interest; and (4) survey data are contaminated by errors in measurement (presumably, to a degree that aggregate statistics are not).

The present study addresses all of these issues. To ameliorate the shortcomings of purely aggregate time series or purely individual-level cross-section analyses (problems 1 and 2, respectively), this study employs a pooled cross-section/time series strategy to examine simultaneously the electoral consequences of longitudinal changes in the national economy *and* cross-sectional, cross-time variations in perceived personal financial situations.

With regard to problem 3, the possible presence of "politically irrelevant" noise in responses to the personal finances question is a concern only if one presumes, as Kramer does, that any changes in personal income not governmentally induced are irrelevant to electoral politics. My own view is that this presumption is almost certainly an inaccurate depiction of reality or, at the least, that its plausibility is an empirical matter—not to mention that daunting question of how citizens might conceivably agree, as economists and politicians cannot, about which economic outcomes should be properly credited to the incumbent administration.

In any event, there is no necessary reason to subscribe to Kramer's particular specification, which aims only at "accounting for the overall relationship between governmentally induced macroeconomic conditions and vote choice, and not in explaining the overall dynamics relating personal well-being to political evaluation" (Feldman, 1985, p. 149). Other investigators (including myself) may legitimately prefer to focus on the latter topic.

Finally, with regard to the status of the personal finances question as a valid and reliable measure of *total* income changes (problem 4), recent work by Rosenstone, Hansen, and Kinder (1986) indicates that the survey item is, in fact, "a respectably valid measure of change in personal economic well-being" (p. 184). It is, however, statistically unreliable, owing to the presence of measurement error, thereby rendering ordinary least squares inconsistent as an estimator of the link between personal economic changes and political outcomes. The textbook solution to this kind of errors in variables problem entails an instrumental variables (or, equivalently, two-stage least squares) estimation strategy, which does yield consistent parameter estimates (Johnston, 1984, pp. 428-35). That estimation strategy is employed here.

Explaining Votes and Explaining Elections

Besides the sociotropic/pocketbook distinction, there is a second criterion by which studies of economic performance and voting may be classified. That criterion is whether the research goal is to account for election outcomes or to explain individual vote decisions. Elections are, of course, aggregations of individual votes. However, explaining differences in individual votes requires attention to *interindividual* differences in relevant causal factors, whereas accounting for variance in election outcomes depends upon *interelection* changes in the distributions of those causal factors (cf. Rosenstone, 1983, pp. 3-4).

For example, it is an article of faith that party identification exerts a powerful influence upon the individual vote decision. Even so, if the distribution of partisanship across voters remains essentially constant throughout a series of elections, it necessarily cannot account for electoral variations in party vote shares.[5] By the same token, actual macroeconomic conditions may be strongly related to the reelection success of presidential incumbents, but such conditions cannot explain differing voter preferences within a single election because they do not vary across voters.

Statements about the electoral "importance" of aggregate or personal economic considerations should, therefore, be explicit about whether the referent is individual behavior or election outcomes. The present study will assess the "importance" of personal and national economics on both electors and elections.

Model, Data, and Estimation Strategy

The model to be estimated here is one of individual choice, but across electoral contexts. More specifically, this study examines the impact of (1) perceptions of recent changes in one's personal financial situation and (2) objective national economic conditions on voting in recent U.S. presidential elections, holding constant long-term factors affecting the vote (represented here by party identification and race).

The survey item discussed above is the measure of personal financial change, with responses scored $+1$ for "better," 0 for "the same," and -1 for "worse." Respondents' party identifications are measured by the traditional SRC/CPS measure, collapsed into five categories.[6] The race variable is coded zero for whites and one for nonwhites.

The annual rate of change in real disposable personal income per capita, denoted $\Delta RDPI_t$ serves as the summary indicator of national economic circumstances. This indicator, or one very much like it, has been used in a number of previous studies of the electoral effects of economic conditions. Bloom and Price (1975, p. 1243) called $\Delta RDPI$ "the best available measure of income as perceived by the voter," since it includes "income from all sources accruing to private individuals" (see also, Lanoue, 1985). This measure is also a useful summary of the national economic situation because inflation, wage rates, hours worked, unemployment rates, and other factors all contribute to the determination of real personal income.

As used here, $\Delta RDPI_t$ refers to change occurring for the year of the presidential election. Other possibilities, including lagged terms and rates computed over longer time spans, were explored and rejected as being inferior to the specification reported here. This result is consistent with that of other research, and there appears to be a consensus that economic conditions prior to the election year do not ordinarily influence voters' decisions (see esp., Fair, 1978; Rosenstone, 1983).

The dependent behavior of interest is individual electoral choice in eight presidential contests, 1956-84. The dependent measure itself is binary, equal to one for respondents who reported voting for the candidate of the incumbent party and zero if they voted for the other major party candidate. To simplify matters, only votes for the two major parties are considered. This decision results in the exclusion of a handful of reported John Anderson voters in 1980 and a somewhat larger number of George Wallace voters in 1968. Together, those two groups of voters accounted for only 1 percent of all reported presidential votes, 1956-84.

The equation for the vote is:

$$VOTE_{it} = \alpha + \beta_1 PERSFIN_{it} + \beta_2 \Delta RPDI_t + (\beta_3 + \beta_4 ID_{it} + \beta_5 RACE_{it}) INCUMB_t + u_{it}$$

where $INCUMB_{it}$ denotes the party of the incumbent president, $+1$ for Democratic and -1 for Republican, and the abbreviations denoting the other variables are self-evident. In the equation the "main effects" coefficient (β_3) for

INCUMB captures any systematic differences in the voting patterns for Democratic and Republican incumbents that are not accounted for by the other variables in the model—most notably, the historically higher defection rates among Democratic identifiers under Democratic incumbents as compared with those rates among Republicans when their party holds the presidency. Consequently, we should expect β_3 to be negative. We should also expect positive values for the interaction coefficients, β_4 and β_5, indicating that increasing strength of Democratic party identification and being nonwhite are associated with comparatively higher probabilities of voting for Democratic presidential candidates, other things being equal.

The vote equation is specified as being linear in probability rather than as a log-odds or probit model. As a practical matter, the choice of specification makes little difference in the present case. Estimated coefficients for a log-odds version of the equation are nearly an exact linear transformation of the coefficients for the dummy dependent variable model—the correlation between the two coefficient vectors is .99.[7] Also, estimated t-ratios are virtually unaffected by the choice of functional form. In this light the linear in probability specification has two principal virtues. First, the straightforward interpretation of the estimated coefficients as probability (or proportion) increments makes for a far simpler discussion and intuitive appreciation of the results than would be the case for logit estimates. Second, by substituting election year means for the regressors in the probability model, one can generate predicted vote shares for the two parties; forecasting election outcomes with the probability model thus requires only aggregate information, not individual-level data. A log-odds specification does not have comparable properties.[8]

As mentioned earlier, I employed instrumental variables/two-stage least squares as an estimator. As any standard econometrics text shows, this method achieves consistency by replacing the error-contaminated regressor (in this instance, the personal finances measure) with a suitable "instrument" formed as a linear combination of exogenous variables. For present purposes, those exogenous variables included respondent's age and sex, family annual income, education of head of household, whether or not the household head was a farmer, whether or not the respondent or household head (if different) had in the year prior to the interview been unemployed, laid off, experienced a pay cut, or had his or her work hours reduced, and responses to questions about recent changes in income and spending patterns—as well as the other exogenous variables on the right-hand side of the vote equation.

Because the coefficients linking the aforementioned variables to the personal finances item undoubtedly change over time (and because some of the measures themselves changed formats across election studies or were omitted entirely in some years), the first-stage regression to form the instrumental variable was specified in a form equivalent to a "saturated" covariance model that included the set of exogenous variables, a set of election year dummy variables, and the cross-products of the dummies and the exogenous variables.

The vote equation was estimated using data from all eight presidential elections, 1956-84, and also excluding the data from 1960 and 1968, the two instances in which no incumbent was seeking reelection. There were no appreciable differences in parameter estimates, so analysis based on the full set of elections is reported here. Also, after the vote equation was estimated, the residuals were examined for evidence of systematic departures from a good fit to the data. In addition, a simple "jackknifing" procedure was employed in which the model was successively estimated, each time with data for a single election year omitted. These analyses indicated that coefficient estimates were not being unduly influenced by any outlier elections.[9]

Results

The results in Table 10-1 show that the long-term factors of party identification and race are (not surprisingly) important determinants of the vote. The probabilities of strong Democrats and strong Republicans voting for a Democratic presidential candidate are approximately .40 greater or less, respectively (i.e., $\pm 3 \times .134$), than the corresponding probability for independents. And the probability of a Republican vote is .18 ($\pm .03$) less for nonwhites than for whites, ceteris paribus.[10]

The coefficient for the incumbent party dummy variable is negative, indicating that for the period under study the probability of white Democratic identifiers supporting their party's incumbent candidates was .148 ($\pm .018$) less (i.e., $-.074$ versus $+.074$) than the probability of white Republicans of comparably strong partisan attachments supporting their own party's incumbents. Of course, the somewhat weaker loyalties of Democratic partisans as a group were offset by their greater numbers.

Regarding the effects of national economic conditions on the vote, the coefficient of ΔRDPI is both statistically and substantively significant. Each 1 percent real increase in per capita disposable personal income raises the vote for the incumbent by a 1.9 ($\pm .4$) percentage points, other things being equal. The qualifying phrase is important because, in actuality, an increase in real DPI would undoubtedly increase the proportion of voters who felt personally better off financially, thereby inducing an indirect as well as a direct effect of ΔRDPI on the vote.[11] The reduced form equation (Table 10-1) provides the best estimate of the *total* (i.e., direct plus indirect) effect of changing macroeconomic conditions on electoral choice. That estimate is a 2.3 percent ($\pm .35$ percent) proincumbent vote shift for each 1 percent change in real DPI.

The analysis also indicates that any advantage of incumbency in a presidential election depends on the prevailing economic circumstances. For a Republican incumbent, the model predicts that a no-growth or negative-growth economy in the year prior to the election would in all likelihood lead to defeat at the polls. For Democratic incumbents the model predicts that preelection annual growth in real DPI of less than 1.5 percent would result in an election loss, other factors held constant at their overall means. In this regard Jimmy Carter demonstrated that a troubled national economy in an election year can transform incumbency into an electoral liability. Except for 1980, however, real DPI grew in every presidential election year in the 1956-84 period. Consequently,

Table 10-1　Parameter Estimates for a Model of the Probability of Voting for the Presidential Candidate of the Incumbent Party

	Full Equation		Reduced Form	
	Coeff.	*S.E.*	*Coeff.*	*S.E.*
Constant	.478	.006	.483	.006
ΔRDPI	.019	.002	.023	.002
Personal finances	.082	.011	—	—
Incumbent party	−.074	.005	−.079	.004
Party ID × incumbent party	.134	.002	.133	.002
Race × incumbent party	.182	.015	.207	.014
R^2	.46		.45	
N	7,777		9,275	

Note: Entries are unstandardized instrumental variables coefficient estimates and their estimated standard errors.

incumbent presidents since 1956 have generally enjoyed a net advantage.[12]

My estimate of the impact of national economic conditions on the presidential vote is larger than that of some other studies. It is, for example, nearly twice the size of Tufte's (1978) estimate, which was based on aggregate statistics from the eight presidential election years 1948-76, and it is greater yet than estimates based on other data sets or model specifications (see Kiewiet and Rivers, 1984).

In part, the discrepancy between the present study's estimate of national income effects on the vote and those of other investigations reflects differences in model specification, choice of indicators, and set of elections under study. For instance, Kramer's (1971) model constrained the impact of macroeconomic conditions on voting to be the same in congressional election years as in presidential ones—a specification that, as Tufte's (1978) work shows, understates considerably the actual effects in the latter context. In addition, few studies other than the present one have incorporated data from elections since 1976, a period in which the state of the economy has been arguably the single most salient electoral issue (cf. Lanoue, 1985).

Some research has also overlooked the distinction between direct effects and total effects. To illustrate, Tufte's report of the impact of real personal income changes on presidential voting was based on a regression equation that included as a "control" variable a measure of voters' comparative evaluations of the incumbent and his challenger. Those comparative evaluations are undoubtedly endogenous. That is, they are partly determined by (voters' assessments of) the nation's current economic health. (In this regard the correlation between Tufte's comparative evaluation measure and percentage growth in per capita real personal income is .38.) Consequently, Tufte's reported estimate of a 1 to 1.32 ratio between percentage income changes and changes in the percentage vote for the incumbent's party reflects only the *direct* impact of the former on the latter, comparative candidate evaluations held constant.

Table 10-2 Perceived Change in Recent Personal Finances and Annual Change in Real Disposable Personal Income (in Percentages)

Year	Worse	Same	Better	N	$\Delta RDPI$
1956	18	42	40	1,254	3.1
1960	18	49	32	880	0.1
1964	14	39	48	1,106	5.4
1968	19	48	33	861	2.8
1972	23	41	36	679	3.2
1976	29	36	35	1,313	2.0
1980	40	26	34	872	−3.4
1984	25	30	45	1,357	2.8

Source: National Election Studies and *Statistical Abstract of the United States*, various years.

Based on Tufte's data, the *total* effect (i.e., including indirect effects via comparative candidate evaluations) is 1 to 2.44, a ratio that is quite compatible with the total effects estimate obtained in the present study. And although Rivers (1987) does not explicitly report his estimate of the total effects of national economic conditions on the vote, the figures he provides (plus a little arithmetic) show that his estimate is virtually identical to mine, even though he uses different measures and a different estimation method.

In addition to the impact of national economic conditions on the vote, Table 10-1 also shows that individuals' perceptions of changes in their personal financial situations are linked to their candidate choices in presidential elections. Among voters, the probability of supporting the presidential candidate of the incumbent party is approximately .164 (±.043) higher for those who believe they are financially better off than it is for those whose self-perceived personal financial circumstances have worsened, other things being equal.[13] Stated another way, *at the individual level* a change from the "same" to the "better" category on the personal economics measure has about the same impact on candidate choice as a 3.6 percent increase in real DPI, which is a rather substantial increase historically (see Table 10-2).

At the level of *elections*, though, the interpretation is different. Changes in real DPI are national-level effects that, according to the model, influence all voters in a given election uniformly. In contrast, changes in personal financial health vary across individuals even within the context of a single election. In any given year some people may feel that their personal situation has improved, while others may believe that theirs has worsened. A *net* change in the distribution of perceived personal financial well-being is necessary for that variable to account for differences in election outcomes.

As shown in Table 10-2, the distribution of perceived financial situations did not fluctuate very much across the elections under study. In seven of the eight election years, the percentage feeling worse off financially did not vary by more than eight points away from 21 percent, and in the pooled survey data only 2

Table 10-3   Incumbent's Share of the Two-Party Vote (in Percentages)

Year	Actual	Predicted	Error
1956	57.4	58.7	−1.3
1960	49.5	51.2	−1.7
1964	61.5	64.4	−2.9
1968	49.6	53.9	−4.3
1972	60.7	57.5	3.2
1976	48.0	54.0	−6.0
1980	44.7	40.3	4.4
1984	59.1	59.0	0.1
Mean absolute error			3.0

percent of the total variation in the personal finances variable was between election variance. As a consequence, changing personal financial attitudes have not accounted for much of the variance in election outcomes, even though they do influence individual voting decisions.

For an intuitive sense of the impact of fluctuations in personal economics on *elections* (as opposed to individual votes), consider that, absent a change in RDPI, shifting from a distribution of perceived personal financial well-being such as occurred in 1976 (a relatively bad year) to a distribution such as that for 1956 (a relatively good one) would increase the incumbent's vote share by only 1.3 percent. That gain is not trivial, but it is nevertheless only a bit more than one-half as large as the net effect of just a 1 percent rise in real DPI. Hence, the relative "importance" of national and personal economic conditions on political choice depends on whether one is accounting for individual votes or election outcomes.

With regard to the model's overall goodness of fit, the R^2 values in Table 10-1 provide some information, but because the dependent variable is dichotomous, other indicators of predictive accuracy are probably superior. One approach is to employ the model to generate for each respondent the predicted probability of voting for the incumbent candidate and then assess how well the observed percentages covary with those predicted probabilities. This is accomplished in Figure 10-1, which displays the incumbent's observed vote share for each of 10 groups that divide the (0, 1) predicted probability domain into equal intervals. As may be observed in Figure 10-1, the correspondence between predicted probabilities and observed percentages is quite good: the correlation between the mean predicted probability and the observed percentage voting Republican for the 10 groups is .99.

This report has noted repeatedly the important distinction between accounting for variation in individual votes versus variation in election outcomes, so it is useful to assess the model's fit to elections as well as to electors. Substituting election year means for the right-hand side variables in the vote equation yields a

Figure 10-1   Correspondence between Predicted Probability and Observed Proportion Voting Proincumbent

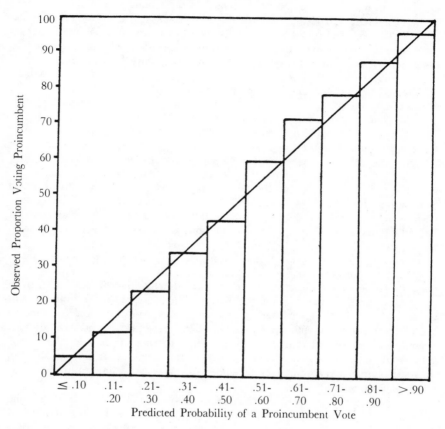

predicted incumbent's share of the two-party vote for each presidential election. Those predictions, along with the actual incumbent vote shares are displayed in Table 10-3. Considering that information about the candidates, their issue positions, the unfolding of the campaign, and a host of other seemingly relevant factors is not incorporated into the predictions, the goodness of fit is impressive.[14] The mean prediction error is three percentage points, a value that compares favorably with that of commercial preelection polls.[15]

Conclusions

This study examined the impact of economic circumstances on electoral choice via an analysis of pooled individual-level survey data from eight presidential election years, 1956-84, augmented by an aggregate measure of objective national economic conditions. This analytical approach was superior to that employed in macro-level econometric studies of the economics-politics connection in that, unlike those investigations, the research design used here could distinguish formally the effects of perceived personal financial circumstances on the vote from those of macroeconomic conditions. This study's approach was also preferable to the purely cross-sectional design utilized by survey researchers in two ways: first, the pooling strategy took into account variation in individuals' attitudes both within and across elections; second, pooling permitted an examination of the effects of the vote of factors (such as incumbency or national economic conditions) that are constants in a cross-sectional design.

The analysis provided support for the "pocketbook" model of voting, with the qualification that the importance of pocketbook considerations depends on whether the referent is individual vote decisions or election outcomes. With respect to the individual vote calculus, personal economic circumstances are moderately influential. From the perspective of accounting for differences in election outcomes, however, voters' feelings of personal financial well-being have been relatively unimportant for the simple reason that the proportion of individuals feeling personally "worse off" has not fluctuated very much from election to election during the period under study.

Consistent with the "sociotropic" thesis, a reliable effect of national economic conditions on the individual vote decision was also detected, even with perceived personal economic circumstances held constant. Each 1 percent real increase in per capita disposable personal income increases the probability of a proincumbent vote by .023 ($\pm$.004), net. Moreover, since objective national economic conditions are identical for every voter in a given election, that effect translates into a 2.3 percentage point change in the incumbent's share of the two-party vote for each 1 percent change in real PDI. Voters in presidential elections are thus sensitive to fluctuations in macroeconomic circumstances as well as to changes in their own financial well-being.

Those are the principal conclusions of this study. There is, however, one other matter that the investigation raises, if not answers directly. Although it was not designed explicitly for predicting presidential election outcomes, the model performed reasonably well in that capacity—especially considering that it ignored any direct reference to the identities and personality traits of the candidates, policy controversies, the nature of the campaign, conventions, presidential debates, vice-presidential nominees, and more. If fairly accurate election predictions can be made without mention of the candidates and their campaign themes, what does that say about the contemporary obsession with candidate images, political marketing, continuous tracking polls, psychographic targeting, and other sophisticated schemes of campaign strategists and media experts?

With particular reference to the 1984 contest, Frankovic (1985) observed (in a piece provocatively subtitled "The Irrelevance of the Campaign") that although media coverage of the Reagan-Mondale match-up was dominated by an array of campaign-generated events and issues, "in the end . . . these events mattered little" (p. 41). Armed with preelection forecasts that ultimately predicted state-by-state voting with great precision, Rosenstone (1985) similarly argued that "President Reagan's victory in 1984 and the margin by which he won were due to conditions that were in place well before the campaign even began" (p. 32). The present study also demonstrated that Reagan's 1984 vote share could have been predicted almost perfectly without referring to any contrasts between his and Walter Mondale's personalities, policy stands, or campaign strategies.

My conclusion, however, is *not* that campaigns are "irrelevant." For one thing, the 3 percent of the vote, on average, that is not accounted for by long-term factors can be—and has been—decisive in presidential contests, and the campaign is probably critical in directing that marginal "floating vote." Moreover, even in instances in which campaigns do not actually convert or mobilize many voters, they undoubtedly provide information to reinforce preexisting dispositions and to structure personal political agendas (Iyengar and Kinder, 1987; Markus, 1982). In particular, the campaign is undoubtedly an important vehicle for heightening voter awareness of prevailing economic conditions and the electoral relevance thereof. Finally, the model's prediction errors for the 1968 and 1976 presidential contests strongly suggest that noneconomic factors (such as Wallace's third-party challenge and racial issues in 1968 and an unelected incumbent burdened by the legacy of "Watergate" in 1976) can sometimes be crucial.

NOTES

1. The sociotropic and pocketbook models are, of course, not mutually exclusive. One possibility is that the population is heterogeneous, with some kinds of voters acting sociotropically while others vote their pocketbooks (Kinder and Mebane, 1983; Weatherford, 1983). Or the individual voter may arrive at a political decision by considering both personal and national economic circumstances.
2. For an important exception, see Rivers (1987).
3. Kramer (1983) has taken this argument to the limit. His position is that actual, governmentally induced change in the economy is the independent variable of interest (to him), and therefore *all* cross-sectional variation in perceptions of national economic conditions is necessarily "*only* . . . perceptual noise" (p. 104).
4. In earlier surveys respondents were asked about the relative change in their financial situations over the past few years.
5. This is strictly true only so long as the coefficients in the structural equation linking partisanship to the vote do not themselves change.
6. Several alternative coding schemes and ways of collapsing categories were evaluated. The scale used here collapses weak identifiers and leaning independents together: Strong Republicans $= -3$, Weak and Leaning Republicans $= -2$, Independents $= 0$, Weak and Leaning Democrats $= +2$, and Strong Democrats $= +3$.
7. A two-stage logit estimation procedure was employed.
8. Assume we have estimated a model for the log-odds of a Republican vote, $L(R_i)$, using data from a sample of voters in an election. Define $\overline{L(R)}$ as the value obtained by substituting mean values for the right-hand side variables in the model. In general,

$\overline{L(R)} \neq \ln(p/(1 - p))$ where p is the observed Republican proportion of the vote for the sample (see Amemiya, 1985, pp. 285-86).

9. In particular, only 1 percent of the residual variation was "between election" variation (in a variance-components sense—see Stimson, 1985). This result indicates that incorporating dummy variables into the model to allow for election year differences in intercepts is unnecessary, a conclusion that was confirmed when such dummies were added and the model was reestimated. A full set of seven election year dummies (plus a constant term) renders the model inestimable, given the presence of the other regressors in the model. However, preliminary analysis indicated that, at most, only dummies for election years 1968-80 were of even marginal importance. When those dummies were added and the model reestimated, no coefficient estimates differed by more than .002 in absolute value from those shown in Table 10-1.

10. Approximate 95 percent confidence intervals are provided in parentheses.

11. In this regard the regression of the percentage of individuals feeling "worse off" on annual percentage change in real per capital disposable personal income is:

$$\text{WORSE} = 28.0 - 2.6 \, \Delta\text{RDPI}$$
$$\phantom{\text{WORSE} = } (2.6) \quad (0.8)$$
$$N = 8, \, R^2 = .69$$

12. Tufte (1978) has advanced the claim that incumbents strategically plump the national economy during election years for political gain.

13. This instrumental variables estimate is approximately twice as large as the estimate obtained via ordinary least squares (OLS). In multivariate models (in contrast to the bivariate case), OLS parameter estimates may be biased upward or downward in the presence of errors in variables, depending on the nature of the errors and the intercorrelations of the regressors; in the present case, though, the evidence indicates that OLS estimates are biased downward substantially.

14. Perhaps it is more accurate to say that "information about the candidates," etc., is not *directly* incorporated into the predictions, since party identifications, especially in the aggregate, are somewhat responsive to the excluded factors.

15. For that matter, the mean absolute difference between candidates' actual ballot shares and respondents' *post*election reports of their votes is 2.4 percent.

11. FOREIGN AFFAIRS AND ISSUE VOTING: DO PRESIDENTIAL CANDIDATES "WALTZ BEFORE A BLIND AUDIENCE"?

John H. Aldrich, John L. Sullivan, and Eugene Borgida

Foreign policy attitudes among most Americans lack intellectual structure and factual content. Such superficial psychic states are bound to be unstable since they are not anchored in a set of explicit value and means calculations or traditional compulsions.

—Gabriel A. Almond

The public's attention span to foreign affairs is strictly limited; elections are not decided on foreign policy issues.

—Deborah Welch Larson

Almond's (1950) research indicated that most U.S. citizens knew very little about the remote issues of foreign policy and instead focused their attention on domestic policies. They did so because domestic issues often have more direct and immediate consequences on people's lives and their material well-being. This view continues to be widely held today, and as a consequence studies of public opinion and voting tend to focus on domestic issues. To be sure, there is a dissenting view, but the study of issues remains primarily the study of domestic issues.

This view that voting ends at the water's edge presents something of an anomaly. Many presidential candidates seem to place considerable emphasis on foreign affairs. If these issues are unimportant to the public, why do candidates waste their scarce time and resources addressing them? Are they basing their campaign behavior on a false assumption? Are they waltzing before a blind audience?

Foreign Policy Attitudes: The Prevailing Scholarly View

Most research on the 1984 election treats foreign policy lightly or ignores it altogether (Abramson, Aldrich, and Rohde, 1987; Boyd, 1985; Burnham, 1985;

Source: *American Political Science Review* (1989) 83:123-141. Reprinted with permission of the publisher.

Ladd, 1985; Shanks and Miller, 1990; Weisberg, 1985). Light and Lake (1985, p. 94), for example, note that "Public opinion polls . . . show that people do not follow foreign affairs closely and often do not know enough about the specifics of a particular issue to form opinions." They conclude that "the [1984] election was clearly a referendum on the state of the economy."

Studies like those of the 1984 election are not unique. As early as 1949, scholars concluded that about 30% of the public was unaware of foreign issues, another 45% was aware but unable to frame an intelligent argument, and the remaining 25% had some knowledge of foreign problems (Almond, 1950). These groups have been labeled the "mass public," the "attentive public," and "opinion leaders" (Hughes, 1978). Rosenau (1961) estimated the size of these three groups at about 75%, 15-20%, and 5-10%, respectively, an even more pessimistic assessment than the one offered more than a decade earlier.

Some scholars have suggested that the public's ill-formed opinions on foreign affairs have no impact on their voting behavior. Kagay and Caldeira (1975), for example, extended Stokes's (1966) analysis of the open-ended likes-dislikes questions and found that foreign policy had a modest effect on the electoral outcomes in 1952 and 1956 but had virtually no impact between 1960 and 1976. Only in 1972, with the Vietnam War so important, did foreign affairs have a significant effect.

Hess and Nelson (1985, pp. 143-44) concluded that foreign policy had a significant impact on electoral behavior only in 1952, 1972, and 1980. In these three elections the Korean and Vietnam Wars and the Iranian hostage crisis exemplified "intermestic" issues: foreign issues that had a strong domestic component that affected daily life. They also argued that foreign policy played its typically minor role in the 1984 election. But it is Hess and Nelson who pose the anomaly reflected in our title. In virtually all recent elections, they argue, foreign policy has been the candidates' dominant concern. While this may have been less true in 1984, they suggest that it was still important during the nomination campaign and in the final Mondale-Reagan debate on foreign affairs. They argue, however, that in no recent campaign, including 1984, did foreign policy issues have a decisive impact on voting behavior.

One way to resolve the anomaly is to conclude that candidates simply misunderstand the role of foreign policy issues in presidential elections.[1] But a second resolution is to conclude that the prevailing scholarly wisdom underestimates the importance of foreign policy attitudes. Reagan, for example, made significant gains in his Florida primary campaign against Ford in 1976 after his decision to shift his emphasis from domestic issues to foreign policy.[2] Richard Wirthlin's polls showed that after the shift in focus, Reagan cut Ford's lead in Florida by 14 percentage points (Witcover, 1977).

There is some scholarly evidence suggesting that foreign policy issues do play an important role in electoral behavior. There have been a few scholars who have argued that foreign policy attitudes play an enduring and important role in electoral behavior. Kessel (1988) analyzed the likes-dislikes data from the 1952-84 period and found that his "international involvement" measure was strongly related to the vote in all but the 1968 and 1976 elections. Its impact exceeded the effect of most issues in virtually all elections and even exceeded "economic management" in several elections (for similar data through 1980 see Miller and Wattenberg, 1981). Hurwitz and Peffley (1987) show that foreign policy, if measured as perceptions of general retrospective "postures" taken by the administration, exerted a substantial impact on Reagan's approval ratings. Other scholars have reported isolated findings suggesting that there are exceptions to the conventional wisdom (Miller and Shanks, 1982; Nie, Verba, and Petrocik, 1976; Page and Shapiro, 1983; Pomper, 1972).

The *prevailing* consensus, however, is that the public possesses little information and only few, ill-formed attitudes about foreign affairs and is concerned deeply about these issues only when their daily lives are directly affected. As a result, such concerns are not terribly consequential in the voting booth. It seems clear, however, that a reexamination of the prevailing consensus is warranted.

Issue Salience, Attitude Accessibility, and Voting Behavior

The prevailing scholarly consensus—that foreign policy attitudes are either nonattitudes or weakly held attitudes—has an intuitive plausibility given the remote and complex nature of foreign policy issues. But there has been no theoretically plausible account of attitude formation and salience that would explain why attitudes on domestic issues—as opposed to foreign policy issues—should be so accessible and so likely to affect voting behavior. We will review recent work in social psychology on attitudes and their relationship to behavior that can provide such an account.

During the late 1960s and early 1970s the conceptual and predictive utility of attitudes was seriously questioned by many social psychologists (e.g., Abelson, 1972). However, a second "generation" of attitude research beginning in the mid-1970s reexamined the relationship between attitudes and behavior by adopting a moderator variable approach (Fazio and Zanna, 1981). Instead of asking the question "Do attitudes predict behavior?" scholars began to investigate more systematically the various conditions, attitudinal qualities, individual differences, and behavioral criteria that moderate attitude-behavior relations. More optimistic assessments of the conceptual and predictive utility of the attitude construct have emerged from these studies.

More recent research examines the *process* by which attitudes guide decision making and behavior. The emergence of these process models may bring some theoretical coherence to the burgeoning set of variables that seem to moderate the relationship between attitudes and behavior. The fundamental assumption underlying the various process models (e.g., Chaiken, 1987; Fazio, 1986; Snyder, 1982) is that available or existing attitudes must first be made accessible from memory if they are to exert any influence on perceptions, judgments, or behavior. *Availability* refers to whether a construct or category is stored in memory (Higgins and King, 1981), while *accessibility* refers to the readiness with which a stored construct like an attitude is retrieved from memory or is used in stimulus encoding.

Thus Fazio's (1986) model of attitude accessibility, the most developed of the attitude-behavior process models in current research on social cognition, posits that available and accessible attitudes are more likely to guide the processing of relevant information and behavior than are less accessible attitudes. Thus attitudes may be thought of as occupying a position on an accessibility continuum. At the lower end of this continuum are nonattitudes, where no evaluation of the attitude object is represented in memory. At the upper end of the continuum are attitudes that are well learned and chronically accessible. In the middle range of the continuum are attitudes that are available but only moderately accessible. Empirical tests of this model have shown that the accessibility of attitudes determines the predictive power of an attitude. Accessibility, in turn, can vary depending on both chronic and temporary factors. The *chronic accessibility* of constructs like attitudes refers to whether the construct is frequently and consistently activated from memory upon mere exposure to the attitude object. This is distinguished from *temporary accessibility*, in which the construct is temporarily "primed," or rendered more accessible, by the current environmental context.

Research in social cognition suggests that both chronic and temporary sources of construct accessibility influence the interpretation of social information (e.g., Bargh et al., 1986). Attitudes that become temporarily accessible, for example, may be particularly important in an electoral context. Candidates or media emphasis on foreign policy issues may temporarily increase the accessibility of such attitudes for members of the public whose attitudes are not chronically accessible. Continuous campaigning on these issues could prolong the otherwise short-term accessibility of situationally primed attitudes. Thus to the extent that foreign policy attitudes are available, attitude accessibility models predict that such attitudes are more likely to influence voter decision making (Fazio and Williams, 1986). In addition, to the extent that foreign policy attitudes are available but are not chronically accessible, process models predict that the impact of these attitudes on voter behavior will be enhanced by environmental factors that increase temporary accessibility.

The method of attitude formation is one important factor that affects the evaluative strength of attitudes (Fazio, 1986; Fazio and Zanna, 1981). Attitudes based on indirect experiences with an attitude object are as available in memory as attitudes based on direct behavioral experiences. But attitudes based on direct experience are more *accessible* from memory; are held with greater confidence and certainty; have more complex, multidimensional attitude structures; have stronger links to behavior; and are more resistant to persuasion than attitudes based on relatively indirect experience (Fazio et al., 1982; Fazio and Zanna, 1981; Schlegel and DiTecco, 1982; Wu and Shaffer, 1987).

One explanation, then, for the conventional wisdom that domestic attitudes are important while foreign policy attitudes are not is that the former are more accessible because they are more likely to be based on direct experience. The public is likely to have direct experience with problems such as inflation and unemployment, but they are unlikely to have direct experience with arms negotiations or U.S. policies toward Central America. The heavily technical nature of military security and international economic issues is also said to play a role.

But this view may be too facile. Many U.S. citizens have experienced, directly and indirectly, the impact of three major hot wars and one prolonged cold war. A significant proportion of us have matured under the anxiety of the bomb and conditions threatening nuclear war. These experiences, whether direct or vicarious, are certainly as potent as ordinary fluctuations in the macroeconomy. Just as a dramatic economic event like the Great Depression shapes the attitudes and behaviors of a generation for a lifetime, so too have war and the presence of nuclear weapons affected all current generations for a lifetime. Since attitudes toward foreign policies are heavily imbued with rather concrete nuclear war images (Fiske, Pratto, and Pavelchak, 1983) and personal fears (Kramer, Kalick, and Milburn, 1983), it is likely that they are as accessible as most attitudes about domestic issues.

Indeed, as Fazio (Fazio 1987; Fazio, Herr, and Olney, 1984) has shown, people can have direct behavioral experience with social issues—foreign or domestic—by virtue of their engaging in some behavior relevant to the issue and having the opportunity to infer their attitudes from their behavior. For example, if an individual has discussed a given foreign or domestic issue, taken a public stand, signed a petition, or done anything of this sort, the person, Fazio would argue, acquires through this process of self-perception direct behavioral experience with the attitude issue. Again, attitudes based on such behavioral experiences have been found to be highly accessible and more predictive of later behavior than are attitudes based on indirect experiences with the attitude object.

This argument suggests that the candidates' assumption that foreign policy issues are important in presidential campaigns is valid. There is little *theoretical* reason to expect large differences in the availability and campaign accessibility of foreign and domestic attitudes. In fact, the candidates' emphasis on foreign policy may *ensure* equal accessibility. First, we will test this expectation by assuming that most people hold basic, general views in foreign affairs, but that they are—and should be expected to be—largely unconcerned about the detailed arguments that characterize elite debate on most of these issues.[3] Such debates matter to the public only if they illustrate the candidates' more general stances or personal qualities.

Second, we will assess whether foreign policy attitudes are available and whether their accessibility varies from election to election. For instance, peace is a central and ordinarily consensual goal. When events, candidates, or media coverage indicate a threat to peace, the salience of this issue increases, which in turn enhances the accessibility of attitudes about peace. Third, above and beyond the availability and accessibility of foreign policy attitudes, we will examine their relevance for models of voting behavior. We will do so by exploring whether the public perceives significant differences between the candidates on foreign policy issues and whether these perceived differences have a direct impact on voting. This allows us to compare the prevalence of "issue voting" on foreign and defense issues with domestic issues. Throughout the analysis, the standard of comparison for the nature and impact of foreign policy attitudes will be the nature and impact of domestic policy attitudes.

The Availability of Foreign Policy Opinions

In order for foreign policy attitudes to play an important role in voting in presidential elections, they must be available to much of the public, that is, they must be represented in memory. We will analyze data from the 1980 and 1984 NES and a 1984 Gallup survey[4] to establish whether foreign policy attitudes are as available as attitudes on domestic issues.[5]

Determining the availability and the "quality" of the public's attitudes is of course problematic. Since we are interested ultimately in the relationship between attitudes and voting behavior, we can assess the set of conditions that Campbell and his colleagues argued were necessary preconditions for issue voting. These conditions are that the issue must (1) be cognized, (2) arouse some effect, and (3) be accompanied by the perception that one party or candidate best represents the respondent's position (Campbell et al., 1960, p. 270). Scholars assessing these conditions have debated whether voters are becoming more issue-oriented (Margolis, 1977; Pomper, 1972, 1975). The conditions themselves represent controversial tests of the voters' competency, and scholars have debated whether these are jointly necessary conditions for issue voting (Abramson, Aldrich, and Rohde, 1983, 1987; Aldrich and Trump, 1986; Fiorina, 1981). These conditions do, however, provide a minimum indication of the quality of the public's attitudes. They are especially useful for the task of comparing the public's foreign and domestic policy attitudes, because the point is not so much the absolute quality of foreign policy attitudes as establishing that these attitudes are available and accessible for use in voting. It is sufficient to demonstrate that these attitudes are available, are as accessible as domestic attitudes, and affect the voting behavior of much of the public.

Campbell's conditions were operationalized using seven-point issue scales (Abramson, Aldrich, and Rohde, 1983, 1987; Aldrich and Trump, 1986). The conditions were measured cumulatively: the first as the percentage of respondents able to place themselves on a seven-point issue scale, the second as the percentage of respondents who were in addition able to place the two major parties' nominees on the scale, and the third as the percentage of respondents who were in addition able to place the two candidates at different scale positions. The last position was also evaluated by examining the percentage of respondents who, in addition to satisfying the three preceding criteria, placed the Democrat at a more liberal position than the Republican. Satisfaction of these criteria is evidence that the issue is available and aroused some affect, while the last two measures also indicate satisfaction of the issue voting condition that respondents must believe that one candidate or party better represents their position on an issue.

Table 11-1 presents data from three data sets on the 1980 and 1984 elections that evaluate these issue voting conditions for both foreign and domestic policies. In each case large proportions of the public satisfied the first criterion: averages of over 80% of the respondents were able to place themselves on each group of seven-point issue scales. With the exception of two items, at least 80% were able to place themselves on each scale.[6] There are no substantial differences between the percentage of respondents able to place themselves on foreign and domestic issues.

Table 11-1 Average Percentages Meeting Various Issue Voting Criteria, 1980-1984

Issue Scale	Placed Self on Issue Scale	Placed Self and Both Candidates	Placed Self and Saw Difference Between Candidates	Placed Self and Saw Democrat as More Liberal than Republican
1980 (NES)				
Foreign (2 scales)	84.8	70.2	61.2	52.6
Domestic (5 scales)	80.9	64.1	53.7	44.4
Average difference[a]	3.9	6.1	7.5	8.2
1984 (NES)				
Foreign (3 scales)	83.7	72.0	62.8	54.5
Domestic (4 scales)	86.4	75.7	63.3	53.2
Average difference[a]	−2.7	−3.7	−0.5	1.3
1984 (Gallup)				
Foreign (2 scales)	92.6	83.1	76.1	68.0
Domestic (6 scales)	91.8	76.9	63.1	51.7
Average difference[a]	.8	6.2	13.0	17.4

[a] Foreign minus domestic.

There are differences between foreign and domestic issues in the three criteria that involve perceptions of candidate positions. The criteria listed in Table 11-1 are cumulative, so the last column shows the percentage of respondents in each survey who (1) placed themselves, (2) placed both candidates, (3) perceived differences between both candidates, *and* (4) placed the Democrat at a more liberal position than the Republican. In 1980, for example, over 8% more respondents satisfied the cumulative criteria on the foreign than did so on the domestic issues, while over 17% did so on the 1984 Gallup survey.[7] In each of the three surveys, the largest percentage of respondents satisfied the full set of criteria on the defense spending item. That figure ranges from 54% in the 1980 NES survey to 76% in the 1984 Gallup survey (see Appendix 11-1). Foreign policy attitudes and perceptions *are* as available and appear to be as meaningful as attitudes on domestic issues.

But what about earlier elections? In 1976 the NES survey included *no* foreign or defense policy scale. In 1972 there was one scale about the Vietnam War, and on that item, 73% satisfied all four criteria listed in Table 11-1, exceeding all of the scales included in the NES surveys from 1972 through 1984.

On all of the issue scales there is a large proportion of respondents who satisfy the issue-voting criteria. Direct comparisons to Campbell and colleagues' (1960) findings are inappropriate because the measuring instruments changed significantly. Still, one suspects that Campbell and associates would have drawn quite a different conclusion had they analyzed seven-point issue scales and found that an average of over half of the respondents met their three criteria on both foreign and domestic issues.

The Accessibility of Foreign and Defense Policy: Most Important Problems

Available political attitudes must also be accessible to have an impact on voting behavior. Most of the public receives its information about candidates and issues from the mass media, which serve as the key priming agent for accessibility. Coverage of events, personalities, and issues serves to heighten the accessibility of political attitudes. Conventional measures of "issue salience" should therefore be conceptually related to the concept of construct accessibility.

To investigate the accessibility of foreign and defense issues, we present data from a number of surveys that asked respondents to indicate what they thought was "the most important problem facing the country today" or, in one instance, "the most important political problem facing them personally." [8] Turning first to the 1984 election, we present results from two surveys. The data in Table 11-2 are from the Gallup survey noted earlier. Respondents were asked to select, from a list of 12, the most important problem facing the nation. They were also asked which political problem on the list was most important to them personally. Table 11-3 indicates comparable results from the 1980 and 1984 NES surveys (Abramson, Aldrich, and Rohde, 1987).

Over a third of the respondents in both surveys selected foreign and defense issues as the most important problem facing the country. The Gallup data indicate that they were most concerned about nuclear weapons and the arms race—fully one quarter of the respondents picked that issue, greater than any of the other 12 problems. A fifth of the respondents selected a foreign or defense concern as the most important political problem facing them personally, indicating that such problems are *not* remote to many people's lives. Overall, 40% of the public cited foreign or defense issues as most important to the country, to themselves, or to both.

In the 1980 NES survey (Table 11-3), nearly a third of the respondents cited a foreign or defense issue as the most important problem facing the country. Their concern was heavily focused on the Iranian hostage crisis, although 17% cited another foreign or defense issue. Whether a third is high or low is a relative judgment, of course, but in 1980 the economy was problematic, with double-digit inflation and interest rates. It is, therefore, unsurprising that over half of the public cited economic problems as the most important problem; nor is it surprising that far fewer people did so in 1984, given the vast improvement in the economy. Clearly, concern about foreign and defense affairs was relatively high in both elections. While the target of that concern varied, so did the relative salience and targets of concern on domestic issues.

In 1976, by striking contrast, only 4% cited a foreign or defense issue as the most important national problem (see Abramson, Aldrich, and Rohde, 1987). Concern in that year was almost exclusively domestic and, in particular, economic. It is hard to imagine a better single indication of change in attitude

Table 11-2 The Public's Views of the Most Important Problems
Personally and Nationally (Percent)

Issue Area	Nationally Most Important	Personally Most Important
Foreign and defense		
Soviet Union	9	4
Spending for defense	3	2
Nuclear weapons and the arms race	25	14
Subtotal	37	20
Government and economics		
Taxes	6	16
Budget deficits	13	6
Unemployment and jobs	24	17
Subtotal	43	39
Social issues		
Race discrimination	2	3
Women's rights	1	2
Abortion	3	4
Subtotal	6	9
Government domestic programs		
Pollution and environment	5	8
Social Security	5	16
Spending on social services	5	8
Subtotal	15	32
Total	100	100
Number of cases	1,418	1,358
Percentage of total cases (1,509)	94	90

Source: 1984 national survey conducted by Gallup poll for the authors.

accessibility with change in political and economic circumstances. More importantly for our purposes, the accessibility of foreign and defense issues is highly variable. In the 1972 election, for example, nearly a third of the public cited foreign affairs or defense as the most important problem, virtually all of them focusing on Vietnam. Thus, not only is public concern about foreign policy highly variable and systematically related to changing political circumstances but in 1976 this concern was unusually low.

The conclusion that 1976 was atypical is confirmed by an examination of responses to the long-running Gallup most-important-problem question (Smith, 1985). From 1947 to the end of U.S. involvement in the Vietnam War in 1973, the smallest proportion of the entire sample selecting a foreign policy issue as *the* most important problem was *never* lower than 22%; the proportion rarely

Table 11-3   The Public's Views of the Most Important Problem Facing the Nation, 1980 and 1984 (NES) (Percent)

Issue Area	1980	1984
Foreign and defense		
Foreign	9	17
Defense	8	17
Iran	15	—
All others	—	9
Subtotal	32	34
Government and economics		
Unemployment and recession	10	16
Inflation and prices	33	5
Deficit and government spending	3	19
All others	10	—
Subtotal	56	49
Social issues		
Social welfare	3	9
Public order	1	4
All others	3	—
Subtotal	7	13
Functioning of government	2	2
All others	3	3
Total	100	101
Number of cases	1,352	1,780
Total cases	1,408	1,943
Percentage of total cases	96	93

Source: Adapted from Abramson, Aldrich, and Rohde (1983, 121; 1987, 166).

dropped below one-third of all respondents, and it often approached or exceeded the proportion who selected a domestic problem. Even in the period between the Korean and Vietnam Wars, in only 7 of 54 polls did less than 30% of the public select a foreign policy issue. Twenty-one times in this period, this percentage exceeded 50. From the end of World War II to the end of the Vietnam War, foreign affairs was a truly major concern to much of the electorate. It was only somewhat less so in the 1980s, and it was of central concern in both the 1980 and 1984 elections. Conversely, the 1973-79 period stands out as a time when the public was not very concerned about foreign or defense issues. Between February 1973 and January 1980, foreign problems were cited by more than 10% of Gallup's sample only *once* (Smith, 1985).

In sum, foreign problems were exceptionally salient to the public throughout the post-World War II era until about 1973. Attitudes on foreign affairs, therefore, were often as or more accessible than attitudes on domestic issues. In the midsixties concern was heavily focused on the Vietnam War, but Vietnam was obviously a *foreign* problem. Vietnam, Korea, Iran, nuclear weapons, and the arms race are of major public concern in ways commensurate with domestic policies. In short, foreign and defense issues are ordinarily highly accessible political concerns. As such, the electorate's foreign policy attitudes are just as accessible during most presidential elections as their attitudes on domestic issues. Moreover, specific international problems, or "hot spots," tend to dominate the public's foreign policy concerns at various times in an ebb and flow not fundamentally different from that characteristic of domestic issues. In 1980, for instance, the most commonly cited concern was inflation or prices. In 1984 inflation was seldom mentioned, but concern about unemployment, recession, and deficit spending increased dramatically (see Table 11-3). The domestic "hot spots" had shifted.[9]

Candidates and Issues: Perceptions in 1980 and 1984

We have established that the public's foreign policy attitudes are available and are accessible during most campaigns. In addition, much of the public perceives systematic differences between the presidential candidates on foreign policy issues. A remaining question is whether the perceived differences between candidates are as great on foreign issues as they are on domestic issues. Theoretically, even accessible attitudes will affect voting behavior only if people perceive clear choices between the candidates.[10] At the extreme—when candidates are perceived to adopt the same position—there is no issue basis for choice. We assess whether the public perceived differences between Reagan and his Democratic opponents that were as great on foreign as on domestic issues.

Perceptions of candidates' positions on issues are subject to rationalization. For example, a liberal may favor a candidate and therefore be likely to perceive that the candidate is also liberal on particularly salient issues (Brody and Page, 1972; Page and Brody, 1972). For this reason we adopt the procedure used by Page (1978) and examine only the median perception of candidate positions. In using this procedure, we assume that rationalization works in both directions and is averaged out. Moreover, there is no particular reason to believe that rationalization is more likely to occur on foreign than on domestic issues. Rationalization is probably greater for less-informed citizens (Berelson, Lazarsfeld, and McPhee, 1954), on less well formed attitudes, and on more-ambiguous candidate positions (Page and Brody, 1972). As we have seen, foreign issues were as salient as domestic issues in these two elections, suggesting that rationalization will not differentially affect perceptions on these two sets of issues. Furthermore, on the basis of campaign rhetoric in 1984, it is reasonable to assume that Reagan and Mondale differed considerably in their issue positions on both sets of issues.

Table 11-4 presents median perceptions on foreign and domestic issue scales for the three surveys. In all three surveys, respondents perceived greater differences between the candidates on foreign and defense issues than on domestic

Table 11-4 Average of Median Perceptions of Candidates on Seven-Point Issue Scales, 1980-1984

Issue Scale	Reagan	Carter (1980)/ Mondale (1984)	Difference between Candidates
1980 (NES)			
Foreign (2 scales)	5.19[a]	3.09	2.10
Domestic (5 scales)	4.67	3.07	1.60
Difference	—	—	.50
1984 (NES)			
Foreign (3 scales)	5.56	3.39	2.17
Domestic (4 scales)	4.94	3.05	1.89
Difference	—	—	.28
1984 (Gallup)			
Foreign (2 scales)	5.96	3.05	2.91
Domestic (6 scales)	5.05	3.04	2.01
Difference	—	—	.91

[a] These are the average medians for domestic and foreign issues within each survey. For example, medians were computed for all five domestic issues in 1980, and the average of these medians computed and presented.

issues. In the 1980 NES data the difference is ½ point. In the 1984 NES data the difference between foreign and domestic issues is slight, about ¼ point. In the 1984 Gallup data the difference is close to a full point. It is striking how far apart Reagan and his opponents were on all of these issues, from an average of over 1½ points (out of a maximum of 6 points) on domestic issues in 1980 to nearly 3 points on foreign issues in the 1984 Gallup data. In the latter data set the candidates were at least 2½ points apart on every issue.[11]

Foreign Policy Issues and the Vote

If the claims advanced so far are true, attitudes on foreign affairs should have a significant effect on electoral choice, as great or greater than that of domestic issues.

We have specified a vote choice model that includes the three most proximate "causes" of the vote: attitudes on parties, candidates, and issues. All three surveys include the standard party identification question. Attitudes toward the candidates are measured in the two NES surveys by the difference between perceptions of the two candidates' leadership qualities (with a four-point response scale). In the 1984 Gallup data, the comparable difference measure is based on seven-point like-dislike ratings.[12]

To assess the importance of foreign issues, an international policy scale was created in each data set by summing self-placement scores on the relevant items, six from the 1984 Gallup data (alpha = .66), three from the 1984 NES survey (alpha = .51), and two from the 1980 NES survey (r = .12). There was, of course, greater flexibility in creating domestic scales. In each data set, we created domestic scales with the same number of variables as the international policy scales. We also selected domestic issues that were among those most strongly related to the vote.[13] The dependent variable is whether the respondent reported voting for Reagan or for his Democratic opponent.[14] The equations were estimated using probit analysis.

The results are reported in Table 11-5. In each instance all four independent variables are strongly related to candidate choice. The overall fit of each model is impressive, R-squared analogues between .76 and .89, large chi-squared goodness-of-fit measures, substantial percentages of correct predictions (between 78% and 91%), and very strong correlations between actual and probit-predicted vote (.73 to .81). As expected, comparative candidate evaluations and partisan identification are very strongly related to the vote, but so too is the overall impact of issues on the vote. In the last column for each data set in Table 11-5, there is a probit analog to the standardized beta (see Kessel, 1988 for details). The joint impact of the two issues is in each case almost as strong as that of either party identification or candidate evaluations.

In 1984 the impact of international issues was slightly greater than that of domestic issues, while in 1980 the opposite was true. In both cases the important point is that in a reasonably fully specified model foreign and defense issues appear to be very important influences on the choices voters make. When taken in combination with the results of the previous sections, the evidence that foreign and international issues were important to the public in 1980 and 1984, were based on available and accessible attitudes and perceptions, and were at least as important as domestic issues in their impact on voting behavior is compelling.

Summary and Conclusions

Our data do not allow us to test the accessibility of foreign policy attitudes directly. We cannot, therefore, establish whether such attitudes are chronically accessible in politics or whether they are only accessible when they are primed by candidates and, more generally, by national election campaigns. One might suspect, however, that such attitudes are chronically accessible and that the chronic accessibility of such attitudes is enhanced by campaign priming. First, peace stands with prosperity as an outstanding example of enduring goals held by the public (see Ostrom and Simon, 1985). Second, with the exception of the period between 1973 and 1980, foreign issues have been commonly cited as among the most important problems facing the nation. Third, the importance of Vietnam in 1972 parallels the importance of foreign and defense affairs in 1980 and 1984. There was a decreased number of citations of foreign and defense problems in 1976, but data are not available to determine whether there was also a decline in the structure or impact of foreign policy attitudes. We can conclude that in the elections for which we have appropriate data, attitudes about foreign affairs have been consequential. The resolution of the anomaly is simply that candidates do *not* waltz before a blind audience. Ironically, it

Table 11-5 Probit Estimated Vote Equations

Independent Variable	1980 NES Data			1984 NES Data			1984 Gallup Data		
	MLE	t-ratio	"Standardized Beta" Analog	MLE	t-ratio	"Standardized Beta" Analog	MLE	t-ratio	"Standardized Beta" Analog
International	−.78 (.037)	−2.13*	−.093	−.107 (.021)	−5.13**	−.184	.068 (.014)	5.02**	.168
Domestic	−.084 (.034)	−2.53**	−.114	−.070 (.023)	−2.99**	−.114	.054 (.014)	3.73**	.133
Party identification	−.359 (.047)	−7.60**	−.367	−.449 (.041)	−11.04**	−.477	.500 (.040)	12.62**	.474
Candidate evaluation	.736[a] (.075)	9.80**	.521[a]	.525[a] (.067)	7.82**	.345[a]	.319[b] (.037)	8.62**	.372[b]
Constant	2.37 (.384)	6.17		3.18 (.343)			−5.33 (.504)	−10.58	
Goodness of fit									
−2 × LLR[c]	434.9**			771.6**			838.4**		
Pseudo R^2	.76			.89			.84		
Percentage correctly predicted	87			78			91		
Correlation, actual & predicted	.73			.78			.81		

Note: Standard errors are in parentheses.

[a] Based on difference of candidates as "providing strong leadership."

[b] Based on the difference in responses to like-dislike evaluations of the two candidates.

[c] χ^2, df = 4.

* Significant at .05.

** Significant at .01.

appears that the only blind audience has been a significant portion of the scholarly community.

That candidates do campaign on foreign policy themes is itself a source of attitude accessibility for much of the public. Campaigns may temporarily activate foreign policy attitudes, although they may not change many minds. Indeed, the stronger the attitudes, the more immune they are to change. Further, priming or other means of attitude activation, have been shown to activate other, closely related constructs. If, therefore, candidates emphasize or discuss a particular foreign policy issue, attitudes about other foreign policy issues may also be activated. The candidates' campaign strategies may help, in part, to ensure a potent role in electoral choice for attitudes about foreign policies.

This argument suggests that candidates can manipulate the degree to which particular attitudes are activated. Greater discussion and coverage should accentuate—while lesser discussion will reduce—the accessibility of foreign policy attitudes. Of course, external events, news media, and the competition—as well as individual differences in members of the public—may overshadow a candidate's efforts. Elections vary in the salience of foreign policy issues, and candidates can, within limits, address these issues to create greater or lesser differences between themselves. Accordingly, we have created a twofold election typology by examining two dimensions: the degree of emphasis on foreign and defense policies, and the differences between the candidates on these issues. The greater the foreign-defense attitude accessibility and the greater the distinctiveness of the candidates, the more important foreign and defense issues will be in voter choice.

The data suggest that the 1972 and 1984 elections maximized both the accessibility of foreign policy attitudes and the differences between the candidates on these issues. Foreign policy attitudes were also important determinants of the vote. The 1980 election was only slightly below these two elections on both criteria. In 1968 the accessibility of attitudes on Vietnam was high, but candidate differences were low. As a result, that issue was not so important in explaining voting behavior. In the absence of appropriate data, the indirect evidence reviewed above suggests the hypothesis that in 1976 accessibility of foreign policy attitudes was very low and candidate differences were not especially sharp. These attitudes, therefore, probably played only a minor role in voting. The 1960 election was one in which accessibility was probably high (Smith, 1985), and, assuming that differences between Nixon and Kennedy were not particularly great, this election was probably more similar to that of 1968 than to that of either 1972 or 1984. The 1952 and 1964 elections, conversely, were probably similar to those of 1980 and 1984, with large differences between the candidates and relatively high salience. The closest possible example of a relatively high-candidate-difference, low-accessibility election might be 1956. After all, the two candidates were the same as in 1952; but with the end of the Korean War and McCarthyism the role of foreign affairs was probably reduced from 1952.[15] These speculations are summarized in Figure 11-1; and if this election classification is correct, foreign and defense attitudes have had a strong impact on voting in most of the recent elections and have played at least some role in virtually all presidential elections during the previous thirty-odd years.

Figure 11-1 A Typology of Elections and Foreign Policy Issues

	Small Difference Between Candidate Stances	Large Difference Between Candidate Stances
Low Salience and Accessibility	Low Effect of Foreign Issues 1976	Low to Some Effect 1956?
High Salience and Accessibility	Low to Some Effect 1968 1960?	Large Effect 1972 1952? 1980 1964? 1984

Thus the anomaly—why candidates often campaign on foreign policy issues when so many scholars claim that the public does not respond to these appeals—has been resolved. The candidates are acting reasonably, because voters do in fact respond to their appeals. The candidates are waltzing before a reasonably alert audience that appreciates their grace. And, given a choice, the public votes for the candidate who waltzes best.

NOTES

1. One could also argue that presidential candidates emphasize foreign affairs to appeal to small but important groups and leaders. Here we seek to demonstrate that the presidential campaign appeals to the general public, as well as to key groups or leaders.
2. He paid particular attention to the Panama Canal Treaty and later to détente and Kissinger's stewardship of foreign policy. John Sears made this strategic decision, and Reagan concurred because of the emotional and supportive audience reaction to mention of the treaty.
3. Very few citizens relished the details of debates over Quemoy and Matsu in 1969, the B-1 bomber or MX missile debates of more recent vintage, or Reagan's SDI plan.

Many of them were interested, however, in the *general* issues involved in SDI. Concern over nuclear weapons and the arms race, defense spending, and relations with Russia were indeed important concerns in 1984 (Table 11-3). Just as many people have general views about inflation and unemployment but know little about the technical details of fiscal and monetary policy, so also do they have general views about foreign policy without detailed knowledge.

4. The survey was conducted for the authors between 9 and 15 November 1984. We interviewed a total of 1,509 respondents, using standard Gallup procedures.

5. There were no foreign or defense issue scales included in the 1976 NES survey, while in 1972 there was only the Vietnam War scale.

6. All three surveys include more domestic than foreign policy items. It might therefore be that two or three domestic items meet the conditions much better than the foreign affairs items but that this information is lost in the averaging process. We have presented the scale-by-scale data in Appendix 11-1.

   The averages do not distort the data. The differences between the Gallup and NES surveys are not due to differences in screening procedures, since they were identical.

7. The items that measure defense spending, government services, jobs, and aid to minorities were worded identically in the 1984 NES and Gallup surveys.

8. The question arises whether this "importance" operationalization captures the accessibility of the issue. Recent data from Fazio (personal communication) show that what people indicate to be the most important social issue may indeed be the most accessible as measured with reaction time data. In addition, there are data suggesting that the accessibility of an issue is related to the accessibility of one's *attitude* towards that issue.

9. The NES data reported in Table 11-3 report only the percentages selecting an issue as the single most important problem. Examining the fuller array shows that somewhat larger percentages cited foreign and defense concerns as *one* of the most important problems. Thus our measurement can underestimate, but not overestimate, issue accessibility.

10. Perceiving differences between the candidates is a necessary but not sufficient condition for issue voting, because moderate voters may be indifferent between a very liberal and a very conservative candidate. In the aggregate, however, the greater the differences between the perceived positions of the candidates, the larger the proportion of voters who will *not* be indifferent.

11. The medians are presented separately for each issue in the Appendix 11-2. There is a clear pattern.

    There are large interelection differences on domestic issues. In 1976, the candidates were perceived to be much less distinct on domestic issues than in the 1980 and 1984 elections, virtually issue by issue. In 1972 McGovern was seen to be very liberal on nearly every issue while Nixon was perceived to be moderately conservative on most issues, producing differences that were actually slightly smaller than in 1984. The 1972 NES data included the Vietnam issue, upon which the public saw differences between the two candidates at least as great as those perceived on most domestic issues (Aldrich and McKelvey, 1977; Miller et al., 1976).

12. This equation is well specified only in the sense of controlling for other proximate factors in the vote equation. Furthermore, both sets of issue measures would be more strongly related to voter choice if we had relied on measures of the voters' proximity to their perceptions of the candidates' positions on these issues (Rahn et al., 1990). We did not do so, however, wishing to minimize rationalization. They would also show a

stronger relationship if we included retrospective measures, such as Carter's handling of the Iranian crisis.

13. The six issues in the 1984 Gallup data were government services versus spending, the impact of recent government programs on minorities, budget deficit reduction, women's roles, aid to minorities, and jobs and standard of living (alpha = .66). The three issues from the 1984 NES survey were government services versus spending, aid to minorities, and jobs and standard of living (alpha = .59). The last two were also used to create the domestic policy scales in the 1980 data (r = .43). Since the reliabilities are at least as high on the domestic scales as on the international scales, measurement error attenuates the relationship between voting and international issues at least as much as that between voting and domestic issues.

14. Therefore, those who reported abstaining or voting for some other candidate—like John Anderson—are excluded.

15. Kessel's (1988) results on the salience and impact of international involvement are broadly consistent with these speculations, even for 1976 and 1968. The 1960 election is an exception because he found a large impact on the vote.

Appendix 11-1   Percentages Meeting Various "Issue Voting" Criteria, 1980-1984

Issue Scale	Placed Self on Scale	Placed Self and Both Candidates	Placed Self and Saw Difference Between Candidates	Placed Self and Saw Democrat As More Liberal Than Republican
1980 (NES)				
Foreign				
Defense spending	85.1	69.5	63.5	54.1
Russian relations	84.5	70.8	58.8	51.0
Domestic				
Government services and spending[a]	81.5	64.2	56.8	46.8
Inflation and unemployment	59.5	46.5	38.3	26.7
Aid to minorities	85.9	69.1	61.1	52.8
Women's rights	93.6	72.2	54.4	46.9
Jobs and standard of living	84.2	68.3	57.4	48.6
1984 (NES)				
Foreign				
Central America[a]	77.7	64.5	55.2	45.5
Defense spending	88.0	77.9	71.3	65.2
Russian relations	85.3	73.7	62.0	52.9

Appendix 11-1 *(continued)*

Issue Scale	Placed Self on Scale	Placed Self and Both Candidates	Placed Self and Saw Difference Between Candidates	Placed Self and Saw Democrat As More Liberal Than Republican
Domestic				
Government services				
and spending[a]	85.5	76.2	69.7	60.0
Aid to minorities	87.9	76.5	62.9	49.6
Aid to women	85.2	74.0	59.8	49.4
Jobs and standard				
of living	87.1	76.0	60.7	53.6
1984 (Gallup)				
Foreign				
Strong or tough				
stance[a]	91.9	80.6	71.1	60.8
Defense spending	93.4	85.5	81.2	76.2
Domestic				
Government services				
and spending[a]	89.6	80.4	76.4	66.9
Affirmative action	92.9	74.7	61.2	50.3
Government and				
morals[a]	90.0	73.5	53.4	39.0
Aid to minorities	92.9	78.0	65.2	53.7
Jobs and standard				
of living	93.7	79.5	65.9	58.0
Government and				
religion[a]	91.7	75.1	56.4	42.5

Note: Table presents scale-by-scale the data for the averages in Table 11-1.

[a] Denotes scales with scoring reversed so that 1 = most liberal and 7 = most conservative.

Appendix 11-2   Median Self-Placement and Perceptions of Candidates on Seven-Point Issue Scales, 1980-84

Issue Scale	Self	Reagan	Carter and Mondale
1980 (NES)			
Foreign			
Defense spending	5.37	5.76	3.70
Russian relations	3.93	4.62	2.48
Domestic			
Government services and spending[a]	3.68	4.68	2.89
Inflation and unemployment[a]	3.92	4.36	3.65
Aid to minorities	4.46	5.00	3.01
Women's rights	2.40	4.28	2.67
Jobs and standard of living	4.43	5.04	3.14
1984 (NES)			
Foreign			
Central America[a]	3.24	5.51	3.53
Defense spending	4.05	5.96	3.32
Russian relations	4.16	5.22	3.32
Domestic			
Government services and spending[a]	3.97	5.41	2.86
Aid to minorities	4.09	4.63	3.07
Aid to women	3.88	4.58	3.02
Jobs and standard of living	4.23	5.14	3.24
1984 (Gallup)			
Foreign			
Strong or tough stance[a]	4.46	5.86	3.24
Defense spending	3.83	6.06	2.86
Domestic			
Government services and spending[a]	3.72	5.41	2.52
Affirmative action	6.13	5.34	3.28
Government and morals[a]	2.43	4.44	3.39
Aid to minorities	4.13	4.91	2.82
Jobs and standard of living	4.86	5.71	3.25
Government and religion	2.29	4.48	2.98

Note: Table presents scale-by-scale the data for the averages in Table 11-4.

[a] Denotes scales with scoring reversed so that 1 = most liberal and 7 = most conservative.

12. A SOCIAL-COGNITIVE MODEL
OF CANDIDATE APPRAISAL

Wendy M. Rahn, John H. Aldrich, Eugene Borgida, and John L. Sullivan

How individuals perceive and think about candidates, issues, and political events has been the focus of considerable research and theoretical development in political cognition (Lau and Sears, 1986). Researchers in political cognition, drawing on theoretical models from cognitive psychology (Hamill, Lodge, and Blake, 1985; Hastie, 1986; Lau, 1986; Lodge and Hamill, 1986), behavioral decision theory (Iyengar, chapter 7, this volume), and social cognition (Conover and Feldman, 1984; Iyengar, Kinder, Peters, and Krosnick, 1984), have conceptualized the domain of political behavior as a particularly rich, naturalistic context in which to examine theoretical issues that are central to an understanding of human cognition. At the same time, these investigations have also begun to contribute new insights to, and perspectives on, long-standing concerns in political science such as the nature of public perceptions and evaluations of political candidates.

Until recently, political scientists, while recognizing the importance of candidate images, have not provided theoretical or rigorous empirical analyses of the role of candidates and their images in electoral choice. In the predominant view presented in *The American Voter* (Campbell, Converse, Miller, and Stokes, 1960), attitudes toward the candidates were seen primarily as projections of partisan bias, although individual candidates could interject dynamism into presidential contests that prompted short-term deviations from normal partisan voting patterns (e.g., Stokes, 1966). In reaction to this view, scholars in the late 1960s began to analyze the impact of short-term forces on the vote, looking especially at the role of issues. The central argument was that issues, instead of being short-term disruptions of otherwise stable partisan choices, could be seen as systematic determinants of voters' decisions (for a review of the issue-voting literature in this period, see Kessel, 1972). One theoretical approach to explain issue voting is the spatial model of electoral competition (see Downs, 1957; Davis, Hinich, and Ordeshook, 1970). Herstein (1981) critiqued this theory, arguing that such spatial-like calculations are too demanding cognitively, and he demon-

Source: *Information and Democratic Processes*, John Ferejohn and James Kuklinski, eds. Urbana: University of Illinois Press, 1990.

strated experimentally that people do not employ such a complex reasoning process. One important contribution of the spatial approach, however, was the emphasis on choice as based on a comparison between the two alternative candidates, seen in that case as collections of policy alternatives.

Other models of voter choice posited less demanding calculations than the spatial model, in which summary candidate assessments played a critical role (Brody and Page, 1973; Kelley and Mirer, 1974). Indeed, the decision rule in these models is that individuals vote for the candidate receiving the highest net evaluations. More methodologically complicated models have been developed to examine the causal determinants of these summary assessments (Markus and Converse, 1979; Page and Jones, 1979; G. Markus, 1982), but they have lacked a systematic theoretical account of the processes that underlie voters' impressions of political candidates. Given these results, scholars of political behavior have recognized for some time that the focus should shift from predicting vote choice per se, as reflected in the component models of voter choice (Stokes, Campbell, and Miller, 1958; Stokes, 1966; Kagay and Caldiera, 1975), to understanding the nature of the candidate appraisal process.

In this chapter we first develop a social-cognitive model of the process of candidate appraisal and then test it using a national survey conducted for the authors by the Gallup poll immediately after the 1984 presidential election. A central part of the theory underlying the model concerns the role of information in forming these assessments. We will argue that the rich and often redundant flow of political information in a presidential election year, combined with the relative simplicity of a choice between two presidential candidates, leads to relatively similar assessment and decisional processes for most individuals. We will test this argument by estimating the model for respondents who are relatively high in political sophistication and those relatively low in sophistication.

Candidate Appraisal

Research in political cognition has stimulated renewed interest in the study of candidate images as preeminent factors in the voters' world (Kinder and Sears, 1985). Lau (1986) and Miller, Wattenberg, and Malanchuk (1986), for example, rely on an understanding of information processing based on schema theory (e.g., Taylor and Crocker, 1981) and use responses to the open-ended, like-dislike questions from the University of Michigan Center for Political Studies (CPS) national election surveys to identify "information processing proclivities" among the mass public. Lau argues that individuals appear to rely on four broad classes of schemata, or organized structures of knowledge, to process political information (groups, issues, parties, and candidate personalities). These relatively stable categories, he contends, influence the vote decision. For individuals who possess a well-developed party schema, for example, Lau finds that party identification is nearly twice as important in determining candidate evaluations as it is for individuals without a fully developed schema. Even for the latter voters, however, party identification is relevant to their vote.

Similarly, Miller and his colleagues (1986) categorize citizen responses to the open-ended, like-dislike questions into those dealing with candidates, issues, and groups. They find that candidate-directed comments cluster in five generic dimensions (competence, integrity, reliability, charisma, and personal characteristics) that are stable at the individual level across elections, suggesting that individuals do not respond to candidates as idiosyncratic figures. Both Lau (1986) and Miller, Wattenberg, and Malanchuk (1986) find that higher levels of education are associated with the use of a candidate schema, a finding that Miller and his colleagues attribute to well-educated voters' ability to consider the dispositional qualities of the candidates. Less well-educated voters, by contrast, concentrate on readily observable characteristics of the candidates such as physical attractiveness and background.

Work by Kinder and others (Abelson, Kinder, Peters, and Fiske, 1982; Kinder, 1986; Kinder and Fiske, 1986) has examined the candidate appraisal process. This work has made extensive use of the new CPS candidate appraisal batteries (e.g., asking respondents to rate how well such attributes as "strong leader," "moral," or "inspiring" describe the candidates) to develop a theoretical framework for understanding the perception and evaluation of presidential candidates. In particular, Kinder's analysis (1986) of these measures reveals that individuals think about the candidates in stable, structured ways, following a process that resembles that used to think about ordinary people. Although the assessment of ordinary people and of political candidates is similar, attributions about presidential candidates will be appropriate to the task of assessing presidential character and performance. Judgments of presidential character, therefore, will be structured around particularly central and relevant traits (competence, leadership, integrity, and empathy). Some of these traits (e.g., empathy) can be viewed as germane for assessing any individual, whereas others (e.g., competence and leadership) will receive special emphasis due to the political nature of the task. Moreover, these judgments can be influenced by political predispositions such as ideology, partisanship, and policy preferences.

Thus, in contrast to the early perspectives on vote choice, recent research suggests that the candidate appraisal process does not represent an idiosyncratic response to the vagaries and particular characteristics of a given election contest. Rather, these findings support the notion that, when thinking about political candidates, people tend to rely on the same information processing capabilities that guide their thinking and actions in other, nonpolitical domains (Feldman and Conover, 1983; Kinder and Fiske, 1986; Sullivan, Aldrich, Borgida, and Rahn, forthcoming). When people think about political events and make voting decisions in presidential elections, they first rely on the well-developed set of inferential strategies and processes for assessing character that they use in everyday life (Nisbett and Ross, 1980; Ostrom, 1984; Sherman and Corty, 1984). In this respect, we will argue that individual differences in political expertise or interest (Fiske and Kinder, 1981; Fiske, Kinder, and Larter, 1983) should not result in different candidate appraisal processes because all citizens have sufficient practice in evaluating others in the course of their daily lives. But it is also clear that political expertise affects the processing of information for other political tasks (Zaller, 1986).

In most elections, as in everyday life, a great deal of information, much of which is complex, becomes available to individuals. Voters are deluged with comparative information, especially in presidential elections, about the candidates' personal characteristics and qualities, their competencies, their stands on various issues that are salient in the campaign, as well as other, nonverbal cues presented by the candidates and their campaigns (see, e.g., Rosenberg, Bohan, McCafferty, and Harris, 1986; Sullivan and Masters, 1988). Research in social cognition suggests that, under such conditions, people perforce simplify the information environment, and, in doing so, they are likely to rely on the familiar cognitive routines that they employ in other decision-making contexts. The presidential campaign itself facilitates impression formation by emphasizing particular personal qualities such as leadership. Media coverage of the campaign may prime individuals to consider such traits in their evaluations of the candidates (Iyengar and Kinder, 1986). Also fortunately for voters, in virtually all presidential election contests, many political cues point in the same direction, reinforcing one another. In other words, the political characteristics of the candidates, including their party affiliations, their ideologies, and their issue positions, are often highly "correlated." This redundancy offers an additional reason for the similarity of the candidate appraisal process across all types of voters, even those with relatively low levels of political sophistication.

More specifically, in the candidate appraisal process, individuals quickly make some basic judgments about the candidates, particularly with respect to their competencies as potential leaders and their individual qualities. In 1984, for example, voters may have learned that there were vast differences between Ronald Reagan and Walter Mondale on the defense spending issue, with Reagan preferring significantly more spending than Mondale. This information could be expected to have an impact on perceptions of the two candidates as differentially strong or weak, depending on the voters' own positions on this issue and on their partisan predispositions. Likewise, other issues and other types of political information feed into judgments of the candidates' characteristics that help to define each candidate as more or less competent in the mind of a particular voter. Thus, although we agree with others (e.g., Hamill, Lodge, and Blake, 1985; Lau, 1986) that different individuals may rely on different types of schemas (e.g., parties, groups, ideology) for processing political information, we suggest that in the electoral context, a wide variety of political cues and other kinds of information are abundantly available to the voters, and potentially all of it can be used when evaluating candidates.[1]

These assessments about personal competencies, in turn, influence how voters feel about each candidate—whether, for example, they feel pride or shame when confronted with a particular candidate, or whether they like or dislike the candidate.[2] In 1984, a voter may have thought that Reagan was very strong based on his positions on defense and other issues, and thus the voter may have concluded that Reagan was competent because of the perceived connection between competence and strength in a political leader. This in turn made the voter feel pride when confronted with the image of Ronald Reagan. Similarly, in 1988, George Bush used the defense and crime issues to dispel his "wimp" image and establish an image of personal weakness for Michael Dukakis. In this fashion, issues can structure candidate images, which in turn influence feelings about the candidates. A person who supports a greater role for the government in helping the poor and destitute, when presented with Reagan's views on welfare, may conclude that Reagan was selfish and politically untrustworthy. Thus issues can affect judgments of personal qualities as well as judgments of political competencies, and, in turn, these judgments influence feelings about the candidates.

The candidate appraisal process, by which personality assessments are made in combination with the electoral campaign that primes certain issues as well as partisanship and ideology, leads to an overall evaluation of presidential candidates' competency and leadership, their personal qualities, and the voters' feelings about the candidates. In a context as complex as a presidential election, candidates portray these qualities in part on the basis of their own personalities, background, and experiences, and in part on features unique to the political arena, such as policy, party, and ideology.

Unlike judgments about people in everyday settings, however, the decision task confronting the voter is ultimately a choice between two candidates. Therefore, the question is not simply whether Mondale was perceived to be competent or not, but whether he was seen to be more or less competent than Reagan.

A Model of Candidate Appraisal

The model of candidate appraisal is based on several basic assumptions. First, we assume that images of presidential candidates can be formed in two ways. Images of candidates can be formed by a process similar to that used to form impressions of people encountered in everyday life. The alternative— attending to and processing the large amounts of information available in every new setting—contradicts the assumptions of cognitive economy that characterize normal cognitive functioning (Fiske and Taylor, 1984; Markus and Zajonc, 1985). This assumption therefore leads us to expect that, even for those citizens relatively unconcerned about politics, the formation of candidate images will be a relatively easy task, one not dependent upon a vast store of political awareness and knowledge. Moreover, to the extent that people's initial impressions of and beliefs about candidates are bolstered as they learn more about the candidates during the course of the campaign, new information is often perceived to be largely confirmatory (Lord, Ross, and Lepper, 1979; Ross and Anderson, 1982).

Voters can also derive images of candidates based upon their perceptions of the candidates' stands on key issues, partisanship, and ideology. In this sense, the political context primes political cues that are considered in varying degrees in the development of candidate images. This context creates an appraisal process that can include factors common to everyday appraisals, as well as factors unique to national election campaigns.

A second basic assumption of the model is that most voters are capable of distinguishing between the political characteristics of candidates and the candidates' personal qualities. We make this assumption because in everyday life, in a variety of formal and informal settings, people are called upon to distinguish between the professional and personal qualities of individuals. They notice, for example, that some people are fine human beings, even though they may not be highly competent at their chosen occupations; others are not as personally appealing, but are incredibly competent. In this respect, elections represent a setting in which these types of judgments will come quite naturally to most voters. The electoral process is clearly an arena in which citizens will wish to select leaders who will competently run their government *and* whose personal qualities will evoke trust and confidence in their personal motives.

A third assumption, consistent with recent work in social cognition (Berscheid, 1984; Fiske and Pavelchak, 1986), is that feelings about candidates are developed as a natural part of this candidate appraisal process.[3] These assessments can be conceptualized as an overall, affective summary toward each candidate that has its basis in cognitive appraisal. In presidential elections, of course, feelings toward the candidates will also be grounded in political issues, ideology, and partisanship.

Finally, we assume that, in this context, voting is a relatively uncomplicated decision for most people. It really can be "the simple act of voting" (Kelley and Mirer, 1974). If overall affect about the candidates summarizes judgments and feelings about issues, parties, and the competence and personal qualities of the candidates, it leads in a relatively straightforward fashion to a voting decision. One votes for the candidate one likes best (or dislikes least). It is this assumption in particular that leads us to predict that the process of voting is based on a comparative assessment of the candidates and is similar for people who are heavily involved in politics and those for whom politics is more incidental.

Measurement

In order to test the preceding theory, we specify a model relating the exogenous variables of partisanship, ideology, and issues to the three dimensions of candidate image that we have discussed—competence, personal qualities, and affect or feelings about candidates. We then need to estimate the parameters in this model separately for people who are heavily involved and those who are less involved in politics. This theoretical model is depicted in Figure 12-1. A more detailed discussion of measurement follows. The data for estimation of these models are drawn from a postelection survey conducted by the Gallup poll for three of the authors in November 1984. There were 1,509 respondents included in the national sample.

Domestic Issues

In selecting issues for the domestic scale, we initially selected six items that formed a scale as reported in Aldrich, Sullivan, and Borgida (1989). However, because we have argued that the process of deciding for whom to vote is a comparative one, the model could only be tested if we could compare respondents' attitudes on these issues with their perceptions of where each candidate stands on

Figure 12-1 A Model of Candidate Appraisal

Political Information   Candidate Assessments   Affect Generation   Vote Choice

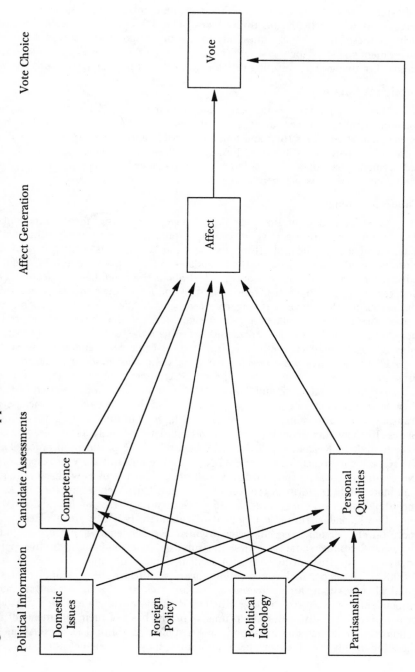

the same issues. Of the original six items in the domestic issues scale, candidate perceptions were solicited on three issues. The domestic issues scale therefore includes these three items—questions measuring respondents' attitudes toward government spending for social services in general, aid to minorities, and jobs and standard of living. The resulting reliability, measured by coefficient alpha, is .60.

Foreign Affairs Issues

The foreign affairs issues scale has two items, one dealing with defense spending and the other measuring respondents' views about whether our government should be strong and tough or flexible and understanding in dealing with other nations. We were limited to these two items because of the requirement that data be available on respondents' perceptions of the two candidates as well as on their own positions.

Candidate Image

As we have conceptualized candidate image, it consists of three components.[4] Two components are cognitive, including respondents' perceptions of the candidates' competence and leadership qualities, and respondents' perceptions of the more personal characteristics of the candidates. The third and final component is affective, referring to how respondents feel about the candidates as people. The first component, competence, represents perceptions of the candidates' personal characteristics that have a strong role component. We measured respondents' perceptions of the candidates' personal characteristics that have a clear professional component by asking respondents to evaluate the candidates on three sets of adjective pairs: ineffective-effective, incompetent-competent, and strong-weak.

These adjectives were selected from the basic potency dimension from the original evaluative, potency, and activity (EPA) dimensions of person perception discussed by Osgood, Suci, and Tannenbaum (1957). They were selected because they have obvious connections to perceptions of how personal characteristics translate into professional competencies in high political office in the United States. Respondents undoubtedly react to candidates not only as people, but also as potential (in Reagan's case, actual) occupants of the presidential office. Thus the respondents' reactions to these adjectives represent a mixture of responses to the candidate as a person and more abstract judgments of how this particular candidate might perform in the role of president. Coefficient alpha for this scale, including these three measures, is .76 for Reagan and .78 for Mondale.

The second cognitive component of candidate image is constructed to be more purely personal and character-oriented. Respondents were asked to judge the candidates' personal qualities, measured by the following adjective pairs: trustworthy-untrustworthy, selfish-unselfish, and cool and aloof-warm and friendly. These particular perceptions are less affected by the nature of the political role than are perceptions of competence. We assume that most respondents, when asked to judge whether Reagan or Mondale is cool and aloof or warm and friendly, will react primarily on the basis of their judgments of the candidates' characteristics as persons, not as potential political leaders. Although these judgments are of a more personal nature, they are nonetheless grounded in the information available to the voter, much of which is expressly political. Images of candidates' personal characteristics are almost always created within an expressly political presentation of self and context. Therefore, this component of candidate image is also expected to be influenced by the exogenous, political variables. Coefficient alpha for scales based on these three items is .69 for Reagan and .63 for Mondale.

The last dimension of candidate image is affective. We asked respondents how they felt about each of the two candidates, by inquiring whether thinking about Reagan (and then Mondale) made them feel ashamed or proud, whether it made them feel relaxed and confident or tense and uneasy, and the extent to which they liked or disliked each candidate. These questions represent self-described emotional, or affective, reactions to the candidates as persons. Coefficient alpha for scales based on these three items is .90 for Reagan and .83 for Mondale.[5]

All of the adjective pairs are seven-point scales. Therefore, when combined to form three measures of candidate image, the resulting range of values for each measure is 3-21.

Other Measures

Party identification was measured with the usual seven-point scale, ideology was measured with the seven-point self-identification scale, and the vote was simply "who did you vote for in the 1984 election?"

Results

We have argued that the decision-making process that most voters follow in arriving at a choice for president is comparative. In order to examine that claim, we tested the model illustrated in Figure 12-1 in several different ways. First, we used the simple values on each item or scale for each respondent and ran separate equations for Reagan and Mondale. In the Reagan equation, for example, the variables measure respondents' positions on domestic and foreign policy issues, their perceptions of Reagan's competence and personal qualities, their feelings toward Reagan, and the respondents' partisan and ideological self-images. The model was estimated first using perceptions of Reagan's character and then using perceptions of Mondale's character. The parameters from these "self-placement" models are not shown, but are available on request. Consistent with the claim that voters cue most heavily on the incumbent, the R^2 for the Reagan equations is generally larger than that for the Mondale equations. Consistent with information processing notions, voters had accumulated more information about Reagan because he was the incumbent.

Respondents' own attitudes on issues, however, are only one potential source of information. The political environment also provides information about the candidates' issue stands, partisanship, ideology, and so on. It is the proximity of the candidates' stands to the individual's own preferences, rather than these preferences per se, that relates the political information environment to individuals' perceptions of the competencies and personal qualities of the candidates.

Therefore, we constructed distance measures for each candidate by taking the absolute value of the difference between respondents' own positions and their placements of the candidates on the same issue scales. The same was done for the ideology scale. The differences on issue scales were summed separately across the three domestic and two foreign policy issues and averaged, thus forming two average distance scales for each candidate. We estimated the model a second time, again separately for each candidate, using the issue and ideology distance scales. The adjusted R^2's for the four equations in these separate-candidate models are reported in Table 12-1.

We are able to explain a considerable amount of the variance in the competence and personal qualities equations for the two candidates, using the ideology and issue-distance scores as well as party identification (and more variation than when only self-placements were used), with one exception. The R^2 for the Mondale personal qualities equation is quite a bit smaller (.16) than that for the same equation for Reagan (.42). This suggests that the electorate's perceptions of Reagan as a person were structured largely by political predispositions, no doubt due to his status as the incumbent. Images of Mondale as a person, on the other hand, were less rooted in the political variables in our model and apparently derived on the basis of other aspects of the challenger's behavior. Both dimensions of the candidates' images—their professional competence and their personal qualities—were very powerful predictors of respondents' emotional reactions to the candidates, with the political variables explaining some of the remaining variation. For competence, the betas were .26 for Reagan and .31 for Mondale; for personal qualities, .34 for Reagan and .41 for Mondale.

Recall, however, the claim that voters attempt to arrive at a summary judgment of the candidates that in turn provides an efficient basis in deciding for whom to vote. This is, clearly, a comparative judgment, and the separate analysis of each candidate, reported above, is misspecified. Comparisons are made, of course, not only in judgments about issues and ideology, but also in the cognitive images and the feelings that voters develop about the two candidates.

Therefore, we developed a fully comparative model of candidate images. For this model, we constructed issue and ideological distance scores by subtracting the Reagan proximity scores from the Mondale proximity scores. For the ideology, foreign policy, and domestic issue scales, the relative distance scores could range from -6 to +6, with a score of 0 indicating a respondent equally close to the two candidates, a score of +6 indicating maximum distance from Mondale relative to Reagan, and a score of -6 indicating maximum relative distance from Reagan. Our assumption is that the farther individuals perceive themselves from a candidate, the less inclined they are to view him or her in a favorable light.[6] Similarly, we measured the perceived differences between the two candidates on competence, personal qualities, and affect. The scores were created by taking respondents' perceptions of Mondale on each scale and subtracting them from those of Reagan. The scores therefore represent the degree to which Reagan is perceived as more competent, as possessing more positive personal qualities, and as more affectively appealing than Mondale.[7] Both candidates may be perceived as competent, both as incompetent, or one as competent and the other as

Table 12-1 Adjusted R^2 for Various Models

	Model				
	Candidate Only		Full Candidate Comparison		
	Reagan	Mondale	Whole Sample	High Sophisti- cation	Low Sophisti- cation
Dependent Variable in Equation[a]					
Competence:					
Adjusted R^2	.36	.40	.55	.57	.43
N	(1076)	(997)	(974)	(431)	(243)
Personal qualities:	.42	.16	.46	.45	.41
	(1015)	(921)	(897)	(395)	(222)
Affect:	.76	.67	.84	.85	.78
	(969)	(847)	(819)	(360)	(203)
Vote:					
Probit pseudo R^2	.82	.75	.87[b]	.85	.88
Regression R^2	.70	.62	.70	.68	.69
	(1009)	(925)	(911)	(406)	(233)

Note: The last three columns are the results for the comparison scores, presented for the whole sample, the high-sophistication group, and the low-sophistication group.

[a] See Figure 12-1 for a listing of independent variables included in each equation.

[b] 94 percent of the two-candidate vote was correctly predicted by the probit model. The correlation between actual and predicted vote was .88.

incompetent. Which of these conditions occurs most often in a particular election affects the importance of the competence dimension in arriving at feelings about the candidates and in deciding how to vote. A similar logic underlies the other distance and difference measures.

We estimated the model in Figure 12-1 using comparative differences for all of the variables except party identification and the vote.[8] As the results in Table 12-1 show, this improved the fit of the model significantly. The R^2's for leadership and for affect are increased the most by conceptualizing the entire decision-making process as a comparative one. Issue distances provide better explanations of perceived differences in competence than do isolated perceptions of Reagan's or Mondale's competence. In turn, perceived differences in competence and in the personal qualities of the candidates provide much better explanations of the differences in feelings toward the candidates than do isolated perceptions and feelings about one particular candidate, even the incumbent. The entire judgment process appears to be comparative.

We earlier developed an information redundancy argument based on the simplicity of the decision-making task facing the voter. Information about the candidates is abundant and relatively cost-free. It is increasingly presented in formats that are at least marginally entertaining. We therefore do not expect the most highly involved and informed segments of the electorate to process information much differently from the less interested and informed segments. By definition, the more sophisticated are more interested, informed, and politically involved, but they must narrow their focus in roughly the same way that the less sophisticated do in order to cast a ballot. Both groups must arrive at some sort of summary, comparative judgment about how they feel about the two candidates— Do they feel better about Reagan or about Mondale? They then cast their ballots largely on this basis, all else equal. If the process we have outlined is at all characteristic, issues will be summarized and simplified into a series of judgments about the candidates, particularly with respect to their competence and their personal qualities. Regardless of whether these judgments are based on knowledge (or at least perceptions) of one or two key issues, or whether they are based on many issues, the information processing is similar, and the resulting judgments have the same status. It results in a set of summary perceptions that one candidate is more competent or possesses more favorable personal qualities than the other candidate. These in turn are summarized as a set of feelings—strongly defined by a like-dislike judgment—about the candidates, leading finally to a vote choice. The process therefore narrows the relevance for voting behavior of the initial gap in sophistication among voters.

To examine this thesis, we reestimated the four equations of the model for two groups of voters: those highest and those lowest in apparent political sophistication. The estimates for the whole sample and each subgroup are reported in Tables 12-2, 12-3, 12-4, and 12-5. The measure of high and low sophistication is based on respondents' levels of education, their knowledge about politics, and their expressed level of interest in politics.[9]

The results are largely supportive of this theoretical approach.[10] The unstandardized and standardized coefficients are reported on each variable for the three ways in which the fully comparative model was estimated, that is, for the whole sample and for the low- and high-sophistication groups. Because there are differences between the high- and the low-sophistication subsamples on several of the variances, when we compare the high and low groups, the discussion focuses on the unstandardized coefficients. In comparing the relative impact of one set of variables with another set within any one sample, we will focus on the standardized coefficients.

Examining the results in Table 12-2, the impact of issues on perceptions of competence is strong for both groups of respondents. The unstandardized coefficients for the high group are .67 for domestic issues and .82 for foreign policy issues; for the low group, these coefficients are .62 and .83. The near equivalence of these coefficients indicates that foreign and domestic issues were important to both groups. As can be seen by the betas, for example, the impact of issues nearly rivals or exceeds that of party identification on the comparative perceptions of candidate competence. The major conclusion to be drawn from these results is that comparative perceptions of candidate competence appear to be equally (and strongly) affected by issues for both groups of respondents.

Perceptions of competence are also affected by partisanship and by perceived

Table 12-2 Competence Equation—Full Comparative Model

	Whole Sample		*High Sophistication*		*Low Sophistication*	
	B	Beta	B	Beta	B	Beta
Domestic issues	.68	.21	.67	.20	.62	.18
	(.11)		(.15)		(.23)	
Foreign policy	.88	.29	.82	.27	.83	.27
	(.09)		(.13)		(.19)	
Political ideology	.44	.16	.49	.18	.35[a]	.12
	(.09)		(.13)		(.18)	
Party ID	.72	.23	.71	.23	.88	.28
	(.09)		(.13)		(.18)	
Constant	−.032[b]		.251[b]		−1.38[b]	
Adjusted R^2	.55		.57		.43	
N	974		413		243	

Note: Standard errors are in parentheses.
[a] Significant at .05 level; all other coefficients significant at $p < .05$.
[b] Not significant at .05 level.

Table 12-3 Personal Qualities Equation—Full Comparative Model

	Whole Sample		*High Sophistication*		*Low Sophistication*	
	B	Beta	B	Beta	B	Beta
Domestic issues	.66	.25	.65	.25	.85	.26
	(.10)		(.15)		(.23)	
Foreign policy	.45	.18	.33	.13	.50	.18
	(.09)		(.13)		(.19)	
Political ideology	.41	.16	42	.19	.31[a]	.12
	(.08)		(.13)		(.17)	
Party ID	.53	.21	.50	.20	.74	.26
	(.08)		(.13)		(.17)	
Constant	−1.89		−1.73		−2.98	
Adjusted R^2	.46		.45		.41	
N	897		395		222	

[a] Not significant at .05 level; all other coefficients significant at $p < .05$.

differences in political ideology. Partisanship seems to have a somewhat stronger impact for the low group, whereas ideology has a slightly greater impact for the high group. But these differences are not substantial. In fact, comparative judgments of the competence of Reagan and Mondale—for both groups of respondents—appear to be first a function of foreign policy issues, second a projection of partisanship, and third a function of domestic issues. Ideology plays only a minor role. (See the standardized coefficients in Table 12-2 for these comparisons.) Individuals thus appear to have emphasized how the candidates would conduct themselves as leaders with regard to our nation's foreign and defense policies when they arrived at judgments of the candidates' personal competencies.

In the equation for personal qualities, the unstandardized coefficients for both foreign policy and domestic issues—as well as that for party identification—are greater for the low- than for the high-sophistication group (see Table 12-3). Thus issues appear to have a marginally greater role in determining the lower group's images of the candidates as people than is true of the higher group's images. But these differences are not as striking as the strong impact issues have for both subgroups, and this underlying similarity is the more important point. The standardized coefficients show that for the high group, domestic issues, ideology, and partisanship have approximately the same impact on comparative perceptions of personal qualities. For the low group, the conclusion is similar except that foreign issues appear to play a somewhat greater role than ideology.

In the affect equation, the impact of competence and of personal qualities, ideology, and partisanship all play a similar role for the high and low groups. Domestic and foreign policy issues have a greater impact in the low group, whereas perceptions of competence are more important to individuals with more political sophistication. Thus, in general, it appears that foreign policy perceptions are more important in the perceptual process for the less sophisticated respondents, in comparison to the more sophisticated group, a somewhat surprising twist. Political ideology is more important to the highly sophisticated respondents in perceptions of the candidates' competencies and personal qualities (see Tables 12-2 and 12-3), although the impact of ideology is nearly even for both groups in the affect equation. In 1984, the candidates took clearly distinct positions on foreign policy issues, particularly on the defense spending issue. Our results suggest that less sophisticated voters could readily detect this difference, but that ideological information was less important to them than to the more highly sophisticated members of the electorate. Thus, although the focal point and perspective may differ somewhat between our two groups of respondents, the redundancy in the political information environment makes for a candidate appraisal process that, we argue, is quite similar for the two groups. Note that in Table 12-4, the relative impact of personal qualities on affect is greater than the impact of competence.[11] This suggests that feelings about the candidates are more firmly grounded in reactions to the candidates as people than they are in reaction to the candidates' competencies. Issues, ideology, and partisanship play little direct role, although they do shape perceptions of competence and personal qualities.

Finally, the vote equations were estimated twice, once using regression

Table 12-4 Affect Equation—Full Comparative Model

	Whole Sample		High Sophistication		Low Sophistication	
	B	Beta	B	Beta	B	Beta
Domestic issues	.56	.15	.41	.11	.58	.14
	(.09)		(.13)		(.20)	
Foreign policy	.18	.05	.22[a]	.06	.36	.10
	(.07)		(.11)		(.17)	
Political ideology	.34	.11	.31	.10	.33	.10
	(.07)		(.10)		(.14)	
Party ID	.47	.13	.50	.14	.53	.15
	(.07)		(.11)		(.15)	
Competence	.32	.28	.36	.31	.24	.21
	(.03)		(.04)		(.06)	
Personal qualities	.53	.37	.52	.36	.51	.41
	(.03)		(.05)		(.06)	
Constant	−1.59		−2.03		−1.64	
Adjusted R^2	.84		.85		.78	
N	819		360		203	

[a] Significant at .05 level; all other coefficients significant at $p < .05$.

Table 12-5 Vote Equation—Full Comparative Model

	Whole Sample		High Sophistication		Low Sophistication	
	B	Beta	B	Beta	B	Beta
Affect	.03	.50	.03	.48	.03	.51
	(.001)		(.002)		(.002)	
Party ID	.08	.41	.08	.40	.09	.40
	(.005)		(.009)		(.010)	
Constant	.174		.175		.171	
Adjusted R^2	.70		.69		.69	
N	911		406		233	
			Probit Coefficients			
Affect	.22	.67	.22	.70	.24	.69
	(.019)		(.028)		(.040)	
Party ID	.34	.32	.29	.27	.43	.34
	(.040)		(.058)		(.086)	
Pseudo R^2	.87		.85		.88	

analysis and once using probit analysis. These results are presented in Table 12-5.[12] The impact of affect and partisanship on voting behavior is quite similar for the two groups. Furthermore, within each group, these two variables appear to have very similar impacts on voting, so that partisanship and feelings about candidates (as a summary of perceptions of competence, personal qualities, and issues) are equally important proximal determinants of voting behavior. The correlation between predicted and actual vote was .88, quite high by most standards. Feelings about the candidates appear to be a very powerful summary of other perceptions and attitudes that influence political behavior such as voting.[13]

Our central point is that there are generally small differences in the fit of the model or in individual parameter estimates between the more and less sophisticated respondents. The R^2 values reported in Table 12-1 show an equally good fit for the four equations in the two groups, with the exception of a somewhat lower R^2 value for the leadership equation for the low-sophistication group. Major individual differences with respect to political sophistication do not generally appear in the assessment of presidential character nor in the relationship between comparative judgments of character and the vote. In both cases, we suggest, complex and redundant information is simplified to make the act of voting a relatively easy task.

Summary

Our theoretical account of the candidate appraisal process is composed of three key elements. First, we have argued that the process of forming assessments of the professional and personal qualities of candidates plays a central role in determining the final vote decision. In our view, person-oriented responses to presidential candidates are neither idiosyncratic nor superficial. Rather, such assessments are grounded in daily processes of impression formation and are, in fact, quite reasonable given the nature of the judgment task and of the information environment. The presidential campaign is, after all, a contest between two highly visible people. The campaign itself and the media that cover the campaign make person-related information easily available and thus highly accessible. This availability, together with the fact that individuals naturally make personality judgments every day, serves to make personal assessments of candidates ubiquitous and unavoidable.

Ordinary processes of impression formation, however, are not directly transferred to the political domain. The political context works, we believe, to modify the process of character assessments in important ways. The use of certain kinds of personality constructs becomes more crucial and more appropriate to the task of choosing the country's leader than it does in assessing character in other daily contexts. In this vein, we have argued that individuals structure their assessments of the candidates' professional qualities in broad terms of political leadership and competence. In turn, these judgments are related to such political variables as partisanship, issue positions, and ideology. Individuals also develop candidate assessments that are more personal in nature. These more personal assessments also are related in part to political variables appropriate to the task of assessing two people running for the presidency, but as our results for Mondale show, they can be derived from other sources as well. The role of these other types of information in character assessments may be more important when candidates are less well known to voters as political figures. Recent research on the presidential nomination campaign (Aldrich, Lin, and Rahn, 1987; Rahn, 1987; Bartels, 1988) has begun to explore this issue.

The political setting of presidential campaigns creates what is fundamentally a choice problem. Thus, the process of impression formation is, from the beginning, a task that must result in a choice between two individuals. This setting means that candidates will be evaluated and comparatively assessed on the key dimensions of competence and personal qualities. We have argued, therefore, not only that the voter must ultimately decide which candidate is the better choice, all things considered, but also that he or she forms assessments of both candidates' leadership abilities and personal qualities. In turn, these assessments lead potential voters to develop feelings about both candidates, and these affective summaries then form the basis for voters' decisions.

We have also suggested that individual differences in political expertise, although important in some kinds of tasks, do not result in different processes of candidate appraisal for two reasons. First, assessment of the personal qualities of individuals occurs naturally and spontaneously in the social world. When confronted with a similar task in politics, individuals will rely on these regularly employed strategies, regardless of their abstract knowledge of or interest in politics. We do not suggest, however, that presidential elections are superficial personality contests. Indeed, the political basis of voters' judgments provides a second rationale for not expecting subgroup differences in the candidate appraisal process. Individuals do have a variety of sources of information to draw upon to make character assessments, information that is explicitly political in nature. Some of this political information, notably partisanship, is conveyed as strong, clear, and simple informational cues. Other information, such as the issue positions of candidates, is quite consistent across issues, especially in 1984. Knowledge of even one or two issue positions would therefore lead most people to the same assessment as would one based on substantial knowledge about many issue positions. An important feature of the full set of information is that much of it is redundant; that is, partisanship, ideology, and the issue positions of the candidates all generally point in the same direction, reinforcing one another and thus the assessments to which they are related. Therefore, individuals may attend to any or all of these sources to guide their assessments and, in many cases, would be led to the same assessments from each source. The result is a candidate assessment process that is remarkably similar across different strata of the electorate.

In this chapter we have placed the candidate appraisal process in a broader theoretical framework by drawing on a perspective derived from research on social cognition. We have extended the work of others in several ways. First, we have argued that the electoral setting makes the candidate appraisal process a comparative one, and we have seen that a model based on comparative judgments outperforms models based on separate assessments of the individual candidates. Second, we have related the model of comparative character assessments to important political variables, illustrating the inherently political nature of such judgments, and we have completed the model by demonstrating its very strong relationship to the vote decision. Finally, in support of our arguments about the repetitiveness of the information environment and about the regularity with which people make character assessments, we have found variations in political expertise to be of strikingly little importance.

NOTES

1. Recall that the analyses of both Lau and Miller, Wattenberg, and Malanchuk were based on the open-ended, like-dislike questions. Respondents' comments to these questions may reflect what type of information is most accessible in memory to the individuals at that moment, but may not necessarily reflect the full range of information available to the voters for their judgments about the candidates.
2. At the individual level, the process leading to these affective responses can be understood in terms of several models of social information processing (e.g., Wyer and Srull, 1986). In a general model like the two-stage "schema-triggered affect" model proposed by Fiske and Pavelchak (1986), for example, initial categorization and schematic processing of the target individual is followed by an affect-generation stage. Affective responses to the target may be cued by a broader social category label (e.g., "Democrat or "conservative"), or they may reflect a summary impression based on an attribute-by-attribute appraisal of the target's personal qualities and competencies. Affective responses are "category-based" in the former mode and "piecemeal" in the latter mode of processing, according to the schema-triggered affect model. Although the predominant mode of processing may vary by the type of electoral setting, our view of candidate appraisal in presidential elections would suggest that affective responses in this contest primarily reflect category-based processing. Thus, successfully categorizing a candidate as competent or trustworthy leads to a quick affective response, rather than this response being based on the sum of the valences associated with each aspect of the candidate's behavior that led to the category-based inferences.
3. Political feelings and emotions are under increasing scrutiny by political scientists, many of whom are beginning to suspect that we have seriously underestimated their role in the understanding of political behavior. See Conover and Feldman (1986), Marcus (1986), and Chubb, Hagen, and Sniderman (1986).
4. Earlier work on the semantic differential by Osgood, Suci, and Tannenbaum (1957) reveals three independent dimensions of person perception: the evaluative (E), potency (P), and activity (A) dimensions. Their research suggests, however, that in the political arena, these dimensions tend to collapse into one overarching perceptual dimension. Watts (1974) shows that the (E) and (A) dimensions converge and are correlated with the (P) dimension when people perceive political objects. This research on the dimensions of perception did not relate the dimensions to voting or to candidate assessment in the way we do, but it did influence our efforts to conceptualize and measure candidate images.
5. We are making a conceptual distinction among the three components of candidate image. The three sets of measures for each candidate are, of course, highly correlated,

although they probably share some method covariance which, when partialed out, would reveal greater distinctiveness among the components.

6. Thus, by construction, all signs of the coefficients for the political variables are expected to be positive in the comparative model.

7. Perceptions of candidates' positions on issues and ideology may be subject to misperception bias or a projection effect. If so, the direction of causality assumed here may be questioned. To investigate this possibly we reran our model substituting the sample median placements of the candidates on issues and ideology scales for the respondents' reported perceptions. In estimating this model, the impact of comparative ideological distance was reduced, while that of party identification was increased slightly. The parameter estimates of the two issue variables were essentially unchanged. Overall, the adjusted R^2's were about 10 percent lower in the competence and personal qualities equation. The results can be used to infer some, but relatively minor, amounts of rationalization. Therefore, these results, by themselves, do not seriously contradict the direction of influence specified in our model. With candidates as distinctive as Reagan and Mondale on so many dimensions, we believe that individuals' perceptions of their positions had a substantial basis in reality, certainly in comparison to, for example, the similarity and ambiguity that characterized Humphrey and Nixon on the Vietnam War in 1968, as analyzed by Page and Brody (1972).

   With a cross-sectional (and postelection) "snapshot" of a dynamic process, it is, of course, exceedingly difficult to disentangle empirically what may be the mutually causative nature of our major variables. Nothing in the theory prohibits nonrecursive relationships, but we believe in principle that the process occurs as modeled. If our model is misspecified, it is not in its failure to specify nonrecursive links; rather, the absence of time-series data makes it impossible to include individuals' initially diffuse reactions to candidates, which are then interpreted with political information to form the more abstract and structured judgments of the candidates that are modeled in our equations.

8. The party identification scale already incorporates a comparative judgment because the two parties are implicitly compared. Thus this measure is in fact similar to the others used in our comparative model.

   The reliabilities (coefficient alpha) for the difference scores are as follows: domestic policy .60; competence .84; personal qualities .78; and affect .92. Because foreign policy is measured by two variables, coefficient alpha is undefined.

9. A sophistication index was constructed by summing respondents' level of political interest (3-point scale), years of education (8-point scale), and number of correct answers to four general political knowledge questions. Those who scored 8 or less (on the 15-point index) were put into the low-sophistication group (36.2 percent of the sample), while those who scored 11 or higher (39.3 percent of the sample) were put into the high-sophistication group. Although this measure is less than ideal, experimental studies (e.g., Hamill and Lodge, 1986) have shown that cognitive ability and political experience are important components of political sophistication.

10. The four equations were estimated for three groups of respondents: the whole sample and the high- and low-sophistication groups. The number of respondents in the high group ranged from 360 in the affect equation to 431 in the competence equation. The number in the low group ranged from 203 in the affect equation to 222 in the competence equation. The total sample size was 1,509, of which 819 appear in the affect equation and 974 in the competence equation.

    The high-sophistication subsample started with 594 respondents and the low-sophistication subsample started with 543 respondents. The number of cases for the low group was reduced considerably because of nonvoting, and also because of missing data on some variables. So the proportion of missing cases is much higher for the low group, and the resulting estimates, which are based on the low group, are not necessarily representative of all low-sophistication voters. They represent the low-sophistication voters able to answer our questions about issues and candidates, and who, in the vote equation, also reported having voted for Reagan or Mondale. In an effort to retain as many cases as possible in order to reduce the possibly unrepresentativeness of the low-sophistication group, the issue distance measures were calculated for all respondents who could place themselves and the candidates on at least one issue. That is, the respondents' distance scores were based on the number of issues on which there was complete information. This procedure helped us to retain cases, although the failure to perceive positions for candidates did eliminate quite a few respondents. In addition, we estimated each equation separately (using listwise deletion for missing data) in order to retain as many cases per equation as possible. Consequently, the results in Tables 12-2 to 12-5 cannot be interpreted in path-analytic terms. We did run the model as a full system, where a case having missing data on any variable in the full system, including vote choice, was eliminated for all equations. The results were virtually identical to those reported here.

11. This difference is underestimated because the reliability for personal qualities is lower than that for competence. A correction for measurement error would therefore undoubtedly increase the importance of personal qualities relative to competence in determining feelings about the candidates.

12. The results from the regression analysis and the probit analysis cannot be directly compared. The standardized and unstandardized regression analogues are reported.

13. The results in Table 12-5 were initially estimated with an equation that included all possible recursive paths. In the vote equation, ideology had a small impact on the vote for the more sophisticated group, while foreign policy issues had a small effect for the less sophisticated group. However, neither personal qualities nor competence was significant, and thus affective reactions to the candidates fully capture perceptions of professional and personal qualities.

PART IV: CONGRESSIONAL AND STATE ELECTIONS

13. WHAT DETERMINES CONGRESSIONAL AND STATE-LEVEL VOTING?

When we compiled the second edition of this book, we described the controversy over the congressional vote as one over the relative importance of national versus local factors. This remains the dominant issue, but the emphasis as well as the details have changed considerably. First, there is now widespread agreement that local factors are important, surely more important than in earlier periods of our political history. Second, the disagreements now focus as much on *which* national factors or *which* local factors are important as on whether one or both types are significant.

Research about nonpresidential voting has also expanded in scope. One can now point to a reasonable body of literature analyzing elections to the U.S. Senate and to state legislatures as well as to a growing literature on gubernatorial elections. Each of these extensions has been stimulated by new, ongoing data collections. Finally, as in other areas of political science, there is greater concern with institutions. Here this interest manifests itself in a concern with possible reforms (such as term limitations) and with an effort to use our greater understanding of multilevel voting to explore the electoral foundations of divided government.

National Factors Influence House, Senate, and Even State Elections

Midterm elections in the United States are routinely marked by a decline in voting turnout and by losses of seats by the president's party in Congress. In 1960 Angus Campbell attributed this regularity to a "surge and decline" pattern of participation in presidential versus midterm elections. According to his version of surge and decline, presidential election years are high-stimulus events; they evoke considerable public interest, so that independents, who are relatively uninvolved in politics, turn out to vote. Swayed by current public opinion trends, these independents tend to favor one presidential candidate, producing a vote surge in that candidate's direction and a corresponding surge in support of that candidate's party for Congress. By contrast, congressional election years are low-stimulus events, so there is a decline in turnout. The voters who remain are a core group of partisans. As a result, the congressional vote more closely parallels the underlying partisan division of the electorate, with a loss of seats for the president's party. The surge and decline rhythm was thus claimed to account for the observed patterns of turnout and vote changes between presidential and midterm elections (compare Wolfinger, Rosenstone, and McIntosh, 1981, who find virtually no difference between presidential-year and midterm electorates).

In 1975 Tufte (see *Classics in Voting Behavior,* chap. 19) offered an alternative explanation of the same midterm elections—that they were a referendum on presidential popularity and the state of the economy. When public approval ratings for the president are low and when the economy is doing poorly, the president's party loses seats at the midterm elections.

While Campbell's and Tufte's explanations differ sharply in some respects, they share the fact that they in no way depend on the identity of the congressional candidates. Rather, they identify changes occurring exclusively at the national level as the crucial determinants of the congressional vote. Indeed, both concentrate more on presidential factors than on congressional factors in explaining the vote for Congress. In the wake of the landmark 1978 National Election Study, which revealed greater public awareness of congressional candidates than was previously thought (Mann and Wolfinger, 1980; in *Classics,* chap. 20), no one would assert that such models are complete explanations of subpresidential votes. But are these factors important at all, and if so, which ones are most important and how do they operate?

Perhaps the strongest proponent of the importance of national factors is James Campbell, who has developed a revised theory of surge and decline. The essence of James Campbell's theory—and the differences between the original and revised theories—are nicely captured by Figure 13-1. As Campbell (1987, p. 969) notes, in presidential election years "the original theory suggested a surge in turnout among independents [whereas] the revised theory hypothesizes that the vote choice of independents would be influenced." Independents "should be swayed by the short-term forces of the presidential election" and "should divide disproportionately in favor of the advantaged party." Conversely, the original theory suggested that short-term forces in presidential elections would alter the vote choice of partisans, whereas the revised theory hypothesizes that the turnout of partisans is affected. "There should be a surge of turnout among partisans of the advantaged party [the party winning the presidency] and a relative depression of turnout for cross-pressured partisans of the disadvantaged party."

In the most complete test of the revised theory, Campbell (1992) draws on the referendum theory as well and extends the analysis to other subpresidential elections. Thus, he includes surge and decline, presidential popularity, and economic conditions in studies of House, Senate and state legislative elections. The results lend strong support to the idea of national forces affecting all three types of elections, but they are especially interesting in the congressional case because of the well-known consistency of losses sustained by the president's party at midterms. For that reason, and because it incorporates evidence about the referendum theory as well, we reprint a portion of Campbell's test of congressional elections as Chapter 14.

Figure 13-1   A Comparison of the Original and Revised Theories
of Surge and Decline in Congressional Elections

		Voters	
		Independents	Partisans
Effects of Short-Term Presidential Election Forces	Turnout Effect	Original Theory	Revised Theory
	Vote Choice Effect	Revised Theory	Original Theory

Source: Campbell (1987, p. 969).

While evidence for the existence of *some* national forces is strong, there is considerable controversy about the precise nature of those forces. When Tufte published his work in the mid-1970s, evidence seemed incontrovertibly to support the significance of both presidential popularity and the midterm economy for congressional elections. With the addition of data from more recent elections, that conclusion is much less clear. For example, updating the Tufte series through 1986 reduces the apparent effect of presidential popularity to the point of statistical insignificance (Erikson, 1990, p. 380). On the other hand, in Campbell's formulation presidential popularity remains highly significant statistically (see Table 14-3), and in Jacobson's marginally so (1990a, p. 402), though one might argue about the meaningfulness of the one percentage point vote gain associated with a 10 percentage point increase in presidential approval (Erikson, 1988, p. 1020). Likewise, individual-level models have found conflicting evidence. Born (1986), for example, found that presidential popularity remained significant—though his measure of popularity was not the standard Gallup approval question—while Ragsdale (1980) found no such effect.

The most heated controversy about national effects, however, concerns the state of the economy. In a recent exchange, Erikson (1990) argues that this effect has also dwindled to the point of statistical insignificance, while Jacobson (1990a) vigorously defends its significance; Campbell, meanwhile, finds it has virtually no effect on the vote (see Table 14-3) and Marra and Ostrom (1989) found it has no *direct* effects. The argument about statistical significance is in part over how to use such tests.[1] Radcliff (1988) accounts for part of this puzzle by showing a decreasing importance of economic conditions in House elections (though they remain important in Senate elections). What is also important, as Erikson (1990, p. 406) points out, is that there is a growing consensus that the size of the effect is lower than the original Tufte estimate, resulting in lower explanatory power altogether for national factors.

The controversy over the effect of the economy is partly over how best to control for electoral history. Erikson (1990), for example, includes in his model the congressional vote in the prior presidential election, whereas Jacobson (1990a), following Tufte, defines the dependent variable as a deviation from one or more past elections. It turns out that this choice makes little substantive difference in the estimated effect of the economy.[2] Using the previous *presidential* vote, however, changes the result considerably (Campbell, 1992). Use of some sort of control is generally regarded as appropriate, but there is obviously considerable disagreement about just what that control should be and how it should be interpreted.

There is also disagreement about the appropriate time lag to use in modeling the effects of the economy. This is more than an esoteric point; it goes to the heart of an explanation of how the state of the economy affects congressional votes. Jacobson and Kernell (1983) argued that national-level factors could affect the congressional outcome even if they had no direct effect on individual voters' decisions. Their argument was that potential challengers would base their decisions on factors such as the economy, with high quality candidates tending to run only when conditions were favorable. For example, during a Republican presidency a well-known Democratic local politician might take on a Republican member of Congress if the economy is weak and the president is unpopular, while that same politician might decide to keep her present office and wait for a later election to run for Congress if the economy is strong and the president is very popular. They called their explanation the strategic politicians hypothesis.

One implication of the strategic politicians hypothesis is that presidential popularity and the state of the economy *at the time candidates are making their decisions about whether to run* should be good predictors of the election outcome. Thus, when the economy is strong a year and a half prior to a congressional election and then sours close to the election, the out-party might not make many gains because its best potential challengers decided to sit out the race. In fact, if politicians (plus the contributors and PACs, who provide them resources) respond to national-level factors more strongly than voters, measurements at the time candidates make their decisions should be better predictors than measurements close to the election itself. Born (1986, p. 602) and Marra and Ostrom (1989) tested this notion by using alternative specifications of the basic model; their results were not supportive of the strategic politicians hypothesis.[3] Jacobson (1989) argued for a slightly different time period (p. 779) and presented a new analysis, with quality of the challenger as the dependent variable. From this analysis, and more forcefully in an update through the 1988 elections (see Chapter 15), Jacobson notes that Democratic challengers seem to have responded more to national forces than have Republican challengers. While this partisan difference yields an impressive interpretation of the difficulties of Republican House candidates in the post-World War II period, it weakens support for the notion that candidates in general use national-level conditions as a way of making strategic decisions about whether or not to run.

There seems to be considerable agreement that the effects of national factors have declined in recent years, especially since the weakening of party ties in the

1960s (see Chapter 16). In the models reviewed here, Campbell (Tables 14-7 and 14-8) finds that surge and decline effects are smaller from the mid-1960s to the present than in the prior three decades, though he emphasizes (1992, chap. 9) that "wasted presidential coattails" (in uncontested congressional elections) are a partial explanation and that national factors are still quite evident. Similarly, Jacobson (Chapter 15) reports that the effect of presidential popularity was considerably weaker after 1966 and that the absence of strategic thinking on the part of Republican candidates is especially apparent in the more recent period. And Ansolabehere, Brady and Fiorina (1992, pp. 29-34) estimate that since the mid-1960s congressional incumbents have been only half as vulnerable to national party tides as incumbents in the 1950s.

Part of the reason for controversy about the influence of national factors lies in differences over the appropriate way to model them. We have already called attention to some differences across models, but there are others. For example, Oppenheimer, Stimson, and Waterman (1986) offered a highly intuitive "exposure" thesis to help explain congressional elections, especially the seat distribution as opposed to the vote outcome. They argued that the higher a party's seat total going into an election, the harder it was for that party to gain seats, or, conversely, the easier it was for the underexposed opposition to gain seats. Regression analyses, with the exposure variable alone or in conjunction with presidential popularity and economic performance, seem to support their argument (see also Marra and Ostrom, 1989). Yet Campbell (1992, chap. 4) argues that they should have tested their thesis on midterm elections alone, and he finds that the exposure variable is statistically insignificant when such a test is made.

Given the number of cases involved—only 23 midterm elections since 1900, for example, and only 12 since 1946, when presidential popularity scores became available—along with differences over how to operationalize the relevant variables[4] and disagreements about appropriate models, we do not expect an easy resolution of these controversies. Indeed, Erikson (1988) reflects this frustration when he argues that *none* of the national-level explanations are really supported by available data. However, his own explanation of midterm losses—that there is a "presidential penalty" with voters routinely trying to weaken the president at the midterm, possibly because their policy positions are between the Republican and Democratic positions—is strikingly atheoretical.[5]

Despite these difficulties, the arguments in support of national-level factors are sufficiently persuasive that they are now being incorporated into models of voting at levels other than the U.S. House. Abramowitz and Segal (1986), for example, found that both presidential popularity and economic conditions were significant in a model of Senate voting. As we already noted, Campbell (1992) extended his surge and decline model both to U.S. Senate and state legislative elections. In a similar fashion, Chubb (1988) reported that presidential coattails and the performance of the national economy affect state legislative races and that the national economy affects gubernatorial voting. Stein (1990) used 1982 CBS/*New York Times* exit polls to show that how voters assign responsibility for the economy in our federal system affects their voting: responsibility for the economy was primarily assigned to the president rather than to state governors, and the voters who blamed President Reagan for the economic downturn at that time penalized Republican Senate and gubernatorial candidates. Prediction models of subpresidential voting also rely successfully on national factors (for example, Lewis-Beck and Rice, 1992).[6]

What is most notable about the research about subpresidential voting reviewed in this section is that virtually all of it is at the aggregate level rather than at the level of the individual voter. These studies may try to incorporate what we know about mass voting behavior, but they analyze election outcomes and seat changes rather than votes and attitudes. There is, of course, a literature about the effects of respondents' economic well-being on their voting, as reviewed in our discussion of vote determinants generally in Chapter 9. Still, caution is appropriate in developing aggregate models that do not have individual level parallels.

As an example of the potential problems involved in matching aggregate models and individual data, let us take the new literature that is developing around the theme of "divided government." Since 1954, the United States has frequently had a Republican president facing a Democratic Congress. The only cases during this period of one-party control of both branches were those of Democratic ascendency in 1961-68 and again in 1977-80. Even when Presidents Reagan and Bush sat in the White House in the 1980s and early 1990s, the House of Representatives was Democratic (as was the Senate, except for 1981-86). This prevalence of divided government at the aggregate level has led to new explanations of voting for Congress. For example, Fiorina (1992, chap. 5) models this by assuming that voters whose policy preferences are between those of the two parties will vote for a Republican for president and a Democrat for Congress to moderate policies. Less formal claims are that voters like Republican presidents for foreign policy but Democratic Congresses for domestic policy. Jacobson's (1990b, chap. 6) variant is that voters want the low taxes and strong defense provided by Republican presidents while feeling that a Democratic Congress would better deliver programs that would benefit their districts. Each of these explanations posits a national factor in voting for Congress—that many individual voters vote Democratic for Congress because they prefer a divided government to single-party control. What is missing to date, however, is actual incorporation of these factors in an analysis of individual voting. People may have inconsistent preferences, but that does not prove that they consciously vote so as to achieve all of those preferences at once. In other words, divided government may have more to do with local factors in voting for Congress than national forces that motivate individual voters to try to have their cake and eat it too.

While we have doubts about the divided government argument, the other studies reviewed in this section represent a strong endorsement of the proposition that national factors influence congressional and state elections.[7] The exact mechanisms involved (for example, whether the state of the economy affects voters directly, indirectly through its influence on presidential approval ratings, or only through its effects on prospective candidates) are difficult to disentangle. But it is almost inconceivable that theoretically based, parsimonious equations could accurately predict so many elections over so long a period were there not considerable reality to the processes underlying the models outlined above.

"All Politics Is Local" [8]

Empirical work on congressional voting initially suggested that there was little value in studying individual districts; the elections were thought to have such low visibility that voter knowledge of candidates and issues was almost nonexistent. By the mid-1970s this view was seriously questioned, and as reports began to appear based on the 1978 National Election Study, the word was out that local factors were of considerable, even paramount, importance (see *Classics in Voting Behavior*, chap. 15).

Interest in local factors began, in part, in an effort to explain decreasing electoral competition faced by House incumbents—the so-called "vanishing marginals." Research focused first on incumbent characteristics, especially on their constituency service. By the mid-1980s, however, the emphasis shifted to the challengers, and "challenger quality" became a frequent research topic as well as the favored explanation for variations in district outcomes.

Before describing that work, it is important to take note of questions about the underlying premise—that the incumbency advantage has in fact increased or, alternatively, that the vanishing marginals were real. The most severe challenge was mounted by Jacobson (1987a), who argued that interelection swings have become more heterogeneous, so that candidates with relatively large vote margins were more likely to lose in the 1970s than in earlier years. A quick response to Jacobson's argument came from Bauer and Hibbing (1989). They argued that the decade of the 1970s was an aberration, especially in the face of the 1974 elections, in which a number of otherwise safe Republicans lost in the wake of the Watergate scandal; results of the first three elections of the 1980s differed little from those of the 1950s and 1960s. Moreover, most of the defeated congressmen from previously safe districts had been involved in scandals. Even so, the average number of formerly safe losers per election increased only from 2.4 and 3.0 in the 1950s and 1960s, respectively, to 7.6 in the 1970s, a change of only 4 or 5 of the 435 seats at stake. They concluded that there has been "no meaningful increase in the chances of big winners subsequently losing" (p. 262).

Bauer and Hibbing's numbers are convincing, but they do not undercut another of Jacobson's points: ignoring the margin of victory, incumbents were no more likely to win reelection in the 1970s (and the 1980s) than earlier.[9] Consequently, despite increasing vote margins, incumbent security has not increased. Has nothing, then, changed since the 1950s? Has there, in fact, been no increase in the incumbency effect?

The question is deceptively simple, but there now seem to be two good answers. A first answer is given by Gelman and King (1990), who developed a new method of estimating the incumbency advantage that eliminates a number of biases inherent in previous measures. Their estimate of incumbency advantage shows a sudden, sharp increase in the mid-1960s, thus confirming the conventional wisdom. A second answer, referred to by Bauer and Hibbing (p. 270) but perhaps most clearly stated in Ansolabehere et al. (1992), is that what the increased incumbency advantage means is that incumbents are now less vulnerable to party tides. In that particular sense, they are safer than before. But they are not safer overall, as Jacobson wisely points out. They still have to be concerned with reelection, but their fate is to a larger extent in their own hands. In other words, local factors, not national forces, are now the more powerful determinants of incumbent reelection rates.

What are these local factors? The most obvious are also the most idiosyncratic—scandals, "special conditions" (often health-related), or, on the positive side, visibility gained through sports, military involvement, or family connections. Almost by definition, these factors are difficult to work with. They can be hard to detect, at least with any degree of certainty. They are fairly infrequent. They are difficult to rate vis-à-vis one another or other factors. Not surprisingly, however, when incorporated into models of the vote, they have a considerable effect on the outcome (Peters and Welch, 1980). These factors influence voting at all levels of elections; Abramowitz's (1988) analysis provides examples involving both incumbents and challengers in Senate elections.

At a more systematic level, local factors might be divided into those that most affect incumbents and those that most affect challengers. In the early 1980s, more emphasis was placed on incumbents, and constituency service was identified as a prominent contributor to continued incumbent success (see *Classics in Voting Behavior*, chap. 15). Members who do more casework are more likely to be reelected, possibly because their reputations for constituent service discourage strong challengers from opposing them (though see below for an opposite argument). More recently, challenger quality has been the dominant interest, as reflected in work by Jacobson, reprinted here as Chapter 15. According to this argument, well-known, experienced challengers are likely to do better in congressional campaigns than political unknowns. Of course, the quality of the challenger is not determined exclusively by local conditions, but tests of the "strategic politicians" hypothesis based on national factors have met with mixed success (see above), and, in any case, candidate characteristics are obviously a district-specific variable. Therefore, challenger quality has been regarded as primarily a local factor.

Challenger quality has been measured in a variety of ways, typically with only passing attention to differences resulting from the conflicting measures. Quality measures are always based, at least in part, on whether or not an individual has held elective office. Most often the measure is simply whether or not the person has held such an office (for example, Ragsdale and Cook, 1987, p. 53; Born, 1986; Jacobson, Chapter 15, this volume). Sometimes, however, a distinction is made between those who have held no office, a "local" office, or a major office (for example, Abramowitz, 1988; Bond, Covington, and Fleisher, 1985), and occasionally a hierarchy of offices is defined (e.g., Squire, 1989). A major reason for adopting measures based on elective office is that other information on challengers is difficult to gather, especially if one studies elections over a long period of time. Yet this treats prominent elected officials as being no more qualified than holders of obscure local elective offices, and it treats candidates who are famous for other reasons (such as national heroes, actors, and children of well-known politicians) as being no more qualified than political unknowns. Certainly, other characteristics and abilities are related to quality, and some researchers have incorporated additional information into their measures (Squire, 1989; Krasno and Green, 1988). Even so, even the best measures of challenger quality miss much of the richness of the concept, which probably makes the effect of challenger quality seem weaker than it actually is.

However it is measured, research on challenger quality has centered around two themes—the conditions that lead to high quality challengers, and the effects of challenger quality on election outcomes. With respect to the former, the most powerful predictor of whether or not elected officials challenge congressional incumbents appears to be the recent electoral history of the district—operationalized variously as the vote margin in the previous election, the "normal vote" in the district, change in party control of the seat in the previous election, and past challenger resources (Bond, Covington, and Fleisher, 1985; Ragsdale and Cook, 1987; Krasno and Green, 1988; Jacobson, chap. 15). In Jacobson's model, for example, vote margin and change in party control, included in a single equation, are both significant for Republicans and Democrats alike, while national factors are much less consistently significant.

A variety of other predictors have also been considered. For example, Jacobson (Chapter 15) also finds the size of the challenger pool, as measured by the number of seats the challenger's party holds in the state legislature, to be significant (see also Krasno and Green, 1988, p. 931). Most interesting of these additional tests is the finding of Bond et al. (1985) and Ragsdale and Cook (1987) that incumbent advertising and constituency service have no effect on challenger quality. This suggests, of course, that not all local-level factors influence challenger quality. But these findings also relate to the abundance of earlier studies on casework, suggesting that casework may be important to the vote—for example, by making the incumbent more visible—but that it does not assist the incumbent in the most immediate way by discouraging high quality challengers.

Do high quality challengers attract more votes? Not surprisingly, most analyses show that they do (Jacobson and Kernell, 1983, p. 46; Ragsdale and Cook, 1987; Green and Krasno, 1988, 1990; Jacobson, 1990a; Chapter 15, this volume). Indeed, having previous political experience often contributes to the vote margin even in the presence of controls for challenger spending.[10] It is disconcerting that Born's (1986) individual-level analysis showed no impact whatsoever of challenger quality.[11] However, such a result is highly reminiscent of the differences between aggregate- and individual-level studies of economic voting (see *Classics*, chap. 15) and will perhaps be accounted for in future theoretical work.[12]

Just as surge and decline and referendum models of congressional voting are being extended to other subpresidential elections, researchers have asked about the impact of local factors in Senate and state elections. The findings were somewhat unexpected with respect to the Senate. It was conventional wisdom in the early 1980s that Senate challengers were prominent while House challengers were often invisible. This seemed to explain the higher rate of reelecting incumbents who run to keep their seats in the House (typically over 90 percent, see note 9) than in the Senate (much more variable, but often no more than 75 percent). As one author put it, the distinction between House and Senate elections is that "there are two candidates competing in the [Senate] contests" (Hinckley, 1980, p. 458). Recent work, however, has emphasized the variety of Senate races, calling attention to both idiosyncratic and systematic local variations.

The fundamental point of Westlye's (1991) work, for example, is that "not all Senate campaigns are highly visible, hard fought affairs" (p. 11); indeed, he finds that a fifth of Senate challengers between 1968 and 1984 had no political experience at all (p. 27). Squire (1992b), in turn, finds that high quality Senate challengers command more voter awareness and attract more votes. Variety is also the theme of Hibbing and Alford's (1990) study of large versus small states and of Stewart and Reynolds's (1990) analysis of the structure of television markets and Senate elections. We expect to know much more about the importance of these and other factors in Senate elections when the 1988-90-92 NES Senate election study is fully analyzed.

State legislative and gubernatorial studies have only begun truly systematic exploration, and, as is not surprising, they confirm that local factors play an important role in these elections. Much of the initial work on legislatures has been related to electoral competition, confirming, for example, that incumbent resources are related to the level of competition (Weber, Tucker, and Brace, 1991; Holbrook and Tidmarch, 1991). Because of their variety, the effects of electoral structures are also a major topic (for example, in Niemi, Jackman, and Winsky, 1991). It is readily apparent that one type of structural difference—use of single-member or multimember districts—plays a major role in the election of minority representatives (Grofman and Handley, 1991). For gubernatorial elections, Squire (1992a) uses much the same approach as in congressional studies and finds some evidence of the importance of challenger characteristics.[13]

Overall, the evidence is considerable that local factors play a major role in subpresidential elections, including not only lower-salience House and state legislative elections but relatively high visibility elections of U.S. senators and state governors.

Conclusion

Since the 1978 National Election Study altered the focus of congressional voting studies, the overriding theme of research on subpresidential voting has been the importance of local factors. Constituency variables, state-level features, incumbent characteristics, and challenger quality have all received attention. National factors have not been set aside, however, even when analyzing voting down to the level of the state legislature. Rather, researchers have come to realize that both levels are crucial to a complete understanding of subpresidential voting. With that realization have come more focused studies at each level, resulting in greater detail but also greater controversy about the precise mechanisms at work. Just how to model the influence of the economy or how to measure challenger quality are now more likely to be the issue than whether each belongs in the analysis.

Despite the continuing presence of controversies, explanations of subpresidential elections are now very different from the days when congressional elections were viewed as little more than low-information, partisan contests and other elections were viewed not at all. Few researchers would now deny the importance of both national and local factors. In addition, we now have a more differentiated picture of subpresidential elections. We are now equally aware that Senate elections are a mixture of high- and low-salience contests and that, on average, Senate races are of greater visibility than congressional or state legislative elections.

There remains controversy as to the reasons behind continued divided government and why the president's party invariably loses seats during midterm elections. At the same time, we are understanding better the consequences of these phenomena. Divided government is no longer viewed as an aberration. And continued Democratic party dominance in Congress is increasingly being explained as a result of these processes.[14]

One continued need is for more good studies of voting below the presidential level. The voting literature initially focused on the presidency, but most voting in the United States is for lower offices. It may be more difficult to conduct good research about state voting, especially at the individual level, but these elections often pose important theoretical matters that cannot be fully researched in the high-stimulus environment of a presidential election. Often these studies yield surprising results, as when Baum (1987) found that 70 percent of voters in each of two *nonpartisan* state judicial races voted for their party's candidate even though party was not on the ballot, or when Beck, Baum, Clausen, and Smith (1992) found that two-thirds of the voters in Ohio voted for different parties in choosing five officials in a state election. Contests like these can be used to show how voters make decisions in low-information contests, and this furthers our understanding of voting behavior more generally.

We concluded the congressional voting chapter (15) in *Classics in Voting Behavior* on a normative note, and we return to that point here. Finding that local factors were important, we argued, affirmed the meaningfulness of congressional elections. Above all, it rescued voters from the charge that they are so inattentive that they vote mechanically on the basis of partisanship and incumbency. In short, it makes a difference who the candidates are and what they do. Interestingly, recent work reiterates that point but emphasizes a contrary point as well. Writers now wonder aloud whether localism has gone too far, whether local factors are now so dominant that there is little collective responsibility. Individual responsiveness may remain, as representatives of all sorts pay increasing attention to the policy preferences and individualistic needs of their constituents, but alongside this there is a decreasing responsiveness to national moods. As one set of authors said of Congress, "individual responsiveness waxes, collective responsiveness wanes" (Ansolabehere, Brady, and Fiorina, 1992, p. 36). Of course, empirical studies of the sort we have reviewed cannot resolve the question of how much localism and how much national influence are ideal. What they have done is to provide a greater understanding of the need for both.

NOTES

1. Erikson uses a more conservative two-tailed test while Jacobson uses a one-tailed test. One could also argue that statistical tests are not especially appropriate since the data set includes the universe of results.

2. However, given the marginality of the claim of statistical significance for the economy variable, using a deviation from past votes saves a degree of freedom and helps Jacobson substantiate his claim for significance. The argument remains a theoretical one; using Erikson's results to justify formulating the dependent variable as a deviation from past votes (Jacobson, 1990a, p. 403) is questionable statistical procedure.

3. Krasno and Green (1988), using a very different approach, also found that challenger quality is not very responsive to national tides.

4. Jacobson (1989, p. 780), for example, introduces one variable to do "double duty," capturing the effects of both exposure and surge and decline. Similarly, Abramowitz and Segal (1986) use a simple exposure variable but identify it as "analogous" to surge and decline.

5. On the other hand, "penalty" or "balancing" theories are becoming more popular in an effort to explain divided government. Alesina and Rosenthal (1989), for example, develop such a model for midterm House and Senate elections.

6. As with studies of the House, there are mixed results. Squire (1992a; 1991, note 11), for example, finds little evidence to support the strategic politicians thesis in either Senate or gubernatorial voting.

7. Moreover, Wright (1990) finds that misreports of the vote choice due to the time elapsed between the election and NES interviews leads many studies to underestimate the significance of national factors.

8. The phrase is generally attributed to former House Speaker "Tip" O'Neill.

9. Since 1950, over 90 percent of incumbents seeking reelection have won except for 1958 (89.9%), 1964 (86.6%), 1966 (88.1%), and 1974 (87.7%). The number seeking reelection has, if anything, declined very slightly over that time. Figures for individual years are given in Stanley and Niemi (1992, p. 204).

10. When Jacobson (1992, pp. 134-35) included informational variables (candidate likes/dislikes) in a multivariable model of voter choice, the variable for incumbency had little impact, suggesting that the key point is voter knowledge, not incumbency or challenger quality per se.

11. Jacobson (1990a, note 1) severely criticizes Born's model, especially his inclusion of the vote margin in the previous election. One might grant Jacobson's concern over including this variable in an individual-level model, yet wonder why he lends no credence to Born's (note 13) contention that excluding it makes little difference.

12. There is, in addition, a narrower controversy over the role of candidate spending. Jacobson (for example, 1980) has long argued that incumbents gain little or nothing from their spending efforts and only spend large amounts in reaction to challenger expenditures. Green and Krasno (1988, pp. 898, 900) argue that the effect of incumbent spending "is much greater than originally estimated" and is "a significant determinant of the vote." In a long exchange (Jacobson, 1990c; Green and Krasno, 1990), they agree that challenger spending typically has a greater marginal effect on outcomes, though Green and Krasno (1990, p. 369) maintain that this difference is made up for by greater amounts of incumbent spending.

13. Interestingly, there is one type of local factor that seems to have a limited impact. Chubb (1988) found that state (as opposed to national) economic conditions had no effect on state legislative elections and only a limited impact on gubernatorial elections.

And contrary to popular wisdom, evidence suggests that governors suffer little from increasing taxes, despite some widely publicized cases to the contrary (Pomper, 1968, chap. 6; Winters, 1991).

14. For example, Erikson (1989b) views Democratic strength in Congress as a natural consequence of electing Republican presidents. After all, from what we know, large Republican gains in a midterm election would be unlikely under a Republican president. Thus, electing a Democratic president could actually result in weakening Democratic control of Congress. With tongue in cheek, Erikson then suggests that Democratic leaders purposely have run losing presidential campaigns so as to maintain their grip on Congress. As far as we can tell, interviews with Democratic leaders have not yet substantiated Erikson's claim.

FURTHER READINGS

Competition in Congressional and State Elections

Monica Bauer, and John R. Hibbing, "Which Incumbents Lose in House Elections: A Response to Jacobson's 'The Marginals Never Vanished,'" *American Journal of Political Science* (1989) 33:262-71. Jacobson's finding that big winners lose more frequently is an artifact of the 1970s.

Andrew Gelman, and Gary King, "Estimating Incumbency Advantage Without Bias," *American Journal of Political Science* (1990) 34:1142-64. An improved method of estimating incumbency advantage; reestimates incumbency advantage in the House since 1900.

James Garand, "Electoral Marginality in State Legislative Elections, 1968-86," *Legislative Studies Quarterly* (1991) 16:7-28. Incumbent vote proportions have increased; very high proportions of incumbents win.

Ronald E. Weber, Harvey J. Tucker, and Paul Brace, "Vanishing Marginals in State Legislative Elections," *Legislative Studies Quarterly* (1991) 16:29-47. Legislative resources, but not compensation or performance, help explain the decline in the numbers of marginal and contested seats.

Mark C. Westlye, *Senate Elections and Campaign Intensity* (Baltimore: Johns Hopkins University Press, 1991). Distinguishes between hard-fought and low-key Senate races and examines their differences in terms of news coverage, issue voting, and so forth.

Stephen Ansolabehere, David Brady, and Morris Fiorina, "The Vanishing Marginals and Electoral Responsiveness," *British Journal of Political Science* (1992) 22:21-38. Individual House incumbents remain responsive to constituents, but Congress as a whole is less responsive to public opinion.

Effects of the Economy, Presidential Approval, and Other National Factors

Raymond E. Wolfinger, Steven J. Rosenstone, and Richard A. McIntosh, "Presidential and Congressional Voters Compared," *American Politics Quarterly* (1981) 9:245-56. No major differences in presidential-election and midterm electorates.

John E. Chubb, "Institutions, the Economy, and the Dynamics of State Elections," *American Political Science Review* (1988) 82:133-54. The national economy, not the state economy, influences state legislative and gubernatorial elections.

Robert S. Erikson, "Economic Conditions and the Congressional Vote: A Review of the Macrolevel Evidence," *American Journal of Political Science* (1990) 34:373-99. The condition of the national economy does not significantly influence the congressional vote.

Gary C. Jacobson, "Does the Economy Matter in Midterm Elections?" *American Journal of Political Science* (1990) 34:400-04. Erikson's conclusion is premature; the economy has a modest influence on congressional elections.

Robert M. Stein, "Economic Voting for Governor and U.S. Senator: The Electoral Consequences of Federalism," *Journal of Politics* (1990) 52:29-53. Voters attribute responsibility for the economy to the President, and therefore do not hold senators or governors to blame for poor economic performance.

James E. Campbell, *The Presidential Pulse of Congressional Elections* (Lexington: University Press of Kentucky, 1992). Theory of and evidence for surge and decline in congressional, senate, and state legislative elections.

Effects of Candidate Policies

Jon R. Bond, Cary Covington, and Richard Fleisher, "Explaining Challenger Quality in Congressional Elections," *Journal of Politics* (1985) 47:510-29. National forces and incumbents' ideology affect the likelihood of facing high quality challengers in U.S. House elections; casework does not.

Gerald C. Wright, Jr., and Michael B. Berkman, "Candidates and Policy in United States Senate Elections," *American Political Science Review* (1986) 80:565-88. Candidates' policy positions have a strong impact on voter decisions in Senate elections.

Effects of Challenger Quality

Richard Born, "Strategic Politicians and Unresponsive Voters," *American Political Science Review* (1986) 80:599-612. Challenger quality has a weak influence on individual voters.

Jonathan S. Krasno, and Donald Philip Green, "Preempting Quality Challengers in House Elections," *Journal of Politics* (1988) 50:920-36. Apparent invincibility in the form of large past victories are the best deterrent against high quality challengers.

Peverill Squire. "Challenger Quality and Voting Behavior in Senate Elections," *Legislative Studies Quarterly* (1992b) 17: forthcoming. High quality Senate candidates are better known and better liked by voters and attract more votes.

Effects of Campaign Spending

Donald Philip Green, and Jonathan S. Krasno, "Salvation for the Spendthrift Incumbent: Reestimating the Effects of Campaign Spending in House

Elections," *American Journal of Political Science* (1988) 32:884-907. The marginal effect of incumbent spending is substantial.

Gary C. Jacobson, "The Effects of Campaign Spending in House Elections: New Evidence for Old Arguments," *American Journal of Political Science* (1990) 34:334-63. Challenger spending has a greater impact than incumbent spending. See also Green and Krasno (1990) rebuttal in the same issue.

Peverill Squire. "Preemptive Fundraising and Challenger Profile in Senate Elections," *Journal of Politics* (1991) 53:1150-64. Raising large sums of "early" money does not produce weak challengers.

14. SURGE AND DECLINE:
THE NATIONAL EVIDENCE

James E. Campbell

In presidential election years, congressional candidates of the party winning the presidency have an advantage over their opponents. Metaphorically, some of these congressional candidates ride their presidential candidate's coattails into office. Two years later at the midterm, however, presidential coattails are unavailable. As a result, the presidential party loses congressional votes and seats. In essence, midterm elections are, at least in part, repercussions from the previous presidential election.

The Revised Theory of Surge and Decline

The revised theory of surge and decline, building on Angus Campbell's original theory (Campbell, 1960), offers an explanation of how the temporary surge of support for the winning presidential party and its subsequent midterm decline play out in the behavior of citizens, in their decision of whether to vote, and in their choice of which candidate to support. The elements of the revised theory of surge and decline are set forth in Figure 14-1 for three segments of the potential electorate—independents, advantaged and disadvantaged partisans.

Sources of the Surge

In presidential election years, according to the theory, the short-term forces (reactions to candidates and issues) favoring the winning presidential party are translated into a surge of votes for that party in two ways. *Short-term forces manifest themselves in the vote choices of independents and in the turnout of partisans.*

Independents are the most open of all voters to campaign influence. Their perceptions of the campaign—its candidates, issues and events—are likely to be less biased than others, and these perceptions affect evaluations of the parties, evaluations that are nearly neutral at the campaign's outset. Given this, it is quite

Source: Adapted from James E. Campbell, *Congressional Elections: The Presidential Pulse* (Lexington: The University Press of Kentucky, 1993).

Figure 14-1 The Revised Surge and Decline Sequence

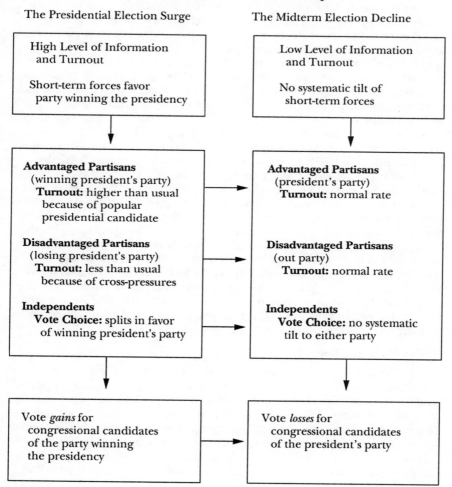

The Presidential Election Surge

High Level of Information
and Turnout

Short-term forces favor
party winning the presidency

Advantaged Partisans
(winning president's party)
Turnout: higher than usual
because of popular
presidential candidate

Disadvantaged Partisans
(losing president's party)
Turnout: less than usual
because of cross-pressures

Independents
Vote Choice: splits in favor
of winning president's party

Vote *gains* for
congressional candidates
of the party winning
the presidency

The Midterm Election Decline

Low Level of Information
and Turnout

No systematic tilt of
short-term forces

Advantaged Partisans
(president's party)
Turnout: normal rate

Disadvantaged Partisans
(out party)
Turnout: normal rate

Independents
Vote Choice: no systematic
tilt to either party

Vote *losses* for
congressional candidates
of the president's party

likely that for independents the campaign makes the difference between voting for Democrats or voting for Republicans. Since campaign influences systematically favor the party able to win the presidential race, independents cast a disproportionate share of their votes for the congressional candidates of the winning presidential party (even with the currently high rates of ticket-splitting).

Partisans contribute to presidential coattails or the presidential surge primarily through their turnout decisions. Within the general rise in turnout associated with a highly charged presidential election, there are systematic differences in the turnout of the two parties. Partisans of the advantaged party, the party winning the presidency, should turn out at *higher* than expected rates because of their enthusiasm for their party's popular standard-bearer. Those in the disadvantaged or losing party in presidential elections, on the other hand, may be expected to turn out at a *lower* than usual rate because of cross-pressures. A significant number of disadvantaged partisans feel cross-pressured, pulled one way because of loyalty to their party and in the opposite direction by short-term positive evaluations of the opposing party and its more popular presidential candidate. These voters face the unpleasant choice of reluctantly voting for their party's unpopular presidential candidate or reluctantly defecting from their party to vote for the opposition's candidate. Given this dilemma, many may simply decide not to vote.[1] The result is a partisan turnout gap. The winning presidential party wins, in part, because of an especially heavy turnout of its own partisans and a lighter than otherwise expected turnout among opposition partisans.

One important caveat about the contribution of partisan defections to the presidential election surge is in order. Partisan defections may also contribute and, on occasion, contribute significantly to the surge. Defections are likely to make the greatest difference in landslide presidential elections. Most partisans do not defect easily. Defection is an extreme response. Most partisans give their party the benefit of the doubt. A certain amount of displeasure with their party can be tolerated or even avoided by nonvoting, but all partisans have a breaking point beyond which they are provoked to defection. When it becomes obvious to most that a party has put forward the inferior offering—as voters themselves judge to be the case of a party on the short side of a landslide—a significant number of its partisans may be driven past the point of mere abstention to outright defection (see Boyd, 1969; DeVoursney, 1977).

Variations in the Decline

In the midterm, with short-term forces diminished and less systematically advantageous to it, support for the president's party and its congressional candidates declines. The extent of this decline depends in part on the extent of the prior surge of support for the party. The independent vote advantage and the partisan turnout advantage are greatest for the president's party in presidential elections in which short-term forces are most strongly in its favor, in landslides. It follows that the loss of both temporary advantages would be most deeply felt by the president's party in midterms following these strong surge presidential elections.

The strength of the prior presidential election surge, however, is not the only factor affecting the extent of the midterm decline for the president's party. Although the revised theory contends that national short-term forces are somewhat weaker and less systematic with respect to the president's party in midterm elections than in presidential elections, national short-term forces in midterm elections are by no means inconsequential. Midterm elections are also in part referenda on the performance of the president (Tufte, 1975, 1978; Campbell, 1985). A popular president can shorten his party's midterm fall and an unpopular president can lengthen it. The president's party may lose less of its independent vote advantage and its partisan turnout differential advantage if the president is very popular at the midterm. Favorable midterm short-term forces, presumably expressed in support for the president, may continue to attract independent votes, sustain enthusiasm among the president's partisans, encouraging them to turn out, and maintain cross-pressures among the opposition's partisans, discouraging them from turning out.

While the referenda aspect of the midterm affects the extent of midterm losses, even in the best of circumstances it does not turn potential losses into gains. A positive midterm referendum for the president's party means only that its losses are less than they would have been otherwise. The midterm referendum is unable to pull the president's party into the gain column because the effects of the midterm are circumscribed by the low stimulus character of the nonpresidential campaign. Whether the president is very popular or unpopular, he is not on the ballot and is not engaged in an aggressive campaign. Midterm elections lack not only the intensity of presidential campaigns but the *explicit* focal point of presidential campaigns. As such, though the midterm is undoubtedly in part a referendum on the president, it is a *muted* referendum.

Evidence from National Elections

Since the theory of surge and decline was originally proposed to explain national midterm losses of the president's party, an appropriate starting point in examining the revised theory is to determine how well it explains the pattern of national electoral change.[2]

There are three parts to this analysis of national evidence. The first examines national evidence of the midterm decline. How well does the revised theory explain variation in both midterm seat and vote losses for the president's party? The second part examines evidence of the presidential surge in the prior presidential election. According to the theory, an initial presidential-year surge sets up the subsequent midterm year decline. Evidence of the presidential surge is as important to the theory as evidence of the midterm decline. How well does the theory explain variation in partisan seat and vote changes in the prior presidential election years? The tracks of presidential election short-term forces, factors generally benefitting the winning presidential party, ought to be evident in the congressional election results of the prior presidential election year. The third part examines how both presidential surge and midterm decline effects have changed over time. Have surge and decline effects weakened? Do they still exist in contemporary elections or are they only a matter of electoral history?

The theory of surge and decline, in both its original and revised forms, claims to explain the consistency as well as the variation in presidential midterm losses. Before proceeding to analyze variation in midterm losses, we ought to make note of the obvious common thread running through all midterm seat and vote losses by the president's party—they happen to the president's party, the party that won the presidency in the prior election. The president's party may or may not be popular at the midterm and it may or may not have a healthy economy after two years in office, but it has always won the prior presidential election. This pattern of presidential victories followed quite consistently by congressional midterm losses (29 of 30 midterms from 1868 to 1990) does not necessarily indicate the validity of surge and decline. However, it lends some additional credibility. We now turn to the national level evidence of partisan seat and vote change in midterms. How well does "surge and decline" stand up to the evidence?

Explaining Midterm Losses

According to surge and decline, midterm seat and vote losses should be proportional to the short-term forces favoring the president's party in the prior presidential election. In normal times (without a critical realignment), the direction and force of short-term forces can be measured as the presidential vote. Examining even crude evidence of midterm decline effects, one can observe that midterm seat losses are, as expected, substantially greater following presidential landslides (Campbell, 1993, chap. 3). The following analysis examines evidence of *both* midterm seat and vote losses in greater depth, with greater precision and statistical reliability.

Before proceeding to the data, we should note that surge and decline in its revised form claims that while midterm losses are largely a function of the prior presidential surge, they are not solely a function of that surge. They are also affected by the public's evaluations of the in-party at the midterm itself (Tufte, 1975). Midterms are in part referenda on the president's performance and his party's performance. While the analysis will take this referenda adjustment to the midterm decline into account, the analysis begins by examining only the midterm repercussions of the presidential election surge. This initially more restricted analysis permits an examination of a longer series of elections, since Gallup poll approval ratings of the president measuring the public's midterm evaluations have only been available since 1946.

The Basic Association.   The analysis begins by examining the fundamental association between the short-term forces of the presidential election, as captured by the presidential vote, and the change in the number of seats won by each party after the midterm election. Figure 14-2 displays midterm Democratic *seat* gains or losses plotted against the Democratic share of the two-party presidential vote in the prior presidential election for the 23 midterms between 1900 and 1990. The number of seats held by the Democrats at each election are calculated from the series in Ornstein, Mann and Malbin (1990). For the sake of comparability, the number of seats won or lost in the early elections of this century are adjusted to reflect a House size of 435 members. The number of congressional seats grew until 1912 and has since been set at 435. Seats held by third parties (primarily in elections early in the series) are equally divided between the two major parties, again for purposes of comparison.

As is apparent from the figure, a party's midterm fate is cast by how well it did in the prior presidential election. The plot indicates a strong negative association between a party's presidential vote and the change in its share of seats and votes in the subsequent midterm, much as anticipated by both the original and revised theory of surge and decline. A companion analysis of midterm

Figure 14-2   Midterm Congressional Seat Change and the Prior
Presidential Vote, 1902-1990

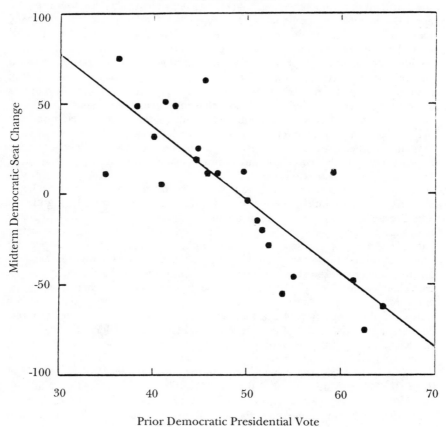

Prior Democratic Presidential Vote

congressional vote change produces essentially the same negative and expected
plot (Campbell, 1993, chap. 6).

Regression Analyses.   Regression analysis offers a more rigorous assessment of the basic proposition of a negative association between the prior
presidential vote and the following midterm loss of congressional votes and seats.
There are two dependent variables. The first is the midterm change in the
number of seats (adjusted to a constant House size of 435) held by Democrats.
The second is the midterm change in the Democratic party's share of the
congressional vote. Different regression analyses are performed on both of these
dependent variables to ensure the reliability of the findings. In both the seat
change and vote change regressions, the independent variable of principal interest

is the Democratic presidential vote, a measure of the general direction and magnitude of short-term forces in the prior presidential election year.[3]

For both the seat change and vote change dependent variables, four separate regression analyses are conducted. The two sets of regressions, one with vote change as the dependent variable and one with seat change, are identical in all ways. The differences among these regressions are intended to take into account the idiosyncratic aspects of several of the elections and changes in electoral volatility or stability over time. The first regression of both sets examines all midterm elections from 1902 to 1990 (n = 23). This regression involves only a single independent variable, the prior Democratic presidential vote.

The second regression is conducted on the same series of elections but includes a dummy variable for the New Deal realignment midterm of 1934 (1 in 1934 and 0 otherwise), a midterm that there is good reason to believe was quite atypical. This variable should, in an admittedly rough way, control for the jolt of the critical New Deal realignment.[4]

The third regression *excludes* four pairs of presidential and midterm elections in which nonmajor party presidential candidates received a significant vote. Presumably, a party's share of the two-party presidential vote would not as accurately reflect the tilt of short-term forces when there is a large third-party vote. The two-party presidential vote implicitly assumes that the popular sentiment behind third-party votes is proportionate to the vote division between the two major-party candidates. However, in some cases, this may be an erroneous assumption. The error would be especially severe when most of the third-party vote would have gone to the losing major-party presidential candidate and when the proportion of the total vote going to the minor parties is large. Given this potential source of error, presidential elections in which the Democrats and Republicans jointly received less than 93 percent of the total presidential vote were excluded from the third regression. Excluded are 1912-14 because of Theodore Roosevelt's second place finish in the popular vote; 1924-26 because of Robert LaFollette's 17 percent of the vote; 1968-70 because of George Wallace's 14 percent; and 1980-82 largely because of John Anderson's 6.6 percent of the vote. After excluding these potentially confounding cases, the third regression with the single independent variable of the Democratic presidential vote is estimated on the remaining nineteen elections. The fourth regression examines these same major-party elections, but includes the New Deal dummy variable along with the Democratic presidential vote. The regression results for the seat change and vote change analyses are presented in Tables 14-1 and 14-2, respectively.[5]

Both sets of national seat change and vote change regressions strongly support surge and decline claims about midterm losses. All estimates of the midterm repercussions of the presidential vote consistently lead to the same conclusion: *a party's congressional midterm losses are proportional to its presidential vote in the previous presidential election.* The estimated effects of the presidential vote on the extent of midterm seat and vote losses remain strong under a variety of specifications and over the different series of examined elections. Whether or not all elections are included in the analysis and whether or

Table 14-1 The Presidential Vote's Effect on Midterm Change in the Democratic Congressional Vote, 1902-1990

	Dependent Variable: Change in the Democratic Congressional Vote from the Presidential to the Midterm Election			
	All Midterm Elections Included		*Third-Party Elections Excluded*	
Independent Variables	*(1)*	*(2)*	*(3)*	*(4)*
Prior Democratic presidential vote	−.45	−.49	−.54	−.60
	(6.77)	(7.39)	(8.83)	(12.69)
New Deal	—	4.94	—	6.34
		(1.86)		(3.96)
Constant	21.73	23.19	25.66	28.37
Number of cases	23	23	19	19
R^2	.69	.73	.82	.91
Adjusted R^2	.67	.71	.81	.90
Standard error	2.63	2.49	2.00	1.47
Mean absolute error	1.98	1.75	1.51	1.17

Note: t-ratios are in parentheses. The Democratic presidential and congressional votes are the Democratic share of the two-party vote. The New Deal variable is a dummy taking on a value of 1 for 1934 and zero otherwise. The significant third-party elections excluded from regressions 3 and 4 are 1912, 1924, 1968, and 1980.

not the New Deal realignment jolt is taken into account, a two percentage point gain in a party's presidential vote is associated with about a one percentage point loss in its midterm congressional vote (b = −.45 to −.60). In terms of seats, a one percentage point increase in the presidential vote sets the party up to sustain a loss of four to five seats in the next midterm (b = −4.06 to −5.31). In all eight regressions over the century, the coefficients are at least five times their standard errors (easily surpassing conventional significance levels) and, moreover, each regression estimated accounts for no less than two-thirds of the variance in the Democratic party's midterm change in votes or seats.

The Referenda Component. The revised theory of surge and decline argues that midterm changes are *not entirely* repercussions of the presidential surge but are a result of the withdrawal of the strong and positive short-term forces of the prior presidential election year and the public's midterm judgment of the administration's performance. Much goes on in the midterm election itself that undoubtedly has national partisan ramifications. Sometimes the midterm

Table 14-2 The Presidential Vote's Effect on Midterm Change in
Democratic House Seats, 1902-1990

	Dependent Variable: Change in the Democratic Congressional Seats from the Presidential to the Midterm Election			
	All Midterm Elections Included		*Third-Party Elections Excluded*	
Independent Variables	*(1)*	*(2)*	*(3)*	*(4)*
Prior Democratic presidential vote	−4.06 (6.58)	−4.48 (7.86)	−4.63 (6.45)	−5.31 (8.81)
New Deal	—	59.72 (2.61)	—	68.35 (3.35)
Constant	199.03	216.65	227.85	257.03
Number of cases	23	23	19	19
R^2	.67	.76	.71	.83
Adjusted R^2	.66	.73	.69	.81
Standard error	24.27	21.48	23.68	18.72
Mean absolute error	17.02	14.57	16.41	11.94

Note: t-ratios are in parentheses. The Democratic presidential vote is the Democratic share of the two-party vote. The number of seats has been adjusted to a constant House size of 435 seats. Seats held by third parties have been divided equally between the two major parties for comparability across years. The New Deal variable is a dummy taking on a value of 1 for 1934 and zero otherwise. The significant third-party elections excluded from regressions 3 and 4 are 1912, 1924, 1968, and 1980.

climate hurts the president's party. For instance, it is hard to imagine that the Watergate scandal, President Nixon's resignation and subsequent pardon by President Ford within three months of the 1974 midterm, failed to hurt Republican congressional candidates. In a more mundane "crisis," it is a good bet that Democrats in 1946 were hurt by the public's displeasure with meat shortages caused by post-war price controls. *Newsweek* (October 21, 1946, p. 31) reported that President Truman attempted to diffuse the issue by decontrolling meat prices just three weeks before the election, but the damage had already been done. In other midterms, the political climate is favorable to the president's party. For instance, it is difficult to believe that Democrats in 1962 were not helped greatly in November's election by President Kennedy's handling of October's Cuban missile crisis. While each midterm does not have an issue of this intensity associated with it, the prevailing political climate of any midterm adds to or subtracts from the losses the president's party are positioned to sustain by the prior presidential election.

The fully specified midterm equation, incorporating the midterm referenda perspective into the analysis, includes three independent variables: the prior presidential vote, the public's approval rating of the president, and the annual change in real disposable income. The analysis of this full midterm equation is conducted on the twelve midterms from 1946 to 1990 since the midterm approval ratings or presidential popularity measure, obtained from Gallup surveys, is only available since 1946. The variables in this portion of the analysis are oriented in terms of the presidential party rather than in terms of Democrats and Republicans in order to simplify the interpretation of the two variables measuring the referenda evaluations of the in-party. The full midterm equation is estimated for both the midterm congressional vote and seat change. Since significant negative autocorrelation was found in the initial OLS regressions, a companion regression was estimated after taking first differences of all variables with their lagged values.[6] The regression estimates are presented in Table 14-3.

Several aspects of these results deserve note. First, consistent with the findings above and the expectations of the revised theory, the presidential vote has the expected significant and negative effect on both midterm vote and seat changes after controlling for possible referenda effects. Every percentage point added to the presidential vote margin sets the stage for nearly two-tenths of a percentage point drop in the party's midterm congressional vote and a loss of about two seats.[7]

Second, consistent with both the midterm referenda research (Tufte, 1978) as well as the revised theory of surge and decline, presidential popularity has a significant positive effect on both midterm vote and seat changes for the president's party. Presidents popular at the midterm are able to cut their party's losses. A one percentage point increase in approval ratings cut congressional vote losses by about one-tenth of a percentage point and saved one seat from being lost.

The third finding from Table 14-3 was not expected. Although the estimated effects of economic growth on midterm vote and seat changes were positive, as expected, in neither case were they statistically significant (see Erikson, 1990; Jacobson, 1990a), though they approached significance in the first difference equations.[8] This does *not* mean that economics are irrelevant to midterm changes. There is substantial research to indicate that economic change matters. However, there is reason to believe that it matters somewhat less than some have supposed; that its effects occur earlier in the process and these effects are more indirect in nature (Campbell, 1993, chap. 4). There is a good deal of other research to show that the health of the economy may influence midterm change by affecting presidential approval ratings and that this effect has some significant lag associated with it (Campbell, 1985, p. 1148; Norpoth and Yantek, 1983; Jacobson and Kernell, 1981; Monroe, 1979). Presidents get credit for prosperity and take the blame for recession but the public is not so attentive as to grant credit or place blame immediately.

Two cases illustrate the point: 1946 and 1982. In both cases the economy went into recession before the midterm. These recessions were translated into political terms. The public assigned blame for the economic downturns to the incumbent administrations. Truman's approval rating among the public sank to a

Table 14-3   The Presidential Vote and Midterm Referenda Effects on
Midterm Change in Congressional Votes and Seats for the
President's Party, 1946-1990

| Independent Variables | Dependent Variable | | | |
| | Vote Change | | Seat Change | |
	OLS	First Differences	OLS	First Differences
Prior presidential vote	−.21	−.21	−2.26	−2.47
	(2.02)	(4.93)	(2.42)	(5.71)
Midterm presidential popularity	.11	.10	1.11	1.15
	(2.79)	(4.17)	(3.15)	(4.77)
Midterm economic change	.06	.11	1.23	1.20
	(.35)	(1.67)	(.88)	(1.74)
Constant	2.04	.30	37.58	1.25
Number of cases	12	11	12	11
R^2	.63	.91	.71	.93
Adjusted R^2	.48	.88	.61	.90
Standard error	1.36	.94	11.99	9.69
Mean absolute error	.86	.56	7.60	5.51

Note: t-ratios are in parentheses. First difference estimates are based on taking the difference of each variable's value with its lagged value and using these differences in place of the simple variables.

mere 32 percent and Reagan's rating dropped to just 42 percent. With the leaders of the parties in disrepute, owing in no small part to the state of the economy, both parties suffered substantially greater midterm losses.

While it is now clear that midterm losses are a product of *both* the withdrawal of the prior presidential surge and the public's midterm referenda appraisal of the administration's performance, which matters more? This is not as easy a question to answer as it might seem. On the one hand, the effect of a one percentage point change in the prior presidential vote is two to three times as great as the effect of a one percentage point change in midterm presidential approval ratings. On the other hand, presidential approval ratings are more than twice as variable as the presidential vote margin. That is, a two percentage point change in presidential approval ratings is about as likely as a one percentage point change in the winning presidential vote margin.

While it might be tempting to conclude simply that the two effects are of approximately equal strength, we should remember that in orienting the analysis in terms of the president's party the variance of the presidential vote has been artificially restricted. Unlike either major party's popular vote, the presidential vote of the winning presidential party effectively has a lower bound of 50 percent. This restricted variation is reflected in the standard deviations of the two votes. While a standard deviation of the presidential vote of the winning party in this period was 4.1 percentage points of the vote, the standard deviation of the Democratic and Republican presidential votes was 6.4 percentage points. Moreover, this restricted variance attenuates the estimated effect of the presiden-·tial vote. This attenuation is evident in estimating the simple bivariate equations in Tables 14-1 and 14-2 both ways, orienting variables in terms of the Democratic and Republican parties and in terms of the winning and losing presidential parties. Both sets of regressions were estimated over the same set of post-war elections (1946-90). The estimated effects of the winning presidential candidates' vote were substantially greater ($-.60$ versus $-.23$ in the vote change equations and -4.57 versus -2.51 in the seat change equations) when variables were oriented in terms of the Democratic and Republican parties rather than the winning and losing presidential parties.

If we proceed on the premise that the earlier estimates of presidential vote effect (oriented by Democratic and Republican parties) are more appropriate (in displaying the true variation in the presidential vote) as well as more accurate (unattenuated compared to the later estimates), the presidential vote would appear to be more influential in midterm seat and vote changes than the midterm referendum. The presidential year short-term forces, measured by the presidential vote, not only account for a party being in the midterm win or loss column, but greatly affect the size of the gains or losses. Dividing the question of midterm change into its two components, the consistency and variability of presidential party losses, it now seems clear that the president's party consistently loses in the midterm because of the prior presidential surge; its losses vary a good deal because the public's midterm judgments vary, but also, at least as importantly, because the magnitude of the prior presidential surge varies.

Finding Prior Presidential Gains

Given the above findings of midterm decline effects, we ought to find the mirror-image surge effects in the previous presidential election years. Both versions of surge and decline contend that congressional elections in on-years are affected by presidential coattails or, at least, short-term causes that affect both presidential and congressional elections. As an examination of seat changes in landslide and non-landslide presidential election years suggests (Campbell, 1993, chap. 3), presidential coattails, or something like them, exist. The winning president's party is more likely to gain seats and gain more seats in landslide elections.

The Basic Association. Democratic seat changes in presidential election years are plotted against the Democratic share of the two-party presidential vote in Figure 14-3. The generally positive association between a party's presidential vote and the change in its congressional fortunes is clearly suggested by the plot

Figure 14-3 Congressional Seat Change and the Presidential Vote, 1900-1988

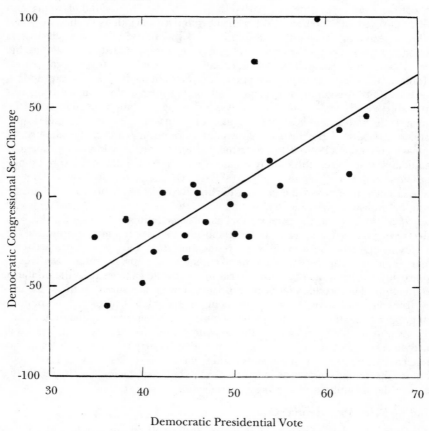

and appears as well in a companion analysis of on-year congressional vote gains (Campbell, 1993, chap. 6). A more precise reading of this relationship is offered by regression analysis.

Regression Analyses. As in the examination of midterm losses, the analysis of presidential election years considers four different regressions for both seat and vote changes. Two equations examine all elections in this century. Two equations exclude from this series those four elections in which there was a substantial third-party presidential vote. Like the midterm analysis, two of the equations also control for the relatively abrupt change in the partisan base caused by the New Deal realignment.

There is one difference in the presidential year equations other than the expectation of a positive effect of the presidential vote. That difference is the inclusion of the party's initial vote or seat share going into the presidential election, its percentage of the congressional vote or number of House seats held after the prior midterm election. The rationale for the inclusion of a party's initial holdings is that it is more difficult to gain votes or seats when a party already holds a large proportion of them. A party cannot gain what it already has. At the extreme, it is impossible for a party having previously won all votes and seats to do any better. Conversely, at the other extreme, it is impossible for a party without votes or seats to lose. Between these extremes, a party holding a large majority of votes and seats would do well just to hold that majority. It might do well and still lose votes and seats if it just isn't quite as popular as it had been. A party with a minority of votes and seats doing just as well in its next election ought to expect to register gains. Given this logic, a party's initial vote and seat holdings ought to be *negatively* associated with vote and seat changes. This initial holding variable will be included in three of the regressions.[9]

Tables 14-4 and 14-5 present the presidential year regression results for congressional vote change and seat change. The single most important finding here is that, regardless of the election series considered or the additional variables included in the analyses, *in presidential election years a party gains both seats and votes in proportion to its presidential vote.* The results are strong, consistent, statistically significant and support the theory of surge and decline. For every additional percentage point of the presidential vote, the party can expect typically to gain approximately two-fifths of a percentage point in the national congressional vote and better than three House seats. There are essentially no differences among estimates of the presidential vote coefficients in the vote change analysis and only very slight differences in the seat change analysis, a range of just one-quarter of a seat (b = 3.16 to 3.43). Moreover, the equations fit the data quite well, accounting for between about one-half and three-fourths of the variation in on-year seat and vote changes. The coefficients are nearly four to more than six times their standard errors and easily surpass conventional standards of statistical significance.

While not integral to the surge and decline proposition, the two "control" variables, the New Deal realignment variable and the prior congressional holdings variable, had their expected effects. As a result of the New Deal realignment, Democrats won an additional 5 percentage points of the congressional vote and about 61 or 62 more seats. Also, as expected, a party's initial seat and vote holdings reduced any expected gains it might have made. For every additional percentage point of the congressional vote it had won before the presidential year election, its expected vote gains were reduced by about a third of a percentage point. Initial seat holdings also limited seat gains. Every four additional seats held prior to the election reduced potential seat gains by one seat. While the inclusion of these "control" variables did not, as noted above, clarify or significantly alter estimates of the surge effects, they did contribute to more completely accounting for variation in both seat and vote changes.

Table 14-4   The Presidential Vote's Effect on Presidential Year Change in the Democratic Congressional Vote, 1900-1988

	Dependent Variable: Change in the Democratic Congressional Vote from the Prior Midterm to the Presidential Election			
	All Presidential Elections Included		Third-Party Elections Excluded	
Independent Variables	(1)	(2)	(3)	(4)
Democratic presidential vote	.40	.40	.41	.39
	(5.61)	(6.70)	(4.40)	(4.86)
New Deal	—	5.15	—	5.15
		(2.13)		(1.85)
Prior Democratic congressional vote	—	−.31	—	−.30
		(2.71)		(2.30)
Constant	−19.16	−3.58	−19.47	−3.38
Number of cases	23	23	19	19
R^2	.60	.79	.53	.75
Adjusted R^2	.58	.76	.51	.70
Standard error	2.82	2.15	3.09	2.40
Mean absolute error	2.17	1.43	2.45	1.64

Note: t-ratios are in parentheses. The Democratic presidential and congressional votes are the Democratic share of the two-party vote. The New Deal variable is a dummy taking on a value of 1 for 1932 and zero otherwise. The significant third-party elections excluded from regressions 3 and 4 are 1912, 1924, 1968, and 1980. The prior Democratic congressional vote is the party's share of the vote in the previous midterm.

Surge and Decline Over Time

While the above analysis indicates that national electoral change in both presidential and midterm elections in the twentieth century has been generally consistent with the theories of surge and decline, the question remains as to whether surge and decline structures electoral change in recent elections as it has in the past. Is the process of surge and decline a relic of the past, when parties were parties and their congressmen hung on to their presidential candidate's coattails for dear life? Have local or district factors such as incumbency, campaign spending by the candidates and the relative appeal of congressional candidates come to dominate congressional races to such an extent that presidential coattails are no longer relevant?

To assess the possible change in surge and decline effects, the presidential and midterm change equations were reestimated on three subsets of presidential

Table 14-5 The Presidential Vote's Effect on Presidential Year Change in Democratic House Seats, 1900-1988

	Dependent Variable: Change in the Democratic Congressional Seats from the Prior Midterm to the Presidential Election			
	All Presidential Elections Included		Third-Party Elections Excluded	
Independent variables	(1)	(2)	(3)	(4)
Democratic presidential vote	3.16 (4.71)	3.18 (4.98)	3.43 (4.01)	3.30 (3.81)
New Deal	—	61.73 (2.62)	—	60.97 (2.28)
Prior Democratic House seats	—	−.24 (1.74)	—	−.22 (1.36)
Constant	−152.82	−98.23	−164.81	−109.10
Number of cases	23	23	19	19
R^2	.51	.72	.49	.69
Adjusted R^2	.49	.67	.46	.63
Standard error	26.38	21.13	28.20	23.22
Mean absolute error	19.51	14.71	21.04	16.22

Note: t-ratios are in parentheses. The Democratic presidential vote is the Democratic share of the two-party vote. The number of seats has adjusted to a constant House size of 435 seats. Seats held by third parties have been divided equally between the two major parties for comparability across years. The New Deal variable is a dummy taking on a value of 1 for 1932 and zero otherwise. Significant third-party elections excluded from regressions 3 and 4 are 1912, 1924, 1968, and 1980. The number of prior Democratic seats are from the previous midterm election.

and midterm elections. These are (1) the first eight pairs of presidential and midterm elections in this century up to the New Deal realignment (1900-30), (2) the seven pairs of elections following the New Deal realignment (1936-62) and (3) the most recent seven pairs of elections (1964-90). These regressions will help us determine how surge and decline effects may have changed over time.

Table 14-6 presents the midterm decline equations for the three subsets of elections. As in the first general equations of Tables 14-1 and 14-2, the prior Democratic presidential vote is used to explain midterm congressional vote and seat change. There are three important findings: (1) The most notable finding is that the prior presidential vote has the expected significant negative effects in each series. In each series, including the most recent, the prior presidential vote coefficient is at least three times its standard error. (2) While significant and strong in each era, midterm decline effects are somewhat smaller in recent years

Table 14-6   Trend in the Presidential Vote's Effect on Midterm Change in Democratic House Votes and Seats, 1902-1990

	Dependent Variables: Change in the Democratic Congressional Votes or Seats from the Presidential to the Midterm Election					
	1902-1930		1938-1962		1966-1990	
Independent variables	*Votes*	*Seats*	*Votes*	*Seats*	*Votes*	*Seats*
Prior Democratic	−.39	−3.77	−.67	−6.25	−.50	−3.59
presidential vote	(3.20)	(3.20)	(6.73)	(7.99)	(3.85)	(4.62)
Constant	18.48	189.82	31.80	301.67	24.63	175.18
Number of cases	8	8	7	7	7	7
R^2	.63	.63	.90	.93	.75	.81
Adjusted R^2	.57	.57	.88	.91	.70	.77
Standard error	3.09	29.91	1.64	12.94	2.42	14.53
Mean absolute error	1.96	20.55	1.14	9.16	1.75	10.20

than they were in mid-century. They declined by 25 percent in the case of vote change and 43 percent in the case of seat change. (3) Although midterm decline effects are weaker now than they were from the late thirties through the early sixties, they are not appreciably weaker than they were in the elections earlier in this century. Midterm effects on seat changes were slightly stronger in the earlier period but midterm effects on vote changes were actually weaker in early elections. While recent midterm decline effects may compare favorably with effects early in the century because of complications from third-party elections, the comparison suggests that, though diminished, midterm decline effects remain potent by historical standards.

The analysis of surge effects in presidential election years in the three subsets of elections generally reinforces the above findings. These regressions are presented in Table 14-7. Like midterm decline effects, presidential surge effects are significant and positive in all three eras, including the most recent elections. Also, as in the case of the midterm decline, presidential surge effects, though significant, are generally somewhat weaker now than in the past (see also Campbell, 1991, 1992). There is very little difference in the effects of the presidential surge on vote change, but its effects on seat change were just more than half its previous magnitude.

The apparent weakening of surge and decline effects may reflect, in part, trends in voting behavior. Partisan dealignment may have weakened coattails (accounting for the drop in the presidential vote coefficients) and increased incumbency advantages may account for the reduced vote and seat changes (accounting for the increased effects of the initial vote and seat holdings). It is also

Table 14-7   Trend in the Presidential Vote's Effect on Presidential Year Change in Democratic House Votes and Seats, 1900-1988

	Dependent Variable: Change in the Democratic Congressional Vote or Seats from the Prior Midterm to the Presidential Election					
	1900-1928		*1936-1960*		*1964-1988*	
Independent variables	*Votes*	*Seats*	*Votes*	*Seats*	*Votes*	*Seats*
Democratic presidential vote	.55 (5.69)	3.48 (2.58)	.31 (4.00)	4.19 (3.15)	.29 (3.61)	2.34 (3.21)
Prior Democratic congressional vote or seats	−.83 (2.84)	−.32 (.58)	−.67 (5.23)	−.72 (3.60)	−.31 (1.20)	−.39 (1.05)
Constant	13.06	−108.02	20.47	−26.12	2.41	−11.52
Number of Cases	8	8	7	7	7	7
R^2	.87	.72	.90	.79	.81	.74
Adjusted R^2	.82	.60	.85	.68	.72	.61
Standard error	1.92	20.61	1.26	18.31	1.44	13.59
Mean absolute error	1.09	14.09	.83	12.75	.92	9.07

likely that some portion of this apparent weakening of presidential coattails may be unrelated to voting behavior. Presidential coattails in several recent elections have been "wasted" by the absence of congressional candidates to ride them. In elections since the late 1960s, favorable Republican short-term forces in many southern congressional districts have not helped Republican congressional candidates because there were no Republican candidates in these districts, Democratic congressional candidates ran unchallenged (Campbell, 1992, 1993).

While there is no doubt that surge and decline effects are weaker than they once were, one point should be emphasized: *presidential surge and decline effects on congressional elections remain substantial.* Even in recent years, a party's success in presidential elections helps it win more congressional votes and seats. As in the past, these are short-lived gains. As in the past, a party should reasonably expect to lose congressional votes and seats in proportion to how well its presidential candidate performed in the previous election. There is a presidential pulse to congressional elections.

NOTES

1. This abstention effect of cross-pressures has been well documented. It was observed in the earliest voting studies (Lazarsfeld, Berelson, and Gaudet, 1944, p. 64) and is also

evidenced in more recent work, including Zipp (1985), Brown (1991, p. 153), and Campbell (1987).

2. Note that the original and revised theories of surge and decline lead to identical hypotheses regarding national aggregate congressional vote and seat change, though the revised theory explicitly acknowledges an additional referenda component to midterm change. The differences between the original and revised theories emerge most clearly at the micro-level (see Campbell, 1993, chap. 8; 1987).

3. A parallel analysis with dependent and independent variables oriented in terms of the presidential party rather than the Democratic party was also conducted. The analysis generally supports the main analysis reported below, though the results were somewhat weaker because orienting variables in terms of the presidential party restricts or truncates variance in both dependent and independent variables. When oriented in terms of the presidential party, the lower bound of the prior presidential vote is 50 percent and, with very rare exceptions, vote and seat changes are losses.

4. Because the dependent variable is a change variable, consideration of change in the normal vote only makes a significant difference to estimates when the normal vote change is substantial and abrupt. When change is more gradual, any change in a party's base vote within the two-year interval should be fairly small and should not obscure the surge and decline effects.

5. There is a definite pattern of narrowing variance in both midterm vote and seat changes since 1900. If the narrowing variance pattern were severe enough through the century to cause distortions in the estimates, we would expect the equations to significantly underestimate early presidential party midterm losses and overestimate later losses. However, neither the vote loss nor seat loss residuals displayed trends of this sort.

6. Negative autocorrelation indicates non-random errors that tend to alternate in sign (for example, positive errors following negative errors). This may inflate standard errors thus biasing significance testing against inferring statistically significant coefficients.

7. These estimates are a good bit smaller than those in Tables 14-1 and 14-2. While one might suspect this reduction is a result of including the midterm popularity consideration into the multivariate analysis, this is not the case. A president's vote and later popularity during this period have been remarkably unrelated ($r = .001$). The difference is due to some decline in effects in recent years but mostly to the attenuation caused by orienting variables in terms of the winning and losing presidential parties rather than the Democratic and Republican parties (see Campbell, 1991).

8. Given the lack of significant direct economic effects in Table 14-3, the prior literature in support of this finding, and the small number of cases considered in this portion of the analysis, the equation was reestimated after dropping the economy variable. The parameters of the reestimated equation did not differ appreciably from the equation that included economic conditions.

9. Initial vote and seat holdings were not included in the midterm analysis because presidential coattails had already built in "slack" for midterm vote and seat change. Also, initial seat and vote holdings going into midterms are themselves partially a result of presidential coattails, proportionate to the presidential vote (which is included in the equation). In any case, adding the initial vote in seat holdings in the midterm analysis to equation 2 in Tables 14-1 and 14-2 does not yield significant effects. In the seat change equation, the initial seat holdings have the expected negative effects but do not reach statistical significance ($b = -.21$, $t = 1.41$). The initial vote share, the Democratic congressional vote percentage in the presidential election year, does not have the expected negative effect ($b = .03$, $t = .20$).

15. YOU CAN'T BEAT SOMEBODY WITH NOBODY: TRENDS IN PARTISAN OPPOSITION

Gary C. Jacobson

In the previous chapter [of Jacobson's book], we observed that by several standards—not least by the crucial standard of winning reelection—the electoral value of House incumbency reached a new plateau in the 1984-1988 period. The 1988 election was particularly striking in this respect: Despite George Bush's decisive victory in the presidential contest, incumbent Democrats as well as Republicans actually improved on their 1986 vote. A curious thing about this change is that it was not associated with any of the other trends that have been offered as explanations for the earlier expansion of the incumbency advantage. It was not associated with any growth in ticket splitting or divided outcomes, because partisan consistency edged upward in all the figures during this period. Nor can it be attributed to further growth in congressional office and staff resources, because growth in perks flattened out in the 1980s under the pressure of tight budgets and, perhaps, natural saturation (Ornstein, Mann, and Malbin, 1990, pp. 132, 134, 144-145).

I shall argue in this chapter that the explanation is not to be found in the behavior of incumbents or voters, but in the quality and vigor of challenges to incumbents. House incumbents did unusually well in these elections because their opposition was unusually feeble. House Republicans took little advantage of their 1984 and 1988 presidential victories because they did not field enough challengers capable of exploiting favorable partisan trends. The strength of the challenges is endogenous, of course, so the explanation cannot stop here. But it is an essential starting point. To understand what has happened, we need to examine changes over the past forty years in both the intensity and electoral importance of local opposition to incumbents. Trends in opposition go far to explain why recent House elections have produced so few incumbent defeats, and they also help to account for the Republicans' failure to make gains in the House during the 1980s.

Source: Gary C. Jacobson, *The Electoral Origins of Divided Government: Competition in U.S. House Elections, 1946-1988* (Boulder, Colo.: Westview Press, 1990).

Unopposed Candidates

The initial requirement for competitive elections is that both parties field candidates.[1] Incumbents are certainly secure if no one chooses to challenge them; a party cannot lose an open seat if the other party does not field a candidate. The incidence of unopposed candidacies has undergone at least two significant changes during the postwar period. These changes are the subject of this section.

The broad pattern of change over time in uncontested seats is revealed in Figure 15-1, which shows how the proportion of unopposed incumbents and uncontested open seats has varied in elections from 1946 through 1988. Few open seats are ignored by either party; since 1954, no election year has produced more than 2 uncontested open seats. A much higher proportion of incumbents go unopposed, and two clear trends appear in the data. The first is a precipitous drop in the proportion of unopposed incumbents between 1958 and 1964; the 1964 election featured the smallest number (forty-three) and proportion (11%) of unopposed incumbents in any postwar congressional election. After 1964, this trend reversed; the incidence of unopposed incumbents rebounded to the point where, in 1988, the number (seventy-nine) and proportion (19.4%) of incumbents given a free ride reached levels not approached since the 1950s.

The sharp drop in unopposed incumbents through 1964 has a ready explanation. It signals the rapid emergence of two-party competition in parts of the South where Republicans had not run candidates since Reconstruction.[2] In retrospect, the 1964 election was a decisive moment in the breakup of the New Deal coalition; Barry Goldwater's conspicuous opposition to the Civil Rights Act of 1964 accelerated the movement of southern politicians as well as voters into the Republican party. With the spread of Republican candidacies across the South, neither party enjoyed unchallenged dominance in any region.

The South's contribution to increased House competition in the early 1960s

Figure 15-1   Unopposed House Candidates, 1946-1988

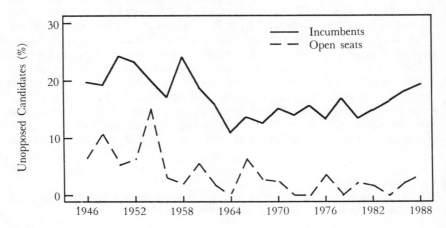

Figure 15-2 Uncontested Southern and Non-Southern House Seats, 1946-1988

is clear from Figure 15-2, which tracks the number of unopposed incumbents within and outside the South since 1946. Figure 15-2 also shows that, despite more frequent opposition, southern incumbents are still considerably more likely to run unopposed and that competition for southern House seats has, by this measure, changed little since 1964. The growth in uncontested seats since 1964 has occurred in regions outside the South. By 1988, major-party challengers were absent in almost as many districts outside the South as in it, although unopposed incumbents are still a good deal more common in southern districts, because the region holds only about one-fourth of all House seats.

The emergence of two-party competition in the South inevitably had partisan repercussions, because the Democrats initially held almost every uncontested southern House seat. Through 1964, more competition meant more challenges to Democratic incumbents. After 1964, the number of uncontested incumbents of both parties drifted irregularly upward, as Figure 15-3 demonstrates. Democrats still maintain a substantial advantage in free rides, but Republicans have narrowed the gap considerably since the 1950s.

Again, however, strong regional differences emerge. Through 1964, few (11%) uncontested Republican seats were located in the South; since then, a

Figure 15-3 Unopposed House Incumbents, 1946-1988

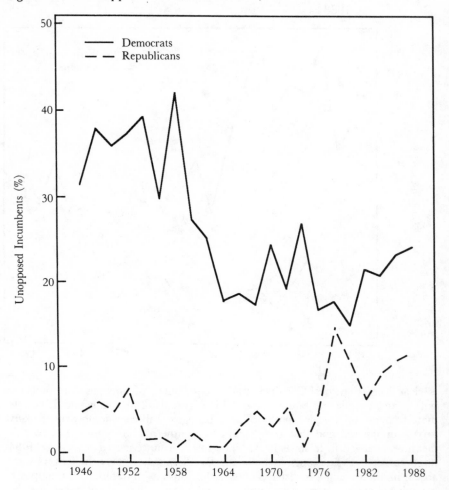

majority of them (57%) have been located there. By winning seats in the South, Republicans have inherited some of the benefit of the region's propensity to leave incumbents alone. Outside the South, however, Democratic incumbents have reaped the lion's share of the growing number of uncontested seats. Figure 15-4 presents the evidence (in raw seats—percentages would make the same general point, but seats tell the politically more important story). As we shall see, this is but one sign of the Republican party's growing weakness in House elections outside the South.

Figure 15-4 Unopposed Non-Southern Incumbents, 1946-1988

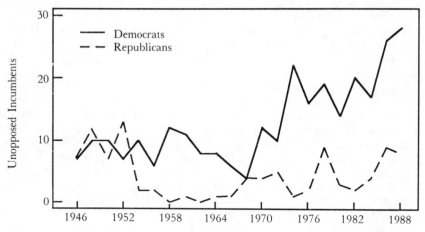

Measured by the presence of candidates from both major parties, competition for House seats expanded sharply in the early 1960s, then subsequently atrophied. How do these changes relate to other measures of competition? Intuitively, the average vote for challengers ought to decline when challengers begin to appear in large numbers in districts once monopolized by the incumbent's party. Because initial challengers win a smaller share of the vote than average—the mean vote for challengers in districts where the incumbent was unopposed in the previous election is less than 30% for the postwar period— expanded opposition ought to be associated with a decrease in the average challenger's vote.

Through 1964, this was indeed the pattern. Since then, however, the challenger's share of the vote in contested elections has continued to decline, while the proportion of unopposed incumbents has grown. The 1988 election occasioned a low point in the first trend and a high point in the second. Not only were there proportionately fewer major-party challenges than at any time in thirty years, the share of votes won by the challengers who did run was among the lowest on record. This brings us back to the question posed at the beginning of this chapter: Why have challenges seemed so futile in recent House elections? The answer requires a look at challengers.

The Challengers

Insofar as House elections are candidate rather than party centered, competition depends on the political talents and resources, not merely the presence, of challengers. To the degree that voters' decisions are shaped by their responses to the choice offered between a particular pair of candidates at the district level, the individual characteristics of the candidates, the extent and content of their campaigns, are crucial. With few exceptions, House incumbents are accomplished campaigners with adequate resources to conduct full-scale campaigns. Usually their challengers are not. Under all but the most unusual circumstances, only attractive, well-funded challengers pose a serious electoral threat to incumbents (Jacobson, 1987b). The growth of candidate-centered electoral politics has thus enhanced the importance of the challenger during the postwar period.

To demonstrate that the quality of the challenger makes a difference, and that the difference quality makes has grown over the past four decades, a measure of quality is required. For this analysis, I resort to a simple dichotomy: whether or not the candidate has ever held elective public office of any kind. Candidates who have held elective office are considered high-quality, experienced candidates; the others are not. Notice that by this standard, all House incumbents are, by definition, high-quality candidates. More elaborate and nuanced measures of candidate quality have been developed, but I stick with this simple dichotomy because it is objective, noncircular, and, most crucially, available for the entire postwar period.[3]

If quality matters, and if experience in elective office indicates quality, then, at minimum, experienced candidates ought to win more victories than inexperienced candidates. Table 15-1 shows that they do. Candidates who have held elective office are much more likely to win. Experienced challengers are four times as likely as inexperienced challengers to defeat incumbents. Candidates for open seats with prior experience in elective office are also more likely to win, their chances depending also on whether their opponents are similarly experienced (as well as on which party already held the seat). For (new) open seats held by neither party, experienced candidates win four of five contests against candidates who have never held elective office (N = 59, data not shown).

Of course, if high-quality challengers follow rational career strategies, they do not appear randomly. Other things equal, the better the odds on winning, the more likely they are to run. Ambitious, experienced career politicians make the most formidable candidates for Congress because they have the greatest incentive and opportunity to cultivate the political skills and connections that lead to effective candidacies. They also risk the most in trying to move to higher office, for defeat may retard or end their career. Thus the best potential candidates are also the most sensitive to the odds on winning and so to conditions that affect the odds.

One major consideration is the availability of money and other campaign resources. Astute career politicians do not enter contests without some reasonable expectation that they can assemble the wherewithal to mount a full-scale campaign. People who control campaign resources also deploy them strategically. They do not invest in hopeless causes; more favorable prospects inspire more generous support. Among the things they consider is the quality of the candidate. Better candidates attract more resources, just as the availability of resources attracts better candidates (Jacobson, 1980; Jacobson and Kernell, 1983).

A simple demonstration that high-quality candidates make strategic career decisions based on the prospects for advancement is presented in Table 15-2.

Table 15-1   Political Experience and Frequency of Victory in House
Elections, 1946-1988

Type of Race	Number of Cases	Winners (%) [a]
Open seats		
Incumbent party candidate experienced	361	87.0
Neither candidate experienced	194	76.8
Both candidates experienced	206	66.5
Challenging party candidate experienced	101	50.4
Challengers to incumbents		
Candidate experienced	1,769	17.3
Candidate not experienced	5,334	4.3

[a] For open seats, percentage of victories for party currently holding the seat.

Open seats attract the largest share of experienced candidates, but within this category, it makes a great deal of difference which party holds the seat because this has such a large effect on the chances of winning. Candidates for open seats who are unopposed always win, of course, and high-quality candidates are most common in these races. Among challengers, the incumbent's margin of victory in the previous election is strongly related to the proportions of both victories and high-quality challengers.

Clearly, career politicians are acutely sensitive to local conditions that affect electoral odds.[4] They are also sensitive to national conditions—the state of the economy, the performance of the administration, scandals, and crises—that promise to help or hinder candidates of their party, though, as we shall see, Democrats are far more responsive to national conditions than are Republicans (Jacobson and Kernell, 1983; Jacobson, 1989). Electoral expectations, then, have a powerful effect on candidacies: The better the prospects, the better the challengers and the more resources they have for their campaigns; the bleaker the outlook, the more feeble the challenge. Thus we would expect an inverse relationship between the strength of a challenge and the incumbent's electoral performance even if the strength of the challenge had no independent effect on the outcome.

In fact, however, the strength of the challenge has, by itself, a major impact on election results. The success enjoyed by high-quality candidates is not merely a consequence of more careful selection of targets, though such strategic behavior certainly contributes to it. Higher quality candidates run when the chances of winning are better, but they contribute independently to the outcome. Much of the evidence for this conclusion is available elsewhere (Jacobson and Kernell, 1983; Jacobson, 1989), but I shall summarize they key results here, because understanding this connection is central to understanding changes in postwar electoral competition.

The equations in Table 15-3 show that experienced candidates win a larger share of the votes and enjoy a higher probability of winning, even when local and national political circumstances are taken into account. The table reports results

Table 15-2 Probability of Victory and Quality of Nonincumbent Candidates for the House, 1946-1988

Type of Race	Number of Cases	Winners (%)	Former Officeholders (%)
Open seats			
No general election opponent	34	100.0	82.4
Held by candidate's party	862	79.7	65.7
Held by neither party	194	50.0	52.1
Held by opposite party	862	20.3	35.6
Challengers to incumbents			
Incumbent's vote in last election (%)			
50.0-54.9	1,546	20.2	45.3
55.0-59.9	1,467	8.6	28.9
60.0-64.9	1,338	3.8	19.7
65.0-69.9	1,124	2.3	14.6
70.0 or more	1,670	0.6	8.9

from two models. The first regresses the challenger's percentage of the vote on a constant and three variables: the vote for the candidate of the challenger's party in the previous election (a measure of the incumbent's local vulnerability), the national two-party vote shift for the challenger's party in the election year (a measure of national trends), and whether or not the challenger has held elective office. In the second model, the independent variables are the same, but the dependent variable is categorical (whether the challenger won or not), so the coefficients are estimated by probit rather than regression.

The results indicate that experience has a significant impact on votes and victories controlling for the kind of local and national political conditions that would affect career strategies. According to the regression coefficient, other things equal, a high-quality candidate was worth an additional 2.8% of the vote. The probit coefficient cannot be interpreted so directly, because its effect depends on the probability of victory established by the other variables. The appropriate computation shows that conditions giving an inexperienced challenger a .05 probability of victory would give a high-quality candidate a .11 probability of victory; in the same fashion .10 would grow to .20, .20 to .34, for a high-quality compared to a low-quality challenger.

Table 15-3 also reports equations covering the 1972-1988 period that include as independent variables campaign spending by the challenger and the incumbent (usable campaign spending data have been available only since 1972). Because diminishing returns applies to campaign spending, the expenditure variables are entered as the natural log of spending in $1,000s.[5]

The inclusion of campaign spending reduces the coefficient on quality, as theory would suggest. Because contributors also act strategically, quality and

Table 15-3 Elective Office Experience and Challenger's Success in House Elections, 1946-1988 and 1972-1988

	Regression		Probit	
Variable	1946-1988 (1)	1972-1988 (2)	1946-1988 (3)	1972-1988 (4)
Intercept	9.87***	9.19***	−5.65***	−5.53***
	(.34)	(.76)	(.23)	(.50)
Vote of challenger's party in last election (%)	.70***	.34***	.09***	.03***
	(.01)	(.01)	(.01)	(.01)
National shift in two-party vote (%)	.95***	.69***	.18***	.14***
	(.02)	(.03)	(.01)	(.02)
Challenger is experienced	2.77***	1.56***	.44***	.29**
	(.19)	(.27)	(.06)	(.11)
Challenger's spending (log $1,000s)		3.73***		.95***
		(.10)		(.09)
Incumbent's spending (log $1,000s)		−.48**		−.45***
		(.16)		(.10)
Adjusted R^2	.58	.68		
Log likelihood			−1,219	−363
Number of cases	6,453	2,667	6,453	2,667

Note: The dependent variable for the regression equations in columns 1 and 2 is the challenger's percentage of the two-party vote; its coefficients are regression coefficients. The dependent variable for the probit equations in columns 3 and 4 is 1 if the challenger won, 0 otherwise; its coefficients are maximum likelihood estimates. The national shift in the two-party vote is the change in the percentage of votes won nationally by the challenger's party in the election. Experienced challengers are those who have previously held elective offices (scored 1, otherwise, 0). Spending is entered as the log of spending in $1,000s, with a minimum of $5,000 assumed for each candidate. Standard errors are in parentheses.

**p < .01, one-tailed test.
***p < .001, one-tailed test.

campaign spending are positively correlated; experienced challengers, on average, spend more than twice as much as inexperienced challengers. But even controlling for spending, experienced challengers do significantly better than inexperienced challengers in winning votes and victories. Clearly, both money and quality contribute to the strength of a challenge.

Notice also that the marginal returns on spending are much larger for challengers than for incumbents. This is not at all surprising (Jacobson, 1980, 1985, 1990a); the surprise is finding that spending by incumbents has *any* significant effect on the vote share or probability of winning in a model of this sort. When analyses are confined to single election years, as has been customary in studies of campaign spending effects, none of the coefficients on incumbent spending in either equation achieves significance (p < .05), and incorrect signs are not uncommon (Jacobson, 1985). Results of this sort have been puzzling: If spending by House incumbents really had no effect, why would they put so much effort into raising funds, and why would they invariably spend more money the more seriously they were challenged? In an earlier paper, I speculated that

> [o]ne possible explanation is that spending by incumbents provides tiny but positive marginal returns, so that it makes perfect sense for incumbents to spend large amounts of money to counteract serious challenges. After all, when an incumbent is defeated, it is normally a close contest; small shifts in the vote make the difference between victory and defeat. Even if the ... effects of spending [on votes] are too small to be measured amid the noise in the data, they may be large enough to be worth the effort (1985, p. 41).

The results of equations 2 and 4 in Table 15-3 are consistent with this view. The large number of observations produced by combining all nine election years mitigates the problem of noisy data, and a more precise estimate of how spending by incumbents affects the vote emerges in equation 2. The marginal return in votes on campaign expenditures is still almost eight times greater for challengers, but spending by incumbents does have a significant payoff in votes as well. The coefficient in equation 4 indicates that spending by incumbents has a relatively stronger effect on the electoral bottom line—winning or losing—though the impact of spending by challengers remains considerably larger. By this evidence, it is not at all irrational for incumbents to spend large sums in response to vigorous challenges. Despite the fact that, in simple terms, the more incumbents spend, the worse they do on election day (the simple correlation between the incumbent's level of expenditures and share of votes or probability of victory are $-.38$ and $-.14$, respectively), reactive spending can partially offset the challenger's gains from more vigorous campaigning.

The Growing Impact of the Challenger

By the logic of the arguments advanced in [Jacobson's] book, the impact of the challenger's personal quality should have grown as electoral politics became more candidate-centered over the postwar period. In an earlier era of stronger party attachments and longer presidential coattails, local outcomes were more subject to district partisanship and national political tides. Strategic decisions were at least as critical to successful electoral careers, but the personal quality of individual candidates was of smaller electoral consequence. Over time, the emergence of a more candidate-centered style of electoral politics reduced the electoral importance of partisan forces while enhancing that of specific candidates and campaigns. Thus the resources and talents of challengers should have an increasing impact on district-level results.

Evidence that the expected change did occur is found in Table 15-4. The table presents a regression model equivalent to equation 1 and a probit model equivalent to equation 2 in Table 15-3, but with the addition of a trend term (1946 = 1, 1948 = 2, ... , 1988 = 22) and interactions between the trend term and the vote of the challenger's party in the previous election and the challenger's quality. The first equation in Table 15-4 indicates that the payoff for quality in

Table 15-4 Growing Impact of Quality of Challengers in House Elections, 1946-1988

Variable	Regression (1)	Probit (2)
Intercept	8.37***	−7.96***
	(.78)	(.50)
Vote of challenger's party in last election (%)	.80***	.15***
	(.02)	(.01)
National shift in two-party vote (%)	.94***	.18***
	(.02)	(.01)
Experienced challenger	1.17**	.44***
	(.38)	(.11)
Election year	.18***	.19***
	(.05)	(.03)
Election year × vote of challenger's party in last election (%)	−.011***	−.005***
	(.001)	(.001)
Election year × experienced challenger	.14***	−.001
	(.03)	(.009)
Adjusted R^2	.60	
Log likelihood		−1,198
Number of cases	6,453	6,453

Note: The dependent variable for the regression equation in column 1 is the challenger's percentage of the two-party vote; its coefficients are regression coefficients. The dependent variable for the probit equation in column 2 is 1 if the challenger won, 0 otherwise; its coefficients are maximum likelihood estimates. The national shift in the two-party vote is the change in the percentage of votes won nationally by the challenger's party in the election. Experienced challengers are those who have previously held elective offices (scored 1, otherwise, 0). The values of "election year" are 1946 = 1, 1948 = 2, ... 1988 = 22. Standard errors are in parentheses.

**p < .01, one-tailed test.
***p < .001, one-tailed test.

terms of votes increased significantly between 1946 and 1988. According to the regression coefficients, its value grew from 1.2 percentage points in 1946 to 4.3 percentage points in 1988. At the same time, consistent with the evidence of dissociation examined in [Jacobson's] Chapter 2, continuity between elections has diminished significantly; the impact of the prior vote fell from .78 to .57.[6] Prior results also have a smaller impact than they once did on the challenger's prospects of victory (equation 2 in Table 15-4), but the impact of quality on victory has not changed at all. Evidently, a high-quality challenge made as large a contribution to the probability of victory forty years ago as it does now.

Although the regression and probit findings might appear at odds with one another, they make sense in the light of the postwar electoral trends we have discussed. In the 1940s and 1950s, contests between challengers and incumbents were typically closer than they are today; electorates were more loyally partisan, and district vote swings tracked national vote swings more faithfully. The presence of a high-quality challenger may have had a smaller direct effect on the vote, but in the more competitive electoral environment, it was sufficient to raise the probability of victory substantially. Since the 1950s, electoral competition between House incumbents and challengers, as measured by vote margins, has diminished. The increment in votes enjoyed by experienced challengers has grown, but the distance challengers must make up to overtake the incumbent has grown even more.

Measured in votes, the increased value of a high-quality challenge almost matched the increased value of incumbency from the 1950s to the 1970s. This helps to explain why, despite wider average vote margins, House seats did not become significantly more secure over these decades. But it indicates that a successful challenge is now far more contingent on local circumstances—on particular candidates and campaigns—than it once was.

Changes in the Quality of Challengers

The quality of candidates and campaigns has a major effect on House election results, and the effect has, in some respects, grown over the past forty years. How has the quality of candidates changed over the postwar period? And how have these changes affected competition for House seats?

Although the importance of a strong challenge has increased over the postwar period, the incidence of strong challenges changed little—until very recently. Figure 15-5 displays the percentage of experienced challengers taking on incumbents in elections from 1946 through 1988. The lower line includes all incumbent-held seats in the denominator; the upper line presents the proportion of high-quality candidates among all major-party challengers that did appear. The two measures of aggregate quality track each other closely.

There is no sign of a trend other than the notable drop in the aggregate quality of House challengers in the late 1980s. Again the 1988 elections stand out: Not only was the number of unopposed incumbents the highest in thirty years, the proportion of high-quality candidates among all major-party challengers who did run was only 12.3%, more than two standard deviations below the 1946-1986 mean of 21.3%.

Another key difference between the 1984-1988 election period and earlier periods is that *both* parties fielded relatively weak challengers. This is unexpected, because strategic considerations should normally lead the parties' potential candidates to opposite decisions. When national conditions— the economy, popular ratings of the president's performance—favor a party, more of its experienced, high-quality candidates should run, because the chances of winning are assumed to be better. The other party's experienced candidates should be more inclined to wait for a more propitious year. And, indeed, the *relative* aggregate quality of a party's challengers has been strongly related to national conditions over the postwar period (Jacobson, 1989). But most of this has been the Democrats' doing; Republican challengers have been consistently less sensitive to national conditions than have their Democratic

Figure 15-5 Quality of House Challengers, 1946-1988

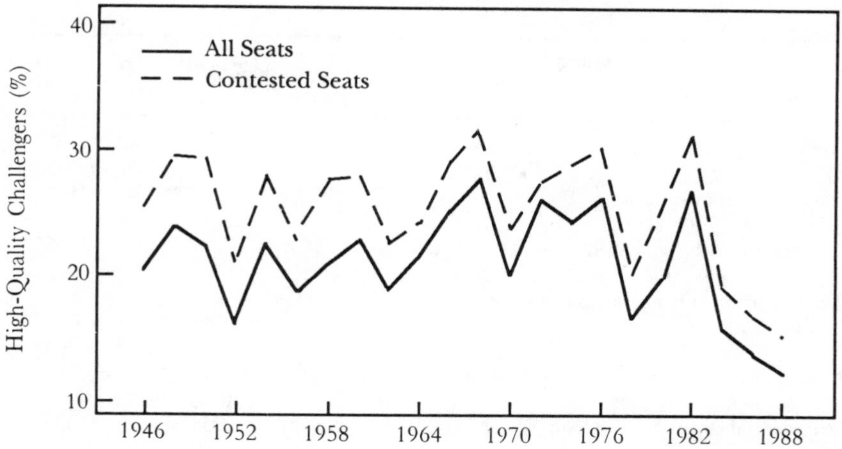

counterparts, and they have been particularly insensitive in recent elections.

Two types of evidence establish these points. Table 15-5 presents probit equations estimating the probability that an experienced challenger opposed the incumbent, given local and national conditions. Local opportunities expected to influence career moves are measured by the percentage of votes won by the candidate of the challenger's party, and whether the seat switched party hands, in the previous election. The economy and the president's level of popular approval measure the national conditions. A fifth variable, the party of the administration (scored 1 if Democratic, 0 if Republican) must be entered as a control because of the way some of the other variables are scored.

The state of the economy is measured as the percentage change in real disposable income per capita over the year ending in the second quarter of the election year.[7] Because the administration's party (not just the Democratic party) is supposed to be rewarded or punished for its management of the economy, this variable is multiplied by −1 when a Republican is in the White House (this is why the administration dummy is required). Presidential approval is scored as the mean percentage of citizens approving of the president's performance in Gallup Polls taken during the second quarter of the election year.[8] Again, this variable is multiplied by −1 under Republican administrations. National conditions are measured in the second quarter (April-June) of the election year because this is the period during which most *final* decisions about candidacy must be made.[9]

Finally, a party should field experienced challengers more frequently when it has a larger pool of experienced candidates from which to draw. We would not, for example, expect to find many experienced Republican challengers in the South prior to the mid-1960s because Republicans held so few elective offices in the region. For convenience (the data are readily available) and because by far the

Table 15-5   Estimates of Probability That House Challenger Has Held
Elective Office, 1946-1988

Variable	Democrats (1)	Republicans (2)
Intercept	−2.25***	.70**
	(.19)	(.25)
Party of administration	−.79***	.49*
	(.20)	(.22)
Change in party control of seat last election	.51***	.53***
	(.08)	(.08)
Votes won by Democratic candidate in last election (%)	.038***	−.037***
	(.004)	(.003)
Change in real income per capita (2nd quarter)	.047***	−.012
	(.010)	(.010)
Presidential approval (2nd quarter)	.005*	−.003
	(.002)	(.002)
Candidate pool	.235***	.301***
	(.031)	(.035)
Log likelihood	−1,718	−1,618
Number of cases	3,349	3,729

Note: See text for a description of the variables; standard errors are in parentheses.

*p < .05, one-tailed test.
**p < .01, one-tailed test.
***p < .001, one-tailed test.

most common stepping-stone to Congress is the state legislature, I estimate the
size of the pool as the ratio of the total number of seats a party holds in the state
legislature at the time of the election to the number of House seats in the state.
The distribution of this ratio is highly skewed—New Hampshire, for example,
currently has 524 state legislators squeezed into its two House districts—so this
variable is entered as its natural logarithm.[10]

The first equation in Table 15-5 indicates that all of the local and national
conditions significantly affect the probability that a high-quality Democratic
candidate challenged the Republican incumbent. All of the coefficients have the
appropriate sign and are more than twice their standard errors. Republican
challengers, in contrast, appear to be sensitive only to local circumstances, though
the coefficients on the items measuring national conditions show the correct signs,
and presidential approval does not fall too far short of conventional levels of
statistical significance.

Aggregate data tell a similar story. In Table 15-6, the dependent variables are
the percentages of Democratic and Republican challengers who have held elective
office, and the difference between these two percentages, in postwar House

Table 15-6 Determinants of Percentage of Experienced House Challengers, 1946-1988

Variable	Democrats (1)	Republicans (2)	Democrats - Republicans (3)
Intercept	53.05***	−11.44	64.49***
	(12.74)	(11.68)	(14.01)
Party of administration	−27.67**	12.28	−39.95***
	(8.90)	(8.15)	(9.79)
Seats won by Democrats last election (%)	−.22	.36*	−.58**
	(.19)	(.17)	(.21)
Change in real income per capita (2nd quarter)	1.44**	.23	1.20**
	(.44)	(.40)	(.49)
Presidential approval (2nd quarter)	.20*	−.11	.31**
	(.09)	(.08)	(.10)
Adjusted R^2	.52	.12	.60
Durbin-Watson	1.23	1.59	1.56
Number of cases	22	22	22

Note: The dependent variable in equations 1 and 2 is the percentage of challengers of the designated party who have held elective office; for equation 3, the dependent variable is the difference between the two; the independent variables are described in the test; standard errors are in parentheses.

*p < .05, one-tailed test.
**p < .01, one-tailed test.
***p < .001, one-tailed test.

elections. They are regressed on the economic and presidential approval variables, plus the current partisan division of House seats. This last variable serves double duty in these equations. It acknowledges that the more seats a party holds, the greater the number of inviting targets it presents to the opposing party regardless of other circumstances (Oppenheimer, Stimson, and Waterman, 1986). But it also serves as a more general measure of opportunity: Substantial gains by a party in one election are commonly followed by substantial losses in the next (a majority of which do *not* consist of seats captured from the other party in the previous election), and strategic politicians should take this cycle of "surge and decline" (Campbell, 1960) into account. As before, the scoring of the other independent variables makes it necessary to control for the party of the administration.

Again, economic conditions and the level of public approval of the president have a significant and substantial impact on the quality of Democratic challengers. Neither one matters for Republicans, who are sensitive only to the opportunities offered by the current level of Democratic strength in the House. However, a composite variable measuring the relative quality of challengers is affected significantly by all of these variables. This is the key variable, because relative quality is what matters on election day (Jacobson, 1989).

By these measures, Democratic challengers are, individually and in aggregate, clearly more "strategic" than Republican challengers. The difference is even more pronounced when analysis is confined to the 1966-1988 period. *None* of the coefficients is significant (t-ratios all below 1.0) when equation 2 in Table 15-6 is reestimated for elections since 1966. The probit coefficients representing national conditions in equations like those in Table 15-5 also have larger standard errors (and income shows the wrong sign) when analysis covers only the past two decades. Thus the quality of Republican challengers has not varied systematically with the party's national electoral prospects, particularly during the recent period of Republican presidential ascendancy. But the quality of Republican challengers has just as strong an impact on election results as does the quality of Democratic challengers. The coefficients on terms interacting party and quality in alternative versions of the equations in Table 15-3 are substantively small and statistically insignificant for the 1968-1988 period; analysis of aggregate data sustains the same point (Jacobson 1989, p. 784). One reason for the Republican party's inability to advance in the House thus may be its failure to field candidates of sufficient quality to take full advantage of favorable conditions. Let us investigate further.

Partisan Trends in the Quality of Challengers

Throughout the postwar period, Republicans have, in every year save 1966, fielded proportionately fewer experienced challengers than have Democrats, as Figure 15-6 demonstrates. The average difference is substantial: For the entire period, 27.0% of Republican incumbents faced high-quality challengers, compared to only 16.5% of the Democratic incumbents. And although no general trend in the incidence of experienced challengers over the entire postwar era is evident for either party (regression slopes for the data points connected in Figure 15-6 are not significantly different from zero), there is some evidence that the Republican party has found it increasingly difficult to recruit experienced challengers during the last two decades. Table 15-7 shows the results of regressing the percentage of Democratic incumbents facing experienced Republican challengers on time (1966 = 1, 1968 = 2, ... 1988 = 12), and whether the election is a midterm election, from 1966 through 1988. The coefficients indicate that the Democratic incumbents have faced increasingly weak Republican challenges (by the criterion of experience) during the period of Republican presidential dominance, though high-quality Republican challenges are significantly more common in presidential election years.

The falloff of experienced Republican challengers has been especially noticeable in districts outside the South. The dramatic growth in the number of Republicans challenging southern Democrats in the early 1960s was accompanied by a sharp increase in the number of high-quality Republican House candidates in the region; the party went from fielding virtually no experienced challengers in the 1940s and 1950s to fielding an average of 9.0% in the 1960s. But since that time, the average quality of Republican House challengers in the South has changed very little; it was no higher in the 1980s (8.8% with experience) than in the 1960s. Meanwhile, however, the quality of Republican challengers outside the South has

Figure 15-6 Quality of Democratic and Republican House Challengers, 1946-1988

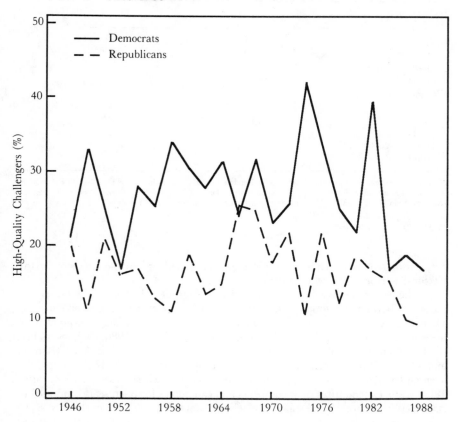

declined. Republicans are less than half as likely as they were forty years ago to field an experienced challenger against a Democratic incumbent outside the South. Their average for the 1946-1950 period was 29.3%; for 1984-1988 it was 13.0%. While the party became more competitive in the South, it became less competitive elsewhere in terms of the quality of its challengers as well as by the measure of running any candidate at all.[11]

The Collapse of Competition, 1984-1988

The growth of the incumbency advantage through the early 1980s cannot be attributed to any systematic decline in the aggregate quality of House challengers, because the aggregate quality of challengers did not decline. Since 1984, however,

Table 15-7   Decline in Quality of Republican Challengers, 1966-1988

Variable	(1)
Intercept	27.63***
	(2.37)
Midterm election	−4.43*
	(1.92)
Election year	−1.27***
	(.28)
Adjusted R^2	.66
Durbin-Watson	1.97
Number of cases	12

Note: The dependent variable is the percentage of Republican challengers who had held elective office; "midterm election" takes the value of 1 for midterm election years, 0 for presidential election years; the values of "election year" are 1966 = 1, 1968 = 2, ... 1988 = 12; standard errors are in parentheses.

*p < .05, one-tailed test.
***p < .001, one-tailed test.

extraordinarily weak challenges have coincided with a notable increase in the electoral performance of incumbents.

The aggregate weakness of challengers in these elections is indicated by measures beyond the simple index of experience in elective office. For example, Donald Green and Jonathan Krasno have developed an elaborate nine-point scale measuring challenger quality in elections from 1972 through 1986; challengers had the lowest mean quality on this scale in 1986, the second lowest in 1984 (Krasno and Green, 1988; Green, 1989, personal communication). In real dollars, the average challenger's campaign spending declined in each successive election after 1982, while expenditures by incumbents and candidates for open seats continued to rise steeply. Figure 15-7 displays the relevant data. The average challenger spent less money on the campaign in 1988 than in any election since 1976; fewer challengers spent beyond $300,000—a conservative threshold for a serious challenge (Jacobson, 1987c)—in 1988 than in any election since 1978.

Republican challenges were especially feeble in 1988. Measured by experience, the quality of Republican challengers reached a postwar low; the average Republican challenger spent less money, and fewer Republican challengers exceeded the $300,000 threshold for an adequately funded campaign, than in any election since 1974. Over the entire twenty-year period of Republican presidential ascendancy, only in 1974, the worst Republican year in two decades, did Republicans mount weaker challenges than in 1988. No wonder George Bush's victory failed to increase Republican representation in the House.

The aggregate weakness of Republican challenges is a genuine puzzle. The boost given to the party's long-term prospects by growing Republican partisanship in the electorate and a succession of presidential victories should, one would think, encourage challengers to take on Democratic incumbents and spur

Figure 15-7 Campaign Spending in House Elections, 1972-1988

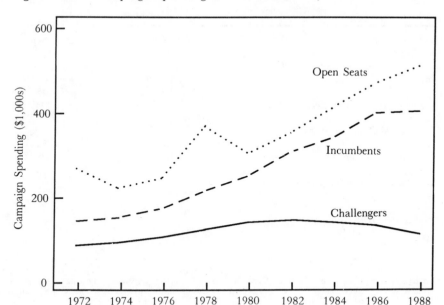

Republican donors to finance their campaigns. Why have Republicans not fielded more experienced, well-funded challengers in recent years? We do not know yet; I shall examine some possible explanations in [Jacobson's] final chapter.

Quality Candidates in Open Seats

The data in Table 15-1 suggest that the quality of candidates also makes an important difference in contests for open seats. Candidates for open seats who have held elective office win more frequently, with their chances depending also on whether their opponents are high-quality candidates. This relationship survives when the appropriate controls are imposed, and, as the equations in Table 15-8 reveal, the quality of the candidate representing the party *not* currently holding the seat makes the most difference.

The first equation in Table 15-8 displays the results of regressing the share of votes won by the candidate of the party currently holding an open seat on its vote in the previous election, the national two-party vote swing, and the quality of the two candidates. Notice that the coefficient on the quality of the out-party's candidate is almost five times as large as that on the quality of the in-party's victory or defeat as the dependent variable and using probit to estimate the

Table 15-8   Impact of Quality of Challengers in House Elections for Open Seats, 1946-1988

Variable	Regression (1)	Probit (2)
Intercept	24.58***	−1.65***
	(2.34)	(.43)
Winner's vote in last election (%)	.54***	.039***
	(.04)	(.007)
National shift in two-party vote (%)	.70***	.106***
	(.08)	(.015)
Experienced challenger, in-party	1.25*	.39***
	(.70)	(.12)
Experienced challenger, out-party	−6.11***	−.74***
	(.68)	(.11)
Adjusted R^2	.37	
Log likelihood		−329
Number of cases	694	694

Note: The dependent variable for the regression equation (1) is the percentage of the two-party vote won by the candidate of the party currently holding the open seat; its coefficients are regression coefficients. The dependent variable for the probit equation (2) is 1 if the in-party's candidate won, 0 otherwise; its coefficients are maximum likelihood estimates. "National shift in two-party vote" is the change in the percentage of votes won nationally by in-party from the last election. Experienced challengers are those who have previously held elective offices (scored 1, otherwise, 0). Standard errors are in parentheses.

*p < .05, one-tailed test.
***p < .001, one-tailed test.

parameters. The quality of both candidates has a substantively large and statistically significant impact on the outcome. Again, the quality of the out-party's candidate makes the larger difference in the results. In contests for open seats, the coefficients on candidate quality do not change over time (the interaction terms are insignificant), but there is a similar decrease in the coefficient measuring the effect of the vote in the previous election, which falls from .82 to .37 over the postwar period (equation not shown).

I argued in [Jacobson's] Chapters 2 and 3 that, while competition for seats held by incumbents has, by some measures, declined, competition for open seats has increased. Incumbents may have tightened control of their seats; their parties have not—rather the contrary. If open seats have become more competitive, then we should expect an increase in the quality of candidates in these races—and vice versa. With improved chances of victory, the out-party ought to field more high-quality challengers; with opportunities to take seats held by incumbents declining, we would expect an increasing concentration of high-quality candidates in the contests for open seats. This is precisely what has occurred. Figure 15-8 displays the increase in the percentage of experienced open-seat candidates representing both the party currently holding the seat and the out-party. Although the pattern

Figure 15-8 Quality of Candidates for Open House Seats, 1946-1988

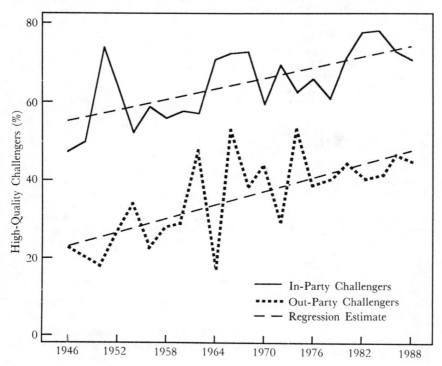

is, as usual, noisy, a significant increase is evident in both cases (see equations 1 and 4 in Table 15-9). The increase in high-quality candidates fielded by the out-party has been steeper, more than doubling (from about 22% to about 47%) over the postwar period.

Recall from the regression equations in Table 15-8 that the quality of the out-party's candidate has a greater impact on the vote and on who wins or loses. This implies that the trends displayed in Figure 15-8 should, other things equal, have made open seats more competitive, which is just what we observed. We cannot from these data untangle cause and effect. A more competitive environment should attract stronger candidates to open-seat contests; stronger candidates should make these contests more competitive. What we observe is the consequence of a mutually reinforcing set of processes: more competition in contests for open seats.

There are notable partisan differences in the incidence of high-quality candidates in contests for open House seats. An increased concentration of experienced candidates in open seats is characteristic of both parties, regardless of which party currently holds a seat. The difference is that Republicans are more likely than Democrats to field experienced candidates when they already hold the

Table 15-9   Increase in Quality of Candidates for Open House Seats, 1946-1988

Variables	In-Party Candidates			Out-Party Candidates		
	All (1)	Democrats (2)	Republicans (3)	All (4)	Democrats (5)	Republicans (6)
Intercept	53.56***	51.13***	57.45***	21.48***	27.13***	16.89***
	(3.11)	(5.36)	(4.74)	(3.57)	(5.56)	(4.38)
Election year	.92***	.89*	.91*	1.17***	1.46**	.88**
	(.24)	(.40)	(.36)	(.27)	(.42)	(.33)
Adjusted R^2	.40	.15	.20	.46	.34	.22
Durbin-Watson	1.64	1.83	1.97	3.07	2.43	2.66
Number of cases	22	22	22	22	22	22

Note: The dependent variable is the percentage of candidates for open seats in each category who have held elective office; the value of "election year" is 1946 = 1, 1948 = 2, ... 1988 = 22; standard errors are in parentheses.

*p < .05, one-tailed test.
**p < .01, one-tailed test.
***p < .001, one-tailed test.

seat, while Democrats are more likely than Republicans to field experienced candidates when the other party currently holds the seat. The percentage of experienced Democrats has also grown faster then the percentage of experienced Republicans in such contests. The regression slopes on time from the equations in Table 15-9 indicate that the expected percentage of experienced out-party Democrats increased from 28.5% to 59.4% over the period, while the same figure for out-party Republicans grew from 17.8% to 36.3%. The increase in the quality of in-party candidates was nearly identical for both parties, rising from 58.4% to 77.5% for Republicans and from 52.0% to 70.7% for Democrats.

The comparatively low quality of Republican candidates for open seats that the Democrats currently hold probably contributes to the Republicans' inability to take more open seats from Democrats, because the effects of quality on election results are identical for the two parties (the coefficients on quality in the models estimated in Table 15-8 are not distinguishable by party). Clearly, Democrats have done the better job of fielding experienced candidates able to exploit the changes that have given parties greater access to each other's open seats.

The Concentration of Competition

Several strands of evidence point to the conclusion that competition for House seats has become ever more concentrated in a smaller number of more intensely contested districts over the past two decades. High-quality candidates are increasingly clustered in contests for open seats. Campaign money, too, is increasingly concentrated in open seats; recall from Figure 15-7 that spending by candidates for open seats has grown steeply since 1972, while spending by challengers has, in real terms, scarcely grown at all. Another perspective on this trend is presented in Figures 15-9 and 15-10, which trace changes in the distribution of campaign money available to nonincumbent House candidates. Figure 15-9 shows that the share of total spending accounted for by the top one-tenth of spenders rose steadily, from less than 30% to nearly 50%, between 1972 and 1988. In the meantime, the share spent by the lowest-spending six-tenths fell from 30% to less than 10%. Figure 15-10, which includes only challengers to incumbents, shows a similar pattern of change.

Why have campaign resources become so much more concentrated? A reflexive reference to the incumbency advantage will not suffice. The trend occurred after the mid-1960s, when the value of incumbency, in votes, had already had its sharpest increase; it continued regardless of whether the election year was particularly bad for one party's incumbents. Indeed, causation probably runs more strongly in the opposite direction: Concentration of resources raises the average incumbent's vote.

Although my view is admittedly speculative, I think the principal reasons for the growing concentration of campaign resources are better intelligence and higher campaign costs. Technology has reduced the cost of polling, and more money is available to pay for polls. The national party campaign committees have been particularly aggressive in exploring the prospects for taking particular seats from the opposition (Herrnson, 1988). District electorates are subject to much more research than before, both prior to and during election campaigns. Thus strategic politicians and their potential supporters and contributors are better informed about the prospects for success than ever before. With a more refined idea of the possibilities, fewer resources are wasted on hopeless causes, and more are channeled into the tightest races.

The high price of competitive campaigns also leads to a bifurcation of effort. The costs in money, time, energy, privacy, and family life of a serious challenge are formidable and growing; the level of commitment necessary to take on an incumbent has grown with the length and cost of campaigns. Unless a potential candidate can convince him- or herself—and others—that he or she has a fighting chance and so can raise the very large sums needed to *have* a fighting chance, there is little point in making the other sacrifices a candidacy entails.

It is easy to understand how greater concentration of campaign resources would increase the incumbency advantage as it is customarily measured. A large majority of incumbents, appearing very safe indeed, face increasingly feeble opposition—or no major-party opposition at all—and so win even larger margins than before. Those who show signs of weakness continue to face full-scale challenges resulting in hard-fought, close races, some of which they lose. The average vote for incumbents grows, but this does not represent an increase in the value of incumbency *to those incumbents who are seriously challenged.* Concentration of resources makes incumbents who convince the opposition that they are unbeatable even safer (by the criterion of vote margin), but it also makes life

Figure 15-9 Growing Concentration of Campaign Money Spent by Nonincumbent House Candidates, 1972-1988

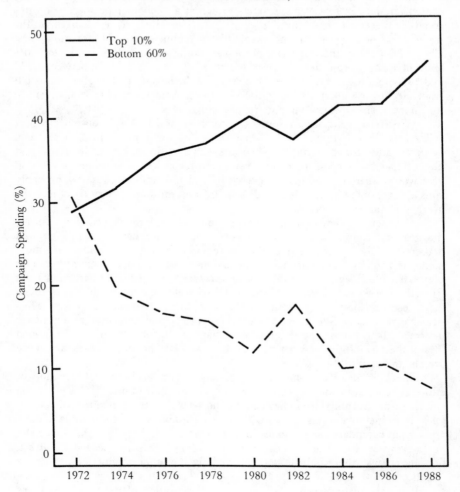

more difficult for incumbents who appear sufficiently vulnerable to invite an all-out challenge.

The concentration of resources may, however, diminish competition and protect incumbents by prematurely closing off the possibility of a competitive challenge. Election forecasts made months in advance of election day are subject to considerable error; bleak prospects can suddenly brighten if national or local

Figure 15-10 Growing Concentration of Campaign Money Spent by House Challengers, 1972-1988

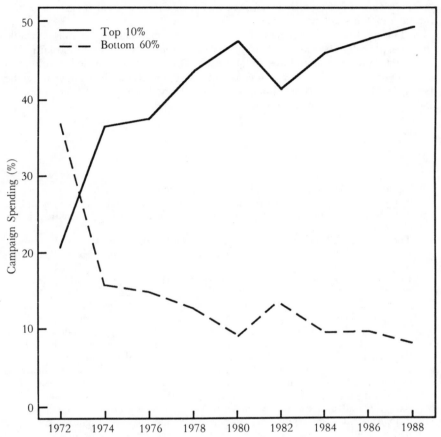

events break for the challenger. Voters do change their minds during the course of campaigns (Jacobson, 1990b). More challenges may appear hopeless than turns out to be the case; too much information, too early, may discourage the kind of risk taking that is occasionally rewarded with unanticipated success.

Conclusion

As the electoral importance of incumbency grew over the postwar period, so did the electoral importance of the opposing campaign, and for the very same reasons. With a growing fraction of the electorate choosing between candidates rather than parties, the individual characteristics of candidates and their campaigns became more salient. Just as what incumbents did in office could have an increasing impact on their support in the district, so could the persona and message of the challenger.

The quality of challengers and vigor of their campaigns are more variable than partisan habits, and so their increasing impact also helps to explain why interelection vote swings have become more variable and election results less stable over the period. It also points to a major reason Republicans have not done better in the most recent House elections: They have fielded comparatively inexperienced, underfinanced, nonincumbent candidates.

NOTES

1. To be sure, primary elections and independent candidates may offer some choice, but their contribution to electoral competition in postwar House elections has been limited; incumbents are four times more likely to be defeated in general than in primary elections.

2. The South is defined as the eleven states of the Confederacy: Alabama, Arkansas, Florida, Georgia, Louisiana, Mississippi, North Carolina, South Carolina, Tennessee, Texas, and Virginia.

3. In addition to local newspapers (the Library of Congress has on microfilm at least two newspapers from each state) and all of the *Congressional Quarterly Weekly Report*'s reviews of individual House races since Congressional Quarterly, Inc., began publishing them, background information on candidates comes from *Election Index* (1966, 1968, 1970, 1972, 1974, 1976, 1978, 1980, 1982), *Biographical Directory of the American Congress* (1971), various regional and occupational editions of *Who's Who*, the *New York Times* (using the obituary index as well as the regular index), various state election pamphlets, and numerous other miscellaneous sources. I also checked state yearbooks to determine whether any of the candidates about whom I could find no information had held any state office; for some states, lists of local elected officials were also available for examination. About 5% of the cases remain uncertain from lack of information (some highly partisan newspapers did not even deign to mention the names of losing candidates representing the unworthy party). I have assumed that these candidates had not held elective public office. Given their obscurity and that only about one-quarter of the known challengers have held elective office, the number of errors produced by this assumption should be quite small; overall accuracy probably exceeds 99%. In any case, all of the substantive results are replicated if the definition of high-quality candidates is narrowed to include only candidates who have held seats in state legislatures or, formerly, the U.S. Congress; for this classification, information is virtually complete and errors are minimal.

4. See also Bianco (1984); Bond, Covington, and Fleisher (1985); Canon (1985); and Krasno and Green (1988).

5. All candidates are assumed to have spent a minimum of $5,000. I make this assumption for two reasons. One is that expenditures totalling less than this sum need not be reported to the Federal Election Commission. The second is that the assumption produces results that closely approximate those attained when the Box-Cox procedure is used to find the appropriate functional form for modeling the

diminishing returns on campaign spending; see Jacobson (1990b) for the details. The spending data are from Common Cause (1974, 1976); the Federal Election Commission (1979, 1982, 1983, 1985); and Barone and Ujifusa (1987, 1989).

6. The positive sign on the election year variable indicates that, while the impact of the prior vote has diminished, the challenger's share of the vote independent of the prior vote has actually increased. The net effect of these two trends puts challengers in a worse position, however, unless the prior vote is less than 16%.

7. The data to compute quarter-to-quarter changes in real income per capita through 1976 are from *The National Income and Product Accounts of the United States, 1929-1976, Statistical Tables* (U.S. Department of Commerce, 1981). Data for later years are taken from various issues of *The Survey of Current Business* (U.S. Department of Commerce). Year-to-year changes are computed from data in *The Economic Report of the President, 1989*. Quarterly data are not available for 1945-1946, so the yearly figure is substituted for that observation for analyses reported in Tables 15-5 and 15-6.

8. Presidential approval data are from King and Ragsdale (1988).

9. Of course, decisions to run for Congress are sometimes taken months or even years earlier (Maisel, 1982; Born, 1986)—though most nonincumbent House candidates do not register with the Federal Election Commission until March of the election year or later (Wilcox, 1987; Wilcox and Biersack, 1990). The choice of a time frame over which to measure for real income change makes little difference, however; all of the plausible alternatives are so highly correlated that it is impossible to distinguish alternative models statistically (Erikson, 1990).

10. I set the minimum value of this variable at 0, which is the natural logarithm of 1, because the log of 0 (the actual ratio for Republicans in some Southern states prior to the 1960s) is undefined.

11. Regional differences in the quality of Democratic challengers have disappeared. In the 1950s and 1960s, experienced Democratic challengers were somewhat more common in the South—not surprising at a time when local offices were monopolized by Democrats, and Republican incumbents seemed aberrant and therefore relatively easy targets. Since the 1960s, the proportion of experienced Democratic challengers has not differed by region.

PART V: PARTY IDENTIFICATION

16. IS PARTY IDENTIFICATION STABLE?

Empirical studies of voting behavior have from the beginning had to account for the considerable stability of individual and aggregate voting patterns. To be sure, there is change from election to election, but this change is typically within a fairly limited range. The underlying stability has been mapped to the individual level by postulating the existence of a long-term factor in voting. The long-term factor could be seen as demographic (as in the Columbia studies' use of an Index of Political Predispositions based on social class, religion, and place of residence) or as ideological (typically a liberal-conservative dimension), but most often it has been seen as partisan. Individual citizens are seen as identifying psychologically with one of the political parties, using that partisanship as a factor in deciding how to vote, and maintaining that party loyalty across a series of elections. The value of the concept as a long-term factor in voting is clearly tied to how stable it is: the more changeable partisanship is, the less of a long-term baseline it provides for voting. The stability of partisanship has ever been the subject of controversy (see *Classics in Voting Behavior,* chap. 21), and that controversy has been reinvigorated in recent years.

The traditional measure of party identification in National Election Studies surveys is based on a set of three questions that yield a seven-point classification ranging from strong Democrats to strong Republicans. This same wording has been used without alteration for several decades. Time trends in the aggregate distribution of partisanship since 1952, along with the exact wording of the questions, are shown in Table 16-1.

Party Identification Is Affected by Short-Term Factors

In recent years there has been an increased challenge to the claim that party identification is stable. Many European scholars earlier came to the conclusion that partisanship was unstable in their countries (see *Classics,* chap. 25), but the most vigorous assault on the claim of stable partisanship in the United States has come only in the past few years. Innovative research designs permitted new tests

Table 16-1 Party Identification in the United States, 1952-1988

Party Identification	1952	1956	1960	1964	1968	1972	1976	1980	1984	1988
Strong Democrat	22	21	20	27	20	15	15	18	17	17
Weak Democrat	25	23	25	25	25	26	25	23	20	18
Ind. Democrat	10	6	6	9	10	11	12	11	11	12
Independent	6	9	10	8	11	13	15	13	11	11
Ind. Republican	7	8	7	6	9	10	10	10	12	13
Weak Republican	14	14	14	14	15	13	14	14	15	14
Strong Republican	14	15	16	11	10	10	9	9	12	14
Apolitical	3	4	2	1	1	1	1	2	2	2
Democratic presidential vote	44%	42%	50%	61%	43%	38%	50%	42%	41%	46%
Republican presidential vote	55	57	50	38	43	61	48	52	59	54

Note: The classification is based on the following question series: "Generally speaking, do you usually think of yourself as a Republican, a Democrat, an Independent, or what?" (If partisan:) "Would you call yourself a strong Republican/Democrat) or a not very strong (Republican/Democrat)?" (If not partisan:) "Do you think of yourself as closer to the Republican or Democratic Party?"

Source: Computed from data collected in the 1952-1988 Center for Political Studies/National Election Studies election surveys, University of Michigan.

of its stability, and the accumulation of long time series provided unexpected evidence of instability.

The most theoretically significant work to argue that party identification is changeable is the MacKuen, Erikson, and Stimson work reprinted here as Chapter 17. These authors analyze Gallup opinion poll data over a lengthy time period, finding systematic changes in aggregate party identification, which they term "macropartisanship." Macropartisanship varied about 20 percentage points during the period of their study, from Democratic strength among major party identifiers in the low 50 percent range in the late 1940s to nearly 70 percent in the mid-1970s and then back down to the low 50 percent range around the 1984 election. They demonstrate that a quarterly measure of macropartisanship varies in response to changes in presidential popularity and in public sentiment about the health of the national economy.

Other studies, using different polls, have found similar shifts in aggregate party identification. Weisberg and Smith (1991) located sufficient commercial polls (including Gallup, Roper, CBS News/*New York Times*, NBC News, and ABC News/*Washington Post*) measuring party identification in the early 1980s to construct a monthly composite measure. The Democratic lead among major party identifiers increased from about 17 percent in mid-1981 to nearly 25 percent in mid-1983 before falling to about 10 percent through 1985 and most of 1986. Weisberg and Smith demonstrate that this monthly measure varied in response to changes in presidential approval and in objective indicators of the economy (inflation and unemployment rates). Additionally, Allsop and Weisberg (1988) were able to take advantage of nightly tracking polls conducted by Decision/Making/Information for the Republican National Committee in the 1984 presidential election. They found systematic changes in partisanship across the June-November campaign period, with the Republicans gaining about seven percent more identifiers at the end of the campaign than at their low point in mid-June. The changes correspond to shifts in presidential vote intention, suggesting that party identification is at least partly responsive to campaign events. Converse (1976) argued that instability of partisanship would be confined to the least involved citizens, but Weisberg and Allsop (1990) reported that the systematic instability in the 1984 data was actually greater among respondents who were registered to vote than those who were not. Overall, these studies show that there is genuine variation in partisanship, though the changes are not vast.

Note that the above studies are all at the aggregate level, comparing polls at different times based on different respondents rather than looking at partisan changes for the same respondents in panel studies. Yet there are few processes by which change could occur at the aggregate level without corresponding change at the individual level. If the changes across time were so small as to be at the level of sampling error, then change might appear to exist at the aggregate level even though no individual-level change was occurring. Or if there was considerable population replacement between the surveys (older people with one set of partisan beliefs leaving the electorate and being replaced by young people with different partisan beliefs), then change might appear to exist at the aggregate level even though no individual-level change was occurring. However, the changes between polls are greater than sampling error, and the polls have been spaced too close together to be seriously affected by population replacement, so the changes observed at the aggregate level imply corresponding changes at the individual level.

Indeed, a few studies at the individual level have shown partisanship to be unstable. Perhaps the most striking finding, though based on only about two dozen people, is that of Flanigan, Rahn, and Zingale (1989), who found very high partisan instability over a year of repeated interviewing of Twin Cities respondents. Similarly, Brody and Rothenberg (1988) found what they considered a great deal of individual change between January and September in the 1980 NES panel study.

These studies of party identification fit well into the research of the late 1970s and early 1980s that suggested that party identification was endogenous to the vote decision. The original 1950s work had suggested an "exogenous" role for partisanship in which it is the "unmoved mover." That is, party identification was seen as affecting attitudes toward candidates and issues as well as votes, but these factors were not seen as affecting partisanship. In contrast, Jackson (1975), Page and Jones (1979), and Fiorina (see *Classics*, chap. 24) found effects of issue positions and of previous votes on partisanship. More recent studies, including those by Howell (1981), Franklin and Jackson (1983), and Brody and Rothenberg (1988), show that such changes can be found over shorter periods of time and, as in the aggregate analyses noted above, that they are systematic in nature. For example, Franklin and Jackson use the NES 1956-60 and 1972-76 panel studies to demonstrate that party identification is affected by election-specific evaluations and that this effect diminishes with age so that partisanship is more stable for older people. Likewise, Brody and Rothenberg show that changes in partisanship in 1980 could be accounted for by short-term factors associated with that election.[1]

Another challenge to the stability of partisanship was a series of studies suggesting that party identification was less universal in the United States than it first seemed to be. After all, if for many respondents the very existence of partisanship is questionable, it cannot be expected to be highly stable. The original reports of the success of the party identification measure derived much of their power from the fact that over 95 percent of the respondents could be located on the scale (Campbell, Gurin, and Miller, 1954; Campbell, Converse, Miller, and Stokes, 1960). Now, however, several studies have found a far greater level of "partisan misfits" (a term coined by Niemi, Reed, and Weisberg, 1991): 10 percent of those responding to the standard question are either apolitical or feel neither partisan nor independent (Miller and Wattenberg, 1983); 28 percent responding to follow-up questions indicate no attachment to partisanship (Dennis, 1988a); 28-30 percent are neither partisan supporters nor independents when asked separate questions on both (Weisberg, 1980, Table 2; Kessel, 1984, Table 16-3A); 24 percent either do not think of themselves in partisan terms or answer three partisanship questions in inconsistent ways (Niemi, Reed, and Weisberg, 1991). The definitions used in these different studies vary considerably, but they agree in suggesting that the fit of the party identification scale is much less complete than it first seemed and that, as is the case for other survey questions, a substantial part of the citizenry may lack a meaningful position on the scale. As a result, the upper limit on the stability of partisanship may be lower than it was once thought to be.[2]

Another facet of partisan stability is intergenerational: to what extent do people follow the partisanship of their parents? The original *American Voter* view of partisanship—supported by early work on political socialization (for example, Jennings and Niemi, 1974)—was that it was highly stable across generations. However, the growth in independents among young people in the 1960s and 1970s resulted in a challenge to that position. Carmines, McIver, and Stimson (1987), for example, concluded that the growth in independents during this period was due mainly to "unrealized partisans," people whose parental partisanship (as recalled by NES respondents) led to predictions that they too would be partisan but who were instead independent. They also explored the issue basis of unrealized partisanship, suggesting that unrealized partisans were people whose issue positions differ from those of their "natural" party, with unrealized Democrats more conservative than Democrats and unrealized Republicans more liberal than Republicans. Luskin, McIver, and Carmines (1989) further explored the dependence of intergenerational change on issues, particularly the role of "hard" issues, which require considerable political knowledge, versus "easy" issues, which do not. Unrealized partisanship was found to depend on an easy issue—race—while conversion of people across partisan boundaries was found to depend on a hard issue—economics.

The intergenerational stability of partisanship was assessed more directly in a multiwave "socialization study" in which a national sample of high school seniors and their parents were interviewed in 1965, with reinterviews in 1973 and 1982. Franklin (1984) used the 1965-73 data and found that party identification was not fixed, but changed in response to issue preferences that did not reinforce earlier partisanship. Niemi and Jennings, in an article reprinted here as Chapter 18, used the full three-wave data to assess the attitudinal basis of such transmission further. They found that the greatest similarity in partisanship between the high school seniors and their parents was immediate, with a decrease in that similarity over the years of their panel study. Issues proved important in explaining the deviations, as when offspring who opposed a federal role in integrating schools proved to be less Democratic than those who favored such a role.

The evidence of instability of party identification detailed in this section undermines the usefulness of partisanship as a long-term factor in models of voting, suggesting that party identification may not be as meaningful as it was first believed to be. If individual party ties sway with the political winds, they may not be a major factor in explaining the vote and in creating political stability.

Party Identification Is Stable

The studies described above have not been regarded as definitive. To the contrary, they have led to a series of articles arguing that partisanship, though not unmovable, is highly stable.

MacKuen, Erikson, and Stimson's analysis of trends in macropartisanship has been challenged most directly by Abramson and Ostrom (1991). They found that the Gallup party identification question analyzed by MacKuen and colleagues has greater variability than the NES measure (see Figure 16-1). The NES data are also less responsive to changes in the economy or in presidential approval than are the Gallup data. Abramson and Ostrom suggest that the differences are due to subtle differences in the wording of the party identification questions, with the Gallup wording ("In politics, as of today, do you consider yourself a Republican, a Democrat, or an Independent?") being more susceptible to short-term fluctuations than the more long-term NES wording ("Generally speaking, do you usually think of yourself as . . .").

In their response to Abramson and Ostrom, MacKuen, Erikson, and Stimson (1992a) show that party identification varies in the CBS News/*New York Times* surveys in the same way as it does in the Gallup Poll (see Figure 16-2). And the CBS News/*New York Times* party identification question ("Generally speaking, do you consider yourself a . . .") is virtually identical to the NES question wording. Yet even this added evidence does not fully settle the debate. After all, party identification *is* less variable in the academic-based NES and GSS surveys than in the media polls, though it is not obvious whether this is due to the

Figure 16-1 Gallup Measure of Partisanship Compared with NES₁ and NES₂, 1952–1988

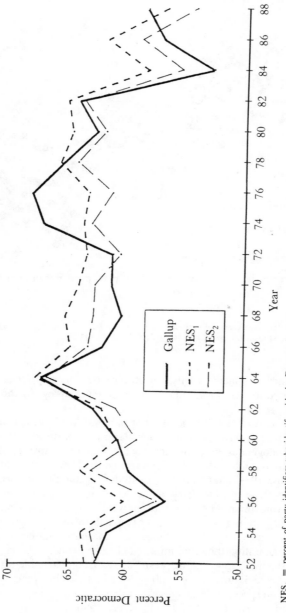

NES₁ = percent of party identifiers who identify with the Democratic party.
NES₂ = percent of party identifiers and independent leaners who identify with, or lean toward, the Democratic party.

Source: Adapted from Abramson and Ostrom (1991)

Figure 16-2 Monthly Gallup and CBS/*NYT* Readings of Micro-partisanship, 1976-1988

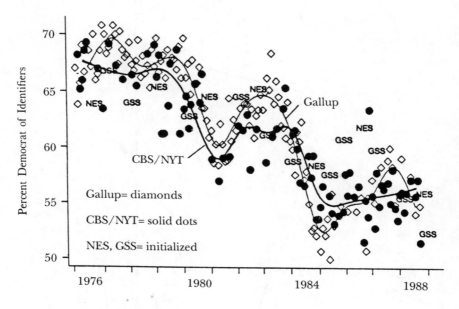

Note: Trend lines are computer-generated cubic splines.
Source: Adapted from MacKuen, Erikson, and Stimson (1992).

greater frequency of media polls, to differences in sampling frames and interviewer procedures, to the greater use of telephone surveys by the media, or to other causes.

Indeed, the debate as to the stability of partisanship has intensified on other fronts. Several studies have challenged the claim that party identification should be treated as endogenous because they do not find partisanship changing as a result of political variables. Whiteley (1988) used the NES continuous monitoring study through the 1984 campaign year to study the stability of partisanship. He did not find partisanship to vary as a result of changing views of issues, candidates, or vote intentions over the one-year period. Green and Palmquist (1990) argue that findings of endogeneity of partisanship are largely artifactual. Every survey question inevitably includes some measurement error; after correcting for limited reliability, they find minimal effects of candidate evaluations, issue proximity, presidential approval, or presidential vote on party identification in the surveys that NES took during the 1980 presidential election year. However, care is necessary in interpreting these studies, as they inevitably depend on how error terms are specified (compare Smith and Reed, 1990).

Additionally, Warren Miller (1991), one of the authors of the Michigan party identification scale, has recently contended that part of the apparent instability in partisanship may be due to use of the wrong measure. He suggests that the original treatment of party identification in *The American Voter* is more compatible with just using the first partisanship question (asking people whether they consider themselves Republicans, Democrats, or Independents). He argues that researchers should use a categorization of Republicans versus Democrats, as proportions of the total sample, rather than the seven-point party identification scale because the latter introduces irrelevant considerations of strength of partisanship. Miller demonstrates that partisanship thus defined was stable from 1952 to after 1980 for northern white voters. There was realignment for white male southerners during that period, plus significant changes for African-Americans. Miller interprets this stability for northern white voters as countering the claim that national changes in partisanship in those years were due to changes in the economic health of the nation. However, his use of just three categories could be masking variability even for northern white voters, and his focus on the Republican-Democratic difference misses the considerable growth in independents over this period.

As to the intergenerational stability of partisanship, Mattei and Niemi (1991) have taken issue with the Carmines, McIver, and Stimson (1987) analysis. Mattei and Niemi pointed out that Carmines, McIver, and Stimson omitted a quarter to a third of respondents who did not know their parents' partisanship. Within this expanded framework, the unrealized partisans amount to less than half of the independents. Furthermore, partisan parents might be less successful than in the 1950s in transmitting their partisanship across generations, but independent parents are more successful than in the 1950s in transmitting their position on partisanship. Thus, there is greater stability in transmission of partisanship and independence than Carmines, McIver, and Stimson located. Additionally, Niemi and Jennings (Chapter 18) find in the 1965-73-82 socialization panel study that the deviation from parental partisanship occurs by the mid-twenties, with no further loss in the 1982 interviews than found in the 1973 wave. This suggests considerable stability in partisanship, albeit after some initial change.

While we have reviewed the debate on the stability of partisanship only for the United States, the same considerations are relevant in other countries. Indeed, the usual view is that party identification is even less stable outside the United States, with party identification shifting as a result of changes in vote intention rather than vice versa as for the United States. Richardson (1991), however, has suggested an important variant on this argument. He examined different types of parties, contrasting traditional cleavage-based parties, which evoke inter-party hostilities based on a century of conflict, with newer noncleavage parties. Panel studies showed greater vote stability for followers of cleavage-based parties in the Netherlands, Germany, and Britain than for followers of non-cleavage parties. Further, supporters of cleavage parties in Britain and the Netherlands had high levels of hostility toward the other cleavage parties. Thus partisan stability may be prevalent for particular types of parties, even in Europe.[3]

In short, this line of argument implies that partisanship is stable enough for the party identification concept to remain meaningful as a long-term component of the vote decision. Party identification is not totally stable, but it is sufficiently so as to preserve its preeminent status in understanding voting.

Measurement Questions: What Does the Party Identification Question Measure?

In addition to controversy over the stability of party identification, there has been considerable debate about its measurement. We focus here on three measurement topics: question wording effects, the dimensionality of partisanship, and the meaning of independence.

The measurement of party identification became a lively source of dispute in the 1970s (see *Classics*, chap. 21). In recent years, attention has turned to the exact wording of the party identification question, partly to see whether a different wording would yield better results and partly to understand the differences that arise when commercial polls use different wordings. The original NES wording is still used today in the NES studies, but researchers have become more sensitive as to how the wording of the party identification question affects the results.

Studies have now examined the time frame in which the question is asked, the effects of different response categories, the level of government for which the question is asked, and the effects of different types of partisanship questions. We now know that commercial polls that ask people their partisanship "as of today" obtain a greater advantage for the party ahead in the presidential race by about five percent as compared to polls that ask about partisanship "usually" or "generally" (Borrelli, Lockerbie, and Niemi, 1987).[4] We know that not providing the "independent" option yields fewer claiming independent status (Kenney and Rice, 1988; Niemi, Reed, and Weisberg, 1991). We know that many citizens in federal systems identify with different parties at different levels of government (Niemi, Powell, and Wright, 1987), a phenomenon described by Wekkin (1991) as "segmented partisanship."[5] And we know that asking people to place themselves directly on a 1 (strongly Republican) to 7 (strongly Democrat) scale yields a less reliable measure than the usual party identification scale (Krosnick and Berent, 1991).[6]

One of the more elaborate question wording experiments was designed to test the commitment of respondents to their partisanship. The 1987 NES Pilot Study asked respondents the traditional party identification question, a "forced-choice" version without the "independent" option, and a "filtered" version with the extra option of permitting people to say that "they don't think of themselves that way." Niemi, Reed, and Weisberg (1991) show that only two-thirds of the respondents were "committed" to their partisanship, either giving the same response all three times or answering independent when that option was offered but a partisan response otherwise. A quarter of the respondents were apartisan (not thinking of themselves as partisans or independents) or gave inconsistent answers (Democrat on some versions of the question and Republican on others). Another question wording experiment was designed to see how well the "party closeness" question that is commonly used in other countries would work in the United States (Barnes, Kaase, et al., 1979, p. 577; Converse and Pierce, 1986, p. 52). In this form of the question, people are asked to which party they feel closest, and then whether they feel very close, fairly close, or not very close to that party. Barnes, Jennings, Inglehart, and Farah (1988) found that that scale has desirable properties even in the United States, with four-fifths of Americans considering themselves closer to one of the parties and with the responses being a good predictor of the presidential vote (though that may mean that the party closeness question is closer to being a surrogate measure of vote intentions than is the usual party identification scale).

Several of these studies of wording effects were designed to show that changes in the usual NES party identification question would be desirable. However, the major result of this work has just been to increase our sensitivity to the inevitable effects of wording choices. Survey results are always dependent on how poll questions are phrased, and that is as true for party identification as for any other question. What you get always depends in part on how you ask for it.

A special measurement issue examined at length in the past decade is the dimensionality of party identification. Following work by Weisberg (see *Classics*, chap. 27) and by Valentine and Van Wingen (1980), there has been debate as to whether there is a single Republican-Democratic dimension with independence as the neutral point or whether partisanship should be seen as multidimensional with a separate independent-partisan dimension. In support of the latter position, Kamieniecki (1985; 1988) demonstrated that the usual strength of partisanship scale and a separate strength of independence scale had the same sign correlations with several variables instead of the expected opposite signed correlations. Also, Alvarez (1990) found that most party identifiers did not have transitive preferences over the parties and independence—fewer than two out of five identifiers had ranked their own party highest on the thermometers, independence second, and the opposite party lowest. Alvarez concluded from this test and others that party identification is multidimensional.

The use of party thermometers in many of these studies has proved controversial. Alvarez confirmed Weisberg's (see *Classics*, chap. 27) initial report that thermometer ratings of the political parties better predict the vote than does the usual party identification scale and that Republican and Democratic partisanship are not polar opposites because the correlation between the party thermometers is often near zero. However, the counterargument (McDonald and Howell, 1982; Converse and Pierce, 1985) is that the party identification scale may be a better long-term measure. Converse and Pierce (1985), for example, found that the 1976 vote could be better predicted from 1972 party identification than from 1972 party thermometers (even though the 1972 vote could be better predicted from 1972 thermometers than from the party identification scale). This echoes a McDonald and Howell (1982) finding that, taking into account the thermometer's lower reliability and stability, party thermometers in 1972 have less effect on 1976 party identification than does the usual party identification scale, when 1972 presidential vote is controlled. These findings imply both that the party identification scale performs better for long-term analysis and that the party thermometers are contaminated by short-term political forces.

Also, Green (1988) and Krosnick and Weisberg (1988) argue that the lack of correlation between the party thermometers is partially due to measurement artifacts. Green (1988) used confirmatory factor analysis to analyze 1976 responses, controlling for the bias introduced by the fact that some respondents give uniformly high thermometer scores and others give uniformly low thermometer scores. Correcting for both random and nonrandom measurement errors, the correlation between the latent Republican and Democratic factors was $-.81$, compared to $-.30$ when only nonrandom errors were considered, and an observed correlation of just $-.03$. As a result, Green argues that the party thermometers are actually unidimensional, even if measurement error makes them look independent. Krosnick and Weisberg (1988) obtained similar results using confirmatory factor analysis with a methods factor on which all of the thermometers load equally. With that extra methods factor included, the Republican and Democratic party factors were negatively correlated enough to suggest unidimensionality. Yet, these models are based on assumptions about measurement error that can be challenged, and the quality of fit of the confirmatory factor analysis models is not excellent. These limitations argue that the Republican and Democratic thermometers should be viewed as neither totally unidimensional nor totally independent.

The debate as to the dimensionality of partisanship continues. In their influential books, Kessel (1984) and Fiorina (1981) found the multidimensional view unnecessary. Yet the recent journal articles by Kamieniecki (1988) and Alvarez (1990) reveal a continuing fascination with the multidimensional approach. A final conclusion may depend on which aspect of partisanship is at issue. In particular, the usual measurement of partisanship seems to confound strength of partisanship with political independence, rather than measuring independence separately.

This leads us to the third concern of this section: the meaning and measurement of political independence. The original work on party identification virtually treats independence as a residual category, rather than examining its basis in depth. Furthermore, the coding of independents has proved controversial.

The major change in party identification from 1952 through 1980 was an increase in political independents. Keith et al. (1986) find that this growth was most heavily due to "leaners" (those who respond Independent to the first party identification question but then say they are closer to one party than the other), and they argue that leaners should really be treated as partisans. Furthermore, Miller and Wattenberg (1983) point out that some people who are coded as independents actually have answered that they are not Republican, Democratic, or Independent. (NES surveys code as independents those who avoid answering the first party identification question, who are not closer to the Republicans or the Democrats on the follow-up question, but who are interested in politics; they code as "apoliticals" those respondents who give the same pattern of answers except that they are not interested in politics.) Miller and Wattenberg (1983) demonstrate that the increase in independents from 1968 through 1980 was largely due to these no-preference independents. Further, they show that these respondents differed from self-proclaimed independents in political involvement and in attitudes toward political independence. Craig (1985), however, sharply disagrees, discovering that no-preference independents and self-proclaimed independents differ on attitudes toward symbols of independence.

Paralleling the growth in independents, Wattenberg (Chapter 22) has shown that there has been a considerable growth since 1952 in the proportion of the public whose open-ended comments are neutral to both parties. This greater neutrality toward parties could represent balanced views of each party with equal numbers of like and dislike comments, but Stanga and Sheffield (1987) show that it is mainly composed of what they term "artificial neutrals," respondents who make no comments at all when asked what they like and dislike about each party, and that this category is the one that has increased over the years. Thus, there may seem to be a growth over the years in independents and also in people who are neutral toward the parties, but both of these points can be challenged on the basis of coding issues.

The more fundamental issue is what political independence means. Analysis by Dennis (1988b) reveals that there are four aspects of independence: political autonomy (viewing independence positively in terms of such values as individualism), antipartyism (being independent because of a negative view of parties), partisan neutrality (being independent because of neutrality between the parties), and partisan variability (seeing oneself as switching between the parties). Factor analysis of 1980 NES data shows that these are four separate factors. Furthermore, Dennis shows these four factors have different relationships to other variables. For example, people with more education are higher on autonomy and variability but lower on antipartyism and neutrality. Those who are high on variability are more likely to vote. All in all, neutrality is related to lower political awareness and involvement (and antipartyism has a somewhat similar pattern), while variability has positive correlations with those variables.

These several measurement disputes have important substantive implications. Minimally the "official" distribution of party identification in the electorate should be seen as dependent on the question wording, and probably on the mode of interviewing as well. Additionally, our limited understanding of independence, whether as a separate dimension or as a composite for several different syndromes a la Dennis, means that the potential support for a nonparty candidate (such as Ross Perot in 1992) may be much higher than was realized.

Conclusion

The terms of the debate over the stability and measurement of partisanship are important, even if it may be impossible to reach consensus on some of the most vital concerns. Party identification is so important to actual politicians that the debates of this chapter cannot be dismissed as merely methodological or viewed as only of academic interest.

Let us begin with whether party identification is stable in the short term. The Republican party in 1984 tried targeting particular groups of voters with their appeals, and it financed an expensive nightly polling operation to monitor changes in vote intention and in party identification. Party identification moved sharply in the Republican direction during this campaign (Allsop and Weisberg, 1988), and Republican campaign advisers wanted to take credit for that change. They clearly saw partisanship as being affected by the political forces unleashed in an election year and as something they could manipulate in that atmosphere. The short-term stability of partisanship can thus be important to political practitioners.

Similarly, both party pollsters and political scientists must be able to count on the validity of some measure of party identification, rather than just wonder which measurement is correct. The debate over the measurement of partisanship has been vexing. On the one hand, most researchers in voting behavior seem content to continue using the usual party identification scale. On the other hand, the questioning of that measure continues unabated. If there is a middle ground here, it is that the usual measure does fine in measuring partisan direction, but it confounds political independence with strength of partisanship rather than measuring independence sufficiently in its own right. Still, it is particularly regrettable if independence has not been measured well, given that one of the most interesting political changes in the last half century has been the growth in independents (see also Chapter 19).

The theoretical importance of studies of partisanship in the 1980s and early 1990s is considerable, but these studies are limited intrinsically by the time span they cover. Most of these studies show only that partisanship was changeable during the 1980s, which does not indicate whether this was always the case or whether it is a new development. Has the meaning of partisanship changed, with that accounting for the ability of parties to move partisanship in their direction during a political campaign, or has partisanship always been volatile, with our measurements being too infrequent to tap that change? Was the measurement of independence better suited to tapping 1950s-style independence? Has independence always been multifaceted, or is that a new development based on a more educated electorate? Have parties simply receded in importance as a means of thinking about elections? Perhaps some of the debates as to the stability and measurement of partisanship will someday be answered, but we suspect we shall never know whether the current set of findings is a new one or if partisanship has always been the way it is today.

NOTES

1. Of course, almost no one sees partisanship as entirely short term but rather as a mixture of long- and short-term aspects. An estimation by Smith and Reed (1990) of the relative sizes of long- and short-term components found that the long-term factor predominates in the usual party identification scale, but with a short-term factor that leads to some instability.
2. Over-time panel studies have traditionally found party identification to be more stable

than other political attitudes. However, Krosnick (1991) shows this is due to the higher reliability of the party identification measure. Indeed, he argues that the usual finding that party identification explains candidate preferences and other dependent variables better than other attitudinal predictors may be due to its being measured with greater reliability.

3. This question is still open to debate with respect to Great Britain; Heath and Pierce (1991) argue that the greater movement of party identification with the vote in Britain is due to asking people their partisanship directly after asking them about their vote. As Heath and Pierce recognize, however, their effort is weakened by the limited experimentation with alternative partisanship questions.

4. This is in accord with Abramson and Ostrom's (1991) suggestion that the greater variance in partisanship for the Gallup question than for the Michigan wording is due to a shorter time frame in the Gallup question. (See also Nie, Verba, and Petrocik, 1979, p. 421).

5. This topic has also been extensively studied in Canada. See Blake (1982) and Uslaner (1990).

6. We also know that Gallup—in a series of comparisons beginning in 1985—has consistently found a greater percentage of Democrats in personal than in telephone interviews, a discrepancy that is only partly explained by socioeconomic differences in the two types of surveys. See "Birth of a Question" (1991) and Hugick (1991b).

FURTHER READINGS

Aggregate Stability and Change

Dee Allsop and Herbert F. Weisberg, "Measuring Change in Party Identification in an Election Campaign," *American Journal of Political Science* (1988) 32:996-1017. Partisanship changes during 1984, showing responsiveness to events of the presidential campaign.

Herbert F. Weisberg and Charles E. Smith, Jr., "The Influence of the Economy on Party Identification in the Reagan Years," *Journal of Politics* (1991) 53:1077-92. Partisanship changes through the early 1980s, showing responsiveness to economic events.

Paul R. Abramson and Charles W. Ostrom, Jr., "Macropartisanship: An Empirical Reassessment," *American Political Science Review* (1991) 85:181-92. Apparent macropartisanship changes due to question wording effects.

Michael B. MacKuen, Robert Erikson, and James A. Stimson, "Question-wording and Macropartisanship," *American Political Science Review* (1992) 86:475-81. Macropartisanship changes hold regardless of question wording.

Warren E. Miller, "Party Identification Realignment and Party Voting: Back to the Basics," *American Political Science Review* (1991) 85:557-68. Party identification was highly stable from 1952 to 1980 among non-Southerners.

Warren E. Miller, "Generational Changes in Party Identification," *Political Behavior* (1992) 14:forthcoming. Comparison of party change for pre- and post-New Deal generations.

Individual Stability and Change

Richard A. Brody and Lawrence S. Rothenberg, "The Instability of Partisanship: An Analysis of the 1980 Presidential Election," *British Journal of Political Science* (1988) 18:445-65. Issues caused partisanship changes in the 1980 NES panel study.

Paul F. Whiteley, "The Causal Relationships Between Issues, Candidate Evaluations, Party Identification, and Vote Choice—the View From 'Rolling Thunder'." *Journal of Politics* (1988) 50:961-84. Issues do not cause partisanship changes in the 1984 NES continuous monitoring study.

Donald Philip Green and Bradley Palmquist, "Of Artifacts and Partisan Instability," *American Journal of Political Science* (1990) 34:872-901. Findings of partisan stability are due to measurement error.

Intergenerational Transmission of Partisanship

Charles H. Franklin, "Issue Preferences, Socialization, and the Evolution of Party Identification," *American Journal of Political Science* (1984) 28:459-78. The partisanship of young adults changes in response to their issue positions.

Edward G. Carmines, John P. McIver, and James A. Stimson, "Unrealized Partisanship: A Theory of Dealignment," *Journal of Politics* (1987) 49:376-400. The growth of independents is due to "unrealized partisans," whose issue positions are unlike those who follow their parents' partisanship.

Robert C. Luskin, John P. McIver, and Edward G. Carmines, "Issues and the Transmission of Partisanship," *American Journal of Political Science* (1989) 33:440-58. Conversions are heavily influenced by "hard" issues while movement toward independence is less often based on issues.

Franco Mattei and Richard G. Niemi, "Unrealized Partisans, Realized Independents, and the Intergenerational Transmission of Party Identification," *Journal of Politics* (1991) 53:161-74. The number of unrealized partisans has not increased, but political independence has been successfully transmitted between generations.

Cross-National Perspectives on Partisanship

Lawrence LeDuc, "The Dynamic Properties of Party Identification: A Four Nation Comparison," *European Journal of Political Research* (1981) 9:257-68. Party identification changes with the vote in some European nations.

Samuel H. Barnes, M. Kent Jennings, Ronald Inglehart, and Barbara Farah, "Party Identification and Party Closeness in Comparative Perspective," *Political Behavior* (1988) 10:215-31. Cross-national differences in party identification reflect question wording, particularly providing the Independent option in American studies.

Bradley M. Richardson, "European Party Loyalties Revisited," *American Political Science Review* (1991) 85:751-75. Stable partisanship exists in three major European nations.

Measurement of Partisanship

Philip E. Converse and Roy Pierce, "Measuring Partisanship," *Political Methodology* (1985) 11:143-66. The party identification scale is a better long-term predictor of the vote than are thermometers.

Stephen Borrelli, Brad Lockerbie, and Richard G. Niemi, "Why the Democrat-Republican Partisanship Gap Varies from Poll to Poll," *Public Opinion Quarterly* (1987) 51:115-19. Analysis of question wording effects on party identification.

Donald Philip Green, "On the Dimensionality of Public Sentiment toward Partisan and Ideological Groups," *American Journal of Political Science* (1988) 32:758-80. Partisanship is unidimensional, once measurement error is taken into account.

R. Michael Alvarez, "The Puzzle of Party Identification," *American Politics Quarterly* (1990) 18:476-91. Party identification is indeed multidimensional.

Richard G. Niemi, David Reed, and Herbert F. Weisberg, "Partisan Commitment," *Political Behavior* (1991) 13:213-20. Low level of commitment to partisanship answers across multiple wordings of the question.

Political Independence

Bruce E. Keith, David B. Magleby, Candice L. Nelson, Elizabeth Orr, Mark C. Westlye, and Raymond E. Wolfinger, "The Partisan Affinities of Independent 'Leaners,'" *British Journal of Political Science* (1986) 16:155-85. Independent leaners resemble partisans more than independents.

Jack Dennis, "Political Independence in America, Part II: Towards a Theory," *British Journal of Political Science* (1988) 18:197-219. The many dimensions of political independence.

Bruce E. Keith et al. *The Myth of the Independent Voter* (Berkeley: University of California Press, 1992). Independents have not increased in strength as is commonly believed.

Symposium on Party Identification

Political Behavior (1992) vol. 15. Research articles on a variety of aspects of party identification.

17. MACROPARTISANSHIP

Michael B. MacKuen, Robert S. Erikson, and James A. Stimson

Party identification is the key concept of U.S. electoral research. Always in the forefront in the analysis of individual behavior and attitudes, it is all but obvious that its aggregate, the national partisan balance, should be a central barometer of the party system. But owing to an early consensus that individual identifications did not respond to the current issues, personalities, and conflicts of politics, its aggregate was presumed to be a constant, not a variable. That early consensus, we now know, was wrong. And if individual party ties respond to issues, performance, or whatever, the partisan balance ought to vary over time. We assert that it does, that the variation is patterned, that it has electoral consequences, and that it can be explained.

Just as party identification is the key concept in studies of the individual voter, its aggregate—what we term macropartisanship—is central to theories of party system and voter alignment.[1] For macropartisanship, constancy is the norm. Change is expected only during the rate realigning transition to a new party system. And any such epochal change in macropartisanship that has occurred has gone unobserved for the reason that even the most recent supposed realignment (of the early 1930s) predates modern survey research measurement of party identification. Macropartisanship in the current era is agreed to be marked by stability. More specifically, the consensus is that changes in macropartisanship should be infrequent, small, and of brief duration. That too is wrong.

Previous Work

What is party identification? The standard view, traced to *The American Voter* (Campbell et al., 1960) is that identification is a stable psychological attachment to one's favored political party. The evidence that party identification is stable, particularly when compared to other political attitudes, appears to be quite strong. Over time, the directional component of the distribution of party

Source: *American Political Science Review* (1989) 83:1125-42. Reprinted with permission of the publisher.

identification shows a Democratic advantage of seemingly constant magnitude that varies only slightly in response to political events like landslide elections. At the individual level, changes in party identification are uncommon, at least in comparison with the turnover of responses to other political items, such as those intended to tap preferences on policy issues (Converse, 1976; Converse and Markus, 1979). Panel studies show that no more than about 4% of the electorate changes identification from Republican to Democratic or vice versa over a four-year period (although more will move in and out of the Independent category). Analysts have suggested that even these changes reflect measurement error more than true attitude change (Achen 1975; Green and Palmquist, 1990).

It was standard, until recently, to model the attitudinal variables affecting the vote decision to give party identification the status of the ultimate independent variable in the causal hierarchy (Declerq, Hurley, and Luttbeg 1975; Goldberg 1966; Miller et al. 1976; Schulman and Pomper 1975). Party identification was assumed to affect candidate evaluations, issue positions, and certainly the vote— but not to be affected by them. Citizens, it seemed, did not change their party preferences except during realignment events or perhaps when undergoing major changes in demographic attributes.

The reason for party identification's secure place in the voting paradigm is its stability. Voting decisions and candidate evaluations cannot cause major changes in party identification because, in the aggregate, the former variables are unstable over time while party identification is supposed not to be. Similarly, analysts have resisted the notion that issue attitudes have much influence on party identification because measures of issue attitudes are notoriously unstable while party identification is not.

Is party identification in the United States the stable psychological attachment that we have described? Over the past decade or so, party identification has been subject to some revisionary thinking (see Shively, 1980 for an early history). In part, the revised view is based on growing awareness that party identification is far from perfectly stable and is indeed somewhat responsive to short-term political forces. Some evidence for revised thinking comes from simultaneous equation models of political attitudes and the vote that (with appropriate identifying assumptions) test the possibility of simultaneous effects of two variables on each other (Erikson, 1982; Franklin and Jackson, 1983; Markus, 1982; Markus and Converse, 1979; Page and Jones, 1979). These studies suggest that a major causal flow is from other variables to party identification.

Still other evidence comes from panel studies where change in party identification is seen as a function of short-term influences (Brody, 1977, 1978; Fiorina, 1981). The 1972-76 National Election Study provides evidence that changes in party identification were associated with perceived economic satisfaction, attitudes toward Richard Nixon, and attitudes toward Gerald Ford's pardon of Nixon (Brody, 1978; Fiorina, 1981). Moreover, in the 1960 wave of the earlier national panel, Catholic Democrats and Protestant Republicans tended to strengthen their identifications and Catholic Republicans and Protestant Democrats tended to do the opposite—exactly as one would expect if people adjusted their identifications in response to the religion issue of the Kennedy-Nixon campaign (Brody, 1977). Both Brody and Fiorina suggest that party identification has both a short-term and long-term component.

It is unclear how much revision in our thinking about party identification is required from such studies. It has long been known (Knoke and Hout, 1974), for instance, that the aggregate distribution of party identification does change over time in response to short-term forces, but the change is thought to be slight (Campbell et al., 1960; Converse, 1976; Markus, 1982). Moreover, some doubt can be cast on the findings of simultaneous equation models because the models are identifiable only on the basis of assumptions that themselves are open to question. And while panels show some responsiveness of partisanship to short-term forces, it is not clear whether this responsiveness is extensive enough to be of much substantive significance.

Macropartisanship as Time Series

Some of the apparent stability of party identification is a result of how we look at it. We normally see the frequency distribution of party identification presented as a time series with two- or four-year intervals between readings.[2] Such a series looks much like the concept originally developed in *The American Voter*. Because they do not appear systematic, its year-to-year fluctuations do not draw our attention. For that we need a finer time scale.

Party identification may be treated as a continuous macro phenomenon measured through time. We have gathered data for such a series, presented here as a quarterly compilation of the Gallup identification measure from 1945 through 1987. This series is presented in Figure 17-1 as the Democratic percentages of the major party identifiers. Impressionistic examination of this series suggests the presence of important systematic variation over time.

From Figure 17-1, Democrats can be seen to achieve "governing" majorities in the early 1960s and for most of the 1970s, with less secure, but still majority, standing at other times. But the Republicans now challenge for ascendancy, as they did once before in 1945-47. These movements in partisanship are often of a magnitude large enough to suggest electoral realignment.

Note that these shifts are not temporary but persist from quarter to quarter. Yet they have nothing like the permanence envisioned in realignment notions. The partisan balance is not nearly so stable as *The American Voter* or critical realignment theory would lead us to expect of this "normal" postwar period. Instead, macropartisanship appears to be a midrange phenomenon, one that appears and disappears in a time frame of a year or two rather than a month or two or, alternatively, a decade or two. The movements within this stable alignment period appear substantial, both in magnitude and duration.

Is Macropartisan Movement Systematic and Does It Matter?

Before pursuing macropartisanship in earnest, we must first be sure that the movement we observe is more than the inevitable random fluctuations from sampling error. In principle, this question can be answered by a simple

Figure 17-1   Macropartisanship, 1945-1988

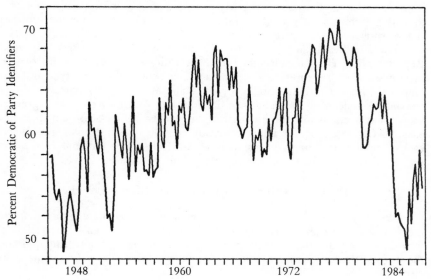

application of sampling theory to estimate the reliability of our aggregate measure. All we need is the average number of cases for our quarterly readings.

The average N is unavailable for the full set of Gallup surveys, because the provided number of cases in many instances is weighted by multiple counting of certain cases to achieve a representative sample. A conservative estimate, however, is a typical N of at least fifteen hundred partisans per quarterly reading. Given this approximate N, the average error variance is only about 1.67 percentage points. The observed variance for the quarterly series is 25.44. Dividing the former by the latter and subtracting from one yields an approximate reliability estimate of .93 for the time series.[3] Thus, the observable trends of the party identification time series cannot be accounted for by sampling or measurement error, a statistical conclusion that matches visual evidence.

What the series seems to indicate is that we have a phenomenon— multiquarter, multiyear systematic movements of partisanship—for which there is no obvious explanation. We have not tried but failed to account for it; instead it has gone pretty much unnoticed (but see Maggiotto and Mishler, 1987). It is by no means a small matter. Given the often overwhelming causal power of micro party identification, knowledge of the secular movement of this macro series could give us purchase on all sorts of electoral phenomena.

The Electoral Importance of Macropartisanship

Party identification is a variable little in need of defense. At the individual level its explanatory power is thoroughly tested. But we might ask whether macropartisanship matters. That question, too, will provoke little skepticism. But it might be argued that the aggregated series contains no meaningful variation—that its movements are statistical flukes without consequences for the supposed stable patterns of U.S. party politics.

For an illustration that macropartisanship matters, we regress House of Representatives election outcomes (in Democratic seats won) on third quarter macropartisanship (expressed as percentage Democratic of two party identifiers). National House elections, both relatively stable and relatively partisan, should respond to underlying movements in partisanship. And they do. The regression shows that a one-point shift in partisanship yields a three-seat gain in House elections ($R^2 = .38$). Alternatively we can focus on votes instead of seats, where each one-point gain in partisanship is worth .31% of the national House vote ($R^2 = .23$).[4] Movements in macropartisanship do matter.

Party Identification Dynamics: Micro Level

We focus here on the partisan movement of the electorate rather than the more typical focus on the changing partisanship of individual citizens. To ask why the individual citizen sometimes changes identifications is a worthy question, the subject of a vast literature. But it is not our question. We wish to know about electorates, about net change.

To ask about net movements in partisanship is to ask only part of the micro behavior question, for we do not presume that the individual changes that produce net movements of one or two percentage points from one month to the next are more than a fraction of all individual partisan changes. But for the larger story of politics—the interaction of citizens and governing apparatus—they are the meaningful part. For that percentage or two has consequences; it builds or undermines electoral coalitions and it alters election outcomes.

Of course, the relationship between micro-level party identifications and our aggregated measure of macropartisanship can be a matter for interesting speculation. The systematic movements of macropartisanship do not by any means require that the citizens who comprise the electorate behave uniformly, that an increase, say, in proportion Democratic implies that each citizen individually becomes more likely to answer *Democrat* to the party identification query; for systematic macro patterns easily emerge from situations where only a relative handful behave systematically. It is the familiar story of aggregation gain. Where most are either fixed or changing in a noisy randomlike fashion and a few are systematic, the signal is wholly the behavior of the few.

One implication of this point is that our findings will neither support nor undermine particular models of individual partisanship. For those models are couched in the language of modal patterns and typical behaviors. Thus, an *American Voter* sort of model that posits partisanship prior to political evaluation could, for example, be fundamentally accurate with but a handful of exceptions. And yet that handful is enough to produce the macro behavior that we shall model.

Consider economic evaluations. A question often raised in the context of·

economics and politics is whether the average citizen can ever be adequately equipped with either the information or analytic tools necessary for economic evaluation. We don't know. Nor need we. For if we posited a hypothetical world in which, say, the daily subscribers to the *Wall Street Journal* alone made political judgments driven in part by economic performance, we would expect to see systematic movement in the aggregate.[5] It matters that *some* be capable of economic evaluation, not all.

This is little different from the original Downs (1957) formulation of the voter calculus. Our departure from Downs is agnosticism about whether rational and informed citizen behavior is typical or exceptional. Taking account of aggregation gain vitiates much of the three-decade conflict over citizen capabilities for rational action. The survey research tradition might be quite on the mark in asserting that average citizens do not so behave. But if only some do, the systemic consequences follow. "Thus it is quite possible," Converse similarly concludes, "to have a highly rational system performance on the backs of voters most of whom are remarkably ill-informed much of the time" (1986, p. 17).

Party Identification Dynamics: Macro Level

We now consider the causes of macrolevel movements in partisanship. The most obvious source for theoretical guidance is Fiorina's (1981) theory of cumulative updating. According to Fiorina's model, citizens use partisan orientation as a shorthand device for making sense of the political world. Citizens continually evaluate their political environments and adjust their views of the political parties accordingly. They alter their own partisan attachments as their comparative judgments of the parties' merits change over time. (More formally, this can be understood as a Bayesian updating model; see Calvert and MacKuen, 1985).

The electorate's collective judgments about various aspects of the incumbent party's performance thus become the leading candidates to explain shifts in macropartisanship. When the incumbent administration fares well, its party should attract supporters. When the administration encounters disaster, it should lose its numbers. Our historical data allow us to test this proposition, as they provide periods of palpable good and bad times for both Democrats and Republicans. Gallup's measure of presidential approval is one obvious and important indicator of the incumbent party's perceived performance. Economic performance could matter too. But which economic indicator should we use?

For a clean measure of citizen economic evaluations, we use the well-known (Michigan) composite Index of Consumer Sentiment (ICS). This index is available on a quarterly basis for 1953 onward. It taps perceptions of how well things have gone, are going, and (most important) are likely to go. It is a summary of the state of confidence citizens express in the economy. It is a short step to postulate a likely relationship between confidence in the economy and confidence in the economic managers—the president and his party. We presume—and have elsewhere (MacKuen, Erikson, and Stimson, 1988) demonstrated—the index to be intermediate between objective economic indicators and political response. It taps the state of the economy as perceived by those same citizens from whom political response is expected. Clearly, it is a direct measure, purged of the usual slippage between what indicators show and what citizens feel. ICS is a composite of five separate items tapping retrospective and prospective evaluations of both the respondents' personal economic situation and the national economy.

We posit that macropartisanship responds to presidential approval and economic perceptions as registered by the Index of Consumer Sentiment. As numerous studies show (Hibbs, 1982a, Kenski, 1977, Kernell, 1978, MacKuen, 1983, Monroe, 1981, Ostrom and Simon, 1985, and others in support; Norpoth and Yantek, 1983 in dissent), economic sentiment exerts its own direct effect on presidential approval. Thus a major portion of the effect of economic perceptions on macropartisanship may be indirect—with economic perceptions affecting presidential approval, which in turn affects partisanship.

The Correspondence of Consumer Sentiment, Presidential Approval, and Macropartisanship

We begin our analysis with a visual "test" of the responsiveness of macropartisanship to presidential approval and consumer sentiment. In Figure 17-2, we track partisanship (as support for the president's party), presidential approval, and ICS for 1946-86 (ICS from only 1953 on). Each is presented on a separate metric. In order that the eye not be distracted by random movement, this data display has been smoothed by taking a simple three-quarter moving average (the average of the preceding, current, and following quarter) for each time point.[6]

The data bear close inspection. It is clear that both approval and partisanship move in step with economic perceptions. Both rise with perceived prosperity and fall with perceived depression. The translation is sometimes loose. Not every twist in the economic series is mimicked in the partisanship series. Nor is it clear that the turning points in each series coincide exactly. As economists are apt to moan, it looks like the lags are long and variable.

Yet we should not lose sight of the overall pattern. At the level of, say, yearly movements, the consumer sentiment series appears to translate directly into both approval and partisanship. While the precision of a mathematical representation has yet to be demonstrated, the plausibility of modeling partisanship as a function of economic well-being is apparent. The relationship is evident to the naked eye. And even the loose translation is partly reassuring evidence. The notable mismatch of economic perception and political response, for example, occurs during the Johnson administration, where generally strong economic performance could not hold up political support in the face of foreign war and domestic turmoil, a pattern none will find surprising.

The pictures show that macropartisanship responds to historical forces. We need to know that the apparent relationships are more than optical illusions and that they reflect a plausible causal ordering. The first matter is measuring the extent to which macropartisanship coincides systematically with our measures of environmental conditions. After all, many tendencies fall to careful statistical scrutiny.

Figure 17-2 Macropartisanship, Presidential Approval, and Consumer Sentiment: Truman to Reagan

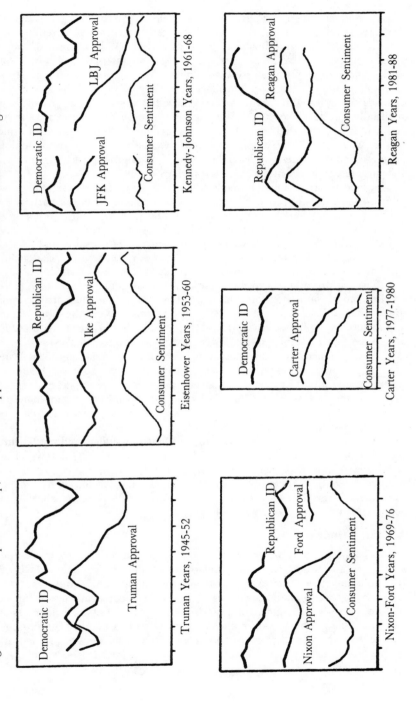

Fortunately, we can apply a formal "exogeneity" test to see whether the temporal correlations shown in Figure 17-2 can be attributed to genuine causal connections. A Granger-Sims test[7] proceeds as follows: First, each of the three series is whitened. The problem is that each series (as is typical of this sort of work) reflects its own previous values. The dependence process, an autoregressive function, is often similar in form across different series. It is the case that independent series with similar autoregressive functions will be substantially but artificially correlated over time. The solution is to *whiten* each series at the outset; that is to say, each variable is modeled as a function of its own previous values in such a way that the resulting series has (virtually) no autocorrelation. Each manifestation therefore represents the "innovation" in the series at that time point and does not reflect continuations of previous inputs.

Second, each variable is modeled as a transfer function of the previous *prewhitened* values of the other variables. For example, *whitened* partisanship is modeled as a function of previous values of *whitened* approval in order to see if the "innovations" in approval may be said to have caused subsequent innovations in partisanship. Post hoc propter hoc is no assurance of causality and its absence no sure disconfirmation, but our argument about meaningful relationships is substantially strengthened when such an exogeneity test is passed.

The results of the exogeneity tests are shown in Table 17-1. Here all possible causal connections are estimated, though of course some are theoretically implausible. Entries in the table are the correlations between the estimated model and the observed series. Equally important are the significance tests in parentheses. (Note that the table is asymmetric: temporal ordering makes a difference.)

Three connections show statistical strength. Consumer sentiment "causes" both approval and macropartisanship. Approval then goes on further, and independently, to affect macropartisanship. Our statistical apparatus also allows us to test the reverse causal flows. Happily, the evidence sustains none of the contrary linkages. Macropartisanship does not cause approval and neither macropartisanship nor approval shapes economic perceptions.[8]

Again, this more skeptical scrutiny sustains our understanding that macropartisanship varies in an interesting and theoretically meaningful way. This type of Granger-Sims exogeneity test can be overly tough (it is given to false negatives), so that our discovering substantial causal connections among the prewhitened variables is strong statistical evidence. The fact that it makes common sense is all the more appealing.

A Causal Model

All this suggests that we may be able to account for changes in macropartisanship with a substantially interesting empirical model. We should like to offer a plausible and interesting example of how this might be accomplished.

The preceding analyses were essentially bivariate in character. Yet it is clear that our variables are highly collinear. Thus, if we seek unbiased estimates of our empirical relationships, proper model specification is a matter of the first order.

With our major theoretical specification complete, we add to our quiver a couple of additional series. First, it is clear from models of presidential approval

Table 17-1   Exogeneity Tests

Dependent Variable	Partisanship[a]	Presidential Approval	Consumer Sentiment
		Independent Variable	
Partisanship	—	.28	.25
		(.00)	(.00)
Presidential approval	.12 [b]	—	.27
	(.18)		(.00)
Consumer sentiment	.08 [b]	.06	—
	(.34)	(.51)	

Note: Entries are multiple correlations (root of R^2) for a model fitting the "dependent" variable to a simple AR(1)—"first order" in Box-Jenkins (1976) terminology—transfer function of the "independent" variable. Contemporaneous observations are omitted so that only previous observations of the "independent" variable are used. All variables are prewhitened by an ARMA process. Numbers in parentheses represent the probability that the correlation could be ascribed to chance.

[a] Partisanship is the percentage Democratic of the two party identifiers. Each of the remaining variables has been recoded (multiplied by −1) for Republican administrations so that the sign works in the expected direction. All variables are scored as mean deviates.

[b] The substantive coefficients of this model are of the wrong sign (negative).

that specific political *events*, such as the Hungarian revolt and Suez crisis of late 1956, the Cuban Missile Crisis in 1962, and so on,[9] register in the public's psyche. What is not clear is whether they affect partisanship as well. One might guess that the connection would be less direct, but that is an empirical matter.

In addition, we include a set of *administration*-specific dummy variables to capture the public's long-term reaction to each particular presidency. This scheme has proven itself valuable in modeling presidential approval. Much previous work has suggested that this medium-term movement may be attributed to a dissolving coalition of minorities (Mueller, 1970, 1973) or to a comparison with the failures of previous regimes (Hibbs, 1982a, 1982b; Keech, 1982). The importance for macropartisanship remains to be seen. For each administration we add a separate constant term and a template that begins with a score of one at the president's (initial) inauguration and then declines exponentially throughout his tenure in office. In order to avoid overfitting these specific data, the speed of the decline is here specified a priori from previous work (MacKuen, 1983) better suited for this specific purpose, thus leaving only the magnitudes for estimation.

These two sorts of variables, the events and administration dummies, do not represent substantive theory (their specification is essentially ad hoc) but instead serve to avoid underspecification. This turns out to be important because our ability to get crisp estimates for the substantive variates depends on our not asking those variables to account for variances more directly attributable to the event and administration variables. Further, while not a priori measures of observable conditions, these variables are specified in a systematic fashion. To the extent that macropartisanship may be successfully modeled as a function of their manifestation, as well as that of the approval and consumer sentiment variables, our case is strengthened.

Putting all these pieces together requires two steps. First, we model presidential approval as a function of consumer sentiment, historical events, and administration dummies. Second, we model macropartisanship as a function of the *political* part of approval, as well as consumer sentiment, the historical events, and administration dummies. These successive stages are indicated by the model's recursive form. The results for the first part, presented in Table 17-2, show the sort of pattern obtained in much previous work. Importantly, we get a very crisp estimate of the effect of economic judgments on approval. Both the immediate impact (what would be an unstandardized regression coefficient in a contemporaneous analysis) and the dynamic coefficient are estimated with good precision. (The overall fit, an R-squared of .94 and a standard error of the estimate of 2.68, indicates that we have specified the model with some completeness.) Getting good estimates here is important for the second step.

Approval is clearly a function of economic evaluations. We observe a direct translation of a shift of one point in consumer sentiment into a shift of .32 points in presidential approval. Thus, we need to eliminate the economic portion of approval to get clean estimates of the distinct effects of economics and of presidential approval. (In this sort of dynamic work collinearity makes simultaneous estimates pretty dicey.) Here we generate a political approval series that is purged of the effects of consumer sentiment, but that includes all other variance components.[10] Thus, we may contrast the impacts of (1) economic conditions (measured by consumer sentiment) and (2) politics of the dramatic sort (measured by political approval with the economic component extracted).

Joining the components produces the estimates shown in Table 17-3.[11] First note the fit. A substantive model allows us to model 84% of the variance in partisanship over time.[12] This, of course, beyond what one might do by chance alone. Notwithstanding the usual provisos about overinterpreting goodness of fit, here there is an important message about our variable of interest: it must move quite systematically in order to be explainable by any model. Any hypothesis that the movement in partisanship over time is essentially random can no longer be sustained.[13]

But the fit is much better than that. Here the standard error of the estimate (1.83) is pretty close to a minimal sort of sampling error that one might expect from these data. Thus, another way of looking at the results is to guess that about five parts of six in macropartisanship's variance are substantively interesting.

We wish to do more than reject the straw man of randomness. These data suggest that a very large portion of the movement in macropartisanship is of substantive interest. The nature of the empirical estimates for consumer sentiment and for presidential approval encourage further understandings. The numbers are fairly large, are estimated with some precision, and are robust against alternative specifications (not shown).

Our dynamic specification requires interpretation to consider both how much influence each of the two variates has on partisan shifts and how that

Table 17-2 Presidential Approval (1953-87) as a Function of Consumer Sentiment, Events, and Administration Dummies

Variable[a]	Immediate Impact (ω_0)[b]	Dynamic Parameter (δ_1)[c]
Consumer sentiment	.32	.61
	(.04)	(.05)
Historical events		
Watergate	12.94	.28
Vietnam troops	−1.87	—
Iran crisis	15.07	.64
Reagan assassination attempt	−12.48	.77
Event series	5.10	—
Presidential administration intercepts and dynamic parameters		
Eisenhower	−.30	—
	−28.60	.85[d]
Kennedy	−1.38	—
	20.63	.85
Johnson	−12.86	—
	24.71	.85
Nixon	—	—
	−7.39	.85
Ford	10.96	—
	−22.98	.85
Carter	−19.13	—
	28.90	.85
Reagan	5.62	—
	−6.72	.85
Noise model		
Constant	.62	—
	(1.51)	
Disturbances	—	.33
		(.10)
Measures of fit		
R^2		.94
Standard error of estimate		2.68
N		140

[a] Each of the variables has been recoded (multiplied by −1) for Republican administrations so that the sign works in the expected direction for the subsequent partisan analysis. All variables are scored as mean deviates.

[b] These are the scalar translations, equivalent to "regression" coefficients. For the critical variables the standard errors of the estimators are given in parentheses. Other coefficients are statistically discernible from zero.

[c] These parameters are the AR(1) transfer function parameters.

[d] This value and those below it are fixed a priori.

Table 17-3 Macropartisanship (1953-87) as a Function of Consumer Sentiment, Presidential Approval, Events, and Administration Dummies

Variable [a]	Immediate Impact (ω_0) [b]	Dynamic Parameter (δ_1) [c]	Time Constant (Quarters) (T_k)	Gain
Consumer sentiment	.10	.84	6.09	.59
	(.01)	(.02)		
Presidential approval (political) [d]	.22	.35	1.55	.34
	(.04)	(.09)		
Historical events				
Watergate	−5.69	—	—	—
Vietnam troops	.56	—	—	—
Event series	−1.38	—	—	—
Presidential administration intercepts and dynamic parameters				
Eisenhower	4.71 [e]	—	—	—
	−5.11 [f]	.85 [g]	—	—
Carter	17.91	—	—	—
	−15.86	.85	—	—
Reagan	−5.26	—	—	—
	12.33	.85	—	—
Noise Model				
Constant	−2.78	—		
	(.46)			
Disturbances	—	−0.04		
		(.10)		
Measures of Fit	.84			
R^2	1.83			
Standard error of estimate	140			
N				

[a] Each of the variables has been recoded (multiplied by −1) for Republican administrations so that the sign works in the expected direction for the subsequent partisan analysis. All variables are scored as mean deviates.

[b] These are the scalar translations, equivalent to "regression" coefficients. For the critical variables the standard errors of the estimators are given in parentheses. Other coefficients are statistically discernible from zero.

[c] These parameters are the AR(1) transfer function parameters.

[d] Presidential political approval has the consistent component due to consumer sentiment's being removed before analysis. It represents the dramatic portion of presidential performance.

[e] Intercept.

[f] Decay parameter.

[g] This value and those below it are fixed a priori.

influence is felt over time—how quick the onset, how long-lasting the effect. The immediate impacts for both consumer sentiment (.10) and for approval (.22) are substantial. Roughly speaking, for every 10 people who move one unit on ICS (for example, from neutral to positive on all items), 1 of them changes parties in the next quarter. For every 10 who switch to or from approval of the president, 2 change parties.[14]

This immediate influence is easy to understand and appreciate. The long-range impact is more difficult to see. We need to turn to dynamics. The exponential declines—in this case estimated, not prespecified—for the impacts of consumer sentiment and approval allow for direct interpretation (see MacKuen, 1981, chap. 2). Each represents a continuous process in which its initial impact dissipates or reequilibrates over time. The dynamics for each process may be characterized by a measure T_k, called a time constant or the mean lag, that fits the reequilibration speed for each variable to an empirical time scale. Formally, about 63.2% of the contemporary impact dissipates in the amount of time calibrated by one T_k. Thus, the estimated T_ks shown in Table 17-3 tell us how fast macropartisanship reacts to changes in approval and also how fast it reacts to changes in consumer sentiment. The time constant, $T_k = 1.0/(1.0 - \delta_{k1})$, is about six quarters (6.09) for consumer sentiment and a little more than a single quarter (1.55) for approval.

This means that current partisanship reflects (mostly) the impact of the current *quarter's* approval but the last *year-and-a-half's* economic conditions. Put another way, current economic conditions will continue to be felt for six quarters, but current approval will be mostly forgotten in six weeks. The difference in the persistence of each component's immediate impact is shown clearly in the upper half of Figure 17-3. This picture draws the response, over time, of a single-point, single-quarter shift in either consumer sentiment or approval. In this case the exogenous shift is followed directly by a return to the previous level—an impulse in exogenous change—and we see the reaction dynamics. Partisanship quickly "forgets" approval while it evinces a more elephantine memory for previous economic conditions.

An equally useful way of seeing the same story lies in the equilibrium impact coefficient. This is the change in partisanship that would be produced if either approval or consumer sentiment changed by one point and then remained at that new level indefinitely. In this case, we have a "step function" as the exogenous change, and we calculate the response level reached in the long run.[15] This abstraction provides a more comprehensive view of empirical influence (*how much* taking into account *how fast*). Our estimates suggest that each one point change in approval ultimately results in about one-third of a one-point change in partisanship. In contrast, a point shift in consumer sentiment produces about .59 points response in partisanship. The equilibrium responses for the two variables are shown in the lower portion of Figure 17-3. Once we take into account response dynamics, it becomes apparent that economic influence is much greater.

In summary, the causal forces of political and economic evaluations have distinctive and substantial dynamic profiles. The impact of approval is sharp but transitory while that of economic evaluations is gradual and more enduring. Thus, assessing the relative contribution of politics and economics to macroparti-sanship is a matter of hare and tortoise. In the short run the impact of politics appears more important, but in the medium and long run the cumulative impact of previous economic perceptions becomes decisive. More significant for present

Figure 17-3   Response of Micropartisanship to Changes in Presidential Approval and Consumer Sentiment

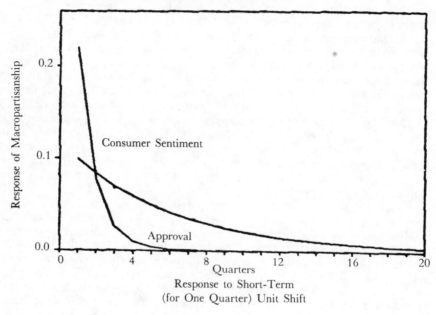

Response to Short-Term
(for One Quarter) Unit Shift

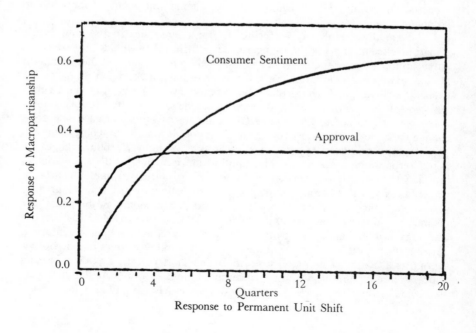

Response to Permanent Unit Shift

Figure 17-4   Macropartisanship: Actual and Predicted

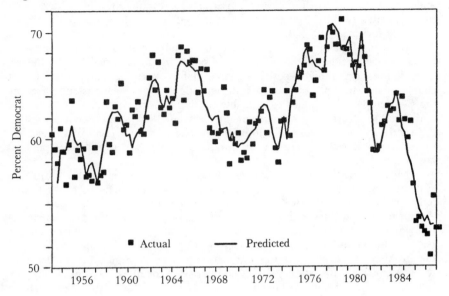

purposes, the equilibrium impact of *each* of these causal variables is of appreciable weight. We have known for some years that approval and consumer sentiment rise and fall over time; it now becomes apparent that this movement translates into the dynamic of macropartisanship.

The main point of this exercise is to see that a substantive model can account for the evident fluctuations in partisanship. The fit statistics certainly confirm the message. But, of course, statistics can lie. Examine the graph in Figure 17-4. The series of solid black squares represents the actual readings on partisanship over time. The solid line tracks the prediction produced by our estimated model. It is clear that (1) the movement of macropartisanship is as complex as we would expect from the history of these four decades—this is no secular trend; (2) macropartisanship clearly incorporates factors that vary and vary irregularly. This is nothing like a realignment scenario. Gains and losses are "permanent" on a scale of months, not decades. Like economic cyclicality, there appears to be a regular back and forth dynamic to partisanship but with irregular amplitude and irregular duration.

On What We Know Now

We now know that partisanship moves and that the economy moves it. More precisely, we know that the aggregate division of partisanship has fluctuated over the past 40 years, that those fluctuations have been substantial, and that they have had political consequences. Finally, we now know that partisanship's twisting course has been shaped by the winds of political and economic fortune.

Knowing that the public's partisanship is subject to considerable variation forces us to reconsider the standard view of party systems and realignment theory. The dominant paradigm posits a stable self-maintaining party system that changes character only in sudden transfigurations. This theory is supported by the twin empirical regularities of stable partisanship in the individual's psyche and of stable partisanship in the aggregate distribution. While we do not question the centrality of partisanship within the individual's own political garden, we now perceive a very different place for partisanship on the collective political landscape.

More formally, the realignment view posits a punctuated equilibrium system: a system that yields a pattern of stable partisan conflict that only rarely—but dramatically—responds to changing historical circumstance. As normally understood, this system performance relies on the permanence of individual partisanship. A party system may withstand most political storms because individual citizens, who may be buffeted about momentarily, hold fast to their partisan ties. For the postwar United States the model predicts an essentially stable division in party loyalties, a stable division that is notably absent in our data. Instead, we discover that the partisan balance varied according to the political and economic performance of various governments.

The direction for further theoretical work is not obvious. As pre-Copernican astronomers preserved the Ptolemaic system, we may simply add medium-term partisan shifts to the longer-run cycles implicit in current party systems theory. The data mandate nothing more. By itself, this addition to party systems theory recasts our understanding about the flow of politics. The mid-range dynamics we highlight are of tangible importance. They yield partisan movements of realignment magnitude (though not realignment duration) that require neither miracles nor catastrophes but instead arise from the routine success and failure of ordinary politics. We argue for a quotidian, as well as a chiliastic, view of political change.

More speculatively, the dynamics of macropartisanship may indicate a deeper look at party systems theory. For some time now we have had considerable evidence that the ideological and social bases of the party division shift continually (e.g., Carmines and Stimson, 1989; Petrocik, 1981). We add our voice to those who argue that our theoretical challenge transcends that of cataloging electoral history into periods of realignment and periods of partisan stability. We must focus more clearly on the constancy of change. Rather than worry whether political changes are large enough to signal a realignment, we ought to wrestle with their cause and consequence.

NOTES

1. Sophisticated and forceful statements of the realignment literature can be found in Sundquist (1983) and Clubb, Flanigan, and Zingale (1980).
2. Allsop and Weisberg's (1988) demonstration that partisanship fluctuated meaningfully during the course of the 1984 election campaign is a notable exception.
3. This reliability estimate assumes a simple random sampling. Failure to approximate this assumption may cause the reliability estimate to err on the conservative side. As compensation, the assumption of an average N of 1,500 is probably overconservative. The quarterly Gallup readings are themselves aggregated from bimonthly readings. Measures of macropartisanship were obtained from the Roper Center as a systematic sampling of party identification from the first Gallup survey of every odd-numbered month. We reaggregated to quarters because key economic indicators are measured quarterly.
4. Predicting popular vote in contests for the presidency is yet another test, if a less desirable one (for want of cases). Here the translation is .55 points of the popular vote for a 1% change in macropartisanship with standard error .22 and $R^2 = .85$ for a model including also disposable income change and policy mood. In a bivariate (under) specification, the same coefficient (.56) is obtained, but with larger standard error (.44) and considerably lower explanatory power ($R^2 = .17$).
5. An alternative and wholly contrary scenario is that those minimally informed and minimally involved in political life learn the social consensus that one of the parties is doing a good or bad job with the economy and, in lieu of policy or ideological commitment, base their weakly determined partisanship on that knowledge.
6. Each of the three variables (Democratic macropartisanship, presidential approval, and consumer sentiment) is calibrated so that one unit represents the standard error of estimate from an equation predicting the variable from a series of administration dummies. Thus, each is measured as a deviation from the administration mean, with each having the same variance when summed across administrations. To avoid visual overlap of the three scales, 2½ units are subtracted from approval and 5 units are subtracted from consumer sentiment. Please note that the smoothing and this rescaling are intended to make the timing and the dynamics clear to the eye. In the statistical analysis we employ the original series.
7. Exogeneity tests of this sort have received more attention in economics than in political science. See, for example, Granger (1969) and Sims (1977). For a good expository discussion in political science see Freeman (1983). Similar applications can be found in Norpoth and Yantek (1983) and Alt (1985). The models used here are simple linear filters: the persisting effects of the past are assumed to dissipate in an exponential fashion. Experience suggests that this simple model captures the main direct effects of most dynamic models.
8. This result is generated by a restricted form of exogeneity test in which the impacts of previous innovations are modeled to disappear in a smooth exponential fashion. We have examined these same propositions (among others) with a more powerful test, the unrestricted direct Granger test, and obtained substantively similar results (MacKuen, Erikson, and Stimson, 1988).
9. Events are all coded in a single variable made up of unit impulses (that is to say, a set of zeroes except at the designated time points where a score of one or minus one is substituted) and are thus treated equivalently. While this constrained estimation produces some inaccuracies, it avoids the trick of fitting dummies to error terms and calling it a model.

The pro-Republican events are Eisenhower's heart attack (3rd quarter 1955, 4th quarter 1955), Hungary-Suez (4th quarter 1956), Khruschev's visit to the United States (4th quarter 1959), the civil rights march on Washington (3rd quarter 1963), the Newark-Detroit riots (3rd quarter 1967), the Vietnam peace declaration (1st quarter 1973), the Mayaguez incident (2nd quarter 1975), the *Achille Lauro* terrorist capture (4th quarter 1985), and the *Challenger* explosion (1st quarter 1986). The pro-Democratic events are the army-McCarthy hearings (2nd quarter 1954), the KAL007 shoot-down (3rd quarter 1983), and the TWA hijacking in Beirut (2nd quarter 1985). Also added, separately, are the Iran Crisis (4th quarter 1979, 1st quarter 1980) and the Reagan assassination attempt (2nd quarter 1981).

10. This is simply approval minus that part of approval forecasted from the economic component alone, with other parts of the model zeroed out.

11. Note that the events and administration dummies are included for reasons of specification. The event series negative sign suggests that particular events are less compelling stimuli for partisan shift than for change in approval, as we might expect. The dummies for the Carter and Reagan administrations are not mere corrections for approval. They indicate some other phenomenon, perhaps a Watergate disillusionment of Republicans that was relieved with Reagan's assertive entrance stage right. This component of the model, while systematic, is an explicit description of ignorance.

12. The R-squared is simply the squared correlation between the actual percentage Democratic and the predicted percentage Democratic, with the noise portion of the model zeroed out. Thus, the model is not self-correcting. Lagged values of the dependent variable do not appear on the right-hand side of the prediction equation.

13. These results are no artifact of our dynamic modeling. If we use ordinary least squares (OLS) and specify the same two models (for approval and macropartisanship), we produce a similar inference. The OLS equation for approval has, on the right-hand side, the same specification variables (the events and administration dummies) and also a single, lagged value for approval and for consumer sentiment. And a similar model for macropartisanship uses lagged political approval (actual approval minus .29 lagged consumer sentiment) and lagged macropartisanship (see Table N-1). These estimates are comparable to those in Table 17-2 and Table 17-3. These simple OLS models neither cope with autocorrelated disturbances nor allow different dynamics for approval and consumer sentiment. And their fit appears inflated by including the

Table N-1   OLS Models for Presidential Approval and Macropartisanship

Variable	b	$SE (b)$
Presidential approval[a]		
Presidential Approval (lagged)	.31	.05
Consumer sentiment (lagged)	.29	.04
Macropartisanship[b]		
Macropartisanship (lagged)	.26	.09
Political approval (lagged)	.13	.04
Consumer sentiment (lagged)	.10	.03

[a]R^2 = .94; Mean squared error = 3.14.
[b]R^2 = .81; Mean squared error = 2.17.

measured lagged macropartisanship on the right-hand side. Nevertheless, their overall form shows that our substantive inferences are not mere technical wizardry.

14. The immediate impact of economic evaluation may be larger than it appears here. Following convention, the consumer sentiment items are measured with a range of 2 points (0 negative, 1 neutral, 2 positive) while approval is scored as a dichotomy (0 or 1). One unit of ICS marks the movement from negative to neutral or from neutral to positive. One unit of approval reflects the complete change from a negative response to an approving one. Because these metrics are not the same, any claim about which variable shows a "bigger" impact on macropartisanship must be ambiguous. To make scores more nearly equivalent, the reader may want to double the coefficients associated with ICS.

15. Mathematically, for this simple linear filter, the equilibrium impact is simply $T_k \omega 0$ (the time constant [or mean lag] times the immediate impact). It appears that empirical estimates of the equilibrium impact are more robust than are the separate estimates of the immediate impact and how it gets distributed over time.

18. ISSUES AND INHERITANCE IN THE FORMATION OF PARTY IDENTIFICATION

Richard G. Niemi and M. Kent Jennings

The initial interpretation of party identification as an effective, nearly immutable, emotionally based orientation has given way to a view of partisanship as instrumental, changeable, and responsive to events and to individuals' attitudes on contemporary political issues. In particular, a number of studies have shown that partisanship is endogenous to political preferences, changing over the years in response to current attitudes (Markus, 1979; Fiorina, 1981; Franklin, 1984; MacKuen, Erickson, and Stimson, 1989) and even in response to the events of a single presidential campaign (Allsop and Weisberg, 1988). Likewise, the inheritance of partisanship from one's parents is not absolute—or altered only by catastrophic events at the time of coming of age—but is affected by evolving issue preferences, expected benefits, and transactions with the political environment throughout adulthood (Carmines, McIver, and Stimson, 1987; Luskin, McIver, and Carmines, 1989; Achen, 1989).

This revised interpretation notwithstanding, it remains the case that party affiliations are relatively stable, both in an absolute sense and in comparison to other political orientations (Converse and Markus, 1979). Similarly, among adults, both young and old, "realization" of parents' partisan or independent positions remains a dominant mode (Carmines, McIver, and Stimson, 1987, p. 388; Mattei and Niemi, 1991) and surely more frequent than adoption of parents' issue positions (Jennings and Niemi, 1981). Moreover, this relative stability and inheritability was preserved even during the dealignment period of the 1970s.

The overall view—of endogeneity, yet with relative stability and inheritability—raises a number of questions, such as the extent to which partisanship structures issue preferences (Franklin, 1984, pp. 472-73), the responsiveness of party identification to alternative survey questions (Borrelli, Lockerbie, and Niemi, 1987; Barnes et al., 1988), and the extent and rate of decay of intergenerational continuity. It is this last topic that concerns us here. How great

Source: *American Journal of Political Science* (1991) 35:970-88. Reprinted with permission of University of Texas Press. Copyright © 1991 by the University of Texas Press.

is the decline in inherited partisanship over time? How quickly do issues begin to affect the decline? And what kinds of issues are most likely to drive offspring away from parental partisanship?

We shall use three-wave, parent-offspring panel data to address these matters. We shall find that parental influence is, indeed, very high at the onset of adulthood, though opinions on current issues begin to intrude even at that stage. The effects of issues increase rapidly, with a notable decline in parental influence by the time offspring are in their mid-twenties. As offspring move into their mid-thirties, new and continuing issues exert still more influence, but the impact of parents remains strong.

The data come from a longitudinal study carried out by the Survey Research Center and Center for Political Studies of the University of Michigan. It began with personal interviews of a national probability sample of high school seniors and one or both of their parents in the spring of 1965. In 1973 and again in 1982, as many as possible of these youths and as many as possible of one randomly chosen parent were questioned again. Retention rates were unusually good even by comparison with shorter panels. In all, 70% of the surviving younger sample and nearly two-thirds of the surviving parents were surveyed. Bias owing to panel mortality was minimal (Jennings and Markus, 1984).

When analyzing early waves of panel data, we find that there is inevitably a choice about whether to maximize cases at a given time or to use the set of respondents available for all waves. Because our interest in this paper is in individual-level dynamics involving parent-child pairs, rather than in making the best population estimates for each year, we have elected to use throughout a single set of respondents—namely, all offspring for whom three-wave data are available and for whom 1965 parent data are available ($N = 1,074$). One consequence of this decision is that even the simplest figures reported here (e.g., the correlation between parent and youth party identification) are likely to differ slightly from earlier reports based on this study.

Partisanship Inheritance

A common expectation is that parental influence will be highly significant in the late teens but will decline with age. As expressed by Fiorina (1981, p. 90): "When a citizen first attains political awareness, socialization influences may dominate party ID. But as time passes, as the citizen experiences politics, party ID comes more and more to reflect the events that transpire in the world." What is left unsaid is just when and to what degree parental influence declines and youthful opinions take effect, and the types of events and experiences that affect this process.

It is well known that late adolescents are relatively uninvolved in the political world—participating less, expressing less interest in issues, and so on. It would not be surprising, therefore, if at age 18 issues played almost no role in pulling youths away from their parents' partisan feelings. On the other hand, generational theories emphasize the impact of events that occur as young people come of age, suggesting not only that young adults will be very sensitive to extant issues but that, as time goes on, newer issues will have less effect than those that were initially influential.

Later in adulthood there is the question of how much atrophy occurs in the parental tradition. The view that partisanship responds to contemporary issues implies, at least on the surface, a continual decline until at some point parents' effects become vanishingly small. On the other hand, at least two factors work against this. First, partisanship becomes less responsive to current political forces as individuals age (Markus, 1979; Franklin and Jackson, 1983; Jennings and Markus, 1984), suggesting that there might be a leveling-off point at which ordinary issues are less and less likely to pull people away from their parents' positions. Second, current political forces may redirect offspring partisanship back toward parents' views, which also suggests that apparent parental influence will not vanish. The potency of these arguments is suggested by the fact that respondents' party identification is strongly correlated with parents' partisanship even among middle-aged and elderly individuals (e.g., Beck and Jennings, 1975).

We need first, then, to put in place the over-time partisan similarity between parents and their children in order to gain a first approximation of the degree to which issues might have influenced the course of intergenerational transmission. We are interested, of course, not so much in contemporary similarity as in the persistence of parental influence exerted on youths up to the time they entered adulthood. Hence, the most relevant correlations are those between parents' partisanship in 1965 and youths' partisanship in each of the three waves of the panel. These product-moment correlations are .61, .38, and .38, for youths in 1965, 1973, and 1982, respectively.

Two key points emerge from these coefficients. First, the initial similarity between parents and offspring is indeed much higher than any subsequent observation. The early social learning model has much to recommend it as young people begin their partisan trek through adulthood. Second, if these results are any guide, the great bulk of movement away from inherited partisanship occurs during the early years of adulthood, for the correlation for the 1965-82 pairing is just as strong as that for 1965-73. The major point, however, is that substantial erosion occurs in parental partisanship, and our task is to examine the role that issues play in fostering and abetting that erosion.[1]

Issues and Party Identification

Along with most other scholars who have treated this topic, we rely on inferential evidence when we assert that issue preferences affect the shifting of partisanship. Inasmuch as preferences on issues change simulatneously with alterations in party identification, it is virtually impossible statistically to sort out the precise causal mechanisms that govern relationships between the two. In addition, other attitudes, such as those toward candidates, may also play a role in partisan development.

What we can show is that initial transmission of partisanship as well as movement away from parental feelings over a long portion of the life span are consistent with a model of issue preferences similar to models that are now commonplace in explaining short-term partisan change. In this effort we are aided by the fact that a key variable, parents' partisanship, remains unchanged because throughout the analysis we rely on 1965 reports.

Our choice of issues was governed by two main factors. One was to utilize, where possible, the same issues across time. The other was to employ issues that were both salient and important, issues that represented domains that seemed likely to have impinged upon partisan dispositions in the period covered by our study. Four issues were ultimately used, although, as we report below, a number of others were examined and found wanting. (In addition, we shall later report on the use of self-placement on a liberal/conservative scale as an imperfect surrogate for still other issues.) Of the issues used, attitudes toward racial integration of the schools and use of prayers in schools were ascertained in each wave; attitudes about the correctness of entering the Vietnam War and about the government's role in ensuring jobs and a good standard of living were asked about in the last two waves. To help control for the presence of nonattitudes, three of the questions included filters designed to eliminate respondents who had no opinion.

The federal government's role in school integration was a critical issue throughout the period and for some time was virtually a litmus test for liberal credentials. Although the prayers in school issue has not had that kind of prominence, it has surfaced from time to time, and attitudes on the issue clearly serve as a barometer of civil libertarian predispositions. The divisive Vietnam War had barely begun in earnest in the spring of 1965; by 1973 the war was nearly over, but strong feelings continued to exist then and well into the future. Finally, a traditional, ongoing liberal-conservative issue is represented in the form of government help versus individual initiative in achieving jobs and a good standard of living (hereafter called jobs). More than the previous three issues, this one is probably very sensitive to the life stage changes experienced as our cohort aged from around 18 years of age to around 35, though the transition from the Carter years to the Reagan years also made the general attitude domain highly salient.

In assessing defection from the parental tradition, the most appropriate test lies in taking 1965 parental partisanship as the baseline. To the degree that adolescents enter young adulthood with an "inherited" partisanship, it is most evident at that point. Subsequent measures of parental partisanship, while useful for some purposes, are tainted by the fact that the socializer-socializee relationship has altered drastically and that both parents and offspring may be responding to the same forces in the environment. For offspring party identification, however, we shall use all three points of observation (1965, 1973, 1982) to capture the dynamics of the deviation process. Major attention will be given to the 1982 report, in large part because party identification has approached mature adult levels of stability by that time (Jennings and Markus, 1984). Similarly, issue preferences at all three times will be utilized, with more emphasis on those from 1982.

That there is a relationship between offspring issue positions and changes both in their own party identification and in their deviation from parental partisanship is no longer surprising. Nonetheless, it is useful to begin with some

Table 18-1　Offspring Party Identification as a Function of Parent Party Identification and Offspring Attitude on School Integration

Offspring Opinion on School Integration	Offspring Party Identification				
	Democrat %	Independent %	Republican %	N	Marginal %
Democratic parents*					
Oppose	35	41	23	164	37
Depends	39	49	12	94	21
Favor	53	41	6	180	41
Independent parents*					
Oppose	14	47	38	77	42
Depends	32	58	9	53	23
Favor	35	48	16	79	34
Republican parents*					
Oppose	5	42	54	111	44
Depends	13	54	33	54	22
Favor	30	37	33	86	35

Note: Data in Tables 18-1 through 18-4 are from the 1965 parent wave and the 1982 offspring wave. Independents include pure independents and leaners. A small number of respondents volunteered intermediate responses on the prayer and Vietnam issues. They are deleted from the tables but retained in the regression.

*$p < .01$ using a chi-square test.

Source: All tables based on 1965-73-82 Socialization Study, University of Michigan.

simple tables showing the relationship between issue preferences and offspring partisanship, controlling for parental party identification. These findings are all the more significant because, as we shall see, the basic relationships survive multivariate analysis.

Tables 18-1, 18-2, 18-3, and 18-4 show that attitudes in 1982 on each of the issues were related in the expected ways to offspring party identification. In Table 18-1, for example, those who opposed a federal role in integrating the schools were less often Democratic and more often Republican than those who favored that role. The same is true of those who opposed prayers in school, who thought that the United States did the right thing in Vietnam, and who felt that the government should let individuals get ahead on their own (Tables 18-2 to 18-4). Reversals in the pattern are almost nonexistent, and the differences are often quite large.

Significantly, the pattern holds for all categories of parental partisanship, an especially compelling point in locating the sources and magnitudes of defection from parental partisanship. Illustratively, if the offspring of Republican parents subscribed to an active government role in ensuring employment, they were three times more likely to identify with the Democratic party by 1982 than were those

Table 18-2 Offspring Party Identification as a Function of Parent Party Identification and Offspring Attitude on School Prayers

| Offspring Opinion on School Prayers | Offspring Party Identification | | | | |
	Democrat %	Independent %	Republican %	N	Marginal %
Democratic parents**					
Favor	42	41	17	281	71
Oppose	52	41	7	115	29
Independent parents**					
Favor	20	54	27	123	63
Oppose	32	49	18	71	37
Republican parents***					
Favor	14	40	46	155	67
Oppose	21	47	32	77	33

**p < .05 using a chi-square test.
***p < .10 using a chi-square test.

Table 18-3 Offspring Party Identification as a Function of Parent Party Identification and Offspring Attitude on Vietnam

| Offspring Opinion on Vietnam | Offspring Party Identification | | | | |
	Democrat %	Independent %	Republican %	N	Marginal %
Democratic parents*					
Right thing	31	46	24	85	20
Stayed out	48	41	11	331	80
Independent parents*					
Right thing	14	46	40	35	16
Stayed out	27	54	19	182	84
Republican parents*					
Right thing	6	30	64	50	19
Stayed out	18	46	36	215	81

*p < .01 using a chi-square test.

Table 18-4 Offspring Party Identification as a Function of Parent Party Identification and Offspring Attitude on Jobs and Standard of Living

Offspring Opinion on Jobs	Offspring Party Identification				
	Democrat %	Independent %	Republican %	N	Marginal %
Democratic parents*					
Up to individual	33	49	18	217	61
Mixed	61	32	7	85	19
Government role	59	35	5	91	20
Independent parents*					
Up to individual	20	54	26	153	64
Mixed	38	50	12	48	20
Government role	41	49	11	37	16
Republican parents*					
Up to individual	10	42	48	192	70
Mixed	27	40	33	45	16
Government role	30	54	16	37	14

*$p < .01$ using a chi-square test.

who said that jobs are the responsibility of the individual (Table 18-4). Similarly, those offspring with Democratic parents and who also approved of the U.S. entry into the Vietnam War were about twice as likely to be Republican as were those who disapproved of the action (Table 18-3).

At the same time, the results also show that these issues, at least when taken one at a time, by no means eliminate the impact of parental partisanship. If anything, variations in offspring party identification are even stronger when holding issue position constant than when comparing across categories of parental partisanship. Among those favoring school prayers, for example, almost half of those with Democratic parents are themselves Democratic, which is true of only 14% of those with Republican parents. This difference is considerably larger than that between offspring with opposing views on any of the issues.

Although it is not the main focus here, it is also relevant to note that offspring issue preferences are themselves not closely related to parents' partisanship. Consider the marginal percentages in Table 18-3, for example. Among offspring of Democratic parents, only one in five thought the United States did the right thing in going to Vietnam. However, almost identical proportions held this opinion among offspring of independent and Republican parents. Indeed, out of 30 comparisons involving matched response categories across the four issues, the largest single difference was but 9%. The effect of parental partisanship, if it retains its impact in a multivariate model, appears to be limited to partisanship itself (and perhaps voting choices). By the time they are in their mid-twenties and continuing into their thirties, the effect of parental partisanship of offspring issue positions is muted or nonexistent.[2]

It is also important to note that a variety of issues are *not* associated with defection. A number of additional issue questions were asked in both the 1973 and 1982 surveys. These include such topics as equal roles for women, legalization of marijuana, federal aid to minorities, abortion, and protecting the rights of the accused. All of these at one time or another were visible controversies during the study period. However, even when they were related to deviation from parental partisanship at the bivariate level (which was rare), that relationship evaporated when placed in a multivariate context. Thus, even though our four issues do not capture all of the relevant domains that might have figured in the general deterioration of the parental tradition, they do perform that role much better than several other prominent issues of the day. They appear to represent rather well attitudinal domains associated with movements away from parental partisanship.

Issues and Intergenerational Partisanship over Time

The results in the previous section show strong presumptive evidence that parental partisanship retains a significant though diminished impact on offspring party loyalties even as high school seniors mature into mid-thirties adults. By considering issues one at a time, however, we have left open the collective impact of issues on the diminished intergenerational partisan similarity. We have also left unanswered the question of the relative importance of the issues over time. A multivariate model is called for. Turning to such a model has the added advantage of enabling us efficiently to study parental impact at multiple time points (i.e., to observe the changing legacy of parental partisanship as the offspring age). To explore these matters—the impact of multiple issues, changes in the influence of issues over time, and the possible leveling off of parental influence—we ran a series of regressions in which offspring party identification for each observed year was the dependent variable. Independent variables consisted of parents' 1965 party identification[3] and the offsprings' contemporaneous positions on the issues described above (two in 1965, four in the last two years). Thus, the primary model is intended to recognize and reflect the fact that although parents' partisanship is not entirely static and that offspring are not completely removed from parental influence at age 18, the baseline for assessing the decay of intergenerational agreement should be 1965 parental party identification.

The model is not intended to reflect precisely the process by which parental influence is exercised. Except for one's early, initial sense of party identification, parental influence at any one point is presumably channeled through one's own partisanship at a prior time. A model including both parents' identification and an earlier measure of one's own identification (e.g., Franklin, 1984) better reflects this process, whereas ours more directly assesses overall parental influence (see note 5).

Initial results are shown in Table 18-5. The first equation is a kind of baseline result that reflects the situation at the time of high school graduation. As expected, it shows the strong connection between parent and offspring party identification. Even at age 18, however, attitudes on one of the two issues are significantly related to youths' affiliations. It is likely that school integration is the influential issue because race is, in Carmines and Stimson's (1980) words, an "easy" issue, one on which individuals are inclined to have opinions whether or not they are interested and involved in politics. Despite the presence of only one significant issue, the equation explains much of the variance in offspring partisanship, but largely because of parental identification.

For 1973 we add Vietnam and jobs to our short list of issues. Because the inclusion of these variables could affect the results for the "holdover" variables, we present two equations: one with only variables used in 1965 and one with the added issues. Whichever of these results one considers, four conclusions stand out.

First, the relative standing of parents' partisanship drops considerably from what it was eight years earlier. Second, despite this drop, parents' affiliations are still a greater influence on the offspring than any single issue, with a standardized coefficient over twice as high as that for jobs. Third, it is clear that the importance of issues is growing. In the equation that matches 1965, both variables are now significant. When Vietnam and jobs are added, school prayer again becomes insignificant, but the new issues take its place. Finally, the explanatory power of the model drops sharply from what it was in 1965.

The last point deserves additional emphasis. In 1973 three issues are significant, as opposed to only one in 1965; yet that is not enough to make up for the declining force of parental partisanship. It seems likely that as newly minted adults are suddenly released from close parental contact and supervision, a variety of factors (friends, spouses, and perhaps even a touch of rebellion) impinge on their partisan inclinations and make them temporarily less responsive to both parents and their own political opinions. In any event, parent party identification and offspring issue positions on four salient issues do not account for the partisanship of offspring in their mid-twenties as well as parental affiliations and one issue eight years earlier.

The results for 1982 are similar in some respects but also supply additional information. What is perhaps most striking is that the impact of parental party identification is virtually unchanged from what it was in 1973. The lowered responsiveness of partisanship to current political forces as adults age, along with the impact of common environmental influences acting on parents and offspring, evidently prevent a continuing slide in parental tradition despite the continued growth in the role of issues. Though we cannot be certain, it is likely that a kind of plateau has been reached and that there will be little further erosion in the coefficient that represents parental partisanship.

Alongside the leveling off of parental influence, the results for 1982 show yet another increase in the influence of opinions on current issues. In the two-issue model, both school prayers and school integration are significant, and the coefficients are substantially greater than in previous years, both in absolute and relative terms (i.e., both unstandardized and standarized forms). But now, adding

Table 18-5 Regression Estimates for Offspring Party Identification as a Function of Parent Party Identification and Offspring Attitudes

Year	Constant	Parents' Party Identification	School Integration	School Prayer	Vietnam	Jobs	R^2
1965	.40	.54/.57 [a]	.16/.13	−.02/−.02			.34
	(.15)	(.03)	(.03)	(.03)			
1973	1.41	.31/.38	.12/.13	−.08/−.08			.17
	(.15)	(.03)	(.03)	(.03)			
	1.05	.30/.38	.08/.08	−.05/−.06	−.07/−.09 [a]	.16/.15	.21
	(.23)	(.03)	(.03)	(.03)	(.03)	(.03)	
1982	1.31	.31/.36	.25/.24	−.13/−.13			.22
	(.16)	(.03)	(.03)	(.03)			
	.54	.30/.35	.16/.16	−.08/−.08	−.16/−.14	.33/.26	.30
	(.28)	(.03)	(.03)	(.03)	(.04)	(.04)	

Note: Signs of the coefficients for issues reflect their wording and are all in the expected direction. Pairwise deletion of missing data. N = 867 for 1965; 866 and 765 for 1973; 805 and 738 for 1982.

[a] Unstandardized coefficient/Standardized coefficient; standard errors are in parentheses.

Vietnam and jobs to the equation does not render either of the other variables insignificant. By the same token, all four issues are now significant. In addition, the apparent effect of opinions of the jobs issue increased very substantially between 1973 and 1982. The increased impact of jobs would seem to be a consequence of life stage developments and the polarizing effect of the issue as ushered in during the 1980 presidential campaign and the ensuing Reagan years.

Finally, note that the explanatory power of the equation, especially with all four issues, is edging back up to where it was in 1965. Now, as the youths have become mature adults, issues are perhaps showing their full strength as explanatory factors. It is ironic in a way that issues should continue to become more consequential inasmuch as it is also the case that partisanship becomes more stable and less influenced by current opinions as people age (Markus 1979; Franklin and Jackson 1983). What appears to be happening is that, by the time individuals are in their mid- to late-twenties, most of the deviation from parental partisanship that is going to occur has in fact transpired, as we demonstrated earlier by noting that the 1965-73 and 1965-82 parent-offspring correlations were identical. Issues continue to be a factor, and indeed their direct impact grows at least until the mid-thirties, but further environmental influences do not reduce the continuing effects of parental identification as observed some 17 years earlier.

As noted above, other issues available in the 1973 and 1982 waves did not have a noticeable impact on offspring partisanship. Nor did they reduce the impact of parental partisanship. Of course, even the more issue-filled 1973 and 1982 interviews do not exhaust the supply of topics that could conceivably pull youths away from parental feelings. We may have missed important issues in spite of efforts to include those that were most salient at the time of the interviews. So, as a final and quite demanding check on the relative importance of parents' partisanship versus contemporary attitudes, we ran a further regression in which the offspring's self-placement on a seven-point liberal/conservative scale was added to the equation. This scale was not included in the first-wave question- naire, so the analysis is limited to 1973 and 1982.[4]

The results are shown in Table 18-6. Not surprisingly, inclusion of this broad ideological scale effaced some of what was previously explained by separate issues, in part because the scale undoubtedly captures much more than general- ized issue positions (e.g., Conover and Feldman, 1981). Still, the results are very much of a piece with what we have seen up to this point. Of the single issues, in 1973 only jobs is significantly related to offspring partisanship; in 1982 the coefficient for that issue increased, but simultaneously the coefficients for two other individual issues are now significant. Liberalism/conservatism itself is clearly important, but it, too, increased in magnitude between 1973 and 1982. In fact, in that year its standardized coefficient is the largest of any of the variables in the equation. What is most important, however, from our perspective of judging whether or not parental influence remains a factor, is that the coefficient for parental partisanship is nearly as high as when we included only the four specific issues, and it is almost unchanged from 1973 to 1982.[5]

It is also true, as in the earlier results, that the explanatory power of the equation rises considerably between the two surveys. With liberalism/conserva-

Table 18-6 Regression Estimates for Offspring Party Identification as a Function of Parent Party Identification and Offspring Attitudes and Ideology

Year	Constant	Parents' Party Identification	School Integration	School Prayer	Vietnam	Jobs	Liberalism/ Conservatism	R^2
1973	.03	.29/.36[a]	.05/.05	−.01/−.01	−.04/−.04	.11/.10	.30/.23	.24
	(.29)	(.03)	(.03)	(.03)	(.03)	(.04)	(.05)	
1982	−.76	.27/.31	.10/.10	−.02/−.02	−.13/−.12	.16/.13	.53/.38	.41
	(.31)	(.03)	(.03)	(.03)	(.04)	(.04)	(.05)	

Note: Signs of the coefficients for issues reflect their wording and are all in the expected direction. Pairwise deletion of missing data. N = 681 for 1973; 661 for 1982.

[a] Unstandardized coefficient/Standardized coefficient; standard errors are in parentheses.

Figure 18-1 Offspring Party Identification by Level of Parental Partisanship and Offspring Position on Issues

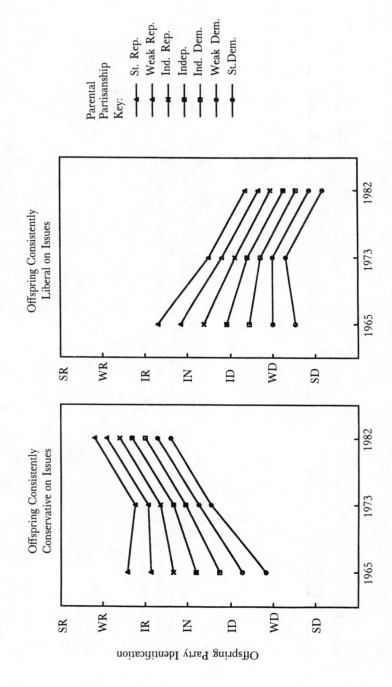

tism added, the predictive power finally surpasses what it was in 1965. Thus, contemporary attitudes eventually come to mean as much as parental partisanship did at the onset of adulthood. Even so, a conclusion of continuing parental influences seems secure.

One can breathe life into the regression models with examples that show both the pull of issue positions and the inertia created by parents' partisanship in the determination of offspring party identification. Based on the models in Table 18-5, Figure 18-1A shows, for all levels of parental partisanship, the party identification score in each year for offspring who consistently take the most conservative position on each issue. Figure 18-1B shows the same for offspring who take the most liberal position. The upsloping lines in the left-hand picture and downsloping lines on the right indicate the pull of issues over time. For example, very conservative offspring of strong Democrats begin adult life as weak Democrats but move sharply in a Republican direction in 1973 and again in 1982, ending up as independent with a slight tendency toward the Republican party. In contrast, very liberal such children are initially rather strong Democrats (thus showing the effects of issue positions even in 1965) and end up slightly closer to the Democratic party as their attitudes reinforce their partisanship over the years.

At the same time, the multiple lines within each box show the effects of parental partisanship. In 1965 very conservative offspring range from a weak Democratic position to a weak Republican position depending on their family background; in 1982 they cover a reduced range, but those who come from strong Democratic backgrounds are pulled only to the middle of the scale. A similarly differentiated pattern characterizes very liberal offspring.

Parental Partisanship and Offspring Voting

One needs no convincing that contemporary issues influence voting behavior. Nor is it surprising that presidential preferences are strongly related to parental partisanship when offspring are on the verge of adulthood (Jennings and Niemi 1981, p. 90). But are there any signs of parental influence three elections later, when the offspring are in their early thirties?

We duplicated the preceding regression analysis using reported presidential preferences for 1964, 1972, and 1980. For ease of comparability, because we are interested in the general patterns rather than the specific sizes of the coefficients, and because the preferences were not extremely one-sided, we used ordinary least squares rather then probit analysis despite the fact that vote is a dichotomous variable.

The results are remarkably similar to those for party identification except that the relative influence of parental partisanship is lower and that of issues generally higher at every point. As expected, the standardized coefficient for parents' party identification is greatest for 1964 preferences (.31). It drops considerably in 1972 (.14) but remains at that level (.15) in 1980 and is clearly significant in all three elections. Despite the political maturation process and the idiosyncrasies of particular elections, voting behavior in adulthood continues to bear the imprint of parental partisanship.

On a relative basis, parental identification shares influence with offspring opinions from the very outset. Thus, the standardized coefficient that represents the association between opinions on the school integration issue and the 1964 vote is almost identical with that for parental party identification (.30 vs. .31). This strong showing reflects the highly salient and party-connected nature of the integration issue in the 1964 contest. In succeeding elections, opinions on at least two issues are more closely linked to the vote than is parent party preference.[6]

The issues themselves vary in their importance over time and, not surprisingly, a bit more so than was the case with offspring party identification. School integration is most visible during the 1964 election whereas the prayers in school issue is most pronounced in 1972. As should be the case, the Vietnam issue has by far its greatest impact in 1972 ($-.30$), although it remains significant eight years later ($-.16$). Least affected by the peculiarities of specific election years is the apparent effect of the traditional issue about the government's role in providing jobs and a good standard of living. In both 1972 and 1980, the standardized coefficient was substantial and similar in magnitude (.22 in 1972 and .27 in 1980).

Conclusion

The parent-youth socialization study began in an earlier research era, in which it was widely believed that party identification was more or less inherited from one's parents. Despite these roots the current analysis strongly supports the revised view, in which partisan shifts during adulthood as well as between generations are influenced by individual policy preferences. Indeed, what we referred to as baseline results, involving only 1965 data, suggest that issues play some role in the determination of partisan preferences even as individuals are just embarking on adulthood. The number of issues that impinge on partisanship, and the magnitude of their effect, then grow rapidly as adults move into their twenties and thirties. There is no turning back, in these results, to the earlier view.

Given what can now be characterized as overwhelming support for the revised view of partisanship, it may be worthwhile to conclude by calling attention to the remnants of the older perspective. While the partisanship of the 1965 high school seniors was not simply inherited—even as they were taking their first steps into the adult world—parental party loyalties surely had much to do with the direction of their children's initial pathways. As the offspring became adults in their mid-twenties, parental influence was left behind to a degree. The apparent imprint of parental partisanship decreased substantially, in both absolute and relative terms, from what it had been just eight years earlier. And taken altogether, even with the addition of self-location on the liberal/conservative scale, the combination of parental identification and offspring issue preferences was not as powerful a predictor as parental identification alone in 1965. Yet parental influence did not vanish.

As the offspring reached greater political maturity in their mid-thirties, issues were more closely linked to offspring partisanship, especially if the overall liberalism/conservatism scale is included as an indicator of general issue orientation. Predictability of offspring loyalties had now virtually returned to its original 1965 level, thereby supporting the understanding of party identification as a "running tally" and the place of issue stances in the calculation of that tally. Yet parental influence still did not vanish; in fact, it demonstrated as much strength as in 1973. Thus the gain in the inferred impact of policy preferences does not come at the expense of the parental partisan tradition.

It is also worth recalling that the general contours of the results were the same for presidential preferences. The relevance of policy preferences for voting has never been in dispute, so what is of greatest interest here is whether parents' party preferences are of any consequence whatsoever, at least after age 18. It turned out that the influence of parental partisanship, though lower than for offspring partisanship itself, was always present to a significant degree.

Lest anyone misread these comments as an attempt to resurrect the assumptions extant when the socialization study began, our final emphasis is again on the fine fit of the present results to the view of partisanship as subject to the continuing influence of policy preferences and the association of these preferences with party and candidate positions. That we could hardly be disappointed by this turn of events can be understood if one recalls that the first report of the socialization study noted that parent-youth transmission was imperfect (Jennings and Niemi, 1968), even though it provided little understanding of why that imperfection existed or just what it meant. Nevertheless, just as others have emphasized that partisanship, for all its endogeneity, is one of the most stable of political orientations, it is satisfying to come full circle by observing that the family of origin plays a major role in determining the initial political direction of their offspring and that this influence, though reduced, continues to play a significant role in the over-time partisan development of their adult children.

Appendix

Party identification (scored 0-6) and liberal/conservative self-placement (1-7) were the standard CPS items. Wording of the issue questions follows.

School prayers: Some people think it is all right for the public schools to start each day with a prayer. Others feel that religion does not belong in the public schools but should be taken care of by the family and the church. Have you been interested enough in this to favor one side over the other? (If yes) Which do you think—schools should be allowed to start each day with a prayer (scored 5) or religion does not belong in the schools (scored 1)? Intermediate responses (volunteered) scored 3.

Integration: Some people say that the government in Washington should see to it that white and black [Negro in 1965] children are allowed to go to the same schools. Others claim that this is not the government's business. Have you been concerned enough about this question to favor one side over the other? (If yes) Do you think the government in Washington should see to it that white and black children go to the same schools (1) or stay out of this area as it is none of its business (5)? "Depends" scored 3.

Vietnam: [Slightly different introductions were used in 1973 and 1982.] Do you think we did the right thing in getting into the fighting in Vietnam (1) or should we have stayed out (5)? Intermediate responses (volunteered) scored 3.

Jobs: Some people feel that the government in Washington should see to it that every person has a job and a good standard of living (scored 1). Others think the government should just let each person get ahead on his own (scored 7). And other people have opinions somewhere in between. Where would you place yourself on this scale, or haven't you thought much about this?

NOTES

1. Utilizing the 755 pairs available for all three time points reveals correlations of .61 in 1965, .44 in 1973, and .46 in 1982. Thus, contemporaneous similarity is always greater than lagged similarity, suggesting that parents and their offspring are responding similarly to forces in the political environment and in their personal circumstances. In view of the greater individual-level stability of the parental generation (Jennings and Markus, 1984), it is likely that this response consists primarily of offspring moving toward their parents' partisanship.

2. The apparent absence of parental influence on issue positions can be traced to the fact that young adults' feelings in 1973, at least about Vietnam and about race relations, were not influenced by their own prior partisan ties (Markus, 1979, p. 353).

3. The 1965 self-report is highly related to subsequent ones. Correlations were .78 and .83 for 1965-73 and 1973-82, respectively. Most changes over both time periods are between strong and weak partisanship of the same party; very few parents change from one party to the other.

4. One drawback to using the scale is that the number of cases drops off because many individuals fail to place themselves. Compare the N's in Table 18-6 with those in Table 18-5.

5. When we rerun the 1973 and 1982 models but incorporate respondents' earlier partisanship as well as parents' partisanship, both variables are statistically significant. Coefficients for parents' partisanship are larger than those for most individual issues. The coefficients were as follows for 1973 and 1982, respectively (showing only statistically significant values): 2.95 + .12 (parents' partisanship) −.06 (school prayer) −.07 (Vietnam) +.16 (jobs) +.35 (R's 1965 partisanship), with R^2 = .30; .20 + .15 (parents' partisanship) +.12 (school integration) −.12 (Vietnam) +.19 (jobs) +.53 (R's 1973 partisanship), with R^2 = .50. Parents' partisanship remains virtually the same even when liberal/conservative self-placement is added to these equations. Two other extensions of the model were considered. One was to use a nonrecursive model in which current issue positions are dependent on current party identification. However, the assumptions required to specify such a model are quite stringent. A second extension was to use lagged issue positions. That procedure is not at all possible for 1965, of course, or for new issues introduced in subsequent years.

6. With offspring vote, in contrast to party identification, the effect of parents' partisanship is channeled entirely through offspring partisanship. Thus, when we control for both parents' and prior offspring partisanship, the coefficient for the parent variable is not significant.

PART VI: HISTORICAL PERSPECTIVES

19. DEALIGNMENT AND REALIGNMENT IN THE CURRENT PERIOD

In Chapter 28 of *Classics in Voting Behavior* we reviewed work on historical realignments of the party system, especially those of the 1850s, 1890s, and 1930s. We noted briefly that there is controversy over the concept of realignment and about the nature of political change in the period since 1960. Here we take up these matters directly.

Why controversy exists is strikingly clear. General agreement that realignments took place possibly in 1828 and then in or about 1860, 1896, and 1932 suggests a striking periodicity of 32-36 years. Simple extrapolation led researchers to expect a realignment in the 1960s. While much happened during that tumultuous decade, there was no change in the parties contesting major offices and almost no shift in the balance of party identifiers (see Table 16-1). Does that mean that a realignment did not occur? If none happened, is the concept of continuing use? If a realignment did occur, what were its characteristics, and what does it tell us about the general concept? And, finally, what about more recent decades? These are the questions we take up here.

The controversy discussed here is slightly different from those reviewed in previous sections. There is broad agreement on the type of change considered first—what has been called dealignment. Disagreement occurs when we try to interpret that change in the realignment framework.[1]

Dealigning Politics

Most observers agree that there has been meaningful partisan change in recent decades, at least in terms of movement toward more volatile politics. Voting patterns that once seemed totally stable have now become remarkably fluid. In particular, party ties weakened (see below). Political scientists coined the term "party dealignment" to describe this movement of the electorate away from political parties.

The beginning point for understanding this argument is Lipset and Rokkan's (1967) classic treatment of cleavage structure. Writing in a political sociology tradition, Lipset and Rokkan were intrigued by the development of conflicts in Western societies and their translation into party systems. First, according to their analysis, nation-building proceeded. In many countries, the national revolution led to conflict between the "central nation-building culture" and ethnic, linguistic, and religious minorities in the peripheries, conflict that remains especially apparent in Scottish and Welsh separatist movements in the United Kingdom and in linguistic conflict in Belgium and Canada. In some nations the conflict was between the government and the established church, as in disputes in France over the demands of the church for control over education, marriage and divorce law, and other moral matters. Still other conflicts were associated with the coming of the Industrial Revolution, which created cleavages between urban and rural elements in many nations as well as between employers and workers.

To Lipset and Rokkan, writing in the mid-1960s, the party systems of European nations still reflected the interactions of those earlier cleavage patterns. They saw a "freezing" of major party alternatives that resulted in contemporary party systems mirroring in many ways those of nearly a century ago. For example, the Christian Democratic, Calvinist, Agrarian, Labour, and many other parties in European countries even today are based on cleavages of long ago. The parties may even reflect those divisions more than contemporary societal cleavages. Nations like France, Germany, and Italy, whose democratic experiences were interrupted by fascist rule and by war, retained party systems that reflected the conflicts of the 1920s. Thus, the beginning point of understanding contemporary partisan change was to realize the extent to which political alternatives had become frozen across a number of countries.[2]

About the time that Lipset and Rokkan were writing, there appeared numerous indications that the grip of old conflicts on the contemporary party system was loosening. In the United States the clearest indicator was the increase in political independence that was pointed out in Table 16-1. In the 1950s most Americans considered themselves either Republicans or Democrats, with little more than a fifth calling themselves Independents. By the late 1970s more than a third of the population called themselves Independents, while the proportion of Republicans had fallen almost to the level of Independents in the 1950s.

Both the increase in the proportion of Independents and several other aspects of this decline in partisanship were dramatically apparent in *The Changing American Voter* (Nie, Verba, and Petrocik, 1976, chap. 23 in *Classics*). Beginning in the 1960s, fewer citizens considered themselves strong partisans. More partisans defected to vote for the other party. Increasingly, people voted split tickets rather than voting for candidates of only one party for every office. Presidential candidates were less often evaluated in terms of their party affiliation than in terms of their personal characteristics. Overall, the ties of partisanship were weakening. Party dealignment was under way.

The initial response to the appearance of these trends was to search for their causes, especially with an eye toward determining their permanence. Above all, there were efforts to determine the age-related character of the weaker partisanship. *The Changing American Voter* (chap. 4), for example, charted the dealignment with graphs depicting voters by when they entered the electorate.

This soon led to efforts to determine whether the changes were due to period or generational effects. If, for example, the changes could be traced exclusively to the Vietnam War period, the thought was that "normal" partisan strength might return as soon as the war ended.

As it turned out, the initial increase in the proportion of Independents was clearly attributable to period effects. Abramson (1975, 1976), for example, found that declining numbers of strong partisans could be found among all age groups in the mid-1960s. In addition, he found only a weak tendency for individuals to become stronger partisans as they aged, thus closing off the possibility that the younger generation would "automatically" become more partisan over time (Abramson, 1979).[3] Finally, a variety of analyses (for example, Nie, Verba, and Petrocik, 1976, p. 63) pointed to a generational difference as well, with younger generations clearly more independent than older ones. Altogether, the prospects for a quick return to a high level of partisan strength were not very great.[4]

Once it was determined that dealignment was not going to disappear momentarily, researchers began to assess the nature and extent of change and, ultimately, its consequences. Wattenberg was foremost in arguing that what had happened did not so much represent negativity toward the parties as neutrality.[5] In *The Decline of American Political Parties*, a portion of which we reprint here as Chapter 22, he makes extensive use of the open-ended "likes" and "dislikes" questions that form the opening of each of the National Election Study interviews. What comes through is a picture of an electorate much more concerned with candidates and much less anchored by their long-term attachments to political parties than in the 1950s. Expanding on these observations, Wattenberg (1991) has recently argued that voting is more "performance based"—attributable to what the authors of *The American Voter* might have called "the nature of the times."[6]

It was also clear by the 1970s that dealignment was not limited to the United States. Indeed, Särlvik and Crewe (1983) used the title *Decade of Dealignment* to describe politics in Great Britain during that period. Since then, in a number of European countries, long-established voting patterns have given way to greater volatility, and new parties have gathered enough votes to gain seats in national legislatures. Most notable, perhaps, are the various environmental Green parties as well as a number of small, right-wing parties.

Rather than view declining partisanship across a number of countries as coincidental, at least a partial accounting can be made with a common cause—a decline in the importance of class divisions in Western societies. According to this argument, class distinctions were of crucial importance immediately after the Industrial Revolution as well as in the aftermath of the Great Depression. But the 1950s and 1960s were marked by greater affluence among all classes, so there was less of a basis for class voting by the 1970s and 1980s. Indeed, trend data for several countries show a decline in class voting in recent times—though there are occasional increases during periods of economic distress. Declining class voting corresponds well with Inglehart's (1977, 1990) finding of a shift from materialist to post-materialist perspectives in Western European nations. Of course the decline in class voting does not mean that Lipset and Rokkan's other cleavages have also declined, but there is evidence of at least some drop-off in the importance of religious differences as well.[7]

As to the consequences of dealignment, speculation has taken at least two directions. First, some observers feel that the decline in the strength of partisanship and increased electoral volatility have a potential for leading to an "end of parties." Burnham (1970), in fact, speaks of long-term electoral disaggregation and party decomposition. He and others have noted that parties—both as organizations and as electoral aggregations—have been weakened in this century. That weakening has been due to the decline of the urban political machine, the advent of popular primaries that take decision-making away from party bosses, the institution of federal job and welfare programs that take away many of the benefits that parties could once dispense to the faithful and, especially in parts of Europe, the massive growth of government bureaucracies to support increasingly socialized public policies.[8]

According to this view, the New Deal represented a temporary strengthening of party feelings in the electorate, but by the 1960s the decline of party was again in full swing. Fueling this decline was the replacement of party-based campaigns with candidate-oriented media campaigns (Wattenberg, 1991, chap. 22). Television provided the initial shock by allowing candidates to reach large audiences quickly and essentially independently of party workers and leaders. The "Great Debates" between Kennedy and Nixon in 1960 demonstrated that appearance and media "presence" were important, creating a need for campaign media consultants. Later, the development of campaign polls and computer-assisted fund raising called for still more specialized knowledge. Distributing candidate videotapes to voters in 1988 and candidate appearances on television talk shows in 1992 are further instances of new technologies strengthening candidates vis-à-vis the party.[9]

One other probable consequence of partisan dealignment is divided government. In recent decades Republicans have dominated the presidency while Democrats have continued to control Congress. At the same time, unified state governments have become much more scarce (Fiorina, 1992, p. 25). In one sense, the connection between dealignment and divided governments is obvious. When partisanship is strong, voters tend to cast straight tickets, so a party's candidates rise or fall together. With the weakening of party ties, the possibility that one party wins the legislative branch while another wins the executive branch increases. However, as Fiorina notes (1992, p. 45), "party decline is a precondition rather than an explanation." That is, the weaker role of parties permits, but does not guarantee, split control of governments.

Efforts to explain divided government have just begun (see Mayhew, 1992). Thus far, there seems to be consensus that structural factors such as gerrymandering and campaign finance laws do not adequately explain divided control; nor is an increased rate of incumbency reelection the explanation (Jacobson, 1990b, chap. 5; Fiorina, 1992, chap. 2). There also seems to be some agreement that Republicans have fielded weaker legislative candidates, perhaps because of changes in legislative professionalization (see Chapter 15; Fiorina, 1992, chap. 4). Beyond this, there are two competing explanations. Fiorina (1992, chap. 5) suggests that voters consciously opt for divided government, or at least act as if they do. Either to prevent waste, fraud, and abuse or to achieve policy moderation, voters give up the efficiency of unified government in favor of divided control. Jacobson (1990b, chap. 6), in contrast, argues that divided government may be the result of voter approval of presidential candidates (generally Republican) who will "keep taxes low and defense strong and . . . govern competently" and House candidates (generally Democratic) who will "deliver local benefits and . . . protect their favorite programs" (p. 119).

Interestingly, these two presumed consequences of dealignment are rather contradictory. The concept of divided government depends on the existence and meaningfulness of parties, which is contrary to the claim of an end to parties. The fact that both divided government and the end of parties are said to result from dealignment is an indication of considerable uncertainty over the interpretation of this relatively new phenomenon of dealignment. In any case, we may have time to sort it all out, for it now seems obvious that dealignment has a good deal of staying power. Weakened partisan affiliations and their consequences will be around for a while longer.

Realigning Politics in the 1960s and 1970s

While most political scientists agree that party dealignment has been occurring since the mid-1960s, there is a lively controversy as to how to interpret this in the realignment framework. Has a realignment occurred since the New Deal period? If not, why not?

To some extent the disagreements are "simply" matters of definition. Everyone agrees that realignment is concerned with enduring partisan change— that is, long-term shifts as distinguished from short-term fluctuations. But is a realignment a switch in which party is in the majority? Or does it only require a movement in levels of party support? Can a realignment be defined as a transformation in the support coalitions for the parties? A shift in the issue bases of the parties? Or a change in public policy direction following a change in party control of the presidency? Does it require changes in political behavior in Congress and the Supreme Court?[10] Or some combination of the above? As we shall see, all of these questions have been raised in the realignment debates of recent decades.

A little reflection makes it clear how these differing definitions lead to alternative interpretations. It is obvious, first of all, that no major shifts occurred in the party balance in the 1960s or 1970s. The number of Independents increased considerably between 1965 to 1972, but the ratio of Democratic to Republican identifiers remained relatively constant. Democrats, who had dominated elective offices since the 1930s, continued to dominate congressional and state legislative offices. Thus, if one requires as part of a definition of realignment that a "decisive, unidirectional shift occurs in partisan control over the agencies of government, as a new majority party appears at all levels and relegates its predecessor to the dustbin of history" (Ladd, 1991, p. 27), a realignment obviously did not occur in the 1960s. This, then, destroys the periodicity that many had seen in past realignments and suggests that we still require more understanding of their expected timing.

But, as noted, there are alternative ways of thinking about the concept of realignment. One way is to think of realignments as including changes in the coalitions supporting each of the parties (Sundquist, 1983, chap. 2; Petrocik, 1987, p. 353). Thus, for example, if one social group suddenly switched from the Democratic party to the Republican party while another group of the same size switched in the opposite direction, there would be a realignment of sorts even without change in the overall amount of support for each party.

We present arguments based on the support-coalition concept with an updated version of work by Stanley, Bianco, and Niemi, included here as Chapter 22. In one sense, the work of Stanley and his coauthors follows a lengthy, sometimes sterile tradition of determining group support for the parties. Their work is subtly different from earlier studies, however, in that it allows one to estimate the incremental impact of multiple group characteristics. For example, blacks were far more likely than the general population to vote for Democrats as early as 1952 (Axelrod, 1972), but they find that race (that is, the marginal impact of being black) did not contribute strongly to being Democratic until 1964.[11]

A potential problem with realignment theory, whether defined as changes in party majorities or support coalitions, is that changes may not occur precipitously. In the 1930s, for example, partisan changes occurred throughout the Depression period (see *Classics in Voting Behavior*, p. 291). Indeed, ambiguity over the length of time over which changes occur led Carmines and Stimson (1989) to suggest that "issue evolution" is a more appropriate concept than realignment. Still, despite their ultimate rejection of the term, they are fascinated with a transformation they document in the American electorate in the 1960s: race came to dominate the way in which voters thought about issues and influenced the division between the parties. Thus, under the realignment heading, we include here a portion of their work (Chapter 21) in which they test between several realignment models.[12] Significantly, the Carmines and Stimson and the Stanley et al. findings, though very different in their approaches, strongly reinforce the idea that major partisan and ideological shifts occurred in the 1960s.[13]

Carmines and Stimson's work serves another useful purpose—namely, to remind us that realignments are usually thought to involve more than just a change in partisanship, and, indeed, more than just changes the electorate. One of the strengths of their analysis, in fact, is that they discuss changes at the level of congressional voting on racial issues and relate those elite changes to later shifts among ordinary voters (1989, chaps. 3, 4, 8). Indeed, others have discussed the relationship between realignments and a broader range of changes in Congress (Brady, 1988), changes in the Supreme Court (Adamany, 1991), and changes in the governmental system (Beck, 1979).[14]

Another interpretation of the current period begins with the observation that past realignments were not all the same. In the Jacksonian period, a new party (the Whigs) was created in what had been a one-party system; in the 1850s one party (the Whigs) disappeared and another (the Republicans) emerged; in the

1890s an existing party (the Republicans) rose from near equality to a clear majority; and in the 1930s the minority party (the Democrats) became the majority party. Given the different character of these past realignments, why should one expect a realignment in the 1960s to mirror that of the 1930s? All that may be important about the past is that a major change took place with a considerable degree of regularity.

From this perspective, the most surprising thing about the 1960s is that political scientists failed to recognize what occurred as a major system shift. It was widely recognized that there were important changes away from parties and toward candidate-centered elections. However, we were looking for a change in the majority party, so we somehow thought that there was more to come. In fact, the realignment—in the sense of "a set of rapid changes in a broad range of crucial political variables, where these changes, once made, endure" (Aldrich and Niemi, 1989, p. 6)—had occurred.[15]

This argument is made by Aldrich and Niemi (1989), who then draw together time series data covering a large number of indicators related to voters and voting. Many of the individual patterns are themselves quite clear, but when combined (using deviations from mean levels for each indicator), they yield a convincing picture of an equilibrium during the 1950s and into the 1960s, a disequilibrium through 1972, and a new equilibrium from 1972-1988. Interestingly, in arguing that a new party system was created in the 1960s—a "candidate-centered party system"—they fully embrace the dealignment described in the first section of this chapter. The dealignment, properly interpreted, constituted a realignment.

Realignment in the 1980s?

While the primary change in the partisan distribution during the 1960s was an increase in the number of Independents, the party balance itself appears to have shifted significantly in the 1980s. Judging solely by data from the National Election Studies surveys, it would appear as if the Republicans have narrowed the gap from about a 17-point margin prior to 1984 to about 10 points thereafter (Table 16-1). While the initial changes were met with some skepticism, the shift has now been sustained for about eight years and is evident in a wide variety of polls (see, for example, Niemi, Mueller, and Smith, 1989, p. 17; Hugick, 1991a; *Public Perspective*, 1992). Moreover, data from a number of sources suggest that the shift has been particularly significant among young adults (for example, Norpoth, 1987; Miller, 1990; Hugick, 1991b; *Public Perspective*, 1992); simply a continuation of such a shift would inexorably (as the more Democratic depression-generation ages and leaves the electorate) lead to an even greater shift toward the GOP.

Does this mean that a realignment—at least in the constrained sense of a shift in the party balance—has occurred? Is this the long-awaited realignment of the parties? If so, does it, coming some 20 years after the 1960s, destroy the 32-36 year periodicity that has been so attention-grabbing?

Perhaps the most unequivocal statements that realignment occurred in the

1980s are those of Shanks and Miller (1991). They detail a two-phase realignment: movement of less politicized younger voters toward the Republicans between 1980 and 1984 due to attraction to Reagan's leadership followed by movement of older, more politicized citizens to the Republicans between 1984 and 1988 as they began to consider themselves conservatives. What is missing, however, at this stage is any demonstration that these partisan shifts are actually enduring changes rather than instances of the instability of partisanship discussed in Chapter 16.

On the one hand, the preponderance of data suggests a noticeable and relatively durable shift toward the Republicans. On the other hand, the Republicans do not appear to have achieved majority status, and, at the end of 1991, the Republican shift seems to have stalled (Hugick, 1991a; *Public Perspective*, 1992). Indeed, the shift could prove to be transitory. If macropartisanship is as dependent on the state of the economy—as MacKuen, Erikson, and Stimson suggest in Chapter 17—the pro-Republican shift could just reflect the economic growth of the 1980s and could vanish with more difficult economic times under a Republican president in the 1990s. Moreover, if realignment requires major changes in a variety of indicators, the increase in the proportion of Republicans is insufficient. The variety and depth of changes in the 1960s are, it seems to us, a better indicator of system-wrenching alterations than is a downshift only in the Democratic/Republican margin.[16] If that is so, however, it is still important that such an alteration occurred. Whatever next month's polls show, and whatever the historical judgment on the 1980s, even a decade-long Republican shift may lead to still further revisions in our understanding of what constitutes an electoral realignment.[17]

Conclusion

That dealignment has occurred since the mid-1960s is beyond question. That a modest, but reasonably durable shift in the Democratic/Republican balance took place in the mid-1980s is increasingly so. What is less clear is the meaning of each development for the party system, for the political system, and for the concept of realignment.

At the end of the "partisan change" chapter in the second edition of this book, we wrote: "the pity is that for all our interest in long-term political change, it can only be assessed in the long-term—after it has become old news . . . . By [the time we are able to judge whether a realignment occurred], the topic will be the meat of historians, rather than whetting the appetites of political scientists." Perhaps we were wrong. The empirical, especially survey-based, study of mass electorates is now 40 years old, and interest in the entire period remains high. It now appears to us as if unresolved questions about the meaning of dealignment and realignment will keep it so.

NOTES

1. Our coverage of the literature also differs from that in other chapters; we consider here all writings about aggregate partisan changes in the electorate after the New Deal rather than focusing only on writings since the mid-1980s. However, the readings will be quite recent.

2. In the United States, the shape of the party system of the 1950s could easily be traced to the experiences of the Civil War and to the class conflict of the 1920s and 1930s.

3. There was a considerable debate about the strengthening of partisanship with age. Converse (1969) had earlier claimed that voters develop stronger partisan ties as they age, and he later (1976) found evidence of life-cycle effects in the "steady-state" period (1952-1964). However, Abramson (1979) showed that some of the increased partisan strength could be explained by the increasing politicization of African-Americans in the 1960s and that for whites the evidence of strengthening partisanship was much weaker. In any event, there was no doubt that whatever life-cycle effects existed were overwhelmed by the period effects in favor of independence.

4. Another possibility that received some attention was that youthful independence along with the large size of the baby boom population (which began entering the electorate in the 1960s) could account for decreasing partisanship. However, Norpoth and Rusk (1982) found that the changing age composition of the electorate did little to explain the change in partisanship.

5. Part of the argument dealt with the measurement of party identification, and what Miller and Wattenberg (1983) argued was a growth after 1964 in the number of "no preference" responses. See Chapter 22.

6. However, current writings, such as Wattenberg's, generally do not convey anything like the negative overtones to nature-of-the-times-voting found in *The American Voter*. When its authors first discovered the limited knowledge and skills of the ordinary citizen in the late 1950s, they tended to regard voting on the basis of anything less than clearly understood issues as undesirable or even "irrational." See *Classics*, chap. 4.

7. Dalton (1988, chap. 8) provides a succinct summary of these arguments as well as data on the United States, Great Britain, (West) Germany, and France. His book is also a useful starting place for references to other countries. A rather complete, though undifferentiated, list of sources on non-U.S. elections is given by de Guchteneire, LeDuc, and Niemi (1991).

8. The foremost popularization of this view was through David Broder's (1971) aptly titled book, *The Party's Over*.

9. Increasingly, candidate-centered campaigns have led to new master's programs in campaign techniques, new journals, such as *Campaigns and Elections*, and new texts and readers, such as Salmore and Salmore (1989) and Sabato (1981; 1989). All of these have focused on campaigns and candidates; there has been relatively less attention to the effects of the media on the electorate. Recently, however, better descriptive information about media content has been collected (Lichter, Amundson, and Noyes, 1988), and Iyengar and Kinder (1987) and others have begun imaginative studies of the impact of the media. Graber (1989) provides a good summary of the literature on the media and elections.

10. At least two schemes have been proposed for counting realignments. One is to categorize a set of "party systems" in American history—the first through 1824, the second 1828-56, the third 1860-92, the fourth 1896-1928, the fifth beginning in 1932 (Chambers and Burnham, 1967), and possibly a sixth beginning in the mid-1960s (see

below). Another is to categorize "political systems"—the prealignment period through 1838, an alignment/realignment phase from 1838-93, a realignment/dealignment era from 1893-1948/52, and a postalignment period since 1948/52 (Silbey, 1991). It is not obvious to us that the latter categorizations provide any fewer problems than does the usual concern with realignments. See *Classics*, chap. 28.

11. Stanley, Bianco, and Niemi used party identification as their indicator of group support; Erikson, Lancaster, and Romero (1989) found generally similar results using the presidential vote.

12. Previously they heartily embraced the realignment concept (for example, Carmines, Renten, and Stimson, 1984). In fairness to them, we note that in Chapter 20 of the present volume, Carmines and Stimson attempt a serious effort to distinguish "realignment"—by which they mean a sudden change from one steady-state to another—from "dynamic growth"—by which they mean a sudden shift followed by continued change over an extended period. They find support for the latter and attribute the slower, gradual change to population replacement.

13. In recognition of the possibility that not all changes would be sudden and brief, Key (1955) coined the term "secular" realignment to indicate slower, extended changes that nonetheless amounted to a major shift over some extended period of time. We recognize, of course, that such types of changes may occur (for example, the shift to post-materialist outlooks among European electorates). Carmines and Stimson discuss this type of change further in Chapter 20.

14. Another way of searching for realignments is to determine whether there has been a shift in the dimension underlying states' presidential votes. Rabinowitz, Gurian, and Macdonald (1984) have factor analyzed these votes from 1948 through 1980 and found such a shift. In the non-southern states, in particular, the voting dimension starting in 1968 is orthogonal to that through 1960, consistent with a realignment in the 1960s.

15. Perhaps the confusion would have been avoided if researchers had focused on the term used by Key (1955) in his original article title—critical elections—instead of realigning elections.

16. Wattenberg (1990, p. 167) makes much the same point: " . . . even assuming that the Republican surge is a long-lasting one, it will be of limited importance as long as partisan attitudes remain so weak and split-ticket voting so prevalent." Earlier Wattenberg (1987) dubbed the party identification shift not matched with corresponding changes in control of Congress or in other attitudinal data a "hollow realignment."

17. In his analysis of partisan changes in the South, Stanley (1988) accepts the possibility that both a dealignment and a realignment have occurred there, but he makes the important point that the volatility inherent in the dealignment of a one-party system can look like a realignment. More work is required on the interconnections between these two change processes.

FURTHER READINGS

The Realignment Concept

V. O. Key, Jr., "A Theory of Critical Elections," *Journal of Politics* (1955) 17:3-18. Classic theoretical statement of realigning elections.

Walter Dean Burnham, *Critical Elections and the Mainsprings of American Politics* (New York: Norton, 1970). Burnham's full analysis of historical trends in voting. The end of parties?

James Sundquist, *Dynamics of the Party System: Alignment and Realignment of Political Parties in the United States* (Washington, D.C.: Brookings, 1973, 1983). Historical and theoretical perspective on U.S. realignments.

Paul Allen Beck, "The Electoral Cycle in American Politics," *British Journal of Political Science* (1979) 9:129-56. A theory of cycles of realignments, stable alignments, and dealignments.

Byron E. Shafer, *The End of Realignment? Interpreting American Electoral Eras* (Madison: University of Wisconsin Press, 1991). Essays pro and con on the utility of the realignment concept for studying both early and contemporary party history.

Dealignment Since the 1960s and Its Consequences

Norman H. Nie, Sidney Verba, and John R. Petrocik, *The Changing American Voter* (Cambridge: Harvard University Press, 1976, 1979). Initial book-length statement of the weakening of partisanship and its consequences.

Helmut Norpoth and Jerrold G. Rusk, "Partisan Dealignment in the American Electorate," *American Political Science Review* (1982) 76:522-37. Decomposes the sources of the dealignment.

Martin P. Wattenberg, *The Decline of American Political Parties* (Cambridge: Harvard University Press, 1984, 1990). Decline of partisanship and increasing emphasis on candidates and some of the consequences.

Martin P. Wattenberg, *The Rise of Candidate-Centered Politics* (Cambridge: Harvard University Press, 1991). Analysis of presidential elections in the 1980s, emphasizing the consequences of weak parties.

Divided Government

Gary C. Jacobson, *The Electoral Origins of Divided Government: Competition in U.S. House Elections, 1946-1988* (Boulder, Colo.: Westview Press, 1990). Tests various explanations for Democratic dominance in House elections.

Morris P. Fiorina, *Divided Government* (New York: Macmillan, 1992). Theoretical explanation of why voters might be choosing divided government.

Realignment in the 1960s

John R. Petrocik, "Realignment: New Party Coalitions and the Nationalization of the South," *Journal of Politics* (1987) 49:347-75. Analysis of changes in party coalitions, especially in the South.

Harold W. Stanley, "Southern Partisan Changes: Dealignment, Realignment or Both," *Journal of Politics* (1988) 50:64-88. Both a dealignment and a realignment occurred in the South.

John Aldrich and Richard G. Niemi, "The Sixth American Party System: The 1960s Realignment and the Candidate-Centered Parties," manuscript, 1989. Analysis of multiple time series; stable equilibrium-disequilibrium-stable-equilibrium characterizes the past forty years.

Edward G. Carmines and James A. Stimson, *Issue Evolution: Race and the Transformation of American Politics* (Princeton. N.J.: Princeton University Press, 1989). Study of parties at the elite and mass level and their changing relationship to the issue of race in American politics.

Partisan Realignment in the 1980s

Helmut Norpoth, "Under Way and Here to Stay: Party Realignment in the 1980s?" *Public Opinion Quarterly* (1987) 51:376-91. Republican gains in the 1980s, especially among young voters.

Merrill Shanks and Warren E. Miller, "Partisanship, Policy, and Performance: the Reagan Legacy in the 1988 Election," *British Journal of Political Science* (1991) 21:129-97. Analysis of the 1988 election describes party realignment in the 1980s.

20. MODELING CHANGE IN MASS IDENTIFICATION WITH THE PARTIES

Edward G. Carmines and James A. Stimson

Let us review the evidence [of previous chapters of Carmines and Stimson]. We saw in Chapter 3 a striking issue polarization in the pattern of roll-call votes on racial issues in the U.S. Senate and the House. In Chapter 4 we saw similar evidence of change in popular perceptions of where the parties stood, led by the changing attitude composition of party activists on both sides. And we saw in Chapter 5 that racial concerns have moved to a central position in the constellation of attitudes ordinary Americans hold toward political life, a position usually reserved for orientations of considerably greater abstraction. We have seen that much of the actual connotation of the popular concepts of liberalism and conservatism is racial in character.

Taken as a whole, this evidence suggests change of far-reaching character. It suggests redefinition of the normal grounds of political debate, a changing character of the experience of politics. At the beginning of our period racial issues were not aligned with the party system; they cut across it. Now they clearly are aligned. Racial issues have become an integral part of the normal struggle for political power.

The ultimate evidence of an issue evolution, however, is not to be found in the halls of Congress, the behavior of party activists, or even the ideological orientations of the electorate. It is to be found in the link between issues and citizens' partisan identifications. An issue evolution implies that the emergence of a new issue conflict has severed the connection between citizens and the ongoing party system—that, to be more precise, a mass partisan polarization has occurred along the new dimension of conflict. Have racial issues created a new partisan division in the electorate, overlaying the New Deal issue constellation? This is the question we will discuss in this chapter—the final piece of the issue evolution puzzle.

We posit three models of issue evolution: critical election, secular growth, and dynamic growth. All three lead to permanent changes in the issue basis of the party system, but they do so at different rates and involve different causal mechanisms. Here we focus on which model most accurately characterizes the evolution of racial issues. To address this question we construct hypothetical models of issue evolution, adding a fourth variation, temporary effect, to round out the hypothetical issue possibilities.

Models of Partisan Change

Imagine for the moment that we can measure polarization between parties over a particular issue, candidate, or event. A variety of techniques might be employed; the one we shall later use is the simple difference between the aggregate (mean) issue attitudes of the party groups (i.e., party identifiers) over time. Polarization might or might not exist before the process begins, but the increase[1] in polarization is important. Thus, we can presume without loss of generality a zero base-line. The models of Figure 20-1 track four hypothetical patterns of polarization of a party system to new issue conflict. The impulse-decay model of Figure 20-1 illustrates dramatic but transitory change. As soon as the temporary stimulus is removed, the system rapidly returns to its preexisting level of stability. The temporary nature of this change rather than its abruptness is its most distinctive characteristic.

Many different kinds of political phenomenons, especially presidential candidates, presumably have this type of dramatic but momentary effect on the party system. John Kennedy's nomination for the presidency by the Democrats in 1960, for example, led to a polarization of the electorate on the religious issue (Converse et al., 1961). Catholics became more heavily Democratic, just as Protestants became more Republican. But this increased partisan differentiation between religious groups was transient. It is convenient to digress to our underlying conception of causality in partisan change to explain why this must be the case.

We assume that the American party system exists in a state of equilibrium.[2] Because it has powerful implications, the equilibrium assumption is not to be taken lightly; equilibriums do not exist accidentally. Systems acquire that property when built-in causal forces tend to restore them after deviation (Stokes and Iversen, 1966). We will not speculate here—in part, to be candid, because we do not know—about which particular mechanisms produce equilibrium, but one is hard pressed to account for the lengthy duration of any party system without recourse to the implicit causation of equilibrium.

It follows naturally that any temporary disturbance must have temporary effects. The disturbance can drive the system away from equilibrium, but it cannot keep it there after its causal force is no longer present. There is an important corollary. Two changes are required to alter the equilibrium level: one moves the system from equilibrium to a new level, and a second permanent redefinition of the grounds of party cleavage maintains its new level after the initial stimulus is no longer present.

To the extent that most political issues affect partisan change at all, they are

Figure 20-1 Four Hypothetical Models of Partisan Change

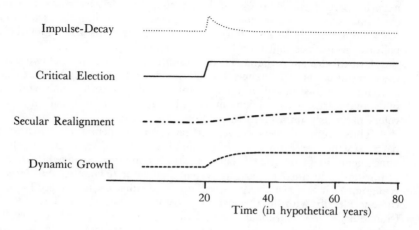

likely to be of the impulse-decay type. Occasionally, the public may become aroused about specific political issues (e.g., Vietnam and Watergate), even to the point of decisive electoral impact. These issues are typically linked to political events that are a major source of disturbance in the existing political environment. Although these issues can be important in a particular election, their effects are short term. They may influence system outcomes, but they do not change the system. They move the system away from its equilibrium level, but they do not keep it away. They have the important limitation of being unable to sustain themselves beyond the events that brought them into being. Thus, as the events fade in public memory, the issues lose their salience and with it their ability to influence citizen party identifications. The dramatic short-term electoral importance of these issues is thus more than counterbalanced by their inconsequential long-term effects on the party system. It is only a matter of time before the effects of these issues decay, leaving no permanent mark on the system.

The second panel of Figure 20-1 models the issue configuration of a classic critical election realignment, the earliest and most simplistic account of a party system change. The party system is in equilibrium prior to the impact of some unspecified event after which it shifts dramatically and permanently to a new equilibrium. A long period of stability is followed by a sudden burst of dramatic change that shifts the party system to a new level of stability. The party system is stationary before the critical election—an intervention that leads to a radical and profound alteration of the system manifested in a sharp and sudden increase in issue polarization.

The scenario is familiar. A divisive political issue emerges that represents a major source of unresolved tension with the majority party's fragile electoral coalition. Despite its most strenuous efforts, the majority party is unable to keep the issue off the political agenda. Indeed, eventually it dominates the agenda.

With the ascendence of the issue comes the inevitable and rapid collapse of the majority party fortunes; it can no longer command decisive support among the electorate. One party's misfortunes are another's opportunities as the minority party or a recently formed third party quickly assumes control of the major political institutions and forges a new direction in public policy.

Critical election realignments can result from either or both of two particular mechanisms of partisan change. The sharply discontinuous and episodic character of change specified in critical realignment models is consistent only with massive individual partisan conversions or equally rapid partisan mobilization of new voters previously uninvolved in politics.

Thus, from this perspective, abrupt and permanent transformation of the party system are caused by large numbers of voters discarding old party attachments in favor of new ones or massive numbers of newly active voters acquiring a distinctive partisan orientation. For example, the New Deal realignment, it is alternatively argued, occurred either because many Republicans came to identify with the Democratic party in response to the Great Depression (Sundquist, 1983; Burnham, 1970; Erikson and Tedin, 1981) or because the ranks of the Democratic party were swelled by the massive mobilization of previously inactive voters, especially immigrants and women (Andersen, 1976, 1979; see also Converse, 1975; Salisbury and MacKuen, 1981; Clubb, Flanigan, and Zingale, 1980).

Population replacement, as we will argue, is capable of profound alteration of the party system, but this mechanism is sharply inconsistent with critical election realignment models. The more obvious inconsistency is that replacement effects by themselves are not large enough to produce dramatic change in a single election. The less obvious inconsistency is a theoretical Achilles' heel of critical election theories: unless conversion or mobilization is total at the time of the critical election, population replacement should cause steady increases in issue polarization in the years immediately after the critical election. Prerealignment cohorts, those least polarized, will be successively replaced by newly eligible young voters who come of age when the alignment is at the peak of salience and should therefore be highly polarized (Beck, 1974, 1979).

Replacement mechanisms entail a dynamic evolution to a new equilibrium level; they are inconsistent with a one-time shift. And if replacement is ruled out, only overnight conversion or implausibly rapid mobilization is left. We are left to postulate an event of such magnitude that it can alter the party system in one election and yet not be decisive enough to create distinctive party alignments of those coming of age in the years thereafter.

The third panel of Figure 20-1 is the political equivalent of Darwinian gradualism. The panel displays a gradual transformation of the party system that takes place over an extended period. The change effected through this transformation is permanent; it leaves an imprint on the political landscape. And the change can be quite substantial, fundamentally altering the complexion of the party system, but the process is slow, gradual, incremental. This is a noncritical, evolutionary model of partisan change, a model consistent with Key's notion of secular realignment. As Key observed:

A secular shift in party attachment may be regarded as a movement of the members of a population category from party to party that extends over several presidential elections and appears to be independent of the peculiar factors influencing the vote at individual elections. . . . A movement that extends over a half century is a more persuasive indication of the phenomenon in mind than is one that lasts less than a decade. (1959, p. 199)

Thus, Key viewed a secular realignment as a gradual shift in the partisan composition of the electorate. Though gradual, the shift is persistent, and herein lies its significance.

Although critical realignments look to individual conversion or rapid mobilization to explain the dynamics of partisan change, secular realignments can be accounted for by the far more common mechanism of normal population replacement. They can result from such essentially nonpolitical forces as differential birthrates between the party coalitions, interregional migration patterns, or economic-technological transformations that gradually produce new political generations exposed to different political forces than their parents. Secular· realignments do not depend upon large-scale changes in individual partisan attachment, a characteristic noted for its substantial level of stability (Converse and Markus, 1979), or upon massive partisan mobilizations of segments of the electorate. Instead, the gradual character of secular realignments means that they can be understood as a not atypical outcome of continuous population replacement.

The fourth panel portrays a dynamic evolutionary model of change in the party system. The model is dynamic because it presumes that at some point the system moves from a fairly stationary steady-state period to a fairly dramatic change; the change is manifested by a "critical moment" in the time series. Significantly, however, the change—the dynamic growth—does not end with the critical moment. Instead, it continues over an extended period, albeit at a much slower pace. This continued growth after the initial shock defines the evolutionary character of the model. The issue polarization, however, does not continue to grow indefinitely. Instead, after an extended period of increase, the polarization decays at a gradual pace. The pattern culminates in the establishment of a new equilibrium—one that shows a clear but lessened degree of polarization.

The dynamic growth and decay pattern of partisan change may be thought of as a synthesis of critical and secular realignment models. The more pronounced the initial step compared to the eventual development of the issue polarization, the more closely the model follows a critical election realignment. Conversely, if the critical moment is modest compared to the continuous long-term component of change, then the model approximates a pure secular realignment. In either case, the main characteristic of the polarization is that it is not a one-shot, large-scale phenomenon but rather follows a discernible pattern over time. The polarization not only sustains itself but grows larger for a lengthy period until it begins a modest decay that eventually leads to a new equilibrium.[3] Thus, studied over a sufficiently long period, the evolutionary character of the change—the fact that the electorate is undergoing small, incremental change after the critical moment—

is most impressive. The initial shock merely sets in motion a pattern of change that continues into the future.

Dynamic evolution is consistent with a variety of causal mechanisms of change. The initial step could be due partly to individual partisan conversions and partly to rapid partisan mobilization. The gradual change over an extended period of time is probably the result of population replacement.

The gradual growth and decay in polarization, a basic characteristic of dynamic issue evolutions, is well accounted for by normal population replacement. The growth in polarization comes about when older voters, relatively unaffected by the new issue cleavage due to their well-established partisan predispositions, inevitably leave the electorate and are replaced by newly eligible young voters whose weak partisan ties are easily influenced by the salience of the new issue. This dual impact of population replacement leads to a predictable increase in issue polarization. The later decay in polarization can be explained by the same mechanism. With the passage of time, the salience of the issue gradually declines as does its influence on mass partisanship. Its major influence is now concentrated among older voters—those whose partisanship was formed during the heat of political conflict. Young voters, having had no direct experience with the issue, are least likely to be polarized by it. Thus, both the gradual growth and partial decay in issue polarization are logical outcomes of normal population replacement.

Of the four models of partisan change we have presented, the first (impulse-decay) is probably the most common issue impact, but it is not lengthy enough to be important in the evolution of party systems. Its fundamental limitation is that the partisan effects are wholly temporary. The second, critical election realignment, is too simplistic to accord with the complexities of partisan change. Resting on assumed massive partisan conversions or equally massive (and sudden) partisan mobilizations, it overestimates the degree of change occurring at a single point and underestimates the amount of change occurring over time. Pure secular realignment, which might be an adequate account of the impact of demographic shifts and the like, cannot explain issue evolution, for it fails to account for the reason why the process begins in the first place. It is a fire with no spark.

The dynamic growth and decay model is the most plausible account of partisan transformations. Where critical election accounts are conversions with no replacement and secular realignment posits replacement but no conversion or (rapid) mobilization, the dynamic evolution model posits all three mechanisms; conversion and mobilization start the process, and replacement sustains it. The "critical moment" of the dynamic growth model must be large enough to be visible—far less, however, than the convulsive change of the critical election. Long-term dynamic growth occurs when that "visible" shift is reinforced by recruitment (and derecruitment) that continues to emphasize the new cleavage in following years; and partial decay occurs when the issue loses its capacity to shape the partisan orientations of the newest members of the electorate.

Although we believe the dynamic evolution model provides a plausible account of issue evolution, it presents difficult problems of estimation. Most important, we lack the necessary information to track any single issue, including race, throughout its extended growth and partial decay. To compensate for this limitation, we will first turn to a limited analysis of an issue that represents the political conflict underlying the New Deal. Then we will conduct a more formal, statistical analysis of desegregation, which shows it still in its dynamic growth phase of partisan development.

The New Deal in Decay: An Empirical Sketch

The New Deal, we all agree, is the basis of the current party alignment. Analysts have predicted its demise for at least three decades, but it seems to persist. Few, however, would disagree that the alignment is in decay.

Decay has another face, the depolarization of attitudes that give policy content to the alignment. For the New Deal was not only a party coalition, an appeal to the common man; it was also a set of programs that reached out to the unemployed working man, saying "It is not your fault, you did not cause the Depression" and, most important, "It is the government's responsibility to do something about it." Thus, government responsibility was then and is still a controversial assertion. More than anything else, this cleavage issue separated partisans; it still does.

Contemporary survey data allow the study of this party cleavage issue. Recalled partisanship permits the reconstruction of parties of the past. Decay of polarization can be loosely estimated, which we will do, and modeled with some precision, which we will not do. The reconstruction methodology demands more than we can reasonably assume (Niemi, Katz, and Newman, 1980). Recovering an event of the 1930s from respondents who lived on to be interviewed in the 1970s asks more than can be expected. Pushed further back in time, our sample becomes ever smaller and progressively age-biased. The technique requires memory of forty-year-old events, when Niemi and coauthors (1980) have found four years problematic. Thus, we shall paint no portrait of the New Deal, only a sketch.

No single issue portrays the New Deal realignment; it was a complex brew of issues, symbols, personalities, and coalitions. But most would concur that, if one issue had to be chosen, it would be the fundamental disagreement over the proper role of government intrusions into the marketplace to provide jobs for those who wanted to work. We, in turn, have chosen to look at its best empirical manifestation in the Center for Political Studies survey item on this question.[4]

Issue alignment is too subtle a phenomenon to tolerate the considerable noise introduced by variations in question wording over time. Thus, we must restrict our analysis to surveys where question wording is identical. We have chosen the CPS cross-sections of 1972, 1976, and 1978 for a reconstruction data base. They are current and present no question wording artifact, but they are long removed in time from many events of interest.

To model the New Deal realignment is a tempting prospect. A series can be reconstructed back to, perhaps even before, the event; however, the data are not good enough to sustain the modeling exercise.[5] Consequently, we settle for the more modest goal of sketching issue depolarization in progress.

Figure 20-2   Mean Party Positions on Government Responsibility for Jobs and Standard of Living: A Reconstructed Time Series

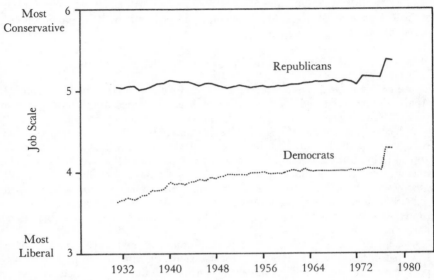

Source: SRC/CPS National Election Studies of 1972, 1976, 1978.

The reconstructed attitudes graphed in Figure 20-2 show the issue dealignment we expected to see. Ignoring the sharp upward changes at the end of the series, attributable to sampling fluctuation, the sketch has some surprising features. For example, the decay of cleavage is asymmetric, accounted for entirely by changes among Democratic identifiers. Republican identifiers show no evidence of shift on New Deal issues from Hoover through Carter. Nothing happens.

Democrats are a more interesting lot. They, too, show no change over the last three decades, which also means that the New Deal cleavage has been stagnant for three decades. These probably conservative estimates, however, show a decay of some 30 to 40 percent of the original party difference, all of which occurs in the 1930s and 1940s. This is unexpected in two regards. First, the method is far more sensitive to recent than ancient changes. Yet Figures 20-2 and 20-3, which shows the interparty difference computed from Figure 20-2, portray remarkable stability for recent decades and change in the past. Second, the pattern of decay could be produced only if the old in the 1970s samples were considerably more liberal than the young, which contradicts our normal expectation.

The pattern of the figures does make sense from another perspective. If one assumes that the generation that experiences realignment is peculiarly sensitive to the party-aligning issue but passes on its partisanship to its children (and they to theirs) more successfully than its issue position, then the gross patterns of Figures 20-2 and 20-3 are what would be expected. Party alignments decay to a new

Figure 20-3 The Decay of Interparty Polarization of the Jobs and
Standard of Living Issue

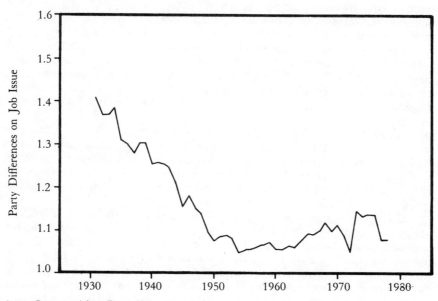

equilibrium as the generation of realignment loses its numbers and its intensity over the years. Our sketch of the New Deal in decay is an unintended confirmation of Beck's (1974) "socialization theory of partisan realignment." It is consistent with the view that the socialization mechanism can pass on partisanship as identification but not the vivid emotional context in which the identification was forged. Where the ties between generations are imperfect, as they surely are, any alignment formed from idiosyncratic events must of necessity decay (Carmines, McIver, and Stimson, 1987).

The Polarization of Desegregation

If an issue persists relatively unchanged for a lengthy period, we can make several cross-sectional estimates of the polarization of issue and party and from these varying readings estimate what a continuous time series might have been if it had existed. That is our method here. We have used all the American national election studies for presidential and off-year elections (1956 through 1980) to construct an "even-year" time series of the desegregation attitudes of party identifiers.

Desegregation attitude scales are constructed for each cross-section by summing attitude items, each weighted equally, and transforming the scales obtained to a common metric (mean: 50, standard deviation: 25) for all years. The years 1945 to 1955 and odd-numbered years thereafter, except 1963, are then reconstructed from respondent reports of party identification change.[6] The intensity and continuity of racial attitudes make us comfortable with this procedure, but the need for intensity and continuity limits the method.

There are probably large numbers of issues of the impulse-decay type, for example, but we cannot study the decay of party alignments on them because questions cease to be asked when they are no longer topical. Other issues may have a lengthy history, but, because attitudes on them are not intense, cross-time measures are highly suspect from the intrusion of the varying cues of question wording.

Niemi, Katz, and Newman (1980) have demonstrated from panel data that recalled party identifications are frequently erroneous. Since the reconstruction methodology rests in part—thankfully not in large part—on the quality of recall, it, too, may be questioned. But we have shown elsewhere (Carmines and Stimson, 1984, pp. 154-58) that the reconstruction methodology is fairly robust when applied to the reconstruction of racial attitudes.

Before proceeding to the business of modeling issue evolution on race, we pause to describe our expectations for the varying models of partisan change. Polarization is measured by the difference between the mean attitudes of the two party groups over time. Operationally, that entails simply computing party means for each year and subtracting one from the other. Arbitrarily, we subtract the Republican mean from the Democratic mean. That leaves us with three time series, one for each party and one for the difference between parties. The party mean series are graphed in Figure 20-4 for a first visual demonstration of the phenomenon.

Figure 20-4 shows a stable and very minor difference in the views of the two parties' identifiers through 1962, followed by the appearance of growing polarization in 1963-1964. A cautious spectator of the civil rights movement before that time, in 1963 the Kennedy administration, and implicitly the Democratic party, took up the cause of civil rights as its own. Whether that by itself would have been sufficient to create a partisan issue evolution we shall never know, for it was quickly followed by Barry Goldwater's abandonment of the pro-civil rights Republican tradition the next year. Taken together, these events and these two years form our critical moment.

All four models of issue evolution may be expressed as variations of the first-order transfer function:

$$Y_t = [\omega_0/(1 - \delta_1 B)]I_t + N_t \qquad [20\text{-}1]$$

where:

Y_t is the interparty difference series to be explained
δ_1 is a first-order growth (or decay) rate parameter
B is the backshift operator such that $BX_t = X_{t-1}$
ω_0 is a zero-order initial impact parameter
I_t is an input series of zeros and ones
N_t is a noise model accounting for residual time dependence in the series.

Figure 20-4 The Desegregation Attitudes of Party Identifiers, 1945-1980

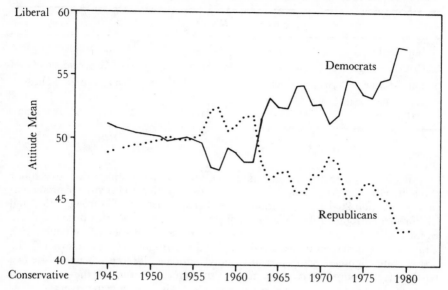

Source: SRC/CPS National Election Study Series, 1956-1980, and Louis Harris and Associates, Study #1285.

Variation in three aspects of the intervention model of equation 20-1 can produce the outcomes of our four models of Figure 20-1. The input series I_t may be either a pulse ("1" for the critical moment and "0" at other times) or a step ("0" before, "1" after). The pulse input is used to model a temporary effect (e.g., impulse-decay), and the step is used to model any of our three permanent effects. The two parameters (ω_0, δ_1) model the size of initial impacts and dynamic effects, respectively.

Thus, for example, a critical election scenario would imply a very large ω_0 with no dynamic term. The pure secular formulation is the opposite combination; incremental change implies a small ω_0 coefficient while continuous growth over a long time span implies a δ_1 approaching the limit of 1.0. Evaluating the four models is an empirical question, given that each has a distinctive pattern of inputs and parameters, as shown in Table 20-1. Two can be ruled out by statistical inference, and the choice between the remaining two is a judgment call but not a difficult one. We consider them in order.

Model 1, the impulse-decay formulation, can be dismissed on visual evidence. It implies a sharp but temporary response of the issue/alignment series. The effect in Figure 20-4 is demonstrably not temporary. We have nonetheless modeled it and found what we expected to find; the decay rate parameter (δ_1) does not indicate decay. It takes on an unacceptable value, greater than 1.0, indicating the inappropriateness of a temporary effects model.

Table 20-1   Four Models of Issue Evolution

Model	Input	Dynamic (δ)	Impact (ω)
1. Impulse-Decay	Pulse		significant
2. Critical realignment	Step	zero	very large and significant
3. Pure secular	Step	large	small but significant
4. Dynamic growth "critical moment"	Step	large	"visible" and significant

Ruling out a temporary effects model, we can now distinguish between our three alternative permanent effects. We do so by fitting the first-order intervention of equation 20-1 with the input series (I_t) specified as "0" through 1962 and "1" in 1963 through 1980. The two parameters (ω_0, δ_1) from this fit and a third, Θ_2 for a second-order moving average noise process, are displayed in Table 20-2. This same information is displayed graphically in Figure 20-5; it shows (1) the actual issue alignment series measured now as the net difference between the two parties; (2) a pure intervention model, the smooth curve, of the series; and (3) the best prediction of the series, including also the moving average noise component.

Reduction in mean square from 24.85 for the unmodeled series to 3.54 for the full model (analogous to an R^2 of about 0.86) indicates a good fit of the model to the issue alignment series.

Few would postulate a critical realignment around racial attitudes, and it comes as no surprise that the evidence at hand rules it out. This model fails both predictive criteria; the initial change ($\omega_0 = 5.42$) is not large enough to be "critical," and the continuing growth rate ($\delta_1 = 0.41$) is clearly significant.

The model of Table 20-2 clearly reflects the dynamic growth variety. The 1963-1964 change reverses the preintervention differentiation between parties,

Table 20-2   The Evolution of Interparty Differences on Desegregation: A Dynamic Growth Model of Issue Evolution

	Parameter	Value	t	Description
Intervention: 1963	δ_1	0.41	2.9	Growth rate parameter
	ω_0	5.42	4.4	Initial impact
Noise Model: $(1 - B)Z_t = (1 - \Theta B^2)a_t$	Θ_2	0.94	40.8	Moving average (2)

Note: Residual Mean Square = 3.535; χ^2_{11} = 7.7 (white noise).

Figure 20-5 The Growth of Party Differentiation on Desegregation: Actual and Predicted

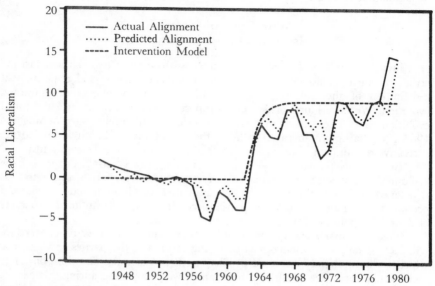

providing an easy distinction between the "visible" change of the dynamic growth formulation rather than the "small" change implied by the pure secular Model 3. The series approximates its asymptotic equilibrium level after approximately seven time points, far too quickly for the long, slow, gradual sort of change expected from pure secular realignment. Issue evolution on desegregation, in short, seems to follow closely a dynamic growth pattern. The fact that it is dynamic growth is far less interesting than why it is.

Earlier we argued that population replacement should play a major role in the dynamic evolutionary model of partisan change because this mechanism can easily account for the steady, continuous, long-term increase in issue polarization following the critical moment. Partisan conversions, or massive mobilizations, associated with the critical moment may set into motion the initial differentiation between partisans on the evolving issue dimension, but the selective, successive recruitment of new partisan identifiers over time drives the system toward a new equilibrium.

This is precisely what we observe in the racial case (Carmines and Stimson, 1981). Throughout the 1960s and 1970s new Republican and Democratic identifiers were substantially more distinctive in their racial attitudes than continuing identifiers. As these new partisans slowly but inevitably became an increasingly larger proportion of each party's base, the parties were driven steadily apart on the racial dimension. The cumulative result is the development of a significant polarization between partisans on racial desegregation largely due to population replacement.

Why Dynamic Growth?
Issue Evolution in Congress

Dynamic growth of issue polarization must consist of two components: the critical moment to account for departure from equilibrium and a permanent redefinition of the meaning of party alignment to account for continuing evolution. We have found evidence in support of both components in the racial evolution case. The critical moment is associated with events surrounding the 1963-1964 flashpoint in racial politics: the continuing evolution is due to the successive recruitment of new partisan identifiers with distinctive racial attitudes.

But we have not yet seen what accounts for the process itself. For mass issue evolutions do not occur within a political vacuum. They can only be understood as a delayed response, the most visible cumulative result of a more basic and profound issue redefinition of the parties occurring in the institutional structures of American politics.

There are many ways to examine the images of parties over time. Here we will look at only one, the aggregated voting records of the parties in Congress, which we have already discussed in Chapter 3 [of Carmines and Stimson]. The racial voting series are a rich data base; much was happening during this period. They can be examined for many purposes, individual and aggregate, internal and external to Congress. Our purpose here is the development of a summary index of issue evolution in the most visible records of the national parties in Washington. Except for the racially turbulent 1960s, we do not think citizens were paying much attention to congressional voting alignments, but the series do index a wide variety of more subtle displays of party image. They reflect the party images conveyed through the media, members' discussions about the relation of race and party with their constituents, and presidents' comments about Congress.

To examine the institutional series along with the mass series, we compute the interparty difference (Democratic minus Republican) of the series for each house. This information is graphed in Figure 20-6 for the 1945-1980 period, where data are available for both Congress and mass public. If citizens had paid attention to Congress, Figure 20-6 suggests they would have witnessed an issue evolution far more striking than what we have observed in the mass series. Both houses of Congress display an unmistakable issue evolution on race. Republicans were unquestionably the more racially liberal party through the 1950s, a pattern probably little changed since Reconstruction, and unquestionably the more conservative party after the transition of the 1960s. That the congressional issue evolution occurs earlier than the mass response is less obvious but likewise important for causal analysis; the two congressional series lead the mass series.[7]

The result in Figure 20-6 easily confirms the image redefinition thesis. And it begins to suggest an answer to a troublesome anomaly—that evolution along racial lines is more striking in the 1970s after racial issues fell from the top of the

Figure 20-6 Growing Party Differentiation on Desegregation: Congress and the Mass Electorate

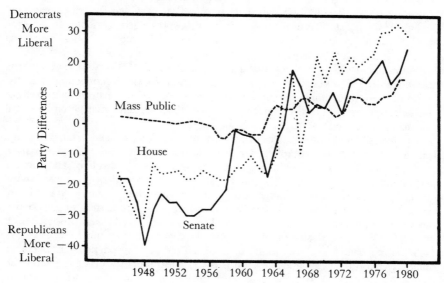

Source: Senate and House series compiled by the authors from analyses of annual roll-call votes of the U.S. Congress, 1945-1980. Mass electorate series compiled by the authors from SRC/CPS National Election Study Series, 1956-1980, and from Louis Harris and Associates, Study #1285.

public agenda than it had been during the peak salience period. If the congressional series are good indicators of party image—and we think they are— the answer is simple: the forgiving force of continuing mass evolution is continuing elite evolution.

And why should party elites, here congressmen and senators, continue to polarize after peak salience? The answer is both predictable and general for all issue evolutions. Most change among a party's visible officials occurs by replace- ment. Where officeholders can rely upon incumbency to retain office, (1) there will be inertial resistance to any new issue cleavage, and (2) the polarization process is likely to continue so long as a sizable proportion of "old" members retain office. For the American Congress, that time span is measured in decades.

Conclusion: Partisan Change Without Critical Elections

Change is a stubborn fact of political life; it is especially pervasive in the electoral arena. Candidates change, issues change, and, on occasion, even the parties change. Not surprisingly there is a rich and varied literature on change in mass party systems. Although this literature abounds in rich historical detail and provides intriguing particularistic accounts, its theory is problematic at its core. It fails to provide a general account of political change.

The standard view of partisan change is that provided by critical election realignment theory. According to this theory, prolonged periods of partisan stability are interrupted by periodic realignments precipitated by critical elections. Thus, a stable party system undergoes a convulsive shock that leads to a sudden and permanent alteration in existing partisan alignment. A new majority party usually emerges in response to the changed political environment and rapidly becomes stabilized along the new issue dimension. The party system is thus characterized by a cyclical pattern of long periods of stability interposed by short but dramatic periods of change.

The problem with this prevailing account is not that it is necessarily wrong, but that it is clearly incomplete. Critical election realignment theory treats all partisan change as a single phenomenon that occurs through an abrupt, permanent transformation of the party system. As a consequence, it must ignore other types of partisan change—most important, change more gradual in character. Moreover, gradual transformations in the party system are probably more typical, occur more frequently, and account for the largest proportion of political change. Critical election realignment theory is thus not only a partial theory of partisan transformation, but it is also partial in a particularly perverse sense: it concentrates on the most unusual and infrequently occurring mode of change. A focus on the unusual and infrequent is unlikely to provide a satisfactory basis for a general theory of partisan change.

In this chapter we have examined a variety of models of partisan change and found the dynamic evolutionary model consistent with both the decay of the New Deal alignment and the growth in issue polarization on race. The model posits that the mass issue evolution begins with a "critical moment"—more visible than the creepingly slow change implied by pure secular realignment but much less pronounced than that presumed by critical election realignments. Equally significant, the initial increase in mass issue polarization does not complete the process but only begins it by setting in motion a change that grows over time.

Dynamic evolutions thus represent the political equivalent of biology's punctuated equilibrium. The critical moment corresponds to the punctuation point—a change of some magnitude but not a cataclysmic adaptation. The slower, continuous change following the critical moment is the drive toward a new equilibrium—the semipermanent redefinition of the link between issues and mass parties.

Dynamic issue evolutions can accommodate a variety of causal mechanisms. Unlike critical election models that imply either massive conversions or equally massive mobilization, normal population replacement plays a central role in issue evolutions. Conversion and mobilization account for the initial partisan differentiation on the issue, but population replacement accounts for its steady and continued growth.

This chapter, then, has provided a revised theoretical framework for understanding partisan change, one that looks to the dynamic evolution of new issues as the stimulus of change and to the continuous replacement of the electorate as its primary mechanism.

NOTES

1. There are conditions under which one would want to model decreasing polarization as well. The decay of old alignments should produce decaying polarization, as we will show later.
2. The equilibrium we presume is a short-term interelection phenomenon. Riker (1982) argues persuasively that disequilibrium in the long run is to be expected from party systems.
3. The process is bounded by an asymptotic equilibrium. The new equilibrium occurs when the electorate becomes sufficiently polarized around an issue that replacement can no longer add to the process.
4. The question is the familiar seven-point forced choice between "The Government should see to it that every person has a job and a good standard of living" and "Each person should get ahead on his own."
5. We are in a much stronger position for the desegregation analysis because the events of interest are contemporary. We can measure alignment from a number of independent cross-sections before and after the beginning of the issue evolution.
6. Party identifier attitudes for 1963 are estimated from a Harris survey of November 1963.
7. Our conceptual framework here is the Box-Jenkins transfer function model, where one dynamic series is postulated to be the causal result of another, after the removal of time dependence processes in both series. We turn to explicit transfer function modeling in the next chapter [of Carmines and Stimson]. See Box and Jenkins (1976, chaps. 10 and 11).

21. PARTISANSHIP AND GROUP
SUPPORT OVER TIME

Harold W. Stanley and Richard G. Niemi

Studies of changes in party coalitions (Axelrod, 1972, 1982; Petrocik, 1981) have focused either on overlapping groups, such as blacks and the working class, or on exclusive groups such as white, middle-class Protestants. Neither approach is adequate. Use of overlapping groups makes it impossible to tell which characteristics are the crucial determinants of party support. Reliance on exclusive groups largely predetermines the outcome, because the critical groups have to be defined a priori.

By analyzing the partisanship of individual group members with multivariate methods similar to those applied elsewhere in the study of political behavior, we provide improved insights into the marginal difference made by membership in each group and into the makeup of a party's support coalition. Here we examine the Democratic and Republican coalitions since 1952. Our results strengthen conventional wisdom about individual partisan changes by blacks and southern whites, but they differ significantly with respect to the strength and timing of changes by these and other groups. In addition, our findings lend support to Carmines and Stimson's (1982, 1984) conclusion that a realignment centering on race occurred in the mid-1960s.

Party Identification: Measurements of Changes in Group Support

We focus on partisanship over the period from 1952 to 1988, with special emphasis on the extent to which the New Deal coalition supporting the Democratic party has deteriorated. We concentrate on party identification as the more durable indicator of partisanship,[1] estimating a total of seventeen equations—one for each of seventeen presidential or congressional elections from 1952 to 1988.[2]

Our basic model includes the core elements of the New Deal coalition: native southern whites (11-state definition), blacks, Jews, the working class, union

Source: Taken from *American Political Science Review* (1986) 80:969-76 (with William T. Bianco) and *American Politics Quarterly* (1991) 19:189-210.

members (in the household), and Catholics. We also included gender. In order to analyze very recent changes in group support, especially with respect to the Republican party, we added several new groups. The availability of data for these groups dictates three separate models:[3]

Model 1 (1952-1988): New Deal elements, gender, church attendance, income.

Model 2 (1972-1988): New Deal elements, gender, white Protestant fundamentalists, church attendance, income.

Model 3 (1980-1988): New Deal elements, gender, Hispanics, white Protestant fundamentalists, church attendance, income, 1943-1958 birth cohort, 1959-1970 cohort.

Our dependent variables throughout are Democratic identification or Republican identification; leaners are not considered partisans, but with one exception (see footnote 6) the results are very similar if one defines partisans to include those leaning toward the parties. The inclusion of variables tapping religion, income, age, and Hispanic origin merits further comment.

In recent years, evangelicals, the Protestant right, fundamentalists, frequent churchgoers, and others have variously been identified as part of the emerging party coalitions (e.g., Edsall, 1988, pp. 9, 25-27). In Model 1, we use frequency of church attendance, which is available from 1952 on and which appears to have a substantial effect on party preference (Petrocik and Steeper, 1987). We are constrained by a change in the survey question in 1970, so that in order to maintain continuity, frequent churchgoers must be defined as a less exclusive category than we would like (attends church regularly or as often as "once a week"). Because of the coding of Baptists, beginning in 1972 it is possible to select fundamentalist Protestants as a separate category. That variable is added to create Model 2.

Much has been made of the recent attractiveness of the Republican party to the wealthy (Edsall, 1988, pp. 9-11). Income, however, is hardly a new factor, so it is useful to gain the perspective that comes from including it throughout the entire period. The problem of cut-points is solved by dividing respondents into thirds on the income distribution in each year. The top third is less exclusive than one might like, but it is surely better than using a constant dollar figure and defines a group that is large enough to carry real political meaning if it tends toward one party.

In recent years new generations of young people seem to have swung toward the Republicans (Norpoth and Kagay, 1989, though see Petrocik, 1989, p. 15). As birth year is most consistent with generational shifts, we define the young as those born in 1959 and later and baby boomers as those born between 1943 and 1958. The fact that the youngest group only began to enter the electorate in the late 1970s, and then in small numbers, is one reason for defining a third model beginning in 1980.

Hispanics are an important group that emerged in the 1980s and are the other reason for establishing the third model. Hispanics are not a unitary force, with Republicans having appealed especially to Cuban-Americans (e.g., Southwest Voter Research Institute, p. 2). Therefore our Hispanic variable excludes those of Cuban origin, and the expectation is that it will push respondents in a Democratic direction.

We use separate models for Democrats and Republicans. To the extent that the New Deal coalition is breaking up, we want to see whether formerly Democratic voters have gone to the Republican party. In addition, for newer groups, we shall see that the hypothesized connections are not always found, and it is useful to see if such groups lean instead to the other party.

The Results

Overall and Incremental Effects of Group Memberships

Axelrod (1972, 1982) found that between 1952 and 1988 three groups had decreasing loyalty to the Democrats: Catholics, southerners, and individuals in households with union members. The poor, blacks, and those residing in the central cities of the nation's 23 largest metropolitan areas showed increasing Democratic loyalty. Petrocik (1981) reported that all groups except blacks shared a marked tendency toward independence and a diminished partisan preference; blacks became much more strongly Democratic.

Our results confirm the sharpest of these movements—especially of blacks and southern whites—but they differ in other respects. First of all, once other variables are taken into account, being poor and residing in metropolitan areas did not incline individuals toward Democratic identification (i.e., they did not achieve statistical significance) in the 1952-1988 period. The tendency of the poor and of metropolitan residents to support the Democrats can be accounted for by their other characteristics. Two indicators of status—education and income— were also not related to Democratic identification, perhaps because subjective identification with the working class better revealed the connections of status to partisanship.

Given the nonlinearity of logit, the original coefficients (not shown) are difficult to interpret. Transforming them into probability values, however, yields two summary values of special significance—the overall predicted mean probability of being a Democrat or Republican for each group, and the incremental probability difference each group membership makes.[4]

Table 21-1 presents the mean and incremental predicted probability that a group member would claim Democratic identification in each of the nine presidential election years and seven off-years. The mean predicted probability gives the frequency of Democratic identification in each group before imposing any controls for other group memberships. Even these initial figures show the plight of the Democrats. Comparisons of the chronological endpoints, for example, show that only for blacks did the probability of Democratic identification increase. Jews declined the most, with the decline particularly steep in the early 1960s and then again after 1984. White southerners also registered a strong decline, with a 29-point drop between 1964 and 1970, and a 10-point drop between 1980 and 1984. The probability of Democratic identification for Catholics, females, individuals in union member households, and self-identified members of the working class, although peaking in 1960 or 1964, later declined to levels below those of the 1950s. Even among the newer groups, where the time span available for analysis is much shorter, Democrats had less support in 1988 than in the first year of the series.

The incremental impact of a particular group membership makes equally apparent the strongest movements over the years. The black increase, the southern white decrease, and the Jewish decline are all evident and are of about the same magnitude as in the overall results.

Significantly, the patterns are not identical to what has been observed using other approaches. Axelrod (1972), for example, found that in 1952 blacks were far more likely (by 38 percent) than the general population to vote for Democrats. That Democratic edge declined until 1964, when it rebounded to the same level as in 1952. Our results are not a direct contradiction, because they involve slightly different questions (i.e., the marginal impact and partisan identification), but they suggest that being black did not contribute strongly to being Democratic until 1964; before that, it had less marginal impact than, for example, being Catholic. In 1964 and later, however, the effect of being black contributed much more significantly to a Democratic identification than it had at any time in the 1950s.

Similarly, the impact of being Jewish declined between the 1950s and 1960s, but unlike Petrocik's (1981) trend, our results show a rebound, even by 1972, when his series ended. After 1984, the marginal impact declined again, leaving it where it had been in the early 1960s.

Though smaller and therefore less noticeable, a contrast with earlier results is also apparent among Catholics. Axelrod (1972) and Petrocik (1981) found the contribution of Catholics declining by 1972 and 1968, respectively. Our data suggest that, except for the special circumstances of 1960, being Catholic stimulated a Democratic identification to about the same degree until 1980.

The sharpest contrast suggested by our approach occurs for members of union households. Here both Axelrod's earlier results and our overall probabilities suggest a decline in Democratic proclivities. In contrast, the incremental push that comes from this characteristic appears to have changed very little over the last four decades. This difference may be identifiable because we are able to separate the effect of being working class from that of being in a union household. Since many union members consider themselves working class, and since there was a drop in the marginal impact of this variable (except for the partial recovery in 1988), exclusion of the working class measure might erroneously indicate a decline in the effect of being in a union household.

Observe also the contrasting images created by the overall versus incremental probabilities for women. Females were less likely to identify themselves as Democrats in the 1980s than they were in the 1950s; at the same time, being female has given an increasingly larger boost to Democratic identification. Note, however, that this increment is not simply a Reagan phenomenon. Marginal

Table 21-1 Mean and Incremental Probabilities of Democratic Identification for Members of Each Group

Group	Year																
	1952	1956	1958	1960	1964	1966	1968	1970	1972	1974	1976	1978	1980	1982	1984	1986	1988
Mean Probabilities[a]																	
Black	.54	.51	.51	.44	.78	.63	.85	.75	.67	.71	.74	.66	.74	.82	.64	.71	.65
Catholic	.56	.51	.58	.65	.60	.54	.52	.51	.50	.51	.50	.50	.43	.54	.43	.45	.39
Jewish	.76	.63	.71	.52	.56	.67	.51	.56	.52	.52	.60	.55	.83	.62	.60	.36	.37
Female	.47	.43	.51	.49	.55	.47	.47	.45	.43	.43	.42	.42	.45	.49	.40	.42	.41
Native southern white	.77	.71	.76	.72	.73	.60	.54	.44	.52	.52	.52	.45	.52	.54	.42	.43	.41
Union household	.54	.51	.60	.57	.64	.56	.50	.54	.46	.47	.47	.50	.47	.52	.46	.45	.43
Working class	.54	.49	.55	.51	.61	.52	.52	.47	.45	.43	.47	.45	.47	.51	.41	.45	.44
Regular church-goer	.50	.47	.47	.49	.54	.48	.47	.45	.44	.40	.43	.43	.40	.47	.37	.43	.39
Income: top third	.43	.40	.46	.44	.43	.42	.39	.39	.34	.31	.31	.33	.35	.36	.32	.33	.29
Wh. Prot. fundamentalist	—	—	—	—	—	—	—	—	.45	.44	.42	.42	.54	.48	.41	.39	.36
Hispanic, non-Cuban	—	—	—	—	—	—	—	—	—	—	—	—	.54	.60	.49	.58	.48
Born 1959-1970	—	—	—	—	—	—	—	—	—	—	—	—	.32	.35	.31	.35	.27
Born 1943-1958	—	—	—	—	—	—	—	—	—	—	—	—	.39	.43	.34	.35	.35

Incremental Probabilities[b]

Black	.16	.17	.13	.08	.32	.23	.49	.38	.36	.41	.43	.35	.46	.46	.35	.42	.37
Catholic	.20	.19	.22	.31	.18	.16	.18	.15	.20	.21	.21	.20	.14	.20	.14	.15	.10
Jewish	.44	.34	.34	.19	.19	.37	.22	.25	.28	.25	.38	.32	.58	.35	.35	.08	.19
Female	−.01	−.04	.04	.04	.02	.03	.03	.03	.05	.04	.03	.04	.09	.06	.06	.05	.10
Native southern white	.44	.42	.41	.41	.33	.26	.20	.10	.19	.22	.22	.13	.18	.19	.10	.12	.13
Union household	.11	.11	.13	.13	.15	.15	.06	.14	.07	.09	.10	.15	.10	.11	.12	.09	.11
Working class	.12	.08	.08	.08	.08	.09	.08	.03	.05	−.02	.07	.06	.06	.04	.03	.04	.10
Regular church-goer	.00	.00	−.09	−.03	−.01	.02	.00	.03	.03	−.03	.03	.02	−.04	.01	−.04	−.01	.03
Income: top third	−.04	−.01	−.02	−.04	−.12	−.03	−.04	−.05	−.06	−.12	−.09	−.10	−.05	−.11	−.06	−.06	−.05
Wh. Prot. fundamentalist	—	—	—	—	—	—	—	—	.08	.04	.04	.08	.21	.07	.09	.05	.03
Hispanic, non-Cuban	—	—	—	—	—	—	—	—	—	—	—	—	.16	.10	.06	.13	.08
Born 1959-1970	—	—	—	—	—	—	—	—	—	—	—	—	−.17	−.17	−.16	−.16	−.19
Born 1943-1958	—	—	—	—	—	—	—	—	—	—	—	—	−.09	−.06	−.10	−.10	−.10

Notes: All three models described in the text were evaluated. However, presentation is greatly simplified by showing only the following: 1952-1970 values are based on Model 1; 1972-1978 values are based on Model 2; 1980-1988 entries are based on Model 3. Values that can be estimated with more than one model seldom differ by more than .01 from one model to another.

[a] Cells are the mean of the predicted probabilities of Democratic identification for all group members in each year.

[b] Cells are the average of the difference, for each group member, between the individual's predicted probability of Democratic identification and what the individual's probability would have been without the effect of the group membership.

female support for the Democrats goes all the way back to 1960 and has been slowly but steadily increasing since then.

As we turn to newer groups and draw on other models, we note first that none of the above conclusions changes with the inclusion of new variables (see note to Table 21-1). In addition, since several of the new groups are said to be attracted to the Republican party, we shall draw on Table 21-1 and on a parallel table for the Republicans (Table 21-2). (Note that the probabilities in Tables 21-1 and 21-2 do not sum to 1.0 because they exclude independents and apoliticals.)

The relationship between religion and partisanship was allegedly reinvigorated during the Reagan years as the president supported traditional moral values consistent with fundamentalist Christianity. However, both measures of religiosity yield some surprises. Church attendance has a relatively minor effect on partisanship throughout the entire period, with what appears to be a Reagan effect in 1980 and 1984. Incremental probabilities for the Democrats (Table 21-1), are mostly insignificant. For the Republicans (Table 21-2) incremental probabilities are small, straddling statistical significance except for 1958 and for a small but meaningful bulge in the two Reagan election years. The fact that the probabilities return to their usual levels in both congressional years in the 1980s and in 1988 suggests that the religious phenomenon was personal and was not transferred to the party. The overall probabilities tell a slightly different story. Between the 1950s and 1980s there was a small but steady decline in Democratic support among regular churchgoers; combined with steady support for the Republicans among this group, the ratio of Democratic to Republican mean probabilities changed noticeably.[5]

When our measure is affiliation with a fundamentalist religion, the results are contrary to popular rhetoric but in line with most scholarly research. Rothenberg and Newport (1984, chap. 6) found that self-described fundamentalists are little, if any more Republican than other respondents. Baptists are more Democratic than any other denomination, with "conservative" denominations relatively Democratic as well. Similarly, Smidt (1983, p. 36) found that white southern evangelicals are more Democratic than nonevangelicals.

Our multivariate results indicate that in every election since 1972, membership in a Protestant fundamentalist denomination has pushed whites away from a Republican identification and uniformly inclined them toward the Democrats (incremental probabilities, Tables 21-2 and 21-2). These forces were especially strong during the first Reagan term. Note, however, that the overall probabilities in recent years show a strikingly different pattern. Since 1980, the likelihood of fundamentalists identifying with the Republican party has increased steadily, while the corresponding figure for the Democrats dropped steadily and even more sharply. Thus, there is an increased relationship between fundamentalism and Republican identification, but in the sense of the partisan push that comes from specific group attachments, religious fundamentalism is not a powerful partisan force.

A key to the divergent mean and incremental probabilities lies, in part, in changes among native southern whites. One of the major groups of white fundamentalists is Southern Baptists. As native southern whites moved away from the Democrats, this coincidentally moved many Southern Baptists from the Democratic to the Republican fold. But that change appears not to have had religious motivation. In fact, as Table 21-1 shows, fundamentalism itself still carries with it a small incremental nudge in favor of the Democrats.

A second group thought to be part of a Republican rejuvenation is the well to-do (Petrocik and Steeper, 1987). Here our results are less at variance with conventional wisdom, though still there are differences. Table 21-2 shows a clear increase in incremental probabilities of Republican identification in the early 1970s and the early 1980s. There is less consistency in Table 21-1, but the numbers there also indicate a major change beginning in the 1970s. Note, however, that the push toward Republican identification did not sustain itself past 1984. Incremental probabilities for 1986 and 1988 retreated to a level not seen since 1970. The change appears to be only a bit more stable if one examines the overall probabilities.

Another group thought to be part of the Republican upsurge is young voters, especially those born after 1958 (Norpoth and Kagay, 1989). Our results suggest that the incremental push from being in the youngest cohort is better described as a strong anti-Democratic force. Indeed, none of the coefficients underlying the incremental probabilities of being a Republican are statistically significant, though most are in the "right" direction. Those relating to Democratic identification are consistently significant and strongly negative.[6] The baby boomers are also anti-Democratic, though to a lesser degree, and are neutral with respect to the Republicans. Both of these groups have consistently high positive increments in favor of independents (not shown), most likely a reflection of the dealigning period in which they became adults.

The final group to gain significance in the 1980s is Hispanics (here excluding those of Cuban origin). Group attachments clearly incline them toward the Democratic party and away from the Republican party. There are too few cases and years to make finer distinctions about country of origin or changes over time.

Before moving on, it is useful to take a global look at the overall and incremental probabilities. The first observation is that for all of the New Deal groups, the Democrats maintain a rather wide advantage, even in those instances in which there have been dramatic changes over the past four decades. Among native southern whites in 1988, for example, twice as many identify with the Democrats as with the Republicans.

Differences of comparable magnitude are found in only one of the newer groups. While frequent churchgoers and those in fundamentalist congregations have at times identified with the Democrats by two to one margins, the current margin is about four to three for both groups. The well-to-do have never split very unevenly. The youngest cohort has not leaned heavily toward either party even though it is potentially significant that the margin has shifted (barely) to the Republicans as of 1988. Baby boomers are more Democratic, but the margin has declined in the last few years. Only among Hispanics is the margin similar to those for the old-line groups.

Of course the size of the group differences is partly a reflection of the

Table 21-2 Mean and Incremental Probabilities of Republican Identification for Members of Each Group

Group	Year																
	1952	1956	1958	1960	1964	1966	1968	1970	1972	1974	1976	1978	1980	1982	1984	1986	1988
Mean Probabilities[a]																	
Black	.14	.19	.15	.17	.06	.09	.03	.05	.08	.03	.06	.06	.04	.02	.03	.05	.06
Catholic	.18	.20	.17	.14	.16	.17	.15	.17	.14	.15	.16	.14	.18	.17	.20	.22	.26
Jewish	.00	.12	.12	.08	.06	.05	.05	.05	.09	.12	.09	.05	.00	.19	.10	.21	.12
Female	.29	.31	.28	.31	.24	.25	.23	.26	.24	.23	.27	.23	.23	.23	.28	.26	.28
Native southern white	.09	.12	.11	.12	.09	.11	.09	.17	.16	.12	.15	.16	.15	.18	.22	.22	.22
Union household	.22	.21	.17	.17	.14	.18	.19	.15	.16	.13	.14	.14	.14	.18	.20	.21	.20
Working class	.21	.23	.23	.24	.16	.20	.20	.20	.21	.19	.19	.16	.18	.17	.22	.20	.19
Regular church-goer	.28	.29	.31	.30	.26	.25	.24	.26	.26	.25	.28	.23	.28	.26	.32	.28	.32
Income: top third	.31	.34	.33	.30	.31	.26	.27	.29	.30	.28	.30	.25	.30	.33	.36	.30	.33
Wh. Prot. fundamentalist	—	—	—	—	—	—	—	—	.20	.16	.21	.18	.17	.20	.22	.26	.27
Hispanic, non-Cuban	—	—	—	—	—	—	—	—	—	—	—	—	.14	.05	.09	.14	.13
Born 1959-1970	—	—	—	—	—	—	—	—	—	—	—	—	.14	.28	.25	.27	.29
Born 1943-1958	—	—	—	—	—	—	—	—	—	—	—	—	.20	.20	.28	.25	.26

Incremental Probabilities[b]

Black	−.24	−.18	−.24	−.23	−.24	−.22	−.32	−.28	−.24	−.28	−.25	−.22	−.26	−.28	−.35	−.29	−.28
Catholic	−.23	−.19	−.25	−.27	−.20	−.18	−.22	−.17	−.19	−.17	−.17	−.18	−.13	−.16	−.17	−.12	−.09
Jewish	−.43	−.32	−.27	−.34	−.35	−.35	−.34	−.34	−.28	−.21	−.29	−.30	−.35	−.23	−.35	−.15	−.33
Female	.03	.06	−.01	.02	.00	−.01	−.02	.01	.01	.00	.05	.02	−.02	−.03	.00	−.01	−.02
Native southern white	−.34	−.30	−.33	−.35	−.28	−.27	−.29	−.19	−.15	−.18	−.16	−.12	−.14	−.13	−.08	−.10	−.14
Union household	−.06	−.10	−.13	−.14	−.11	−.09	−.07	−.13	−.11	−.12	−.13	−.10	−.13	−.09	−.10	−.07	−.11
Working class	−.13	−.09	−.04	−.11	−.11	−.09	−.04	−.07	−.01	−.01	−.03	−.07	−.04	−.07	−.06	−.07	−.12
Regular church-goer	.05	.04	.10	.06	.04	.03	.03	.01	.05	.06	.06	.05	.08	.03	.08	.04	.05
Income: top third	.01	.04	.03	−.02	.05	−.03	.02	.03	.08	.05	.07	.04	.07	.09	.08	.03	.03
Wh. Prot. fundamentalist	—	—	—	—	—	—	—	—	−.06	−.07	−.05	−.07	−.09	−.07	−.13	−.04	−.03
Hispanic, non-Cuban	—	—	—	—	—	—	—	—	—	—	—	—	−.03	−.13	−.11	−.09	−.11
Born 1959-1970	—	—	—	—	—	—	—	—	—	—	—	—	−.06	.04	.02	.04	.04
Born 1943-1958	—	—	—	—	—	—	—	—	—	—	—	—	−.02	−.05	.03	−.01	−.01

[a] Cells are the mean of the predicted probabilities of Republican identification for all group members in each year.
[b] Cells are the average of the difference, for each group member, between the individual's predicted probability of Republican identification and what the individual's probability would have been without the effect of the group membership.

overall numbers of Democrats and Republicans. Because the Democrats are the larger party, it is perhaps not surprising that they hold larger margins in "their" groups than the Republicans hold in theirs. Still, not one of the groups comprising the new elements of the Republican coalition tilts heavily in its direction.

It is worth dwelling on this point for a moment in relation to the concept of partisan realignment. If, as some have suggested, the changes over the past two decades or so constitute a realignment (in the sense of changes in the underlying support coalitions), one can draw at least two inferences. First, the realignment appears to be on shaky grounds because the party that is growing in size lacks a really strong base in any group, old or new. Given the lingering pro-Democratic sentiments in New Deal groups and the absence of similar new Republican support, the Republicans' best hope appears to lie in continuing support from new adults. A generational change is by its nature relatively slow and undramatic; when favorable groups are only marginally so, it will be even slower. The consequence for the Republicans is that, absent a dramatic event or personality, it will take a long time to become a majority party. A consequence for those analyzing group support is that they will find small, sometimes conflicting change until eventually clear trends emerge.

Somewhat contrariwise, one might also conclude that a realignment requires less in the way of "reshuffling" than has been commonly suggested. A significant realignment may occur when there is a major change in only one or two groups (e.g., as occurred among blacks in the 1960s), accompanied by a variety of other changes (Aldrich and Niemi, 1989). In any case, both inferences suggest why the concept of group realignment is so difficult to work with.

It is also noteworthy that the extra push from membership in new groups is generally weaker than that from traditional ones. Note, for example, the 1988 column of incremental probabilities in Tables 21-1 and 21-2. Despite the declining force of the New Deal groups, only age—and then only negatively for the Democrats—has an incremental probability as high as those for any of the older groups. Apart from age, what may be happening is not so much a change in the group basis of support for the two parties as a breakdown of group differences altogether. Weakening ties between group attachments and party loyalties, not simply changes in which groups are allied with which party, may be a partial explanation for the widely observed decline of political parties.

Changing Demographics or Changing Support Levels

In addition to our ability to distinguish overall and marginal effects another way of using our multivariate approach is to ask whether changes in the mix of demographic characteristics have had a significant effect on the probability of claiming Democratic identification. It is possible, for example, that the decline in the number of females identifying with the working class (60 percent in 1952; 50 percent in 1984) and other such changes can largely account for the observed changes. We can apply the coefficients from a later election year to an earlier distribution of individual group memberships and contrast these hypothetical results with the actual ones for the later year. Such a comparison conveys the degree of partisan change arising from shifts in the coefficients (that is, the partisan meaning of group memberships). By similarly varying the distribution of group memberships, one can gauge the degree of partisan change arising from shifting mixes of individual group memberships.

The two sets of coefficients for the endpoints 1952 and 1988 capture the partisan meanings of group memberships for those two years. If we first apply the 1952 coefficients to 1952 or 1988 data, the overall probabilities of Democratic identification are not appreciably different. The changing composition of groups made for very little partisan change. However, major differences in probabilities result from applying the 1988 coefficients to the data from 1952. The shifts in the meaning of group memberships far outweigh the partisan implications of demographic changes. Changes in the partisan meaning of group memberships, not declines in reinforcing group memberships, account for the decreasing probabilities of identifying with the Democrats.

Group Support and the Party Coalitions

Axelrod's (1972) analysis reveals the extent to which the Democratic coalition is made up of blacks, metropolitan residents, and so on. If one wishes simply to know a group's share of the a party's coalition, Axelrod's approach has much to recommend it. However, studying groups within party coalitions does not require us to treat the groups as if they were monolithic. Since most individuals have multiple group characteristics, removing a single characteristic from the mix need not mean that all members of that group desert the party. Axelrod's figures cannot reveal, for example, how many southern whites would remain Democratic if being a southern white gave no nudge toward Democratic identification. Nor can they show what the size of the Democratic coalition would be if that Democratic propensity was lost. Our approach yields both of these results. Such results are hypothetical, of course, but they are what the party strategist would most like to know. If the party stopped appealing to southern whites as such, how many southern whites would remain Democratic, and how much of a loss would the party sustain?

Answers to these questions, along with comparison figures of the type that Axelrod generated, are given in Tables 21-3 (Democrats) and 21-4 (Republicans). In the first two sections of the tables we show the proportion of Democratic and Republican identifiers in the U.S. and, below that, the percentage of the partisan coalition with a given group characteristic. This breakdown of the coalition is in terms of overlapping groups, making these percentages analogous to those presented for the Democratic vote by Axelrod. Not surprisingly (because of their size in the population), working class identifiers and females consistently make up the largest shares of Democratic identifiers, although the proportion of working class identifiers has dropped significantly from what it was in the 1950s. Jews now constitute only one percent of the Democratic coalition, and blacks, thanks to recent increases, now constitute a fifth of the coalition. Of the newer groups, the only striking result is the ragged upward trend in the proportion of the coalition that is Hispanic.[7] With the long-term decline of most New Deal elements and relatively quick, further increases in minority supporters, the

Table 21-3 Size and Composition of the Democratic Coalition, 1952-1988

Group								Year									
	1952	1956	1958	1960	1964	1966	1968	1970	1972	1974	1976	1978	1980	1982	1984	1986	1988
Predicted Probability of Democratic Identification in the U.S.[a]																	
	48	44	50	47	54	46	45	44	41	41	40	40	41	46	38	40	36
Percentage of Democratic Coalition with a Given Group Characteristic[b]																	
Black	10	9	9	7	13	13	16	14	14	14	15	12	14	16	15	21	20
Catholic	25	23	24	24	24	25	24	21	28	25	27	26	21	23	26	23	22
Jewish	4	4	4	3	2	4	3	3	3	3	3	3	5	2	3	1	1
Female	50	50	51	50	52	53	54	51	53	53	50	46	47	48	49	49	53
Native southern white	23	26	25	25	19	18	18	16	19	20	16	13	16	18	16	17	18
Union household	30	29	28	30	27	32	25	25	26	26	23	25	22	20	22	20	20
Working class	65	64	62	64	60	60	55	49	54	50	50	45	43	47	45	46	51
Regular church-goer	38	43	39	42	41	40	37	36	37	33	34	33	29	35	31	36	34
Income: top third	35	26	30	33	27	33	25	30	24	18	23	23	19	23	22	21	27
Wh. Prot. fundamentalist	—	—	—	—	—	—	—	—	15	16	12	12	15	14	13	13	15
Hispanic, non-Cuban	—	—	—	—	—	—	—	—	—	—	—	—	3	2	6	5	8
Born 1959-1970	—	—	—	—	—	—	—	—	—	—	—	—	3	5	10	13	13
Born 1943-1958	—	—	—	—	—	—	—	—	—	—	—	26	28	28	28	28	29
Percentage of Democratic Identifiers in Group Continuing to Claim Democratic Identification After Removing Democratic Tendency of Defining Group Characteristic[c]																	
Black	71	66	75	82	59	64	43	49	46	42	42	48	38	43	44	42	43
Catholic	64	64	63	53	70	70	66	72	61	58	58	59	67	63	68	67	73
Jewish	41	45	53	63	65	44	57	56	45	52	36	41	30	44	41	78	49
Female	103	111	93	91	96	94	93	93	89	91	92	91	79	88	86	88	76
Native southern white	42	41	45	43	55	56	62	77	64	57	58	71	66	65	77	73	67

Union Household	80	79	79	76	77	74	88	74	84	80	78	71	78	78	73	79	74
Working class	79	83	85	87	85	82	85	94	88	105	86	87	87	92	93	92	78
Regular church-goer	100	101	120	102	106	96	101	93	92	107	94	95	110	97	110	98	93
Income: top third	110	104	104	128	110	107	111	113	118	139	128	129	114	130	119	119	117
Wh. Prot. fundamentalist	—	—	—	—	—	—	—	—	83	90	92	80	61	84	78	87	91
Hispanic, non-Cuban	—	—	—	—	—	—	—	—	—	—	—	—	71	83	87	77	83
Born 1959-1970	—	—	—	—	—	—	—	—	—	—	—	—	153	148	152	145	170
Born 1943-1958	—	—	—	—	—	—	—	—	—	—	—	—	122	114	130	134	127

Relative Size (%) of Democratic Coalition After Removing Group Characteristic

Black	97	97	98	99	95	95	91	93	92	92	91	94	91	91	92	88	89
Catholic	91	91	91	88	93	93	92	94	89	90	89	90	93	92	92	92	94
Jewish	97	98	98	99	97	97	99	98	99	99	98	98	96	99	98	100	99
Female	102	105	96	98	97	96	96	96	94	95	96	96	90	94	93	94	88
Native southern white	87	85	87	86	91	92	93	96	93	91	93	96	94	94	96	96	94
Union household	94	94	94	93	94	92	97	94	96	95	95	93	95	96	94	96	95
Working class	86	89	91	90	92	89	92	97	94	103	93	94	94	96	97	96	88
Regular church-goer	100	100	108	102	101	98	100	97	97	102	98	98	103	99	103	99	98
Income: top third	104	101	101	103	107	102	103	104	104	107	107	107	103	107	104	104	105
Wh. Prot. fundamentalist	—	—	—	—	—	—	—	—	97	98	99	98	94	98	97	98	99
Hispanic, non-Cuban	—	—	—	—	—	—	—	—	—	—	—	—	99	100	99	99	99
Born 1959-1970	—	—	—	—	—	—	—	—	—	—	—	—	102	103	105	106	109
Born 1943-1958	—	—	—	—	—	—	—	—	—	—	—	—	106	104	108	108	109

[a] These estimates, derived from the model, are virtually identical to the actual percentage of Democratic identifiers.

[b] Figures derived from taking the mean predicted probability of Democratic identification for a group in a particular year (Table 21-1) multiplied by that group's number of respondents, and dividing this product by the number of Democratic identifiers.

[c] Figures derived by recalculating the probabilities of Democratic identification without the effect of, say, working-class identification, and then taking the mean of these probabilities for all respondents who claimed working-class status. The ratio of this revised mean probability to the mean probability that includes the effect of working class status gives the ratio of the hypothetical size to the actual one.

Table 21-4 Size and Composition of the Republican Coalition, 1952-1988

Group	Year																
	1952	1956	1958	1960	1964	1966	1968	1970	1972	1974	1976	1978	1980	1982	1984	1986	1988
Predicted Probability of Republican Identification in the U.S.[a]																	
	28	29	28	29	24	25	24	25	24	22	24	21	23	25	28	26	29
Percentage of Republican Coalition with a Given Group Characteristic[b]																	
Black	4	5	5	4	2	3	1	2	3	1	2	2	1	1	1	2	2
Catholic	14	14	12	8	14	14	13	12	14	13	16	13	16	14	17	18	19
Jewish	0	1	1	1	1	1	1	1	1	1	1	1	0	1	1	1	1
Female	53	55	48	50	48	53	49	51	52	48	56	47	44	42	46	48	46
Native southern white	5	7	6	6	5	6	6	11	10	8	8	9	8	11	11	14	12
Union household	21	18	14	14	13	19	18	12	16	13	12	14	12	12	13	15	12
Working class	43	46	47	46	33	42	40	37	43	39	35	31	30	29	33	32	29
Regular churchgoer	37	39	45	40	41	38	36	36	39	36	39	34	38	36	36	37	36
Income: top third	44	33	37	36	40	37	33	40	37	29	39	33	31	39	33	31	39
Wh. Prot. fundamentalist	—	—	—	—	—	—	—	—	12	10	10	10	8	11	10	14	15
Hispanic, non-Cuban	—	—	—	—	—	—	—	—	—	—	—	—	1	0	1	2	3
Born 1959-1970	—	—	—	—	—	—	—	—	—	—	—	—	3	8	11	16	17
Born 1943-1958	—	—	—	—	—	—	—	—	—	—	—	—	24	25	31	31	28

[a] These estimates, derived from the model, are virtually identical to the actual percentage of Republican identifiers.

[b] Figures derived from taking the mean predicted probability of Republican identification for a group in a particular year (Table 21-2) multiplied by that group's number of respondents, and dividing this product by the number of Republican identifiers.

Democrats may increasingly be viewed as the party of racial/ethnic minorities and liberal whites (cf. Schneider, 1988, p. 67-68).

As the Democratic coalition lost some of its New Deal elements, one might expect a transfer into the Republican party, either in the form of a direct transfer or by Democrats becoming independents while independents become Republican. Such is the case for no group. Native southern whites come the closest. As the proportion of the Democratic coalition made of up this group dropped by about seven percentage points between 1960 and 1988, the proportion in the Republican party increased by about the same margin (Tables 21-3 and 21-4), though the larger Democratic coalition means these similar percentages do not constitute similarly-sized groups. In contrast, Catholics now make up a slightly larger proportion of the Republican coalition without having decreased their share of the Democratic coalition. Most striking are the declines in working class and union household support in both coalitions. The explanation for these simultaneous declines is quite simple—fewer respondents now classify themselves as working class and union membership has declined. Nevertheless, it suggests that the parties may be able to reduce their appeal to these groups without fearing the same magnitude of negative response that would have occurred in years past.

The Republican coalition has not increased its proportions of new group members except for the young and possibly those in fundamentalist congregations, where there appears to be an increase of four to five percentage points in the last two elections. Non-Cuban Hispanics are no more a part of the Republican coalition than are blacks. Young people constitute a slightly larger proportion of the Republicans than of the Democrats.

The results in the third section of Table 21-3 show what would have happened to each group if the Democratic increment due to the group characteristic were removed.[8] Of the New Deal groups, the working class would have been the least affected. Despite the appeal of Reagan and Bush to the workers, other characteristics of working class individuals are sufficiently pro-Democratic, that even in 1988, 78 percent of this group who identified with the party would have continued to do so if there were no special push due to their class identification. In contrast, less than half of the blacks and Jews would have continued to identify with the party if it lost its special appeal to them as blacks and Jews. Of more interest are the percentages who would remain in the coalition among frequent church goers and among those in fundamentalist congregations. The high percentages, often above 90 percent, reemphasize the small incremental push that comes from membership in these categories. Other groups are much more important for the Democrats to worry about. The 145 + percentages for the youngest cohort indicate that Democrats have a lot to gain even from a neutral, rather than negative, appeal to the young.

What effect would such changes have had on the party coalition? The last section of Table 21-3 shows that the Democrats used to depend more variably and more heavily on limited group appeals. The loss of a given group increment would have reduced the coalition by as little as 2-3 percent or by as much as 14 percent. Recently, however, the overlap among group memberships and the Democratic tendency of each membership has been such that the loss of appeal to any of the characteristics would result in a more uniform 5-12 percent loss in identifiers. This change is significant, but it leaves the Democrats no less vulnerable. The party is no longer so dependent upon a few groups, as it was in the 1950s, but is now almost equally dependent upon six.

Perhaps a bit surprisingly, loss of appeal to Hispanics as such would seem to have very little effect on the coalition. In part this reflects the modest size of the Hispanic group, but it also results from multiple characteristics that push Hispanics toward the Democrats. The number for the post-1958 cohort is as much above 100 as many of the other numbers are below 100. The Democrats could increase their size substantially with direct appeals to the young if those appeals did not somehow undercut the attention they currently pay to their strongest support groups.

Conclusion

At the individual level of analysis, research in the last 10 years has altered the way we view partisanship. We no longer think of party identification as immutable or as unchanging except for sudden upheavals (e.g., Franklin and Jackson, 1983). Change is typically slow and limited to small movements along the partisanship scale, but movement there is. Yet we are only now incorporating this view of individual-level partisanship into models of aggregate change (MacKuen, Erikson, and Stimson, 1989). If individuals change their partisanship in response to on-going political events, we need to ask how these changes alter the group composition of the party coalitions. One inference is that if individual changes are slow, small, and partially self-canceling, changes in group support for the parties will more often be glacial than explosive despite the endogeneity of partisanship.

It is this deliberate, halting manner of aggregate change that most strikes us here. Over the past four decades, changes in the composition of each party's coalition have more often conformed to a pattern of secular realignment than to that of a single, critical election.[9] An explanation for this slowness of group realignment can be tied directly back to the individual-level change. Much of the movement has been limited to partisan-independent or independent-partisan shifts rather than moves from one party to the other. Even the movement of blacks toward the Democrats between 1960 and 1968 lowered the incremental probability of being a Republican (or, actually, raised the negative probability) much less than it increased the probability of being a Democrat (from −.23 to −.32 for Republicans and from .08 to .49 for Democrats). The same was true of the propensities away from the Democrats among native southern whites (−.35 to −.29 for Republicans and .41 to .20 for Democrats). Whether a group realignment has occurred has been so heavily debated in part because the deliberateness of the change has made it very difficult to detect.

If a realignment has indeed taken place, the important questions shift to what the new Republican coalition looks like, whether a Republican majority will result, and why it has taken so long for the Republican coalition to solidify. A partial answer to these questions is found in the fact that the Republicans have not yet found strong support among the traditionally Democratic groups. While the New Deal coalition has weakened, we already noted how little increased support there was for the Republicans (as opposed to decreased support for Democrats). Another part of the answer is that among the "newer" groups, it was only among the post-1958 cohort, the well-to-do, and frequent churchgoers that the incremental probabilities in the 1980s were in a Republican direction; even then, the probabilities for the young cohort were very small and those for the rich and religious were largely unchanged from the 1970s. Such loosening of group ties to the parties may reflect as well as partially effect the candidate-centered politics of recent years.

NOTES

1. On presidential voting, see Erikson, Lancaster, and Romero (1989).
2. Some group memberships were not available for surveys in 1954 and 1962.
3. For precise specification of the variables, see the appendix in Stanley and Niemi (1991).
4. For the first value, we began by calculating a predicted probability for each individual. This required applying the parameter estimates for each variable to data values for each individual. The predicted probability for a group in a given year is then the average of the predicted probabilities for all group members in that year. Similarly, the incremental difference is the average of the difference, for each group member, between the individual's predicted probability and what the individual's probability would have been without the effect of the group membership.
5. Rothenberg and Newport (1984, p. 84) also found little relationship between church attendance and party registration or "usual" vote. Petrocik and Steeper (1987, p. 43) found conflicting results, possibly because they did not control for a variety of confounding factors.
6. Defining partisans to include those leaning toward the party, the coefficients for the Republicans are significant, but the incremental probabilities are still smaller than those for the Democrats in 1982-1988.
7. The increase in the proportion from post-1958 cohorts is explained simply by their increasing numbers as time passes.
8. We show these results for Democrats only. Since most groups we have analyzed tilt strongly away from the Republicans, complete removal of these negative tendencies is highly unlikely.
9. Certain shifts—especially those by blacks and native southern whites in the 1964-1968 period—were quite rapid and are consistent with Carmines and Stimson's (1982, 1984) thesis of a racial realignment of the parties at that time.

22. VIEWS OF THE PARTIES:
NEGATIVITY OR NEUTRALITY?

Martin P. Wattenberg

What has been found thus far [in Wattenberg] about the decline of partisanship in the electorate suggests that political parties are substantially less important to the general public than they were two or three decades ago. Yet much of the literature on party decline in the electorate has postulated disenchantment with the parties as the major causal factor for the decline of partisanship. In *The Changing American Voter,* for example, Norman Nie, Sidney Verba, and John Petrocik (1976, pp. 57-58), argue that voters have come to view the parties in increasingly negative terms.

The two explanations are not, of course, mutually exclusive. One reason the parties are less salient to people could be that they dislike both parties and therefore don't concern themselves much with either. However, it will be argued in this chapter that the increase in dissatisfaction with the parties has been minimal. The major change that has taken place in the public's evaluations of the parties has been that people feel neutral rather than negative. This is not to say that there has not been a decline of partisanship in the electorate, but instead that the nature of the decline has been different from what many have assumed. The distinction is a crucial one for any understanding of the future of American political parties. If voters are actually discontented with political parties, then the parties' chances for recovery in the near future are doubtful; but if people feel only neutral toward them, then the door remains open for party renewal.

Indeed, a good deal of speculation on the future of the political party system rests on the assumption that voters have rejected parties. For example, Kristi Andersen (1976, p. 95) writes that a major difference between the 1920s and the 1970s is that in the twenties those not affiliated with a party were largely apathetic, while in the seventies "there appears to be a more principled rejection of parties." Such a repudiation, she argues, will make the capture of Independents by one of the parties "exceedingly difficult." It is thus crucial to assess

Source: Reprinted by permission of the publishers from *The Decline of American Political Parties, 1952-1988* by Martin P. Wattenberg, Cambridge, Mass.: Harvard University Press, Copyright © 1984, 1986, 1990 by the President and Fellows of Harvard College.

whether such a process has in fact been responsible for party decline in the electorate.

An Examination of the Dissatisfaction Hypothesis

The dissatisfaction hypothesis about party decline in the electorate contains two basic components. The first component is the assertion that voters increasingly see no important differences between the Democrats and the Republicans. It has been said that the issues of the 1960s cut across the traditional line of party cleavages and blurred the distinction between the two major parties (Sundquist, 1973, p. 353). As George Wallace said in 1968, "There's not a dime's worth of difference between the two major parties." Second, it has been presumed that because distrust of the government—that is, political cynicism—has risen concurrently with independence, the two trends are related. One of the clearest arguments for the joint impact of these causal factors has been offered by Nie, Verba, and Petrocik. They attribute the increased expressions of disenchantment with the government to the troubles of the late 1960s and proceed to describe the following sequence of events: "The issues of the 1960s . . . do not clearly coincide with party lines; thus the parties offer no meaningful alternatives that might tie citizens more closely to them. Thus the political parties reap the results of the disaffection. Citizens come to look at the parties in more negative terms; they also begin to abandon the parties in greater numbers" (Nie, Verba, and Petrocik, 1976, p. 283).

The data available from the SRC/CPS election studies do not provide much support for such an interpretation, however. To begin with, as Table 22-1 shows, the proportion of respondents who thought that there were "important differences in what the Republican and Democratic parties stand for" [1] has remained quite stable over the years. Between 1952 and 1976 the proportion seeing important differences fluctuates minimally in the range from 46 to 52 percent. The data for 1980 show a significant change from 1976, but it is in the opposite direction from what would be predicted by the dissatisfaction hypothesis: in 1980, 58 percent perceived important differences between the parties. It is interesting to note that public perception of party differences was more widespread in 1980 than in either 1964 or 1972, years when, as most scholars would undoubtedly agree, the differences were in reality even sharper.

Nevertheless, the fact that the electorate continues to see important differences in what the parties stand for does not necessarily mean that citizens continue to see the differences as meaning anything in terms of government performance. Since 1960 the election studies have asked respondents what they consider to be the most important problem facing the country. Those who mention a problem are subsequently asked which of the two parties would be the most likely to do what they want on this problem.[2] As can be seen in Table 22-2, the percentage who feel that one of the parties will do better on the problem that most concerns them has declined since 1964. In that year 65.7 percent thought that one party would be the more likely to do what they wanted, even though only 50.8 percent said that there were important differences in what the parties stood

Table 22-1 The Electorate's Perception of Differences in What the Two Parties Stand For

Year	Important Differences	No Differences, Don't Know[a]
1952	49.9	50.1
1960	50.3	49.7
1964	50.8	49.2
1968	52.0	48.0
1972	46.1	53.9
1976	47.2	52.8
1980	58.0	42.0

[a] In 1964 and 1968 "don't know" was not on the questionnaire; thus the percentage coded as "no difference" was artificially inflated. To make all results comparable, I have combined responses of "no difference" and "don't know."

for. In contrast, in 1980 only 50.3 percent thought that one party would be better on the problem they considered most important—which for the first time was significantly lower than the proportion seeing important differences between the parties.

One possible interpretation of this finding is that it represents a growing disenchantment with political parties and the government in general. Merle Black and George Rabinowitz, for instance, note that this pattern bears a striking similarity to trends in trust in government. They write, "If neither party can provide desirable alternative solutions to the problems an individual feels are most important for the government to do something about, it is reasonable for the individual to view the parties unfavorably and lose faith in the government" (Black and Rabinowitz, 1980, p. 241). According to such an interpretation, respondents may still see major differences between the parties but many are so dissatisfied with the opposing alternatives that they have become alienated.

However, those respondents who believe that there wouldn't be any difference between the parties in handling the problem they feel is most important are no more cynical than those who believe that there would be a difference. On a cynicism scale ranging from $+100$ to -100, the former group is never more than two points more cynical than the latter. In fact, those respondents who feel that there would be no difference between the parties are actually somewhat less cynical in both 1976 and 1980 than their counterparts in these years.

Such a null finding brings into question whether there is any relationship between the respective declines in partisanship and trust in government, as is often presumed. One simple way to establish whether there is such a relationship is to correlate the cynicism scale with strength of party identification. Only in 1968 is there a relationship worth noting. The Pearson correlation between the two variables varies from a high of .11 in 1968 to a low of $-.02$ in 1972, averaging about .04. It is plausible to infer, therefore, that the initial declines in

Table 22-2 Percent Seeing One of the Parties as Doing the Best Job on the Problem They Considered Most Important

Year	Party Mentioned[a]	About the Same	Don't Know
1960	62.0	25.0	13.0
1964	65.7	25.3	9.0
1968	51.6	38.7[b]	9.8
1972	49.0	42.4	8.6
1976	46.3	46.0	7.7
1980	50.3	42.7	7.1

[a] These respondents mentioned either the Democratic or the Republican party.

[b] Included are those who saw no difference between the major parties but believed that Wallace would do what they wanted.

Source: SRC/CPS National Election Studies.

both party identification and trust in government between 1965 and 1968 were *slightly* interwined, but there has been no consistent relationship between the two variables.

Yet cross-sectional data can hide systematic changes over time. As Nie et al. emphasize, panel data are necessary for establishing or rejecting a causal link. Fortunately, one panel is now available in which there are substantial declines in both party identification and trust in government—the 1965-1973 Jennings-Niemi socialization panel. This dataset is particularly interesting because it contains a large sample of new entrants into the electorate who have contributed so much to the growth of the nonpartisan group (see Abramson, 1976).

If it is true that the decline in party identification is due to the growth of cynicism toward the government, then it would be expected that those in the panel who became more distrusting between 1965 and 1973 would also be the respondents who showed the greatest decline in partisanship. As Table 22-3 demonstrates, however, this was not the case. For example, data on the younger generation (first interviewed as high school seniors in 1965) show that there was a substantial decline in strength of party identification in every cell of the table with very little variation depending on whether the cell represents those whose cynicism score increased, stayed the same, or decreased. Even the youth who were *least* cynical in both years showed a sizable decline of 24.4 points on strength of partisanship. In comparison, those who shifted from trusting to cynical during the eight-year interval showed only an 18.5 point drop. For the parents the decline in strength of party identification was much smaller, but there is a similar lack of any consistent pattern of changes by cynicism scores. Indeed, some of the cells show changes that are the reverse of what would be expected. The absence of any systematic pattern of changes in the data is best demonstrated by the near-zero correlation between each individual's score on a change in strength of party identification measure (ranging from $+3$ to -3) and a change in cynicism score

Table 22-3   Change in Strength of Party Identification by Change in Cynicism Toward the Government

	1973 Cynicism		
Youth	*Trusting*	*In Between*	*Cynical*
1965 cynicism			
Trusting	−24.4[a]	−36.3	−18.5
(N)	(206)	(307)	(281)
In between	−16.3	−29.4	−22.1
(N)	(49)	(108)	(160)
Cynical	—[b]	−24.8	−30.2
(N)	(8)	(28)	(63)

	1973 Cynicism		
Parents	*Trusting*	*In Between*	*Cynical*
1965 cynicism			
Trusting	−9.9	+4.3	−13.9
(N)	(153)	(206)	(137)
In between	+2.1	−12.2	0.0
(N)	(51)	(132)	(157)
Cynical	—[b]	−6.1	−17.7
(N)	(16)	(84)	(154)

[a] Table entries represent change in strength of party identification from 1965 to 1973. Strength of party identification is calculated by scoring the percentage of Strong Democrats and Strong Republicans as +2, Weak Democrats and Weak Republicans as +1, Independent Democrats and Republicans as 0, and Pure Independents and Apoliticals as −1.

[b] Insufficient data.

Source: Jennings-Niemi Socialization Panel Study.

(ranging from +5 to −5). These correlations are .01 for the youth cohort and −.01 for the parents.

Thus there is no evidence in this panel to suggest that the rise in cynicism has been responsible for the decline of party identification. It must be concluded that the growth of cynicism and nonpartisanship are roughly parallel trends that have little relationship to each other in both a static and a dynamic sense.

What has been found thus far in this chapter suggests that a reexamination of citizens' attitudes toward the parties is in order. The dissatisfaction hypothesis depends largely on two assumptions—that voters no longer see important differences in what the parties stand for, and that the decline in strength of party identification has been an outgrowth of the decay of public trust in the government—for which little support has been found here.

It is true that there has been a decline in the percentage of the electorate which believes that one party would do a better job in handling whatever they perceive to be the most important governmental problem. However, the fact that such feelings are not related to political distrust indicates that this trend may not necessarily be a reflection of negative attitudes toward the parties. An equally plausible alternative explanation is that citizens simply see the parties as less relevant than in the past, and hence citizens' feelings toward them are more neutral than negative. With the growth of the mass media and candidate-centered campaigns, the importance of parties in the presidential selection process and in government in general has been weakened. The ideological differences between the parties may remain, but on the crucial short-run policy issues of the day it is the candidates that now matter most. Because of these changes there is reason to expect that the electorate should be less positive about the two parties than in the past but that the shift in attitudes will be toward neutrality rather than negativity. Just such a possibility will be examined next.

An Evaluative Perspective on Party Decline

One major weakness in the literature on party decline is that the research has been nearly wholly concerned with the affective (party identification) and behavioral (voting by party line) aspects of the electorate's relationship to political parties. This is not to demean the importance of the decline in strength of party identification and straight-ticket voting; clearly these trends may have significant systemic consequences, most notably the rise in political volatility and instability in the United States. The problem is that such trends have been grafted onto the description of the evaluative dimension of parties as well without proper evidence. That more people choose not to call themselves Democrats or Republicans may not necessarily mean that they are "rejecting" parties, or, as James Sundquist puts it, "calling down a plague on both their houses" (Sundquist, 1973, p. 343). Similarly, choosing to split one's ticket also may not imply a long-term rejection of the parties, but rather may simply mean that people no longer view the candidates in partisan terms.

What is sorely lacking is an analysis of just how positive, neutral, or negative Americans are toward the parties and what they like or dislike about them. It is such an evaluative approach that will be presented here. In every presidential election year since 1952 the SRC/CPS election studies have asked respondents in the preelection wave what they liked and disliked about the two political parties. Up to five responses have been coded in each year for each of the four questions.[3] By simply subtracting the number of negative comments from the number of positive ones, respondents can then be classified as either positive, neutral, or negative toward each of the parties, depending on whether the number of likes is greater than, equal to, or less than the number of dislikes.

After collapsing the data into negative, neutral, and positive ratings on each of the two parties, a sixfold classification representing respondents' ratings of both parties was created. The six categories are as follows: (1) *negative-negative,* those who have negative attitudes toward both parties; (2) *negative-neutral,* those who report negative ratings of one party, a neutral evaluation of the other; (3) *neutral-neutral,* those who are neutral with respect to both parties; (4) *positive-negative,* those who report a positive evaluation of one party, a negative evaluation of the other; (5) *positive-neutral,* those who are positive toward one party and neutral toward the other; and (6) *positive-positive,* those who rate parties in a positive fashion. It should be noted that in all of these categories which party the respondent feels warm, neutral, or cold toward is irrelevant. For example, some of the positive-negative respondents rate the Democrats positively and the Republicans negatively and some vice versa, but what is important here is that these respondents see the parties in a polarized warm-cool fashion, not which party they feel positive toward.

The percentages of respondents falling into the six categories on the basis of these like/dislike questions from 1952 to 1980 are shown in Table 22-4. If it is true that citizens are disenchanted with the parties and have come to perceive them in far more negative terms than in the past, then we would expect to find a large increase in the proportion of negative-negatives and negative-neutrals in the post-1964 period. Certainly this is the case in 1968, the first measurement point available after party identification began to decline. From 1964 to 1968 there is a 5.6 percent increase in those negative toward both parties and a 2.6 percent rise in the negative-neutral category. Given that party identification continued to erode after 1968, it might be hypothesized that the percentage of the electorate with negative attitudes toward the parties would also continue to rise. However, the data clearly shows just the reverse. Between 1968 and 1980 both the negative-negatives and negative-neutrals declined. Thus, the 1968 election stands out as an aberrant year with respect to negative attitudes about the parties, rather than the beginning of a trend.

What does change dramatically after 1968 involves the large increase of the neutral-neutrals and the decline of polarized partisans, that is, the positive-negatives. In 1968 the proportion of polarized partisans was over twice that of the neutral-neutrals; in both 1972 and 1976 the proportion of neutral-neutrals is roughly equal, and in 1980 over 9 percent higher. But what is most fascinating about Table 22-4 is that the increase of those having neutral attitudes toward both parties is a trend that is evident throughout the entire twenty-eight-year period—in the "steady state" period as well as in the period of weakening ties to the parties. From 1952 to 1964, while strength of party identification showed little change, the proportion of neutral-neutrals increased with each election, from 13.0 percent in 1952 to 20.2 percent in 1964. Only in 1968 is the linearity of the trend broken because of the largely short-term increase in negativity toward the parties in that year.

It is also evident from the table that the decline of polarized partisans began well before strength of party identification started to drop off. This is especially apparent between 1952 and 1956, when the proportion of positive-negatives fell by over 10 percent. One would intuitively have to hypothesize that the issues of the New Deal, which the party system is generally considered to have been

Table 22-4 Trends in the Public's Evaluations of the Two Major Parties

Year	Negative-Negative	Negative-Neutral	Neutral-Neutral	Positive-Negative	Positive-Neutral	Positive-Positive
1952	3.6	9.7	13.0	50.1	18.1	5.5
1956	2.9	9.0	15.9	40.0	23.3	8.9
1960	1.9	7.5	16.8	41.4	24.2	8.3
1964	4.4	11.2	20.2	38.4	20.6	5.0
1968	10.0	13.8	17.3	37.5	17.4	4.1
1972	7.9	12.6	29.9	30.3	14.7	4.7
1976	7.5	11.8	31.3	31.1	13.7	4.5
1980	5.0	8.6	36.5	27.3	17.7	4.8

Source: SRC/CPS National Election Studies.

aligned upon, were sharply declining in salience from 1952 to 1956. Through 1960 many of these positive-negatives apparently moved to the less polarized categories of positive-neutral and positive-positive, both of which reached their high points during the years of the Eisenhower presidency. But after 1960 these groups declined in numbers, as did the positive-negatives. Overall, from 1952 to 1980 the percentage of positive-negatives fell from 50.1 to 27.3 percent. Except for the slight increase during the Eisenhower years, the percentage of those positive toward both parties remained fairly stable at about 5 percent.

Given the evidence from Table 22-4, the reader may wonder how Nie, Verba, and Petrocik concluded that citizens had come to look upon parties in more negative terms—especially because they also analyzed responses to the party like/dislike questions.[4] The answer simply is that Nie et al. combined the categories of negative-negative, negative-neutral, and neutral-neutral into a single group that they labeled variously as "negative evaluations of both parties," "alienated from the parties," or "nonsupporters of the parties." Only the third phrase is an accurate description of what they were measuring. To infer that a neutral evaluation of the parties represents dissatisfaction is to make an extremely tenuous assumption, especially since the growth of neutrality on these open-ended questions has been entirely due to the increase (from 9.7 to 34.3 percent) in the proportion of the population who have nothing at all to say—either positive or negative—about either party, and hence end up being classified as neutral toward both.[5]

Additional Evidence from Feeling Thermometers

Another point that Nie et al. make about the increase in negative attitudes concerns the decline over time in the public's feeling thermometer ratings of the parties. As shown in Figure 22-1, the mean rating of "Democrats" has fallen by about eight points since 1964, and the mean rating of "Republicans" shortly after the Reagan victory in 1980 was actually lower than during the Goldwater debacle in 1964.

Figure 22-1 Feeling Thermometer Ratings of the Parties, 1964-1980

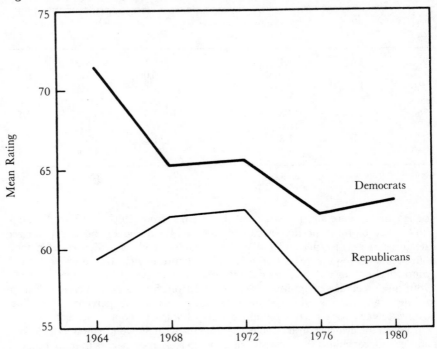

Source: SRC/CPS National Election Studies.

But do lower ratings necessarily indicate the presence of more intense negative evaluations? Because feeling thermometer ratings represent a summary of both positive and negative affect, the trends shown in Figure 22-1 could just as easily be due to a decline in positive feelings as to a rise in negative ones. Furthermore, it is quite possible that if *both* positive and negative feelings were to decline in intensity, the net result would be a lower mean rating. This is because of the positivity bias that is usually associated with the feeling thermometer instrument. For example, on the like/dislike measure one never finds more than 9 percent of the population giving a positive evaluation of both parties (see Table 22-4), while an average of nearly 40 percent rate both parties at above the neutral point—that is, 50 degrees—on the feeling thermometer. Thus one could find people who are positive as well as those who are negative gravitating equally toward the neutral point, but the fact that the distributions are so heavily skewed toward the positive side means that there will be more downward than upward movement.

From Table 22-5 we can see that such a decline in the intensity of *both* positive and negative feelings toward the parties has in fact taken place. Those who give favorable ratings now give less favorable ones than in the past.

Table 22-5 Trends in the Intensity of Feeling Thermometer Ratings of the Parties

	1964	1968	1972	1976	1980
Rating of "Democrats"					
Average distance above 50 degrees for those positive	34.0	29.9	26.2	24.4	25.5
Average distance below 50 degrees for those negative	24.0	22.5	17.1	17.0	18.1
Average distance from 50 degrees (includes those at 50)	26.5	21.3	19.1	15.5	17.5
Rating of "Republicans"					
Average distance above 50 degrees for those positive	28.4	27.2	25.1	21.6	21.8
Average distance below 50 degrees for those negative	26.5	25.1	22.7	19.7	20.6
Average distance from 50 degrees (includes those at 50)	19.6	18.9	18.2	12.7	14.6

Source: SRC/CPS National Election Studies.

Similarly, respondents who give negative ratings are now less intensely negative than in the mid-1960s. These trends are best summarized by taking the absolute value of the distance of the ratings from 50 degrees. In 1964 the average respondent evaluated the two parties such that the combined distance of both ratings from the neutral point was 46.1 points (26.5 for ratings of "Democrats" plus 19.6 for ratings of "Republicans").[6] By 1976 the comparable figure has fallen by nearly 40 percent to 28.2. There is a slight increase between 1976 and 1980 in the intensity of feeling thermometer ratings of the parties, but it hardly represents a major reversal of the trend.[7] The overall picture is clearly one of movement toward the neutral point from both the positive and negative sides of the scale.

In sum, the results from both the like/dislike responses and the feeling thermometers reinforce one another despite their methodological differences. In each the major trend is a growing neutrality in the electorate's perceptions of the parties. The fact that similar trends can be found with disparate sets of data provides a pleasing confirmation of the theoretical framework outlined above.

A Comparison of Party Images in 1952 and 1980

Just how fragile the current party alignment has become because of the rise in neutrality can be illustrated by the lack of substance in respondents' party images, as revealed in the 1980 election study. As Table 22-6 demonstrates, the

Table 22-6   Images of the Political Parties, 1980

	Like Democrats	Dislike Democrats	Like Republicans	Dislike Republicans
Because of:				
The groups they are for or against	25.5	4.2	4.3	19.3
Economic/welfare policy stands	6.2	10.0	8.1	3.9
Social issue stands	0.8	0.7	1.0	1.1
Stands on general philosophy of government activity	8.1	8.2	11.1	5.1
Their ability to manage the government	2.5	9.7	7.2	2.0
Foreign policy	4.2	6.3	7.4	4.5
Carter	0.6	1.9	—	—
Reagan	—	—	1.1	1.5

Note: Table entries are the proportion of the sample offering each given type of response.

Source: 1980 CPS National Election Study.

only major advantage enjoyed by either party is the positive image of the groups that the Democrats are perceived as representing. Similarly, the only major disadvantage for either party is the negative image that people have of the groups popularly associated with the Republican party. These feelings that the Democrats are the party of the common working man while the Republicans are the party of the upper class and big business represent virtually the last remnant of the images of the parties that developed during the New Deal era.

Table 22-7 presents an examination of the party images found in the 1952 election study, which can be directly compared to the percentages displayed in Table 22-6 for 1980. The comparison indicates that there has been a marked deterioration of images that once were highly favorable to the Democrats and of those that once greatly benefited the Republicans. Leaving aside the long-standing impressions of which parties favor which groups, the electorate just no longer has much to say when asked what they like and dislike about the two parties.

In 1952, for example, nearly a third of the respondents stated that they liked the Democratic party because of its economic or welfare policies, while 22 percent made negative comments along those lines in reference to the Republicans. With memories of the Depression now in the distant past, it is probably not too surprising to find that the comparable figures in 1980 were only 6 and 4 percent, respectively. Many observers may be surprised to find, however, that positive comments about the Republican party's economic/welfare policy stands were also

Table 22-7   Images of the Political Parties, 1952

	Like Democrats	Dislike Democrats	Like Republicans	Dislike Republicans
Because of:				
The groups they are for or against	33.1	4.7	3.2	20.3
Economic/welfare policy stands	31.9	16.3	22.1	22.4
Social issue stands	—	—	—	—
Stands on general philosophy of government activity	11.4	8.7	11.0	5.8
Their ability to manage the government	2.3	26.6	18.0	4.3
Foreign policy	4.1	17.1	12.3	3.4
Truman	1.0	7.6	—	—
Eisenhower	—	—	7.7	1.8
Stevenson	1.3	0.9	—	—

Source: 1952 CPS National Election Study.

more numerous in the 1952 sample than in 1980 (22 percent compared to 8 percent). Moreover, despite the poor performance of the economy during the Carter administration, only 10 percent of those interviewed made negative comments about the economic and welfare policies of the Democratic party. In sum, neither party now has a very firmly entrenched positive or negative public image on such issues compared to two or three decades ago.[8]

In the areas of foreign policy and management of the government, the images of the parties are also not nearly as clearly defined as they once were. In both 1952 and 1980 the Republicans were perceived favorably on these dimensions while the Democrats were viewed negatively because of dissatisfaction with the performances of Truman and Carter, respectively. The key difference to note is that in 1980 such feelings were far less salient than in 1952. The fact that only 7 percent of those interviewed made positive comments about the Republicans on each of these dimensions in 1980 hardly constitutes a resounding statement of faith in Republican foreign policies or management capabilities. Nor is there any indication that Carter's failures in these areas are likely to have a long-term negative impact on the Democratic party, as the comparable negative figures in 1952 were nearly three times as high.

That the Democratic party largely escaped blame for the entire range of problems of the Carter administration, from the economy to Iran, might be interpreted as an incredible stroke of good fortune, especially considering that such problems were quite prevalent in open-ended evaluations of Jimmy Carter in 1980. However, such a pattern is more likely a symptom of the dissociation of public perceptions of candidates and presidents from the political parties that they nominally represent. With the rise of the plebiscitary presidency and the growth of the mass media, candidates no longer need the parties to convey their messages and voters are now able to see for themselves just what the candidates are like. A number of recent presidential campaigns—most notably that of Richard Nixon in 1972—have thus been able to consciously downplay partisan appeals.

In 1980 neither candidate really made any effort to avoid party associations, however. Reagan clearly attempted to be more of a Republican team man than any nominee in the party's recent history, and Carter stressed his Democratic affiliation to the utmost given that his low approval ratings made it difficult to offer much else in the way of a positive appeal. In spite of these strategies, very few people evaluated the parties in 1980 on the basis of their standard-bearers, as shown in Table 22-6. For example, only 1 percent of the sample stated that they liked the Republicans because of Ronald Reagan. Whether this figure will be much greater in the future if the Reagan program succeeds remains to be seen, but if so it would mark a reversal of the historical trend that will be the major focus of the following chapter [of Watterberg]. In this candidate-centered media age, people have apparently become less accustomed to praising or blaming the parties for presidential performance.

The results presented in this chapter offer somewhat more hope for the revitalization of American political parties than most previous work on the subject. However, one can also extrapolate reasons to be doubtful about such a prospect, based on the interpretation of party decline that has been argued here.

Taking the positive side first, the most important new piece of data is that there has been little increase in the proportion of the population holding negative attitudes toward the parties. It is conceivable that the initial decline in strength of party identification may have been due to the large jump in negativity apparent in 1968. But since that time negative attitudes toward the parties have subsided. Positive attitudes have also continued to decline, but what has increased has been neutrality rather than negativity.

Besides the fact that parties do not have to overcome largely negative attitudes toward them, it is also encouraging to note that recovery probably does not hinge on a restoration of trust in government. Like other institutions, political parties are viewed more cynically than in the past. However, this sort of cynicism is apparently not being translated into negative attitudes. People may be more skeptical about the motives of parties, but that does not necessarily mean that they dislike parties in general or that they will not identify with a party in the future. This point is supported by the fact that hardly any relationship was found between strength of party identification and trust in government, except for the .11 correlation in 1968. And in a dynamic sense, panel data show that the two trends are quite independent of one another. Given that the decline of partisanship has been a reflection of growing neutrality instead of negativity, such null findings are quite explicable. If negative attitudes about parties were at the root of the rise of nonpartisanship then one would expect that other negative attitudes such as cynicism would be related to it, as indeed the case of 1968 appears to show. But overall the evidence demonstrates that the decline of parties in the electorate has been a function of a reduction in saliency than an increase in negative attitudes.

However, turning to the reasons to be pessimistic about any revitalization of parties in the electorate, there seems to be little prospect for reversing the trend toward neutrality in the immediate future. One of the most important findings in this chapter is that the decline of parties in the electorate can be traced back much further than the mid-1960s in terms of party evaluations. The decline of polarized views of the parties and the increase in neutrality is visible throughout the election study times series. Thus it can undoubtedly be considered a long-term secular trend, and such trends are usually difficult to reverse.

NOTES

1. The wording of this question has changed slightly over the years. Listed below are the different versions that have been asked:

    1952: "Do you think there are any important differences between what the Democratic and Republican parties stand for, or do you think they are about the same?"

    1960, 1964, 1972-1980: "Do you think there are any important differences in what the Republicans and Democrats stand for?"

    1968: "Do you think there are any important differences between the Republican and Democratic parties?"

2. This question has also undergone slight changes in wording over the years. In 1960, 1964, and 1968 respondents were asked which party they thought would be the most likely to do what they wanted on whichever problem they mentioned. In 1972 this was changed to asking which party would be the most likely to get the government to be helpful on the problem, and in 1976-1980 the wording was again changed to which party would be the most likely to do a better job in dealing with the problem.

3. In 1972 CPS originally coded only the first three responses. The fourth and fifth responses were later coded by Arthur H. Miller.

4. Several technical differences between the like/dislike data that I have used and those that Nie et al. use should be noted. First, Nie et al. use only the first three responses in all years while I employ all five. Second, they fail to filter out the 100 respondents in 1952 and the 17 in 1960 who were not interviewed in the preelection wave. As these respondents were not asked the like/dislike questions, they should be excluded from the analysis. Finally, Nie et al. include responses from the black supplements in 1964 and 1968. Subsequent analysis at CPS has shown that these supplements actually introduce a greater degree of bias into the sample. Hence I have not used them.

5. The proportion without any positive or negative comments for each year are as follows: 1952, 9.7%; 1956, 12.9%; 1960, 15.7%; 1964, 17.1%; 1968, 14.0%; 1972, 27.0%; 1976, 28.7%; 1980, 34.3%. The tiny remainder of those who fall under the neutral-neutral category in Table 22-4 express both likes and dislikes, with each like being matched by a dislike of the same party.

6. In the 1964 and 1968 studies those who responded "don't know" were coded at the 50 degree mark. Therefore, I have followed the same coding rule with the 1972-1980 data to ensure consistency throughout the time series.

7. Furthermore, there are two reasons to expect that this jump may be a methodological artifact of changes in the structure of the interview schedule in 1980. First, respondents were also asked to rate the "Democratic party" and the "Republican party" in the preelection interview. And second, the preelection interview in 1980 focused more on political parties than any other in the past. Both of these factors could well have caused respondents to think more about the parties than they would have otherwise and therefore rate them less neutrally. The reason such an effect is not found in the like/dislike questions is that these remained very early in the preelection interview whereas the 1980 feeling thermometer ratings shown in Table 22-5 are from the postelection wave.

8. Similarly, when asked which party would do a better job in handling inflation, only 42 percent of those interviewed in 1980 thought one party would do a better job than the other, and regarding unemployment the comparable figure was just 39 percent.

REFERENCES

Abelson, Robert. "Are Attitudes Necessary?" In *Attitudes, Conflict, and Social Change,* ed. Bert T. King and E. McGinnies. New York: Academic, 1972.

Abelson, Robert P., Donald R. Kinder, Mark D. Peters, and Susan T. Fiske. "Affective and Semantic Components in Political Person Perception." *Journal of Personality and Social Psychology* (1982) 42:619-30.

Abramowitz, Alan I. "A Comparison of Voting for U.S. Senator and Representative in 1978." *American Political Science Review* (1980) 74:633-40.

———. "Explaining Senate Outcomes." *American Political Science Review* (1988) 82:385-403.

Abramowitz, Alan I., and Jeffrey A. Segal. "Determinants of the Outcomes of U.S. Senate Elections." *Journal of Politics* (1986) 48:433-39.

———. *Senate Elections.* Ann Arbor, Mich: University of Michigan Press, 1992.

Abramson, Paul R. *Generational Change in American Politics.* Lexington, Mass.: Lexington Books, 1975.

———. "Generational Change and the Decline of Party Identification in America: 1952-1974." *American Political Science Review* (1976) 70:469-78.

———. "Developing Party Identification: A Further Examination of Life-Cycle, Generational, and Period Effects." *American Journal of Political Science* (1979) 23:78-96.

———. "Measuring the Southern Contribution to the Democratic Coalition." *American Political Science Review* (1987) 81:567-70.

Abramson, Paul R., and John H. Aldrich. "The Decline of Electoral Participation in America." *American Political Science Review* (1982) 76:502-21.

Abramson, Paul R., John H. Aldrich, Phil Paolino, and David Rohde. "'Sophisticated' Voting in the 1988 Presidential Primaries." *American Political Science Review* (1992) 86:55-69.

Abramson, Paul R., John H. Aldrich, and David W. Rohde. *Change and Continuity in the 1980 Elections,* rev. ed. Washington, D.C.: CQ Press, 1983.

———. *Change and Continuity in the 1984 Elections,* rev. ed. Washington, D.C.: CQ Press, 1987.

———. *Change and Continuity in the 1988 Elections,* rev. ed. Washington, D.C.: CQ Press, 1991.

Abramson, Paul R., and William Claggett. "Race-related Differences in Self-reported and Validated Turnout in 1984." *Journal of Politics* (1986) 48:412-22.

Abramson, Paul R., and Charles W. Ostrom, Jr. "Macropartisanship: An Empirical Reassessment." *American Political Science Review* (1991) 85:181-92.

Achen, Christopher H. "Mass Political Attitudes and the Survey Response." *American Political Science Review* (1975) 69:1218-31.

_____. "Prospective Voting and the Theory of Party Identification." Manuscript, University of Chicago, 1989.

Adamany, David. "The Supreme Court." In *The American Court: A Critical Assessment,* ed. John B. Gates and Charles A. Johnson. Washington, D.C.: CQ Press, 1991.

Aitchison, John, and J. A. C. Brown. *The Lognormal Distribution: With Special Reference to Its Uses in Economics.* Cambridge: Cambridge University Press, 1957.

Aldrich, John H., Tse Min Lin, and Wendy M. Rahn. "Learning During the 1984 Nomination Campaign." Manuscript, 1987.

Aldrich, John H., and Richard D. McKelvey. "A Method of Scaling with Applications to the 1968 and 1972 U.S. Presidential Elections." *American Political Science Review* (1977) 71:111-30.

Aldrich, John H., and Richard G. Niemi. "The Sixth American Party System: The 1960s Realignment and the Candidate-Centered Parties." Manuscript, 1989.

Aldrich, John H., and Dennis M. Simon. "Turnout in American National Elections." In *Research in Micropolitics,* vol. 1, ed. Samuel Long. Greenwich, Conn.: JAI Press, 1986.

Aldrich, John H., John L. Sullivan, and Eugene Borgida. "Foreign Affairs and Issue Voting: Do Presidential Candidates 'Waltz Before a Blind Audience'?" *American Political Science Review* (1989) 83:123-41. Chapter 11 in this volume.

Aldrich, John H., and Thomas M. Trump. "Issue Opinions and Perceptions, 1962-1984: Citizen Competence, Campaign Context, and Candidate Behavior." Manuscript, University of Minnesota, 1986.

Alesina, Alberto, and Howard Rosenthal. "Partisan Cycles in Congressional Elections and the Macroeconomy." *American Political Science Review* (1989) 83:373-98.

Allen, Richard L., Michael C. Dawson, and Ronald Brown. "A Schema-Based Approach to Modeling an African-American Racial Belief System." *American Political Science Review* (1989) 83:421-41.

Allsop, Dee, and Herbert F. Weisberg. "Measuring Change in Party Identification in an Election Campaign." *American Journal of Political Science* (1988) 32:996-1017.

Almond, Gabriel A. *The American People and Foreign Policy.* New York: Harcourt, Brace, 1950.

Almond, Gabriel A., and Sidney Verba. *The Civic Culture.* Princeton, N.J.: Princeton University Press, 1963.

Alt, James E. "Political Parties, World Demand, and Unemployment: Domestic and International Sources of Economic Activity." *American Political Science Review* (1985) 79:1016-40.

Alvarez, R. Michael. "The Puzzle of Party Identification." *American Politics Quarterly* (1990) 18:476-91.

Amemiya, Takesh. *Advanced Econometrics.* Cambridge, Mass.: Harvard University Press, 1985.

Andersen, Kristi. "Generation, Partisan Shift, and Realignment: A Glance Back to the New Deal." In *The Changing American Voter,* ed. Norman H. Nie, Sidney Verba, and John R. Petrocik. Cambridge: Harvard University Press, 1976.

_____. *The Creation of a Democratic Majority, 1928-1936.* Chicago: University of Chicago Press, 1979.

Anderson, Barbara A., and Brian D. Silver. "Measurement and Mismeasurement of the

Validity of the Self-reported Vote." *American Journal of Political Science* (1986) 30:771-85.

Andrain, Charles F. *Children and Civic Awareness: A Study in Political Education.* Columbus, Ohio: Charles E. Merrill, 1971.

Ansolabehere, Stephen, David Brady, and Morris Fiorina. "The Vanishing Marginals and Electoral Responsiveness." *British Journal of Political Science* (1992) 22:21-38.

Antunes, George, and Charles M. Gaitz. "Ethnicity and Participation: A Study of Mexican-Americans, Blacks, and Whites." *American Journal of Sociology* (1975) 80:1192-211.

Arseneau, Robert B., and Raymond E. Wolfinger. "Voting Behavior in Congressional Elections." Paper presented at the annual meeting of the American Political Science Association, New Orleans, 1973.

Ashenfelter, Orley, and Stanley Kelley, Jr. "Determinants of Participation in Presidential Elections." *Journal of Law and Economics* (1975) 18:711-21.

Asher, Herbert B. *Presidential Elections and American Politics.* Homewood, Ill.: Dorsey Press, 1980, 1984, 1988; Pacific Grove, Calif.: Brooks/Cole, 1992.

Axelrod, Robert. "Where the Votes Come From: An Analysis of Electoral Coalitions." *American Political Science Review* (1972) 66:11-20.

———. "Communication." *American Political Science Review* (1982) 76:394-95.

Babchuk, Nicholas, and Ralph V. Thompson. "The Voluntary Associations of Negroes." *American Sociological Review* (1962) 27:647-55.

Bargh, John A., Ronald N. Bond, Wendy J. Lombardi, and Mary E. Tota. "The Additive Nature of Chronic and Temporary Sources of Construct Accessibility." *Journal of Personality and Social Psychology* (1986) 50:869-78.

Barnes, Samuel H., M. Kent Jennings, Ronald Inglehart, and Barbara Farah. "Party Identification and Party Closeness in Comparative Perspective." *Political Behavior* (1988) 10:215-31.

Barnes, Samuel, Max Kasse, et al. *Political Action.* Beverly Hills, Calif.: Sage, 1979.

Baron, J. "Personality and Intelligence." In *Handbook of Human Intelligence,* ed. Robert J. Sternberg. Cambridge: Cambridge University Press, 1982.

Barone, Michael, and Grant Ujifusa. *The Almanac of American Politics 1988.* Washington, D.C.: National Journal, 1987.

———. *The Almanac of American Politics 1990.* Washington, D.C.: National Journal, 1989.

Barry, Brian, and Russell Hardin. *Rational Man and Irrational Society?* Beverly Hills, Calif.: Sage, 1982.

Bartels, Larry M. "Issue Voting Under Uncertainty." *American Journal of Political Science* (1986) 30:709-28.

———. "Candidate Choice and the Dynamics of the Presidential Nominating Process." *American Journal of Political Science* (1987) 31:1-30.

———. *Presidential Primaries and the Dynamics of Public Choice.* Princeton, N.J.: Princeton University Press, 1988.

Bauer, Monica, and John R. Hibbing. "Which Incumbents Lose in House Elections: A Response to Jacobson's 'The Marginals Never Vanished'." *American Journal of Political Science* (1989) 33:262-71.

Baum, Lawrence. "Information and Party Voting in 'Semipartisan' Judicial Elections." *Political Behavior* (1987) 9:62-74.

Bean, Clive, and Anthony Mughan. "Leadership Effects in Parliamentary Elections in Australia and Britain." *American Political Science Review* (1989) 83:1165-79.

Beck, Nathaniel. "Parties, Administrations, and American Macroeconomic Outcomes." *American Political Science Review* (1982a) 76:83-93.

——. "Does There Exist a Political Business Cycle? A Box-Tiao Analysis." *Public Choice* (1982b) 38:205-09.

——. "Elections and the Fed: Is There a Political Monetary Cycle?" *American Journal of Political Science* (1987) 31:194-216.

Beck, Paul Allen. "A Socialization Theory of Partisan Realignment." In *The Politics of Future Citizens,* ed. Richard G. Niemi, et al. San Francisco: Jossey-Bass, 1974. Chapter 31 in *Classics.*

——. "The Role of Agents in Political Socialization. In *Handbook of Political Socialization,* ed. Stanley Allen Renshon. New York: Free Press, 1977.

——. "The Electoral Cycle in American Politics." *British Journal of Political Science* (1979) 9:129-56.

Beck, Paul Allen, Lawrence Baum, Aage R. Clausen, and Charles E. Smith. "Patterns and Sources of Ticket-Splitting in Subpresidential Voting." *American Political Science Review* (1992) 86:forthcoming.

Beck, Paul Allen, and M. Kent Jennings. "Parents as 'Middle-Persons' in Political Socialization." *Journal of Politics* (1975) 37:83-107.

Bejar, Issac I. *Achievement Testing: Recent Advances.* Beverly Hills, Calif.: Sage, 1983.

Bennett, Stephen, and David Resnick. "The Implications of Nonvoting for Democracy in the United States." *American Journal of Political Science* (1990) 34:771-802.

Benson, Edward G. "Three Words." *Public Opinion Quarterly* (1940) 4:130-34.

Berelson, Bernard R., Paul F. Lazarsfeld, and William N. McPhee. *Voting.* Chicago: University of Chicago Press, 1954.

Berscheid, Ellen. "Vocabularies of Emotion circa 1984." Presidential Address, American Psychological Association, 1984.

Bianco, William T. "Strategic Decisions on Candidacy in U.S. Congressional Districts." *Legislative Studies Quarterly* (1984) 9:351-64.

"Birth of a Question: An Interview with Alec Gallup." *The Public Perspective* (1991) 2(No.5):23-24.

Black, Merle, and George B. Rabinowitz. "American Electoral Change: 1952-1972." In *The Party Symbol,* ed. William Crotty. San Francisco: Freeman, 1980.

Blake, Donald E. "The Consistency of Inconsistency: Party Identification in Federal and Provincial Politics." *Canadian Journal of Political Science* (1982) 15:691-710.

Bloom, Harold, and H. Douglas Price. "Voter Response to Short Run Economic Conditions: The Asymmetric Effect of Prosperity and Recession." *American Political Science Review* (1975) 69:1240-54.

Bobo, Lawrence. "Attitudes Toward the Black Political Movement: Trends, Meaning, and Effects on Racial Policy Preferences." *Social Psychology Quarterly* (1988) 51:287-302.

——. "Societal Obligations, Individualism, and Redistributive Policies." *Sociological Forum,* forthcoming.

Bolland, John M., James H. Kuklinski, and Robert C. Luskin. "Where's the Schema? Schema Theory in Political Psychology." Paper presented at the annual meeting of the International Society of Political Psychology, 1987.

Bond, Jon R., Cary Covington, and Richard Fleisher. "Explaining Challenger Quality in Congressional Elections." *Journal of Politics* (1985) 47:510-29.

Born, Richard. "Strategic Politicians and Unresponsive Voters." *American Political Science Review* (1986) 80:599-612.

Borrelli, Stephen, Brad Lockerbie, and Richard G. Niemi. "Why the Democrat-

Republican Partisanship Gap Varies from Poll to Poll." *Public Opinion Quarterly* (1987) 51:115-19.

Bostis, David A., and Milton D. Morris. *Black Political Participation*. Washington, D.C.: Joint Center for Political and Economic Studies, 1992.

Bousfield, Weston A. "The Occurrence of Clustering in Recall of Randomly Arranged." *Journal of General Psychology* (1953) 49:229-40.

Box, George E. P., and David R. Cox. "An Analysis of Transformations." *Journal of the Royal Statistical Society*, series B (1964) 26:211-43.

Box, George E. P., and Gwilym M. Jenkins. *Time Series Analysis: Forecasting and Control*. San Francisco: Holden Day, 1976.

Boyd, Richard W. "Presidential Elections: An Explanation of Voting Defection." *American Political Science Review* (1969) 63:498-514.

———. "Electoral Change and the Floating Voter: The Reagan Elections." Paper presented at the annual meeting of the American Political Science Association, New Orleans, 1985.

Brady, David W. *Critical Elections and Congressional Policy Making*. Stanford, Calif.: Stanford University Press, 1988.

Brady, Henry E., and Paul M. Sniderman. "Left-shift: Ideological Maps of Politics." Manuscript, University of California, Berkeley, 1983.

Bransford, John D., and Marcia K. Johnson. "Contextual Prerequisites for Understanding: Some Investigations of Comprehension and Recall." *Journal of Verbal Learning and Verbal Behavior* (1972) 11:717-21.

Broder, David S. *The Party's Over*. New York: Harper and Row, 1971.

Brody, Richard A. "Stability and Change in Party Identification: Presidential to Off-Years." Paper presented at the annual meeting of the American Political Science Association, Washington, D.C., 1977.

———. "Change and Stability in the Components of Party Identification." Paper presented at the National Science Foundation Conference on Party Identification, Tallahassee, 1978.

———. "The Puzzle of Participation." In *The New American Political System*, ed. Anthony King. Washington, D.C.: American Enterprise Institute, 1978.

Brody, Richard A., and Benjamin I. Page. "The Assessment of Policy Voting." *American Political Science Review* (1972) 66:450-58. Chapter 10 in *Classics*.

———. "Indifference, Alienation and Rational Decision: The Effects of Candidate Evaluations on Turnout and the Vote." *Public Choice* (1973) 15:1-17.

Brody, Richard A., and Lawrence S. Rothenberg. "The Instability of Partisanship: An Analysis of the 1980 Presidential Election." *British Journal of Political Science* (1988) 18:445-65.

Brody, Richard A., and Lee Sigelman. "Presidential Popularity and Presidential Elections: An Update and an Extension." *Public Opinion Quarterly* (1983) 47:325-28.

Brody, Richard A., and Paul M. Sniderman. "From Life Space to Polling Place: The Relevance of Personal Concerns for Voting Behavior." *British Journal of Political Science* (1977) 7:337-60.

Brown, Courtney. *Ballots of Tumult*. Ann Arbor: University of Michigan Press, 1991.

Brown, Steven D., Ronald J. Lambert, Barry J. Kay, and James E. Curtis. "In the Eye of the Beholder: Leader Images in Canada." *Canadian Journal of Political Science* (1988) 21:729-55.

Brown, Thad, and Arthur A. Stein. "The Political Economy of National Elections." *Comparative Politics* (1982) 14:479-97.

Browning, Rufus, Dale Rogers Marshall, and David H. Tabb. *Protest Is Not Enough:*

The Struggle of Blacks and Hispanics for Equality in Urban Politics. Berkeley: University of California Press, 1984.

Bullock, Charles S., III. "Is There a Conservative Coalition in the House?" *Journal of Politics* (1981) 43:662-82.

Burnham, Walter Dean. "The Changing Shape of the American Political Universe." *American Political Science Review* (1965) 59:7-28. Chapter 29 in *Classics*.

———. *Critical Elections and the Mainsprings of American Politics.* New York: Norton, 1970.

———. "Insulation and Responsiveness in Congressional Elections." *Political Science Quarterly* (1975) 90:411-35.

———. *The Current Crisis in American Politics.* New York: Oxford University Press, 1982.

———. "The 1984 Election and the Future of American Politics." In *Election 1984.* ed. Ellis Sandoz and Cecil V. Crabb, Jr. New York: New American Library, 1985.

Buschke, Herman. "Learning is Organized by Chunking." *Journal of Verbal Learning and Verbal Behavior* (1976) 15:313-24.

Caldeira, Gregory A., and Samuel C. Patterson. "Contextual Influences on Participation in U.S. State Legislative Elections." *Legislative Studies Quarterly* (1982) 7:359-81.

Caldeira, Gregory A., Samuel C. Patterson, and Gregory A. Markko. "The Mobilization of Voters in Congressional Elections." *Journal of Politics* (1985) 47:490-509.

Calvert, Randall L., and Michael B. MacKuen. "Bayesian Learning and the Dynamics of Public Opinion." Paper presented at the annual meeting of the Midwest Political Science Association, Chicago, 1985.

Campbell, Angus. "Surge and Decline: A Study of Electoral Change." *Public Opinion Quarterly* (1960) 24:397-418.

Campbell, Angus, Philip E. Converse, Warren E. Miller, and Donald E. Stokes. *The American Voter.* New York: Wiley, 1960.

Campbell, Angus, Philip E. Converse, and Willard L. Rodgers. *The Quality of American Life: Perceptions, Evaluations, and Satisfactions.* New York: Russell Sage, 1976.

Campbell, Angus, Gerald Gurin, and Warren E. Miller. *The Voter Decides.* Evanston, Ill.: Row, Peterson, 1954.

Campbell, James E. "Explaining Presidential Losses in Midterm Congressional Elections." *Journal of Politics* (1985) 47:1140-57.

———. "Predicting Seat Gains from Presidential Coattails." *American Journal of Political Science* (1986) 30:165-83.

———. "The Revised Theory of Surge and Decline." *American Journal of Political Science* (1987) 31:965-79.

———. "The Presidential Pulse of Congressional Elections." In *The Atomistic Congress, 1968-1988,* ed. Ronald Peters and Allan Herzke. New York: Sharpe, 1991.

———. "The Presidential Surge and Its Midterm Decline in Congressional Elections, 1868-1988." *Journal of Politics* (1991) 53:477-87.

———. "Forecasting the Presidential Vote in the States." *American Journal of Political Science* (1992) 36:386-407.

———. *The Presidential Pulse of Congressional Elections.* Lexington: University Press of Kentucky, 1993.

Campione, Joseph C., Ann L. Brown, and Nancy R. Bryant. "Individual Differences in Learning and Memory." In *Human Abilities: An Information Processing Approach,* ed. Robert J. Sternberg. New York: W. H. Freeman, 1985.

Canon, David T. "Political Conditions and Experienced Challengers in Congressional Elections, 1972-1984." Paper presented at the annual meeting of the American Political Science Association, New Orleans, Louisiana, 1985.

Carmines, Edward G., John P. McIver, and James A. Stimson. "Unrealized Partisanship: A Theory of Dealignment." *Journal of Politics* (1987) 49:376-400.

Carmines, Edward G., Steven H. Renten, and James A. Stimson. "Event and Alignments: The Party Image Link." In *Controversies in Voting Behavior,* 2d ed., ed. Richard G. Niemi and Herbert F. Weisberg. Washington, D.C.: CQ Press, 1984.

Carmines, Edward G., and James A. Stimson. "The Two Faces of Issue Voting." *American Political Science Review* (1980) 74:78-91. Chapter 12 in *Classics.*

———. "Issue Evolution, Population Replacement and Normal Partisan Change." *American Political Science Review* (1981) 75:107-18.

———. "Racial Issues and the Structure of Mass Belief Systems." *Journal of Politics* (1982) 44:2-20.

———. "The Dynamics of Issue Evolution." In *Electoral Change in Industrial Democracies,* ed. Russell Dalton, Paul Allen Beck, and Scott Flanagan. Princeton, N.J.: Princeton University Press, 1984.

———. *Issue Evolution: Race and the Transformation of American Politics.* Princeton, N.J.: Princeton University Press, 1989.

Carroll, John B., and Scott E. Maxwell. "Individual Differences in Cognitive Abilities." In *Annual Review of Psychology,* ed. Mark R. Rosenzweig and Lyman W. Porter. Palo Alto, Calif.: Annual Reviews, 1979.

Cassel, Carol A. "Issues in Measurement: The 'Levels of Conceptualization' Index of Ideological Sophistication." *American Journal of Political Science* (1984) 28:418-29.

Cassel, Carol A., and Robert Luskin. "Simple Explanations of Turnout Decline." *American Political Science Review* (1988) 82:1321-30.

Castles, Stephan, and Godula Kosack. *Immigrant Workers and Class Structure in Western Europe.* London: Oxford University Press, 1973.

Chaffee, Steven H., Marilyn Jackson-Beeck, Jean Duvall, and Donna Wilson. "Mass Communication in Political Socialization." In *Handbook of Political Socialization,* ed. Stanley Allen Renshon. New York: Free Press, 1977.

Chaiken, Shelly. "Heuristic versus Systematic Information Processing and the Use of Source versus Cur Messages in Persuasion." *Journal of Personality and Social Psychology* (1980) 39:752-66.

———. "The Heuristic Model of Persuasion." In *Social Influence,* ed. Mark P. Zanna, James M. Olson, and C. P. Herman, The Ontario Symposium, vol. 5. Hillsdale, N.J.: Lawrence Erlbaum, 1987.

Chaiken, Shelly, and Mark W. Baldwin. "Affective Cognitive Consistency and the Effect of Salient Behavioral Information on the Self-perception of Attitudes." *Journal of Personality and Social Psychology* (1981) 41:1-12.

Chambers, William Nisbet, and Walter Dean Burnham, eds. *The American Party Systems.* New York: Oxford University Press, 1967, 1975.

Chiesi, Harry L., George J. Spilich, and James F. Voss. "Acquisition of Domain-related Information in Relation to High and Low Domain Knowledge." *Journal of Verbal Learning and Verbal Behavior* (1979) 18:257-73.

Chong, Dennis, Herbert McClosky, and John R. Zaller. "Patterns of Support for Democratic and Capitalist Values." *British Journal of Political Science* (1983) 13:401-40.

Chubb, John E. "Institutions, the Economy, and the Dynamics of State Elections." *American Political Science Review* (1988) 82:133-54.

Chubb, John E., Michael G. Hagen, and Paul M. Sniderman. "Ideological Reasoning." *Brookings Discussion Papers in Governmental Studies,* No. 4, 1986.

Clarke, Peter and Eric Fredin. "Newspapers, Television, and Political Reasoning." *Public Opinion Quarterly* (1978) 42:143-60.

Clausen, Aage R. "Response Validity: Vote Report." *Public Opinion Quarterly* (1968-1969) 32:588-606.

Clubb, Jerome M., William H. Flanigan, and Nancy H. Zingale. *Partisan Realignment: Voters, Parties and Government in American History.* Beverly Hills, Calif.: Sage, 1980.

Common Cause. *1972 Congressional Campaign Finances,* 10 vols. Washington, D.C.: Common Cause, 1974.

_____. *1974 Congressional Campaign Finances,* 3 vols. Washington, D.C.: Common Cause, 1976.

Conover, Pamela Johnston, and Stanley Feldman. "The Origins and Meaning of Liberal/Conservative Self-Identification." *American Journal of Political Science* (1981) 25:617-45.

_____. "How People Organize the Political World." *American Journal of Political Science* (1984) 28:95-126.

_____. "Emotional Reactions to the Economy: I'm Mad as Hell and I'm Not Going to Take It Anymore." *American Journal of Political Science* (1986) 30:50-78.

_____. "Candidate Perception in an Ambiguous World: Campaigns, Cues, and Inference Processes." *American Journal of Political Science* (1989) 33:912-40.

_____. "Critique: Where is the Schema?" *American Political Science Review* (1991) 85:1364-69.

Converse, Philip E. "The Nature of Belief Systems in Mass Publics." In *Ideology and Discontent,* ed. David E. Apter. New York: Free Press, 1964.

_____. "Of Time and Partisan Stability." *Comparative Political Studies* (1969) 2:139-71.

_____. "Some Priority Variables in Comparative Electoral Research." In *Electoral Behavior: A Comparative Handbook,* ed. Richard Rose. New York: Free Press, 1974.

_____. "Public Opinion and Voting Behavior." In *Handbook of Political Science,* vol. IV, ed. Fred I. Greenstein and Nelson W. Polsby. Reading, Mass.: Addison-Wesley, 1975.

_____. *The Dynamics of Party Support.* Beverly Hills, Calif.: Sage, 1976.

_____. "Popular Representation and the Distribution of Information." Paper presented at the Conference on Information and Democratic Processes, Champaign-Urbana, 1986.

Converse, Philip E., Angus Campbell, Warren E. Miller, and Donald E. Stokes. "Stability and Change in 1960: A Reinstating Election." *American Political Science Review* (1961) 55:269-80.

Converse, Philip E., and Gregory B. Markus. " 'Plus ça Change . . .': The New CPS Election Study Panel." *American Political Science Review* (1979) 73:2-49. Chapter 8 in *Classics.*

Converse, Philip E., and Roy Pierce. "Measuring Partisanship." *Political Methodology* (1985) 11:143-66.

_____. *Political Representation in France.* Cambridge: Harvard University Press, 1986.

Conway, Margaret. *Political Participation in the United States,* 2d ed. Washington, D.C.: CQ Press, 1991.

Cover, Albert D. "The Advantage of Incumbency in Congressional Elections." Unpublished Ph.D. dissertation, Yale University, 1976.

Cox, Gary W., and Samuel Kernell, eds. *The Politics of Divided Government.* Boulder, Colo.: Westview, 1991.

Cox, Gary W., and Michael C. Munger. "Closeness, Expenditures, and Turnout in the 1982 U.S. House Elections." *American Political Science Review* (1989) 83:217-31.

Craig, Stephen C. "Partisanship, Independence, and No Preference: Another Look at the Measurement of Party Independence." *American Journal of Political Science* (1985) 29:274-90.

Crewe, Ivor. "Electoral Participation." In *Democracy at the Polls: A Comparative Study of Competitive National Elections,* ed. David Butler, Howard R. Penniman, and Austin Ranney. Washington, D.C.: American Enterprise Institute, 1981.

Crewe, Ivor, and Martin Harrop, eds. *Political Communications: The General Election Campaign of 1987.* Cambridge: Cambridge University Press, 1989.

Crotty, William, and Gary C. Jacobson. *American Parties in Decline.* Boston: Little, Brown, 1980.

Dahl, Robert A. *Modern Political Analysis,* 4th ed. Englewood Cliffs, N.J.: Prentice-Hall, 1984.

Dalton, Russell J. *Citizen Politics in Western Democracies.* Chatham, N.J.: Chatham House, 1988.

Davis, James A., and Tom W. Smith. *General Social Surveys 1972-1987: Cumulative Codebook and Data File.* Chicago: University of Chicago, 1987.

Davis, Otto A., Melvin J. Hinich, and Peter C. Ordeshook. "An Expository Development of a Mathematical Model of the Electoral Process." *American Political Science Review* (1970) 64:426-48.

Declerq, Eugene, Thomas L. Hurley, and Norman R. Luttbeg. "Voting in American Presidential Elections: 1956-1972." *American Politics Quarterly* (1975) 3:247-83.

de Guchteneire, Paul, Lawrence LeDuc, and Richard G. Niemi. "A Compendium of Survey Studies of Elections around the World, Update 1." *Electoral Studies* (1991) 10:231-43.

DeNardo, James. "Turnout and the Vote: The Joke's on the Democrats." *American Political Science Review* (1980) 74:406-20.

Dennis, Jack. "Political Independence in America, Part I: On Being an Independent Partisan Supporter." *British Journal of Political Science* (1988a) 18:77-109.

———. "Political Independence in America, Part II: Towards a Theory." *British Journal of Political Science* (1988b) 18:197-219.

Denver, D. T. and H. T. Hands. "Marginality and Turnout in British General Elections." *British Journal of Political Science* (1975) 4:17-35.

DeVoursney, Robert M. Issues and Electoral Instability: A Test of Alternative Explanations for Voting Defection in the 1968 American Presidential Election. Unpublished Ph.D. thesis. Chapel Hill: University of North Carolina, 1977.

Dinkel, Reiner. "Political Business Cycles in Germany and the United States: Some Theoretical and Empirical Considerations." In *Contemporary Political Economy,* ed. Douglas A. Hibbs, Jr., and Heino Fassbender. Amsterdam: North-Holland, 1981.

Dooling, D. James, and Roy Lachman. "Effects of Comprehension on Retention of Prose." *Journal of Experimental Psychology* (1971) 88:216-22.

Downs, Anthony. *An Economic Theory of Democracy.* New York: Harper and Row, 1957.

Duncan, Otis Dudley. "Ability and Achievement." *Eugenics Quarterly* (1968) 15:1-11.

Edsall, Thomas Byrne. "The Reagan Legacy." In *The Republican Legacy,* ed. Sidney Blumenthal and Thomas Byrne Edsall. New York: Pantheon, 1988.

Eisenger, Peter K. "Black Employment in Municipal Jobs: The Impact of Black Political Power." *American Political Science Review* (1982) 76:380-92.

Erikson, Robert S. "The 'Uncorrelated Errors' Approach to the Problem of Causal Feedback." *Journal of Politics* (1982) 44:863-81.

———. "The Puzzle of Midterm Loss." *Journal of Politics* (1988) 50:1011-29.

———. "Economic Conditions and the Presidential Vote." *American Political Science Review* (1989a) 83:567-73.

———. "Why the Democrats Lose Presidential Elections: Toward a Theory of Optimal Loss." *PS: Political Science and Politics* (1989b) 22:30-35.

———. "Economic Conditions and the Congressional Vote: A Review of the Macrolevel Evidence." *American Journal of Political Science* (1990) 34:373-99.

Erikson, Robert S., Thomas D. Lancaster, and David W. Romero. "Group Components of the Presidential Vote, 1952-1984." *Journal of Politics* (1989) 51:337-46.

Erikson, Robert S., and Kent L. Tedin. "The 1928-1936 Partisan Realignment: The Case for the Conversion Hypothesis." *American Political Science Review* (1981) 75:951-62.

Erskine, Hazel G. "The Polls: The Informed Public." *Public Opinion Quarterly* (1962) 26:669-77.

———. "The Polls: Textbook Knowledge." *Public Opinion Quarterly* (1963a) 27:133-41.

———. "The Polls: Exposure to Domestic Information." *Public Opinion Quarterly* (1963b) 27:491-500.

———. "The Polls: Exposure to International Information." *Public Opinion Quarterly* (1963c) 27:658-62.

Fair, Ray C. "The Effects of Economic Events on Votes for President." *Review of Economics and Statistics* (1978) 60:159-73.

———. "The Effect of Economic Events on Votes for President: A 1984 Update." *Political Behavior* (1988) 10:168-79.

Farkas, Steve, Robert Y. Shapiro, and Benjamin I. Page. "The Dynamics of Public Opinion and Policy." Paper presented at the annual meeting of the American Association for Public Opinion Research, Lancaster, PA., 1990.

Farley, Reynolds, and Walter R. Allen. *The Color Line and the Quality of Life in America.* New York: Russell Sage, 1987.

Fazio, Russell H. "How Do Attitudes Guide Behavior?" In *The Handbook of Motivation and Cognition,* ed. R. M. Sorrentino and E. T. Higgins. New York: Guilford, 1986.

———. "Self-Perception Theory: A Current Perspective." In *Social Influence,* ed. Mark P. Zanna, James M. Olson, and C. P. Herman, The Ontario Symposium, vol. 5. Hillsdale, N.J.: Lawrence Erlbaum, 1987.

Fazio, Russell H., J. Chen, E. C. McDonel, and S. J. Sherman. "Attitude Accessibility, Attitude-Behavior Consistency, and the Strength of the Object-Evaluation Association." *Journal of Experimental Social Psychology* (1982) 18:339-57.

Fazio, Russell H., Paul M. Herr, and Timothy J. Olney. "Attitude Accessibility Following a Self-Perception Process." *Journal of Personality and Social Psychology* (1984) 47:277-86.

Fazio, Russell H., and C. J. Williams. "Attitude Accessibility as a Moderator of the Attitude-Perception and Attitude-Behavior Relations: An Investigation of the 1984 Presidential Election." *Journal of Personality and Social Psychology* (1986) 51:505-14.

Fazio, Russell H., and M. P. Zanna. "Direct Experience and Attitude-Behavior Consistency." In *Advances in Experimental Social Psychology,* vol. 14, ed. L. Berkowitz. New York: Academic Press, 1981.

Federal Election Commission. *FEC Reports on Financial Activity, 1977-1978, Interim*

Report No. 5: U.S. Senate and House Campaigns. Washington, D.C.: Federal Election Commission, 1979.

————. *FEC Reports on Financial Activity, 1979-1980, Final Report: U.S. Senate and House Campaigns.* Washington, D.C.: Federal Election Commission, 1982.

————. *FEC Reports on Financial Activity, 1981-1982, Interim Report No. 3: U.S. Senate and House Campaigns.* Washington, D.C.: Federal Election Commission, 1983.

————. *FEC Reports on Financial Activity, 1983-1984, Interim Report No. 9: U.S. Senate and House Campaigns.* Washington, D.C.: Federal Election Commission, 1985.

Feldman, Stanley. "Economic Self-interest and Political Behavior." *American Journal of Political Science* (1982) 26:446-66.

————. "Economic Self-interest and the Vote: Evidence and Meaning." In *Economic Conditions and Electoral Outcomes*, ed. Heinz Eulau and Michael S. Lewis-Beck. New York: Agathon, 1985.

Feldman, Stanley, and Pamela Johnston Conover. "Candidates, Issues and Voters: The Role of Inference in Political Perception." *Journal of Politics* (1983) 45:810-39.

Ferejohn, John A. "On the Decline of Competition in Congressional Elections." *American Political Science Review* (1977) 71:166-76.

Field, John Osgood, and Ronald E. Anderson. "Ideology in the Public's Conceptualization of the 1964 Election." *Public Opinion Quarterly* (1969) 33:380-98.

Fiorina, Morris P. *Congress: Keystone of the Washington Establishment.* New Haven, Conn.: Yale University Press, 1977.

————. *Retrospective Voting in American National Elections.* New Haven, Conn.: Yale University Press, 1981.

————. *Divided Government.* New York: Macmillan, 1992.

Fiske, Susan T., and Donald R. Kinder. "Involvement, Expertise, and Schema Use: Evidence from Political Cognition." In *Personality, Cognition, and Social Interaction*, ed. Nancy Cantor and John F. Kihlstrom. Hillsdale, N.J.: Lawrence Erlbaum, 1981.

Fiske, Susan T., Donald R. Kinder, and W. Michael Larter. "The Novice and the Expert: Knowledge-based Transmission Strategies in Political Cognition." *Journal of Experimental Social Psychology* (1983) 19:381-400.

Fiske, Susan T., and Mark A. Pavelchak. "Category-Based versus Piecemeal-Based Affective Responses: Developments in Schema-Triggered Affect." In *Handbook of Motivation and Cognition*, ed. Richard M. Sorrentino and E. Tory Higgins. New York: Guilford, 1986.

Fiske, Susan J., Felicia Pratto, and Mark A. Pavelchak. "Citizens' Images of Nuclear War: Contents and Consequences." *Journal of Social Issues* (1983) 39:41-66.

Fiske, Susan T., and Shelley E. Taylor. *Social Cognition.* New York: Random House, 1984.

Flanagan, Scott. "Electoral Change in Japan: A Study of Secular Realignment." In *Electoral Change*, ed. Russell J. Dalton, Scott C. Flanagan, and Paul Allen Beck. Princeton, N.J.: Princeton University Press, 1984.

Flanigan, William H., Wendy M. Rahn, and Nancy H. Zingale. "Political Parties as Objects of Identification and Orientation." Paper presented at the annual meeting of the Western Political Science Association, Salt Lake City, March, 1989.

Flanigan, William, and Nancy Zingale. *Political Behavior of the American Electorate*, 4th ed. Boston: Allyn & Bacon, 1979.

Fleishman, John A. "Trends in Self-Identified Ideology from 1972-1982: No Support for the Salience Hypothesis." *American Journal of Political Science* (1986) 30:517-41.

Franklin, Charles H. "Issue Preferences, Socialization, and the Evolution of Party Identification." *American Journal of Political Science* (1984) 28:459-78.

Franklin, Charles H., and John E. Jackson. "The Dynamics of Party Identification." *American Political Science Review* (1983) 77:957-73.

Franklin, Mark, Tom Mackie, Henry Valen, et al. *Electoral Change: Responses to Evolving Social and Attitudinal Structures in Western Countries.* Cambridge: Cambridge University Press, 1992.

Frankovic, Kathleen A. "The 1984 Election: The Irrelevance of the Campaign." *PS* (1985) 18:39-47.

Freeman, John R. "Granger Causality and the Time Series Analysis of Political Relationships." *American Journal of Political Science* (1983) 27:327-58.

Fuchs, Dieter, and Hans-Dieter Klingemann. "The Left-Right Schema." In *Continuities in Political Action,* ed. M. Kent Jennings, Jan W. van Deth, et al. Berlin: deGruyter, 1990.

Gallup, George H. *The Gallup Poll: Public Opinion 1935-1971.* New York: Random House, 1972.

Garand, James. "Electoral Marginality in State Legislative Elections, 1968-86." *Legislative Studies Quarterly* (1991) 16:7-28.

Gelman, Andrew, and Gary King. "Estimating Incumbency Advantage Without Bias." *American Journal of Political Science* (1990) 34:1142-64.

Gibson, James L., and Richard D. Bingham. *Civil Liberties and Nazis: The Skokie Free Speech Controversy.* New York: Praeger, 1985.

Gibson, James L., and James P. Wenzel. "Intelligence, Cognitive Sophistication, and Political Tolerance." Paper presented at the annual meeting of the Midwest Political Science Association, 1988.

Gilliam, Franklin D. "Influences on Voter Turnout for U.S. House Elections in Non-Presidential Years." *Legislative Studies Quarterly* (1985) 10:339-51.

Gilliam, Franklin D., and Lawrence Bobo. "The Motivational Bases of Black Political Participation in the 1980s." Paper presented at the annual meeting of the National Conference of Black Political Scientists, Washington, D.C.: 1988.

Gilliam, Franklin D., and Kenny J. Whitby. "Race and Attitudes toward Social Welfare Spending." *Social Science Quarterly* (1989) 70:86-100.

Glass, David P., Peverill Squire, and Raymond E. Wolfinger. "Voter Turnout: An International Comparison." *Public Opinion* (1984) December/January 49-55.

Glenn, Norval D. "Problems of Comparability in Trend Studies with Opinion Poll Data." *Public Opinion Quarterly* (1970) 34:82-91.

Glenn, Norval D., and Michael Grimes. "Aging, Voting, and Political Interest." *American Sociological Review* (1968) 33:563-75.

Goldberg, Arthur S. "Discerning a Causal Pattern Among Data on Voting Behavior." *American Political Science Review* (1966) 60:913-22.

Goldberger, Arthur S. *Econometric Theory.* New York: Wiley, 1964.

――――. *Topics in Regression Analysis.* New York: Macmillan, 1968.

Goldberger, Arthur S., A. L. Nagar, and H. S. Odeh. "The Covariance Matrices of Reduced Form Coefficients and of Forecasts for a Structural Economic Model." *Econometrica* (1961) 29:556-73.

Golden, David G., and James M. Poterba. "The Price of Popularity: The Political Business Cycle Reexamined." *American Journal of Political Science* (1980) 24:696-714.

Graber, Doris A. *Processing the News: How People Tame the Information Tide.* New York: Longman, 1984.

――――. *Mass Media and American Politics,* 3d ed. Washington, D.C.: CQ Press, 1989.

Granberg, Donald, and Sören Holmberg. *The Political System Matters: Social Psychology and Voting Behavior in Sweden and the United States.* New York: Cambridge University Press, 1988.

Granger, Clive W. J. "Investigating Causal Relations by Econometric Models and Cross Spectral Methods." *Econometrica* (1969) 37:424-38.

Green, Donald Philip. "On the Dimensionality of Public Sentiment toward Partisan and Ideological Groups." *American Journal of Political Science* (1988) 32:758-80.

Green, Donald Philip, and Jonathan S. Krasno. "Salvation for the Spendthrift Incumbent: Reestimating the Effects of Campaign Spending in House Elections." *American Journal of Political Science* (1988) 32:884-907.

_____. "Rebuttal to Jacobson's 'New Evidence for Old Arguments'." *American Journal of Political Science* (1990) 34:363-72.

Green, Donald Philip, and Bradley Palmquist. "Of Artifacts and Partisan Instability." *American Journal of Political Science* (1990) 34:872-901.

Greir, Kevin B. "On the Existence of a Political Monetary Cycle." *American Journal of Political Science* (1989) 33:376-89.

Grofman, Bernard, and Chandler Davidson, eds. *Controversies in Minority Voting: The Voting Rights Act in Twenty-Five Year Perspective.* Washington, D.C.: Brookings, 1992.

Grofman, Bernard, and Lisa Handley. "The Impact of the Voting Rights Act on Black Representation in Southern State Legislatures." *Legislative Studies Quarterly* (1991) 16:111-28.

Grofman, Bernard, Lisa Handley, and Richard G. Niemi. *Minority Representation and the Quest for Voting Equality.* New York: Cambridge University Press, 1992.

Guterbock, Thomas M., and Bruce London. "Race, Political Orientation, and Participation: An Empirical Test of Four Competing Theories." *American Sociological Review* (1983) 48:439-53.

Hagner, Paul R., and John C. Pierce. "Correlative Characteristics of Levels of Conceptualization in the American Public, 1952-1976." *Journal of Politics* (1982) 44:779-807.

_____. "Liberal Is a Four-Letter Word: Campaign Rhetoric and the Measure of Political Conceptualization." Paper presented at the annual meeting of the Midwest Political Science Association, Chicago, 1991.

Hamill, Ruth, and Milton Lodge. "Cognitive Consequences of Political Sophistication." In *Political Cognition,* ed. Richard R. Lau and David O. Sears. Hillsdale, N.J.: Lawrence Erlbaum, 1986.

Hamill, Ruth, Milton Lodge, and Frederick Blake. "The Breadth, Depth, and Utility of Class, Partisan, and Ideological Schemata." *American Journal of Political Science* (1985) 29:850-70.

Hamilton, Charles V. "Political Access, Minority Participation, and the New Normalcy." In *Minority Report,* ed. Leslie W. Dunbar. New York: Pantheon, 1984.

_____. "Social Policy and the Welfare of Black Americans: From Rights to Resources." *Political Science Quarterly* (1986) 101:239-55.

Harman, H. H. *Modern Factor Analysis.* Chicago: University of Chicago Press, 1976.

Harvey, S. K., and T. G. Harvey. "Adolescent Political Outlooks: The Effects of Intelligence as an Independent Variable." *Midwest Journal of Political Science* (1970) 14:565-94.

Hastie, Reid. "A Primer of Information-Processing Theory for the Political Scientist." In *Political Cognition,* ed. Richard R. Lau and David O. Sears. Hillsdale, N.J.: Lawrence Erlbaum, 1986.

Hastie, Reid, and Bernadette Park. "The Relationship between Memory and Judgment

Depends on Whether the Task Is Memory-Based or On-line." *Psychological Review* (1986) 93:258-68.

Heath, Anthony, John Curtice, Roger Jowell, et al. *Understanding Political Change: The British Voter 1964-1987.* Oxford: Pergamon Press, 1991.

Heath, Anthony, and Roy Pierce. "It Was Party Identification All Along: Question Order Effects on Reports of Party Identification in Britain." Paper presented at the annual meeting of the American Political Science Association, Washington, D.C., 1991.

Herman, Valentine, with Françoise Mendel. *Parliaments of the World.* London: Macmillan, 1976.

Hero, A. O. *Americans in World Affairs,* vol. 1: *Studies in Citizen Participation in International Relations.* Boston: World Peace Foundation, 1959.

Herrnson, Paul S. *Party Campaigning in the 1980s.* Cambridge, Mass.: Harvard University Press.

Herstein, John A. "Keeping the Voter's Limits in Mind: A Cognitive Process Analysis of Decision Making in Voting." *Journal of Personality and Social Psychology* (1981) 40:843-61.

Hess, Stephen, and Michael Nelson. "Foreign Policy: Dominance and Decisiveness in Presidential Elections." In *The Elections of 1984,* ed. Michael Nelson. Washington, D.C.: Congressional Quarterly, 1985.

Hibbing, John R., and John R. Alford. "Constituency Population and Representation in the U.S. Senate." *Legislative Studies Quarterly* (1990) 15:581-98.

Hibbs, Douglas A. "Political Parties and Macroeconomic Policy." *American Political Science Review* (1977) 71:1467-87.

———. "Contemporary Political Economy: An Overview." In *Contemporary Political Economy,* ed. Douglas A. Hibbs, Jr., and Heino Fassbender. Amsterdam: North-Holland, 1981.

———. "The Dynamics of Political Support for American Presidents Among Occupational and Partisan Groups." *American Journal of Political Science* (1982a) 26:312-32.

———. "Economic Outcomes and Political Support for British Governments Among Occupational Classes: A Dynamic Analysis." *American Political Science Review* (1982b) 76:259-79.

Hicks, Alexander M., and Duane H. Swank. "Politics, Institutions, and Welfare Spending in Industrialized Democracies, 1960-1982." *American Political Science Review* (1992) 86:forthcoming.

Higgins, E. T., and G. King. "Accessibility of Social Constructs: Information Processing Consequences of Individual and Contextual Variability." In *Personality, Cognition, and Social Interaction,* ed. N. Cantor and J. Kihlstrom. Hillsdale, N.J.: Lawrence Erlbaum, 1981.

Hinckley, Barbara. "House Re-elections and Senate Defeats: The Role of the Challenger." *British Journal of Political Science* (1980) 10:441-60.

Holbrook, Thomas M., and Charles M. Tidmarch. "Sophomore Surge in State Legislative Elections." *Legislative Studies Quarterly* (1991) 16:49-63.

Holm, John D., and John P. Robinson. "Ideological Identification and the American Voter." *Public Opinion Quarterly* (1978) 42:235-46.

Holmberg, Sören. *Svenska Väljare.* Stockholm: Lieber, 1981.

Howell, Susan E. "Short Term Forces and Changing Partisanship." *Political Behavior* (1981) 3:163-80.

Hughes, Barry. *The Domestic Content of American Foreign Policy.* San Francisco: W. H. Freeman, 1978.

Hugick, Larry. "Party Identification Stable Since the Mid-1980s." *The Gallup Poll Monthly.* (1991a) 311 (Aug.):47.

———. "Party Identification: The Disparity between Gallup's In-Person and Telephone Interview Findings." *The Public Perspective* (1991b) 2(No.6):23.

Hurwitz, John, and Mark Peffley. "The Means and Ends of Foreign Policy as Determinants of Presidential Support." *American Journal of Political Science* (1987) 31:236-58.

Hyman, Herbert H., and Paul B. Sheatsley. "Some Reasons Why Information Campaigns Fail." *Public Opinion Quarterly* (1947) 11:412-23.

Inglehart, Ronald. *The Silent Revolution: Changing Values and Political Styles Among Western Publics.* Princeton, N.J.: Princeton University Press, 1977.

———. "Political Action: The Impact of Values, Cognitive Level and Social Background." In *Political Action: Mass Participation in Five Western Democracies.* ed. Samuel Barnes and Max Kaase. Beverly Hills, Calif.: Sage, 1979.

———. *Culture Shift in Advanced Industrial Society.* Princeton, N.J.: Princeton University Press, 1990.

Irvine, William P. "Testing Explanations of Voting Turnout in Canada." In *Party Identification and Beyond,* ed. Ian Budge, Ivor Crewe, and Dennis Farlie. London: Wiley, 1976.

Iyengar, Shanto. "Shortcuts to Political Knowledge: The Role of Selective Attention and Accessibility." In *Information and Democratic Processes,* ed. John Ferejohn and James Kuklinski. Urbana: University of Illinois Press, 1990.

Iyengar, Shanto, and Donald R. Kinder. "More Than Meets the Eye: TV News, Priming, and Public Evaluations of the President." In *Public Communication and Behavior,* Vol. 1. ed. George Comstock. New York: Academic Press, 1986.

———. *News That Matters.* Chicago: University of Chicago Press, 1987.

Iyengar, Shanto, Donald R. Kinder, Mark D. Peters, and Jon A. Krosnick. "The Evening News and Presidential Evaluations." *Journal of Personality and Social Psychology* (1984) 46:778-87.

Iyengar, Shanto, Mark D. Peters, and Donald R. Kinder. "Experimental Demonstrations of the Not-So-Minimal Consequences of Television News Programs." *American Political Science Review* (1982) 76:848-58.

Jackman, Robert. "Political Institutions and Vote Turnout in the Industrial Democracies." *American Political Science Review* (1987) 81:405-23.

Jackson, Byran O., and Melvin L. Oliver. "Race and Politics in the Advanced-Industrial City: A Critical Assessment of Los Angeles Mayor Tom Bradley's Job Performance." Paper presented at the annual meeting of the American Political Science Association, Washington, D.C., 1988.

Jackson, John E. "Issues, Party Choices, and Presidential Votes." *American Journal of Political Science* (1975) 19:161-85.

Jacobson, Gary C. "The Effects of Campaign Spending in Congressional Elections." *American Political Science Review* (1978) 72:469-91.

———. *Money in Congressional Elections.* New Haven, Conn.: Yale University Press, 1980.

———. "Money and Votes Reconsidered: Congressional Elections, 1972-1982." *Public Choice* (1985) 47:7-62.

———. "The Marginals Never Vanished: Incumbency and Competition in Elections to the U.S. House of Representatives." *American Journal of Political Science* (1987a) 31:126-41.

———. *The Politics of Congressional Elections.* Boston: Little, Brown, 1987b.

_____. "Enough Is Too Much: Money and Competition in House Elections, 1972-1984." In *Elections in America,* ed. Kay L. Schlozman. New York: Allen and Unwin, 1987c.

_____. "Strategic Politicians and the Dynamics of U.S. House Elections." *American Political Science Review* (1989) 83:773-94.

_____. "Does the Economy Matter in Midterm Elections?" *American Journal of Political Science* (1990a) 34:400-04.

_____. *The Electoral Origins of Divided Government: Competition in U.S. House Elections, 1946-1988.* Boulder, Colo.: Westview Press, 1990b.

_____. "The Effects of Campaign Spending in House Elections: New Evidence for Old Arguments." *American Journal of Political Science* (1990c) 34:334-63.

Jacobson, Gary C., and Samuel Kernell. *Strategy and Choice in Congressional Elections.* New Haven, Conn.: Yale University Press, 1981, 1983.

Jacoby, William G. "Levels of Conceptualization and Reliance on the Liberal-Conservative Continuum." *Journal of Politics* (1986) 48:423-32.

_____. "The Sources of Liberal-Conservative Thinking." *Political Behavior* (1988) 10:316-22.

Janda, Kenneth. *Political Parties: A Cross-National Survey.* New York: Free Press, 1980.

Jennings, James. "Blacks and Progressive Politics." In *The New Black Politics,* ed. Rod Bush. San Francisco: Synthesis, 1984.

Jennings, M. Kent, and Gregory B. Markus. "Partisan Orientations over the Long Haul: Results from the Three-wave Political Socialization Panel Study." *American Political Science Review* (1984) 78:1000-18.

Jennings, M. Kent, and Richard G. Niemi. "The Transmission of Political Values from Parent to Child." *American Political Science Review* (1968) 62:169-84.

_____. *The Political Character of Adolescence.* Princeton, N.J.: Princeton University Press, 1974.

_____. *Generations and Politics.* Princeton, N.J.: Princeton University Press, 1981.

Johnston, J. *Econometric Methods,* 3rd ed. New York: McGraw Hill, 1984.

Joint Center for Political Studies. *Black Elected Officials: A National Roster.* Washington: JCPS, 1986, 1988.

Jones, Mack H. "A Frame of Reference for Black Politics." In *Black Political Life in the United States,* ed. Lenneal J. Henderson. San Francisco: Chandler, 1972.

Junn, Jane. "Participation and Political Knowledge." In *Political Participation and American Democracy,* ed. William Crotty. Westport, Conn.: Greenwood, 1991.

Kagay, Michael R., and Greg A. Caldeira. "I Like the Looks of His Face: Elements of Electoral Choice, 1952-1972." Paper presented at the annual meeting of the American Political Science Association, San Francisco, 1975.

Kamieniecki, Sheldon. *Party Identification, Political Behavior, and the American Electorate.* Westport, Conn.: Greenwood, 1985.

_____. "The Dimensionality of Partisan Strength and Political Independence." *Political Behavior* (1988) 10:364-76.

Katosh, John P., and Michael W. Traugott. "Consequences of Validated and Self-reported Voting Measures." *Public Opinion Quarterly* (1981) 45:519-35.

Keech, William R. "Of Honeymoons and Economic Performance: Comment on Hibbs." *American Political Science Review* (1982) 76:280-81.

Keith, Bruce E., David B. Magleby, Candice L. Nelson, Elizabeth Orr, Mark C. Westlye, and Raymond E. Wolfinger. "The Partisan Affinities of Independent 'Leaners'." *British Journal of Political Science* (1986) 16:155-85.

Kelley, Stanley, Jr., and Thad W. Mirer. "The Simple Act of Voting." *American Political Science Review* (1974) 68:572-91.

Kenney, Patrick J., and Tom W. Rice. "The Effect of Primary Divisiveness in Gubernatorial and Senatorial Elections." *Journal of Politics* (1984) 46:904-15.

———. "The Evaporating Independents." *Public Opinion Quarterly* (1988) 52:231-39.

Kent, K. E., and Ramona R. Rush. "How Communication Behavior of Older Persons Affects Their Public Affairs Knowledge." *Journalism Quarterly* (1976) 53:40-46.

Kernell, Samuel. "Presidential Popularity and Negative Voting: An Alternative Explanation of the Midterm Congressional Decline of the President's Party." *American Political Science Review* (1977) 71:44-66.

———. "Explaining Presidential Popularity." *American Political Science Review* (1978) 72:506-22.

Kessel, John H. "Comment: The Issues in Issue Voting." *American Political Science Review* (1972) 66:459-65.

———. *Presidential Parties.* Homewood, Ill.: Dorsey, 1984.

———. *Presidential Campaign Politics.* Homewood, Ill.: Dorsey Press, 1980, 1988; Pacific Grove, Calif.: Brooks/Cole, 1992.

Key, V. O., Jr. *Southern Politics in State and Nation.* New York: Knopf, 1949.

———. "A Theory of Critical Elections." *Journal of Politics* (1955) 17:3-18.

———. "Secular Realignment and the Party System." *Journal of Politics* (1959) 21:198-210.

———. *The Responsible Electorate.* Cambridge, Mass.: Harvard University Press, 1966.

Kiewiet, D. Roderick. "Policy-Oriented Voting in Response to Economic Issues." *American Political Science Review* (1981) 75:448-59.

Kiewiet, D. Roderick, and Douglas Rivers. "A Retrospective on Retrospective Voting." *Political Behavior* (1984) 6:369-93.

Kinder, Donald R. "Diversity and Complexity in American Public Opinion." In *Political Science: The State of the Discipline,* ed. Ada W. Finifter. Washington, D.C.: American Political Science Association, 1983.

———. "Presidential Character Revisited." In *Political Cognitions,* ed. Richard R. Lau and David O. Sears. Hillsdale, N.J.: Lawrence Erlbaum, 1986.

Kinder, Donald R., Gordon Adams, and Paul Gronke. "Economics and Politics in the 1984 American Presidential Election." *American Journal of Political Science* (1989) 33:491-515.

Kinder, Donald R., and Susan T. Fiske. "Presidents in the Public Mind." In *Political Psychology,* ed. Margaret G. Hermann. San Francisco: Jossey-Bass, 1986.

Kinder, Donald R., and D. Roderick Kiewiet. "Economic Discontent and Political Behavior: The Role of Personal Grievances and Collective Economic Judgments in Congressional Voting." *American Journal of Political Science* (1979) 23:495-527.

———. "Sociotropic Politics." *British Journal of Political Science* (1981) 11:129-61.

Kinder, Donald R., and Walter R. Mebane, Jr. "Politics and Economics in Everyday Life." In *The Political Process and Economic Change,* ed. Kristen Monroe. New York: Agathon, 1983.

Kinder, Donald R., and David O. Sears. "Public Opinion and Political Action." In *Handbook of Social Psychology,* vol. 2, 3d ed., eds. Gardner Lindzey and Elliot Aronson. New York: Random House, 1985.

King, Gary, and Lyn Ragsdale. *The Elusive Executive.* Washington, D.C.: Congressional Quarterly Press.

Klingemann, Hans D. "Measuring Ideological Conceptualizations." In *Political Action: Mass Participation in Five Western Democracies,* Samuel H. Barnes et al. Beverly Hills, Calif.: Sage, 1979a.

———. "The Background of Ideological Conceptualization." In *Political Action,* Samuel H. Barnes et al. Beverly Hills, Calif.: Sage, 1979b.

_____. "Ideological Conceptualization and Political Action." In *Political Action*, Samuel H. Barnes et al. Beverly Hills, Calif.: Sage, 1979c.

Knight, Kathleen. "Ideology in the 1980 Election: Ideological Sophistication Does Matter." *Journal of Politics* (1985) 47:828-53.

_____. "Ideology and Public Opinion." *Micropolitics* (1990) 3:59-82.

Knoke, David, and Michael Hout. "Social and Demographic Factors in American Party Affiliation: 1952-1972." *American Sociological Review* (1974) 39:100-13.

Kramer, Bernard M., S. Michael Kalick, and M. A. Milburn. "Attitudes Toward Nuclear Weapons and Nuclear War: 1945-1982." *Journal of Social Issues* (1983) 39:7-24.

Kramer, Gerald H. "Short-Term Fluctuations in U.S. Voting Behavior." *American Political Science Review* (1971) 65:131-43.

_____. "The Ecological Fallacy Revisited: Aggregate- versus Individual-Level Findings on Economics and Elections and Sociotropic Voting." *American Political Science Review* (1983) 77:92-111.

Krane, Ronald E. *International Labor Migration in Europe*. New York: Praeger, 1979.

Krasno, Jonathan S., and Donald Philip Green. "Preempting Quality Challengers in House Elections." *Journal of Politics* (1988) 50:920-36.

Kriesberg, Martin. "Dark Areas of Ignorance." In *Public Opinion and Foreign Policy*, ed. Lester Markel. New York: Harper, 1949.

Krosnick Jon A. "The Role of Attitude Importance in Social Evaluation: A Study of Policy Preferences, Presidential Candidate Evaluations, and Voting Behavior." *Journal of Personality and Social Psychology* (1988) 55:196-210.

_____. "Government Policy and Citizen Passion: A Study of Issue Publics in Contemporary America." *Political Behavior* (1990) 12:59-92.

_____. "The Stability of Political Preferences: Comparisons of Symbolic and Nonsymbolic Attitudes." *American Journal of Political Science* (1991) 35:547-76.

Krosnick, Jon A., and Matthew K. Berent. "Comparisons of Party Identification and Policy Preferences: The Impact of Survey Question Format." Manuscript, Ohio State University, 1991.

Krosnick, Jon A., and Herbert F. Weisberg. "Ideological Structuring of Public Attitudes toward Social Groups and Politicians." Presented at the annual meeting of the American Political Science Association, Washington, D.C., 1988.

Kuklinski, James H., Robert C. Luskin, and John M. Bolland. "Where's the Schema? Going Beyond the 'S' Word in Political Psychology." *American Political Science Review* (1991) 85:1341-55.

Ladd, Everett Carll. "On Mandates, Realignments, and the 1984 Presidential Election." *Political Studies Quarterly* (1985) 100:1-25.

_____. "Like Waiting for Godot: The Uselessness of 'Realignment' for Understanding Change in Contemporary American Politics." In *The End of Realignment? Interpreting American Electoral Eras,* ed. Byron E. Shafer. Madison: University of Wisconsin Press, 1991.

Lane, Robert E. *Political Ideology*. New York: Free Press, 1962.

Langton, Kenneth P., and M. Kent Jennings. "Political Socialization and the High School Civics Curriculum in the United States." *American Political Science Review* (1968) 62:852-67.

Lanoue, David J. "Modeling Presidential Popularity: Do Real Disposable Income Levels Matter?" Paper presented at the annual meeting of the Midwest Political Science Association, Chicago, 1985.

Larkin, Jill, John McDermott, Dorothea P. Simon, and Herbert A. Simon. "Expert and Novice Performance in Solving Physics Problems." *Science* (1980) 208:1335-42.

Lau, Richard R. "Political Schemata, Candidate Evaluations, and Voting Behavior." In *Political Cognition,* ed. Richard R. Lau and David O. Sears. Hillsdale, N.J.: Lawrence Erlbaum, 1986.

Lau, Richard R., and David O. Sears. "Cognitive Links Between Economic Grievances and Political Responses." *Political Behavior* (1981) 3:279-302.

———, eds. *Political Cognition.* Hillsdale, N.J.: Lawrence Erlbaum, 1986.

Lazarsfeld, Paul F., Bernard Berelson, and Hazel Gaudet. *The People's Choice.* New York: Duell, Sloan and Pearce, 1944, 1948.

Lazarus, Richard. "Thoughts on the Relations Between Emotions and Cognition." *American Psychologist* (1982) 37:1019-24.

LeDuc, Lawrence. "The Dynamic Properties of Party Identification: A Four Nation Comparison." *European Journal of Political Research* (1981) 9:257-68.

Lee, L. F. "Simultaneous Equations Models with Discrete and Censored Dependent Variables." In *Structural Analysis of Discrete Data with Econometric Applications,* ed. C. F. Manski and D. McFadden. Cambridge, Mass.: The MIT Press, 1981.

Leighley, Jan E. "Social Interaction and Contextual Influences on Political Participation." *American Politics Quarterly* (1990) 18:459-75.

Leighley, Jan E., and Jonathan Nagler. "Individual and Systemic Influences on Turnout: Who Votes? 1984." Presented at the annual meeting of the Midwest Political Science Association, Chicago, 1990.

Levine, Stephen, and Alan Robinson. *The New Zealand Voter.* Wellington, New Zealand: New Zealand University Press and Price Milburn, 1976.

Levitin, Teresa E., and Warren E. Miller. "Ideological Interpretations of Presidential Elections." *American Political Science Review* (1979) 73:751-71.

Lewis-Beck, Michael S. *Economics and Elections: The Major Western Democracies.* Ann Arbor: University of Michigan Press, 1988.

Lewis-Beck, Michael S., and Brad Lockerbie. "Economics, Votes, Protests: Western European Cases." *Comparative Political Studies* (1989) 22:155-77.

Lewis-Beck, Michael S., and Tom W. Rice. "Are Senate Election Outcomes Predictable?" *PS* (1985) 18:745-54.

———. "Forecasting Presidential Elections: A Comparison of Naive Models." *Political Behavior* (1984) 6:9-21.

———. *Forecasting Elections.* Washington, D.C.: CQ Press, 1992.

Lichter, S. Robert, Daniel Amundson, and Richard Noyes. *The Video Campaign: Network Coverage of the 1988 Primaries.* Washington, D.C.: American Enterprise Institute, 1988.

Light, Paul C., and Celinda Lake. "The Election: Candidates, Strategies, and Decision." In *The Elections of 1984,* ed. Michael Nelson. Washington, D.C.: Congressional Quarterly, 1985.

Linz, Juan. "The New Spanish Party System." In *Electoral Participation: A Comparative Analysis,* ed. Richard Rose. Beverly Hills, Calif.: Sage, 1980.

Lipset, Seymour Martin, and Stein Rokkan. "Cleavage Structure, Party Systems and Voter Alignments." In *Party Systems and Voter Alignments,* ed. Seymour M. Lipset and Stein Rokkan. New York: Free Press, 1967.

Lockerbie, Brad. "The Influence of Levels of Information on the Use of Prospective Evaluations." *Political Behavior* (1991) 13:223-35.

Lodge, Milton G., and Ruth Hamill. "A Partisan Schema for Political Information Processing." *American Political Science Review* (1986) 80:505-19.

Lodge, Milton, and Kathleen M. McGraw. "Critique: Where is the Schema?" *American Political Science Review* (1991) 85:1357-64.

Lodge, Milton, Kathleen M. McGraw, and Patrick Stroh. "An Impression-Driven Model of Candidate Evaluation." *American Political Science Review* (1989) 83:399-419.

Lord, Charles G., Lee Ross, and Mark R. Lepper. "Biased Assimilation and Attitude Polarization: The Effects of Prior Theories on Subsequently Considered Evidence." *Journal of Personality and Social Psychology* (1979) 37:2098-2109.

Lord, Frederick M., and Melvin R. Novick. *Statistical Theories of Mental Test Scores.* Reading, Mass.: Addison-Wesley, 1968.

Luskin, Robert C. "Explaining Political Sophistication." Paper presented at the annual meeting of the Midwest Political Science Association, 1987a.

_____. "Measuring Political Sophistication." *American Journal of Political Science* (1987b) 31:856-99.

_____. "Explaining Political Sophistication." *Political Behavior* (1990) 12:331-61. Chapter 8 in this volume.

_____. "Abusus Non Tollit Usum: Standard Coefficients, Correlations, and R^2s. *American Journal of Political Science* (1991) 35:1032-46.

Luskin, Robert C., John P. McIver, and Edward G. Carmines. "Issues and the Transmission of Partisanship." *American Journal of Political Science* (1989) 33:440-58.

Mackie, Thomas, and Richard Rose. *The International Almanac of Electoral History,* 2d ed. New York: Free Press, 1982.

MacKuen, Michael B. "Social Communication and the Mass Policy Agenda." In *More Than News: Media Power in Public Affairs,* ed. Michael B. MacKuen and Steven L. Coombs. Beverly Hills, Calif.: Sage, 1981.

_____. "Political Drama, Economic Conditions, and the Dynamics of Presidential Popularity." *American Journal of Political Science* (1983) 27:165-92.

MacKuen, Michael B., Robert S. Erikson, and James A. Stimson. "On the Importance of Economic Experience and Expectations for Political Evaluations." Paper presented at the annual meeting of the American Political Science Association, Washington, D.C., 1988.

_____. "Macropartisanship." *American Political Science Review* (1990) 89:1125-42. Chapter 17 in this volume.

_____. "Question-Wording and Macropartisanship." *American Political Science Review* (1992a) 86:475-81.

_____. "Peasants or Bankers? The American Electorate and the U.S. Economy." *American Political Science Review* (1992b) 86:forthcoming.

Madsen, Henrik Jess. "Electoral Outcomes and Macro-Economic Policies: The Scandinavian Cases." In *Models of Political Economy,* ed. Paul Whiteley. London: Sage, 1980.

_____. "Partisanship and Macroeconomic Outcomes: A Reconsideration." In *Contemporary Political Economy,* ed. Douglas A. Hibbs, Jr., and Heino Fassbender. Amsterdam: North-Holland, 1981.

Maggiotto, Michael A., and William Mishler. "Tracing the Economic Roots of Partisanship: A Time Series Analysis, 1946-1984." Paper presented at the annual meeting of the Midwestern Political Science Association, Chicago, 1987.

Maisel, Louis Sandy. *From Obscurity to Oblivion: Running in the Congressional Primaries.* Knoxville: University of Tennessee Press, 1982.

Mann, Thomas E. *Unsafe at Any Margin: Interpreting Congressional Elections.* Washington, D.C.: American Enterprise Institute, 1978.

Mann, Thomas E., and Raymond E. Wolfinger. "Candidates and Parties in Congressional Elections." *American Political Science Review* (1980) 74:617-32. Chapter 20 in *Classics.*

Marcus, George, "A Theory and Methodology for Measuring Emotions in Politics." Manuscript, 1986.

———. "The Structure of Emotional Response: 1984 Presidential Candidates." *American Political Science Review* (1988) 82:737-62.

Margolis, Michael. "From Confusion to Confusion: Issues and the American Voter (1956-1972)." *American Political Science Review* (1977) 71:31-43.

Markus, Gregory B. 'The Political Environment and the Dynamics of Public Attitudes: A Panel Study." *American Journal of Political Science* (1979) 23:338-59.

———. "Political Attitudes During an Election Year: A Report on the 1980 NES Panel Study." *American Political Science Review* (1982) 76:538-60.

Markus, Gregory B., and Philip E. Converse. "A Dynamic Simultaneous Equation Model of Electoral Choice." *American Political Science Review* (1979) 73:1055-70. Chapter 14 in *Classics*.

Markus, Hazel, and Robert B. Zanjoc. "The Cognitive Perspective in Social Psychology." In *Handbook of Social Psychology*, vol. 1, 3d ed., ed. Gardner Lindzey and Elliot Aronson. New York: Random House, 1985.

Marquette, Jesse, and Katherine Hinckley. "Voter Turnout and Candidate Choice." *Political Behavior* (1988) 10:52-76.

Marra, Robin F., and Charles W. Ostrom, Jr. "Explaining Seat Change in the U.S. House of Representatives, 1950-1986." *American Journal of Political Science* (1989) 33:541-69.

Marshall, T. R. *Presidential Nominations in a Reform Age*. New York: Praeger, 1981.

Mattei, Franco, and Richard G. Niemi. "Unrealized Partisans, Realized Independents, and the Integenerational Transmission of Partisan Identification." *Journal of Politics* (1991) 53:161-74.

Matthews, Donald R. " 'Winnowing': The News Media and the 1976 Presidential Nominations." In *Race for the Presidency: The Media and the Nominating Process*, ed. James David Barber. Englewood Cliffs, N.J.: Prentice-Hall, 1978.

Matthews, Donald R., and James W. Prothro. *Negroes and the New Southern Politics*. New York: Harcourt Brace, 1966.

Mayhew, David R. "Congressional Elections: The Case of the Vanishing Marginals." *Polity* (1974) 6:295-317. Chapter 18 in *Classics*.

———. *Divided We Govern: Party Control, Lawmaking, and Investigations, 1946-1990*. New Haven, Conn.: Yale University Press, 1991.

McClosky, Herbert. "Consensus and Ideology in American Politics." *American Political Science Review* (1964) 58:371-82.

McClosky, Herbert, and John R. Zaller. *The American Ethos: Public Attitudes Toward Capitalism and Democracy*. Cambridge, Mass.: Harvard University Press, 1984.

McClure, Robert D., and Thomas E. Patterson. "Print vs. Network News." *Journal of Communication* (1976) 26:18-22.

McDonald, Michael D., and Susan E. Howell. "Reconsidering the Reconceptualization of Party Identification." *Political Methodology* (1982) 8:73-91.

McGraw, Kathleen M., Milton Lodge, and Patrick Stroh, "On-Line Processing in Candidate Evaluation: The Effects of Issue Order, Issue Importance and Sophistication." *Political Behavior* (1990) 12:41-58.

McKelvey, Richard D., and Peter C. Ordeshook. "Sequential Elections with Limited Information." *American Journal of Political Science* (1985) 29:480-512.

McPherson, J. Miller. "Correlates of Social Participation: A Comparison of the Ethnic Community and Compensatory Theory." *Sociological Quarterly* (1977) 18:197-208.

Meehl, Peter E. "The Selfish Voter Paradox and the Thrown-Away Vote Argument." *American Political Science Review* (1977) 71:11-30.

Merelman, Richard. *Political Socialization and Educational Climates: A Study of Two School Districts.* New York: Holt, Rinehart and Winston, 1971.

———. "Communication." *American Political Science Review* (1981) 74:319-32.

Merriam, Charles E., and Harold F. Gosnell. *Non-Voting: Causes and Methods of Control.* Chicago: University of Chicago Press, 1924.

Metzner, C. A. *Interest, Information and Attitudes in the Field of World Affairs.* Ann Arbor: Survey Research Center, University of Michigan, 1949.

Milbrath, Lester W., and M. L. Goel. *Political Participation,* 2d ed. Chicago: Rand McNally, 1977.

Miller, Arthur H. "Critique: Where is the Schema?" *American Political Science Review* (1991) 85:1369-77.

Miller, Arthur H., Patricia Gurin, Gerald Gurin, and Oksana Malanchuk. "Group Consciousness and Political Participation." *American Journal of Political Science* (1981) 25:494-511.

Miller, Arthur H., and Warren E. Miller. "Ideology in the 1972 Election: Myth or Reality—A Rejoinder." *American Political Science Review* (1976) 70:832-49.

Miller, Arthur H., Warren E. Miller, Alden S. Raine, and Thad H. Brown. "A Majority Party in Disarray: Policy Polarization in the 1972 Election." *American Political Science Review* (1976) 70:753-78.

Miller, Arthur H., and Martin P. Wattenberg. "Policy and Performance Voting in the 1980 Election." Presented at the annual meeting of the American Political Science Association, New York, 1981.

———. "Measuring Party Identification: Independent or No Partisan Preference?" *American Journal of Political Science* (1983) 27:106-21.

———. "Throwing the Rascals Out: Policy and Performance Evaluations of Presidential Candidates, 1952-1980." *American Political Science Review* (1985) 79:359-72.

Miller, Arthur H., Martin P. Wattenberg, and Oksana Malanchuk. "Schematic Assessments of Presidential Candidates." *American Political Science Review* (1986) 80:521-40.

Miller, Mark J. *Foreign Workers in Western Europe.* New York: Praeger, 1981.

Miller, Warren E. "The Electorate's View of the Parties." In *The Parties Respond,* ed. Sandy Maisel. Boulder, Colo.: Westview, 1990.

———. "Party Identification, Realignment, and Party Voting: Back to the Basics." *American Political Science Review* (1991) 85:557-68.

———. "The Puzzle Transformed: Explaining Declining Turnout." *Political Behavior* (1992a) 14:1-43.

———. "Generational Changes in Party Identification." *Political Behavior* (1992b) 14:forthcoming.

Miller, Warren E., and Teresa E. Levitin. *Leadership and Change.* Cambridge, Mass.: Winthrop, 1976.

Miller, Warren E., Arthur H. Miller, and Edward J. Schneider. *American National Election Studies Sourcebook, 1952-1978.* Cambridge, Mass.: Harvard University Press, 1980.

Miller, Warren E., and J. Merrill Shanks. "Policy Directions and Presidential Leadership: Alternative Interpretations of the 1980 Presidential Election." *British Journal of Political Science* (1982) 12:357-74.

Miller, Warren E., and Santa M. Traugott. *American National Election Studies Data Sourcebook.* Cambridge, Mass.: Harvard University Press, 1989.

Mock, Carol, and Herbert F. Weisberg. "Political Innumeracy: Encounters with Coincidence, Improbability, and Chance." *American Journal of Political Science* (1992) 36:forthcoming.

Monroe, Kristen. "Economic Analysis of Electoral Behavior: A Critical Review." *Political Behavior* (1979a) 1:137-73.

——. "'Gods of Vengeance and of Reward:' The Economy and Presidential Popularity." *Political Behavior* (1979b) 1:301-29.

——. "Presidential Popularity: An Almon Distributed Lag Model." *Political Methodology* (1981) 7:43-70.

Moore, W. John. "From Dreamers to Doers." *National Journal* (1988) 20:372-77.

Morton, Rebecca B. "Groups in Rational Turnout Models." *American Journal of Political Science* (1991) 35:758-76.

Mueller, John E. "Presidential Popularity from Truman to Johnson." *American Political Science Review* (1970) 64:18-34.

——. *War, Presidents, and Public Opinion.* New York: Wiley, 1973.

Myrdal, Gunnar. *An American Dilemma: The Negro Problem and Modern Democracy.* New York: Pantheon, 1944.

Nelson, William, and Phillip Meranto. *Electing Black Mayors.* Columbus: Ohio State University Press, 1977.

Neuman, W. Russell. "Pattern of Recall Among Television News Viewers." *Public Opinion Quarterly* (1976) 40:115-23.

——. "Differentiation and Integration: Two Dimensions of Political Thinking." *American Journal of Sociology* (1981) 86:1236-68.

——. *The Paradox of Mass Politics.* Cambridge, Mass.: Harvard University Press, 1986.

Nie, Norman, Sidney Verba, Henry Brady, Kay Schlozman, and Jane Junn. "Participation in America: Continuity and Change." Paper presented at the annual meeting of the Midwest Political Science Association, 1988.

Nie, Norman H., Sidney Verba, and John R. Petrocik. *The Changing American Voter.* Cambridge, Mass.: Harvard University Press, 1976, 1979.

Niemi, Richard G., and Larry Bartels. "New Measures of Issue Salience: An Evaluation." *Journal of Politics* (1985) 47:1212-20.

Niemi, Richard G., and Patrick Fett. "The Swing Ratio: An Explanation and an Assessment." *Legislative Studies Quarterly* (1986) 11:75-90.

Niemi, Richard G., Simon Jackman, and Laura Winsky. "Candidacies and Competitiveness in Multimember Districts." *Legislative Studies Quarterly* (1991) 16:91-109.

Niemi, Richard G., Richard S. Katz, and David Newman. "Reconstructing Past Partisanship: The Failure of the Party Identification Recall Questions." *American Journal of Political Science* (1980) 24:633-51.

Niemi, Richard G., John Mueller, and Tom W. Smith. *Trends in Public Opinion.* Westport, Conn.: Greenwood, 1989.

Niemi, Richard G., Lynda Powell, and Stephen G. Wright. "Multiple Party Identifiers and the Measurement of Party Identification." *Journal of Politics* (1987) 49:1093-103.

Niemi, Richard G., David Reed, and Herbert F. Weisberg. "The Nature and Measure of Partisanship." *Political Behavior* (1991) 13:213-21.

Niemi, Richard G., Harold Stanley, and Charles L. Evans. "Age and Turnout Among the Newly Enfranchised." *European Journal of Political Research.* (1984) 12:371-86.

Niemi, Richard G., and Herbert F. Weisberg. *Classics in Voting Behavior.* Washington, D.C.: CQ Press, 1993.

Niemi, Richard G., and Anders Westholm. "Issues, Parties, and Attitudinal Stability: A

Comparative Study of Sweden and the United States." *Electoral Studies* (1984) 3:65-83.

Niemi, Richard G., Guy Whitten, and Mark Franklin. "Constituency Characteristics, Individual Characteristics, and Tactical Voting in the 1987 British General Election." *British Journal of Political Science* (1992) 22:229-54.

Nisbett, Richard, and Lee Ross. *Human Inference: Strategies and Shortcomings of Social Judgment.* Englewood Cliffs, N.J.: Prentice-Hall, 1980.

Norpoth, Helmut. "Under Way and Here to Stay: Party Realignment in the 1980s?" *Public Opinion Quarterly* (1987) 51:376-91.

Norpoth, Helmut, and Michael R. Kagay. "Another Eight Years of Republican Rule and Still No Partisan Realignment?" Paper presented at the annual meeting of the American Political Science Association, Atlanta, 1989.

Norpoth, Helmut, Michael S. Lewis-Beck, and Jean-Dominique Lafay, eds. *Economics and Politics.* Ann Arbor: University of Michigan Press, 1991.

Norpoth, Helmut, and Jerrold G. Rusk. "Partisan Dealignment in the American Electorate." *American Political Science Review* (1982) 76:522-37.

Norpoth, Helmut, and Thom Yantek. "Macroeconomic Conditions and Fluctuations of Presidential Popularity: The Question of Lagged Effects." *American Journal of Political Science* (1983) 27:785-807.

Norrander, Barbara. "Explaining Cross-State Variation in Independent Identification." *American Journal of Political Science* (1989) 33:516-36.

Olsen, Marvin E. "Social and Political Participation of Blacks." *American Sociological Review* (1970) 35:682-97.

Oppenheimer, Bruce I., James A. Stimson, and Richard W. Waterman. "Interpreting U.S. Congressional Elections: The Exposure Thesis." *Legislative Studies Quarterly* (1986) 11:227-47.

Ornstein, Norman J. "The House and the Senate in a New Congress." In *The New Congress,* ed. Thomas E. Mann and Norman J. Ornstein. Washington, D.C.: American Enterprise Institute, 1981.

Ornstein, Norman J., Thomas E. Mann, and Michael Malbin. *Vital Statistics on Congress 1989-1990.* Washington, D.C.: Congressional Quarterly, 1990.

Orum, Anthony M. "A Reappraisal of the Social and Political Participation of Negroes." *American Journal of Sociology* (1966) 72:32-46.

Osgood, Charles F., George J. Suci, and Percy H. Tannenbaum. *The Measurement of Meaning.* Urbana: University of Illinois Press, 1957.

Osterlind, Steven J. *Test Item Bias.* Beverly Hills, Calif.: Sage, 1983.

Ostrom, Charles W., and Dennis M. Simon. "Promise and Performance: A Dynamic Model of Presidential Popularity." *American Political Science Review* (1985) 79:334-58.

Ostrom, Thomas M. "The Sovereignty of Social Cognition." In *Handbook of Social Cognition,* vol. 1, ed. Robert S. Wyer, Jr., and Thomas K. Srull. Hillsdale, N.J.: Lawrence Erlbaum, 1984.

Page, Benjamin I. *Choices and Echoes in Presidential Elections: Rational Man and Electoral Democracy.* Chicago: University of Chicago Press, 1978.

Page, Benjamin I., and Richard A. Brody. "Policy Voting and the Electoral Process: The Vietnam War Issue." *American Political Science Review* (1972) 66:979-95. Chapter 11 in *Classics.*

Page, Benjamin I., and Calvin Jones. "Reciprocal Effects of Policy Preferences, Party Loyalties and the Vote." *American Political Science Review* (1979) 73:1071-89. Chapter 13 in *Classics.*

Page, Benjamin I., and Robert Y. Shapiro. "Effects of Public Opinion on Policy." *American Political Science Review* (1983) 77:175-90.

———. *The Rational Public: Fifty Years of Trends in American's Policy Preferences.* Chicago: University of Chicago Press, 1992.

Paldam, Martin. "How Robust is the Vote Function? A Study of Seventeen Nations over Four Decades." In *Economics and Politics,* ed. Helmut Norpoth, Michael S. Lewis-Beck, and Jean-Dominique Lafay. Ann Arbor: University of Michigan Press, 1991.

Parker, Frank R. *Black Votes Count: Political Empowerment in Mississippi After 1965.* Chapel Hill: University of North Carolina Press, 1990.

Patchen, Martin. *The American Public's View of U.S. Policy Toward China.* New York: Council on Foreign Relations, 1964.

Patterson, Samuel C., and Gregory A. Caldeira. "Getting Out the Vote: Participation in Gubernatorial Elections." *American Political Science Review* (1983) 77:675-89.

Patterson, Thomas E. *The Mass Media Election: How Americans Choose Their President.* New York: Praeger, 1980.

Patterson, Thomas E., and Robert P. McClure. *The Unseeing Eye: The Myth of Television Power in National Politics.* New York: G. P. Putnam's Sons, 1976.

Perlez, Jane. "Does Voter Registration Cut Two Ways?" *New York Times,* April 13, 1984.

Persons, Georgia. "Blacks in State and Local Government: Progress and Constraints." In *The State of Black America,* ed. Janet Dewart. New York: National Urban League, 1987.

Peters, John G., and Susan Welch. "The Effects of Charges of Corruption on Voting Behavior in Congressional Elections." *American Political Science Review* (1980) 74:697-708.

Petrocik, John R. *Party Coalitions.* Chicago: University of Chicago Press, 1981.

———. "Realignment: New Party Coalitions and the Nationalization of the South" *Journal of Politics* (1987) 49:347-75.

———. "Issues and Agendas: Electoral Coalitions in the 1988 Election." Paper presented at the annual meeting of the American Political Science Association, Atlanta, 1989.

Petrocik, John R., and Frederick T. Steeper. "The Political Landscape in 1988." *Public Opinion* (1987) 10(5):41-44.

Petty, Richard E., and John T. Cacioppo. "Issue Involvement Can Increase or Decrease Persuasion by Enhancing Message-relevant Cognitive Responses." *Journal of Personality and Social Psychology* (1979) 37:1915-26.

———. The Effects of Involvement on Responses to Argument Quantity and Quality: Central and Peripheral Routes to Persuasion." *Journal of Personality and Social Psychology* (1984) 46:69-81.

Piazza, Thomas. "The Analysis of Attitude Items." *American Journal of Sociology* (1980) 86:584-603.

Pierce, John C. "Party Identification and the Changing Role of Ideology in American Politics." *Midwest Journal of Political Science* (1970) 14:25-42.

Pierce, John C., and Paul R. Hagner. "Conceptualization and Party Identification: 1956-1976." *American Journal of Political Science* (1982) 26:377-87.

Political Action: An Eight Nation Study 1973-1976. Zentralarchiv für empirische Sozialforschung. Machine Readable Codebook. Cologne: University of Cologne, 1979.

Polsby, Nelson W., and Aaron Wildavsky. *Presidential Elections,* 8th ed. New York: Free Press, 1991.

Pomper, Gerald M. *Elections in America.* New York: Dodd, Mead, 1968, 1970.

_____. "From Confusion to Clarity: Issues and American Voters, 1956-1968." *American Political Science Review* (1972) 66:415-28.

_____. *Voters' Choice.* New York: Dodd, Mead, 1975.

Popkin, Samuel, John W. Gorman, Charles Phillips, and Jeffrey A. Smith. "Comment: What Have You Done for Me Lately? Toward an Investment Theory of Voting." *American Political Science Review* (1976) 70:779-805.

Powell, G. Bingham, Jr. "Voting Turnout in Thirty Democracies." In *Electoral Participation,* ed. Richard Rose. Beverly Hills, Calif.: Sage, 1980.

_____. *Contemporary Democracies: Participation, Stability and Violence.* Cambridge, Mass.: Harvard University Press, 1982.

_____. "American Voter Turnout in Comparative Perspective." *American Political Science Review* (1986) 80:17-43. Chapter 5 in this volume.

Presser, Stanley. "Is Inaccuracy on Factual Survey Items Item-specific or Respondent-specific?" *Public Opinion Quarterly* (1984) 48:344-55.

The Public Perspective (1992) 3(No.2):95.

Rabier, Jacques-René, and Ronald Inglehart. *Euro-Barometer 11-April, 1979.* Ann Arbor, Mich.: Inter-University Consortium for Political and Social Research, 1981.

Rabinowitz, George, Paul-Henri Gurian, and Stuart Elaine Macdonald. "The Structure of Presidential Elections and the Process of Realignment." *American Journal of Political Science* (1984) 28:611-35.

Rabinowitz, George, and Stuart Elaine Macdonald. "A Directional Theory of Issue Voting." *American Political Science Review* (1989) 83:93-121.

Rabinowitz, George, James W. Prothro, and William Jacoby. "Salience as a Factor in the Impact of Issues on Candidate Evaluation." *Journal of Politics* (1982) 44:41-63.

Radcliff, Benjamin. "Solving a Puzzle: Aggregate Analysis and Economic Voting Revisited." *Journal of Politics* (1988) 50:440-48.

Ragsdale, Lyn. "The Fiction of Congressional Elections as Presidential Events." *American Politics Quarterly* (1980) 8:375-98.

_____. "Strong Feelings: Emotional Responses to Presidents." *Political Behavior* (1991) 13:33-65.

Ragsdale, Lyn, and Timothy E. Cook. "Representatives' Actions and Challengers' Reactions: Limits to Candidate Connections in the House." *American Journal of Political Science* (1987) 31:45-81.

Rahn, Wendy M. "Candidate Image During Nomination Campaigns." Manuscript, 1987.

Rahn, Wendy M., John H. Aldrich, Eugene Borgida, and John L. Sullivan. "A Social-Cognitive Model of Candidate Appraisal." In *Information and Democratic Processes,* ed. John A. Ferejohn and James H. Kuklinski. Urbana: University of Illinois Press, 1990. Chapter 12 in this volume.

Rawls, John A. *A Theory of Justice.* Cambridge: Harvard University Press, 1971.

Reed, David R., and Charles E. Smith, Jr. "Estimating the Separate Effects of Party Identification and Short-Term Partisan Orientations on the Vote." Paper presented at the annual meeting of the Southern Political Science Association, Atlanta, 1990.

Renshon, Stanley Allen. "Assumptive Frameworks in Political Socialization Theory." In *Handbook of Political Socialization,* ed. Stanley Allen Renshon. New York: Free Press, 1977.

Richardson, Bradley M. "European Party Loyalties Revisited." *American Political Science Review* (1991) 85:751-75.

Riker, William H. *Liberalism Against Populism.* San Francisco: Freeman, 1982.

Rivers, Douglas. "Heterogeneity in Models of Electoral Choice." *American Journal of Political Science* (1988) 32:737-57.

Robinson, John P. *Public Information About World Affairs.* Ann Arbor: Survey Research Center, University of Michigan, 1967.

———. "Mass Communication and Information Diffusion." In *Current Perspectives in Mass Communication Research,* ed. F. Gerald Kline and Philip J. Techenor. Beverly Hills, Calif.: Sage, 1972.

———. *How Americans Use Time: A Social-Psychological Analysis of Everyday Behavior.* New York Praeger, 1977.

Rogers, Joel. "The Politics of Voter Registration." *The Nation,* July 21, 1984.

Rosenau, James N., ed. *Public Opinion and Foriegn Policy.* New York: Random House, 1961.

Rosenberg, Shawn W., Lisa Bohan, Patrick McCafferty, and Kevin Harris. "The Image and the Vote: The Effect of Candidate Presentation on Voter Preference." *American Journal of Political Science* (1986) 30:108-27.

Rosenstone, Steven J. *Forecasting Presidential Elections.* New Haven, Conn.: Yale University Press, 1983.

———. "Why Reagan Won." *Brookings Review* (1985) 3:25-32.

Rosenstone, Steven J., John Mark Hansen, and Donald R. Kinder. "Measuring Change in Personal Economic Well-being." *Public Opinion Quarterly* (1986) 50:176-92.

Rosenstone, Steven J., and Raymond E. Wolfinger. "The Effect of Registration Laws on Voting Turnout." *American Political Science Review* (1978) 72:22-45.

Ross, Lee, and Craig A. Anderson. "Shortcomings in the Attribution Process: On the Origins and Maintenance of Erroneous Social Assessments." In *Judgment Under Uncertainty: Heuristics and Biases,* ed. Daniel Kahneman, Paul Slovic, and Amos Tversky. New York: Cambridge University Press, 1982.

Rothenberg, Stuart, and Frank Newport. *The Evangelical Voter.* Washington, D.C.: Free Congress Research & Education Foundation, 1984.

Rousseuw, Peter. J. "Least Median of Squares Regression." *Journal of the American Statistical Association* (1984) 79:871-80.

Sabato, Larry J. *The Rise of Political Consultants.* New York: Basic Books, 1981.

———. *Campaigns and Elections.* Glenview, Ill.: Scott, Foresman, 1989.

Salisbury, Robert H., and Michael MacKuen. "On the Study of Party Realignment." *Journal of Politics* (1981) 43:523-30.

Salmore, Barbara G., and Stephen A. Salmore. *Candidates, Parties, and Campaigns,* 2nd ed. Washington, D.C.: CQ Press, 1989.

Särlvik, Bo, and Ivor Crewe, *Decade of Dealignment: The Conservative Victory of 1979 and Electoral Trends in the 1970s.* Cambridge: Cambridge University Press, 1983.

Schlegel, Ronald P., and Don DiTecco. "Attitudinal Structures and the Attitude-Behavior Relation." In *Consistency in Social Behavior,* ed. Mark P. Zanna, Edward T. Higgins, and C. P. Herman. The Ontario Symposium, vol. 2. Hillsdale, N.J.: Lawence Erlbaum.

Schneider, William. "The Political Legacy of the Reagan Years." In *The Republican Legacy,* ed. Sidney Blumenthal and Thomas Byrne Edsall. New York: Pantheon, 1988.

Schram, M. *Running for President: A Journal of the Carter Campaign.* New York: Pocket Books, 1977.

Schroder, Harold, Michael Driver, and Siegfried Streufert. *Human Information Processing.* New York: Holt, Rinehart, and Winston, 1967.

Schulman, Mark A., and Gerald M. Pomper. "Variability in Electoral Behavior:

Longitudinal Perspectives from Causal Modeling." *American Journal of Political Science* (1975) 19:1-18.

Scott, William A. "Conceptualizing and Measuring Structural Properties of Cognition." In *Motivation and Social Interaction: Cognitive Determinants*, ed. O. J. Harvey. New York: Ronald Press, 1963.

Shafer, Byron E. *The End of Realignment? Interpreting American Electoral Eras*. Madison: University of Wisconsin Press, 1991.

Shaffer, Stephen D. "A Multivariate Explanation of Decreasing Turnout in Presidential Elections." *American Journal of Political Science* (1981) 25:68-95.

Shanks, J. Merrill, and Warren E. Miller. "Policy Direction and Performance Evaluation: Complementary Explanations of the Reagan Elections." *British Journal of Political Science* (1990) 20:143-235.

———. "Partisanship, Policy and Performance: The Reagan Legacy in the 1988 Election." *British Journal of Political Science* (1991) 21:129-97.

Shanks, J. Merrill, and Bradley Palmquist. "Intra-party Candidate Choice in 1980: An Early Portrait of Pre-convention Preference." Paper presented at the annual meeting of the Midwest Political Science Association, Cincinnati, April 1981.

Sherman, Steven J., and Eric Corty. "Cognitive Heuristics." In *Handbook of Social Cognition*, vol. I, ed. Robert S. Wyer, Jr., and Thomas K. Srull. Hillsdale, N.J.: Lawrence Erlbaum.

Shingles, Richard D. "Black Consciousness and Political Participation: The Missing Link." *American Political Science Review* (1981) 75:76-91.

Shively, W. Phillips. "The Nature of Party Identification: A Review of Recent Developments." In *The Electorate Reconsidered*, ed. John C. Piece and John L. Sullivan. Beverly Hills, Calif.: Sage, 1980.

Silbey, Joel H. "Beyond Realignment and Realignment Theory: American Political Eras, 1789-1989." In *The End of Realignment? Interpreting American Electoral Eras*, ed. Byron E. Shafer. Madison: University of Wisconsin Press, 1991.

Silver, Brian, Barbara Anderson, and Paul Abramson. "Who Overreports Voting?" *American Political Science Review* (1986) 80:613-24.

Sims, Christopher R. "Exogeneity and Causal Ordering in Macroeconomic Models." In *New Methods of Business Cycle Research*, ed. Christopher R. Sims. Minneapolis: Federal Reserve Bank, 1977.

Smidt, Corwin. "Born-Again Politics: The Political Behavior of Evangelical Christians in the South and Non-South." In *Religion and Politics in the South*, ed. Tod A. Baker, Robert P. Steed, and Laurence W. Moreland. New York: Praeger, 1983.

Smith, Charles E., Jr., and David Reed. "Estimating the Separate Effects of Party Identification and Short-term Partisan Forces on the Vote." Paper presented at the annual meeting of the Southern Political Science Association, Atlanta, 1990.

Smith, Don D. " 'Dark Areas of Ignorance' Revisited: Current Knowledge About Asian Affairs." In *Political Attitudes and Public Opinion*, ed. Dan D. Nimmo and Charles M. Bonjean. New York: David McKay, 1972.

Smith, Eric R. A. N. "The Levels of Conceptualization: False Measures of Ideological Sophistication." *American Political Science Review* (1980) 74:685-96.

———. "Communication." *American Political Science Review* (1981) 75:152-54.

———. *The Unchanging American Voter*. Berkeley: University of California Press, 1989.

Smith, Eric R. A. N., and Michael Dolny. "Modeling the Decline of Turnout in American Elections." Manuscript, University of California, Santa Barbara, 1989.

Smith, Tom W. "The Polls: America's Most Important Problems," pt. 1. *Public Opinion Quarterly* (1985) 49:264-74.

Sniderman, Paul. *Personality and Democratic Politics.* Berkeley: University of California, 1975.

Snyder, Mark. "When Believing Means Doing: Creating Links Between Attitudes and Behavior." In *Consistency in Social Behavior,* ed. Mark Zanna, E. Tory Higgins, and C. P. Herman. The Ontario Symposium, vol. 2. Hillsdale, N.J.: Lawrence Erlbaum, 1982.

Southwest Voter Research Institute. *Research Notes.* California edition, 2 (No. 3), 1988.

Squire, Peverill. "Challengers in U.S. Senate Elections." *Legislative Studies Quarterly* (1989) 14:531-47.

_____. "Preemptive Fundraising and Challenger Profile in Senate Elections." *Journal of Politics* (1991) 53:1150-64.

_____. "Challenger Profile and Gubernatorial Elections." *Western Political Quarterly* (1992a) 45:125-42.

_____. "Challenger Quality and Voting Behavior in U.S. Senate Elections." *Legislative Studies Quarterly* (1992b) 17:247-63.

Squire, Peverill, David P. Glass, and Raymond E. Wolfinger. "Residential Mobility and Voter Turnout." Paper presented at the conference: Where Have All the Voters Gone?, Chicago, April 26-28, 1984.

Squire, Peverill, Raymond E. Wolfinger, and David P. Glass. "Residential Mobility and Voter Turnout." *American Political Science Review* (1987) 81:45-65.

Stanga, John E., and James F. Sheffield. "The Myth of Zero Partisanship: Attitudes Toward American Political Parties, 1964-84." *American Journal of Political Science* (1987) 31:829-55.

Stanley, Harold W. "Southern Partisan Changes: Dealignment, Realignment or Both." *Journal of Politics* (1988) 50:64-88.

Stanley, Harold W., William T. Bianco, and Richard G. Niemi. "Partisanship and Group Support over Time: A Multivariate Analysis." *American Political Science Review* (1986) 80:969-76.

Stanley, Harold W., and Richard G. Niemi. "Partisanship and Group Support, 1952-1988." *American Politics Quarterly* (1991) 19:189-210.

_____. *Vital Statistics on American Politics,* 3rd ed. Washington, D.C.: CQ Press, 1992.

Stein, Robert M. "Economic Voting for Governor and U.S. Senator: The Electoral Consequences of Federalism." *Journal of Politics* (1990) 52:29-53.

Stephenson, William. *The Play Theory of Mass Communication.* Chicago: University of Chicago, 1967.

Stevenson, Robert L., and Kathryn P. White. "The Cumulative Audience of Network Television News." *Journalism Quarterly* (1980) 57:477-81.

Stewart, Charles, III, and Mark Reynolds. "Television Markets and U.S. Senate Elections." *Legislative Studies Quarterly* (1990) 15:495-523.

Stimson, James A. "Belief Systems: Constraint, Complexity, and the 1972 Election." *American Journal of Political Science* (1975) 19:393-417.

_____. "Regression in Space and Time: A Statistical Essay." *American Journal of Political Science* (1985) 29:914-47.

_____. *Public Opinion in America.* Boulder, Colo.: Westview, 1991.

Stokes, Donald E. "Some Dynamic Elements in Contests for the Presidency." *American Political Science Review* (1966) 60:19-28.

Stokes, Donald E., Angus Campbell, and Warren E. Miller. "Components of Electoral Decision." *American Political Science Review* (1958) 52:367-87.

Stokes, Donald E., and Gudmund Iversen. "On the Existence of Forces Restoring Party

Competition." In *Elections and the Political Order,* ed. Angus Campbell, Philip E. Converse, Warren E. Miller, and Donald E. Stokes. New York: Wiley, 1966.

Stokes, Donald E., and Warren E. Miller. "Party Government and the Saliency of Congress." *Public Opinion Quarterly* (1962) 26:531-46.

Stone, Walter, and Alan I. Abramowitz. "Winning May Not Be Everything, But It's More Than We Thought: Presidential Party Activists in 1980." *American Political Science Review* (1983) 77:945-56.

Sullivan, Denis, G., and Rodger D. Masters. " 'Happy Warriors': Leaders' Facial Displays, Viewers' Emotions and Political Support." *American Journal of Political Science* (1988) 32:345-68.

Sullivan, John L., John H. Aldrich, Eugene Borgida, and Wendy M. Rahn. "Candidate Appraisal and Human Nature: Man and Superman in the 1984 Election." *Political Psychology* (forthcoming).

Sundquist, James L. *Dynamics of the Party System,* rev. ed. Washington, D.C.: Brookings, 1983.

Tate, Katherine. "Black Political Participation in the 1984 and 1988 Presidential Elections." *American Political Science Review* (1991) 85:1159-76.

Taylor, Charles, and David A. Jodice. *World Handbook of Political and Social Indicators III.* New Haven, Conn.: Yale University Press, 1983.

Taylor, Shelley F., and Jennifer Crocker. "Schematic Basis of Social Information Processing." In *Social Cognition: The Ontario Symposium,* vol. 1, ed. E. Tory Higgins, C. Peter Herman, and Mark P. Zanna. Hillsdale, N.J.: Lawrence Erlbaum.

Teixeira, Ruy A. *Why Americans Don't Vote: Turnout Decline in the United States 1960-1984.* Westport, Conn.: Greenwood, 1987.

Tetlock, Philip E. "Accountability and Complexity of Thought." *Journal of Personality and Social Psychology* (1983) 46:365-75.

———. "Cognitive Style and Political Belief Systems in the British House of Commons." *Journal of Personality and Social Psychology* (1984) 46:365-75.

Thernstrom, Abigail M. *Whose Votes Count?* Cambridge, Mass.: Harvard University Press, 1987.

Thomas, Melvin E., and Michael Hughes. "The Continuing Significance of Race: A Study of Race, Class, and Quality of Life in America, 1972-1985." *American Sociological Review* (1986) 51:830-41.

Thompson, Dennis F. *The Democratic Citizen: Social Science and Democratic Theory in the Twentieth Century.* New York: Cambridge University Press, 1970.

Thompson, William R., and Gary Zuk. "American Elections and the International Electoral-Economic Cycle: A Test of the Tufte Hypothesis." *American Journal of Political Science* (1983) 27:464-84.

Tingsten, Herbert. *Political Behavior.* Totowa, N.J.: Bedminster, 1937.

Torney, Judith V., A. N. Oppenheim, and Russell F. Farnen. *Civic Awareness in Ten Countries.* New York: Wiley, 1975.

Tufte, Edward R. "Determinants of the Outcomes of Midterm Congressional Elections." *American Political Science Review* (1975) 69:812-26.

———. *Political Control of the Economy.* Princeton, N.J.: Princeton University Press, 1978.

Tulving, Endel. "The Effect of Alphabetical Subjective Organization on Memorizing Unrelated Words." *Canadian Journal of Psychology* (1961) 16:185-91.

Uhlaner, Carol J. "Rational Turnout: The Neglected Role of Groups." *American Journal of Political Science* (1989) 33:390-422.

United Nations. *Demographic Yearbooks.* New York: United Nations, 1979, 1981, 1983.

University of Michigan Center for Political Studies. *Codebooks for the National Election Studies, 1960-1980.* Ann Arbor, Mich.: ICPSR, 1961-1982.

U.S. Bureau of Census. "Voting and Registration in the Election of November, 1976." *Current Population Reports.* Ser. P-20, no 322. Washington, D.C.: Department of Commerce, 1978.

U.S. Bureau of Census. "Voting and Registration in the Election of November, 1980." *Current Population Reports.* Ser. P-20, no 370. Washington, D.C.: Department of Commerce, 1982.

Uslaner, Eric M. "Splitting Image: Partisan Affiliations in Canada's 'Two Political Worlds'." *American Journal of Political Science* (1990) 34:961-81.

Valen, Henry. "Structural Change and Ideological Dimensions in a Multiparty System: The Case of Norway." Paper presented at the International Political Science Association World Congress, Moscow, August 1979.

Valentine, David C., and John R. Van Wingen. "Partisanship, Independence, and the Partisan Identification." *American Politics Quarterly* (1980) 8:165-86.

Verba, Sidney, and Norman H. Nie. *Participation in America.* New York: Harper & Row, 1972.

Verba, Sidney, Norman H. Nie, and Jae-on Kim. *The Modes of Democratic Participation.* Beverly Hills, Calif.: Sage, 1971.

———. *Participation and Political Equality.* Cambridge, Mass.: Cambridge University Press, 1978.

Walton, Hanes. *Invisible Politics.* New York: State University of New York Press, 1985.

Wattenberg, Martin P. *The Decline of American Political Parties.* Cambridge, Mass.: Harvard University Press, 1984, 1990.

———. "The Hollow Realignment: Partisan Change in a Candidate-Centered Era." *Public Opinion Quarterly* (1987) 51:58-74.

———. *The Rise of Candidate-Centered Politics.* Cambridge, Mass.: Harvard University Press, 1991.

Watts, Meredith W. "Semantic Convergence in the Measurement of Political Attitudes." *Political Methodology* (1974) 1:133-48.

Weatherford, M. Stephen. "Economic Voting and the 'Symbolic Politics' Argument: A Reinterpretation and Synthesis." *American Political Science Review* (1983) 77:158-74.

Weber, Ronald E., Harvey J. Tucker, and Paul Brace. "Vanishing Marginals in State Legislative Elections." *Legislative Studies Quarterly* (1991) 16:29-47.

Weisberg, Herbert F. "A Multidimensional Conceptualization of Party Identification." *Political Behavior* (1980) 2:33-60. Chapter 27 in *Classics.*

———. "The Electoral Kaleidoscope: Political Change in the Polarizing Election of 1984." Manuscript, Ohio State University, 1985.

Weisberg, Herbert F., and Dee Allsop. "Sources of Short-Term Change in Party Identification." Paper presented at the annual meeting of the Midwest Political Science Association, Chicago, 1990.

Weisberg, Herbert F., and Charles E. Smith, Jr. "The Influence of the Economy on Party Identification in the Reagan Years." *Journal of Politics* (1991) 53:1077-92.

Wekkin, Gary D. "Why Crossover Voters Are Not 'Mischievous Voters'." *American Politics Quarterly* (1991) 19:229-47.

Westholm, Anders, and Richard G. Niemi. "Political Institutions and Political Socialization: A Cross-National Study." *Comparative Political Studies* (1992) 25:forthcoming.

Westlye, Mark C. "Competitiveness of Senate Seats and Voting Behavior in Senate Elections." *American Journal of Political Science* (1983) 27:253-83.

_____. *Senate Elections and Campaign Intensity*. Baltimore: Johns Hopkins University Press, 1991.

Whitby, Kenny J. "Measuring Congressional Responsiveness to Policy Interests of Black Constituents." *Social Science Quarterly* (1987) 68:367-77.

White, Elliot S. "Intelligence, Individual Differences, and Learning: An Approach to Political Socialization." *British Journal of Sociology* (1969) 20:50-66.

Whiteley, Paul F. "Politics-Econometric Estimation in Britain: An Alternative Interpretation." In *Models of Political Economy,* ed. Paul Whiteley. London: Sage, 1980.

_____. "The Causal Relationships Between Issues, Candidate Evaluations, Party Identification, and Vote Choice—The View From 'Rolling Thunder.' *Journal of Politics* (1988) 50:961-84.

Wilcox, Clyde. "The Timing of Strategic Decisions: Candidacy Decisions in 1982 and 1984." *Legislative Studies Quarterly* (1987) 12:565-72.

Wilcox, Clyde, and Bob Biersack. "Research Update: The Timing of Candidacy Decisions in the House, 1982-1988." *Legislative Studies Quarterly* (1990) 15:115-26.

Williams, Eddie N., and Milton D. Morris. "Is the Electoral Process Stacked Against Minorities?" In *Elections American Style,* ed. A. James Reichley. Washington, D.C.: Brookings, 1987.

Williams, John. "The Political Manipulation of Macroeconomic Policy." *American Political Science Review* (1990) 84:767-96.

Wilson, William J. *The Declining Significance of Race,* rev. ed. Chicago: University of Chicago Press, 1980.

_____. *The Truly Disadvantaged.* Chicago: University of Chicago Press, 1987.

Winters, Richard F. "Taxing Choices: Mapping the Electoral Costs of Increasing Taxes." Paper presented at the annual meeting of the American Political Science Association, Washington, D.C., 1991.

Witcover, Jules. *Marathon: The Pursuit of the Presidency 1972-1976.* New York: Viking, 1977.

Withey, Stephen B. *The U.S. and the U.S.S.R.* Ann Arbor: Survey Research Center, University of Michigan, 1962.

Wolfinger, Raymond E., and Steven J. Rosenstone. *Who Votes?* New Haven, Conn.: Yale University Press, 1980.

Wolfinger, Raymond E., Steven J. Rosenstone, and Richard A. McIntosh. "Presidential and Congressional Voters Compared." *American Politics Quarterly* (1981) 9:245-56.

Wright, Gerald C. "Misreports of Vote Choice in the 1988 NES Senate Election Study." *Legislative Studies Quarterly* (1990) 15:543-64.

Wright, Gerald C., Jr., and Michael B. Berkman. "Candidates and Policy in United States Senate Elections." *American Political Science Review* (1986) 80:565-88.

Wright, Gerald C., Robert S. Erikson, and John P. McIver. "Measuring State Partisanship and Ideology with Survey Data." *Journal of Politics* (1985) 47:479-89.

Wu, Cheng-huan, and David R. Shaffer. "Susceptibility to Persuasive Appeals as a Function of Source Credibility and Prior Experience with the Attitude Object." *Journal of Personality and Social Psychology* (1987) 57:677-88.

Wyckoff, Mikel. "Belief System Constraint and Policy Voting: A Test of the Undimensional Consistency Model." *Political Behavior* (1980) 2:115-46.

_____. "Issues of Measuring Ideological Sophistication: Level of Conceptualization, Attitudinal Consistency, and Attitudinal Stability." *Political Behavior* (1987) 9:193-224.

Wyer, Robert S., Jr., and Thomas K. Srull. "Human Cognition in Its Social Context." *Psychological Review* (1986) 93:322-59.

Zajonc, Robert B. "Attitudinal Effects of Mere Exposure." *Journal of Personality and Social Psychology Monograph Supplement* (1968) 9 (2, Part 2):2-27.

———. "Feeling and Thinking: Preferences Need No Inferences." *American Psychologist* (1980) 35:151-75.

Zaller, John. "The Effects of Political Involvement on Public Attitudes and Voting Behavior." Paper presented at the annual meeting of the American Political Science Association, Washington, D.C., 1986.

———. "Vague Minds Versus Vague Questions." Manuscript, University of California, Los Angeles, 1988.

Zipp, John F. "Perceived Representativeness and Voting: An Assessment of the Impact of 'Choices' and 'Echoes'." *American Political Science Review* (1985) 79:50-61.

NAME INDEX

SUBJECT INDEX

Abortion, 175
Abstention. *See* Voting turnout
Age. *See also* Party identification, and the life cycle; Voting turnout, and the life cycle
  correlates of, 132
  and political sophistication, 119-132
Aggregate versus individual analysis
  of congressional voting, 212, 215
  and effects of the economy, 138-139, 154, 212
  of party identification, 270, 288-289
  of turnout effects, 73-74
Attitude stability. *See* Ideology
Australia, 12, 60, 80, 145, 150
Austria, 57, 60, 71-72, 80, 92

B-1 bomber, 182n
Bandwagon effects. *See* Primary elections
Belgium, 60, 80, 83, 322
Belief systems. *See* Ideology
Blacks. *See also* Civil rights; Race; Realignment, and race
  black empowerment, 39-55
  and participation, 39-55
  and party identification, 326, 329n, 351-355, 358-367
  restrictions on voting, 21n
  and voting choice, 18, 159
  and voting turnout, 2, 15, 17-20, 25, 29, 38n, 84n

Campaign spending, and turnout, 18, 215, 218n, 220-221. *See also* Congressional elections, and campaign expenditures
Campaigns, importance of, 164-165
Canada, 8, 61, 77, 80, 82, 84n, 145, 281n, 322
Candidates. *See also* Congressional elections, importance of candidates; Voting choice, determinants of
  comparative studies, 145
  images of, 3, 143-145, 150, 187-204, 204n-205n
  perceived differences, 172-173, 177-178, 181, 183n
  personal qualities, 133n, 142-143, 190-204
  and voting choice, 133n, 137-138, 142-146, 148, 178-181, 200-202
Casework. *See* Congressional elections, and constituency service
Catholics, 285, 334
CBS/*New York Times* poll, 7, 211
Census Bureau, 15, 19
China, 101-102, 110
Civil rights, 88, 175, 184-186, 307-308, 312-313, 315, 318-319, 320n. *See also* Realignment, and race
Class voting. *See* Socioeconomic status; Voting turnout, and social class
Cleavages
  and the party system, 275, 321-323, 329n, 339